Discourse on History, Law, and Governance in the Public Career of
John Selden, 1610–1635

Discourse on History, Law, and Governance in the Public Career of John Selden, 1610–1635

Paul Christianson

UNIVERSITY OF TORONTO PRESS
Toronto Buffalo London

© University of Toronto Press Incorporated 1996
Toronto Buffalo London
Printed in Canada

ISBN 0-8020-0838-0

Printed on acid-free paper

Canadian Cataloguing in Publication Data

Christianson, Paul, 1937–
    Discourse on history, law, and governance in
    the public career of John Selden, 1610–1635

    Includes bibliographical references and index.
    ISBN 0-8020-0838-0

    1. Selden, John, 1584–1654.   2. England – Constitutional
    law.   3. Great Britain – Politics and government –
    1603–1649.   I. Title.

    JX2148.C57 1996   342.42'0092   C96-930182-0

University of Toronto Press acknowledges the financial assistance to its
publishing program of the Canada Council and the Ontario Arts Council.

This book has been published with the help of a grant from the Humanities and Social Sciences Federation of Canada, using funds provided by the
Social Sciences and Humanities Research Council of Canada.

To the memory of
Kristin Wigley Fleming

Contents

Preface

The research for this study was carried out at the Bodleian Library, the Douglas and Stauffer Libraries at Queen's University, the Cambridge University Library, the Henry E. Huntington Library (especially in the Homer D. Crotty Collection of John Selden), the House of Lords Record Office, the Libraries of Lincoln's Inn and the Inner Temple, and the Yale Center for Parliamentary History; I would like to thank the staff at these institutions for their courteous help. Funding for my research was provided by the generosity of the Social Sciences and Humanities Research Council of Canada (grant no. 410-790262), the Henry E. Huntington Library, the Liberty Fund, and the Advisory Research Committee at Queen's University; the Principal's Development Fund at Queen's University generously provided me with released time for the writing of the first chapter; much of the research for the final chapter and the revision of the whole manuscript were done during sabbatical leaves also provided by Queen's University; all of these institutions receive my thanks. Among those many friends and fellow scholars who have kindly listened to, read, and commented upon various portions of this book, I would like to single out for thanks Professor J.G.A. Pocock and Professor Kevin Sharpe, for their comments on chapter 1; Professor Conrad Russell and Dr Thomas Cogswell, for theirs on chapter 2; Professor Louis Knafla, for his on portions of chapter 3; and Dr Glenn Burgess, Professor Daniel Woolf, and the readers for the University of Toronto Press and the Aid to Scholarly Publications Program, for theirs on the whole manuscript. I would also like to thank Professor Ross Kilpatrick for his expert help in untangling a number of complicated Latin passages. Any mistakes which remain are mine.

In carrying out my research for this book, I have deliberately followed a strategy of reading and analysing Selden's publications and speeches in chronological order. This approach represented an attempt to read and write history forwards, as it occurred, instead of backwards, as it has often appeared in retrospect to historians. This strategy also made it easier to portray Selden's ideas as they developed over time and in reaction to the discourse of his contemporaries. It meant refraining from drawing upon Selden's posthumously published *Table Talk* (London, 1689) to 'clarify' his earlier works; the remarks in the *Table Talk* date mainly from the 1640s and reflect the views of a more middle-aged John Selden than that persona discussed in these pages. The final text of this study has incorporated numerous revisions since the first research and writing. After completing the first version of chapter 1, I felt uneasy about the way in which it situated Selden's earliest publications and I went back to make a more thorough search of English constitutional discourse during the first two decades of the seventeenth century. Anyone wishing to establish a grid of this mental archaeology can compare the final text with the earlier versions that appeared in print. Likewise, after completing the first version of chapter 3, I decided to add the section on *Mare Clausum*; however, this meant only adding to, not disturbing, the chronology. I hope that these revisions have solidified the interpretation.

During the many years it has taken to complete this book, an earlier version of the first chapter appeared as 'Young John Selden and the Ancient Constitution, ca. 1610–1618,' in *Proceedings of the American Philosophical Society* 128 (1984), 271–315; an earlier version of portions of the second chapter was first delivered as a paper at a conference held at the Folger Library in April 1985 and then appeared as 'John Selden, the Five Knights' Case, and Discretionary Imprisonment in Early Stuart England,' in *Criminal Justice History* 6 (1985), 65–87; I would like to thank Professor Donald R. Kelley for inviting me to share my research on this occasion, and Professor Louis Knafla for encouraging me to publish it. Revised versions of research overlapping with portions of the first two chapters were presented as papers at the conference 'The Mental World of the Jacobean Court,' held at the Folger Library in March 1988, and at the Liberty Fund Symposium 'Magna Carta and Ancient Constitution: Medieval and Renaissance Roots of American Liberty,' held at St George's House, Windsor Castle, on 15–19 June 1988, and appeared in 'Royal and Parliamentary Voices on the Ancient Constitution, ca. 1604–21,' in *The Mental World of the Jacobean Court*, ed. Linda Levy Peck (pp. 71–95) (Cambridge, 1991), and 'Ancient Constitutions in the Age of Sir Edward Coke and John Selden,' in *Magna Carta and Ancient Constitution: Medieval and Renaissance Roots of American Liberty*, ed. Ellis Sandoz (pp. 89–146) (Columbia, 1993). As well as the sponsors, I would like to thank Professors Linda Levy Peck and Ellis Sandoz, the organizers of these events, for inviting me to share my research on those occasions and for editing the volumes in which the resulting papers appeared, and those who attended for their helpful comments. Finally, I would like to thank my mother, my brothers and sister, their spouses and children, and my wife and two stepsons for their support over recent years and to dedicate this book to the memory of my niece, whose beauty, talent, wit, intelligence, and sparkle brought great joy to all who knew her.

In quotations, spelling, capitalization, and punctuation follow the original, except for the normal expansions of contractions and such normal emendations as the changing of 'u' to 'v.' Dates follow the 'old style' calendar used in England during the seventeenth century, except for representing a new year as starting on 1 January.

DISCOURSE ON HISTORY, LAW,
AND GOVERNANCE IN
THE PUBLIC CAREER OF
JOHN SELDEN, 1610–1635

Introduction

In early-seventeenth-century England, many able magistrates, artists, divines, lawyers, and scholars spoke, wrote, created, and acted to uphold what they conceived of as the proper governance of the commonwealth. A multitude of voices, in parliaments, in publications, and in paintings, debated such interrelated theoretical and practical issues as what kind of monarchy England possessed and how the king's servants should behave in governing the realm. Apart from some theoretical treatises dealing with the relationship of English monarchs to the papacy,[1] discussions on governance centred on expressions of moral and legal rule by the king and his servants, stretching from the court through the great officers of state, and judges down to local justices of the peace and constables. In order to deal with all aspects of governance, Englishmen could and did draw upon a wide range of discourse, from domestic Protestant sermons to Continental Catholic treatises; from the classic texts of Roman law (the *Corpus Juris Justiniani* and the Theodosian Code), and the myriad commentaries which interpreted and applied them (especially the former) to contemporary situations, to the treatises, reports, statutes, and customs of the English common law; from treatises upholding the traditional Christian values of 'mirrors for princes' to those supporting the necessity of 'reason of state'; and from practical guidebooks for moral decisions to utopian visions.[2]

Despite this abundance of discourse, few Englishmen living in the first four decades of the seventeenth century engaged in what some of their Continental contemporaries would have recognized as the 'up-to-date' political theory of 'reason of state.' Instead, they articulated constitutionalist principles of governance in the discourse of the English common law and disputed particular policies in royal courts and parliaments. In a fitful, sometimes unintended manner, criticism of the behaviour of the king's servants led to a series of profound disputes over governance during mid- and late-seventeenth-century England which, in turn, gave rise to the formal statements of political theory and prudential statements verging on political platforms published during the 'Great Rebellion' and 'Glorious Revolution,' and to the creation of party politics, with its characteristic contests for power and office, by at least two reasonably organized groups with rival programs.[3] Even after the start of party or proto-party activity, politics often retained its earlier aim of moral consensus and its earlier method of personal rivalries. Increasingly expressed in a secularized discourse of natural law assembled by Hugo Grotius (with strong inflections of civil or Roman law), political thought remained a branch of moral philosophy and retained significant portions of earlier discourses of history, religion, and common law.[4]

Before the 'fall' of the British monarchies during the mid-seventeenth century, the discourse of the common law, intertwined with history and kept in creative tension during what Glenn Burgess has called the 'Jacobean consensus' by theological and civil-law discourses operating in their appropriate spheres, exercised a hegemonic, if not unchallenged, position in English discussions of governance.[5] Of course, common lawyers and their followers could speak with more than one accent, and this study will argue that competing representations of the English constitution played a large role in the constitutional disputes of early Stuart England. These disputes were founded on theoretical differences over the extent and distribution of political authority and were not just practical conflicts 'over access to power or wealth.'[6] During the first three decades of the century, natural law had infused some of the arguments voiced by Roman or civil lawyers and divines, and reason of state had resonated in the arguments of some royal counsellors, but the seemingly insular voices of common lawyers dominated most of the debates which took place in court, country, and parliaments. Many years ago, Margaret Judson and J.G.A. Pocock established the importance of common-law discourse in seventeenth-century English political thought. More recently, Johann Sommerville has stressed the contributions of civil lawyers and divines, and Glenn Burgess has mapped the interrelationships and appropriate audiences addressed by the political discourses of theology, civil law, and common law.[7] A host of recent scholars have started to map the discourse of visual and literary artists on the holding and exercise of power involved in governance.[8] In addition, social historians have given voice to the moral concerns which informed both the prudential pronouncements of working magistrates – justices of the peace, constables, and jurymen – and the conceptions of 'folk justice' enforced in local communities.[9] The extension of the history of political thought into areas outside of its earlier boundaries – far beyond an attempt to establish the linguistic, political, and social contexts for the ideas of those recognized as 'great political theorists' – has enriched our understanding of historical discourse in general.[10]

In an attempt to interpret aspects of political and historical thought in early Stuart England, especially in relationship to English common-law discourse, Continental customary- and civil-law discourse, Grotian natural-law discourse, and the history of Europe and England, this study concentrates on the relevant ideas and actions of the young to middle-aged John Selden. It discusses the interpretations of governance – organized around the images of the ancient constitution, the feudal law, and the Roman law – put forward in Selden's early published works (ca 1610–18), in his legal and parliamentary career in the 1620s, and in his relevant publications in the 1630s, and attempts to interpret his writings and speeches within the linguistic and political context provided by comparable contemporary works. Since reading all of the published sources and treatises cited in the margins of Selden's books would take an incredible number of additional years, I have relied on recent secondary works to fill in much of that context. Despite some early indications of a sceptical and Tacitist bent, Selden continued to articulate his model of governance in constitutionalist terms into the early 1630s (strongly opposing arguments based on 'reason of state' and 'necessity' in the Parliament of 1628–9), and only began a shift to the discourse of Grotian natural law in the mid-1630s. From 1610 to 1618, Selden assembled and defended one of the three major interpretations of the 'ancient constitution' most frequently voiced in the debates over governance which took place in early-seventeenth-century England. In the parliaments of 1621, 1624, 1626, and 1628–9, he attempted to put the newest version of this interpretation into action. Ironically, Selden's profound mastery of Continental humanist legal-historical methods and perspectives helped him to reassert the 'traditional liberties' of Englishmen, most notably in the Petition of Right, and to expand the evidential and interpretative horizons of the practice and history of the common law and governance of England.[11] In 1631, he published his most sophisticated work on European and English history, which provided a defence of his interpretation of the English constitution by projecting an ancient constitution for each of the European societies which succeeded the Roman Empire. In 1635, Selden produced his last piece of English constitutional history and the first of his treatises on natural law, combined together in his famous text on the law of the sea.

An antiquary and historian both of the ancient Near East and of medieval and early modern western Europe (including England); a common and civil lawyer well read both in the treatises and in the codes of the Roman, canon, and customary laws of western Europe; a member of Parliament; and an author in both Latin and English, Selden was a major scholar and a more than minor political figure.[12] A full understanding of his interests lies outside of the scope of this limited study – indeed, beyond my linguistic and scholarly skills. Concentrating upon Selden's historical representations of the feudal laws and the ancient constitutions of western Europe (including England), this study presents a partial reading of those books and speeches which enter the discussion. Recent accounts have stressed Selden's contributions in a number of areas: Arthur Ferguson, F. Smith Fussner, and Daniel Woolf have documented his originality as a historian; Christopher Brooks, Donald Kelley, Kevin Sharpe, Richard Tuck, Martha Ziskind, and I have singled him out as a leading English common-law attorney who absorbed the learning and methods of the Continental humanist legal historians; and Richard Tuck and Johann Sommerville have discussed his impact upon natural-law traditions of English political thought.[13] The recent book by David Berkowitz centred upon Selden's political career in the 1620s, while portions of books by Burgess, Colin Tite, and Stephen White, and articles by Linda Popofsky and myself, have also detailed some of his early political ideas and actions.[14] None of these works, however, has presented a systematic reading of Selden's parliamentary and legal speeches in relation to his own and other contemporary constitutionalist interpretations of governance. This study attempts to represent both the written and the vocal sides of Selden's conversation with contemporaries, and his dialogue with his own texts on these topics.

The first chapter deals with Selden's early interpretations of the

English constitution. Applying Continental humanist legal-historical methods to English and European evidence, the most important of these treatises, *Jani Anglorum Facies Altera* (London, 1610), *Titles of Honor* (London, 1614), an edition with notes and a translation of Sir John Fortescue's, *De Laudibus Legum Angliæ* (London, 1616), and *The Historie of Tithes* (London, 1618), helped to establish Selden's scholarly reputation as a leading legal historian and antiquary. Attempting to establish the truth about controversial topics, all of these profoundly historical treatises followed Renaissance and Reformation polemical traditions. In response to the 'constitutional monarchy created by kings' voiced by King James in March 1610 and the 'constitutional monarchy governed by the common law' argued in the House of Commons by Thomas Hedley and others in the following June, the *Jani Anglorum* detailed an extensive history of the laws and constitution of England as a 'mixed monarchy.' Demonstrating the relevance of Continental methods and materials for a 'proper' understanding of European (including English) history and society, *Titles of Honor* demythologized the whole question of titles, honour, and gentility; royal and noble titles and families had not existed from time out of mind, but arose and altered over time in relation to changes in specific societies. Reflecting Continental scholarship, *Titles of Honor* also argued that William the Conqueror had transformed the basic nature of the English common law by introducing the feudal tenures of the Continent, thus threatening to subvert Selden's earlier image of the English constitution as a mixed monarchy. Reacting against this cataclysmic interpretation of the Norman Conquest, Selden's edition of Fortescue's popular apology for England's constitutional monarchy established a critical text and, in extensive notes, both corrected the historical account offered by the fifteenth-century master and fashioned a theory which reduced all law to the 'state' (or fundamental distribution of powers) and customs of a particular jurisdiction. Subordinating divine law in its practical application to the laws of particular jurisdictions, *The Historie of Tithes* plunged into a very terrestrial and often bitter dispute over the nature and ownership of ecclesiastical tithes. All of these works integrated Continental humanist philological methods with English and European evidence to establish and refine a historical interpretation of the English constitution as a mixed monarchy in which the king, nobles, clergy, and freemen had shared sovereignty from the very beginning. All also helped to establish the independence of the English common law from the universalist claims of canon and civil lawyers.

The second chapter examines Selden's political career in the 1620s, which began with his appointment as a consultant to the House of Lords in 1621 and continued with his selection as a member of the House of Commons in 1624, 1626, and 1628. Dependent upon aristocratic patronage, he sat in the parliaments of 1626 and 1628–9 for boroughs controlled by the Earl of Hertford and worked together in the House with other members of the Seymour connection – Edward Kirton in both of these parliaments, and Sir Francis Seymour in 1628–9. Selden's training as a lawyer, knowledge of the history of English law (including parliaments), and refined interpretation of the English constitution as a mixed monarchy gave him distinct advantages in becoming a leading speaker and trusted and active committee member in the House of Commons. These skills also made him a valuable member of a team. Through words and deeds, Selden attempted to put his interpretation of the English constitution into action, if necessary by binding the king's servants to act in what he believed were proper and appropriate ways. This involved working to obtain the privilege of Parliament for Sir Robert Howard and advancing the impeachment of the Duke of Buckingham in 1626, acting as one of the attorneys for the defence in the Five Knights' Case of 1627, playing a leading role in the debates and proceedings which led to the passage of the Petition of Right in 1628, and advocating the privilege of Parliament for Robert Rolle and attacking royal servants in 1629. In part, Selden's advocacy of liberties took the form of a series of disputes over the nature of the English constitution with the attorney general, Sir Robert Heath. Ironically, some of Selden's speeches and actions, especially in 1629, helped to break down that mutual trust between the king's servants and members of the House of Commons so necessary for the day-to-day working of mixed monarchy.

The third chapter opens with a discussion of Selden's historical method and with a reading of his most sophisticated English historical text, the second edition of *Titles of Honor* (London, 1631), and moves on to a reading of his famous natural-law and historical treatise on dominion over the seas, *Mare Clausum* (London, 1635). In *Titles of Honor* (1631), Selden expanded his common-law representation of the ancient constitution into a intricate comparative account which dealt with European and British societies. He marshalled masses of historical evidence and insightful medium-range and micro-historical interpretations to demonstrate that all European societies formed since the collapse of the Roman Empire in the West – and, by implication, all other jurisdictions in the world – consisted of a 'state' (or firm constitutional distribution of powers) and customary laws. By tracing feudal tenures back to the lands held by thegns in Anglo-Saxon England and construing them as just another local example of northern European custom, *Titles of Honor* (1631) subverted attempts to derive the common law either from the will of the Conqueror or from the purportedly universal principles of jurisprudence embodied in the Roman law. With a similar pattern applied to the Continent, the feudal law of the civilians no longer remained a unitary appendix to the *Corpus Juris Justiniani*; it became a patchwork of feudal laws and ancient constitutions, laws appropriate to each of the successor societies. A great compendium of learning, but no impartial work, this weighty treatise remained the crowning glory of Selden's attempt to establish his interpretation of the English constitution as a mixed monarchy through historical scholarship. Although historical in much of its argument and evidence, *Mare Clausum* opened with close definitions of dominion and of the laws of God, nature, nations, and individual realms. In this first section, inspired by the ideas of Grotius, Selden argued that the laws of God and nature became enforceable only by integration into the laws of particular societies and he erected an orderly law of nations out of the practices and treaties of European maritime states. In doing so, he not only demoted the Roman and canon laws to a theoretical status inferior to that of the English common law and eliminated the need for an abstract law of nature as a foundation for international law, but also provided the basis for a refutation of the principle of communal ownership of the sea and for the ensuing historical demonstration of the exercise of dominion over the adjoining seas by the rulers of Britain from the time of the Romans to the seventeenth century. As well as being the last treatise by Selden on European history, *Mare Clausum* drew upon natural-law Grotian discourse to devise a radical subversion of the universalist perspective displayed by Grotius.

The conclusion provides a reflection upon the major themes in the mental and political world of John Selden during the first four decades of the seventeenth century, especially his conceptions of the research and writing of history; his interpretations of the common, canon, civil or Roman, and natural laws; his model of the ancient constitutions of England and Europe; and his role in the changing shape of parliamentary politics. It ends with a major subversion of Selden's interpretation of the ancient constitution in a law case which referred to his early works and with a reinterpretation of mixed monarchy by royal servants to show how the careful constructions of even the most scholarly authors escape their control.

CHAPTER ONE

Young John Selden and the Ancient Constitution, *ca* 1610–1618

During the period from 1610 through 1618, John Selden published a series of works which not only established his reputation as a scholar, but also provided historical representations of the ancient constitution of England and the feudal law of Europe. Selden's works more than rivalled those advanced by other leading common lawyers such as Sir Edward Coke, Sir John Davies, Thomas Hedley, and Sir Henry Spelman, and challenged those of civil lawyers, who viewed the English common law as a 'municipal custom' subject to correction from the universal principles and practices of the law of nations.[1] Selden's representation of England's ancient constitution as a 'mixed monarchy' in which monarchs, nobles, clergy, and representatives of the people had shared sovereignty from the very beginning of the society openly competed with the interpretations of 'constitutional monarchy created by kings' and 'constitutional monarchy governed by the common law' articulated by James VI and I, and by Thomas Hedley in 1610, as well. The influence of the ancients and of Continental scholars appeared in the text and marginal notes of Selden's earliest publications and increased thereafter. Richard Tuck's recent sketch of Selden as a Tacitist sceptic, a common lawyer who did not share Sir Edward Coke's vision of the rationality and certainty of English law, and an English analogue of his famous Dutch contemporary, Hugo Grotius, will find some resonance in the following pages. After all, Selden cited Tacitus, Seneca, and Justus Lipsius quite frequently in his early works. To look at them alone, however, would not do justice to the range of Selden's reading; in the pages of *Jani Anglorum* (1610) and *Titles of Honor* (1614), for example, Plutarch received as many citations as Tacitus, and Joseph-Juste

Scaliger more than Lipsius.[2] Despite one early reference, the impact of Grotius did not seriously manifest itself in print until the 1630s, and even then Selden retained more of the particularist perspective of a common lawyer than of the universalist perspective of many Roman lawyers echoed by Grotius. As Selden's mastery of English and European primary sources for legal history and of a humanist philological method of analysis matured, his scholarship became much more bold, inclusive, and complex.

Unlike many common lawyers, Selden did not stress the immemoriality of the ancient constitution and, although he did believe that the common law fitted the character of the English people, he did not characterize it as embodying reason.[3] Writing from a profoundly acute historical perspective and starting from the earliest reliable surviving evidence, Selden constructed his accounts as moving forward. This guarded against anachronism. A chronological recital of the customs which governed the southern part of Britain from the time of the ancient Britons onward, *Jani Anglorum* presented a detailed historical model of the ancient constitution in which the fundamental shape of mixed government endured, while particular laws, practices, and institutions slowly changed over time to accommodate various shifts in society. Embracing both historical continuity and change, this basic interpretation guided Selden's later accounts and became more defined and refined as his scholarship matured. After a great deal of ambiguity over the question of whether the Norman Conquest represented a major break in continuity (including an explicit portrayal of the introduction of the feudal law into England by William as a conqueror), Selden eventually argued that the Anglo-Saxon constitution prescribed bounds to and legality upon the Conquest, that even the Conqueror had to employ a parliament as the means for continuing old laws and introducing new ones and, thereby, had confirmed the fundamental shape of the ancient constitution. Although custom and statute played a central place in Selden's interpretation of the English common law, in 1618 he reduced all law to customary adjustments to the founding 'state' or distribution of powers within each particular jurisdiction, and thereby laid the theoretical foundations for the historical account of Europe's ancient constitutions eventually detailed in his second edition of *Titles of Honor* (1631). By placing the English constitution firmly within a European context, this theory of judicature strengthened his interpretation of England as a 'mixed monarchy' and guarded the English common law from the universalist claims of Roman, or civil, and canon lawyers. Just prior to the start of his parliamentary career in the 1620s, Selden had constructed and illustrated a sophisticated historical representation of the ancient constitution which took into full account relationships between the common and the canon, feudal, and Roman laws. The foundations for this vision appeared in his first books.

SELDEN'S PUBLICATIONS

Down from Oxford and resident at the Inner Temple (but not yet called to the bar), Selden formally opened his career as an author in 1610 with the publication of two brief treatises, one on the antiquity of judicial and private combat – *The Duello or Single Combat* – and the other on the ancient laws of southern Britain – *Jani Anglorum Facies Altera*. As early as 1607, he had written a historical account of the governance of ancient Britain and England, the *Analecton Anglobritannicon*, and shortly thereafter had produced a similar work in English, *England's Epinomis* – the last of these, however, did not reach print until 1683. The *Duello*, *Jani Anglorum*, and *Analecton* treated the English past with a command of English and Continental learning, a careful scrutiny of primary sources and leading secondary works that would come to characterize Selden's scholarship. A set piece written to display a young man's erudition before the eyes of leading scholars, *The Duello* dealt with a topic previously handled at length by the Society of Antiquaries. Drawing upon scholarly treatises and the Law Books of the common law, it demonstrated that trial by combat entered England only after the Norman Conquest. The firm sense of chronology and accompanying awareness of anachronism which provided the foundation for Selden's historical discourse received an early exposition here.[4] A greater and more complex body of sources and interpretations informed the other early works.

Analecton Anglobritannicon undertook a much more ambitious project, the history of government in southern Britain from the time of its original inhabitation through the Norman Conquest. Drawing upon the works of ancient, medieval, and modern historians, and occasionally quoting from medieval legal documents, it took the form of a conventional chronological account organized largely around the reigns of particular rulers. With no elaborate English model to follow, Selden appears to have patterned his book upon that famous portrayal of the ancient constitution of France, François Hotman's *Francogallia* (1573, 1576, 1586 ff.), a work that the Cambridge scholar and civil lawyer Gabriel Harvey could call, in 1584, Hotman's 'preamptorie and almost seditious Francogallia' a 'dangerous' pamphlet 'in a monarchie or politique kingdom; and flat opposite to the imperiall civil lawe of the prudent, valorous, and reputed just Romans.'[5] The similarities extended far beyond the respective titles of the books; both authors described the polity of the ancient inhabitants, both portrayed the Roman Conquest as an enslavement of the native people and a break in constitutional development, and both reserved the bulk of their attention for the German kings who succeeded the Romans.[6] Here Selden sketched out much of the interpretation that he would develop more systematically and with greater detail in *Jani Anglorum*. Hence, he characterized the ancient British polity as an 'aristocratic commonwealth,' noted the presence of a paramount king of the Anglo-Saxons, even during the earliest days of the heptarchy, and displayed an ambiguous view of the Norman Conquest which sought to combine the arbitrary power held by the Conqueror with evidence for the continuity of Saxon laws and institutions. Clearly the first of these points aimed at subverting traditional derivations of royal rule in Britain from the sons of the Trojan refugee Brutus and undermining the credibility of British poets as sources for the history of the ancient Britons – hence, Selden's argument that 'it is right to contradict those who derive this monarchy from remote stock: for the type of government under the Britons was quite different from monarchy, if Caesar is to believed, and if we follow the conjectures of recent scholars, as we should'; among those recent scholars was William Camden, who had argued that 'they were called kings, but their realms ... were of such size that they might better be characterized as nobles.'[7] The *Analecton* retained lasting interest as an elegantly composed history of the early governance of *Anglobritannica*, available in Latin for an international audience; however, as a detailed and systematic guide to Selden's early representations of the ancient constitution, it took second place to *Jani Anglorum* even before reaching print.

Jani Anglorum Facies Altera (1610)

Selden's early works arose within a context of complex patterns of discourse on governance which stretched back at least as far as the debates of the French religious wars of the sixteenth century, continued with arguments over the succession to Queen Elizabeth I of England, and gained added urgency with quarrels over the proposed union of England and Scotland in the first parliament of James VI and I.[8] The influence of French models, especially those of the Huguenot constitutionalists, and of Continental humanist legal-historical traditions operated not only directly, but also indirectly – for example, in setting standards of historical veracity and in stimulating refutations of particular constitutional positions. As Pocock has suggested, constitutional theories which restrained monarchs not only gained supporters, but also engendered – in reaction – more rigid royalist positions.[9] Illustrating this particular point dialogically, Julian Franklin has demonstrated that Jean Bodin formulated his doctrine of sovereignty as a refutation of the writings of François Hotman, Theodore Beza, Philippe du Plessis-Mornay, and other so-called monarchomachs. With the emergence of a Protestant heir to the French throne, Huguenots became the absolutists and Catholics the constitutionalists. Historical accounts could just as easily stress the powers of kings as those of the clergy, nobles, or freemen, and natural-law arguments could support either absolute monarchs or those deriving power from the people. Various stages of the arguments presented by both sides soon spread across Europe and became entangled with local concerns and with other international traditions of discourse on governance. As Franklin, Quentin Skinner, Richard Tuck, and others have shown, a complex set of competing scripts on the distribution and exercise of power had entered print by the late sixteenth century.[10]

Although drawing upon Continental traditions of legal humanism and scepticism, Selden also wrote within a tradition of English common-law discourse and used it to address issues of great importance to governance. *Jani Anglorum* arose in good part as an answer to interpretations of the ancient constitution made earlier in 1610 by King James and members of the House of Commons during debates over such issues as the Crown's right to levy impositions without parliamentary approval and the interpretations of governance contained in *The Interpreter* by Dr John Cowell.[11] In a speech made to Parliament on 21 March 1610, James VI and I abandoned the application of his earlier writings on absolute monarchy to the governance of England, appropriated one tradition of common-law discourse, and fashioned a theory of 'constitutional monarchy created by kings.' A transitional sentence, which distinguished between the unlimited powers of 'Kings in their first originall' and the limited powers of 'setled Kings and Monarches, that doe at this time governe in civill Kingdomes,' marked the shift. Just as God had come to govern 'his people and Church within the bounds of his reveiled will,'

so in the first originall of Kings, whereof some had their beginning by Conquest, and some by election of the people, their wills at that time served for Law; Yet how soone Kingdomes began to be setled in civilitie and policie, then did Kings set down their minds by Lawes, which are properly made by the King onely; but at the rogation of the people, the Kings grant being obteined thereunto. And so the King became to be *Lex loquens* ['a speaking law'], after a sort, binding himselfe by a double oath to the observation of the fundamentall Lawes of his kingdom: *Tacitly*, as by being a King, and so bound to protect aswell the people, as the Lawes of the Kingdome; And *Expresely*, by his oath at his Coronation: So as every just King in a setled Kingdome is bound to observe that paction made to his people by his Lawes, in framing his government agreeable thereunto, according to that paction which God made with *Noe* after the deluge, *Here after Seed-time, and Harvest, Cold and Heate, Summer and Winter, and Day and Night shall not cease, so long as the earth remaines.* And therefore a King governing in a setled Kingdome leaves to be a King, and degenerates into a Tyrant, as sone as he leaves off to rule according to his Lawes.[12]

This passage worked the themes and imagery of earlier speeches and writings into a new representation of the constitution. The stress placed upon the covenants of God and kings, a covenant made by the ruler of the universe to restrict the exercise of his powers within the laws of grace and nature and the corresponding covenant made by kings with themselves and their successors to exercise their powers within the laws and institutions of the realm, changed the relationship of an individual king to the law in a 'civil kingdom.' Kings ruled by arbitrary will only at the start of societies; in making law and creating civil polities, they restricted their own freedom of action and that of their successors. Just as God chose to channel his grace through the church, so kings chose to exercise their power through courts of law and parliaments; like God, they could not go back on their word.

During debates over impositions on 28 June 1610, Thomas Hedley answered with his representation of 'constitutional monarchy governed by the common law' in a speech to the House of Commons. Drawing its wisdom 'strength, honor, and estimation' from the test of time, Hedley argued, the common law embraced both reason and immemorial custom: 'the common law is a reasonable usage, throughout the whole realm, approved time out of mind in the king's courts of record which have jurisdiction over the whole kingdom, to be good and profitable for the commonwealth.'[13] A subtle interplay of maxims and immemorial custom built continuity and flexibility into the laws. The rationality of maxims assured that 'no unreasonable usage will ever make a custom (pleadable in law),' while the ability to overrule judgments assured that the mere 'reason or opinion of 3 or 4 judges' could not make law.[14] The unwritten nature of the common law produced greater certainty than either statutes or civil law, which needed continual interpretation.[15] 'Confirmed by time,' immemorial custom far better upheld the liberties of freemen and 'establisheth kings and their regal power' than could any law created by 'the wisest lawgivers or parliament or council,' for such law was not 'reversible by that power that made it.'[16] The common law stood above and distributed power to both kings and parliaments. This meant that any attempt to replace the refined wisdom of generations with the fallible judgments of one parliament, as in the 'reforms' advocated by King James and Attorney General Bacon, threatened the very nature of the common law.[17]

Before the end of 1610, John Selden registered another major representation of the ancient constitution in his *Jani Anglorum*. Dedicated to the Earl of Salisbury, this short treatise of 133 pages of text in the original Latin marked a major event in the representation of England's ancient constitution as a 'mixed monarchy.'[18] Covering the laws of southern Britain from the days of the ancient Britons to the death of Henry II, it was the first substantial published history of the early English constitution. Nothing of similar scope would appear until after the outbreak of the English Civil War in 1642. As late as the 1680s, publishers found it profitable to reprint the Latin text and to produce an English translation. During the early seventeenth century, most competing historical interpretations of the ancient constitution remained relatively hidden in unpublished manuscripts; in the prefaces of legal treatises; in the speeches of judges, lawyers, officials, and members of Parliament; and in the dense accounts of massive histories.[19] The original probably appeared in Latin in order to attract attention in the international scholarly community and because of the profound debt that Selden felt to William Camden's *Britannia* (London, 1590 ff.). In contrast to King James and Thomas Hedley, Selden fashioned an image of the ancient constitution as a mixed government in which kings, clergy, nobles, and freemen had shared sovereignty from the earliest days.

The Ancient British Constitution

From a limited range of literary sources and the secondary accounts of leading scholars, Selden created a persuasive reconstruction of pre-Roman customs, one which left little room for any historical assertion that kings had initiated civil society or ordained the earliest laws in southern Britain. Debunking earlier historians who had accounted for the origins of government in Britain by the myth of a founding monarch, Selden disowned the derivation from Samothes (purportedly the son of Japhet, son of Noah) as totally lacking in evidence and dismissed the legend of the Brut (that Brutus and his sons, refugees from Troy, established the kingdoms of England, Scotland, and Ireland) with indirect derision: 'There are some both very Learned and very Judicious persons, who suspect that the story is patched up out of Bards Songs and Poetick Fictions taken upon trust, like *Talmudical* Traditions, on purpose to raise the *British* name out of *Trojan* ashes.'[20] Rejecting all earlier attempts to write the history of ancient Britain from the stories of medieval chroniclers (men who lived long after those events), the humanist scholar based his account upon contemporary, or as close as possible to contemporary, evidence. This meant a strong reliance upon the British portions of Julius Caesar and Tacitus. In addition, Selden followed the lead of such scholars as William Camden, who had argued that the institutions, customs, and laws of the early Britons resembled those of their contemporaries in Gaul to round out sketchy portions of their texts with details drawn by analogy from the better-documented descriptions of Gallic (and sometimes Germanic) society.[21] The evidence appeared to reveal a considerable dispersion of political power.

The pages of *Jani Anglorum* portrayed an ancient constitution in which sovereign power resided outside of the hands of any single monarch. Ruled by petty kings or queens, the Britons met together in assemblies ('per concilium') to discuss public affairs and to decide such crucial matters as foreign relations or war and peace. So small were these kingdoms that southern Britain seemed best understood as an aristocracy, rather than a monarchy:

The *Kings* were neither Monarchs of the whole Island of Anglo Britannia. For there were at the same time over the single County of *Kent* four Kings; to wit *Cyngotorix*, *Carvilius*, *Taximagulus*, and *Segonax*: and at the same rate in other Counties. Wherefore we have no reason to make any question, but that part wherein we live, now called *England*, was governed by several persons, and was subjected to an Aristocracy: according to what *Polydore Virgil*, *John Twine*, *David Powell* and others have informed us.[22]

British society gained its unity from a common law and religion, not from any single political authority. Religious leaders, the Druids, acted as the guardians of ritual, morals, and law. Led by one chief Druid who, elected or recognized by the others as the most learned, held this position for life, they trained their own successors in oral schools. Portrayed as judiciously combining the salient characteristics of Catholic priests and common-law judges, the Druids gathered at a central meeting-place to make, interpret, and preserve the laws for all of Britain: 'The Druids were wont to meet, to explain the Laws in being, and to make new ones as occasion required, as is most likely, in some certain place designed for that purpose; as now at this very time all matters of Law go to be decided at *Spire* in *Germany*, at *Westminster*-Hall in *England*, and *Paris* in *France*.'[23] Not written down, the laws of the ancient Britons perforce sprang from custom. They seem to have owed little to the will of a royal lawgiver. Selden's interpretation of the pre-Roman period left even less room for a powerful monarchy than had Hotman's account of ancient Gaul.[24]

This subtle section of *Jani Anglorum* must have caused rage among absolute-monarchists or even supporters of 'constitutional monarchy created by kings,' for Selden seems deliberately to have pre-empted any historical claim that kings founded the English portion of the ancient constitution of Britain.[25] With the Druids preserving and creating laws in their meetings, and assemblies of armed warriors (sometimes with their wives) deciding matters of war and peace, only a limited, mainly executive power remained to the pre-Roman British kings and queens. More like aristocrats than monarchs, they exercised a limited authority over areas smaller than an English county.[26] This historical account of the creation of a common law, however, still needed to show how England had become a single monarchy.

Despite the fact that the Romans first had brought southern Britain under one jurisdiction, Selden devoted few pages to Roman Britain. With Camden's *Britannia* and the works of such Roman historians as Tacitus readily available, this brevity hardly sprang from a scarcity of sources. Selden mentioned the expedition of Julius Caesar, explained the casting off of early Roman rule as a British revolt against the introduction of Latin laws, and recorded the Claudian conquest and the impact it produced, including the settlement of Romans in cities under their own law and government in various parts of Britain. The insight that 'the *Romans*, as in other places, so in *Britany*, made use of even Kings for their instruments of slavery' was not allowed to undermine the precedence of King Lucius, a British client of the Romans, as the first Christian king in the world.[27] However, since Selden skipped lightly over the claim that Emperor Constantine the Great was born in Britain of a mother who was a British princess, one suspects that he wished to avoid even the smallest opportunity for a Roman Imperial entry into the ancient constitution.[28] Any impact of Roman upon common law came long after the ancient Romans left Britain. Roman rule, then, left little constitutional legacy in England. In profound contrast stood the enduring character of Saxon law and institutions.

The Anglo-Saxon Constitution

Monarchy and law arrived with the Saxon invasion and fashioned the fundamental distribution of powers and privileges within the English monarchy – what Selden would later call a 'state' – an ancient constitution which survived the buffeting of the Norman Conquest and continued to Selden's own day. Although seven Saxon kingdoms existed in the early days, only one king had held a recognized position of suzerainty: 'The *King* was alwayes one amongst the *Heptarchs* or seven Rulers, who was accounted (I have *Beda* to vouch it) the *Monarch of all England*.'[29] Unlike ancient Britain, Saxon England possessed a true monarchy. Saxon kings proclaimed law with the advice of the leading men of the realm, as seen in the preamble to the laws of King Ine: '*I Ina by the grace of God King of the West-Saxons, by the advice and order of Kenred my Father, and of Hedda and Erconwald my Bishops, and all of my Aldermen* ['ealdor mannum' in Anglo-Saxon and 'Aldermannorum' in Latin], *and of the Elders and Wise Men of my people, do command*, &c.'[30] Similar phrases occurred frequently in other laws. On the basis of this and other evidence, Selden concluded that such consultation took place within a system of assemblies, that the Germanic *wapentakes* described by Tacitus became the *witans* of the Anglo-Saxons and that these, in turn, became parliaments: 'These Assemblies were termed by the *Saxons*, Wiδδena ʒemoδeʒ, i.e. Meetings of the Wise Men, and ꟿicil ʒinoδeʒ, i.e. the Great Assemblies. At length we borrowed of the *French* the name of *Parliaments*, which before the time of *Henry* the First, Polydore Virgil sayes, were very rarely held. An usage, that not without good reason seems to have come from the ancient *Germans*.'[31] In addition to declaring or making the law, such bodies chose those who enforced the law locally. ' "There are also chosen at the same Councils or Meetings, chief persons (as Justices) to administer Law in the several Villages and Hamlets. Each of those have a hundred Associates out of the Commonalty for their Counsel and Authority." '[32] The precedent of selecting local officials in assemblies would later form part of the justification for parliamentary approval of royal ministers (in at least two pamphlets in 1642) and for the Leveller program of local election of such officials as the justices of the peace, but Selden – apparently not interested in such aims in 1610 – employed it merely to indicate the antiquity of hundreds.[33] However, it also helped to establish the crucial pattern that the king-in-parliament had exercised a supreme governing authority in the ancient constitution since the earliest days of the English monarchy.

In *Jani Anglorum*, Selden represented the constitution within the context of a compact, detailed, documented description of Saxon society. Reaping the benefits of the pioneering generation of Anglo-Saxon scholarship, he could draw upon collected manuscript versions or printed editions of the Saxon laws and of such early historians as Bede, Ingulf of Croyland (whom he thought had lived in the time of William the Conqueror), and William of Malmesbury.[34] These provided a great deal of evidence. Organized into the four ranks of nobles, freemen, freedmen, and slaves, the Saxons followed many customs that remained 'still in use with the *English*' or at least 'lawful with us down to our Grandfathers time.'[35] Saxon aristocrats received the grant of arms in a special ceremony as young men ('the right ancient pattern of dubbing *Knights*'), balanced portion and jointure in marriage agreements ('contrary to what the *Roman* Law saith'), and held their lands by military tenure ('knight's fees,' but not the 'more modern form,' derived from 'the *Huns* and *Lombards*,' that came in with the Norman kings).[36] The lower orders rented their farms from lords in return for payments in kind. Lands passed to all of one's children by succession, not by will.[37] In such practices, the reader could discern the foundations of English medieval and early modern society. The more exotic extirpation of crime, especially murder, by the payment of 'Head-mony' ('wergild') or 'a certain number of some head of Cattle' made to 'the whole Family of the murdered Person' and the use of trial by ordeal struck just those notes of discontinuity which underlined the continuity of other customs and institutions.[38] Indeed, such central and local offices as king, lord high constable, chancellor, treasurer, deputy lieutenants ('vicedomini'), justices ('justiciarios'), and sheriffs ('vicecomites') originated under the Saxons.[39] Society and government worked together in many subtle ways. The warrior aristocrats who held their lands on military tenure also filled local offices and sat in the assemblies. This symbiotic fit between social and political patterns made for a firm but flexible sharing of powers, one continually adjusting to new circumstances by dropping old and adding new laws. The ancient constitution could accommodate considerable change without endangering its fundamental shape.

Two major challenges to the Saxon system, the victory of Christianity and the near triumph of the Vikings, posed a weighty challenge to continuity. The first of these, the conversion of the Saxons and its effects, received considerable direct and indirect attention in *Jani Anglorum*. Christian priests transformed much more than the worship and ethics of the Saxons. Quoting from Bede, Selden credited King Ethelbert with the reintroduction of Christianity and explained that '"he did also with the advice of wise men, appoint for his peoples use the orders of their proceedings at Law, according to the example of the *Romans*. Which having been written in the *English* tongue (says he [Bede]) are hitherto, or at this time kept and observed by them."'[40] From the time of their conversion, then, Saxon kings and their advisers drew upon foreign precedents to integrate the new religion into their old law. The penalties imposed required the multiple restoration of goods robbed from church and churchmen and, with payment in coin substituted for that in kind, continued in effect for centuries. Drawing upon his comparative study of law codes, Selden showed how stability over time sprang from one king borrowing from the laws of another. 'In the Laws of some that came after him, as those of King *Alured* [Alfred] (who cull'd out of *Ethel-*

bert's Acts to make his own) and those of King *Athelstan*, Thieves make satisfaction with mony ...'[41] The conversion of the Saxons to Christianity, however, not only created new laws, but also provided a whole new group of educated advisers. As valued counsellors on moral and legal matters, Christian priests became integrated into royal governance. They sat with sheriffs to hear cases in the shire courts and counselled kings on the codification of law.[42] Without any real sense of disruption, Saxon law and society assimilated the new religion. Could it as easily handle pagan invaders?

The Viking invasions posed a serious problem, for the Danes long held sway over large portions of England, and at least one Danish king, Cnut, ruled over all of the kingdom. In his history of Great Britain, John Speed ranked the Danish with the Saxon and Norman invasions in importance, while both Camden and Arthur Hall also had dealt seriously with the Danes.[43] Selden solved the problem largely by ignoring it. For example, he did not relate King Alfred's creation of shires, hundreds, and tithings to the struggle against Viking invaders, nor did he point out that the kings of Wessex unified England by reconquering the Danelaw.[44] The only concession came in several references to the laws of King Cnut, whom Selden portrayed as preserving the ancient constitution by confirming the laws of earlier Saxon kings and passing them on intact to his successor:

There are a great many Laws of King *Ina*, *Alfred*, *Edward*, *Athelstan*, *Edmund*, *Edgar*, *Ethelred*, and *Knute*, the *Dane*, written in the *Saxon* language which have lasted till these very times. 'For King *Knute* gave order ('tis *William* of *Malmesbury* speaks) that all the Laws which had been made by former Kings, and especially by his Predecessor *Ethelred*, should under pain of his displeasure and a Fine, be constantly observed; For the keeping of which, even now in the time of those who are called the *Good*, people swear in the name of King *Edward*; not that he appointed them, but that he observed them.' The Laws of *Edward*, who for his piety has the sirname of *Confessor*, are in Readers hands. These of the *Confessor* were in *Latin*: those others of *Knute* were not long since put into *Latin* by *William Lambard*, a learned man, and one very well vers'd in Antiquity ...[45]

Selden's case for continuity, while buttressed by the authority of early historians such as William of Malmesbury, rested primarily upon his analysis of the Anglo-Saxon laws, expecially those in Lambarde's collection. From these, came the evidence which revealed both the interpenetation of Saxon law, religion, and social custom and the observation that 'a greate many laws ... written in the Saxon language ... have lasted till these very times.' The framework of the Saxon constitution – with its royal rule and consultation with clergy, nobles, and freemen – proved strong and flexible enough to absorb one group of foreign invaders and the potentially disruptive change of religion. The greatest challenge came neither from Rome nor from Denmark, however, but from Normandy.

The Norman Influence

The undeniable reality of the Norman Conquest posed more of an obstacle for Selden than it had for Hedley, who saw it as a break in the continuity of the constitution, but argued that Magna Carta represented 'a restoring or comfirming of the ancient laws and liberties of the kingdom, which by the Conquest before had been much impeached or obscured,' or for Coke, who minimized the discontinuity involved.[46] Ignoring the canons of humanist legal-historical scholars, Coke overcame the problem by accepting at face value the pre-Norman origins of the *Mirror of Justices* and the claim of the *Modus Tenendi Parliamentorum* to describe parliamentary procedure as it existed in the days of Edward the Confessor. Since the *Modus* actually gave a reasonable account of the parliaments of the fourteenth century, it deftly bridged the gap between the Saxon and the early-seventeenth-century constitution.[47] Rejecting the *Modus* as a source for Saxon assemblies and pushing aside the *Mirror*, Selden faced the issue of a fundamental break at the conquest much more squarely than had the famous attorney general and chief justice.[48]

Selden opened his discussion of the Normans by drawing upon such medieval historians as the early-twelfth-century William of Malmesbury, the late-twelfth-century Roger of Hoveden, the early-thirteenth-century Matthew Paris, and the fourteenth-century forgery that claimed to be the eleventh-century Ingulf of Croyland, and upon an analysis of the laws contained in Lambarde's *Archaionomia* to portray Duke William's invasion as a real conquest.[49]

Upon pretence of a double Right, both that of Blood (inasmuch as *Emme* the Mother of *Edward* the *Confessor* was Daughter to *Richard* the first Duke of the *Normans*) and withal that of Adoption, having in Battel worsted *Harald* the Son of *Godwin* Earl of *Kent*, *William* Duke of *Nor-*

mandy obtain'd a large Inheritance and took possession of the Royal Government over all *England*.

'After his Inauguration he liberally bestowed the Lands and Estates of the *English* upon his fellow-soldiers; that little which remained (so saith *Matthew Paris*) he put under the yoke of perpetuall servitude.' Upon which account, some while since the coming of the *Normans*, there was not in *England* except the King himself, any one who held their Land by right of *Free-hold* (as they term it), since in sooth one may well call all others to a man only Lords in trust of what they had, as those who by swearing fealty and doing homage did perpetually own and acknowledge a Superior Lord, of whom they held and by whom they were invested into their Estates.[50]

Clearly this change included more than the substitution of one set of lords for another; it involved a significant shift in the nature of lordship and a major modification of the system of landholding. The cautiously sceptical language echoed that of Tacitus. By branding the attempt of William to legitimate his claim to the English throne as a pretense ('obtenso'), Selden appeared to suggest that the Duke of Normandy extended his rule over England by little more right than mere force.

Aware of the arguments over the origins of feudal tenure presented by members of the French historical school of legal studies, Selden stood on the brink of applying these insights to England by arguing that the feudal law arrived with the Conqueror.[51] Not only did William I introduce new laws and customs, such as the curfew (fires out at a particular time signalled by the ringing of a bell), the authentication of charters and other documents with a seal, the protection of deer and boars for royal hunting, the creation of separate church courts, and the substitution of French for English in all legal proceedings, he employed old procedures and laws in new ways.[52] Matthew Paris reported that William I had extended military tenure to church lands, '"enrolling every Bishoprick and Abbacy according to his pleasure, how many Souldiers he would have each of them find him and his successors in time of Hostility or War."'[53] Gervase of Tilbury recorded that the Conqueror decided which English laws to keep and which to reject or modify: '"Some of these *English* Laws he disliked and laid aside; others he approved of and added to them some from beyond the Sea out of *Neustria* (he means *Normandy* ...) such of them as seemed most effectual for the preserving of the Kingdom's peace."'[54] Such passages suggested that William I held, if only for a moment, an absolute power at the time of the Conquest.

Just as Selden appeared to have argued in favour of a Norman origin for English feudal institutions and an arbitrary foundation for the post-Saxon English monarchy, however, he drew back from unequivocal support for such an interpretation. In part, this derived from his humanist historical method. The evidence which portrayed William I as an absolute conqueror came from the testimony of historians who themselves lived more than a century later. Other evidence purportedly closer to the event – such as the laws of Kings Cnut, Edward the Confessor, and William the Conqueror as printed by Lambarde – pointed to a less catastrophic view of the Conquest than that presented by Matthew Paris and Gervase of Tilbury. Hence, philological concerns led Selden to downplay the interpretation put forward by these medieval historians:

Now this is no rare thing among Writers for them to devise that *William* the Conqueror brought in as it were a clear, new face of Laws to all intents and purposes. 'Tis true, this must be acknowledged, that he did make some new ones (part whereof you may see in *Lambard's Archaeonomia* and part of them here subjoyned), but so however that they take their denomination from the *English*, rather than from the *Normans*; although one may truly say, according to what Lawyers dispute, that the *English* Empire and Government was overthrown by him.[55]

Although Anglo-Saxon kings and lords no longer ruled England, the case for a sharp break remained ambiguous, especially since the laws of William the Conqueror appeared to differ little from those of Cnut or Edward the Confessor. Indeed, a careful comparison of Norman offices of state and early titles of honour with those of the Saxons, one that noted that earldoms became hereditary only after the Conquest, led to the conclusion stated in the last sentence of *Jani Anglorum*: 'As to doing Justice, as in all other Cases, and managing of Publick Affairs, the *Normans* had almost the same names and Titles of Officers and Offices as the *Saxons* had.'[56] Not much room for major innovation here! The Saxon constitution appeared to have triumphed over the Norman Conqueror and to have imposed limits to his actions.

The final words of *Jani Anglorum*, however, did not contain Selden's last word on the subject, not even in 1610. A long explanatory passage in the preface attempted to resolve a number of seeming contradictions while keeping the ambiguities in his treatment of the

Norman Conquest. The result neatly, if somewhat cynically, synthesized conquest and custom into one coherent interpretation:

But however to refer the original of our *English* Laws to that Conquest (as some make bold to do) is a huge mistake; forasmuch as they are of a far more ancient Date. For it is a remark amongst Statesmen, That new acquired Empires do run some hazard by attempting to make new Laws; and the *Norman* did warily provide against this danger, by bestowing ['impertiuit'] upon the yielding conquered Nation the requital of their ancient Law, a requital, I say, but more, as it should seem for shew than use; and rather to curry favour with the people at the present, than in good deed for the advantage of the *English* name ... For the times on this side the *Normans* entrance are so full of new Laws, especially such as belong to the right of Tenancy and Vassalage, though other Laws have been carefully enough kept up from the time of the *Saxons* and perhaps from an earlier date.[57]

In a rare Machiavellian moment marked by a marginal note to the *Prince* and the *Discourses*, Selden solved the problem of combining evidence for the continuity of Anglo-Saxon laws and institutions with the equally compelling evidence that Continental feudal practices entered England only with the Normans by arguing that William I brought in many new laws, especially those governing military tenure, but that he also allowed the English, if more 'for shew than for use,' to retain many of their ancient customs. Little confirmation or covenant here, the Conqueror bestowed 'the requital of their ancient Law' upon the conquered as a matter of grace. This tentative theme of a major break at the Conquest so ambiguously announced in the preface found less than persuasive support in the detailed discussion of the text; rather, it awaited Selden's future publications.[58] Overall, in *Jani Anglorum*, William I, while often acting for somewhat expedient reasons, paradoxically preserved not only a large number of Saxon laws, but the fundamental shape and character of the Saxon constitution.

The Ancient Constitution Modified

During the following centuries, the successors of William I continued both to cherish and to modify the ancient constitution, Feudal laws blended with Saxon customs to produce a potent, vital polity. In *Jani Anglorum*, Selden detailed the development of this pattern up to the death of Henry II.[59] At times, the English Janus focused on the past to explain the historical present. For example, Henry I, while bringing in such Norman customs as the payment of a feudal aid upon the marriage of the oldest daughter of one's lord, even more firmly strengthened the Saxon elements in the constitution by restoring the coinage and reaffirming the laws (as modified by the Conqueror) of Edward the Confessor.[60] Even Henry I's innovation of the feudal service of relief (a payment made to one's lord at the succession of an heir to land held on military tenure) appeared to stem from the Saxon custom of heriot (a payment of weapons, armour, and one or more horses made to one's lord upon the death of a thegn who held land on military tenure) and, thus, to represent the modified restoration of an old law, not the creation of a new one.[61]

At other times, bringing in evidence from future centuries afforded a clearer view of constitutional development. For example, discussion of the problem of whether King Stephen 'banished' the Roman civil law or the Roman canon law from England posed the puzzle of relating the English common law to other legal systems. Although Selden would discuss this question at great length in later works, he had begun to work out an answer. After explaining that John of Salisbury's remark that '"the *Roman* Laws were banisht the Realm"' under Stephen applied to 'the Decrees of the Popes' (that is, to canon law), he argued that a definitive statement on 'the Laws of the Empire' followed at a much later date.[62] The case brought forth against the favourites of Richard II, recorded in the *Rotuli Parliamentorum*, provided the crucial evidence:

... They being intrusted with the management of the Kingdom, by soothing up the easie and youthful temper of the King, did assist one another for their own private interest, more than the publick ['privatem rem prae publicâ'], well near to the ruine and overthrow of the Government itself; the Common Lawyers and Civilians are consulted with, about the form of drawing up the Charge; which they answer all as one man, was not agreeable to the rule of the Laws. But the Barons of Parliament reply, That they would be tyed up to no rules, nor be led by the punctilioes of the *Roman* Law, but would by their own authority pass judgement ... *inasmuch as the realm of* England *was not before this time, nor in the intention of our said Lord the King and Lords of Parliament ever shall be ruled or governed by the Civil Law.* And hereupon the persons impleaded are sentenced to be a banished.[63]

This passage showed how the common law towered over its potential rivals within the realm and upheld the sovereign place of the king-in-parliament within the constitution. With the discussion of the private 'interest' of the courtiers, it echoed Tacitean tones. The hedge against external legal systems also linked Selden's mixed monarchy with the model of 'constitutional monarchy governed by the common law.'

Firmly rooted in the English antiquary and common-law traditions, *Jani Anglorum* patiently presented a new historical account of English legal customs. Pieces of the mosaic lay scattered elsewhere, for example, in Camden's *Britannia* and in the unpublished papers of the Society of Antiquaries, but Selden carefully assembled the bits of evidence into a pattern which varied considerably in perspective and interpretation from the rival versions advocated by contemporaries. Selden eschewed the embarrassing anachronism of some common-law colleagues, the uncomfortably unmixed sovereignty of the absolutists, and the unfailing initiative of monarchs accorded by 'constitutional monarchy created by kings.'

Selden's Method

Laying aside the notion of immemoriality as a major tool of analysis, Selden absorbed Continental, humanist, philological historical methods and applied them to English materials. Even the earliest works contained enough Continental learning and a sufficient selection of primary evidence to display the author's mastery of a critical apparatus and a comparative point of view. Paying careful attention to chronology, comparing different sources for the same event, and noting both the form and the content of documents, Selden built his account as much as possible from carefully winnowed contemporary evidence. To establish their authenticity, he compared the documents under analysis with other documents from the same era. For example, a charter purporting to bear the seal of King Arthur had to be a forgery because the earliest sealed documents in England came from the Norman period; Saxons had used crosses, not seals, to authenticate their charters.[64] As we shall see, Selden would later call this comparative method, derived from humanist philologists, 'synchronisme.' His sceptical, contextual approach contrasted with Coke's confident, closely argued lawyer's brief. It exhibited a different, more sophisticated, historical sensibility than that which characterized Coke's version of the common-law mind.

Instead of projecting the present back into the past, Selden made a challenging shift in perspective which significantly shaped his perception and presentation of interpretations and evidence. Starting with the most ancient point recoverable from reliable sources, his representation moved forward. This critical procedure not only alerted him to the vast differences between his own society and those which had existed in earlier times, but also helped him to perceive history as a series of discrete periods, each with its own appropriate social, religious, political, and legal practices. Hence, *Jani Anglorum* focused on three separate phases of historical development, the ancient British, Saxon, and Norman. Selden showed how changes in one aspect of a society, such as religion, led to numerous adjustments elsewhere; for example, how the introduction of Christianity seriously restructured Saxon society by bringing in a new set of literate royal advisers. Such significant shifts as language, the inheritability of social status and political power, and the form of military tenure marked the change from one cultural complex to another. Within a given era, the constitution often evolved through 'the gradual accretion of new laws and the loss of old ones'; however, from time to time, it also made rapid adjustments.[65] Selden's relatively refined historical awareness allowed him to build into this representation of the English constitution both a toughness that contributed to continuity and a flexibility that helped to accommodate alterations. This constituted a superlative accomplishment.

Throughout the millennium of history surveyed in *Jani Anglorum*, England had lived under a polity in which various social orders shared sovereignty, a mixed aristocracy under the ancient Britons, a mixed monarchy under the Saxons and Normans. Here lay the foundation for Selden's historical subversion of rival representations. From the days of the Druids onward, laws came from assemblies. The Ოicil ɣinoδeɣ of the Saxons translated into the parliaments of the Normans, which, in turn, gradually evolved into the parliaments of the early seventeenth century. Few of the most ancient laws remained in force, but the fundamental configuration of shared power had survived. Selden summed up his historical analysis in an arresting image of the parliaments of his own day: 'These Assemblies do now sit in great State, which with a wonderful harmony of the Three Estates, the *King*, the *Lords*, and the *Commons*, or Deputies of

the People ['Trium Ordinum, Regis, Magnatum, remque plebis pro-
curantium harmoniâ'], are joined together to a most firm security of
the publick ...'[66] This image refurbished the medieval ideal of the
three estates by substituting the monarch for the clergy as the first
estate. In addition, it included that Polybian or Aristotelian version
of mixed polity earlier applied to the English constitution by John
Aylmer.[67] The fusion of these two traditions in an extended historical account established the foundation for a practical and powerful
theory of mixed monarchy.

Competing Common-Law Voices

In 1610, King James VI and I, Thomas Hedley, and John Selden gave
public voice to three rival representations of the ancient constitution, James articulating that of a 'constitutional monarchy created by
kings,' Hedley that of a 'constitutional monarchy governed by the
common law,' and Selden that of a 'mixed monarchy' in which kings,
nobles, clergy, and representatives of freemen shared power from the
formation of the society. The speech by James not only received a
hearing in Parliament, but rapidly appeared in print in three editions;
that by Hedley remained in manuscript; while Selden's book received
a single printing.[68] As well as providing competing models for understanding the laws, statutes, and legal writings from the past, these
interpretations also supported divergent distributions of power in the
present, with 'constitutional monarchy created by kings' empower-
ing creative initiatives for the Crown, 'mixed monarchy' for parliaments, and 'constitutional monarchy governed by the common law'
for judges and juries. Each representation carried practical implications for contemporary understanding of the emergency powers of
the Crown, the liberties of the people, and the governance of the
realm.[69] The 'Jacobean consensus' did map out which political discourse applied to which issues and audiences, as Glenn Burgess has
argued, but it did not include a consensus on historical representations of the exercise of governance in England, including the history
of the common law.[70] As with other voices on matters of pressing
concern, the representations articulated in 1610 by James VI and I,
Thomas Hedley, and John Selden did not remain static, but provided
the closure which made possible competing traditions of constitutional discourse in the decades that followed.

Although opening his scholarly career in 1610, Selden established his solid scholarly reputation as a result of treatises published in the following decade. Four of these works, his notes to Michael Drayton's *Poly-Olbion* (London, [1612]), the first edition of *Titles of Honor* (London, 1614), his annotated critical edition of Sir John Fortescue's *De Laudibus Legum Angliæ* (London, 1616), and his brilliantly contentious *Historie of Tithes* (London, 1618), illustrate a maturing erudition, especially a growing grasp of Continental scholarship and English manuscript evidence. While none of these writings presented a systematic account of the ancient constitution, all modified or spelled out some of the interpretations of *Jani Anglorum*. In addition, *Titles of Honor* contained a brief exposition of the feudal law and its relationship to England. Each of these works displayed Selden's increasingly sophisticated view of politics and understanding of history.

Selden on Michael Drayton's *Poly-Olbion* (1612)

The earliest treatise, his 'illustrations' of Michael Drayton's *Poly-Olbion*, followed an unusual format as annotations to a scholarly, topographical, historical poem. Drayton, more than twenty years the senior of and much better known than his young friend, gave Selden an opportunity to display his learning. In the text of the poem, Drayton drew on the traditional British history for his view of the early Britons and on a variety of histories for later periods. Clearly, the poet had done a good deal of reading, especially of secondary works, and wrote with some authority. In the notes, Selden added relevant illustrative material turned up by recent research, including portions of *Jani Anglorum* now translated into English, and evaluated Drayton's evidence critically, where 'upon weighing of the Reporters credit, Comparison with more perswading authority, and *Synchronisme* (the best Touch-stone in this kind of Triall) I leave note of Suspicion, or adde conjecturall Amendment.'[71] By 'synchronisme' Selden meant making sure that the source was as closely contemporaneous as possible to the events that it purported to detail and that fit together with other authenticated contemporary sources. Openly avowing an active role for the historian, he commented, 'after *Explanation*, I oft adventure on *Examination*, and *Censure*.'[72] It took a great deal of courage for Drayton to submit his poem to such scrutiny. The whole work formed a lovely baroque conceit, with poet and historian, medievalist and humanist antiquary, engaged in friendly discourse and debate.

To support the interpretation that the Trojan Brutus and his sons had founded the monarchies of Britain, the voice of the wandering river Wye launched a 'bitter' attack on 'those fooles that all Antiquitie defame, / Because they have found out, some credulous Ages layd / Slight fictions with the truth,' and further lashed out against scholars who preferred the account of ancient society offered by Julius Caesar: 'Unskilfull of our tongue but by Interpreter, / Hee nothing had of ours which our great Bards did sing, / Except some few poore words,' a skimpy outside source in comparison with the epics of the Welsh poets.[73] Of course, Drayton sang on behalf of Wales and the muse of poets in this section. Still, Selden took embellishments and anachronisms as signs that the sources containing them needed the most careful sifting. 'And indeed my Jealousie hath oft vext me with particular inquisition of whatsoever occurrs, bearing not a marke of most apparant Truth, ever since I found so intollerable Antichronismes, incredible reports, and *Bardish* impostures, as well from Ignorance as assum'd liberty of Invention in some of our Ancients; and red also such palpable Fauxeties, of our Nation, thrust into the World by Later Time ...'[74] In part, this represented the historian's rather heavy-handed attempt to humour the poet, but below the surface lay a serious point.

On the basis of synchronism, Selden rejected the legend of the Brut and accepted Caesar as the earliest reliable, detailed source for the history of the British Isles. Although the British monarchy founded by Brutus had supposedly lasted from the time when Samuel was judge of Israel until 54 B.C., when Caesar invaded Britain, the earliest reports of its history came from a much later date. 'How then are they, which pretend Chronologies of that Age without any Fragment of Authors before *Gildas*, *Taliessin* and *Nennius* (the eldest of which was since D. [500] of *Christ*) to be credited?'[75] Clearly not much, especially when earlier sources existed. The sceptical current of much late-sixteenth- and early-seventeenth-century criticism, moderately applied, strongly informed Selden's approach to historical evidence. Although some Greek and Roman writers had discussed the ancient Britons, 'untill *Cæsar's* Commentaries, no piece of description was known, that is now left to posterity. For the time therefore preceding *Cæsar*, I dare trust none, but with Others adhere to *Conjecture*.'[76] As the earliest surviving eyewitness account of British society, then, Caesar took precedence for Selden. For the Roman, Saxon, and Norman eras as well, Selden also listed the historians upon whom he most relied and added the general rule that 'in all, I beleeve him most which freest from *Affection* and *Hate* (causes of corruption) might best know, and hath, with most likely assertion, delivered his report.' [77] Taken together, these remarks and his stress upon philology – all appearing in Selden's portion of the preface – added up to a brief but relatively comprehensive explication of his historical method: the application of scepticism, a careful comparison of all of the available evidence for a particular event, a reliance as much as possible upon evidence contemporary with the events under consideration, and a trust of moderate above highly partisan accounts. Of course, Selden had employed this humanist form of source criticism in his earlier works, but it seems to have taken the challenge of Drayton's arguments to entice such an explicit articulation of it into print.

While the notes to *Poly-Olbion* contained coherent expressions of Selden's historical method, they dealt in a less systematic manner with the ancient constitution. After all, he 'illustrated' the poem written by Drayton; naturally, the poem dictated the order and scope of the notes. Coming shortly after his earlier works, these comments largely reflected the contents of the earlier treatises. Indeed, Selden advertised *Jani Anglorum* in the preface and drew upon it for much of his evidence, sometimes lifting whole passages, now translated into English, for this purpose.[78] Still, these 'illustrations' brought Selden's scholarship and constitutional interpretation to a wider public. In addition, material not in *Jani Anglorum* appeared in several sections. For example, Selden had read the sources on the ancient Britons more carefully and included much more information on the Druids; he also used coins from before the Roman Conquest to correct Caesar's account of British customs.[79] The sections on Saxon England drew upon the *Analecton* to include more material on the Vikings and to discuss at greater length the laws of King Cnut, compared here with those of King William to illustrate the continuity of Saxon law over the Conquest.[80]

While retaining some of the ambiguities of his earlier interpretation, Selden moved closer to portraying William I as a conqueror who held supreme power and who granted law to his new English subjects as a matter of grace. Since Drayton repeatedly stressed the traumatic nature of the Conquest, one might have expected Selden to lean in the opposite direction, if only to keep up the dialogue. Instead, a slightly expanded translation of one of the more decisive passages of

Jani Anglorum upheld the idea of a real conquest in one portion of the illustrations.[81] In another place, the will drawn up by the Conqueror appeared to support the contention that William obtained England by right of military might. Discussing this document and a court case cited by Camden in which the tenurial claim of a Saxon dating from before the Conquest was upheld against a grant of the same manor made by the Conqueror to a Norman after the Conquest, Selden concluded:

But, (admit this case as you please, or any cause of right beside his sword), It is plaine that his will and imperious affection (mov'd by their rebellions which had stood for the sworne *Harold*) dispos'd all things as a Conqueror: Upon observation of his subjection of all Lands to tenures, his change of Lawes, disinheriting the English, and such other reported (which could be but where the profitable Dominion, as the Civillians call it, was universally acquired into the Prince's hand) and in reading the disgracefull account then made of the English name, it will be manifest.[82]

Despite its complicated structure, this passage clearly supported the contention that William ruled England, if only for a short time, by his arbitrary will. It also contained the germ of an interpretation that he introduced the feudal law into England at the Conquest. Not all of the notes reported so fundamental a break, however. Remnants of the earlier stress upon continuity remained in the clearly stated judgment that the laws of the Conqueror and the Confessor essentially repeated the code created by King Cnut out of the laws of Mercia, Wessex, and the Danelaw.[83] Despite a greater stress on the changes brought in by the Conquest, then, Selden's account retained some of the earlier tensions.

Because Drayton's poem extended well into the history of medieval England and Wales, Selden took the opportunity to move his representation of the ancient constitution up to the reign of Edward I. A substantial section on the struggle for Magna Carta spelled out some of the faults of King John, but blamed most of the troubles of his reign upon the 'undigestable incentives of the Clergy with traiterous confidence striking at his Crown, and in such sort, as humanity must have exceeded itselfe, to have indured it with any mixture of patience.'[84] Accordingly, Archbishop Stephen Langton stirred up 'the hearts of the Barons against *John*, by producing the old Charter of liberties granted by *Henry* I, comprehending an instauration of St

Edwards lawes, as they were amended by the Conqueror, and provoking them to challenge observation thereof as an absolute dutie to subjects of a free State.'[85] This led to the mustering of armies and the granting by King John in 1215 of 'two Charters; the one, of Liberties generall, the other of the Forest: both of which were not very different from our *Graund Charter* [and that] of the *Forrest*.'[86] All seemed lost, however, for the clerics betrayed the Barons by allying with John and persuading the Pope to issue a bull against both charters. The death of the king in 1216 ended this attempted evasion and brought to power a moderate regency for his young son, Henry III.

In the ninth year of his reign, Henry III confirmed the charters and sent copies into every county in England. While Selden did not explicate the contents in detail, he did point out that the charters issued by Henry III differed from those of John in several ways, including the treatment of the Jews and the addition of the commons to those who needed to consent to the levying of tallages and other duties. Among 'the Petitions, and Grievances of the Commons at the time of his instauration of this Charter to them, one was thus consented to'; the chapter of Magna Carta opening – '*Nullum Tallagium vel Auxilium*' – had added to it the words '*aliorum liberorum hominum*.' Still, these charters of liberties remained uncertain during the long reign of Henry III. For example, he withdrew that of the forest at the Oxford Parliament. As a result, these 'controverted Charters had not their setled suretie untill Edward I. Since whom they have been more than XXX. times, in Parliament confirmed.'[87] This account, while not fully discussing the contents of Magna Carta, linked its provisions to the laws of the Saxons and to the liberties of free Englishmen.

By bringing forward Selden's earlier history of the common law to the restoration of English liberties in Magna Carta, these notes integrated much of historical and constitutional value into an awkward format; 'teaching primarily by example,' Selden showed the reader 'how to do good history' and also how to appreciate the delights of poetry.[88] In addition, the preface took a step towards spelling out Selden's historical method in explicit terms. Although the representation of the Norman Conquest offered in the preface seemed to contradict the continuity stressed elsewhere in the 'illustrations,' it pushed a bit further that idea of a real conquest expressed in the introduction of *Jani Anglorum* and prepared the way for Selden's radical reassessment of the relationship of the feudal law to the ancient constitution published just two years later. In addition, Selden's partnership with Drayton both raised the younger man's scholarly prestige and revealed to him the market in patronage and sales for works published in English.

Titles of Honor (1614)

By far the most ambitious of his earliest works in terms of its subject-matter and the breadth of its visible scholarship, *Titles of Honor* provided an analytic historical account of current titles such as King, Duke, Count, Baron, and Knight. Selden dedicated this treatise, first to his 'most beloved Friend and *Chamberfellow*, M. *Edward Heyward*,' the gentleman with whom he shared his chambers at the Inner Temple, and second to 'that singular Glory of our Nation, and Light of *Britain*, M. Camden Clarenceulx,' the famous antiquary William Camden.[89] Although concentrating upon western Europe, the work also included special chapters on '*The beginning of* Feuds' and 'Turkish *dignities*' and touched upon many other related problems.[90] Selden claimed: '*I vent to you nothing quoted at second hand, but ever lov'd the Fountain, and, when I could come at it, usd that Medium only, which would not at all, or least, decieve by Refraction.*' In cases where he could not consult the primary sources, he quoted from reliable secondary works and referenced them with marginal notes: '*But where ever I was driven to take up on other mens credits, I acknowledged it.*' In matters of '*Storie* [history] and *Philologie*,' he passed over the '*old* Civilians (*I mean the elder* Doctors *and* Commentators)' – such as Bartolo di Sassoferrato (Bartolus) and Baldus – and drew strongly upon such moderns as '*the most learned* Budé, Alciat, Hotoman, Cuias, Wesenbeck, Brisson, *the* Gentiles, *and some few more of this Age.*'[91] The '*few more*' included such well-known scholars as Jean Bodin, William Camden, Issac Casaubon, Justus Lipsius, Charles L'Oyseau, and Joseph-Juste Scaliger. The marginal notes read like a roll-call of ancient, medieval, and contemporary luminaries, including the leading English and Continental antiquaries of the late-sixteenth and early-seventeenth centuries; the 'Table of Authors' at the back provided a bibliographical index to citations from classical and medieval sources, while the general index, and indices of words in 'Eastern Tongues,' Greek, and topics on the English common law, made the scholarship of the treatise even more accessible.[92] Evidence of cosmopolitan learning abounded throughout this book.

The modernity of *Titles of Honor* emerged in its detached tone and its refusal to deal with such chivalric romances as King Arthur and the Knights of the Round Table or even such beloved topics as the numerous European honorary orders of knighthood, such as the Order of the Golden Fleece and the Order of the Holy Spirit.[93] Selden's strongly historical account did not savour of heralds and kings of arms. However, any reader who wishes to grasp the difference between even the most scholarly of early-modern versus modern historical writing need only turn to the preface of *Titles of Honor*, a twenty-page *Wunderkammer* of miscellaneous learning. It explained that the following account '*extended from the* Highest title *to* Gentrie, *exclusively,*' defined the gentry as the 'Civill Nobility,' those who held '*the first degree above the Multitude ... either by* aquisition *from the Prince ... or by* Discent *from Noble Ancestors,*' and added that even '*a Gentleman by birth, is not only so in regard of his Ancestors,* Sed qui, ob eam Originem, Princeps illum suis legibus nobilitat, *as Bartol will have it. The Prince, as it were, supposing that if the Father be Noble, the issue will resemble him.*'[94] It may have sounded like a poor boy's definition and raised the question of how one, '*bred from the bottome of Obscuritie, and so farre from Court-Custome, should dare at these* Honors'; as his answer, Selden quoted Robert Grosseteste, '*Bishop of* Lincoln *under* Henrie III,' who argued: '*That there was, in* Libraries, *greater aid to the true understanding of Honor and Nobilitie, then mongst* Gold *and* Purple outsides.' Still, neither scholarship nor any other form of virtue could create civil nobility: '*Virtue plainly ennobeleth not civilly, but is a deserving cause of it only, whereof the Prince must judge. If* Honor *and deserving* Vertue *accompanie not each other, its his Fault or Error. They should alwaies so.*'[95] This subverted any claim to a hereditary nobility independent of the state, the mystique of blood so favoured by some Renaissance European nobles and their apologists. All civil honours derived from the prince.

Nobility as a recognition of honour and virtue had arisen in an earlier era and had undergone a number of changes of emphasis over time and space. In ancient Republican Rome,

their Nobiles *(a thing not unworthie to be here noted) were only those which could shew the* Images *of such their Ancestors as had born a State Office (the Ædilitas Curulis, or any above it) which were of Wax expressing the Face and Bodie only to the shoulders, kept every one in severall cases of*

Wood or Closets, and subscirb'd with the name of the Dead (they calld it
Titulus *or* Index) *and additions of his Place or particular Worth ...*

Those first raised to such honours remained 'homines Novi, *and this distinction was both in the* Patricij *and* Plebeij'; only their descendants became nobles.[96] As with the '*Reversing of Coats*' of arms in '*later Times*,' the images inherited by '*men condemned capitally for matter against the State ... were broken, or, at lest, omitted in their pompous Funeralls.*' The comparison to the formal derogation of offending vassals of the Middle Ages and of nobles and gentlemen in early modern Europe was deliberate. Although under the Roman Empire, all offices, including those which bestowed nobility, came under the control of the emperors, who '*so did ennoble by* Rescript *or* Patent,' only those with inherited images, '*by the ancienter forme, were Noble*' and those newly raised remained '*only* Novi.'[97] The hereditary nobles of Rome differed in many ways from those of later times.

In ancient Greece, '*Gentlemen*' were either descended from certain '*Noble Tribes*' or other people '*in whose posteritie, was a Concurrence of ...* Birth, Education, *and* continuall affectation of good Studies.'[98] This less formal recognition of a nobility of birth and talent, though not its emphasis on education, was more typical than the formal recognition based upon the holding of particular offices of the Romans:

In most other Nations (I think) untill particular ennobling, by the Princes autoritie, came in use, was a kind of distinction of Nobilitie, and most neer to that in Greece. None so barbarous, but had the like; witnesse the Goth-ique Anses; a Name interpreting Half-Gods, or men above common human fortune, and applied by them to their Chieftains valorously bearing themselves in the Warres, and their posteritie.[99]

Honour won in war remained strong among the successors to the Romans in western Europe; from it came the coats of arms, first as a sign of honour (at the time of the Crusades); then as hereditary, and finally as bestowed by the prince when creating new nobles (in England, during the reign of Henry III). Selden compared coats of arms to other 'hereditarie Ensigns' such as the images of the ancient Roman nobles.[100] As well, considerable material illustrated obsolete customs not relevant to the body of the text, including the long hair of the kings of the Franks, the carrying of a lamp and relics and 'strewing' of 'Gold-Dust' before the German emperors, and the use of white sealing-wax by the kings of France. In comparison to the well-organized chapters of the text, however, the preface remained quite rambling.

After the extensive preface, the treatise divided into two parts, the first on monarchy and the second on other titles of honour. The opening chapter provided both historical and philosophical positions on the origins of monarchy. The former came in a long discussion of the 'first Monarch of a Nation, we read of, is that *Nimrod*, (nephew to *Cham) the mightie hunter before the Lord*,' who founded the Babylonian or Assyrian monarchy by force.[101] The latter marked Selden's initial foray into the more abstract realm of political philosophy and commenced with a complex passage, not without a historical dimension, which seemed to derive royal from patriarchal rule:

Communitie of life, and Civill Societie, beginning first in particular Families, under Oeconomique rule (representing what is now a common-welth) had, in its state, the Husband, Father and Master, *as King*. Hence many Colonies; which, whithersoever deduced, were Cities, Townes, Villages, or such like. In them, deserved Honor added to the eminencie of some fit man's Vertue, made him by publique consent, or some of his own ambition violently got to be what every one of them were in proportion to their owne Families; that is, over the common state, and as for the common good, *King*. Thus came first Cities to be governed by Kings, as now whole Nations are. And in the Heroique times ... such as shewed themselves first publique benefactors to the Multitude, either by invention of Arts, Martiall prowesse, encreasing of Traffique, bettering or enlarging the countrie, or such like, were (saith *Aristotle)* by severall Nations constituted Kings over them, and, by general consent, left lines of hereditarie succession.[102]

'Oeconomic rule' meant government by a patriarch over a self-sufficient household made up of members of his extended family; 'Heroique times' meant the type of society described by Homer. Before civil societies existed, patriarchs ruled over their families. When several families joined together to constitute a village, a town, or, eventually, a classical *polis*, or city-state, whether by common consent or force of arms, states succeeded families as the most important social organizations, and individual patriarchs recognized the overarching power of a single monarch, who governed for the 'common good.' This quasi-historical interpretation of the origins of kingship sounded very much like the arguments employed by some writers who favoured absolute monarchy.[103]

To provide the grounds for a constitutionalist position, Selden turned to reason. Patriarchy only covered 'Oeconomic rule'; it could not form the basis of government in a 'civil society' and, therefore, monarchy could have neither a chronological nor a logical precedence over democracy and aristocracy:

I know the usuall assertion, that makes the *first* of those three kindes of States a *Monarchie*. Great Philosophers dare affirm so ... . But that cannot, in my understanding, be conceived as truth, otherwise then with a presupposition of a Democracie, out of which, as is related, a Monarchie might have originall: no more than can bee imagined how an Aristocracie should be before the Multitude; out of which, such, as make in their lesse number the Optimacie, must be chosen.[104]

Both monarchy and aristocracy presupposed the prior existence of democracy, the form of government most naturally derived from patriarchy. By 'state,' Selden meant what Aristotle had called a 'polity,' the form of government or constitution established in a particular jurisdiction and the means by which the people constituted rule by one, few, or many. Starting from the premises that all 'men' (i.e., patriarchs) enjoyed equality in nature and that all people possessed a sociable character, Selden argued for the priority of democracy:

So that naturally, all men, in Oeconomic rule, being equally free and equally possest of superioritie, in those Ancient propagations of mankind, even out of nature it selfe, and that inbred sociablenesse, which every man hath as his character of Civilitie, a Popular state first rais'd it selfe, which, by its owne judgement, afterward was converted into a *Monarchie*; both by imitation of as well the subordinat as Supreme Rule, whereunto the whole Systeme of the world is governed, as taking also example from unreasonable creatures; in whom, because the libertie of discourse was wanting, Nature itself had placed that instinct of chusing alwaies *One* for their Prince or Leader.[105]

Although the earliest governments originated as 'popular' states, both reason and expediency pointed towards the superiority of monarchy. The supreme government of God and the example of such creatures as bees provided a model of rule by one that human reason

grasped, and the 'imperfections' of rule by the 'giddie-headed multi-
tudes' pushed patriarchs to believe that 'if they subjected themselves
to some eminent *One*,' he might better preserve their peace and pros-
perity.[106] Hence, democracies gave rise to monarchies.

This opening chapter of *Titles of Honor* amalgamated philosophical and historical representations of the origins of monarchy into a
complex, many-sided account which moved beyond the derivation of
power from God to portray polities as 'states' created by collections
of human beings. Discussion of the origins of civil society stretched
beyond the Renaissance and the Middle Ages into antiquity. Contesting the representations of such learned sages as '*Aristotles* Com-
menters, *Bodin, Machiavel* on *Livy*,' Selden argued that rule over a
state (as distinct from rule over a family or lineage) always started off
as popular.[107] This meant that monarchies always came later and
kings derived their powers from the heads of families. Although
Selden's problematic account added very little to contemporary
natural-law theories of the origins of government and had not yet
come close to that highly sophisticated political theory based upon
natural rights which Richard Tuck has delineated, these issues were
marginal to his historical concerns in 1614.[108] In the first edition of
Titles of Honor, the historical account of the origins of monarchy not
only held a central place in the narrative, but also informed and
shaped Selden's first, tentative attempt to present a philosophical
political theory.

As soon as Selden finished his philosophical and historical account
of the origins of monarchy, he started to place practical limits upon
the powers of the one and the many, especially in states that moved
from democracy to monarchy. The inherent tensions between the
power of the monarch and the liberty of the democrats soon became
controlled by the rule of law: 'The absolute power of the one, and the
unlimited libertie of the other, were even incompatible, unlesse they
be referred to some short time in the beginning of States, when, by
necessitie, no lawes were but only the Arbitrement of Princes, as
Pomponius speakes of *Rome*.'[109] Historically, such actions took place
at an early date. In answer to those scholars who argued that 'that
Homer, writing of the Heroique times, hath not the word Νομος, i. *a
prescribed law*, but only Θ'εμις, i. *an arbitrary rule*,' Selden argued
that public, prescriptive laws existed in Crete at a time beyond the
memory of the Greeks: 'Read *Plato's Minos*, and there you shall have
Talus his lawes in *Crete* written in Brasse. And *Talus* is made

coetaneall with *Rhadamanth* sonne to *Jupiter*, whose time although uncertain, yet must be farre ancienter then any *Greek* testimony.'[110] Although the general interpretations offered in the first edition of *Titles of Honor* lacked the clarity and sophistication of his later works, Selden would develop the stress upon natural law and the concentration upon the constitutions of individual jurisdictions into a powerful explanatory tool. Philosophical and historical discussion on the origins of government now gave way to chapters on various aspects of royal rule, each based primarily upon historical evidence and filled with all sorts of intriguing information; as a whole, the format of part one set the pattern followed by most of the chapters in part two.

Dukes and Counts

After charting the derivation of a particular title, Selden traced its history and variations within a comparative European context. Usually he began with the Roman Empire and carried developments up to the fringes of his own day. The chapter on Duke, for example, observed that: '*Dux* then properly was at first the *Generall of an Armie* under the Emperor. Afterward it became usually applied to such as had military care of Frontiers.'[111] Even before the late stages of the Roman Empire, the office began its trek towards becoming territorial. Under Constantine the Great, the new office of Count was created by sending out important men from the Imperial court to govern in the provinces. Some rivalry followed among those who held these offices: 'But howsoever the difference of *Duke* and *Count* was at the first institution of the *Comitiua* under *Constantine* or about *Justinian's* time ... it's certain they became not long after *Constantine*, equall.'[112] In the late Roman Empire, Selden suggested, Duke remained a martial office, Count primarily a legal one with an army attached for defence and for the execution of justice. In the following centuries, '(you may understand this of the times twixt D. and C I Ɔ of Christ [A.D. 500–1000]),' many petty counts arose under the jurisdiction of dukes; others continued; however, 'which were the same in honor, power, and jurisdiction with Dukes, and not so much differing from them, as the Counts of Provinces of the first Rank.'[113] Although the earlier equality of Duke and Count still remained, something approaching a hierarchical order had begun to appear. However, these titles remained personal and attached to offices: 'But untill the French Empire, they were rarely more than meer personall, and as much or rather Official then Honorary, when the Government of a Province was annext to them. Neither did the Provinces make them otherwise then Personal. For they were not annext to them as Feudall, but given into their Rule at the Emperors or King's will for a certain time, or at pleasure.'[114] Throughout more than five hundred years, the office of Duke (and that of Count) had retained much of its original character. This would change dramatically, first in France and then in the rest of western Europe.

The shift, according to Selden, started around the time that the Carolingians had replaced the Merovingians as kings of the Franks: 'About this time [A.D. 747–68] of *Pipin* in whom the *Carolin* line had its originall, this dignitie (with that of *Count* equivalent to it) began to be feudall for life, and annext to the Territorie given, for which the Duke or Count did his fealtie or Homage to the Emperor or King.'[115] Selden dated this important change by reference to surviving contemporary evidence such as the formula employed in making Tassilo Duke of Bavaria and a number of enfeoffments made by the Archbishopric of Salzburg.[116] Of course, these documents not only recorded the genesis of feudal titles, but also illustrated the spread of such practices to Germany. The Carolingians had started the process, but not until the time of the Emperor Otto the Great ('c. 940') were such 'honorable titles bestowd in Feudall right of enheritance, his Territories with particular Names of Dignity annext to them.'[117] Now the title became attached to a particular territory held by feudal military tenure and inheritable; in Germany, these officers remained governors of a province 'next under imperiall Power.'[118] In France, however, royal power declined under the later Carolingians and decayed under the early Capetians; as a result dukes and counts made their titles and holdings hereditary.

... First through the weaknesse of the *Carolins*, and then the example of *Hugh Capet* Count of *Paris* which got the Diadem of France, most of those who before were honor'd with the equall titles of Duke or Count for life, extorted or by armes established their Dignities and Territories to themselves and their inheriting posteritie. Yet so, that the more to secure their divided greatnesse, they acknowledged to the King a Supremacie, and did him Homage as for hereditarie and patrimoniall Fiefs. Being, as is said of the Dukes of *Normandie*, different from the King, and in this only that the King did them no homage, as they did to him. But in their Territories, they usurped all kind of soveraignty, as to make laws, Officers of the magistracie, to give judgment not subject to Appeale, levy militarie forces, Coin monie, take imposts, subsidies, and the like and used also a Crown such as in more ancient times the Kings did, that is a *Crown Fleurnoee*, only differing from what is now a Royall one, in that it was not arch't or close. Such kind of Soveraign Dukes were afterward sometime there created.[119]

In less than two centuries, Duke had undergone a transformation from an office held at will from a king or emperor into a hereditary title attached to a territory, which, in France, had usurped most of the marks of sovereignty. It would take nearly five hundred years before such dukes and counts came back under the power of the French Crown, either 'by marriage, Treason committed, or some such cause.'[120] Having detailed the Continental history of the title and traced the origins of feudal institutions, Selden then turned to England.

In that kingdom, the word *Dux* appeared frequently in Anglo-Saxon documents and from the thirteenth century onward, after Henry III applied it to his sons, 'yet hardly twixt him and the *Norman* Conquest. It seems it was the rather abstaind from in that time, because the Conquerors title in *Normandie*, whence he came, was at the best no greater.'[121] Before the Conquest, however, Selden argued: 'I am resolv'd that the Dukes or chiefest princes were in the Saxon idiom known by the name of Ɛoꞃleꝗ, which is our very word *Earles*. Their *Archbishops* and *Earles* were in the same rank of worth; their *Bishops* and Ɛalðoꞃmanneꝗ (*Aldermen*) in another.'[122] By 'rank of worth,' Selden meant the amount of wergild assessed for injuring or killing a person. Since both 'Earl' and 'Ealdorman' frequently appeared in Latin documents as *Comes*, the problem lay in distinguishing one from the other and differentiating both from Prince or Etheling, another high-ranking title. Selden attempted a solution in the chapter on Count.

Deriding those scholars who sought 'to derive into the *Saxons*, their Counts from that of *Tacitus*,' he pointed out that 'those *Comites* can signifie nothing there but meer followers, neither did *Tacitus* ever dream of it as an Honorary Title or Office, by that speciall name. Neither in *Tacitus* his time, was the name at all Honorary or Officiary.'[123] Sychronism applied with devastating effect against anachronism! Clearly, Selden had read Tacitus carefully. The Anglo-Saxon title Earl came from 'Ɛar or Ar, i.e. *Honor*, and Arlíc or

Eorlic, i.e. *Honorable* (and that in *Danish*; some think the name came in with the *Danes*) ...'[124] Earls 'were both Officiary and Honorary, having the government of Provinces,' directly under kings.[125] Ethelings differed only in enjoying hereditary titles. On the other hand, 'Ɛalðoɲmen were merely Officiarie,' and held a lesser rank.[126] Earls and ealdormen, while both officers of the Crown, diverged significantly in power and status, 'the one having suprem government next after the King over the Province ... the other being but Judges, *Judices fiscales*, Shirifes, and like those *Comites minores*, inferior to Dukes ...'[127] Some puzzles remained. In the Saxon laws, only the ranks of Earl and Thegn bore honour; since only 'the *Earle* or *Thane* paid his Lord or King in the nature of a Relief,' the heriot in 'such things as were for martiall furniture, as horses, speares, shields, mony, and the like,' Selden believed that they held land only by military tenure.[128] How did the ealdorman fit in here? Despite such difficulties, however, the main outline seemed clear enough. Before the Conquest, *Dux* and *Comes* translated the officiary and honorary title Earl, while *Comes* also translated the officiary title Ealdorman. Anglo-Saxon usage employed prefeudal categories.

The Norman Conquest, while preserving aspects of past practice, brought England into closer conformity with more recent Continental practice. If during the early Norman period, the Latin *Dux* passed from usage, the Anglo-Saxon title Earl did continue, now translated primarily as *Comites*: 'At the *Norman* invasion (the title of the Conqueror being before but *Dux Normanniæ*, and oftimes *Comes*) to those Saxon *Eorles* were given the names of *Consules* or *Comites* ... But it appears that their Dignitie under the *Normans* was like that of the Dukes and greatest Princes under the *Saxon* Kings, otherwise why should they have retain'd the name of *Eorle*?'[129] This seemed to indicate that Anglo-Saxon offices and honours remained as before the Conquest. More than the translation of the name changed, however, for King William I transformed the substance as well, by making earls both feudal and hereditary. 'The Conqueror, *William* the first, putting all enheritances and possessions both of the Church and Laitie under his suprem dominion, nor permitting any foot of land within this Realme to be free from either a mediat, or immediat Tenure of him, created divers into this title of *Earle*, making it feudall, and hereditarie.'[130] While unequivocally explaining the nature of the innovation, this comment – taken on its own – marked no new insight by Selden into the ancient constitution. *Jani Anglorum* had noted that the Conqueror granted all of the land in England on feudal tenure and it had added that 'their Counts and Earls before the Conquest ... were but Officers, and not as yet hereditary. When William bore sway, they began to have a certain Fee and a descent of Patrimony ...'[131] Although Selden slightly modified the first part of this summary in *Titles of Honor*, the statement as a whole still stood up. In *Jani Anglorum*, it lacked the sort of comparative context which could bring out its significance. Having reached the section on Anglo-Saxon and early Norman earls in *Titles of Honor*, however, the reader would have observed how the Continental titles Duke and Count, after having an officiary and honorary standing for many centuries, had gradually become first feudal, then feudal and hereditary – within the course of somewhat more than a century. A similar shift took place within a few years of the Conquest in England. The structure of the account led to the conclusion that a real conquest with significant results had taken place. Rather than pressing the point, however, Selden stuck to his subtle comparative account of English and Continental titles.

Barons and Knights

The manifold effects of the Conquest unfolded in several additional portions of Selden's treatise, especially in the chapters on Baron and on Knight. That on Baron traced how the title first meant a servant or officer, then came to signify 'the King's *Man, Servant, Tenant,* or *Officer*, of better note, constituted with some kind of Jurisdiction in som Territorie,' and eventually applied to all of those lesser feudal 'Dignitaries or Seigneuries, which were immediat to the Crown of *France* or the Empire.'[132] The title originated on the Continent. 'For England,' in the Anglo-Saxon period, 'the neerest name for Baron was that of *Thane*, anciently writen also *Thegn* þeʒen.'[133] As pointed out above, thegns, with earls, made the payment of heriot and were honorary. Two kinds existed, the '*Kings* Thanes and a *Mean* Thane.'[134] Since he identified thegns with barons and the office of Ealdorman with that of Sheriff, it puzzled Selden that 'in *Athelstans* laws an *Ealdormans* worth is accounted eight times as much as a *Thanes*.'[135] Nor could he unlock the meaning of the Anglo-Saxon unit of the hide, although he knew it formed the basis for taxation and had something to do with the support of thegns.[136] While Selden's understanding of Anglo-Saxon laws and institutions had matured considerably since he had written *Jani Anglorum*, he still ran into serious philological uncertainties, as he readily admitted with regard to one source: 'Some other matters [in addition to hides] in that *Saxon* fragment, ingeniously I acknowledge, passe my conceit; nor can I yet understand them.'[137] Still, he knew full well that when the word *Baron* appeared in King Cnut's laws of the forest and in King Edward's laws, it was a later intrusion: 'I impute both these testimonies to the later time and translation out of the *Saxon* into *Latin* under the *Normans* ...'[138] Clearly, then, the title remained on the Continent throughout the Anglo-Saxon period.

Baron arrived in England with the Norman Conquest as a title for those great landholders who, although lesser than earls, held their lands either directly from the king or indirectly through a great magnate on hereditary feudal tenure.

When the Conqueror subjected most lands in the kingdome to Militarie and Honorarie Tenures, as in making hereditarie Earls; he likewise invested others in smaller Territories, with base jurisdiction, and they were Barons, and had their Courts called *Court Barons*, whence, that name to this day remains as an Incident to every Mannor. Because, such as had not the dignitie of Count, yet had speciall Territories with jurisdiction given them, of part whereof they enfeofft others to hold of them, as they of the King, generally were stiled *Barons*, or *the Kings Barons*, provided that their lands and Manors were of sufficient revenue and qualitie to make what was accounted a Baronie, which was xiii. *knights Fees, and a Third part* ... So that their Honor was not in those ancient times given by writ or Patent, but came *a Censu* or from their possessions, and Tenure. When the beginning of this value of a Baronie was, I find not, but plainly was since the *Normans* ... so some more specially honord by the King's Bounty with so many Knights Fees, or possessing as much (I think) by mesne tenures, were accounted for Honorarie and Parliamentarie Barons.[139]

This rich, complex passage not only explained the origins of such a common-law term as 'court baron,' but more than hinted at the categories of secondary and tertiary vassals, of barons and knights, created by subinfeudation. Once again, the reader obtained a subtle sense of the many innovations introduced by William I.

If early Norman barons obtained that status by possessing large estates on feudal tenure, however, Selden still had to show how this title became attached to membership in the House of Lords and how the Crown came to grant it by letters patent. 'And the ancientest summons of Parlament now remaining mongst the Records,' he noted, came from the forty-ninth year of the reign of Henry III (1266).[140] Antiquaries knew that these were the earliest existing writs and had worked out various interpretations to explain or to explain away this fact. Unwilling to claim that more ancient writs had been lost or destroyed, Selden pointed out that much earlier sources for the history of parliaments had survived.

> But we have Statuts and Parlaments of elder time, as that of the Grand Charter first made in the xvii. of King *John* at a Parlament (or what was in those troubled times as one) held in *Runingmed*, between *Stanes* and *Windsor* xv. of June, and that at *Merton* in the xx. of Henry III. to omit the Testimonies of the *Saxon* Wittenaзemoteɤ or Micil Ɉɣnoðeɤ (as they calld them) and the Parlaments held under the *Normans* of ancienter time, as the I. and II. *Henries*, whereof our Stories enough. And in those Parlaments, as is shewed, so many Barons as would (by *Barons* I understand here all the Greater Nobilitie) after notice of the King's purpose, came and sate with him ...[141]

This linked feudal with Anglo-Saxon institutions in an understated manner and paved the way for future shifts.

In the second half of Henry III's reign, two important modifications took place. Henceforth, barons by tenure were 'taken for *Baronia Capitalis*, and immediat of the King.'[142] Because of the frequent holding of parliaments at that time, it became customary thereafter that 'none have been accounted Barons (as honorarie) but such as have been so called by Writ to Parliament (of what revenue soever they bee) or created into that Dignitie by Patent.'[143] Not until the reign of Richard II, over a century later, however, would creation by royal patent emerge. In this chapter, Selden captured the dynamic, fluctuating meaning of Baron from its introduction by the Conqueror onward, as it accommodated to changes within English society over time. With respect to the titles of the higher nobility, the feudal law had intervened decisively in the history of the ancient constitution. Would this apply equally to those of the lesser nobility, the knights and esquires?

Unlike the titles hitherto discussed, knighthood did not originate as an office and eventually become feudal and hereditary; it remained a personal honorary title. Esquire even lacked the status of a formal title; according to Selden, it had started as the name for the shield-bearer of a fighting man and had become a term 'to distinguish the better sort of Gentlemen from *Knight*, and those (as I may say) of the vulgar Gentrie.'[144] The roots of knighthood lay in the venerable aristocratic puberty rites of northern Europe, analogous to the bestowing of the *virilis Toga* in ancient Rome, in which 'the sonnes of Princes, and others of Noble Rank, usd to receive Armes from a superior, as a token of' their future promise as warriors.[145] '... In the Martiall Nations of *Gaules, Germans*, and some neighboring States, the Honor of taking armes (which in our present idiom may be calld *Knighting*) was in their Aristocracies given to all deserving it by age and worth, in their Publique Assemblies, as expresly that of *Tacitus* shews ...'[146] Medieval ceremony sprang from these venerable practices. 'Out of the customs of these ancient and Northern Nations came it, that afterward Knighthood was by *girting with a sword* ...'[147] Reports from the tenth and eleventh centuries illustrated this. The Emperor Charlemagne, for example, girded the candidate with a sword and gave him a blow on the ear.[148] Anglo-Saxon customs provided just another variation on the northern European theme. Although King Alfred employed a simple ceremony in knighting his nephew Athelstan, 'in succeeding times of the *Anglo-Saxons*, more religion was usd in taking this Order. Neither was it done without a solemne confession of sinnes, receiving the Sword from the Altar at the hands of some Churchman, and such like, which also hath been done in the Empire and *France*.'[149] Although the Normans disliked this practice, they continued it in England. From rites of this sort stemmed the elaborate ceremonies of the later orders of knights.

If knighthood arose from the bestowing of arms upon aristocratic young men, it came to signify a particular sort of military man. At first the Latin word for Knight, *Miles*, had more than one meaning for 'in the Empire as well as elswhere, *Miles* was in the more barbarous times both a Knight and a common Souldier, and one also that held his Fief by Knight service, as out of the Feudalls you are instructed.'[150] However, in time this changed and 'the proper *Furniture*, as a supposed incident to Knighthood, consisted of a *Horse* and *Armor*,' the accoutrements of the mounted warrior.[151] So widespread was this identification that the name for Knight 'in all places except England, hath its originall from a *Horse* ... For to the *Spaniards* they are *Cavalleros*, to the *Italians Cavallieri*, to the *French Chevallers* (all, in their provinciall tongues, from the Latin *Caballus*) and in the British *Margoghs* in like signification.'[152] In this edition of *Titles of*

Honor, however, Selden never explicitly put together the mounted warrior and the feudal knight's fee as a unique sort of military tenure. He seemed to assume the reader's familiarity with the relationships described in the feudal law.

With no historical account of the development of the fief or knight's fee on the Continent, the reader could grasp its introduction to England only with some difficulty. At least Selden tried to define knight service in England. Instead of relating this to his earlier discussion of subinfeudation and fitting it into a whole system of relationships, however, he offered a definition dependent upon income:

The Knights *Fief* or *Fee* is commonly known by name as Knight [service]. But what it was or is, is not to all known. An old testimonie makes it DC. LXXX [680] acres, consisting of IV. Hydes. Of Hydes, before, where of Barons. Other certainties are proposed for a Knights Fee anciently, but in vain. Its neerest truth to set no number of Acres, nor quantitie of Territorie, but only of Revenue out of land, which being xx l^i. yeerly was the value of a Knights Fee.[153]

By arguing that English fiefs had no fixed size, Selden shrewdly anticipated the generally accepted solution offered to this vexing problem in the late nineteenth century by John Horace Round.[154] By opting for an annual income of £20 as the essential characteristic of a knight's fee despite the fact that he knew that this sum did not become fixed until Magna Carta, Selden begged the question for the Norman and early Angevin periods.[155]

His category worked well enough for the later Middle Ages, however. According to the Statute of Westminister I (1275), 'they which had such an estate might be compelled to take, and, it seems, of right to demand a Knighthood.'[156] Illustrations of such distraint of knighthood from the reigns of Edward II, Edward III, and Henry VI underlined the point.[157] Since such modes of holding land as 'Sokeman, Burgensis, Villanus, Tenant in ancien demesne, and Serviens' continued to exist in medieval England, Selden carefully distinguished between these and knight service.[158] *Serviens* came closest, but by 'Servientes (Serjants) were those understood which either by perpetuall covenant, or temporary pay, were bound to the warrs not by Tenure, as the *Milites*, or tenants by Knight's service.'[159] This account of the lesser nobility contained many good insights and made a number of crucial points about knight service, but it lacked the coherence, clarity, and historical precision of the chapters on the greater nobles.

Selden needed to give a more explicit chronological interpretation of how the ancient Germanic honour of granting arms had become a form of feudal tenure at specific times and in particular places. He wrote around this issue, not on it. Fortunately this fogginess about the lower reaches of honour was partially dissipated in a special chapter on the feudal law.

Selden on the Feudal Law

During the sixteenth and seventeenth centuries, the question of the origins and dispersion of the feudal law remained a hotly disputed topic, especially among the historically minded civil and customary lawyers of Italy, France, and Germany.[160] Selden plunged into these disputes by asserting about the origin of feuds that 'the common opinion supposes it in the *Longobards* or *Lumbards* a Northern Nation. Their incursions into *Italie* ... and greatnes there began under *Justin* II, about DLXX. [570] of our Saviour. *Millan* was their seat Royall, and in it their first King *Alboin* inaugurated. And its commonly affirmd, that they brought the more formall and frequent use of Militarie Feuds thither with their other customs: having had mongst themselves the use of them, very ancient.' According to this interpretation, Charlemagne continued these feuds on grants for life when he conquered the Lombard kingdom and they became hereditary under the Emperor Otto the Great: 'The forms of the Fealtie and such like of these times are extant, and inserted in *Sigonius* his Storie de Regno Italiæ.'[161] These customs were not codified into law, however, until around 1150, under '*Frederique Barbarossa*,' when two 'Consuls of *Millan*,' Gerardus and Obertus, carried out this task:

Which, it seems, was the rather done, because about that time the Volumes of the *Roman* (i. [e]. what wee call the Civill laws) began to be newly in request, and, as it were, awakt out of that neglect, wherein they had neer DC. [600] yeers slept, as of no reckoning among the *Lombards*, and were now publiquely read and profest in *Bologna* by *Irnerius* the first publique professor of them after *Justinian's* time. Its quite likely that the *Lombards* thought it presently requisit to put their Feudall customs into Writing and forme, and under Titles, as well as the *Romans* had don their ancient Laws. What was then performed by the two *Millanois*, hath since been betterd, and for publique use inlarged by that most learned Lawier *Cuiacius*, and is as a part of the Civill law, for Feuds.[162]

In summing up this 'common opinion,' Selden followed a historical interpretation which also drew attention to the relationship between the revival of Roman law and the codification of customary feudal law. According to this view, feudal institutions and the feudal law spread from Lombardy to the rest of Europe. Although rejected by Selden, it remained a respectable interpretation well into the future.

Taking the side of Hotman once more, Selden argued against an Italian origin for the feudal law and in favour of a French genesis instead:

For although it be true that mongst the *Lombards* they were, and anciently, yet plainly, before the *French* Empire, in *France* they were, and that hereditarie, if their ancient laws deceive not. For, what els was their *Terra Salica* but as a Knights Fee, or land held by Knights service? It was so adjudged in the Parlament at *Burdeaux* ... And those *Salique* laws are supposed much ancienter then the *Lombardian* Kingdome in *Italie*.[163]

While the Lombards had military tenures at an early time, as did most other northern Europeans, they did not, Selden argued, follow the practices prescribed by the feudal law until '*Charlemagne* according to the custom of his own patrimoniall State, brought them into *Italie* ... But the inheritance of them beeing annext to Honorarie Titles, may well be allowd to *Otho's* time,' as earlier argued.[164]

Although not making the point in this section, Selden had shown previously how the Carolingians had extended the feudal law into Germany and made it the law of the Western Empire. 'Out of the Empire, by imitation, it seems, or by generall consent of Nations, most part of *Europe* took their forms of Feudall possessions: but by imitation, doubtless, those Dignities of Feudall right. The identitie of names in the Empire and other Kingdoms justifies it.' These institutions and their terminology even extended into the Eastern Empire during its later days. 'The Tenants of Feuds in the Western Empire, and now every where in *Europ*, are known by the name of *Fideles*, *Homines*, *Vassi*, *Vassalli*, and the like.'[165] Vassal he derived 'from the old *Gaulish* word *Gues, Gaus,* or *Gais* for a *Valiant* or *Militarie* man,' once again underscoring the French origin of feudal customs.[166] Briefly refuting those who deduced the feudal law from ancient Roman law, Selden capped his interpretation by pointing out that Roman military tenures were quite different, for 'all their old volumes of the Civill law have nothing that touches Feuds, either in name or substance, as they truly are.'[167] All of this added up to a well-protected, coherently argued position which distinguished feuds from other sorts of military service. The feudal law originated among the Franks and spread, first through the conquests of the Carolingian emperors, and later by imitation.

In *England*, before the Normans, plainly were military Fiefs, although not in the like manner as since. That law of King *Knout* for the certaintie of Heriots paid only in Martiall Furniture, proves it; and that their Earls and Thanes were bound to a kind of Knights service. And, in those times so were, it seems, all the lands of the Kingdom (except some priviledged with great immunities) if, at least, held of the King or Crown, mediatly or immediatly.[168]

To make the latter point, Selden discussed several ecclesiastical charters which carried no military service, but did have to provide for the '*repairing of Bridges, Tax for Warre, and Castle gard, or repairing them*'; these provided examples of privileged lands.[169] The European feudal law arrived in England with the Norman Conquest: 'Those kind of Militarie Fiefs or Fees as wee now have, were not till the Normans; with whom the custom of Wardships in Chivalrie (they began not under *Henry* III. as most ignorantly *Ranulph Higden* the Monk of *Chester*, and *Polydore* tells you) came into *England*.'[170] After having derived the English word '*field*' from '*feud,*' Selden finished his account of England by differentiating between feudal and allodial landholding:

Now every *Feud* or *Fief* paid a Relief or Heriot upon the death of the tenant, and the Heir or successor came in alwaies (as at this day) in some fashion of a new Purchase. But where no tenure was, there the enheritance discended freely to the Heire, who claimd it alwaies meerly from his ancestor. Out of this difference, I imagin, the names of *Feudum* and *Alodium* were translated to make that distinction which is usually twixt them: whence *Alodium* now abusively denotes chiefly lands possest without service or subjection, except only acknowledgment of superioritie in the Giver.[171]

Having traced allodial land back beyond the Conquest, Selden left the topic without attempting to establish it as a Saxon survival. The distinction, however, focused additional light on the nature of feudal tenure. This brief section on England clearly and succinctly confirmed the interpretation embedded in the historical details of other chapters in *Titles of Honor*, that William the Conqueror had introduced the feudal law into England and, as a result, had instituted major modifications in the ancient constitution.

After moving towards a catastrophic interpretation of the Norman Conquest, Selden finally took the leap; he turned the hypothesis announced in the preface of *Jani Anglorum* into a full-scale historical interpretation. Comparative Continental scholarship overcame the taboos of the English common-law tradition. Of course, some imperfections remained. For example, the historical origin of Duke as a feudal title under the first of the Carolingians in the mid-eighth century did not square with the assertion that the Franks possessed feudal tenures before the Lombards entered Italy in the late sixth century. The chapters on the lower nobility, especially that on knights, lacked the analytic and chronological clarity of the chapters on the titles Duke and Count. Still, the accomplishment was an impressive one. In the process of giving a historical account of various titles of honour, Selden created a subtle, reasonably sophisticated, historical analysis of the genesis of the feudal law on the Continent and its application to England. *Titles of Honor* displayed a mastery of the humanist historical method, a mature grasp of Continental evidence and scholarship (including works on provincial as well as national history), and an acquaintance with English evidence (including manuscripts) matched by few contemporaries. His originality lay not in creating a historical representation out of primary sources, however, for he relied heavily upon Continental evidence and interpretations found in treatises written by civil lawyers, but in applying this scholarship to English materials. More than a decade before any of Spelman's relevant works had appeared in print, Selden had shown systematically that the Conqueror had introduced the feudal law into England and dramatically shifted the nature of English law. Ironically, the first edition of *Titles of Honor* marked the high point of that interpretation in Selden's works; few traces of it remained in the greatly expanded second edition, published in 1631. The historical search for the fluctuating nature of titles of honour, however, not only brought Selden more firmly into contact with both the feudal and the civil or Roman law, but also forced him to view the English common law in a more comparative context and to reflect upon the nature of law itself.

Selden on the Nature of Law

The common-law model of the ancient constitution so far had received scant notice in print. Several of the prefaces of Coke's early *Reports* (especially the third, fourth, and sixth, all printed before 1610) had differentiated the common law from customs and statutes, and had sketched its continuous history from the time of Brutus to the present. Between 1611 and 1615, portions of Hedley's model of 'constitutional monarchy governed by the common law' received support in the preface of the Irish *Report* of Sir John Davies, attorney general of Ireland, and in the eighth, ninth, and tenth *Reports* of Sir Edward Coke. In his preface, Davies stressed the immemorial nature of the common law, whereas, in his, Coke argued for its antiquity. Both eschewed the violent interpretation of the Norman Conquest put forward by Hedley.[172] Still, they defended in print many of the points and the general interpretation of the ancient constitution that he had articulated in his speech against impositions made in the Commons. However, even when taken together, the prefaces of the *Reports* of Coke and Davies did not add up to an interpretation of the ancient constitution which matched the completeness and coherence of those presented by Hedley and Selden.

Selden's Edition of Fortescue's *De Laudibus Legum Angliæ* (1616)

Within the context of the prefaces of Coke and Davies, the eminence of John Selden's annotated critical edition of Fortescue's *De Laudibus Legum Angliæ* in 1616 takes on added significance. In the preface, Selden explained that Fortescue had held the post of Chief Justice of the King's Bench for many years under Henry VI, 'as the records of the later halfe of his Raigne, every where shew,' and added that 'his bookes which I have seene are three. This now newly publisht, his *Difference* between *Dominium Regale* and *Dominium Politicum* and *regale*, and that *Declaration* touching the title of the Crowne. Neither of the two last were ever publisht, but they remaine Manuscripts in divers hands.'[173] Although earlier editions and translations of this key treatise already existed in print, Selden employed the humanist technique of collating several manuscripts to prepare his Latin text and added an Elizabethan English translation and copious notes, mostly in English. In other words, this fifteenth-century treatise received the respect normally accorded to the classics. The notes brought portions of Fortescue's interpretation more closely in line with recent scholarship, but also worked to subvert both the concept of immemorial custom argued by Davies and the anachronistic historical interpretations displayed by Coke. For a confident, learned young man just starting to become known for his *Titles of Honor*, a new edition of the most prestigious common-law text on governance marked a bold political move.

Selden seems to have worked out many of his interpretations in dialogue with the writings and ideas of other people, reinforcing or contesting other voices. Although this interactive mode appeared in *Jani Anglorum* and in some of the notes to *Poly-Olbion*, it operated even more clearly in the notes to *De Laudibus*. In a stirring, classic passage, Fortescue had characterized the English constitution both as constant despite changes of dominion and as the most ancient known in Europe:

The Realme of *England*, was first inhabited of the *Britons*, next after them the *Romanes* had the rule of the land and then againe the *Britons* possessed it, after whom the *Saxons* invaded it, who changing the name thereof did for *Britaine* call it *England*, after then for a certain time the *Danes* had the dominion of the Realme, and then *Saxons* againe, but last of all the *Normans* subdued it, whose discent continueth the government of the kingdome at this present. And in all the times of these several nations and their kings, this realme was stil ruled with the selfe same customes, that it is now governed withall. Which, if they had not been right good, *some of those kings mooved either with Justice, or with reason or affection*, would have changed them, or els altogether abolished them, and *especially the Romans*, who did judge all the rest of the world by their owne lawes. Likewise would other of the foresaid kings have done, which by the sword, only possessing the realme of England, might by the like power and aucthority have extinguished the Lawes thereof. And touching the antiquitie of the same, neither are the *Romane Civile lawes, by so long continuence of ancient times, confirmed*, nor yet the Laws of the *Venetians*, which, above al other are reported to be of most antiquity, for so much as their Iland in the beginning of the *Britons* was not then inhabited, as *Rome* then also unbuilded, neither the laws of any Paynim nation of the world, are of so old and ancient yeeres: Wherefore the contrarie is not to be said nor thought, but that the English customes are verie good, yea of all other the verie best.[174]

Ironically, Coke had taken this interpretation more or less at face value and had quoted the same passage to demonstrate the antiquity of the common law.[175] Indeed, Fortescue displayed most of the characteristics that Pocock noted as properties of the common-law mind, the immemorial antiquity (here traced back beyond the foundation of Rome to Brutus), the perfection of custom (here tried by kings as well as by continual usage), and the ability of the law to overcome even conquerors. Since Selden sanctioned none of these ideas and could not fully reject Fortescue, the passage posed an interpretive crux.

Selden's quiet scholarship collapsed the whole image of the common law as immemorial custom, unchanged through thousands of years. Carefully drawing upon a wide range of evidence – including such ancient authors as Caesar, Tacitus, and Pliny; the foremost modern expert, Lipsius; and inscriptions found on monuments from Roman Britannia – Selden subverted Fortescue's assertion that the Romans had ruled Britain by the common-law.[176] Nor had the same customs survived unscathed through the succeeding conquests of the Saxons, Danes, and Normans:

> But questionlesse the *Saxons* made a mixture of the *British* customes with their own; the *Danes* with old *British*, the *Saxon*, and their own; and the *Normans* the like. The old laws of the *Saxons* mencion the *Danish* law (*Danelage*) the *Mercian* law (*Mercenlage*) and the *Westsaxon* law (*Westsaxonlage*) of which also some Counties were governed by one, and some by another. All of these being considered by *William* I. comparing them with the laws of *Norway* ... They were you see called St *Edwards* laws, and to this day, are. But cleerly, divers Norman customes were in practice first mixt with them, and to these times continue. As succeeding ages, so new nations (comming in by a Conquest, although mixt with a title, as of the *Norman* Conqueror, is to be affirmed) bring alwaies some alteration, by this wel considered, That of the laws of this realm being never changed will be better understood.[177]

This passage deliberately deconstructed Fortescue's seamless web of law into a series of distinct customs, which kings and conquerors fashioned into suitable collections, such as the laws of King Cnut, King Edward, and King William. Aware of the distinctions which separated the laws of Wessex, Mercia, and the Danelaw, Selden had solved some of the puzzles of Saxon law codes; since Coke had thought that the 'Marchenleg' was a 'Booke of the Lawes of England in the Brittish toong' written by 'Mercia proba,' the wife of 'king

Gwintelin,' some '356. yeres before the birth of Christ,' this represented a considerable scholarly accomplishment.[178] So did the image of law as something altering over time in relation to the changing needs of the community of the realm.

Faced by Fortescue's denial that the Romans had ruled Britain with Roman laws, Selden dealt with this problem at length. None of his sources specifically stated that the Romans had brought their law to Britain, so he resorted to probabilities. Roman law obviously applied in the colonies of Romans planted in Britain: 'For every Colonie was but as an image of the mother Citie, with like holie rites, like Courts, Laws, Temples, places of publique commerce,' and, since both literary and material evidence (inscriptions and coins, for the most part) demonstrated that colonies had existed in Britain, it followed that, at the very least, the Romans settlers there lived under their own law.[179] The Imperial regime extended further, however, to include the native Britons, transformed by Roman rule to accept and learn the customs of their conquerors:

After *Claudius*, the Britons began to learne the arts, to exceed the Gaules in wit and learning ... and this is spoken of naturall Britons, not Colonies. They affected, we see, Roman language, Rhetorique, Roman habit, Roman pleasures, diet, and the like. Neither needed *Tacitus* to have mentioned their affecting the laws of Rome, when they were subject to them as a conquerd people. And no doubt is, but they that imitated their Conquerours, and neighbour Colonies in the rest, were not backward in affecting those laws, for which the languages and rhetorique was most usefull.[180]

Building upon that vision of the law as something that existed only as part of a whole cultural complex, the guiding principle of all of his early historical works, Selden showed how the destruction of British religion also probably involved the loss of their ancient laws.

The easier might the use and studie of the laws of *Rome* be received here, after this *Claudius* his conquest, in regard that those which before and in ancient time had the determining of controversies, and the learning of that kind in their hands, were by him forbidden to use any longer their religion, for which they were most of all reverenced and regarded. I mean the *Druides* and when their holy rites were prohibited by the Emperor, it's likely enough that the nations governed by them in point of law (as the *Gaules* and *Britons* were) grew regardlesse, at lest remain'd nothing so respectfull of them as before, and so became prone to receive the laws of *Rome* which had both conqure'd them, and also taken away the reverence before given to the *Druides*.[181]

The bland assertion by Fortescue that the Romans had not changed British law brought forth an intricate, imaginative historical reconstruction by Selden, one that combined the detection of a declining respect for the Druids, and for native traditions in general, with a growing assimilation of Roman culture by the Britons to explain the triumph of Roman law. The solution raised equally formidable questions, however. If Roman law once governed the southern half of Britain, why did it no longer apply? Why was it not mixed with the laws of the Britons, Saxons, Danes, and Normans as part of the ancient constitution? The answer to this perplexing problem came in a lengthy discussion of the antiquity of various systems of law.

Moving outside of the insular perspective which marked many of the writings of those who defended 'constitutional monarchy ruled by the common-law,' Selden again noted that the Roman civil law had not commanded a continuous allegiance in western Europe from the days of ancient Rome, but had passed from usage from A.D. 565 to 1125, and stressed the implication that the common law was older than the recently revived Roman civil law. In addition, he provided a profoundly historical model for reducing all laws to a combination of the original 'state' of a particular society, rationally tempered over time by statutes and customs. This gave conceptual rigour to the idea of the 'state' employed in the first chapter of *Titles of Honor*. In response to those who asked 'When and how began your common-laws?' Selden replied with a long, reflective discourse on the nature of law:

But in truth, and to speak without perverse affectation, all laws in generall are originally equally ancient. All were grounded upon nature, and no nation was, that out of it took not their grounds; and nature being the same in all, the beginning of laws must be the same. As soone as *Italy* was peopled, this beginning of laws was there, and upon it was grounded the *Roman* laws, which could not have that distinct name indeed until *Rome* was built, yet remaind alwaies that they were at first, saving that additions and interpretations, in succeeding ages increased, and somewhat alterd them, by making a *Determinatio juris naturalis*, which is nothing but the *Civill law* of any Nation. For although the law of nature be truly said Immutable, yet its as true that its limitable, and limited law of nature is the law now used in everie

State. All the same may bee affirmed of our *British* laws, or *English*, or other whatsoever. But the divers opinions of interpreters proceeding from the weaknesse of mans reason, and the several conveniencies of divers States, have made those limitations, which the law of Nature hath suffered, verie different. And hence is it that those customs which have come all out of one fountain, *Nature*, thus varie from and crosse one another in severall Common welths. Had the *Britons* receivd the X. or XII. *Tables* from *Greece* ... cleerly the interpretations and additions which by this time would have been put to them here, must not be thought on as if they would have fell out like the body of the *Roman* Civill law. Divers nations, as divers men, have their divers collections, and inferences; and so make their divers laws to grow to what they are, out of one and the same root. Infinit laws we have now that were not thought on D. [500] yeers since. Then were many that D. yeers before had no being, and lesse time forward alwaies produced divers new; the beginning of all here being in the first peopling of the land, when men by nature being civill creatures grew to plant a common societie. This rationally considered, might end that obvious question of those, which would say somthing against the laws of England if they could. 'Tis their triviall demand, *When and how began your common laws?* Questionless its fittest answered by affirming, when in like kind as the laws of all other States, that is, *When there was first a State in that land, which the common law now governs*: then were naturall laws limited for the conveniencie of civill societie here, and those limitations have been from thence, increased, altered, interpreted, and brought to what now they are; although perhaps (saving the meerly immutable part of nature) now, in regard of their first being, they are not otherwise then the ship, that by often mending had no piece of the first materialls, or as the house that's so often repaired, *ut nihil ex pristina materia supersit*, which yet (by the Civill law) is to be accounted the same still ... Little then follows in point of honor or excellency specially to be atributed to the laws of a Nation in generall, by an argument thus drawn from difference of antiquitie, which in substance is alike in all. Neither are laws thus to be compar'd. Those which best fit the state wherein they are, cleerly deserve the name of the best laws.[182]

This answered the slights of the civilians in their own discourse and also provided a historical model for interpreting the laws of England – indeed, of any other independent European jurisdiction. Instead of reading late medieval common law back into Saxon England, Selden argued that at their origin societies formed a 'state' or distribution of powers or constitution which limited the law of nature through the creation of positive laws and customs. Although various individual laws were added or repealed to adjust to the ever-changing needs of society, the shape of the 'state,' as with the often repaired boat, remained the same. The mutability of laws did not create an impermanent commonwealth. In England, the ship of state took the shape of a mixed monarchy in which the king, nobility, clergy, and freemen had shared in the ability to make law through custom and statute from the very beginning. Other jurisdictions had different distributions of power and different methods for making new and repealing old laws. This meant that each of the kingdoms of Europe possessed its own ancient constitution.[183]

Having laid the groundwork, Selden could now make a historical contribution to the debate over the temporal relationship between the Roman and English common laws, and thus the precedence of the one over the other. This represented but one aspect of the dispute between civil and customary lawyers that raged throughout the Renaissance.[184] Selden showed that the Roman civil law could not claim a continuous usage in Europe stretching from the days of ancient Rome to the present:

For it appears that the Emperors from *Justinian*, who died in D. LXV. [565] of *Christ*, untill *Lothar* the II. in the yeer C I Ɔ.C. XXV. [1125] so neglected the bodie of the Civill law ... that all that time none ever professt it. But when *Lothar* took *Amalfi*, he there found an old copy of the *Pandects*, or *Digests*, which as a precious monument he gave the *Pisans* ... from whom it hath bin since translated to *Florence*, were in the Duke's Palace it is never brought forth but with Torch-light and other reverence. Under that *Lothar*, began the Civill law to be profest at *Bologna*, and *Irner* or *Werner* (as some call him) first made Glosses on it about the beginning of *Frederique Barbarossa* in C I Ɔ.C.L [1150] of Christ ... And this was the first time and place of profession of it in the Western Empire.[185]

Clearly a gap of over five hundred years marked the departure of Roman civil law from western Europe until its return. Selden asked: 'Why were they so neglected neer DC. [600] yeers in the Empire, if their excellency were so beyond others, as is usually said by many, that, to the purpose, know nothing of either them or ours?'[186] Indeed, this gap had already received some brief discussion in the first edition of *Titles of Honor*.[187] Now Selden used it both to contest the claims of the civil lawyers about the excellence of the Roman or civil law and to support the venerability of the common law: 'And cleerly you see the profession of them is not so ancient in the Western Empire, as the latest of time, to which som most ignorantly refer the beginning of the common law; I mean as the Norman *William*, who arrived in the yeer C I Ɔ.LXVI. [1066] ... As if the profession begun under *Lothar*, and since thus continued, were not meerly new, and not a recontinuance of what was in use under *Justinian*.'[188] English common law, while not as venerable as envisioned by Fortescue, had experienced a longer continuous usage and, therefore, a superior prescriptive prestige than had the relatively recently revived Roman civil law. Despite his revision of Fortescue's history, Selden managed to uphold many of the traditional common law assertions about the sagacious and time-honoured nature of the English constitution by building a new, sophisticated, comparative defence. Ironically, this deployed the devices often marshalled by civilians to attack the recent and limited nature of customary laws as means for subverting the ancient universalist claims of the Romanists.

The notes to Selden's edition of Fortescue's *De Laudibus Legum Angliæ*, while brief and somewhat hidden away, included a number of important insights into the nature of jurisprudence and some significant contributions to his historical view of the English constitution. The integration of Roman rule, for example, filled an embarrassing lacuna in his earlier descriptions of British government. The image of the ancient constitution as a ship which retained its shape, although so often repaired that hardly an original plank remained, brilliantly captured that vision of the continuity of the constitution and the mutability of custom already present in the pages of *Jani Anglorum*. Most crucial of all, the encounter with Fortescue – within a freshly acquired Continental context – coaxed from Selden a brilliant account of the nature of law which both converted all law into a polity with its own rationalized customs and revealed the first glimpses of a new theory of natural human rights. Having translated the law of nature, in its practical application, into the basic constitution and customary laws of various jurisdictions, Selden also paved the way for a similar treatment of the law of God. This theme formed the core of his last and greatest book of the decade.

Selden on the Law of God: *The Historie of Tithes* (1618)

An analytic narrative of great imagination and expertise, *The Historie of Tithes* marked Selden's entry into full maturity as a scholar.

Even into the late twentieth century, it has remained a cited historical work on the subject.[189] Dedicated to Sir Robert Cotton, it drew widely upon Cotton's vast collection of medieval manuscripts for evidence and left a lasting monument to the deep friendship shared by the two men.[190] In terms of its sceptical, sometimes cynical exposure of how clergy had preached pious principles while forging and interpreting evidence to fit their own self-interest, it was the most Tacitean of Selden's early books. *The Historie of Tithes* arose within and contributed to a rich polemical context. During the years from 1605 through 1613, such learned authors as George Carleton, Thomas Ridley, and Foulke Robarts had drawn upon the views of medieval canon lawyers and the history of God's people to make increasingly strident attacks upon the lay ownership of tithes; indeed, Robarts's treatise questioned any limitations placed upon the clerical collection of tithes. These publications bestowed strong support upon the campaign of some English ecclesiastical authorities to enforce a fuller payment of tithes to parish churches and to reclaim advowsons and appropriations.[191] The logic of the arguments pressed by Robarts posed a serious challenge to custom, an explicit move to outflank both the canon and the common law as administered in their respective courts by a direct appeal to the law of God. Composing his *Historie of Tithes* as an answer to the extreme claims of his immediate predecessors, Selden sought to uphold the rule of law in general and the supremacy of the common law in England. The outraged responses of his clerical opponents (which apparently began even before the publication of the *Historie*) and the silence of Sir Henry Spelman, whose *The Larger Treatise concerning Tithes* (London, 1646), promised as a 'greater work' on the subject in 1613, appeared only posthumously, provide some measure of Selden's success.[192]

A glimpse at the immediate background should help to establish the context. While debates over the nature and legitimacy of tithes had raged in earnest throughout the Middle Ages, the Reformation of the sixteenth century, with its large-scale secularization of church lands and doctrines of a 'sufficient maintenance' for the clergy, gave a new sense of urgency to such questions. Did tithes belong to the parish clergy by divine right, as argued by the medieval canonists? Could that right be held by other clergy or be circumscribed? Could princes and laymen justly hold the right to collect tithes? Disputes over these contentious issues not only arose in England but engulfed a host of Catholic, Protestant, and Reformed churches, including that in Scotland.[193] Under the Tudors, royal annexation and sale of church properties brought many tithes, especially those formerly belonging to monasteries, into lay hands.[194] By the latter part of Elizabeth's reign, this new order seemed reasonably established at law. Building upon medieval precedent and not disputing the validity of the statutes passed under Henry VIII and Edward VI, authors normally supported the divine origin of tithes and granted the justice of their regulation by both ecclesiastical and common law.

An anonymous treatise from 1595, for example, argued that priests collected tithes by a divine right and that human laws could alter the amount owing and the means of collection: 'The payment of Dismes or Tithes to the Priestes, is of the law of God, and by divine constitution, that they may therof live, and be sustayned: but to assign this portion or that, or to alter the said Dismes or Tithes to other rentes or profites, pertaineth to the Positive lawes of man ...'[195] This took the normal position that the 'Positive lawes of man' made particular those laws of God that society provide for the sustenance of 'Priests.' Attempting to sort out a number of the practical disputes which had arisen between some parish clergy and their parishioners, especially regarding the tithe on wood, this anonymous author systematically listed the tithes due in England, outlined the various means and types of compositions, and quoted at length from the relevant statutes still in force (27 Henry VIII, c. 20; 32 Henry VIII, c. 87; and 2 Edward VI, c. 13).[196] Clearly, this person recognized the ability of the king-in-parliament to regulate tithes.

A few years later, William Fulbecke took up the issue briefly in his dialogues on the civil, canon, and common laws. A civil and common lawyer, Fulbecke sketched out a brief proof for the divine right of tithes from the Bible (citing Exodus, Leviticus, Numbers, Proverbs, and I Corinthians) and from pagan examples (citing Pliny, Livy, Genesis, and Malachi), and briefly listed the canon- and common-law rights of the clergy to tithes in England. Displaying a warmer attitude towards a 'full' collection of tithes than had the anonymous author, Fulbecke still avoided any challenge to the customary and statute law of England.[197] The Elizabethans, it appeared, had confirmed the nature of tithes as an unusual sort of property, a source of revenue held by clergy and laymen alike, partly subject to the ecclesiastical courts, and strongly protected at the common law.

During the reign of James I, however, all of this came into question, as a growing number of scholars forcefully asserted that all tithes belonged by divine right to the parish clergy alone and that other possessors held them against the law of God. In the earliest of the new English treatises, George Carleton set out to refute the view, upheld by Cardinal Bellarmine and by the consensus of Reformed writers, that only a 'competent maintenance is injoyned' for clergy-men in the New Testament and to support the proposition that 'tithes are due to the Ministers of the Church, by the expresse word of God.'[198] Systematically examining 'How Tithes stood before the Law,' 'How Tithes stood under the law,' 'How Tithes stood in the time of the new Testament,' and 'How Tithes stood in the ages of the Church after the Apostles,' Carleton took a historical approach. Even before the Law of Moses, tithes belonged to the Lord. The payment of tithes by Abraham to Melchesedech, the type of Christ, also proved that 'tithes were, and are to be paid to Christ alwayes, aswell after as before the law.'[199] Under Mosaic law, the Levites collected them only so long as they served at the tabernacle.[200] During the early days of Christianity, their collection had lapsed, but 'as soone as it can be shewed that a Magistrate did favour the Church, so soone will it also appeare that tithes were established.'[201] Nor did this await a godly emperor; as early as A.D. 266 'parishes began to be divided and tithes orderly assigned to severall Churches.'[202]

Starting in the late tenth century, however, bad popes had granted away the privileges of parish priests, first to monks and friars, and later to the highest bidder: 'then came in exemptions first, and after-ward impropriations, transfering titles from one another.'[203] This explained the holding of tithes by monasteries, friaries, and laymen as unjust usurpations. Magisterial jurisdiction over tithes represented an indirect enforcement of God's law, one subsequent and inferior to spiritual jurisdiction. 'Some learned men have thought, because some Princes have made constitutions for tithes to bee payed to the Church: that therefore tithes are held by no other right then Princes constitutions. But before this time tithes were alwaies held by the lawes of God and not of Princes.'[204] Historically, the Christian clergy had a right to tithes by the law of God before the laws of princes had assisted in their collection. While Carleton did not expect that 'the thing for which I will plead will or can be effected,' that is, that all tithes should be paid to 'the Ministers of the Church,' his short pam-phlet strongly supported a move in this direction.[205] Carleton said little about England and skipped over the Middle Ages, but he had created a foundation upon which others could easily build.

Within the next decade, several divines, a civil lawyer, and a leading antiquary took up this cause. The most moderate was Thomas Ridley, a prominent civil and canon lawyer. Adding English detail to the picture, he argued that the British had established tithes before the arrival of St Augustine; cited the laws of Athelstan as enforcing their payment; and discussed statutes regulating their collection passed in the reigns of Edward III, Richard II, Henry IV, Henry VIII, and Edward VI.[206] Although sorrowful over the loss to the church by impropriations and sceptical about the restoration of tithes, Ridley accepted compositions as part of the ecclesiastical law.[207] Far more aggressive was Spelman, who mentioned tithes in his strident defence of all church property from lay ownership. Asserting that 'the *Church* for ever, should have of her owne, to maintaine her selfe withall,' Spelman pushed the view that all tithes belonged by divine right to the parish priest to the extreme conclusion that human laws could not justly allow laymen to hold them: 'If then *Tithes* be *things spiritual*, and due *de jure divino*, as great many Clarkes, Doctors, Fathers, some Councels, and (that ever honorable Judge and oracle of Law) my Lord *Coke* himselfe *in the second part of his Reports*, affirme them to be: I cannot see how humane Lawes should make them *Temporal*. Of the same nature therefore that originally they were of, of the same nature doe I still hold them to continue.'[208] The laws of men could not regulate or set aside the law of God. Spelman more than hinted that all former lands of the church should be returned to the clergy and warned lay holders of tithes: 'It is not then a worke of bounty and benevolence to restore these appropriations to the Church, but of duty and necessity so to doe.'[209] Divine retribution awaited those who refused. The pious wish of Carleton was now transformed into an awesome duty! Concerned primarily with church lands, Spelman's tract brought a new, frenetic tone to the debate.

In the weighty compendium compiled by Foulke Robarts, a Norwich divine, the position seemed fully established. Drawing upon the works of Junius, Carleton, Ridley, and Richard Eburne, Robarts buttressed his case with a systematic citation of authorities and evidence.[210] The example of Abraham and payment to the Levites received another detailed discussion. Robarts not only repeated Carleton's view that tithes in the Old Testament represented 'the Lord Gods owne right,' however; he extended it into apostolic times: 'And as thus in the old Testament, so also in the New we find tythes challenged to be the Lords, although not by the very name of tythes, yet under the generall name of the Lords due: as, Matthew 22: 21. *Give unto God that which is Gods.*[211] Supporting Carleton's view that 'ever since the Church had a Christian Magistrate ... there have beene humane lawes to enforce the payment of tythes, which were formerly due by the law of God,' he drew upon Carleton and Eburne to cite the favourable judgments of such church fathers as Ambrose, Augustine, Chrysostom, Cyprian, Jerome, and Origen that all tithes belonged by divine right to the parish clergy.[212] During the Middle Ages, laymen became the owners of tithes 'by fraud and violence' and monks 'sucked the best tythes into their cloysters.'[213] Nor did the Reformation end such expropriation; Henry VIII 'shared' the dissolved monasteries 'among his favourites, for love or for mony, as himselfe thought good; and still the patrimonie of the Lord is detained in the unjust hands of those who can have no true interest therein.'[214]

Moving beyond Carleton and Ridley, Robarts argued that the divine sanction of tithes extended to the proportion, that God 'also determineth the *tenth part* for his own speciall due' and 'it is not in the power of any man to enforce the diminishing of the number.'[215] This led to a strong attack upon composition and other customary constraints recognized by canon and common law.[216] With a passion not dissimilar to that displayed by Spelman, Robarts catalogued the ruination of families who possessed church lands and threatened divine displeasure against all who failed to return tithes to the church: 'Whether men have received the tythes from Bishops, or Kings, or any other persons (except they will restore them to the Church) let them knowe, that they do commit the sinne of sacriledge, and incurre the daunger of eternall damnation.'[217] Fittingly, Robarts ended his treatise with a chapter in which he 'propounded and answered' objections against the doctrine that tithes belonged by divine right to the parish priest.[218] The relatively moderate position put by Carleton in 1605 had turned into a strong denial of legitimacy to the common and ecclesiastical law of tithes in use for several centuries, a denial which subverted the legitimacy of customary law in particular, and which queried the rule of human law in general.

The Collection of Tithes

Into this polemical context came the contentious *Historie of Tithes.* Generally following the pattern used by Carleton, Selden wrote a much more sophisticated historical narrative than any of those dis-

cussed above. Critically examining the evidence cited by his predecessors (and much more), he drew upon documents in Hebrew,
Aramaic, Greek, Latin, French, German, Anglo-Saxon, and English to
depict the practices used by the ancient Jews and pagans, by early and
medieval Christians, in their support of religious institutions. However, Selden broke with Carleton, Ridley, and Robarts by concentrating most of his attention on the theories and practices of tithing
during the Middle Ages.[219] By demonstrating the historical anachronism of the view pushed by Robarts, the resulting treatise seriously
subverted the case presented by canon lawyers since the twelfth century. Because it probed a sensitive point and because it seemed to
chip away portions of the foundations of any theory of divine right,
The Historie of Tithes sparked off several heated replies.[220] The controversy must have opened before the book passed the press, for
Selden, perhaps protesting too much, attacked his critics as moti-
vated by 'distemperd Malice, Ignorance, or Jealousie' and explained
that his history was

not written to prove *that Tithes are not due by the Law of God*; not writen
to prove *that the Laitie may detain them*, not to prove *that Lay hands may
still enjoy Appropriations*; in summe, not at all *against the maintenance of
the Clergie*. Neither is it any thing else but it self, that is, a meer Narration,
and the *Historie of Tithes*. Nor is the law of God, whence Tithes are commonly derivd, more disputed in it, then the Divine Law, whence all Creatures have their continuing subsistence, is inquired after in *Aristotles
historie of living Creatures*, in *Plinies* Naturall historie, or in *Theophrastus
his historie of Plants* ...[221]

Such analogies seem rather forced if tithes derived their binding force
from God's direct command to man; after all, the Scriptures
impressed no such obligation upon plants or animals. One cannot
entirely blame Selden's contemporaries for finding his defence a bit
disingenuous, a number of his prose passages more than slightly sardonic. Still, one must remember that he defended a practical and
legal interpretation not at all unlike that of the anonymous Elizabethan author cited above.

Also impugned was the propriety of an English common lawyer,
rather than a canon or Roman lawyer, writing such a history. Here
Selden saw *The Historie of Tithes* as applying the philological tradition of such Continental legal scholars as Brisson, Budé, Cujas, Gro-

tius, Pierre Pithou, Etienne Pasquier, and others to the English common law.

> For these all were or are practicers of the various *common* or *secular Laws* of their own Nations, although they studied the *Imperialls* and *Canons* in the Universitie and who of the learned knows not what light these have given out of their studies of *Philologie*, both to their own and other Professions? And that in rectifying of Storie [history], in explication of good Autors, in vindicating from the injurie of time both what belongs aswell to sacred as prophan studies? Why then may not equally a *common Lawier* of *England* use this *Philologie*?[222]

For once, Selden seemed too modest, for his history examined both the theory and the practice of the past in all of western Europe. Neither the admonitions of those clerics, doctors, fathers, and councils cited by his predecessors nor the claims of the canon law provided a sufficient guide to historical usage, he argued, for 'the Laitie at pleasure commonly limited the Canon Law especially where it toucht their dignities or possessions ... To argue therefore from affirmative Canons only to Practice, is equall in not a few things (and especially in this of Tithing) to proving the Practice of a custom from consonant Law of Plato's commonwealth, of *Lucian's* men in the Moon, or of *Aristophanes* his Citie of Cuckoes in the clouds.'[223] Here lay the key to Selden's representation of the past and the storm of protest it aroused. The arguments of divines and canon lawyers were treated like any other historical sources, as slanted, perhaps even self-interested, expressions which arose in particular contexts in response to other voices. Here lay the key, as well, to the Tacitism of this treatise. The model of the 'old Sceptiques,' properly applied, provided 'the only way that in all kinds of studies leads and lies open even to the Sanctuarie of Truth, while others, that are servile to common Opinion and vulgar suppositions, can rarely hope to be admitted neerer then into the base court of her Temple which too speciously often counterfaits her inmost Sanctuary ...'[224] By consistently applying critical, sceptical principles, *The Historie of Tithes* demystified much of the aura surrounding the practical application of divine law. As with the law of nature, the law of God received concrete existence only in the customary laws of particular jurisdictions.

Opening with a chronological format, *The Historie of Tithes* surveyed Jewish, pagan, and Christian experience in seven chapters.

Drawing mostly upon the sources employed by Carleton, Selden put his skill in Semitic languages to good use in a humanist philological analysis of the Torah, the Talmud, and other writings. Although admitting that the ancient Syriac and Arabic translations of the Old Testament favoured the opposite conclusion, Selden accepted the reading of Josephus and the author of Hebrews that Abraham had given one-tenth of his spoils, not of the whole of his increase, to Melchesedech and that Jacob had followed suit.[225] Since no 'other expresse mention is of tithes before *Moses* his time,' it seemed reasonable to conclude that Jewish tithes had started with Mosaic law. Levitical tithes fell only upon wheat, barley, figs, grapes, olives, pomegranates, and dates, among plants, and cattle (which included sheep and goats), among livestock. Other payments, such as the first fruits upon grain, wine, oil, and the fleece of shorn animals, increased the burden.[226] Almost all commentators agreed that Mosaic tithes had ceased with the destruction of the second temple in A.D. 64.

Tithing as a command of the law of nations, however, proved more controversial. An examination of the ancient Greek and Roman evidence cited by the earlier writers turned up no indication that these pagans practised any system of proportional religious contributions enforced by legal sanctions, although they sometimes offered tithes of their spoils as a gift.[227] During the first four centuries of the church, early Christian charity displayed no continuity with the payment of Jewish tithes and only a muddled understanding of their collection. 'So liberall, in the beginning of Christianity, was the devotion of beleevers, that their bountie, to the Evangelicall Priesthood, farre exceeded what the Tenth could have been.' Indeed, 'till towards the end of the first foure hundred [years], no *Paiment* of them can be proved to have been in use.'[228] During the following four centuries, such leading church fathers as St Augustine and St Ambrose argued in favour of tithing and collected tithes as freely given offerings in Hippo and Milan.[229] Other clergy carried on the older tradition of encouraging unspecified offerings; for example, Pope 'Leo the Great' preached numerous sermons 'stirring up every mans devotion, to offer, to his Parish Church, part of his receivd fruits, but, speaks not a word of any certain quantitie.'[230] During this period, some pious laymen began to offer a tenth of their increase on an annual basis, and others to attach perpetual endowments, including tithes, to particular churches and monasteries, particularly to sanctuaries built upon their own territories, but they retained control of the patronage and endowments of such institutions.[231] The purported constitutions of the apostles assembled by Pope Clement, and other early medieval popes and councils, which supported the collection of tithes, received a scathing critique:

Those kind of Acts and Legends of Popes and others, are indeed usually stufft with such falshoods, as being bred in the middle ages among idle Monks, not only grow ancient now, but are receivd amongst us with such reverence, that the antiquitie which the Copies have gaind out of later time, is mistook for a Character of truth in them for the times to which they were first, by fiction or bold interpolation, referd.[232]

A scorn for the forgeries of those who claimed a pious, religious calling and for an uncritical acceptance of old documents as authentic empassioned Selden's philological judgment. After these five chapters, little remained of the view that tithes existed by the law of nature and nothing supported the contention that the clergy had collected them by divine right during the first eight hundred years of Christianity. A historical interpretation of the origins of enforced tithes on the annual increase of grains and animals, therefore, seemed in order.

According to Selden, such a system arose during the next four hundred years. Secular laws proclaimed by Charlemagne marked the first recorded attempt to create a legal right to tithes in western Europe. During this period, laymen began to dedicate tithes more frequently to particular churches or monasteries, especially those that they or their ancestors had founded. The lay patron, by a ceremony, conferred the glebe and tithes to the clerical client:

And hence was the name *Benefice*, for a Church and endowments given. For as such lands or annuities, as in the Empire, were given for perpetuall salaries to military persons, had the name of *Beneficia*, so, what was thus conferd upon spirituall souldiers in the Church, had afterward the like title. But, at this Commendation of the temporalities so make only by the Patron, the Bishop indeed had the usual consecration of the Incumbent, but nothing at all to do with the disposition of the church or endowments.[233]

Even the term for an ecclesiastical holding, a 'benefice,' derived from an extension of previous lay practice. Selden conveyed a reasonable understanding of the roots of what would become the investiture struggle. Clergymen, aggressive in their extension of ecclesiastical power, started to claim more frequently and vociferously that all tithes belonged to them by divine right.

> The practice found in the time twixt about D.CCC. [800] and M.CC. [1200] from Christ, consists in some *ordinarie payments* of Tithes, as in former ages; in more *frequent Consecrations* of a perpetuall right of them alone to any Church, or Monasterie, at the owners choice; in *Appropriations* of them with the churches in which they were by *custom* or *consecration* established; in *Infeodations* of them into Lay-hands; and in Exemptions for discharge of paiment. By the more general *Opinion* of the Church, they are exprest to be due *Jure divino*; but that is warily to be interpreted out of the generall practice cleerly allowd by the Clergie. From the beginning of this time *Canons* are very frequent for the right of them. But the *first Law* that may be at all stiled generall for it, was ordained by *Charles* the Great, and receivd, but little practiced, through the Empire.[234]

With the foundation and endowment of parish churches by laymen and the attachment of earlier gifts (previously paid into a common diocesan fund) to such churches, the theory began to arise that tithes belonged to the parish church.

The next four centuries witnessed the spread of enforced tithes over the whole of western Europe, the triumph in canon law of an argument for their parochial right, and the suppression of the evidence for earlier gifts demanded now by the predominance of the claim by divine right. During the same era, however, theologians, especially Dominicans and Franciscans (who had more than the theory at stake), began to challenge the canonists over the exact nature of the divine right to tithes or, indeed, whether it existed. Selden traced three basic theories taught by the schoolmen, mendicants, and canonists. The first interpreted tithes as part of the ceremonial or judicial law of the Jews, not the moral law, and, therefore, applying to Christians only 'by imitation of the *Jewish* state' and not of 'any continuing force of it under the Gospell. And that the Church was not bound to this part, but freely might as well have ordained the payment of a Ninth, or Eleventh, according to various opportunitie.'[235] Selden accepted this view and claimed that such medieval schoolmen as Alexander of Hales and Thomas Aquinas, such late-fifteenth- and early-sixteenth-century scholastics as Cardinal Cajetan and John Major, and such moderns as Cardinal '*Bellarmin, Suarez,* and

Malder, Bishop of *Antwerp* and late professor at *Louvain*, and others accord, and make it the *communis opinio Theologorum*; and some will have it Ceremoniall, rather then Judiciall, but we dispute not thereof.' The second, supported in England by 'John Wyclif, Walter Brute, and William Thorp,' interpreted tithes as alms.[236] The third, which Selden identified with the canonists, argued 'that the right of the *quota* of Tithes immediately is from the *Moral* or *Divine Natural Law*'; as vigorous popes came to enforce the canon law from the eleventh century onward, this interpretation temporarily triumphed as a theory for the divine right of tithes.[237]

Even during these aggressive assertions of clerical 'rights,' the customs of particular jurisdictions continued to govern practice.

In these following times, the *Canon Law* grew to be of more force, and *Parochiall right* (thorough the Decrees made against former course of arbitrarie Conveyances, and from the passages of Canon Law, that supposed the *generall right* of Tithes) became more established. But the Opinions of *Canonists* and *Divines* have been and are much different in the question, upon what *Law* the generall right of them is immediately grounded. But by the *Practice* of the *Common Laws* (for so much as I have read) of all Christian States, they are subject to *Customes*, and that somtimes as well in *non payment* as in *payment of a less part*.[238]

The secular laws of France, Germany, Spain, Italy, Scotland, and other countries decided upon the enforcement of tithes within a given jurisdiction. This historical interpretation of tithes ended where it began, with the customary laws of Europe firmly in control of all aspects of collection. A transition to the common law of England followed easily.

In seven detailed chapters, Selden applied the model worked out for all of western Europe to English historical evidence, including many medieval manuscripts. Starting with the Anglo-Saxon law codes and ending with the commission established by Edward VI to reform the canon law for Protestant England, he systematically discussed some forty-one bills, petitions, acts, ordinances, and other documents dealing with the establishing and limiting of tithes. Here, a humanist philological method paid substantial dividends. After a careful analysis of the Anglo-Saxon material, which included a separating out of later emendations, Selden noted that the earliest reliable references to tithes came in a law made by King Athelstan by the

advice and consent of his bishops in around 930 and in an act of
'*Edmund*, King of *England* in a ⲱicelne Sẏnoδ, that is, a great Synod,
or Councell, a kind of Parliament, both of Lay and Spirituall men ...
held in London' near the year 940, although the 'Laws made between
King *Alfred* and *Guthrun* the *Dane*' (*ca* 900) contained a passage that
may have dealt with tithes.[239] Having demonstrated that secular rulers and laymen played a part in passing laws for the collection of
tithes from the earliest times, as on the Continent, he turned to an
examination of their nature.

The Nature of Tithes

The traditional interpretation of the canonists, revived by Carleton,
Ridley, and Robarts as theological and historical truth, had asserted
that tithes belonged to the parish priest by divine right. In his interpretation of the evidence, Selden found two major barriers to the historical verification of this theory: the changing nature of the parish
and the early ubiquity of tithes as arbitrary consecrations. In Anglo-
Saxon England, tithes could hardly have belonged to that small unit
later called a parish, for parish churches were just coming into existence, usually founded and endowed by laymen, and 'out of these Lay
foundations chiefly, doubtlesse came those kind of Parishes, which
at this day are in every Diocese.'[240] In those days, the word '*Parochia*
usually denoted as well a Bishoprique, or Diocese, or biⲨceope
Ⲩcẏɲe as the *Saxons* called it, as a lesse Parish,' and offerings of land
or income to the church generally applied collectively to the whole
diocese, not to one local congregation.[241] This strongly emphasized
the lay contribution to the structure of the church and it made
anachronistic nonsense of the assumption that tithes had always
belonged of right to the parish priest.

Little evidence for a system of generally enforced tithes came from
the Anglo-Saxon or early Norman periods. Domesday Book, for
example, listed the possessions and estates of many churches, but
'very rarely any Tithes among those church revenues are there
found.'[242] All of the surviving evidence from this era pointed to tithes
as free offerings given at the will of the donor to dioceses or monasteries or attached to a parish church at its foundation. Listing many
examples of such 'arbitrary consecrations' from early manuscripts,
Selden concluded that before the reign of 'King *John*, it was most
commonly practiced by the Laitie to make arbitrarie Consecrations

of Tithes of their possessions to what Monasterie or Church they would' and that many of the so-called appropriated tithes traced their 'chiefe originall from those arbitrarie Consecrations (which you may well call Appropriations of Tithes) and not from the appropriating only of Parish Churches, as some out of grosse ignorance, with too much confidence, deliver.'[243] This involved a dual reinterpretation, for it argued that tithes arose as the offerings by individuals of one-tenth of the annual produce of their own lands (not as one-tenth of the yearly increase of all lands within a parish) and that the dedication of such pious gifts to a diocese or monastery explained how such institutions came to hold many tithes (not just that they had annexed them from a parish). Of course, some parishes that monasteries had appropriated at an early date later obtained the right to collect tithes, as well. Selden took great pride in his discovery that tithes originated in western Europe as freely given arbitrary consecrations, and rightly so.[244] If this brilliant historical interpretation emphasized the creative contribution of laymen to the church, it also displayed a darker side to the forced demands of leading clergymen.

Following from the detection of the arbitrary consecration of tithes came the discovery that the general enforcement of tithes as belonging of right to the parish priest spread across the face of western Europe as the result of a well-planned and executed program of legal innovation carried out by the papacy. This campaign for *jure divino* tithes involved the abolition of all arbitrary consecrations by decretal, the conversion of regularly paid voluntary tithes into ones due by customary right, and the strong concentration of pressure by the papacy upon lay rulers to embed the general collection of tithes by right in secular law. Starting seriously around the year 1200, the enterprise approached a crescendo under Pope Innocent III and coincided with that period in which the papacy reached the zenith of its political power in western Europe. Selden expounded this interpretation in his text, but summarized it in pungent, stinging prose in the 'Review' at the end of *The Historie of Tithes* (a section written after he knew that clerics had penned attacks upon his work):

But we conclude with that of the *Canon Laws* getting such force, *and* making such *alteration in the matter of Tithes* about the yeer M.CC. when through it, *Parochiall payment* became first to be performed here, or elsewhere, generally, and as of common right (where other titles prevented it not) and through it only; not through the ancienter secular Lawes here made for Tithes. For the suits for them in the Spirituall Courts either were all grounded upon the Canons, or the common right of Tithes was now supposed in the Libell as a knowne dutie to the clergie, without secular Law. It may soon be apprehended, that it was much lesse difficult about that time, then any other, for the Popes and the Canon Laws to gaine more obedience among subjects, and execute more autoritie over Lay possessions, when also they so easily usurpt power over supreme Princes, which yeelded to them. For no time ever was, wherein any of them more insolently bare themselves in the *Empire*, never neere so insolently in *England*, as in the continuing times next before and neere about this change. And to all States the Church of *Rome* now grew most formidable. Remember but the Excommunication and Correction suffered by *Frederique Barbarosa, Henry* the sixt, and other Princes of the *Empire*, and by our Henry the second, and King *John*; the stories of them are obvious. And our *Richard* the first, betweene those two, to gratifie the Clergie here for their exceeding liberalitie, in contribution to his Ransome from Captivitie, with great favour gave them an indulgent Charter of their Liberties; which being joind with those other prone and yeelding Admissions of the Ecclesiastique Government over the Crowne (so were the times) doubtless gave no small autoritie to the *Exercise of the Canon Law* in those things, which before about that time were diversly otherwise. Neither was that part of the Canon Law, which would have a *Generall and Parochiall payment of Tithes*, not only second to any, in regard of the Clergie's profit; but also none other, doubtlesse, was so great as it, in gaining the Clergie a Direct and certain Revenue. Therefore it was not without reason on their side, at such time as they saw the Power of *Rome*, that is, the autoritie of Decretals and of the Canons grow most dreadfull to Prince and subject, that they should urge this on to a continuing practice, and that with execution of the raigning Censures of the Church. Hence have the Canons, in this point, hitherto here continued, and have been and are binding Ecclesiastique Lawes, saving wherein the later expresse Laws of the Kingdome crosse them. And thus out of the qualitie of the time, with regard to the practiced insolencie of the *Pope* and *his Clergie*, in putting their *Canons* and *Decretals* in execution, that receivd generall practice of Parochiall payment (neere almost according to the Canons) and other such alterations, that suddenly varied from former use, and from the libertie of the Lay subject, must have its originall; not from any want of the *Canons of the Church of Rome*, as if they had not been at all had or read, before about that time. For doubtless, the Canon Laws were here used and practiced as farre forth as the Clergie could make the Laitie subject to them.[245]

The parochial right to tithes may have derived from God, but it came to be enforced upon laymen only at the height of usurped power by the papacy, when even emperors and kings had to knuckle under to the demands of the clergy.

Through grants both enticed and extorted from the kings of England, this general right entered the common law:

And by the practice of the Kingdome, it became cleer Law (as it remains also at this day) that regularly, if no other title or discharge, to be specially pleaded or shewed in the Allegation of the Defendant, might appeare, every Parson had a common right to the Tithes of all annual encrease (prediall and mixt), accruing within the limits of his Parish, without shewing other title to them in his Libell. That appeares frequently in our Yeer-books, where the Issues, taken upon Parochiall Limits are reported.[246]

The common law also enforced any customary payments of cash in composition for crops, payments of fixed quantities instead of a tenth as an actual proportion, and adjudicated any disputes over the rights of ownership of appropriated tithes. As in other European nations, the collection of tithes remained subject to the customary law and, therefore, to any changes of regulation enacted by statute.

Firmly believing in the supremacy of national law, Selden saw nothing improper about the statutes of the sixteenth century redressing the imbalance created in the thirteenth century. Indeed, the remarks disparaging the annexation of monastery lands sound bitingly ironic.[247] What galled Selden was the sanctimonious self-interest displayed by the clergy in their arguments, a sentiment tellingly revealed in sardonic comments upon the quarrels between friars and priests over the exact divine derivation of tithes:

But see here the effects of perverse opposition on both sides. Some Friers, providing only for their own wealth, would have had them reckond meer Almes, and so have gotten them from the Secular Priests; and others would have had them retaind by Lay men. The Secular Priests on the other side would rather instruct the Laitie with ridiculous falshoods (in the termes whereof they would not spare to abuse the holiest Name) then not seem to say enough for their own gain.[248]

The rapid shift from voluntary offerings to compulsory general tithes seemed upsetting enough, but far worse was the outright fraud practised by the clergy to perpetuate this innovation. '... It seems certain, that the Titles derivd from lay consecrations were after this third CCCC. yeers [A.D. after 1200] carefully concealed by the Possessors of such publike records of their revenues, as were of more common and open use in their legall proceedings at the Canon Law, however they remaind still in their ancienter and more secret Chartularies.'[249] Having discovered that clergymen, after forcing laymen to pay general tithes, protected this right by removing all references to earlier arbitrary consecrations from their public records, Selden waxed indignant at the perpetrators and defenders of this holy imposture.

Underneath the occasionally flaming heat of the account lay an ideal of Christianity which envisaged a church governed by the prince and people, integrated into society, and enriched by the creative talents of laymen, as well as those of the clergy. This Protestant vision helped Selden to reinterpret *The Historie of Tithes*. After the triumph of the canonists, it had become natural, not deceptive, to believe that tithes had always belonged to the parish priest unless appropriated or usurped into other hands. The evidence publicly available in cartularies supported this argument and even as excellent scholars as Carleton and Spelman did not truly discover its flaws. Only through a new vision of the church and the careful examination of earlier manuscript sources and unadulterated cartularies which Selden carried out in Cotton's collection would contrary evidence ever begin to appear. It took a daring leap of imagination to construct such a controversial historical reinterpretation against such odds and from such a limited number of sources. This Selden did. The intellectual excitement of his accomplishment still remains in the fertile, persuasive pages of *The Historie of Tithes*. Never a fluid stylist, Selden's skills as a historical writer abides in his probing imagination and his diligent assembly, critical examination, and inventive interpretation of the sources.

Relationship of Roman to Customary Law

While *The Historie of Tithes* marked the peak of Selden's narrative powers, it also openly launched him upon a polemical political and legal career. As one of its main themes, it tried to demonstrate that the canon law, 'in such things as are not meerly spirituall, is alwaies governed and limited (as with us) by those *Common* laws' of every European state.[250] Having shown how the law of God found practical historical application only by incorporation into the laws of particular jurisdictions, Selden also offered plausible solutions to two other problems that continued to unsettle his account of the ancient constitution: the relationship of Roman to customary law and the impact of the Norman Conquest. Printed only in the 'Review,' these brief discussions appeared as appendages to the main narrative. However, each provided an acutely concentrated expression of Selden's constitutional thought.

The discussion of Roman law, or the 'old Imperialls,' entered as an aside, as it had in the preface. The problem here was to deal with that great prestige held by the *Corpus Juris Justiniani* during the Renaissance and to allay the fear that Roman law might prove a formidable rival to the common law. The solution lay in a refinement of that theory, announced in the notes to Fortescue's treatise, that image which reduced the constitution to a relatively stable framework, all law to changing custom and statute.[251] Even before mentioning the gap of five hundred years when Roman law no longer governed in western Europe, Selden dismissed the notion that any legal system could remain confined to a single codification. Any table, code, or charter needed interpretation and application; in practice, this meant modification. The redaction of Roman laws carried out under the Emperor Justinian, therefore, could claim no special prestige, for even in the Empire and in Italy, it held sway in the same manner as other early codes governed in other countries.

So, that to affirme, that in these places [Germany and Italy] the old Imperialls, or that Civill Law (as they call it) governes, is as if (for example) an equall ignorance shuld tel us, that *Spain* were governed only by *Alfonso's Partidas*, and *Scotland* only by *Malcolms* Laws or the *Quoniam Attachiamenta*; or that in the time of the old Emperors the *Roman* State had been alwaies governed only by the XII. Tables, or that *England* were legally ruled only by the *Grand Charter*, or by the two volumes of old Statutes. Like accession and alteration as any of these have had, is found in the *Empire* and *Italie*, where the Imperialls have, through the power of the Emperors and Popes, any now continuing autoritie.[252]

The ongoing authority of Roman law derived not from ancient Rome, but from a revival carried out by medieval emperors and popes and a continual usage thereafter. Even then Roman law had changed. In Germany and Italy, the feudal law had replaced the provisions of the old imperials in such areas as 'the disposition of Inheritances, punishing of Crimes, course of Proceedings, Dowers, Testaments, and such other, which are of greatest moment under the Legall rule ...'[253] If custom had modified and superseded ancient Roman practice in the heartland of its revived jurisdiction, then the laws of the rest of western Europe must have limited its application even further.

After its revival in the twelfth century, the influence of the *Corpus Juris Justiniani* had grown significantly, especially as a readily digested guide to the law of nature or nations. Studied in the universities, it enjoyed a great deal of prestige. However, its provisions and principles obtained force only by gaining acceptance or incorporation into an existing system of customary or common law.

And the Interpretation of those common Laws in most places, save *England* and *Ireland*, hath of late time been much directed by the reason of the Imperialls, and only by the reason of them (not by their autoritie) and that also in case when they are not opposite at all to the *common Laws*, but seeme to agree with the Law of *Nations* or *common reason*. ... And even here in *England* were, about *Henry* the thirds time, often applied to the common Law in discourse and argument, as you may see in *Bracton* his frequent quotations of them.[254]

Governing authority still resided in the customary laws which incorporated or rejected the reason of Roman law. The English common law stood supreme over both canon and Roman law, but this did not represent a unique or even unusual situation in western Europe, where every 'Christian State hath its owne *Common Laws*, as this Kingdom [of England] hath.'[255] While sometimes subject to shock, such systems generally changed so gradually that they retained an essential continuity with the fundamental principles present at their formation.

The Effect of the Norman Conquest

The English constitution, of course, had faced such a traumatic experience in the Norman Conquest. Selden had to address the question of whether or not Anglo-Saxon titles to tithes had survived the change of regime. Having discussed the particulars in the body of the history, he offered a more compact general interpretation in the 'Review':

The Laws of before, as well as after the *Norman Conquest* (as it is vulgarly called) are here gathered ... For neither were the Laws formerly made, abolisht by that *Conquest*, although, by Law of Warre, regularly all Rights and Laws of the place conquered, be wholly subject to the *Conquerors* will. For in this of the *Norman*, not only the *Conquerors* will was not declared, that the former Laws should abrogated (and untill such declaration, Laws remaine in force, by the opinion of some, in all Conquests of Christians against Christians) but also the ancient and former Laws of the Kingdome were confirmed by him. For in his fourth yeere, by the advise of his Baronage, he summoned to *London, Omnes Nobiles sapientes et lege suâ eruditos, ut eorum leges et consuetudines audiret,* as the words are of the Book of *Lichfield,* and afterward confirme them, as is further also related in *Roger* of *Hoveden.* Those *Lege suâ eruditi* were common Lawiers of that time ...[256]

The first edition of *Titles of Honor,* published just four years earlier, had interpreted the Conquest as a major break; William I had used his military victory to introduce the feudal law into England. Now Selden reversed that position and campaigned firmly on the side of continuity.

After reviewing the standard evidence again, including the deathbed confession by the Confessor that he had won his right to the English throne by the sword and also the case of the Saxon who held his manor after the Conquest by a title deriving from his possession of it under Edward the Confessor, Selden concluded that

this *William* seised the Crown of *England,* not as conquerd, but by pretence of gift or adoption, aided and confirmed by neernesse of bloud; and so the *Saxon* Laws formerly in force could not but continue and such of them as are now abrogated, were not at all abrogated by his Conquest but either by the Parlaments or Ordinances of his time and of his successors, or else by nonusage or contrarie custom.[257]

The language mirrored that from a passage in *Jani Anglorum* quoted earlier in this chapter; now, however, it conveyed a different message. The 'pretence' still remained, but this time it did not apply to the claim by blood, only to 'the pretence of gift and adoption.' Since William did not seize the crown 'as conquered,' he could not change the laws on his own authority. Having earlier considered and accepted an interpretation that the Conquest marked a major constitutional break, Selden had reversed his judgment and joined those common lawyers who argued against any serious disruption. The laws of England provided the Conqueror with his right to the succession; either usage or Parliament (by continuing old or enacting new laws) bridged any potential gap. Selden's interpretation of the ancient constitution, enriched by his comparative studies and his general theory of law, ended the second decade of the century with its fundamentals strengthened and all ambiguity dispelled; now mixed government reigned supreme.

CONCLUSION: THE FIRST DECADE OF SELDEN'S PUBLICATIONS

Looking back upon several significant publications, John Selden must have felt a good deal of satisfaction and a little trepidation. His early works showed great promise; his later ones delivered the solid scholarship which raised him into the ranks of the leading English antiquaries, the distinguished company of Lambarde and Camden. This mastery emerged especially brilliantly in *The Historie of Tithes*, an analytical narrative based upon primary evidence in several languages, including many manuscripts, which employed the skills of philology, paleography, and careful contextual chronological analysis to assemble a sweeping reinterpretation of the history of tithes that contained startling implications both for political thought and for the history of medieval Europe. Even the earlier works illustrated the fruitful results that one could derive from applying Renaissance humanist philological methods to English materials.

As early as the *Analecton Anglobritannicon*, Selden had started to employ that perspective from which he had composed all of his early works, reading history forward from the earliest recoverable point. In *Jani Anglorum*, he fashioned a powerful, if still unpolished, image of the ancient constitution as a mixed aristocracy under the Britons, a mixed monarchy from the Saxons onward, a complex collection of slowly shifting laws which adjusted to fit the ever-changing needs of society while still retaining its fundamental shape. The notes to *Poly-Olbion* added some details to this interpretation; those to *De Laudibus* filled in the period of Roman rule and added refinement to the section on Saxon England. *Titles of Honor*, by turning earlier ambiguities about the nature of the Norman Conquest into a historical representation of William I as marking a major break in constitutional development by introducing the feudal law into England, temporarily subverted portions of the earlier account. If Selden's immersion in Continental and Scottish scholarship brought about this conversion, his preparation of a critical edition of Fortescue forced him to reconsider the English common-law tradition. Out of the dialogue emerged not only a brilliantly refurbished symbol of the ancient constitution as an oft-repaired ship, retaining its shape while adding new materials, but also a new vision that converted English law, in its practical, effective, down-to-earth operation, into customary usage and statute.

Here lay the key to Selden's defence of the ancient constitution in the 1620s and 1630s, but perhaps not to his theory of natural rights, published in 1640.[258] It would take years for Selden fully to spell out the implications of his new vision in a detailed historical account and natural-law justification of the ancient constitution. *The Historie of Tithes*, however, sketched out the whole framework and applied it to a very controversial topic, the problem of working out how the law of God impinged upon the property of individuals. With bold strokes and an imaginative employment of evidence, Selden showed that when it came to real and personal property, the states and customary laws of western Europe had always stood supreme over canon and Roman law. It was probably for this reason that his book was suppressed by the High Commission in January 1619. Having demonstrated this portion of his theory in detail throughout the text of *The Historie of Tithes*, Selden could return again to the relationship of the common law with other legal systems in the 'Review.' The picture of William I, his barons, and those 'learned in the laws' (whom Selden identified as 'the common Lawiers of that time, as *Godric* and *Alfwin*') gathering together as a parliament in the fourth year of the Conquest to hear and confirm the 'former Laws of the Kingdome' succeeded both the earlier ambiguity of *Jani Anglorum* and the view that the Conqueror had used his military victory to introduce the feudal law into England contained in *Titles of Honor*.[259] This historical triumph of the king-in-parliament may well have displeased some of the advisers of King James VI and I more than the more obviously controversial aspects of *The Historie of Tithes*, but it probably pleased other royal ministers just as strongly and it certainly jelled just in time for Selden's political career of the following decade. Selden faced great pressure from King James and his favourite, the Marquess of Buckingham, over *The Historie of Tithes*. What he would not admit was that his book presented false evidence and interpretations, nor would he back off from its central interpretation, that the law of God found enforcement only in the laws of particular jurisdictions: 'I find, that not only in the churches of *France, Spain, Italy, Germany,* and of all other foreign christian commonwealths, whose practice I have read of in their laws and decisions, but also in the laws and practice of this his majesty's great monarchy, that no tythes are at all, or have been for many ages since, paid or to be recovered as due *jure divino,* but only according as the secular laws made for tythes, or local customs, ordain or permit them.'[260] Forced to withdraw his most brilliant book from circulation and to apologize to the privy council for the mistake of its publication, he also suffered the degradation of a royal order forbidding him to answer the attacks made by his critics. This provided a taste of the bitterness which politics could bring and, no doubt, some scores to settle in the future. During the same years, Buckingham, as Lord Admiral of England, asked Selden for a fair copy of his treatise on jurisdiction over the seas – the original version of what would become *Mare Clausum* – and presented a copy to the king, who, along with Sir Henry Marten, Judge of the Admiralty, made some suggestions for revisions. However, the admiral withdrew his backing for the project and it failed, for the time being.[261] The role of Buckingham in these distasteful moments no doubt helped to enroll the young scholar in the ranks of the favourite's enemies. As a result of his early scholarship on England and Europe, Selden could enter the arena of the parliaments of the 1620s with a sophisticated theory of a continuous and a continuously changing ancient constitution, a theory just as serviceable and far more historically accurate than that propounded by Sir Edward Coke in the prefaces of his *Reports,* a theory with the potential immense value to those aristocrats with power and prestige who sought to defend the ancient liberties of Englishmen. Fortified by Continental methods and learning, Selden had worked out an effective articulation of the 'common-law mind.'

CHAPTER TWO

John Selden's Parliamentary Career, 1621–1629

During the second decade of the seventeenth century, John Selden established a solid scholarly reputation with a series of treatises on the history of English laws, the history of European titles of honour, and the history of tithes. Embedded in these works lay a powerful representation of the English constitution as a mixed monarchy in which the king, nobles, clergy, and freemen shared sovereignty from the earliest days onward. This interpretation provided an alternative to that of 'constitutional monarchy governed by the common law' spelled out by such common lawyers as Thomas Hedley, Sir Edward Coke, and Sir John Davies, and clashed with that of 'constitutional monarchy created by kings' articulated by James VI and I. More consistently than any of his rivals, Selden brought a cosmopolitan humanist perspective and deep understanding of the charters, statutes, and legal documents of medieval England to the defence of his profoundly historical interpretation. Strong men of action valued his political vision and mastery of technique, and sought to channel these talents into political action. During the 1620s, they plunged a not-unwilling Selden into the heady, contentious life of parliamentary politics.

In 1621, the Lords hired Selden to codify and establish their privileges, including the revival of judicature; as part of this task, he also helped to establish the standing orders of the Upper House. Such actions impressed influential patrons and secured his selection to borough seats in the parliaments of 1624, 1626, and 1628–9. In 1624, Selden won the respect of fellow members of the Commons by serving on committees concerned with finding precedents for the powers of the Lower House. In 1626 and 1628–9, he sat for a borough controlled by the Earl of Hertford and became a member of the Seymour parliamentary team. In 1626, Selden used his aggressive handling of the case of Sir Robert Howard to extend the parliamentary privilege of freedom from arrest during sessions and took a leading role in initiating and managing impeachment proceedings against the Duke of Buckingham. By 1628, his parliamentary experience and his leading part in the Five Knights' Case raised Selden into a powerful leadership role in the Commons. Again a member of the Seymour connection, he played a major part in drafting what became the Petition of Right and in working out and presenting the arguments which secured its passage. During the second session, Selden became an even more fiery critic of policies initiated by the king's ministers; indeed, his actions helped to force the dissolution and led to his imprisonment in 1629.

'THE PRIVILEDGES OF THE BARONAGE'

While some would date the start of Selden's political career from his affiliation with the Virginia Company, his impact upon national events became manifest by his employment as an expert legal historian by the House of Lords in the Parliament of 1621.[1] The concern for codification of the practices and privileges of the Upper House arose early in the session when a routine reminder by Lord Chancellor Bacon of 'two things' which 'hath ben the ancient maner of this Howse,' the payment to the poor-box made by those who arrived after prayers and the taking of the oath of allegiance by newly sitting peers, brought forth a wide-ranging reply by the Earl of Arundel:

My Lords: besides these things there are many privileges belonging to us and divers orders which were anciently observed in this house that by disuse and want of puttinge in practise are now almost lost and therefore if your Lordships be plesed there be a Comittie for privileges of the House chosen, both these things and many other are considerable to be thought of, which mocion of mine I leave to your Lordships' wisdoms.[2]

The House appointed a thirty-two-member committee of privileges which considered the problem and made its first report three days later, an occasion for much debate. When the large committee proved too cumbersome, the work was taken over by a subcommittee of six members and, eventually, by an even smaller subcommittee of three members; in addition, a levy of funds was raised to pay 'divers gentlemen' already hired 'to search records, and to take notes for their Lordships.'[3] The rough notes made by Henry Elsyng, the Clerk of the parliaments, named Selden as one of those gentlemen; sometime between early February and late March 1621, those 'Defenders of Old English Honour' who dominated the committee and subcommittees on privileges had brought the author of *Titles of Honor* into the employment of the Lords.[4]

The first concrete result of this new association appeared in the draft roll of standing orders for the House produced in March 1621 by Elsyng and Selden. These orders described the sitting, procedure, committees, and other customs of the Lords.[5] As need arose, the House could (and did) easily amend or add items. The speed with which Elsyng and Selden compiled these standing orders reflected the institutional and procedural maturity of the Upper House. The second product, a report on the privileges of the Lords, which included a long section on the judicature of Parliament, bore the marks of Selden's learning. Ironically, before the report reached the floor of the Upper House, Selden, along with the Earl of Southampton and Sir Edwin Sandys, was arrested on 16 June for '"certain reasons of his state known unto his majesty,"' most probably upon the suspicion that he supported the exercise of judicature by the Commons, a position which he had not argued.[6] Perhaps finished in early June and among those papers seized at the time of Selden's arrest during the recess, the report resided in the hands of the Lord Keeper until released after considerable prodding by the Lords; on 30 November 1621, Selden officially presented this report in the form of a book written in a fair hand.[7] The original resides in the record office of the House of Lords; a number of contemporary manuscript copies exist in various libraries; and a modified and expanded version appeared in print as *The Priviledges of the Baronage in England* (London, 1642).[8] The privileges mentioned fell into two groups: first 'those speciall rights which concern them as they are one estate in the upper house of Parliament,' and second those 'special rights that concerne the Barons that have place in Parliament, as they are every one single in their private estates.'[9] The first embraced such perquisites as proxies, freedom from lawsuits during the sitting of Parliament, and the power of judicature, while the second extended to trial by peers; keeping a set number of chaplains; freedom from such civil actions as imprisonment for debt, account, or trespass; and giving evidence by a protestation upon honour instead of upon oath. For each privilege, Selden followed the advice he had given recently to Augustine Vincent and furnished some, often ample, documentation from appropriate primary sources.[10]

The method used to establish the right of proxy (the privilege of a peer to designate another Lord to represent his voice during a prolonged absence from the House) should suffice to illustrate the historical method applied. Noting that the 'first mention of Proxies that occurres in the memories of our Parliaments, is of Carleil under Edward I,' Selden charted the development of this precedent with concrete examples from the reign of Edward II, and then observed that 'in succeeding tymes the testimonies of them, downe to this day, are most frequent.'[11] The personal appearance of the peer in Parliament was, of course, much preferred, and many writs of summons, therefore, included a clause 'to premonish the Baron summoned that his proxie should not bee admitted unles he were compelled to absent himselfe by most inevitable necessitie.'[12] As this privilege became solidified through continued usage, the custom sometimes changed. During the thirteenth, fourteenth, and fifteenth centuries, for example, spiritual Lords often sent men of 'lower condition' as their proxies, 'Bishops, and Parliamentary Abbotts and Priors' giving 'their letters usuallie to Parsons, Prebendaries, Canonists, or such like.'[13] Observing that 'the proxie rolls for the temporall Lords are for the most parte all lost,' Selden refrained from discussing the earliest practice, but noted that the most recent continuous usage called for one peer to hold the proxy of another, temporal peers for temporal nobles and spiritual Lords for their spiritual colleagues:

The following tymes especiallie ever since the first memorie extant of the Journalls of the Upper house (which beginne 1 Henry 8) have kept a constant course of making Parlamentary Barons only Proxies. And it appeares in those Journalls that one, two, or three are joyned in the Letters *conjunctim et divisim*. And most commonlie temporall Lords give their proxies to temporall, and spiritual to spirituall ...[14]

Privileges of this sort, established by custom, presumably could change in the future as well, to adjust to unforeseen circumstances. The proxy reform of 1626 (which limited the number of proxies which could be held by any individual peer) was added to the standing orders of the House and illustrated Selden's vision of privilege, procedure, and law – indeed, of the ancient constitution, as slowly changing custom.[15]

The most sweeping and well-covered privilege was the revival of original and appellate judicature by the Lords. This long section consisted almost wholly of long quotations of relevant precedents from the Rolls of Parliament. The only commentary came in two introductory paragraphs which stood at the opening of the chapter and proclaimed its purpose:

The power of the Judicature belonging to the Lords of Parliament is chieflie seene in their Jurisdiction uppon Writts of Error and their Judgements of offences as well Capitall as not Capitall which tend to any publique mischiefe in the State.

Of their Judgements of such offences manie examples are of former tymes in the Records of Parliament and out of them are here selected some such as most of all conduce to the opening of the course of accusation, the forme of the Defendants answering, the usuall wayes of triall and other incidents in their various kinds of Judgements which are to be found arbitrarie in cases not capitall soe that they extend not to the life or Inheritance, and in capitall offences soe arbitrary that the forme of the death inflicted sometimes varyes from the ordinary course used in the common Law for suche offences.[16]

From such an understated argument sprang the most significant increase in power gained by any of the constituent parts of Parliament during the early seventeenth century, the revival of the judicature of the Lords. This included three main areas: the reversal of cases from the King's Bench on a writ of error, original civil justice upon petition, and, of course, impeachment.[17]

The presumption that someone like James I, Sir Edward Coke, or Selden had to convince the peers of 1621 to take up and defend the privileges which they could claim by historical precedents does scant justice to the evidence. The Lords had started their search for privileges more than a fortnight before Coke delivered his famous speech on the judicature of Parliament in the Lower House; no doubt, they graciously accepted the support given to their position by the king later in the same month, but neither action proves that the initiative lay outside of the Upper House.[18] Accustomed to astute management in all of their affairs, the Lords hired the best help available. Selden, fitting their requests into his own highly sophisticated interpretation of the ancient constitution, acted as the midwife in this rebirth of parliamentary judicature. Henceforth, the power of judgment stood firmly planted in the Upper House. In return for Selden's help, his patrons protected and paid him (and got his papers returned).[19] The Lords must have rejoiced at the ready concurrence of the king and the Commons in such a major acquisition of useful power.

THE PARLIAMENT OF 1624

Having proved his worth in the affairs of Parliament, Selden obtained a seat as a burgess for Lancaster in the next election, that of 1624.[20] Since Sir Humphrey May, Chancellor of the Duchy of Lancaster (who chose to sit for Leicester instead), had vacated this seat, some sort of court connection looks likely, perhaps with May or his patron, the Earl of Pembroke, most probably not one with Prince Charles and the Duke of Buckingham. The seasoned scholar and controversialist soon put his historical knowledge to work on the business of the Commons and became a person of some standing. This Parliament opened on 19 February 1624. Before a month had passed, Selden had served as a delegate at a joint conference of the Lords and the Commons, had reported to the House from a committee established to examine the details of a bill of Wales (this amended the act of 1536 which had incorporated the principality into the realm of England), and had intervened decisively in the heated debate over commitment of the subsidy.[21] Some members, including privy councillors, had pressed to have the subsidy pass all three readings without the normal reference to a committee; others heatedly opposed such departure from customary procedure. Near the end of along debate on a very sensitive issue, Selden cleverly supported commitment in a speech which revealed both his grasp of procedure and his desire to proceed in a fastidious fashion: 'MR SELDEN will not speak to the great matter in hand nor to the orders of the House, being so young a parliament man, but yet he hath been no stranger to the journals of either House and found that the pettiest business hath not been so precipitated.'[22] Thus reported one diarist; two others provided shorter versions of the speech which cut to the substance of the issue: 'MR SELDEN would not have us resolve till we have it debated it at a commitee' and 'MR SHELDEN [sic] saith that it is a parliamentary way to commit all things and this much more.'[23] The House took his advice and sent the subsidy to a committee.[24] Few new members became so readily established in the House of Commons.

Throughout this session, Selden employed his scholarly ability and his knowledge of parliaments to influence the business of the House. Appointed to the potent committee of privileges on 24 March, he also sat on a number of select committees, especially ones searching for precedents.[25] As early as 20 March, 'it is ordered that Sir Robert Cotton and Mr. Selden shall seek forth precedents to shew how moneys have been kept and expended by committees named in parliament.'[26] The antiquaries did their work well, for slightly more than a month later Selden reported back to the House that he 'thinketh the best precedent to lead us in the appointing of treasurers is that of 6° Henry 4, when the treasurers were 2 only, and they were also the Council of War, but he leaveth it to the wisdom of this House.'[27] Another example came in 'An Act for restitution in blood of *Carew Rawleigh*, son of Sir *Walter Rawleigh*, attainted of high treason'; when a question arose as to whether such a bill should originate in the Lords or in the Commons, Sir Edward Coke, William Noy, and Selden were appointed 'to search precedents, what hath been used to be done.'[28] Although all three spoke learnedly on this topic at the second reading, it was Selden who later shepherded the bill through the committee and reported it to the House.[29] In addition, he chaired the committee to search out popish schoolmasters and presented charges in the House against several persons, including Doctor Anyan, president of Corpus Christi College, Oxford.[30] Selden's only recorded part in the trial of Lionel Cranfield, Earl of Middlesex and Lord Treasurer, came when the Commons, disappointed at the punishment meted out by the Lords, named a committee consisting of 'Sir Edward Coke, Mr Noy, Mr Selden, Sir Robert Cotton, and Sir Robert Phelips, to search out former precedents, how judgments have been given, in former times, by the Lords upon complaints made by the Commons.'[31] Respected as a lawyer and savant, Selden readily joined the ranks of more experienced members in the crucial work of committees.

As a new member, Selden seldom spoke. However, he occasionally participated in the debate by making pithy or pedantic remarks on matters of procedural or historical interest. Often these helped to sway the House. During the debate over a bill to abolish all trials by battle, for example, the author of *The Duello* noted that this was 'an ancient fundamental law and not to be taken away with a breath without commitment.'[32] This speech probably aimed at upholding the committee stage of procedure and reminding the Commons to move warily in repealing old customary laws, not at reviving or even continuing trial by battle. Selden's dynamic view of the ancient constitution, after all, welcomed appropriate piecemeal change. On another occasion, in the midst of a discussion over a petition from Mathaias Fowles, one of the patentees of gold and silver thread imprisoned in the Fleet by an order of the Lords in 1621, Selden fetched forth a powerful, if not fully appropriate, precedent for the Commons exercising judicature on its own, the case of Dr Arthur Hall from the reign of Elizabeth I.[33] Since Hall both sat in and attacked the Commons, and Fowles had done neither, this example did not conform to the situation at hand. However, the House appointed a committee to consider the case and named Selden as a member.[34] Only once in 1624, when he defended the actions of Lord Keeper Williams from aspersions presented in a petition from Lady Darcy, did Selden feel the sting of commotion employed by members against unpopular speeches: 'Mr Selden began to strain some reasons so far in justifying my Lord Keeper that he was interrupted.'[35] This would not happen again. On the whole, then, the Parliament of 1624 marked an auspicious start for Selden's career as a member and a reasonably amicable setting for the arduous task of putting his constitutional ideas into action.

THE PARLIAMENT OF 1626

In the 1620s, Selden sat for boroughs controlled by patrons; he could not command enough social standing to get elected to Parliament on his own. Unable to find a seat in the Parliament of 1625, he experienced the riches of two returns in 1626, clearly a sign that his talents stood in some demand. Elected by the boroughs of Great Bedwin (Wiltshire) and Ilchester (Somerset), he chose to sit for Great Bedwin, most probably as a client of the Earl of Hertford. Brian O'Farrell has argued in favour of a connection to the Earl of Pembroke and Conrad Russell for ties with Thomas Howard, the Earl of Arundel. Neither of these seems improbable, especially since Arundel and Pembroke married sisters of the wife of Selden's friend the Earl of Kent. Of the two boroughs that returned Selden, Sir Robert Phelips was High

Steward of Ilchester and exercised influence there, and the earls of Hertford held the manor of Great Bedwin and a lease on the Bedwyn prebendship.[36] Indeed, since Selden represented a Seymour borough and his actions fit into what we know about the aims of that network (including the attack upon the Duke of Buckingham – a mutual enemy – and a shared support for mixed monarchy), he most probably sat as a member of the Seymour network as a political adviser, a spokesman in the Commons, and – for this Parliament – as a replacement for the earl's brother, Sir Francis Seymour. In part, a peer's 'man of business,' in part an learned adviser, he did not neatly fit into the categories recently constructed by historians. Selden knew far more about the English constitution than such Elizabethans as Gabriel Harvey and Thomas Norton (indeed, far more than all of his contemporaries, with the possible exception of Sir Edward Coke and Sir Henry Spelman) and he quickly displayed exceptional skills in the debates and committees of the Commons.[37] Probably looking at his role as a client through his experiences as a barrister, Selden acted on behalf of his patron but expected his advice on mattters within his own expertise to carry great weight. Selden received a seat in the House of Commons and, in return, the Seymours secured an exceptionally able intellectual as their spokesman and aide.

Although Violet Rowe discovered the existence of a major patronage network in the House of Commons many years ago, and more recently Conrad Russell and Thomas Cogswell have incorporated some patron and client relationships into their analyses of English parliaments of the 1620s, historians know little about the detailed working of patronage in parliamentary politics.[38] No recent historian has written in favour of party politics in these parliaments, but Mark Kishlansky and Victor Stater have argued that the contest for policy and power among competing aristocratic networks before 1640, whether in court, parliaments, or countryside, did not normally involve the ruthless tactics of contested elections and exclusion of rivals from office and power practised after 1660.[39] My own preliminary studies on the patronage network of the Duke of Buckingham in the session of 1628 would seem to indicate that he placed his influence behind such administrative supporters as his secretary in the Admiralty, his receiver, one of his gentlemen ushers, a kinsman who was at Ré in 1627, a Clerk of the privy council, an Auditor of the Exchequer, a royal gentleman of the bedchamber, a diplomat, a courtier, the lieutenant of Dover Castle, the victualler of the Fleet, a customs farmer, and various local worthies; on the whole, these were men who acted as his agents for various concerns, including the war effort, in court, country, and abroad.[40] As noted below, the smaller network assembled by the Earl of Hertford and his brother for the session of 1628 clearly made a larger impact upon proceedings in the Commons than did larger connection assembled by Buckingham. Ever since their punishment for Hertford's unauthorized marriage to Lady Arabella Stuart, the Seymours had felt the pains of exclusion from the bounty of the court and frustration at not exercising the power and influence in the country which they believed should accompany their birth and wealth. Blaming the favourite for their lack of preference under Charles I, Sir Francis struck back by attacking the duke in the Commons in 1625.[41] In 1626, the king retaliated by deliberately pricking him as sheriff of Somerset, an unprecedented move of partisanship which prevented him from sitting in the Commons.[42] Perhaps the Seymours recruited Selden to take the place of Sir Frances in 1626 and, when they perceived his effectiveness in the House, kept him on the team for 1628–9. In any case, it seems not unlikely that despite their constitutional leanings and their distaste for the duke, the Seymours largely sought inclusion, a royal recognition of their 'natural' place in society.

In the Commons, Selden worked together with Edward Kirton, Hertford's estate manager, and played a much more important role in this Parliament than he had in that of 1624. In part this stemmed from his own increased political experience and from his membership on a team, but also because other members had to fill the vacuum left by the absence such stalwart leaders as Edward Alford, Sir Edward Coke, Sir Guy Palmes, Sir Robert Phelips, Sir Francis Seymour, and Sir Thomas Wentworth, all pricked as sheriff in 1626 and made ineligible for election. While neither as aggressively active or as socially prominent as such members as Sir Dudley Digges and Sir John Eliot, nor speaking as often as Kirton, Selden still had considerable impact upon the House. Named to the standing committee of privileges during the first days of the session, he also came to sit on no less than twenty-three select committees.[43] A frequent participant in debates and a skilful manager of complex business, he established a reputation as a sound and effective client and Parliament man applying his skills to a variety of causes, including a defence of the privileges of the House of Commons.

When King Charles requested the Commons to issue a new writ for electing a knight of the shire for Norfolk to replace Sir Edward Coke,

Sir George More argued that 'divers sheriffs have sat here,' including his own service in the second session of the Parliament of 1597–8, when pricked as sheriff after his election as a knight of the shire.[44] Examining the principle, Selden queried the exclusion of a sheriff from the House by casting doubt upon the sufficiency of the precedents cited. 'Mr. Selden. 2 things insisted to make this election unlawful, viz., the ordinance and the writ. The ordinance of 46 Edward 3 was not made upon petition of the commons,' he noted, 'being only an ordinance of the Upper House, as appears in the roll.'[45] Drawing effectively upon the Rolls of Parliament, Selden challenged the propriety of allowing an ordinance initiated by the Lords to bind the Commons. Then he fashioned a reinterpretation of the language of the writ: 'For the clause of the writ, there is nothing observed *venire facias* is *per manucaptores* except *libere et indifferenter*,' and moved that 'because it concerns Sir Edward Coke and the whole county, therefore fit Sir Edward Coke should be called to justify his own election.'[46] It was a clever ploy. If Coke could leave his own county to testify, he could leave it to sit. If Coke could sit, then so could other sheriffs. Considerable debate followed, with voices speaking to both sides. Unable to support Selden's motion, the House referred the case to the committee of privileges, which, in turn, established a subcommittee to examine 'the records and precedents.'[47] No unambiguous answer emerged, however. To judge from the report presented by Sir John Finch to the House on 27 February, the committee must have disagreed sharply over the question of whether sheriffs had served in parliaments before the ordinance of 46 Edward III. At the end of Finch's long, ambiguous report, the Clerk tersely noted: 'No opinion from the Committee, delivered.'[48] Selden, who should have supported the exclusion of sheriffs from the House on grounds of precedent, had allowed his advocacy of Coke's cause – and that of other sheriffs elected and excluded – to cloud his historical and legal judgment, acting – not for the last time – as a highly partial advocate. The Commons refrained from following his lead.

Sir Robert Howard and the Liberties of the Commons

In another dubious cause, Selden scored greater success and at least embarrassed the Duke of Buckingham by obtaining admission into the Commons for the man who had sired the heir of the duke's brother John Villiers, Viscount Purbeck. This case, albeit somewhat indirectly, opened the attacks upon the favourite which would escalate during the course of this Parliament. Within the context of a number of claims for freedom from prosecution or arrest made in the Commons during the first fortnight of this Parliament commenced the case of Sir Robert Howard, a member excommunicated by the High Commission in March 1625 'for not taking the *oath ex officio*' on grounds of the privilege of Parliament.[49] Since every member had to receive Holy Communion before taking his seat in the Commons, this plea appeared to pose a serious problem. When the case arose on 17 February, however, Digges – closely connected to the Archbishop of Canterbury – offered a solution by noting 'that he is already absolved by a great assembly at an high committee' (that is, by a full meeting of the High Commission) and presumably, therefore, could commune.[50] Unwilling to see the matter swept aside so easily, however, Selden vigourously pursued Howard's plea by citing the precedent of Hall's Case to argue that a 'breach of privilege in one Parliament may be punished in another succeeding.'[51] Warming to the debate, he presented an outline of Howard's claim and proposed a drastic solution:

Moves that the registrar [of the High Commission] may be sent for, and that entry to be torn out, and that those over whom we have power may be sent for by this House, and punished, and order taken that he may be absolved, with as much honor to Sir Robert Howard and to the House as he was excommunicate with dishonor and indignity.[52]

The speech breathed indignation – the High Commission riding roughshod over the privilege of a member and thereby placing the whole Parliament in danger – but Selden had failed to note that Howard had received the censure of the church for openly living in adultery with Lady Purbeck, the daughter of Sir Edward Coke and the wife of Buckingham's brother.[53] In addition he strained most of the evidence.

Selden's speech placed a more than charitable construction on Howard's plea for privilege and on the power of the House of Commons to overturn judicial decisions. The excommunication had taken place at the time set for the second session of the Parliament of 1624, not during the session of the last Parliament (that of 1625) as stated by Selden. The king had prorogued the Parliament on 29 May until Michaelmas 1624 and then further prorogued it until the spring of 1625; plans to open a second session came to nought when James I became seriously ill early in March, so, on 5 March 1625, he prorogued the Parliament once again, this time until 20 April; the death of King James on 27 March, however, dissolved this Parliament. It took a severe stretching of parliamentary privilege to cover a session never officially opened. When elected for his own borough of Bishops Castle (Shropshire) to the first Parliament of Charles I in 1625, Howard failed to raise the question of his privilege. On 16 February 1626, the day before Howard's case arose in the Commons, the High Commission had absolved him of his excommunication for the duration of this session.[54] Selden had glossed over all of these complications in his presentation. In addition, he had advocated a solution (tearing the entry out of the register of the High Commission) which asserted the juridical superiority of the House of Commons over the most powerful court in the kingdom on ecclesiastical affairs. Perhaps bitter memories of this court's condemnation of his *Historie of Tithes* added to his aggressiveness. Instead of supporting Selden's motion or that of Eliot to refer the case to the committee of privileges, the House named a special committee to 'take consideration of the restraint and excommunication of Sir Robert Howard.'[55] Pending its report, Howard was allowed to take his seat without receiving Communion.[56] This concession, however, failed to end the dispute.

The press of parliamentary business did not prevent the committee from meeting throughout the next month, and on 21 March Selden reported its findings in a detailed speech. He noted: 'How Sir *Robert* stood privileged by this House, when these proceedings against him. – 21 *Jac.* the Parliament began, 19° *Februarii*; before which time Sir Robert chosen a burgess. The parliament began 15° *Martii*. All the proceedings against him between 1 *Martii* and 20 *Martii*.' This introductory part conveyed the gist of the argument; like the longer report, it cleverly conflated the events of two years. The Parliament had opened on 19 February 1624 and the actions against Howard had taken place between 1 and 20 March 1625, a point concealed throughout the report. In the debate which followed, Sir John Suckling – the Duke of Buckingham's spokesman in the Commons – protested that 'he never heard of any claim of privilege of Parliament by Sir Robert Howard.' To the rescue, however, came such able attorneys as William Noy and Christoper Brooke, with the result that the

House passed two motions unanimously:

1. Upon question, Sir Robert Howard ought to have had privilege of parliament; without one negative.

2ly, upon question, Sir Robert Howard claimed his privilege of Parliament, in due manner; without one negative.[57]

Confirmation of Howard's privilege obtained, a full reversal of the judgment still remained. During a debate over how to punish the erring members of the High Commission, Kirton suggested that their repentence match Howard's public condemnation: 'that at Paul's Cross they may declare their errors, where he was publicly disgraced.' Others, more cautiously, realized that punishment could only extended to members of the Commons who also sat on the High Commission.[58] Despite some wishful thinking, the Commons had not fully shared in the revival of judicature started by the Lords in 1621. No contemporary knew this better than did Selden. Not recognized as a court of record, the Commons could neither examine witnesses under oath nor compel others to accept its judgments; it could only persuade. This seriously hampered any attempt to obliterate the judgment against Howard. During April 1626, the committee dealing with this issue apparently examined all of the commoners on the High Commission. On 29 April, it summoned these men before the Commons to make them feel the weight of the full House.

Selden opened his report from the committee by moving that 'Sir H. Marten,' one of those examined and a member of the Commons, 'should withdraw' from the House.[59] However, Sir Henry Marten, a distinguished Doctor of Civil Law and judge who sat on several ecclesiastical and Admiralty courts (including the High Commission), decided 'to speak for himself. That he has neither vilified, in word, nor act, the privileges of this House, in the person of Sir Robert Howard.'[60] Marten established an unequivocal choronology of the excommunication and of the prorogation. The tenuous nature of Howard's plea, blurred (at best) by Selden's earlier reports, emerged more clearly. Cleverly, Marten also defended his own actions by pointing out that 'he knew not privilege of parliament was due to Sir Robert Howard' because the defendant had not 'claimed it' until late in the proceedings 'and it was then disputed.' He also admitted that he 'thinks every man is to take notice of privilege of a parliament man, in parliament time, and *eundo* and *reduendo*,' that is, going to and returning from Westminster.[61] After this speech, Marten withdrew from the House so that his case could be discussed more freely; shortly, he returned for a full interrogation.[62] Although the overall performance brought out new evidence damaging to the construction earlier presented by Selden, it also produced the spectacle of a powerful royal servant affirming the privileges of the Commons as a matter of record.

The great set piece of the Howard Case took place on 3 May, when Sir John Hayward, Dr Edmund Pope (civil lawyers and distinguished members of the High Commission), and Mr Thomas Mottershed (the registrar of that court) presented their testimony to the full House. They confirmed the witness of Marten and provided new evidence with startling consequences. Hayward said 'that he was present at the excommunication. He saw Sir Robert Howard tender a paper to the Lord Keeper, but heard no word of privilege of Parliament spoken of; and that the Lord Keeper gave it to the Lord President, and he heard them tell Sir Robert Howard, it was not worth a straw.' This confirmed Marten's statement that some commissioners had disputed Howard's claim and it pointed specifically at Bishop John Williams, then Lord Keeper, and Henry Montagu, Earl of Manchester and Lord President of the privy council, as those responsible for the dismissal of the plea of privilege. The Commons knew whom to blame! Pope underlined the point by stating that 'he was present 5° *Martii*, and 17 *Martii*. That 1st day he [Howard] claimed no privilege; the 2nd day he did. That 8 Lords there, parliament men. He ignorant of the privileges of parliament. Gave credit to the opinion of those Lords and other which had been parliament men.' Mottershed confirmed that he had entered Howard's claim to the privilege of Parliament in the ledger and that 'the late Lord Keeper and the Lord President said, it was no worth being no record.'[63] This testimony shed new light upon the case. It showed that the initiative for rejecting the claim of parliamentary privilege lay not with the civil lawyers, but with experienced members of Parliament who sat in the Upper House. Clearly, to get at the root of the matter, the Commons would need to examine members of the Lords.

Aware that the Upper House would not allow its members to appear before the Lower House for questioning, Selden tried a frontal assault. After hearing the testimony of the commissioners, the Commons voted 'that all the proceedings in the High Commission Court against Sir *Robert Howard*, from the first of *February*, 22° *Jac.* at which time he ought to have had his privilege of Parliament, declared to be void, and ought to be vacated and annihilated.' A fierce debate followed on how best to enforce this resolution. Many supported the motion that 'a letter to be written by Mr. Speaker to the Lord of Canterbury, and the rest of the Lords, and others to the High Commissioners for annulling of the said proceedings,' the normal way by which the Commons upheld its privilege, but others – including Selden – forced a division and defeated the motion by a vote of 114 to 105.[64] Selden then proposed that the House compel the commoners in the High Commission, who made up a sufficient although small proportion of the membership, to suppress the record of the proceedings on their own: 'That some of those that are within our jurisdiction are of the quorum in the High Commission and any 3 of them may keep a court, whereof one to be of the quorum. Moves we may enjoin three of them within our cognizance to keep a court and suppress the proceedings.'[65] 'If they refuse,' Selden added, 'they are subject to a second censure.'[66] By paying no attention to the peers (who comprised two-thirds of the membership of the High Commission) and by demanding high-handed action, Selden's motion threatened a serious jurisdictional dispute with both the court and the House of Lords. Sir John Lowther put the problem succinctly in commenting upon the insufficiency of one of the precedents cited during the debate: 'our [the Commons'] order neglected and nothing done upon it. For if any court of Westminster break our privilege because they are members of the Lords House it seems we have no remedy but to complain to the Lords.'[67] Selden's attempt to uphold the privileges of the Lower House unassisted by the Crown and the Lords, however, proved too provocative for his colleagues.

As often happened when dissonance menaced the peace of the House, moderate members managed to patch together a compromise, this time one which upheld the order voted earlier in the proceedings:

Upon question, Sir John Hayward, Dr. Pope, and the register called in, and the effect of the said order to be declared to them by Mr. Speaker; and that the House expects it be done, and to hear by Monday next that this be done and, in the meantime, the House will respite any resolution concerning themselves; and that they attend the House again upon Monday morning. And the like notice to be given to Mr. Comptroller and Sir H. Marten by the Serjeant. All which was done by MR. SPEAKER accordingly.[68]

Although this procedure did threaten unspecified punishments, it actually depended much more upon the moral weight of the Commons for enforcement. Significantly, it allowed the commoners on the High Commission enough latitude to work out a method of reversing the proceedings against Sir Robert Howard which would challenge neither the jurisdiction of their court nor the privileges of the Lords. In practice, they were not pressed to report quickly. The wisdom of this approach finally appeared on 10 June, when 'SIR GEORGE MORE informs the House that he was present at a High Commission Court, where seven bishops present; and knows that then all the proceedings against Sir Robert Howard, from the first of February, 22 *Jac.* were frustrated, and made void. And SIR H. MARTEN affirmed that the order of the House there read and allowed; and all ordered to be there done accordingly.'[69] Clearly, members of the High Commission had made a cooperative move. Although the dissolution of Parliament a few days later prevented the formal confirmation of this obliteration, the House had considerably increased the strength of its privileges.

Acting more as Howard's advocate than as a champion of parliamentary liberties, Selden had managed to extend the privilege of freedom from prosecution during the sitting and adjournment of a Parliament into the period preceding and succeeding a day of prorogation. Although straining the evidence and pressing a risky case already rejected by peers on the High Commission, Selden fashioned a formidable defence out of an uncertain cause. Saved in the end from his own cleverness by members more adept at compromise, he had won a marginal case though an unrelentingly aggressive approach. Such skills of advocacy would also prove advantageous in the most dramatic event in the Parliament of 1626, the impeachment of the Duke of Buckingham.

The 'Reformation' of the Duke of Buckingham

The 'reformation of the Duke,' as Conrad Russell has styled this process, ran concurrently with the retraction of Howard's excommunication. Since a number of historians have detailed the complexities of this attempt to curb the power of the royal favourite, my account will concentrate upon Selden's role.[70] What eventually turned into an attack upon the Lord Admiral started out as an investigation of trade and credit restrictions imposed by the French upon British subjects; these sprang from English arrests of French ships – indeed, of one ship, the *St Peter of Newhaven*. Scenting important game when they discovered this, the members of the committee in charge of the investigation began to question its witnesses in the whole House. On 22 February, the Commons heard testimony from Sir Henry Marten, who spoke this time in his capacity as a judge in the Admiralty, and, on the next day, from Sir Allen Apsley, the Lieutenant of the Tower of London, and Sir John Hippisley, the Lieutenant of Dover Castle. After hearing their accounts, some members recommended that the House petition the king to punish any who had mishandled the case of the *St Peter*. Selden opposed this approach, pointing out that 'yesterday the judge of the Admiralty said it was by advice of the Lieutenants; now they on him. Let us not believe one or other. Sir H. Marten, he said he could not do always as he would.'[71] In other words, the parties giving testimony had blamed each other, so before going any farther, the Commons should sort out where the blame lay. Selden seemed to hint that Marten may have made his decision because of pressure from above. All the more reason for probing further. The House expanded the earlier committee and assigned the case of the *St Peter* to it.[72] As a new member of this committee, Selden became actively involved at an early stage.

The Duke of Buckingham's name entered the investigation of the *St Peter* on 1 March and led to an attempt to condemn the 'second stay of the *Peter*, after the decree in the Admiralty' as a 'grievance' on 11 March, in a division of the Commons lost by six votes. Selden spoke in favour of the motion.[73] The 'reformation of the Duke' began in earnest later in that day, when Dr Samuel Turner (a client of the Earl of Pembroke) asked six questions which focused upon Buckingham as the root cause of England's woes, offering common fame as his only proof.[74] Two consequences followed, a royal call for the punishment of Turner and the pursuit by the House of the cause of England's problems at home and abroad. On 14 March, Sir Richard Weston, Chancellor of the Exchequer, twice read a message from King Charles asking the Commons to punish two of its members: Clement Coke, for a seditious speech, and Turner for his articles of inquiry 'against the Duke of Buckingham as he pretends, but indeed against the honor and government of himself and his blessed father.'[75] Coke excused 'himself that he had no intent to say anything that might tend to sedition, and spoke not those things,' and Turner noted that the common law allowed 'common fame to be a way of presentment' and that the Commons had charged the Duke of

Suffolk on these grounds during the reign of Henry VI.[76] On 15 March, in reply to a petition from the Commons explaining why they needed to proceed jointly on supply and 'in discovering the causes and propounding the remedies of these great evils which have occasioned your Majesty's wants and your people's grief,' King Charles personally warned the members of the Commons assembled in the Banqueting House not to proceed against the Duke of Buckingham.[77]

The tensions raised by these disputes continued. On 17 March, a committee of the whole revealed the reactions of sitting members by passing generalized versions of three of Turner's five points as resolutions of grievances and, on 20 March, a committee of the whole established a subcommittee 'to examine the particulares of these several causes before resolved, and the causes of those causes.'[78] When the House discussed Turner's case again in a committee of the whole on 22 March and the precedents for his accusations were fiercely debated, Selden argued: 'The question only whether an accusation grounded upon common fame be in a parliamentary way or not.' This move worked, for the committee posed the question of whether 'the delivery in of accusations by common fame by a member of this House into this House against the subject be a parliamentary way or not.'[79] Two days later, Sir John Eliot reported from 'the subcommittee of causes of causes,' beginning with an accusation that Buckingham had countenanced the increase of popery (which met with great protests from the duke's clients and supporters and from other members, as well), and then accused him of not sufficiently guarding the 'Narrow Seas' (which again met received rebuttals from supporters of the duke), of holding too many offices, of engaging in the sale of offices, and of 'conferring of honors upon men whom the King's revenues must maintain,' including members of the duke's family. All but the first of these accusations were passed as resolutions to be 'reported to the House, that they may have judgment.'[80] On 27 March, after considerable debate, a committee of the whole fixed supply at three subsidies and three-fifteenths to be brought forward as a bill 'as soon as we have preferred our grievances to the King and received his answer' and their report was accepted by the House.[81] The response of Charles came on 29 March in a strong speech behalf of His Majesty delivered by Lord Keeper to the members of both Houses assembled in the hall at Whitehall. Lord Keeper Coventry castigated the Commons for not having taken action against Coke and Turner, warned against attacks on Buckingham and argued again that those who criticized the duke aimed at the king and his father, and pressed for a rapid provision of supply.[82] On the next day, the duke spoke in justification of his actions, supported by Secretary Conway and by Lord Chamberlain Pembroke, in a joint conference of both Houses.[83] After several days of debate, the Commons replied with a remonstrance on 5 April, in which the House explained why they had not proceeded against Coke and Turner and defended 'the ancient, constant, and undoubted right and usage of parliaments to question and complain of any persons, of what degree or quality soever, found grievous in commonwealth and who have abused the trust and power committed to them by their sovereign' and beseeched the king 'not to give ear to the officious reports of private persons for their own ends' instead of listening to the official spokesmen of the House.[84]

The dispute did not die down over the Easter adjournment, but erupted in a great debate on 22 April, three days after the Earl of Bristol had accused Buckingham of treason in the Lords.[85] Thomas Malet, a lawyer and an experienced member of the Commons, opened with a long attack upon proceeding by common fame. A host of common lawyers, however, upheld the procedure. Selden made his most telling point at the very beginning of a long speech on the subject: 'The question is whether a formal accusation in a parliamentary proceeding by common fame may likewise be exhibited to the Lords on common fame. By reason of conveniency it may, or else great men's faults would never come to light. The faults of gods could not be known till fame was born, and then they came to light.'[86] In practical terms, one could not expect most individual witnesses to take the intitiative against any person as powerful as the Duke of Buckingham. Although not mentioning the royal favourite by name, Selden cited several precedents, including the impeachment of the Duke of Suffolk (another royal favourite) in 1450–1, to bolster the motion. At the end of the debate, the House voted that 'common fame a good ground of proceeding of this House, either to inquire of here or transmit the complaint, if the House find cause, to the King or Lords.'[87] The Commons, however, still seemed somewhat puzzled about the mode of procedure to be followed.

To remedy this situation, the House established a subcommittee of twelve (including Selden) 'to consider the state of the great business now in hand, and to reduce it into form; and to search for, and make use of, and apply precedents for it; and to present those things to the

House, with their opinons,' a task eminently suitable to legal antiquaries.[88] On 24 April, this committee received full power to examine witnesses, to investigate new charges, and to prepare a case
against the Duke of Buckingham; on the same day, when the Lords
again would not allow Buckingham to appear before the Commons,
the Lower House voted eight specific charges against the favourite.[89]
Three days later, upon recommendation of the committee of twelve,
a commitee of the whole House decided on a division of 191 to 150 to
add a charge that the duke had administered improper medicine to
'King James in his sickness,' a resolution spelled out in four points
and carried by the House on the next day.[90] After a day set aside for
discussion of Sir Robert Howard's case, the Commons returned to
the 'reformation of the Duke' by adding the second stay of the *St
Peter of Newhaven* as a grievance; this carried on a division of 185 to
148 and completed the assembly of the case which the Commons
would present to the Lords.[91]

On 2 May, Sir Dudley Digges reported the charges against the
favourite from the committee of twelve, noting 'that the Duke of
Buckingham found the cause of these causes.'[92] Without a division,
the Commons agreed to transmit the full set of accusations to the
Lords and, on the next day, appointed eight members of the committee to 'divide the parts amongst themselves; and every one of them to
choose two members to assist them in their preparation of the business.'[93] Selden selected Charles Jones, the Recorder and member for
Beaumaris, and Kirton as his helpers. On 6 May, this committee produced its full report in the form of a bill containing a preamble, thirteen specific charges, and a conclusion – all to be passed by the
Commons and transmitted to the Lords in writing. When Sir Humphrey May, Chancellor of the Duchy of Lancaster, questioned the
form as differing from the verbal charges laid against Bacon and Cranfield, Selden defended the procedure with his legal learning: 'Of late
times, true, we used to make accusation of those persons accused by
word of mouth, and that a good course. But as true that when accusations are of many parts this course was also used, as 50 E 3; 28 H. 6.
Adam de Berry accused by a long bill and 28 H. 6 there a large accusation is called a bill and runs this way with a preamble and a conclusion.'[94] The House passed each charge separately and assigned
specific portions to each of the eight managers. On 8 May, Kirton
asked 'that the gentleman that speaks the conclusion may desire that
the Duke be sequestered according to the precedent of the Duke of

Suffolk in H. 6 time.'[95] Eventually, he moved that Buckingham be committed upon 'the Lord Digby his petition, whereunto articles are annexed, containing High Treason. That the Earl of Bristol (as opened in the House) does charge him with High Treason.'[96] When William Noy wondered whether the Commons ought to give such directions to the Lords, Selden countered with two precedents and argued that 'it is the first time that ever I heard that a man suspected, much more accused, of treason should stand at liberty.'[97] At the end of an exhausting day, the House decided to postpone a decision on this contentious issue. Despite the tactics of royal servants and the duke's supporters, however, the impeachment moved towards a conclusion.

On 8 May, the Commons put its finishing touches on the engrossed bill and finally presented the articles of impeachment to the Lords in a dramatic ceremony. Each of the eight managers read one or more of the charges and defended it in a short accompanying speech. Selden handled those accusing the Lord Admiral with failure to protect the 'narrow seas' and with abuse of his position by recommitting the *St Peter of Newhaven* on his direct authority.[98] The losses brought about from the 'not guarding of the seas' included the 'prevention of trade, which gives life to the wealth of the kingdom' and the 'weakening of naval strength.'[99] The 'unjust stay of the ship *St Peter* of Newhaven' constituted 'a great offense against the marine laws and the laws of this kingdom and against the law of nations.'[100] Having already written the first draft of what would become the *Mare Clausum*, Selden could have demonstrated this point at great length. The reversal by Buckingham of a judgment made by the Court of Admiralty provided 'an example that may serve hereafter to justify all absolute authority in the admiral, without law or legal course, over the ships and goods of all merchants whatsoever, and so not security to merchants.'[101] Since all law came down to custom or statute for Selden, this breach of traditional procedure, while seemingly trivial, posed a serious threat to the rule of law. When authority operated outside of normal channels, it made an existential claim to arbitrary, absolute power, to power unlimited by custom, statute, consensus, or ordinary procedures. The 'reformation of the Duke' had become a much more profound struggle for principle and power.

The managers of the impeachment presented the last five charges against the favourite on 10 May, followed by a dramatic epilogue in which Sir John Eliot both summed up the case for the Commons and compared the duke to Sejanus, the tyrannical favourite of the

Emperor Tiberius.[102] On the previous day, the House had returned to the contentious issue of moving the 'Lords, that the Duke of Buckingham may be committed'; after a heated debate in which Selden provided a pile of precedents to help bury the arguments presented by the duke's friends, the motion passed by a vote of 225 to 106.[103] Having laid charges and requested the imprisonment of Buckingham, however, the Commons had reached the limits of their jurisdiction. The scene of significant action now shifted to the Lords, who would decide upon the innocence or guilt of the favourite. The Commons, therefore, concentrated upon freeing Digges and Eliot from royal imprisonment, protecting the other managers of the impeachment and furthering other business.[104]

As the session drew to a close, however, Selden participated in a last-minute effort to salvage the impeachment of Buckingham. On 9 June, the Commons asked the Lords for a copy of the duke's answer to their charges, in order to make a reply; the Lower House sat for much of the next day as a committee of the whole, working out the text for a declaration to the king in which they hoped that the Lords would join.[105] As the member who reported from the subcommittee drafting the declaration, Selden moved and helped to carry several new propositions which raised the stakes. The first sought to separate the actions of Buckingham from those of King James and King Charles: 'That the Duke does often strive to excuse himself of such things as are laid to his charge by casting an ill odor upon the King that is dead and using likewise the King's name that now is for that end.'[106] This point attempted to make the favourite responsible for his own deeds. The second raised a serious problem, the collection of tonnage and poundage 'since the death of King James, not being confirmed by parliaments.'[107] Or, as another source put it: 'The takinge of the subsidy of tonnage and poundage without consent of parliament as an effect of new counsels.'[108]

The issue of 'new counsels' led the subcommittee to ask the Lords for the record of the duke's speech on the breakdown of the Spanish marriage (made in the Parliament of 1624) and 'to send for the Lord Digby, or his counsel, to make good, by proof, that point which concerns the abuse of this House.'[109] This foray into the tangled thicket of accusation and reprisal involving Charles I, Buckingham, and the Earl of Bristol, combined with the unwillingness of the Lords to take action against Bristol, sealed the fate of the Parliament of 1626. In a speech before both Houses on 12 June, Charles sought to clear the duke of all wrongdoing. On the next day, the Commons, in a committee of the whole, approved of the declaration drafted by the subcommittee and presented by Selden, and Selden reported the declaration to the House in regular session with an 'addition by way of answer to the King's letter.'[110] Two days later, the order of dissolution arrived. Although the Lords had failed to find Buckingham guilty of the charges laid by the House of Commons, his trial by his peers still marked an important stage in solidifying the procedure appropriate in such accusations. Selden intervened in the debate to defend such proceedings as accusation upon common fame, formal presentation of the charges in writing in the form of a bill, and imprisonment of the accused during the course of his trial. Since he knew of precedents for all of these procedures and sat on the relevant committee, Selden may well have moved that the House employ these methods in the first place!

During the course of the Parliament of 1626, John Selden employed his skills as a lawyer and a scholar to move from the fringes of influence into the recognized status of a significant Parliament man. His handling of Howard's Case not only extended the privileges of the Commons and proved that Selden could bring a complicated, equivocal issue to fruition on the floor of the House, it provided a bit of sweet revenge against the High Commission and the Duke of Buckingham. The impeachment of the duke brought Selden into a prominent position as one of the spokesmen of the Commons before the assembled Lords. His chairmanship of the subcommittee which drew up a declaration to King Charles on the Buckingham Case showed that the majority of his colleagues had enough confidence in his ability to place a task of great responsibility into his care. It also attempted to forward the goals of the Seymour network, mixed monarchy and an attack upon the Duke's monopoly of royal favour. The fear of absolute, arbitrary authority, announced in Selden's speech in support of the charge that Buckingham had improperly arrested the *St Peter*, struck a theme which would reverberate with great power in the Parliament of 1628.

SELDEN'S EARLY PARLIAMENTARY CAREER: CONCLUSION

The glory days of John Selden as an antiquary and lawyer in the Parliament of 1628 lay ahead, but he had already begun to move from a career as a writer into one of public service. Of course, the two firmly intertwined; the scholar fashioned a historical interpretation of the ancient constitution and the politician sought to 'maintain' this vision of England's mixed monarchy. Members of both Houses who first respected Selden for his ability to find accurate ancient precedents came to accept his constitutional vision. Even with his fine sense of historical anachronism, Selden shared with his contemporaries the belief that the practices of the past provided a valid guide for the present, for example, that the Commons might appoint treasurers for the subsidy because their predecessors had done this in the reign of Henry IV. Like many others, he also saw limits to the continuance of ancient customs; clearly, trial by battle belonged to an earlier society and no longer provided a method of solving disputes at common law. Indeed, Selden's historical view of the constitution as slowly changing custom and statute, gradually fitting itself to the changes in the society, provided a better explanation of the legitimacy of appropriating one set of precedents and not another than did interpretations based upon the assumption of immemorial custom. Selden quickly moved from the role of an antiquary into that of an advocate. In his handling of Anian's Case in 1624, Howard's appeal for privilege in 1626, and the attempted impeachment of the Duke of Buckingham in 1626, he employed his legal talents to further the privileges of the Commons, and the goals of his patron, sometimes in a not entirely fastidious manner. During the course of the Parliament of 1626, Selden started to detect a threat to his vision of the ancient constitution of England in the actions of leading royal servants, especially the Duke of Buckingham, and acted accordingly.

Attacks upon men of great power, however, had to cease without the protections of parliamentary privilege. At the conclusion of the Parliament of 1626, Attorney General Sir Robert Heath wrote to all twelve members of the committee which had put together the case for the impeachment of the Duke of Buckingham, requesting information about the charges and evidence assembled against the favourite, presumably so that the Crown could continue the prosecution in the Star Chamber. Like that of other members, Selden's reply of 21 June 1626, wisely would not budge beyond matters of record:

Sir

To your questions proposed by his Majesties command touching the proofes that may concerne the charge delivered in the late dissolved parlia-

ment by the commons house to the Lords against the Duke of Buckingham, my answere, in all humble obedience to that command, is, that for
all the articles of that charge or for most of them; divers proofes of record
and publique acts of courts and names of Witnesses and other testimonies
are mentioned or designed in them or in the arguments that were delivered
with them, when the charge was transmitted to the Lords. But what all the
proofes of the generall articles or any of them were either at the time when
they were severally first agreed by the votes of the whole house of commons (as they all were) or when they were afterward agreed to be transmitted, I remember not. And what those further proofes to any of them were
which the house of commons meant to have used according to the liberty
in that behalf referred by them or purposed to have added in their reply, I
know not. Neither do I otherwise, then I have here declared, of my own
knowledge, know any thing which may be usefull to you in providing any
part of that charge.

J. Selden[111]

The trap of asking members of Parliament to speak outside of the
House about proceedings carried on within that body contained too
many dangers, so Selden – like his colleagues – tempered his reply
with prudence. The attempt to curtail the growth of 'absolute, arbitrary' authority, however, would absorb much of his energies for the
next three years, first in the Five Knights' Case and then in the Parliament of 1628–9.

THE FIVE KNIGHTS' CASE

In early Stuart England, legal discourse, as well as particular points
at law, played an essential role in political dispute. While historians recently have investigated some of the practical limits to the
power and authority of the English privy council in the 1620s and
1630s, they have paid less attention to the accompanying debates
over the nature of government.[112] As Johann Sommerville and Glenn
Burgess have forcefully reminded us, disagreements over power –
while inextricably joined with the factional disputes of interpersonal
politics – also found expression in the terms of political and legal
discourse, in detailed assessments of the nature and limits of the
authority of the king and of the liberties of the people, and in general
political theories.[113] However, for precedent-minded contemporaries,

the ancient constitution of England, as reconstructed by common lawyers, defined the permissible boundaries of political practice much more than did abstract theories based upon natural law, especially when spouted by divines or civil lawyers.[114] Natural-law theories, however intellectually coherent and interesting, could not compel people to pay loans to the Crown, or any other form of taxes, nor could they imprison those who refused to pay. In order to become enforceable in common-law courts of England, the practical policies advocated on the basis of such theories needed to become either enacted by statute or incorporated by custom. Neither happened in the 1620s. The issues in dispute remained largely within the compass of the common law and the ancient constitution. The question of the discretionary power of the Crown to imprison English subjects without specifying a charge arose within the context of a government attempting to fight a war with limited resources; it involved much more than technical legal arguments. The Five Knights' Case of 1627 revitalized an ongoing debate over the distribution and exercise of authority which flowed over into debates over the liberties of the subject in the Parliament of 1628 and forced such key spokesmen as John Selden and the attorney general, Sir Robert Heath, to clarify and defend rival interpretations of the ancient constitution which had practical implications for the everyday relationships between the king's servants and the subjects of the realm.[115]

Deliberations about the nature of England's government appeared very germane in the months and years which followed the Parliament of 1626. As the privy council scrambled to find the means, the soldiers, the sailors, the supplies, and, above all, the money, to win the wars against Spain and France, it took actions which, while not completely without precedent, went well beyond the measures of ordinary administrative methods and raised fears about the 'new counsels' to the Crown.[116] A number of these wartime practices stood out as perceived grievances – namely, the billeting of troops in people's homes without their permission, the use of martial law in England to discipline troops, the formal request of loans for stipulated sums from those subjects who would normally pay parliamentary subsidies, and the imprisonment of those who refused to provide such loans. Billeting and martial law pressed upon scattered communities, but the loan of 1626 touched almost all men of property. The vast majority paid; a considerable number of brave gentlemen and

yeomen refused, and faced loss of office, incarceration, or impressment. Among those jailed, five knights sought release on bail
through a writ of *habeas corpus*. Seeking to defend its action, the
privy council instructed the Warden of the Fleet to enter on the
return of these writs that the knights involved were '"committed by
his majesty's special commandment."'[117] Selden had personal experience with a similar charge in 1621. It sufficed for one, Sir Thomas
Darnel, but not for the others: Sir John Heveningham, Sir Walter Erle, Sir John Corbet, and Sir Edward Hampden. Starting on
22 November 1627, learned counsel for the knights presented their
case before the King's Bench; on 26 November, the attorney general
replied with the case for the Crown; and on 27 November, the Lord
Chief Justice, Sir Nicholas Hyde, reported the resolution of the
court.[118] Despite the care of the judges to protect both the prerogative
of the Crown and the liberties of the people, a great debate over the
essence of the common law and the ancient constitution had commenced.

The privy council deliberately decided to proceed in the King's
Bench in order to defend the royal prerogative of discretionary
imprisonment; this calculated manoeuvre forced Attorney General
Heath to defend a view of the constitution which stressed the freedom of the monarch to act without normal restraints, especially
when the realm stood in danger. Deriving the liberties of subjects
from royal grants, Heath argued for a common-law constitutional
monarchy created by kings. When 'that first stone of sovereignty was
... laid,' the sovereign stood alone; kings, having created the law,
could 'do no wrong' and remained free, especially in times of emergency, to step outside of 'legal and ordinary' procedures; the remedy
for the imprisoned knights was 'to go the right way for their delivery,
which is by a petition to the king. Whether it be a petition of right or
grace, I know not; it must be, I am sure, to the king,' the fount of all
law and bounty.[119] This spelled out some of the legal implications of
the theory articulated by James VI and I in 1610; by creating institutions of government and recognized procedures, kings had limited
royal power, but the Crown still retained a great deal of initiative and
discretion in dealing with matters of state.

The attorneys for the defence in the Five Knights' Case, Selden, Sir
John Bramston, William Noy, and Sir Henry Calthorp, argued that
the Crown must follow recognized procedures or else jeopardize the
ancient liberties of free-born Englishmen. This severely diminished

the discretionary power of the Crown, but need not have refuted the model of 'constitutional monarchy created by kings.' While his colleagues advocated a position closest to 'constitutional monarchy governed by the common law' and argued that the Crown had endangered the liberties of freemen by asserting a prerogative right not recognized by the common law, Selden pursued his model of 'mixed monarchy.' For him, the refusal of the Crown to spell out a specific charge against Sir Edward Hampden when presented with a writ of *habeas corpus* represented a move to establish as customary a procedure which endangered the hereditary liberties of freemen. By aspiring to change the law without proper reference to precedent and statute, the communal modes of creating law, Selden argued, these actions challenged the mixed nature of the English monarchy. The legal cases presented by Heath, Selden, and the other attorneys applied the rival interpretations of the English constitution articulated by James, Hedley, and Selden to a concrete issue at law.[120]

Of a far different nature, the sermons of Roger Manwaring and Robert Sibthorpe supported the loan, and the punishment of those who refused to provide money to the Crown on the basis of civil-law arguments. Manwaring, especially, developed the divine right–derivation of royal power from God into an absolutist argument that the English monarch had a prerogative power to tax without the consent of Parliament:

If any King shall command that which stands not in any opposition to the originall lawe of God, nature, Nations and the Gospell (though it be not correspondent in every circumstance to laws Nationall and Municipall) no subject may without hazard of his own damnation in rebelling against God, question or disobey the will and pleasure of his soveraigne. For as the father of his country he commands what his pleasures is out of counsell and judgement.[121]

This raised the laws of God, nature, and nations above the common law of England in a very relevant, practical manner and severely weakened the obedience to the common law covenanted by King James. Although some divines had used similar arguments earlier in the century to defend the rights of the English monarch against claims of papal supremacy, it now served to justify a domestic policy and denigrated the common law. The sermons of the divines raised the spectre of transforming England into an absolute monarchy.

The Case for the Defence in the King's Bench

While the arguments presented by the various lawyers for the defence meshed into a solid-sounding case, each counsel defended his own client in his own manner. Bramston, Noy, and Calthorp each talked at some length and cited a good number of precedents; Selden, however, spoke briefly. As customary with common lawyers, he opened with such technicalities as the lack of an answer in the return to the caption in the writ of *habeas corpus* (that is, it gave no cause for imprisonment at that particular time and place, as it should) and the failure to note when the writ 'came to the keeper of the prison, whether before the return or after.' On these grounds, he concluded that 'the return is faulty in form, and void.'[122] People had escaped the rigours of the law on lesser failures of form. Preliminaries finished, Selden quickly moved to the heart of the matter and argued that imprisonment on the grounds alleged deprived his client of the liberties due to any freeman by the law of the land: 'I think that by the constant and settled laws of this kingdom, without which we have nothing, no man can be justly imprisoned by either of them [the king or the privy council], without a cause of the commitment expressed in the return.'[123] This portion of the case concentrated upon that most crucial law, Magna Carta, and especially upon a portion of chapter 29: '*Nullus liber homo capiatur vel imprisonatur nisi per legem terræ*,' or, as Selden translated it: 'No freeman shall be imprisoned without due process of the law.'[124] At dispute, of course, was the precise intent of the words '*per legem terræ*.' Did this phrase mean 'according to the laws' in general, as Attorney General Heath would claim, or did it intend to guarantee specific procedures at law? Selden argued that 'it must be intended by due course of law,' in Magna Carta, 'to be either by presentment or by indictment.'[125] Had the words meant 'according to the laws' in a less specific sense, chapter 29 would have left 'the matter very uncertain' and 'this act had done nothing.'[126] Placing Magna Carta into its contemporary legal and historical context, he stressed: 'If you will understand these words, "*per legem terræ*", in the first sense, this statute shall extend to villains as well as to freemen; for if I imprison another man's villain, the villain may have an action of false imprisonment.'[127] Neither King John nor his barons could have had such a notion of false imprisonment in mind, however, for 'the lords and the king ... both had villains' whom they 'might imprison' and 'the villain could have no remedy.'[128] Unless chapter 29 guaranteed the accusation of a free-man for a specific offence by presentment or indictment, then, 'the freeman shall have no privilege above the villain.'[129] Given the pre-posterous nature of such a proposition for the thirteenth-century fashioners of Magna Carta, 'due process' must have meant such prac-tical, specific, everyday customary practices such as presentment and indictment. If so, it still did. Therefore, the Crown should follow nor-mal practices and accuse Selden's client of a specific crime. This clever argument drew its strength from the interpretation of the Great Charter as a document which had arisen in a specific historical context, in response to particular circumstances.

In the opening portion of his analysis of Magna Carta, Selden sup-plemented the arguments presented by the other attorneys for the accused; in the next section, however, he took an entirely different tack, one based upon the application of the philological method of Continental legal historians to the understanding of the common law. The most commonly cited version of Magna Carta (that con-firmed in 9 Henry III), he asserted, mistakenly transcribed a crucial phrase from the original charter issued by King John – specifically that 'these words, "*nec super eum mittimus*"; which words of them-selves signify not so much,' so that 'a man cannot find any fit sense for them,' had replaced the original phrase which made much more sense, '"*nec eum in carcerem mittimus.*" We will not commit him to prison; that is, the king himself will not ...'[130] Of course, such an emendation strengthened the case of Selden's client. This purport-edly earlier version of chapter 29 had come from the history of Mat-thew Paris, who reported that the statute of 9 Henry III 'was renewed in the same words with the Charter of King John' and who, according to Selden, 'might know it better than others, for he was the king's chronologer in those times.'[131] Such an argument may have con-vinced some Continental legal antiquaries, but it hardly worked within the canons of evidence usually accepted at common law. Selden knew this and returned to more familiar discourse in a ringing conclusion which stressed that 'the liberty of the subject is the high-est inheritance that he hath; my humble request is, that according to the ancient laws and privileges of this realm, this gentleman, my cli-ent, may be bailed.'[132] Despite this more conventional ending, Selden's lengthy study of Continental law had provided potentially valuable assistance in his attempt to uphold the liberties of English-men.

The Case for the Prosecution in the King's Bench

The learned presentations of Selden, Bramston, Noy, and Calthorp look persuasive when read on their own. However, they presented only one side of the argument. In arguing the case for the Crown in 1627, Attorney General Heath took care to refute the specific objections raised by the counsel for the defence and summarized their arguments under five general headings: first, 'the inconveniences that would fall to the subjects'; second, the view of 'divers authorities out of their law-books'; third, Magna Carta; fourth, 'acts of Parliament in print'; and fifth, 'precedents of divers times ... that men committed by the king's commandment ... had been bailed.'[133] The summary was a fair one. Both now and in the debates in the Parliament of 1628, these reasons, judgments, acts, and precedents provided the basis for the respective arguments put forward by each side.

Having marked the boundaries of the dispute, the attorney general squarely spelled out the grounds of imprisonment:

It appears that the commitment is not in a legal and ordinary way, but that it is *'per speciale mandatum domini regis;'* which implies, not only the fact done, but so extraordinarily done, that it is notorious to be his majesty's immediate act and will it should be so; whether in this case they should be bailable or not in this court, which I acknowledge to be the highest court of judicature for such a case as is in question.[134]

Upon this distinction between the king's 'immediate act' and his actions mediated through such royal servants as justices would Heath build his argument. In general terms, he sketched a model of the English constitution in which all justice and law flowed from the monarch. It opened with a crucial differentiation of the legal commands of judges from 'that *absoluta potestas* that a sovereign hath, by which a king commands,' continued by insisting that this absolute power of the sovereign did not mean arbitrary might (for the king 'hath rules to govern himself by, as well as your lordships, who are subordinate judges under him'), and concluded with a graphic description of the king as the moving force in all law: 'the king is the head of the same fountain of justice, which your lordship administers to all his subjects; all justice is derived from him, and what he doth, he doth not as a private person, but as the head of the common wealth, as *justiciarius regni*, yea, the very essence of justice under

God upon earth is in him.'[135] Although administered through the institutions created by his predecessors, all justice derived from King Charles. In ordinary judgments, the justices of the King's Bench spoke with the voice of the monarch. However, in extraordinary circumstances, such as war, kings could speak on some issues with their own voices.

This view of English monarchy bore directly on the case in hand. The Crown had discretion in exercising its powers. A return spelling out the cause of imprisonment came as a matter of royal grace 'and, therefore, if the king allow and give warrant to those that make the return, that they shall express the cause of the commitment, as many times he doth, either for suspicion of felony, or making money, or the like,' then the court could proceed; in such cases, if returns listing a specific charge also included 'per speciale mandatum domini regis,' the special command of the king was 'not a secret' and the judges should follow normal procedures.[136] On the other hand, 'if there be no cause expressed' in the return except the special command of the king, then 'this court [the King's Bench] hath always used to remand them; for it hath been used, and it is to be intended a matter of state, and that it is not ripe nor timely for it to appear.'[137] The king had the right, Heath argued, to allow or withdraw permission for his servants to 'express the cause of commitment' in a return to a writ of habeas corpus and the King's Bench should grant or deny bail accordingly. The question remained, however, of whether the monarch had agreed to limit his direct exercise of such grace.

Claiming that 'the main fundamental grounds of argument upon this case begins with Magna Charta,' the attorney general quoted the words of chapter 29 and directly challenged that interpretation of 'per legem terræ' offered by Selden: 'that no man should be committed, but first he shall be indicted or presented.'[138] Heath poured scorn upon such a reading: 'I think that no learned man will offer that; for certainly there is no justice of the peace in a county, nor constable within a town, but he doth otherwise, and might commit before an indictment can be drawn or a presentment can be made.' However, the attorney general did not deal with Selden's carefully drawn distinction between the liberties of freemen and those of villeins, and he clearly distorted the point at issue as well, for Selden had not claimed that indictment or presentment must always precede imprisonment.[139]

The next part of the speech criticized Selden's bold emendation to the commonly cited text of Magna Carta:

it was urged by the counsel on the other side, that our printed Magna Charta, which saith, *'nec super eum mittimus'*, is mistaken; and that in divers manuscripts it is expressly set down to be, *'nec eum in carcerem mittimus'*. I cannot judge of the manuscripts that I have not seen; but, my lord, I have one here by me, which was written many years ago, and the words in print are word for word as that which is here written.[140]

Although unaware that Selden had cited a printed – not a manuscript – source, the attorney general had discovered a fatal historical weakness in the great antiquary's case; the emendation taken from Matthew Paris varied significantly from the text of 1215 Magna Carta and the confirmations of 1216 and 1225. Had Heath possessed the humanist philological method of his opponent and had he known where to find and how to authenticate early-thirteenth-century manuscripts, he could have humiliated Selden in public. Instead, he noted that 'we do not govern ourselves by chronicle,' attacked the verity of Matthew Paris on general grounds, and concluded that the Magna Carta 'was but in election in the time of King John, and then it might be, *"nec eum in carcerem mittimus"*, but it was not enacted till the time of Henry 3, and then that was omitted, and the Charter granted as now we have it.'[141] This speculative explanation cleverly and plausibly avoided the conclusion drawn by Selden. Although it rested on assertion with little critical or evidential base, it sufficed for the moment. In these arguments, Selden's Continental legal-historical method contrasted sharply with Heath's more traditional common-law approach. Ironically, by devoting so much attention to source criticism, the attorney general admitted a place at common law for Selden's style of reasoning. His point remained, however, that Magna Carta had guaranteed 'due process' in general, 'according to the laws of the land,' not such specific procedures as presentment or indictment before commitment.

Although Heath questioned the arguments and the interpretations of the precedents presented by all of the defence attorneys in detail, his case for the refusal of bail relied more upon a positive reading of the royal prerogative, a historical vision of the discretionary powers of the monarch which had existed from the beginning of the ancient constitution:

And sure I am, that the first stone of sovereignty was no sooner laid, but this power was given to the sovereign: if you ask me whether it be unlimited; my lord, I say it is not the question now in hand: but the common law, which hath long flourished under the government of our king and his progenitors kings of this realm, hath ever had that reverend respect of their sovereign, as that it hath concluded the king can do no wrong ...[142]

As a subject, the attorney general hesitated to spell out any restrictions placed upon the powers of the monarch at the foundation of the state or any limits to their discretionary powers subsequently sanctioned by English monarchs. Instead, he emphasized the need for discretion. Warning that 'there be "*Arcana Dei, et Arcana Imperii*" [mysteries of God and mysteries of state],' clearly unfit for the prying eyes of subjects, Heath stressed the need to trust kings when they took unusual actions for the common good: 'there is great reason of state so to do, or else they would not do it: many inconveniences may follow, if it should be otherwise. It may be, divers men to suffer wrongfully in prison, but therefore shall all prisoners be delivered? That were a great mischief.'[143] Apart from the reference to 'reason of state,' which struck an ominous note in some English ears, Heath had assembled a plausible common-law case for the discretionary power of the Crown to imprison subjects without specifying a particular cause, especially during times of trouble. The remedy for the prisoners was by a petition of right or grace to the king, not by a writ of *habeas corpus*.[144]

This positive reading of royal discretionary power drew a distinction between the absolute power (absoluta potestas) of the monarch (governed by rules known to the king) and the ordinary power exercised by all other magistrates (governed by the common law). Although Heath brought the absolute power of the king into a domestic legal dispute, he did not construct a theory of absolute monarchy or royal sovereignty upon this basis. Some of his language, especially the references to 'sovereignty' and 'reason of state,' appeared to evoke the discourse of such Continental upholders of princely powers as Bodin and Botero.[145] In the context of this speech, however, the distinction between the absolute and ordinary power of the monarch served two basic purposes: it emphasized the unique position of the monarch within the hierarchy of the realm and it stressed the legal independence of the discretionary powers of the monarch. The ambiguities displayed by Heath on the latter point were not his alone; one common-law tradition had attempted to place the royal prerogative under the common law, but another equally strong one had represented it as standing above the common law. The case neither stood nor fell on this point, however, because sufficient precedents existed to support the imprisonment of suspects by royal command during times of crisis, at least before they were charged. From the premise that subjects had to trust their kings, Heath built his argument upon a reading of specific texts, primarily Magna Carta, chapter 29, and the various answers made by royal servants in returns to writs of *habeas corpus*. Like any good lawyer, he supported the actions of his client, in this case the Crown. But the attorney general also provided an interpretation of the ancient constitution which stressed that the king had held all powers at the beginning of the state and still retained, and needed to retain, sufficient discretionary powers to preserve order and good government during times of crisis. This he accomplished with a minimal and peripheral recourse to civil law, natural law, or absolutist discourse; instead, Heath related the evidence to a theory of 'constitutional monarchy created by kings.'

The justices of the King's Bench attempted to prevent the clash between these rival interpretations of the ancient constitution from heating up into open warfare. One of the real issues involved, the legitimacy of discretionary imprisonment for refusal to lend a specified sum of money to the Crown, never reached the King's Bench because the privy council would not allow it to go forward.[146] Suspects in the Gunpowder Plot were imprisoned by the special command of the king before specific charges against some of them were drawn up, hardly an analogous case. The issue before the court involved only the granting of bail to defendants imprisoned by the discretionary command of the monarch, something much more abstract. Although they ignored most of the constitutional arguments presented by both sides, the judges refused bail and remanded the defendants back to prison, there to remain in custody '"until they have been delivered according to the law."'[147] Chief Justice Hyde also specifically noted that the precedents cited in the case told against the imprisoned knights. In practical terms, they lost. Selden and his colleagues had failed to obtain liberty for their clients, but Attorney General Heath had suffered as well, for he had not secured a judgment recognizing the right of the Crown to imprison solely upon the special mandate of the king. Neither side rested content with this compromise decision. The attorney general sought to have a more sweeping judgment entered on the Rolls of the King's Bench, and

John Selden pressed the case in the high court of Parliament. With a number of the same participants involved, the clash of interpretation involved in the Five Knights' Case became one of the major issues in the Parliament of 1628–9.

THE PARLIAMENT OF 1628–1629: THE SESSION OF 1628

Charles I opened the Parliament of 1628–9 on 17 March with a brief, pithy speech in which he asked for supply and warned against 'distractions'; three days later the Commons began its business in earnest by establishing a standing committee of privileges and a select committee on the election in the county of Cornwall; Selden sat on both, an honour often repeated during the session.[148] He was selected as a member for Ludgershall (Wiltshire), most probably again as a political adviser and client of the Earl of Hertford.[149] The debates of the House of Lords and the House of Commons for the session of 1628 provide a rich vein of constitutional discourse to uphold the prerogative of the Crown and the liberties of English freemen. Concentrating upon Selden, but drawing upon other speeches made in the House of Commons and its committees, the following pages will attempt to give the reader a sense of some of the many voices and contexts involved. Condemnation of the loan and of the billeting of troops raised few problems, but discretionary imprisonment – an issue involving competing interpretations of the common law – and martial law – an issue involving the relationship between the civil and the common law – raised contentious issues which demanded considerable attention. Since both sides tacitly agreed to accept Magna Carta as the practical starting-point for the issues at stake, most of their historical discussions covered that portion of the ancient constitution which had existed from 1215 to 1628.

Opening Moves on the Liberties of the People

On 21 March, Sir Edward Coke preferred a bill 'against long and unjust detainment of men in prison.'[150] On the next day, the Commons heard rousing general speeches on the issue of the liberties of subjects from such experienced orators as Coke, Sir Francis Seymour, Sir John Eliot, Sir Benjamin Rudyard, Sir Thomas Wentworth, and Sir Robert Phelips; the privy councillors in the House, Sir Thomas

Edmondes, Sir Humphrey May, and Sir John Coke, replied by insisting upon supply, with May and Secretary Coke also promising the royal redress of grievances.[151] Seymour and Wentworth challenged the legality of billeting and the forced loan and Phelips rhetorically argued that 'we are almost grown like the Turks who send their Janissaries, who placeth his halberd at the door and there he is master of the house.' Even Secretary Coke openly admitted that 'illegal courses have been taken, it must be confessed'; seeking to create a consensus, he noted that 'every man agrees the King should be relieved, and grievances heard,' optimistically indicating: 'Only the manner, not the matter of the gift is to be argued.'[152] In the committee on religion, complaints arose against the books of such Arminian divines as John Cosin and Richard Montague and such preachers in support of the recent loan as Manwaring and Sibthorp.[153] On 25 March, the issue of discretionary imprisonment arose in a committee of the whole House; Selden laid the bait by suggesting that 'since the business concerns the King and his privy councillors, I desire therefore a day may be appointed for the King's counsel to come in and defend what was done if they can.'[154] On the next day, the committee of the whole voted unanimously that 'the subjects of England have such propriety in their goods and estates that they cannot be taken from them, nor subject to any levies without their assent in parliament.'[155] This struck a blow against the recent loan and paved the way for further expressions of grievance. The business of Manwaring's sermons would remain in the wings for several months, while that of imprisonment, billeting, and martial law dominated centre stage.

Extended debate over discretionary imprisonment opened on 27 March, with a lengthy speech in a committee of the whole by Richard Cresheld, a future sergeant at law, who asked if any of the 'counsel in the late cause adjudged in the King's Bench' would care to show how Magna Carta and the first Statute of Westminster applied to 'the letting of persons to bail.'[156] Selden obliged immediately, listing the 'remedies provided by the common law against imprisonment,' discussing the specific writs involved, stressing that 'it is the body and sole distinction of freemen that they cannot be imprisoned at pleasure,' analysing and applying the relevant statutes (including the Matthew Paris version of Magna Carta, chapter 29), and noting three favourable precedents.[157] This speech included many of the arguments put forward by the attorneys for the defence in the Five Knights' Case and specifically sought to counter the points raised by

Attorney General Heath and Chief Justice Hyde. As for the legal right of kings to imprison freemen without showing cause, Selden drew upon his comparative perspective to produce a firm conclusion against the practice: 'I hear some men tell us of the power of princes abroad. I confidently affirm no prince in Christendom claims that privilege. My reason: no man can know the law of England but by reading, and so I have sought into the laws of foreign nations. You know where they are, both for the Empire, Germany, Denmark, and Poland, and I will promise any man that desires to see the book shall.'[158] This appeal to Continental laws capped Selden's powerful challenge.

This reading of the case would not stand uncontested, however, for Solicitor General Sir Richard Shelton firmly supported the decision made by the King's Bench and pointed out that the case had not dealt with the power of the king and council to commit, but with the granting of bail to people imprisoned on the special command of the king by means of a writ of *habeas corpus*. He noted that 'the judgment was *remittitur quosque, etc.*, which was not to authorize their imprisonment, but that the court would take further time to advise of it' and added that 'Sir Edward Coke had in 12 *Jacobi* done the like,' that is, refused bail in a similar case.[159] Of course, Shelton had received a full briefing for this sort of occasion and he accurately summed up the decision rendered by Chief Justice Hyde.[160] With both sides engaged, a full-scale debate raged in the committee of the whole House for the next two days; a series of lawyers opposed the legality of the Crown to imprison without specifying a cause and some attacked Attorney General Heath's defence of such commitments on the grounds of reason of state; others defended the privy council's reading of the royal prerogative, while Shelton prodded Coke into explaining his change of mind since the judgments of 12 and 14 James I.[161] Selden took part in this debate. On 28 March, when Sir Francis Nethersole, the agent for Elizabeth of Bohemia, drew upon the law of nature and a common-law maxim in a clever defence of royal discretion in imprisonment: 'It is a written law in the common law *salus populi suprema lex est* [the welfare of the people is the supreme law],' Selden reposted by quoting another maxim: '*Salus populi suprema lex, et libertas popula summa salus populi* [the liberty of the people the greatest welfare of the people],' and drew upon the case of the Apostle Paul to add that 'it was the law of the Empire not to send a prisoner without signifying the crimes laid against him.'[162] Those who wished to defend the actions of the Crown on civil- or natural-law principles received a clear warning.

On 29 March, Coke intervened in the debate to attack discretionary imprisonment because of 'the universality of persons' who could suffer from 'this absolute authority that is pretended' and because of the 'indefiniteness of the time' that they could suffer in prison without a charge, for had 'the law given this prerogative it would have set some time to it ...' Such principle went against the reason of the common law. Before making his earlier ruling, Coke also explained, he had only had time to consult one authority; now, after having consulted many more precedents, he admitted his earlier mistake.[163] On the previous day, Selden had moved: 'Let a subcommittee search into those judgments and precedents.' Supported by Phelips and Coke, the motion carried. Now he obtained permission for the subcommittee to enlarge its search by obtaining copies of the relevant documents, and Soliciter Shelton was ordered to 'bring what he thinks fit to the subcommittee' for their consideration.[164] This marked the conclusion of the opening debate.

During the days and months ahead, this subcommittee proved a formidable body; as a subcommittee, it reported back to the committee of the whole without having to pass through the House in session. This made it easier for those pressing for reform to maintain their initiative. Persistent in its probing, the subcommittee unearthed an actual conspiracy on the part of Attorney General Heath to settle 'the substantive issue of discretionary imprisonment for unknown causes permanently in favour of the Crown,' as John Guy has noted.[165] The first intimation of suspicion came in the report made on 31 March, when Selden, after rehearsing the relevant precedents and acts of Parliament found by the subcommittee, ended by quoting a 'judgment in the *habeas corpus* which is not entered in the roll' of the King's Bench, but which Solicitor Shelton, who had provided the copy, 'said he did think ... had been entered.'[166] This unrecorded draft went beyond the issue of bail to support commitment 'generally by mandate of the King' even though 'on the aforesaid return no special cause of detention appears.'[167] Phelips and Coke immediately grasped the disastrous consequences of entering such a judgment; joined by other members, they expressed the hope that the House could prevent its enrolment.[168] On 1 April, Selden reported that Attorney General Heath had repeatedly importuned the Clerk of the King's Bench to enter the purported judgment; despite the intense pressure, however, the Clerk and the Justices had refused such an unusual procedure.[169] The chairman of the subcommittee had put his research skills to good use. The Commons expressed its increased fear over the actions of the king's servants by unanimously passing through the committee of the whole three strong resolutions against discretionary imprisonment.[170] Selden had helped to turn the inquiry into the Five Knights' Case into a major assertion of the liberties of English subjects.

The problem of billeting received attention in both Houses. On 26 March, the Lords received a petition from the constable of Banbury, Oxfordshire, complaining about the behaviour of soldiers billeted in that borough and initiated an examination of all sides of the dispute. On 2 April, they concluded with a resolution which provided a mild rebuke to several of the parties and an order to all to obey the laws of the land.[171] On the afternoon of the latter day, a committee of the whole House of Commons discussed 'the violation of the propriety of goods by loans, taxing of men's goods, and billeting of soldiers'; Rich related the harm wrought by billeting in Essex; Sir John Eliot and Sir Edward Giles followed with horror stories from Plymouth, Sir Henry Wallop – who sat on the commission of martial law – from Hampshire, and Phelips, from Somerset. Sir Edward Rodney, a deputy lieutenant from Somerset and enemy of Phelips, spoke in defence of those county officials who had ordered the billeting of soldiers: 'we heard of the King's absolute power in Westminster, and we know the great power of kings in arms, all which transcends the law. Also we had an inevitable necessity which was apparent and visible.'[172] Rodney received no support from the privy councillors. Instead came a devastating reply from George Browne, the member for Taunton and an experienced common lawyer, who not only provided details from the borough he represented, but attacked the legality of billeting in no uncertain terms: 'Every man knows there is no law for this. We know our houses are our castles, and to have such guests put upon us, our wives, and children, is a violating of the laws.'[173]

During a debate on impressment held on the next day, Selden launched into a long historical account on the raising of troops, showing that 'three courses were used' in the past 'for levying of forces for wars: 1. By calling them together who are bound to serve by tenure. 2. By sending to those who were engaged by covenant to serve the King. 3. By this new way of pressing.'[174] The first predated the Conquest, grew under William I to provide '60,000 knights and armed men,' and still continued in force; the second 'was the frequent way' from Edward II to Henry VIII and usually involved the granting of indentures to 'barons and great men' who 'could raise 1,000 men at any time'; the third became standard only under the Tudors.[175] Although favouring a monetary value for a knight's fee at this time, Selden had worked out the historical meaning of tenures by knight service (i.e., that lords received the use of land in return for providing the service of mounted warriors). Citing statutes from the reigns of Richard II, Henry VI, Henry VII, Henry VIII, and Edward VI, Selden drew the radical conclusion that 'in all these statutes there is not a word of any soldiers pressed or sent away by compulsion, and so the law then knew no pressing.'[176] The normal method of putting together an army for service abroad in early Stuart England had no precedents before the reign of Philip and Mary. For those schooled in any version of the ancient constitution, the conclusion obviously followed that the Crown could not press troops legally.

Faced with the collapse of the regular method of raising soldiers and sailors while England was engaged in war with Spain and France, reformer after reformer, including Phelips, John Pym, Digges, Wentworth, Eliot, and Sir Edward Coke, supported the apprehensions expressed by Solicitor Shelton on this issue and not the historical arguments presented by Selden.[177] Coke directed attention back to the crux of the question, the misuse of power by royal servants: 'The prerogative of the King is like a river which men cannot live without, but if it swell it will overflow, and perhaps run out of the course, and that swelling is caused by misemployment of the power of deputy lieutenants, and this I desire should be examined.'[178] Defusing the issue, Coke moved 'that there may be a select committee to draw a bill for this business.'[179] As one of the few people who had a historical grasp of tenure in 1628, Selden presented the more accurate account; ironically, it clearly overstepped the bounds of parliamentary propriety. Turning back to other business, the House unanimously passed three resolutions against discretionary imprisonment and, for good measure, added a fourth, on the property of the subject.[180] On 4 April, Coke carried a motion to request a conference with the Lords 'concerning certain ancient and fundamental liberties of England'; Sir Dudley Digges would introduce the case of the Commons, and Edward Littleton, John Selden, and Sir Edward Coke, each with two able assistants, would present the recently passed resolutions and the arguments in support of their adoption to the Lords.[181]

The First Joint Conference

This conference took place on 7 April and set much of the tone for the first session of this Parliament. The format followed the outline produced by Attorney General Heath for the Five Knights' Case, the arguments a refined version of those earlier presented by the counsel for the defence. Digges opened with a learned, composite model of the ancient constitution which argued 'that the laws of England are grounded on reason more ancient than books, consisting much in unwritten customs ... so ancient that from the Saxon days, notwithstanding the injuries and ruins of time, they have continued in most parts the same ... By the blessing of God a good king, Edward, commonly called St. Edward, did awaken those laws ... which William the Conqueror and all his successors since that time have sworn unto.'[182] Portions of the interpretations of Coke, Davies, Hedley, and Selden infused this highly public speech, but the spirit and scholarship of Selden prevailed in most places, especially in the absence of any references to Trojan origins, the *Mirror of Justices*, and the *Modus Tenendi Parliamentum*, but not – as we have seen – in the implicit notion that the Saxon laws had remained dormant during the rule of King Cnut. No doubt, Digges added some interpretations of his own, as well as his well-honed sense of rhetorical flourish.

After presenting the background, Digges went on to show how the liberties of English freemen, which stretched back to the days of the Saxons and had received confirmation many times since, had suffered a severe invasion in recent years:

Be pleased then to know, that it is an undoubted and fundamental point of this so ancient common law of England, that the subject hath a true property in his goods and possessions, which doth preserve as sacred that *meum et tuum* that is the nurse of industry, and mother of courage, and without which there can be no justice, of which *meum et tuum* is the proper object But the undoubted birthright of free subjects hath lately not a little been invaded and prejudiced by pressures, the more grievous because they have been pursued by imprisonment contrary to the franchises of this land.[183]

Later in the conference, Coke would take up the theme of industry and courage. The failure of *habeas corpus* in the Five Knights' Case, Digges went on to explain, had enforced an examination of the relevant 'acts of parliaments, precedents and reasons' by the Commons, whose spokesmen now would present the results of their research to the Lords, with Littleton expounding the statutes, Selden the precedents, and Coke the reasons.[184]

The spirit of Selden, and much more, infused all of the learned orations made by the spokesmen of the Commons. Littleton quoted the relevant portions of the statutes, including the Matthew Paris version of Magna Carta, chapter 29, and gave a lengthy explanation of why the word 'repleviable' from the first Statute of Westminster did not mean 'bailable.'[185] Since this speech expanded upon and systematically developed the arguments presented before the King's Bench and the House of Commons by Selden, one may reasonably infer that he had a large hand in its drafting.[186] Selden followed, patiently explaining the procedure used when seeking remedy through a writ of *habeas corpus* and then reciting, one by one, some thirty-one precedents grouped into three categories: 1 / cases where 'persons committed by the command of the King, or of the Privy Council, without other cause shown, have been enlarged upon bail when they prayed it'; 2 / those 'where some assent of the King or Privy Council appears upon the enlargement of a prisoner so committed'; and 3 / 'those which have been urged as express testimonies of the judges denying bail.'[187] Then he read the full text of draft judgment for the Five Knights' Case drawn up at the command of Attorney General Heath and noted that

if it were entered in the roll (as it was prepared for no other purpose), would be as great a declaration contrary to the many acts of parliament already cited, contrary to all precedents of former times, and to all reason of law, to the utter subversion of the chiefest liberty and right belonging to every free man of this kingdom ... therefore, the House of Commons thought fit also that I should ... show this draft also to your Lordships.[188]

After reading the resolution of the judges of 34 Elizabeth I as recorded in the book of selected cases compiled by Lord Chief Justice Anderson, Selden concluded by offering to provide the Lords with authentic copies of all of the precedents, the draft judgment, and the resolution of the Lower House.[189] Throughout, both Littleton and Selden marshalled the research of the subcommittee with clarity, force, and skill.

Last came the chance of former Lord Chief Justice Coke to finish the case of the Commons. After reading the four resolutions passed by the Lower House into the record, he spent the major part of his time developing nine legal reasons to demonstrate: 'That these acts of parliament and these judicial precedents in affirmance thereof (recited by my colleagues), are but declarations of the fundamental laws of this kingdom ...'[190] The first developed the distinction between freemen and villeins, arguing that 'if free men of England might be imprisoned at the will and pleasure of the King by his commandment, then were they in worse case than bondmen and villeins; for the lord of a villein cannot command another to imprison his villein without cause, as of disobedience, or refusing to serve, as is agreed in our law books.' The second reason argued that, in such matters, the king must act 'judicially, by his judges'; the third discussed the remedies to commitment offered by various writs; the fourth opposed 'the extent and universality of the pretended power to imprison'; and and the fifth stressed the 'indefiniteness of time' as stipulated in the return. Selden had used the first and second of these arguments in his presentation before the King's Bench and in his speech in the Commons of 27 March. Coke had already expressed the third, fourth, and fifth in a debate in the committee of the whole House.[191] The sixth portrayed the 'loss and dishonor of the English nation' for their 'valor and prowess' and for their 'industry' from failing to uphold the distinction between *meum et tuum*. As the readers of Fortescue well knew, the power and riches of the realm sprang from the liberties of English freemen. In his last three points, Coke emphasized that 'the pretended power' of discretionary imprisonment 'being against the profit of the King and of his people, can be no part of his prerogative,' that an expression of the cause of commitment provided greater safety to the king should a prisoner escape, and, last, that earlier judgments had ruled against similar actions.[192] The Lords observed an impressive performance. The spokesmen of the Commons, guided in many points by the visible and invisible hand of Selden, had delivered a learned lesson on the nature of the ancient constitution and a powerful defence of the liberty of free-born Englishmen.

Military Matters

While the Lords engaged in their own examination of the resolutions of the Commons and carried out their own investigation of the draft judgment, the Commons returned to the question of grievances over the conduct of troops, which were divided into the categories of billeting and martial law. Debate continued on the contentious issue of martial law, but the House expeditiously heard individual complaints on billeting and established a subcommittee to draft a petition to the king on this issue.[193] On 9 April, for example, it questioned a member, John Baber (the Recorder of Wells, who sat for that borough), about his signing of a warrant to billet soldiers without an express written command from the deputy lieutenants; while Baber defended his actions on the grounds that he had signed the warrant at the command of his mayor and at the behest of the deputy lieutenants, Seymour demanded punishment and Selden uncharitably echoed: 'He says he was afraid. It is the common excuse of all agents. He that for fear in the country will do that which he ought not, may fear to do what is fit here. Therefore, I humbly move he may not sit amongst us.'[194] The House suspended Baber as an example to other magistrates. On the same day, Rich presented a draft petition on billeting; within two days, it passed the final two readings.[195] Accompanied by the Commons, Speaker Finch presented the petition to King Charles on 14 April; it pointed to the unprecedented nature of billeting, noted the grave difficulties that this procedure had created in the country, and asked 'for the present removal of this unsupportable burden, and that your Majesty would be graciously pleased to secure us from the like pressure in time to come.'[196] In his answer, the king promised to examine the petition, but prodded the Commons to vote supply with greater speed and to spend less energy on worrying about their liberties: 'I have faithfully declared that I will be as forward for the preservation of your liberties as yourselves; therefore go on without distrust or more apologies.'[197] Ironically, new evidence revealed in the Lords just two days previously helped to sap the confidence of members of Parliament in the 'forwardness' of Charles and at least some of his ministers for the liberties of Englishmen.

While the Commons prepared its petition on billeting, the Lords pursued the issue of discretionary imprisonment. On 12 April, Attorney General Heath spoke to the Upper House on the latter issue. Since the papers delivered to the Lords on 9 April for examination by the king's counsel contained fourteen acts of Parliament copied from records in the Tower of London, eleven 'several sheets of precedents out of the King's Bench, etc.,' the draft judgment prepared by Attorney General Heath, and reports of the speeches made on 7 April –

with that by Digges running to one sheet of paper, that by Littleton to twelve 'sides close written,' that by Selden sixty sides, and that by Coke nine sides – he did not lack a target.[198] To open his testimony, Heath agreed with the summary of the issues at stake made by the Commons: 'The first, that no free man ought to be imprisoned by the King or Council without cause shown. If he be restrained by the King or Council, etc., being returned by *habeas corpus* ought to be delivered.'[199] Following, however, came a lengthy attack upon the interpretation put forward in the resolutions of the Commons and the arguments presented by Littleton, Selden, and Coke.

After discussing Magna Carta and the statutes cited, the attorney general made the telling point that 'it is strange that there should be no printed book nor statute that positively says the King cannot commit without showing a cause, being it is a thing so much concerns the liberty of the subject.'[200] Turning from statutes to precedents, he explained: 'When we cannot tell what *lex terræ* or *consuetudo Angliæ* is, we resor[t] to the usual practice of former times.'[201] Each case received a careful interpretation which showed how the actions taken did not demonstrate the bailing of a prisoner without some direction from the king or privy council; a comment on the last case underlined his differences with the spokesmen of the Commons by noting that 'the rules laid down by Mr Selden [were] utterly mistaken.'[202] Heath also defended his 'draft of the judgment intended to be entered' in the roll of the King's Bench explaining that, when he compared it with 'the old precedents,' he 'found no difference but a few words more and therefore resolved never to enter it.'[203] At this point, Buckingham supported his client by interceding to note that 'the Attorney had a check from the King because he had not entered that draft.'[204] This intervention hardly reassured those who feared for their liberties.

On 14 and 15 April, the Justices of the King's Bench spoke individually and established a number of points about the Five Knights' Case. First, in the words of Justice Whitelocke, there 'was no judgment, nothing done to derogate from the king or invade' the liberties of the people, only 'a rule in court of *advisari vult*,' that is, the ruling that the prisoners had been remitted until the court should advise on the matter. This meant that the prisoners could seek bail again at any time on a new writ of *habeas corpus*. In the words of Justice Jones, the judges 'all agreed that the next day, or the next term a new *habeas corpus* might have been demanded by the parties, and they must have done justice,' while Whitelocke added: 'I never did read a record that did make it appear to me that the judges of the King's Bench did deliver a man upon the first return of *per mandatum domini regis.*' With regard to the draft judgment, Whitelocke reported the comforting news that the Justices and Clerk had followed the old customs: 'Mr. Attorney did that which beseemed a good servant. We as judges between the King and people. We gave order to the clerk to enter nothing but that which was accustomed to ancient course.'[205] In other words, the Justices had deliberately avoided deciding the issue of discretionary imprisonment and had not allowed the Clerk the enter on the roll the draft judgment presented by Attorney General Heath.

Even before they had heard the Justices, the Lords had debated whether they should allow the Commons a chance to reply to the presentation made by Heath, and they had ordered 'Mr. Attorney to put his arguments in writing so soon as he can' for such purposes; after listening to the Justices and receiving their submission as a written report, many Lords came to see such a meeting as a means for reaching some sort of accommodation between the prerogative of the Crown and the liberties of the people.[206]

The Great Debate

A dramatic joint conference of both Houses, held on the afternoons of 16 and 17 April, gave formal reality to the ideal of the high court of Parliament and capped the debate between Selden and Heath. In attendance, but without voice, sat the members of the Lords and the Commons, plus the Justices of the King's Bench. Attorney General Heath, with Sir Francis Ashley, King's Sergeant, in attendance, presented the case of the Crown, while Sir Edward Coke, Sir Dudley Digges, Edward Littleton, and John Selden, each with an assistant, spoke on behalf of the House of Commons. Lord Keeper Coventry dramatically opened the proceedings by reading the declaration of the Justices of the King's Bench that Magna Carta and the other statutes cited by the Commons 'stand in force,' that they had 'given no judgment at all, but a rule,' that 'the party might have prayed' for 'a new *habeas corpus,*' that there was no difference 'betwixt *remittitur, etc.,* or a *remittitur quosque*' (as Selden had claimed in the Commons), and that they had no 'intention of a new entry or judgment.'[207] Had the conference ended at that point, this declaration may have built the foundation for a satisfactory accommodation, for the liberties which had seemed endangered clearly had remained intact.

Attorney General Heath followed the Lord Keeper, however, and broke the conciliatory atmosphere built up by Coventry. Heath could not resist launching a strong attack upon the substance of the case presented earlier by the spokesmen of the Commons. Although acknowledging that Magna Carta in 'all parts' and the six 'subsequent statutes' still stood in force, Heath correctly noted that a 'difference in the manner of application' of these laws still remained in dispute, and especially the 'great question' of 'how far the words of lex terræ extend.'[208] In reply to the opening orations, Coke explained that the spokesmen of the Commons had 'delegatam potestatem, to hear only,' and not to speak to 'that which is new,' so they would 'not meddle with the resolution of the judges, but report it to the House.'[209] Littleton next agreed that the seven statutes remained in force, but he reiterated that Magna Carta made little sense unless 'per legem terræ' bestowed greater privileges upon freemen than upon villeins.[210] The rest of the discussion for the opening day consisted of a long case-by-case dispute over the precedents; it made accommodation even more difficult.

In this debate, the attorney general sought to prove that none of the precedents cited by the Commons showed that the Crown could not imprison on the special command of the king; in reply, the spokesmen of the Commons interpreted all of these precedents, except a recent one, as showing that the King's Bench had bailed freemen imprisoned by the express command of the king upon application by a writ of habeas corpus. Many of the cases hinged upon technicalities, such as, whether the persons bailed had another charge in addition to the special command of the king, or whether the privy council had requested their release. Heath admitted that those charged with a specific offence had received bail; the spokesmen of the Commons claimed that defendants had received bail even when charged only with the special command of the king. When Heath pointed to an existing letter from the privy council in one case to argue that prisoners received bail upon such a request, Selden's reply left little room for informal cooperation between the privy council and the judges: 'either the prisoner was bailable by the law, or not bailable; if bailable by the law, then was he to be bailed without any such letter; if not bailable by the law, then plainly the judges could not have bailed him upon the letter without breach of their oaths;

which is, that they are to do justice according to the law without having respect to any command whatsoever.'[211] In four other cases, Heath noted, the defendants 'were committed to the marshal of the King's Bench; and that,' although 'this kind of commitment was by the course of that court always done before the bailing of the prisoner, yet that it did not appear that they were bailed.'[212] Selden replied that the court had resolved 'that the prisoners so committed were bailable, otherwise they had been remanded, and not committed to the marshal of the King's Bench.'[213] It all depended upon one's interpretation of the documents; the prisoners, most likely, were bailable, but no record proved that they had gone free on bail. Upon the minute sifting and explanation of such details depended the case of each side, so the assembled Lords and members of the Commons listened to the attorneys argue out case after case for much of the first afternoon.

On the morning of the second day, Attorney General Heath complained to the Lords that the spokesmen of the Commons 'shall have this advantage which never any had before against the King, viz., to be heard last,' but admitted his willingness 'to speak to that which is known already.'[214] The afternoon, opened with a debate over 'the reasons, and resolutions of the judges.'[215] First, Heath discussed the meaning of 'per legem terræ' in Magna Carta. Repeating his earlier position that: 'if lex terræ be taken for due process of law, then none can be imprisoned for felony before indictment,' he admitted that 'by these laws no free man ought to be committed or imprisoned without good cause.' This meant that 'the great question is, if the commitment come from the King or his Council, if the cause be to be expressed, or to say in general per mandatum domini regis or per mandatum concilii, the King need not to set down the particular cause.'[216] Heath admitted that the first Statute of Westminster did not extend to the King's Bench, as he had earlier argued, but he still wanted to maintain that 'in that statute it is said that they that are committed by the King are not repleviable. It is all one with bailable.'[217] Citing many precedents including the resolution of the judges in 34 Elizabeth I, Ruswell's Case in 14 James I, and Sir Edward Coke's speech in the Parliament of 1621, Heath argued that either the special command of the king or the privy council fulfilled the requirement of a general cause for commitment as specified in these considered resolutions.[218]

At this point, Ashley unexpectedly commented upon the meaning of *per legem terræ* in Magna Carta, chapter 29. In those times, 'there were divers laws of this realm, as the common law, the law of the Chancery, the ecclesiastical law, the law of the admiralty, or marine law, the law of merchants, the martial law, and the law of state, and that these words, *per legem terræ*, do extend to all these laws.'[219] This broadened the concept of 'according to the law' well beyond anything earlier advocated by the attorney general. In addition, Ashley returned to the concept that in a 'matter of state' the 'cause ought not to be shown' and employed it as a defence for discretionary imprisonment.

That the King may commit is not to be denied, and this power is committed to him by God. The King hath a scepter and a sword. A leet may commit and so may a constable, and may not the King, who is the fountain of justice? Objection: The cause ought to be shown. The matter of state is cause sufficient, and in those matters the cause ought not to be shown. Every state hath *secreta regni*.[220]

Heath had studiously avoided any reference to 'reason of state' in his presentation and had gone out of his way to base his case on common-law evidence alone, probably in a desire to avoid confrontation over marginal points. Not only had Ashley spoken with 'no authority nor direction' from the Lords, as Lord President Manchester immediately pointed out, he had asserted a number of highly provocative points.[221]

Most common lawyers held that the canon and civil laws exercised jurisdiction in England only to the degree that the common law had incorporated portions of these laws by statute or custom; this meant that the common law was the law of the land and they were laws of the land only by incorporation. Few common lawyers would have agreed that the law of nations (*jus gentium*) should supply any purported 'defect' in the common law; indeed, most would have viewed that assertion, normally forwarded by civil lawyers, as a threat to the supremacy of the common law in England. A 'matter of state,' as if a 'law of state' existed, raised a particularly ominous spectre, because of its almost infinite possibilities of extension. No doubt, Manwaring would have found the loan of 1627 equitable.

The spokesmen of the Commons answered with firm rebuttals. Littleton recited the statutes upon which the Commons had built their case; Coke followed with a demonstration that earlier statutes had limited the royal prerogatives of coinage and pardon and that, therefore, there was 'no incompatibility between the liberty we demand and a monarchy'; Noy reiterated the reasons why 'the King's command is not sufficient' without a specific cause; John Glanville dealt with the extent and limits of the four royal prerogatives; and Selden handled the resolutions of various judges and the meaning of *per legem terræ*.[222] The tone became fiery, however, when Selden opened by informing the Lords that the two sets of spokesmen in the joint conference 'were no way to be so compared or counterpoised as if the one were of no more weight than the other.'

For the King's counsel spake as counsel perpetually retained by fee ... But the gentlemen that spoke in behalf of the House of Commons came there, bound on the one side by the trust reposed in them by their country that sent them, and on the other side bound also by an oath taken every one of them before he sit in the House, to maintain and defend the rights and prerogatives of the crown ...[223]

In other words, Heath and Ashley spoke for Mammon; Littleton, Coke, Noy, and Selden, for king and country! Resisting any attempt to broaden the meaning of the law of the land, Selden retorted 'we read of no law of state' and, as for the other laws mentioned by Sergeant Ashley,

none of these can be meant there [i.e., in Magna Carta] save the common law, which is the principal and general law, and is always understood by the way of excellency when mention is of the law of the land generally. And that though each of the other laws which are admitted into this land by custom or act of parliament may justly be called 'a law of the land', yet none of them can have the preeminence to by styled 'the law of the land'. And no statute, law book, or other authority, printed or unprinted, could be shown to prove that the law of the land, being generally mentioned was ever intended of any other than the common law; and yet even by these other laws a man may not be committed without a cause expressed.[224]

This repeated the analysis published earlier in Selden's notes to Fortescue's *De Laudibus Legum Angliæ* and in various parts of *The Historie of Tithes*.[225]

Employing his philological method to good effect, Selden continued his presentation by reading at length from the notes of Lord Chief Justice Anderson on the resolution of 34 Elizabeth I to show that, in that case, the judges believed that '"the cause of commitment ... upon the return of their *habeas corpus* ... ought to be ... certified to the judges."'[226] As for the judgment of 13 James I and Coke's speech in the Parliament of 1621, both brought forward by the spokesmen for the Crown, Selden patiently undermined the sufficiency of the evidence offered in proof: the reports of the judgment came from the notes of a young law student who so jumbled together three cases that the account could bear no telling weight, while the record of the speech came from the Journals of the House of Commons, which held no authority 'for any particular man's opinion noted in any of them,' but only for resolutions of the House and other decisions of record.[227] Selden next explained why the resolutions of the Commons in the Parliament of 1628 carried greater weight than either the judgment of the judges or the parliamentary speech of the former chief justice; 'this great point' of discretionary imprisonment 'and all circumstances belonging to it, hath within this half year been so fully examined and searched into that it may well be affirmed that the most learned man whatsoever that hath now considered of it hath within that time, or might have, learned more reason of satisfaction in it than ever before he ever met with.'[228] In other words, recent research had turned up considerably more evidence from the ancient constitution on this point than that available to Coke and earlier Justices. In comparison with 'such debates and mature deliberations,' Selden audaciously concluded, 'the sudden opinion of any judge to the contrary is of no value here.'[229] The spokemen of the Commons stood firmly in support of the principles voted earlier by their House.

The heat of the confrontation seemed to dissipate somewhat as seasoned champions from each side put the concluding statements, but even this formality ended in undignified disputes and bickering. Sir Edward Coke summed up the case of the Commons with an eloquent appeal to the lay Lords, whose 'noble ancestors ... were parties to Magna Carta,' and to the bishops, whose predecessors were 'commanded' to excommunicate 'all infringers of Magna Carta,' asking them to weigh on the scales of justice the seven 'acts of parliament, records, precedents, reasons' presented by the representatives of the Commons, against 'what Mr Attorney said, his wit, learning and great endowments of nature.'[230] Equally moderately, Attorney General Heath noted that both sides agreed that 'the King may commit,' that the 'statutes of Magna Carta' remained 'in force,' and that, if 'a general cause expressed, it is sufficient.'[231] He reiterated his view that the command of the king constituted such a general cause and, therefore, that the Crown had supported 'rules subject to the judges of the common law as much as' had the spokesmen 'on the other side.'[232] Heath wisely deserted 'reason of state' and rested the case of the Crown upon the common law. When the attorney general finished, Coke offered some further comments, only to hear an appeal from Heath for 'that privilege of speaking the last word for the King.'[233] One of the delegates of the Commons 'answered no such privilege here in the court of parliament, we stand for knights and burgesses. The privilege good in a court of Westminster Hall.'[234] A confused, virtual shouting match followed, with Heath and Digges arguing over a particular precedent; Noy jumping in; the attorney general moving 'for an accommodation, their Lordships to find out a middle way'; Coke standing firm for 'no accommodation, no dividing of the child,' the 'true mother will not divide the child'; and the Duke of Buckingham, familiar with the famous scene before King Solomon, calling from the benches: 'Not to use such words, compare his master to a whore.'[235] Harmony and consensus looked farther away than at any time since the opening of this Parliament.

The Earl of Suffolk's Threats against Selden

The attempts of the Commons to secure the liberties of English subjects clearly had started to fray the nerves of some of the royal councillors. On the morning of 12 April, the day on which the Speaker presented the petition against billeting to the king, Edward Kirton (a member of the Seymour connection) declared that he had heard of a threat made by a Lord towards a member of the Commons; the House required Kirton to reveal the name of his informant and then ordered that member, Sir John Strangways, to 'declare his knowledge therein.'[236] Strangways related that, 'going into the Committee Chamber of the Lords, to the best of his rememberance, the words used by the Earl of Suffolk were these: "Sir John Strangways, will you not hang Selden?" To which Sir John answering, "My Lord, I know no cause for it", the Earl swore, "By God, he had razed a record, for which he was worthy to be hanged."'[237] Selden immediately denied that he had defaced any document, and the Commons responded by sending a formal complaint to the Lords and by establishing a committee to investigate the incident.[238]

Suffolk had sat on that royal commission which had drawn up the

'Instructions for the Execution of Martial Law in His Majesty's Army' and obviously did not appreciate the work of the legal anti-quaries in the Lower House. He fabricated the charge that Selden had destroyed a record (a crime carrying the death penalty) out of a remark by Heath that the scholar had not included the full text in some of the transcriptions of statutes and precedents handed over to the Lords.[239] After a number of attempts to deny the words related by Strangways and a claim that he had said: 'If this be true, Selden is to be blamed,' Suffolk escaped with an explanation which acknowl-edged that Selden had not committed this particular crime.[240] In order to extract this apology, the Commons had demanded that the Lords proceed against Suffolk.[241] While minor, this incident illus-trated the dangers inherent in taking controversial stands in Parlia-ment, the difficulty of reaching a consensus on controversial matters, and the irritable feelings of those who were administering the war effort.

Debates over Martial Law

The issue of martial law erupted again in the Commons on 18 April with a fiery debate in a committee of the whole which pitted Sir Henry Marten, Judge of the Admiralty and prerogative court of Can-terbury, against a host of common lawyers and other members.[242] In a long, learned speech which started from the premise that 'if a com-pany of soldiers be raised there must be military law' but still attempted to preserve a role for the common law, Marten had sug-gested:

The question is if the martial law be not executed upon soldiers in time of peace. They are subject to the common law without question, but also they are to be ruled by the military law. I agree where the [common] law may be executed with convenience the martial law is not to be executed, as the com-mon law may with conveniency be executed This reacheth not to soldiers in tenure or covenant, but the soldiers *in actu*. Execution of martial law is need-ful where the sovereign and state hold it needful and it impeacheth not the common law.[243]

Careful to limit its application to soldiers under arms, not to men who held land on knight tenures, Marten stressed the sovereign's power to decide when and where to execute martial law. This also led to an extension of the time of war into times of peace: 'War hath many steps, first in preparation. There must be a military law for preparation, for expedition, for battle. So if you understand *tempus belli* in any of these degrees, martial law is then to be used.' Although attempting to take into account the sensitivity of common lawyers by noting that the 'common law permits admiral law,' Marten created discomfort in the minds of other members with his references to convenience, to the discretionary powers of the sovereign, and to the extension of martial law into the preparations for war.[244] Among other voices, Sir Edward Coke replied: 'Sir H. Marten said martial law is to be used in convenient time. Who shall judge of that? It will bring all to an absolute power. He said the laws common and martial may stand together. It is impossible ... If the soldier and the judge should sit both of one bench the drum would drown the voice of the crier.'[245] Coke feared a slide into absolutist practices if convenience were allowed to rule, an overthrowing of common-law jurisdiction were courts-martial and common-law courts to sit at the same time. Let custom continue to rule, Coke advised. If the courts in Westminster stayed open, England remained at peace and commissions of oyer and terminer could take care of any difficult cases in the countryside.

Silent at first, Selden joined in during the second day of this discussion with an impassioned defence of the ancient constitution against any who would make other laws equal and coordinate with the common law of England, he opened and closed with swipes at Marten:

Our question is whether these commissions for martial law are not against law or no. There was no difference between lawyers yesterday. One civilian differed from us, not as a lawyer but as a statesman. A soldier (said he) is subject to the common law and to martial law for conveniency. Convenience does not make a law, neither does civil law govern as it is studied.

This reinforced earlier objections to 'convenience' as a principle of law and reasserted a distinction made in his earlier writings between Roman or civil law as taught in the universities and as enforced in various jurisdictions where it became subject to customs and precedents in its application. Although many Roman lawyers had argued in principle that soldiers came solely under the martial law, they also had recognized that in England these matters belonged to the jurisdiction of the constable and marshal: 'By the civil law a soldier is to be ruled only by martial law, and not by the civil or common law. Whatsoever civilians discourse, they always thus conclude: *hæc omnia constant ad jura Comistabuli et Marescalli Angliæ* [all these things belong to the jurisdiction of the Constable and Marshal of England].' Thus, Selden turned the writings of other civil lawyers against the arguments of Marten.

To counter the assertion of separate but equal jurisdictions for the common law, canon law, law merchant, and martial law, Selden returned to his previously published constitutional principles:

As the canon law, the law of marrying, and the law merchant does stand with the common law, so they say does the martial law. There are but two ways of making laws, custom and act of parliament. Those are laws of custom. Can any man tell me what martial law is, and how to punish men according to the commission only? It hath reference to instructions by the Council, and it was never known in England that any law was made but by custom or act of parliament ... I say this is a third way of making laws; and this is a new law, not heard of before. In the state of Rome no other authority made martial law but that that made the common law. The same is done in the Low Countries. As for our definition of time of war, it was said by one that it was for the preparation to war. Why then war is peace, because it is a preparation to peace, and peace to war. It was said that in former times all men of fashion were soldiers, and if they were all subject to martial law, where was this common law? As for martial law to be exercized upon the marching of an army, it may be done by a commission of oyer and terminer, and so it hath been done in former times ... I avouch 2 passages out of an old book against Sir H. Marten, H[enry] 7: 1, all belongs to the Constable and Marshal when the battles be ordained; 2ly, in the martial court, and when the King is in war, only the Constable and Marshal ought to hold court.[246]

This complex passage contained three main points. First, that neither the civil nor the common law dealt with such major matters as martial law on the arbitrary principle of convenience; both used established procedures for disciplining soldiers under arms: Roman law placed soldiers under a martial law coordinate with civil jurisdiction, and common law offered three choices for the enforcement of order – through a royal commission of oyer and terminer, an act of Parliament, or the court of the constable and marshal. The rule of law had no place for 'convenience.' Second, Selden stressed two legitimate methods of making law within the English constitution, custom and act of Parliament. Since the recent instructions issued by a royal commission upon the mandate of the privy council fulfilled neither of these conditions, they represented a new and dangerous method of attempting to create law. Third, an examination of English medieval evidence revealed that the constable and marshal alone, as allowed by common law, enforced martial law during these centuries. Although addressing the issues at hand, this speech moved well beyond the particular. Drawing upon his knowledge of the civil law, Selden demonstrated that no legal system recognized the validity of 'convenience' in principle or practice. Drawing upon the theory of law announced in the notes to his edition of Sir John Fortescue, *De Laudibus Legum Angliæ* (London, 1616), he also reasserted and applied his interpretation of law as custom or statute, with its implication that in England the king, Lords, and Commons had shared the responsibility for making and interpreting the law from the very beginning. No wonder his colleagues entrusted him to report from the subcommittees on martial law and discretionary imprisonment.[247]

The Five Propositions from the Lords

During the opening stages of the Parliament of 1628, Selden had strongly upheld the liberties of free Englishmen and had played as prominent part in the proceedings of the House as any other member, including Sir Edward Coke. Selden had directed the research upon which the House based its case against discretionary imprisonment, drafted the resolutions against this grievance, prepared many of the arguments used by the spokesmen of the Commons in their presentations to the Lords, and participated effectively in debate on numerous significant topics. Throughout this time, the House of Commons had taken and held the lead in championing English liberties. As the House of Lords became more active in this cause, Selden's level of visible activity would diminish.

On 25 April, the initiative began to shift. In the midst of Selden's lengthy report on the place of martial law in the ancient constitution, a messenger from the Lords interrupted to request a meeting of a committee of members from both Houses.[248] At this gathering, the peers presented five propositions asking King Charles: 1 / to 'declare' that Magna Carta and the six subsequent statutes remained in force; 2 / to 'declare' that 'every free subject of this realm has a fundamental propriety in his goods and a fundamental liberty of his person'; 3 / to 'ratify and confirm' to his subjects 'all their ancient several just liberties, privileges, and rights'; 4 / to pledge that 'his Majesty' would 'proceed according to the common law'; and 5 / 'touching his Majesty's royal prerogative, intrinsical, incident to sovereignty and entrusted him from God,' to 'resolve' that when he 'shall find just cause for reasons of state to imprison or restrain any man's person, that his Majesty would graciously declare that within a convenient time he shall and will express the cause of his commitment or restraint, either general or special.'[249] On the whole, and especially in the fifth point, these statements reflected the language and enshrined the interpretation supported by Attorney General Heath. They also represented a strong concern to uphold the prerogative of the king expressed by many peers during the debates in their House. The Lords had devised a clever set of proposals which appeared to present a viable compromise between the royal prerogative and popular liberties, but, in reality, upheld a moderate version of the case put forward by spokesmen for the Crown.

The Commons opened debates upon these propositions on 26 April. Many members, including not a few with connections in the Upper House – such as Sir Nathaniel Rich, Sir Dudley Digges, and John Pym – favoured some sort of accommodation between the previous resolutions of the Commons and the new suggestions from the Lords.[250] Coke and Selden, however, strongly opposed any such attempt at compromise. Coke attacked each of the resolutions in turn, but saved his greatest fire for the fifth, which would fundamentally alter the distribution of power within the kingdom and give unprecedented powers to the kings of England.[251] Better to confirm old laws, he suggested, than to make new ones which would bind the subject and endanger the nature of the constitution. Starting out on a more technical tack, Selden distinguished firmly between the resolutions of the Commons which declared the law and the propositions of the Lords which attempted to 'explain' the law: 'Our resolutions we sent to the Lords were matters of law; and I think, nay I am sure, no man can question the reason of them. But the Lords l[a]ying by the consideration of our propositions, being law, have proposed these to explain what is law.'[252] Attempts at explanation, no matter how well intended, muddied the situation, because a declaration of the law bore weight in the common-law courts, but an explanation did not. In addition, the particular statements presented serious difficulties:

'Of the first 3 there is no use; the 4th we have already; and the 5th is
not fit to be asked, because it is not fit to be had.'[253] Selden attacked
each in turn: 'Magna Carta has been confirmed 32 or 33 times, and to
have it confirmed 34 times I do not know what good it will do.'[254] As
for the 'fundamental propriety' and personal 'liberty' of the subject,
he retorted: 'I never heard it denied but in the pulpit, which is of no
weight.' A general confirmation of liberties was 'not fit to be asked'
because 'I conceive his Majesty never proceded but according to law.'
The last proposition contradicted the earlier resolution of the Commons on discretionary imprisonment and it would 'destroy our fundamental liberties,' for the wording, with its 'reason of state' and
'convenient time,' allowed 'any person' to suffer commitment 'at
pleasure. By this the cause may be concealed in the breast for a convenient time, and no man is exempted. At this little gap every man's
liberty may in time go out.'[255] Although a number of members felt
that the first three proposals might contain some useful suggestions,
none dared to oppose the powerful condemnation of the fifth made
by Selden and Coke. The two great common lawyers had slowed the
initiative seized by the Lords; in the process, however, they also
stalled the business of the Parliament.

Both sides sought a way out of the impasse. Charles showed his
support for the propositions of the Lords with a personal promise to
work within the law. In a statement read to the two Houses by the
Lord Keeper on 28 April, the king confirmed

that he holds the statute of Magna Carta, and the six other statutes insisted
upon for the subject's liberty, to be all in force, and assures you that he will
maintain all his subjects in the just freedom of their persons and safety of
their estates, and that he will govern according to the laws and statutes of
this realm, and that you shall find as much security in his majesty's royal
word and promise as in the strength of any law you can make, so that hereafter you shall never have cause to complain.[256]

Incorporating the most important statutes cited by the Commons in
support their liberties with a request for members of the Lower
House to press ahead with the provision of supply, this statement
used the careful language of the royal messages drafted by Secretary
Coke. It came as no surprise then when Sir John eagerly urged the
Commons to accept the king's promise as a better alternative to proceeding by bill. Quoting from the parliamentary speech of James VI

and I of 21 March 1610, he attempted to persuade the Lower House to accept the compromise so graciously offered:

We cannot but remember what his father said, 'He is no king, but a tyrant, that governs not by law'. But this kingdom is to be governed by the common law, and his Majesty assures us so much; the interpretation is left to the judges and to his great council, and all is to be regulated by the common law. I mean not Magna Carta only, for that Magna Carta was part of the common law and the ancient laws of this kingdom ... But his Majesty stopped not there ... He assures us our liberties are just: they are not of grace, but of right. Nay, he assures us that he will govern us according to the law of the realm, and that we shall find as much security in his Majesty's promise as in any law we can make.[257]

To one familiar with the constitutional discourse of hard-liners on the council, the public statement that subjects held their liberties as a matter of right and the promise to rule by the common law may have looked like a major concession. In the guise of a compromise, however, the king had offered only his personal promise to the position already defended by Attorney General Heath. During this whole debate, stretching back to the Five Knights' Case, none of the participants had questioned the force of Magna Carta and the six statutes, nor the willingness of the Crown to govern by the law. What stood at dispute was how the king's servants should proceed; on this point the attorneys for the Crown and the lawyers in the Commons had presented two rival interpretations of the ancient constitution. Still, in a world of interpersonal politics, this move had some chance of success.

From the Bill for the 'Liberty of the Subjects' to the 'Petition of Right'

The Commons responded immediately by establishing a committee to frame a bill on 'the liberty of the subjects in their persons and estates.' When this committee met on the afternoon of 28 April, Selden arrived to help with the drafting.[258] On the next morning, Sir Edward Coke reported out a bill 'for the liberties of freemen'; debate on this draft bill stretched over several days. Ever the scholar, Selden made his only contribution on 30 April with a request that the statutes quoted in the bill be read aloud and transcribed from the 'statute roll,' not from printed copies.[259] On 1 May, Secretary Coke interrupted the discussion with another message from the monarch: 'His Majesty would know whether we will rest on his royal word or no, declared to us by the Lord Keeper; which if we do, he assures us it shall be really performed.'[260] Rival loyalties tugged at the knights and burgesses. Caught between the king's insistence that the administration of the law had become a matter of trust and their constituents' demands for redress of grievances, the members of the Commons at first floundered. Gaining back some confidence, they began to draft a reply to the king's speeches on 2 May; despite another message that afternoon in which Charles promised once more to abide by the law and threatened to end the session in slightly more than a week, they pressed forward and presented their answer on 5 May.[261] When the monarch's reply moved little beyond his earlier messages and threatened refusal of the royal assent to a bill on the liberties of the subject, another impasse appeared. After much debate and discussion, the Commons abandoned their attempt to uphold their liberties by statute and decided to proceed by petition of right, a collective version of the procedure recommended by Attorney General Heath in the Five Knights' Case.[262]

During the debates over the king's messages, Selden remained unusually silent. Indeed, between his powerful rebuttal of the five propositions of the Lords on 26 April and his orations on 7 May, he spoke only on two occasions, both on individual cases of parliamentary privilege.[263] This behaviour probably stemmed from a disagreement within the Seymour network. In these debates, Sir Francis Seymour, who had favoured proceeding by petition as early as 1 May, seconded the motion of Sir Edward Coke (who had abandoned his earlier preference) to change from a bill to a petition of right. Although Selden believed that this change of procedure would produce a weaker result, he could not oppose the shift from bill to petition in public without angering his patron.[264] Indeed, until the opening of proceedings against the Duke of Buckingham on 5 June, in which he returned to a more prominent role, Selden played a less visible part in debate; however, he continued to make notable contributions on committees. In addition, he had to prepare copies of the arguments made at the joint conferences of 7, 16, and 17 April. When the House started to move on the Petition of Right, his activity increased; he helped to tighten up the wording of an amendment suggested by Sir Thomas Wentworth and also used the occasion to register his disappointment at the substitution of petition for bill: 'I think no man doubts that this is of equal force with an act of parliament, for certainly it is not.'[265] This warning exemplified Selden's interpretation that all law sprang from either custom or statute. At this juncture, however, the Commons desperately hoped to enshrine on record any particular guarantee of their liberties that could receive the consent of the Lords and Crown. Having finally obtained the opportunity to finish his report on the records of martial law on 7 May, Selden reported a clause on the topic from a subcommittee on the next day; it proved acceptable and completed the text of the Petition of Right just before the Clerk received the direction to prepare a copy in a fair hand for presentation to the Lords.[266]

The Amendments of the Lords

Although the Commons had assembled a petition for the protection of the English liberties, the struggle for its approval by the Lords and by King Charles still loomed ahead. In a meeting of the select committee of members from both Houses, held on 8 May, Coke presented a fair copy of the Petition of Right to delegates of the Lords and, on the same day, the Lower House sweetened the pot by moving forward on the subsidy.[267] Both the king and the peers replied four days later, Charles with a letter to the Lords which claimed that any limitation on the royal prerogative of discretionary imprisonment would 'dissolve the very foundation and frame of our monarchy,' and the Upper House with eight amendments to the text of the petition; the Lord Keeper presented both the letter and the proposed alterations to the Commons in a joint conference of both Houses.[268] The Commons considered these documents on 14 May and decided, after due discussion, not to answer the king's letter, to accept parts of the amendments, and to reject all of the rest.[269] After considerable prompting by the peers, the Commons finally explained why they refused to answer the letter from Charles I: 'first, because it is no parliamentary way, for the King's assent must come after the petition is exhibited; and also that the debate of it would spend time.'[270] Technically, of course, this was correct; the monarch could neither give nor refuse consent until after the bill or petition had passed both Houses, but the Commons had replied to earlier messages from the king. Solicitous to save the honour of the king, the peers suggested an additional clause for the petition, which would explain: 'We present

this our humble petition to your Majesty not only with a care of preserving our own liberties, but with a due regard to leave entire that
sovereign power wherewith your Majesty is trusted for the
protection, safety, and happiness of your people.'[271] The Commons
countered by asking how far the Upper House agreed 'to the petition
in all the parts of it'; when the peers continued to press for their
amendments, a series of conferences between select committees
from each House helped to thresh out the differences.[272]

Selden continued to play a prominent, if somewhat diminished
role in the conferences and debates which led to the passage of the
Petition of Right. Named as one of the four reporters from the Commons for the conference on 12 May and one of the eleven members
from the Lower House for the select committee appointed to treat
with an equivalent committee from the Upper House on 13 May, he
served on numerous occasions at various sorts of conferences
between members of both Houses during this period; he also served
on the committee which drafted replies to points raised by the Lords
and on that which prepared the impeachment charges against
Manwaring.[273] In debate over particular points, he usually opposed
amendments and took particular offence at the additional clause proposed by the peers. When Sir Henry Vane, the Cofferer of the Household and a client of Buckingham, argued that the Petition of Right
contained 'words of larger extent than is in Magna Carta and other
statutes' and that 'we say no more in this addition than is already
delivered by our Speaker to his Majesty,' Selden arose to call for a full
debate and to speak against the addition.[274] It endangered the liberties recited in the petition by deriving them from royal grace:

The sum of this addition is that our right is not to be subject to loans, or
imprisonment without cause, or martial law, but by sovereign power. If it
has no reference to our petition, what does it here? I am sure all others will
say it has reference, and so must we. How far it does exceed all examples of
former times, no man can show me the like. I have made that search that
fully satisfies me, and I find not another besides 28 E[dward] 1. We have a
great many petitions and bills of parliament in all ages, in all which we are
sure no such thing is added. That clause of 28 E[dward] 1, it was not in the
petition but in the King's answer.[275]

Not only did the addition threaten the liberties upheld by the petition, it was also unprecedented. Magna Carta contained no such

clause.[276] Nor did four petitions of right from the reign of Edward III; this left that clause added to 28 Edward I, c. 20 as the only exception.[277] Although 'no parliament roll of that year' survived, a manuscript chronicle from the abbey of Abingdon (available in the library at Cambridge) showed that the king had appended the phrase '*salvo jure coronae regis*' ('saving the right of the King's crown') in his assent; this source also demonstrated that the king's addition had brought forth such protests from the people of London and from prominent peers, that 'at the next parliament' it 'was reformed.'[278] This speech more than answered Vane's slight challenge to the common lawyers. No member dared attempt a refutation of Selden's explanation and, as a result, the Commons refused to accept the addition.[279]

The Passage of the Petition of Right

Not content with a purely defensive role, Selden also helped with the passage of a number of compromises, including the only proposed alterations to the petition accepted by the Commons, the substitution of 'means' for 'pretext,' and of 'an oath not warranted by the laws and statutes of the realm' for an 'unlawful oath.'[280] When, on 23 May, John Glanville defended the legal portion of the arguments posed by the Commons for rejecting the addition proposed by the Lords, he included in his speech almost all of the points raised in earlier debates by Selden.[281] Finally, the Lords agreed that the two amendments accepted by the Lower House formed a basis for joint action, so on 27 May, the Commons passed the final reading of the Petition of Right and the Lords expedited all three readings; on the next day, the Lord Keeper (attended by the members of both Houses) presented it to King Charles.[282] The struggle for the liberties of subjects had finally produced a positive statement of law which gained the approval of both Houses.

Throughout this contest, Selden had taken a leading role, advancing many of the most compelling arguments which eventually led to the passage of the Petition of Right through both Houses, reporting from the subcommittees on discretionary imprisonment and martial law, sitting on many other relevant committees and subcommittees, and speaking on behalf of the Commons in numerous presentations to the Lords. He played as important a role as any member of the Lower House in the composition and passage of the petition. With

Coke, Selden sought to continue to proceed by bill, instead of changing to a petition; indeed, they were probably correct in arguing that a statute held greater force at law, but they lost that battle.[283] Although not as dominant in the latter stages of the struggle, Selden continued to influence the House nevertheless, especially in turning back the addition and putting through two of the amendments suggested by the Lords. It added up to a notable achievement. John Selden had become one of those leaders who held the initiative in the House of Commons.

The Reformation of the Duke

After the passage of the Petition of Right, the later business of the session of 1628 may seem anticlimactic; some important issues remained, however, including the passage of the subsidy, the provision of tonnage and poundage, the redress of grievances, and, of course, the suitable form for royal assent to a petition of right. For some unknown reason, Selden took no recorded part in this last dispute, a natural topic for an antiquary, but he joined heartily in the attack upon royal advisers which arose out of debates over the royal assent. Dissatisfied with the first answer proposed by Charles and blaming it upon bad advice, Eliot delivered a lengthy speech on 2 June in which he recited England's current woes and called for a remonstrance to the king that would list the problems and call for a 'timely reformation' of the causes.[284] The next day, the House decided to devote a morning in committee of the whole to the topic.[285] Charles I riposted on 4 June by announcing that the session would end in a week. Well knowing that Eliot and his friends had plans to attack the Duke of Buckingham, the king sent a message on 5 June and the Speaker relayed it by announcing that His Majesty 'requires us that we enter not into or proceed with any new business which may spend greater time, or which may lay any scandal or aspersion upon the state, government, or ministers thereof.'[286] This put members of the Commons into a state of shock and agitation, an effect not diminished when Speaker Finch interrupted Eliot, who had just begun to speak about one of the king's ministers, with the firm admonition from the chair: 'There lies a command on me: I must command you not to proceed.'[287] After a tense silence, the Speaker asked 'leave, upon the naming of one to sit in the chair for the committee, to leave the House for half an hour.'[288] The House established the committee of the whole 'to consider what is fit for this House to be done upon this message delivered by the Speaker,' but, upon a motion by Selden, the mandate was 'enlarged to give power to consider of the command also, and for the safety of the King and kingdom.'[289] Despite the best efforts of King Charles, a serious attack upon the ministers of the Crown had begun.

In the 'grand committee' members could speak their feelings more freely; Christopher Wandesford opened with a call for action, but posed the question of whether the Commons should 'go to the King' with a remonstrance 'or to the Lords,' presumably with an impeachment.[290] Naming the actual target for the first time in the debate, Sir Edward Coke answered firmly: 'The Duke of Buckingham is the man: as long as he sits in parliament we shall never sit here or go hence with honor.'[291] Considerable discussion followed, including a full reading and examination of the protestation made by the House in 1621. Finally, Selden sought to channel emotion back into action. He urged a return to Eliot's original proposal that the House present a remonstrance to the king and suggested a revival and presentation to the Lords of those charges drawn up by the Commons in 1626 for the impeachment the Duke of Buckingham.

Time goes away, and we seem to be farther off from our purpose than we were in the beginning. The first question was concerning our liberties, whether we should go to the Lords, or the King, or both. I am for going now to the King and personally charging that interposing man. Let a declaration or remonstrance to the King be framed under four heads:

1. Our dutiful carriage towards his Majesty that we have used hitherto this parliament.
2. Of our privileges now infringed, and the protestation in 18 *Jacobi*.
3. What the purpose was yesterday, and how misreported.
4. That the Duke, fearing to have his faults laid open, did interpose and caused this distraction.

Then to go to the Lords. We were willing to lay by old griefs, but now we are enforced to take off that mantle and look upon him with the same eyes the last parliament did. There was then a charge sent up against the Duke; there was an answer and a replication to be sent up but the parliament broke up; there was enough to have demanded judgment upon answer. I humbly move one committee may be appointed for the King and the other for the Lords.[292]

Despite pressure from Coke and Selden, however, impeachment never became a serious issue in 1628. After support shown for the favourite by a number of his clients, the House resolved to draw up a declaration to the king along the lines suggested by Selden, but it made no mention of Buckingham.[293] Selden moved, therefore, that 'the Duke of Buckingham shall be instanced to be the chief and principal cause of all those evils and an enemy to the state.'[294] At that moment, the Speaker returned and, in the subsequent excitement, the House ignored Selden's motion.

Attacks on the actions of the king's servants continued, however. On 6 June, the Commons debated the remonstrance in a long sitting as a committee of the whole. On this occasion and on the next debate on the topic, no diarist recorded a speech by Selden.[295] On 9 June, the House established a subcommittee to draw up the heads of the remonstrance.[296] Two days later, Rich reported their recommendations under eight separate categories, starting with two powerful indictments, 'the fear of innovation in religion' and 'the fear of the alteration of government,' and ending with the 'not guarding of the seas.'[297] The committee of the whole debated and adopted each heading separately. When that on the 'alteration of the government' arose, Selden took the side of those who wished to include protests against the recent proclamation for the observance of Lent and turned it into a general attack upon the improper use of proclamations:

As for proclamations, let us not pitch upon one particular. You have proclamations that take away men's freehold, as that of buildings, which has been of use but of late, and so also the proclamations before Christmas, which is in the nature of a confinement. Nothing changes government more than proclamations. Men are punished for them in the Star Chamber. What a danger is the proclamation for building.[298]

This raised too fundamental a question even for Eliot and Rich, however, who pointed out that the remonstrance dealt only with 'new innovations' and thereby obtained agreement that proclamations be excluded.[299] The rest of the headings passed in turn.

This left only an assessment of responsibility for the problems of the kingdom. Opening the discussion of this point, Walter Long posed the fundamental question of 'the causes of these evils' and concluded: 'the Duke of Buckingham is the cause. I will make this distinction: he is not "the" cause of all, but "a" cause of some, and the only cause of others.'[300] When some members defended the Duke and others argued that he not be named, Selden cleverly supported a specific indictment of Buckingham:

Let us first resolve whether this man be the cause of all these evils or no, and then it may come in question whether he shall be named or no. For my part, the question being whether the Duke be a cause or the principal cause, do but name the heads and they point out the man, that he is the cause. As for change of religion and government, what his religion is I know not. He favors them that are of the contrary. For the alteration of government, he is the principal instrument. He is the chief commander of sea, Cinque Ports, and munition, and the misguiding of these things and the misgovernment of them do point him out to be a prime cause. If any man can give a reason why he is not the cause I will say he is not the cause; else I will say he is the cause.[301]

This threw the burden of proof upon Buckingham's supporters, unfairly so, thought Richard Spencer, the son of Lord Spencer, who argued that 'it must be proved that he is the cause.'[302] Fairness did not match the mood of the Commons and, after considerable further debate, the committee of the whole adopted the conclusion: 'That the excessive power of the Duke of Buckingham, and the abuse of that power, are the chief causes of these evils and dangers to the King and kingdom.'[303] This completed the substance of the declaration.

Selden continued to entice his colleagues into taking more direct action against the favourite. Back in session, the House voted on a division of 235 to 145 to hear the report from the committee of the whole; it then adopted all of the particular heads, including the accusation of Buckingham, and established a committee (including Selden) to work out the wording of the remonstrance.[304] When this committee reported back on 14 June, some debate took place over particulars and, once again, Selden sought to strengthen the clause dealing with Buckingham: 'As for the last clause that touched the Duke, the power of the Duke is the cause of these evils. Now we offer it whether it be fit for so much power to be in one hand, but here all refers to the excess of his power. Let us mention the abuse of his power and pray that this man be removed from his Majesty.'[305] The distinction was a crucial one: the difference between saying that Buckingham had too much power (which the king could remedy by having the duke resign from one or more offices) and asserting that he had abused his power (which carried the more substantial penalty of removal from all of his offices). It represented such an important addition that the House referred it to a committee of the whole, where Selden persistently pressed the point:

After we present the evils, we show that the cause of those evils is the excessive power in the Duke and the abuse of that power. Now, as we have a clause for the excessive power, so let us add the abuse of that power. Let us say somewhat of that, and to beseech his Majesty that since the abuse of that power is the cause of these evils, let us present to his Majesty to consider whether it can be safe that a man of his power should be so near his Majesty.[306]

This addition sought to underline the point that formed the core of the remonstrance for such members as Selden, Coke, Kirton, and William Coryton, the absolute removal of the favourite from his responsibilities. Other members, including moderates, the Pembroke network, and Buckingham's clientage, sought to avoid the explicit avowal of just this point. When the committee of the whole passed a less stark wording which pointed at 'the danger of the abuse of the power of the Duke of Buckingham,' Selden tenaciously insisted upon a stronger statement and, once again, sought to revive the charges passed by the Commons for the duke's impeachment in 1626: 'As for particulars wherein the Duke does thus abuse his power, we may look back to the last parliament and what was then voted in the House. And this is the cry of the commonwealth, and no power under the King ought to be so great as the power that this man has.'[307] A tougher version asking the king to consider the removal of Buckingham still failed to satisfy the House, so this addition was referred to a subcomittee; Selden reported out a new wording: 'And our humble desire is that your Majesty would be pleased to take into your princely consideration whether, in respect the said Duke has so abused his power, it be safe for your Majesty and the kingdom that he continue still in his office of trust or his place of nearness to your Majesty's royal person.' This passed the committee of the whole, proved acceptable to the House, and finally completed the remonstrance.[308] Throughout the drawing up of this text, Selden pressed successfully to hold Buckingham responsible for the woes of the kingdom. Neither he nor his allies, however, could revive the impeachment of the favourite.

The Commons continued to devote the limited time left in the session to business which could not but help to antagonize the king. They formally adopted the remonstrance and passed the subsidy on 16 June. The Speaker presented this protestation to King Charles on 17 June, the day on which the Lords gave their consent to the subsidy. The king, apparently putting aside the lengthy rebuttal drafted for him by Bishop Laud, offered a tactful, but slightly stinging reply in which he promised to 'take it into my consideration, and answer you as it deserves.'[309] No formal answer surfaced during the short time left in the session. The mood in the Commons remained suspicious. Members began to turn the continuing royal request for tonnage and poundage into the drafting of a remonstrance explaining why they had not passed these duties.[310] Selden spoke at great length in one of these debates to show that tonnage and poundage had not been 'granted "time out of mind" to the King,' as stated in statutes from 1 Elizabeth I and 1 James I, but had always come as a 'matter of free gift' from subjects, as proved by the fact that 'it has ever had the same' form of royal 'assent as the bill of subsidy.'[311] A number of less central matters received serious discussion, including Bowdler's Case and the patent as King's Exchanger held by the Earl of Holland, neither of which lay strictly within the jurisdiction of the House.[312] On the question of Holland's patent, Selden used his knowledge of the ancient constitution to argue at length with many precedents that: 'For part, it is not against law, but for part, it is.'[313] These issues illustrated the continuing sense of grievance which permeated the Commons.

Bowdler's Case

Since Selden took a strong interest in Bowdler's Case, it can serve to show how his actions helped to strain the relationship between the the chief servants of the king and the Commons during the last week of this session. Discussion on this complex case opened on 18 June with the reading in the House of a petition from the heirs of one William Bowdler, a man of considerable substance who had died intestate in 1625. The Crown had prohibited the prerogative court of Canterbury from hearing the case in 1625 on the grounds that Bowdler was a bastard and his goods belonged to the king. Even this claim remained unresolved when the heirs turned to the Commons for a remedy. Coke led off the discussion with an attack upon the princi-

ple, and Marten, for once allied with the common lawyers, chimed in
his support.[314] Selden followed with a stinging attack which displayed his suspicions that Continental procedures once again threatened English liberties:

> The law is as was expressed by Sir Edward Coke.
>
> No man can be assured, if he die without a will, but his goods shall be
> seized on into the Exchequer upon pretense of bastardy. That which has per-
> suaded some to think the King [has] interest in bastards' goods: in records of
> King John's time find that the goods of an intestate were taken into the
> King's hand, which was only upon this occasion: those that were treasurers
> or officers of the Exchequer were indebted to the King and they were fre-
> quently churchmen; when they were dead their goods were seized into the
> King's hand to satisfy his debt and the remainder disposed of by the ordinary
> ... This project is fetched from beyond sea. In France the King has the goods
> of men intestate that are bastards. Moved to stop this project else all our
> goods may be seized.[315]

Having broadened the issue into one of principle and of interest to all
men of substance, Selden did not suggest how the House of Commons might stop a case to which the privy council, the prerogative
court of Canterbury, and the Court of Exchequer had already devoted
considerable attention. Faced with this problem, the House referred
the matter to a committee.[316] After several postponements, Selden
reported the findings of the committee to the House on 24 June, giving a lengthy account of the 'proceedings in the Exchequer Chamber,'
of the current 'state of the estate,' and naming a Mr Bland as 'the pro-
jector or propounder of this business.'[317] In response, the House
'interrogated' Bland and voted that 'upon bastards dying intestate the
ordinary ought to commit administration as in other cases where
men die intestate.'[318] On 25 June, Selden sought to consolidate the
ruling of the House by moving 'that since the administrators of
Bowdler are bound by bond not to meddle with the goods, and the
prerogative court bound by the Exchequer not to meddle with them
but as they should order; and therefore that it may be intimated to
the Lord Treasurer the opinion of this House, that the ordinary may
have the ordinary power as in other case.'[319] Of course, this would
have come close to dictating a decision to a court over which the
Commons held no superior claims of judicature, something Selden
had not blanched to do with regard to the High Commission in 1626,

but which Speaker Finch now took as too aggressive: 'Speaker. There is an order in this House to show to my Lord Treasurer. No question [he] will take notice of [it], but I do not know whether you can precribe any court a course to stay or proceed.'[320] Other members must have agreed, for Selden's motion seems to have died without further action. Although he may have pressed his deep distrust of the Buckingham regime too hard on this occasion, Selden's fear of law brought in from abroad and of arbitrary government remained as strong at the end of this session as at the beginning.

The session ended with a prorogation on 26 June, with the Commons still working on their remonstrance against tonnage and poundage. The royal assent extended to the lay and clerical subsidies and four other acts. King Charles used the occasion to display his dislike of the recent remonstrance of the House of Commons against the Duke of Buckingham, the remonstrance on tonnage and poundage working its way through the Lower House, and the 'false constructions' of the Petition of Right already made by the Commons which 'was in no ways to trench upon my prerogative,' for: 'I have granted no new, but only confirmed the ancient liberties of my subjects.'[321] In the last of these complaints, the king had the sympathy of those Lords who had defended discretionary imprisonment as a royal prerogative and of the judges.[322] Many members of the Commons must have returned home fearful of the interpretation given to the Petition of Right by a monarch who had made the unprecedented (and unsuccessful) move of registering upon the roll of the King's Bench a decision not made by the justices of that court. The long anticipated reconciliation had not entirely succeeded.

Mixed Monarchy and Constitutional Monarchy Governed by the Common Law versus Constitutional Monarchy Created by Kings

Despite Selden's personal ascendency in the Parliament of 1628–9, the first session may well have proved a grave disappointment for him. In the previous Parliament, he had expressed fears that the ministers of the Crown had begun to use the exigencies of war as a means for altering the foundations of the ancient constitution and had pointed specifically at the Duke of Buckingham as the source of this ill advice. The attacks upon English liberties which followed the dissolution in 1626 must have confirmed the worst of his fears. In the Five Knights' Case, Attorney General Heath had bent his talents towards justifying the imprisonment of men of substance at the personal command to the king without laying specific charges. A client of the favourite, the attorney general conformed to the perceived pattern of improper government by the king's servants. Throughout the Parliament of 1628–9, Selden sought to redress what he saw as the injustices and dangers of the Buckingham regime: first by forcing it to operate within the boundaries of the ancient law on specific, significant points, and second by a direct attack upon the favourite. This campaign opened as a renewal of the Five Knights' Case, with its crucial constitutional issues, in the high court of Parliament. In lengthy presentations to the Lords and especially in the joint conferences of 7, 16, and 17 April, Selden and Heath (with extremely able legal assistance) again presented their rival views on discretionary imprisonment and on the basic framework of the English constitution, this time with the support of considerably more research. Other lawyers in the Commons supported variations on the interpretation of constitutional monarchy governed by the common law with equal fervour.

The spokesmen for all sides acted as if they argued for the truth, rather than just an interpretation. Selden believed that his version of the ancient constitution represented historical reality as established by the most demanding canons of English and Continental scholarship, while that put forward by the attorney general both misrepresented the past and endangered the nature of England's mixed monarchy. Heath probably believed just as strongly in his model, justified it primarily on the basis of solid common-law tradition, and viewed Selden's arguments as derogatory to royal power. Although sometimes blending it with Selden's model of mixed monarchy, Sir Edward Coke and other common lawyers stood just as strongly for their version. Once engaged, the legal teams representing the Crown and the Commons each put together its own case, in part in reaction to that of the other side. As lawyers who lived on their reputations, they had strong professional reasons for wanting to win such a public contest. These mixed motives may have varnished the truth for which they struggled, but the dispute involved real issues. The stress upon 'reason of state' given by Attorney General Heath and 'matter of state' defended by Sergeant Ashley not only heralded the importation of a dubious Continental principle into the common law, it seemed to threaten to undermine the dominance of common-law rationality by subordinating it to a Roman-law universalist perspective. With other royal servants, Heath and Ashley defended a model of governance which gave greater freedom to the Crown than those interpretations of mixed monarchy and constitutional monarchy governed by the common law upheld by Selden, Coke, and their allies. However, Heath sometimes twisted the interpretation of constitutional monarchy created by kings to escape the boundaries drawn by King James.[323]

The contest involved much more than political theory; indeed, it included many practical, everyday operations of the law. Common lawyers and many other members of both Houses grasped this fact, but they still believed that the king and the principal royal servants remained open to persuasion, that dialogue and debate would carry the day. Early in the session, Selden shared some of this optimism. This spurred him on to greater action, which, in turn, increased his prominence in the House. Hence, the prodigious research into statutes and precedents carried out and the care taken in fashioning the arguments presented before the Lords. Selden's discovery of the attempt to enter a judgment drafted by the attorney general in the rolls of the King's Bench – against the wishes of the justices and against all established practice – must have convinced him even more strongly of the need for restraining royal servants within the limits prescribed by a proper understanding of the law. Selden also must have seen the continued defence by Attorney General Heath and others in their version of the ancient constitution as an annoyingly wilful persistence in error, not as a failure on the part of the Commons to establish the veracity of its case.[324] The agreement of most members to shift from a bill to a petition of right in order to reach an accommodation seems to have affected Selden adversely as well. Having long defended the view that the common law and English constitution consisted of specific laws and procedures established by either custom or statute, he resisted the move away from procedure by bill as a grave mistake. Selden more than suspected that such a flimsy device as a petition of right could not keep royal servants within the confines of the ancient constitution.

As well as principles, the practical trustworthiness of the Buckingham regime remained an issue. In the evasive tactics of King Charles, as in all of England's ills, Selden saw the hand of the duke. The attempt of the members of the Seymour network to revive the impeachment of Buckingham at first received little support. When the House drafted a remonstrance listing England's recent ills, however, Selden insisted upon and carried a concluding section that accused Buckingham of abusing his power and requested his removal. The vehemence of this attack may have stemmed, in part, from the bad taste left in his mouth from the favourite's intervention in the dispute over *The Historie of Tithes*, but here as elsewhere, his personal preferences coincided with the policy of the Seymour connection. While Selden used Parliament as an arena in which he could maintain and increase his own reputation, he also worked as a team member with Sir Francis Seymour and Edward Kirton in the business of the House, and never more than in pursuit of the favourite. This attack stemmed from a mixture of motives, including desires to remove those responsible for ruinous policies, to open up posts for 'proper' advisers to the king (Seymour had hopes that the subsidy 'may take ... that mask from before the King's eyes that keeps him from the sight of those that would faithfully serve him'), and to restore a proper operation of constitutional government.[325]

Selden normally worked closely with Seymour and Kirton throughout the session, and as a team they had even a greater impact than as individuals. As the most loquacious member of the Seymour network, Selden made 98 recorded speeches in the House and committee of the whole, and 26 in the conference of 16 and 17 April, while Seymour made 51, and Kirton 42, in the House and committee of the whole. Selden ranked among the top-five committeemen in the session, with his 57 committees and 6 subcommittees, while Kirton was named to 23 committees, and Seymour to 21.[326] Among the 24 members of the Commons who were elected with assistance from the Duke of Buckingham, in comparison, only 4 members made many speeches: Secretary Coke, leading with 66 recorded speeches in the House and committee of the whole; Solicitor General Shelton, with 32; Sir Robert Pye – an Auditor in the Exchequer and experienced member of Commons – with 28; and Sir William Becher – a Clerk of the privy council – with 20, were the other most frequent participants in debates; the leading committeemen in the Buckingham network were Pye, with 26 committees and two subcommittees; Secretary Coke, with 19 committees and 3 subcommittees; and John Packer, with 15 committees and one subcommittee. In other words, the 191 speeches by Selden, Seymour, and Kirton clearly outnumbered the 174 speeches made by all 24 members of the Buckingham network, but the latter, with their 106 committee memberships slightly outnumbered the former, with their 101. As illustrated at length in the preceding discussions of these debates and the actions of a number of these committees, the aims of the Seymour network came closer to fulfilment than those of Buckingham and his more numerous followers. Throughout the session of 1628, Selden acted with courage to attack the improprieties of royal servants and support a 'return' to mixed monarchy. As the complaints of the Earl of Suffolk demonstrated, this could involve some personal danger, but Selden did have protectors in high places. He sincerely thought that 'innovation and change of government' menaced the liberties of English subjects and worked to force the innovators back within the boundaries of the ancient constitution, but only experienced limited success. Despite his status as one of the leading members of House, however, he had failed to carry two crucial issues: the upholding of liberties by statute and the impeachment of the favourite. As a result, he must have feared, serious dangers continued to threaten England's mixed monarchy.

THE PARLIAMENT OF 1628-1629: THE SESSION OF 1629

Charles I called a second session for January 1629, largely to vote tonnage and poundage. Between the first and second sessions of this Parliament, the murder of the Duke of Buckingham had removed one perceived barrier between the king and the members of both Houses. However, several of those policies strongly condemned by the Lords and Commons had not met with redress. Among these remained the two unresolved problems of 1628, the growth of the Arminian party within the Church of England and the continued exacting of tonnage and poundage without statutory authority. Despite the warnings contained in the incomplete remonstrance of the Commons that the latter constituted a breach of the Petition of Right, collection continued in 1628 and 1629; however, it now met with serious resistance.[327] In his speech to the Houses on 26 June 1628, Charles had refuted this 'misreading.' To assure a proper understanding of the Petition of Right, the attorney general required the king's printer to include His Majesty's speech in the officially published copies. The defender of the Crown's powers to collect money without parliamentary sanction, Dr Roger Manwaring, although impeached and punished by the Houses, received not only a pardon but also promotion to a rich benefice. Despite parliamentary complaints, the power of 'Arminian' divines had continued to increase.[328] Because the warnings and protests of the Lords and the Commons had produced so little visible impact upon religious and constitutional policy, many members of the Commons worried about the practical effectiveness of their renewal of ancient law. The mood of this session remained suspicious. Selden's temperament both matched and helped to shape that of his colleagues. Named to almost all of the important committees, the member who reported to the House from several key committees, and effective in debate, he reached the pinnacle of his influence in the Commons during the session of 1629.[329] Obsessed with the plan of forcing the ministers of the Crown to work within the limits of his interpretation of the ancient constitution, Selden often confronted the privy councillors in the House and enfeebled their efforts to heal the breach between the king and the Commons. Ironically, this, in turn, served to alienate King Charles from parliaments, and thereby to undermine any practical working of mixed monarchy in England.

The Printing of the Petition of Right

In the House of Commons, the new session opened with an investigation of the enrolment and printing of the Petition of Right. On 21 January (the second day of the session), as part of what looks like a carefully prepared campaign, Selden moved the appointment of a committee to investigate the recording of the Petition of Right, 'in the Parliament Roll, and in the Courts at *Westmynster*,' as the king had promised, and 'to search the Journal-book of this House, of the last Session what hath been entered therein sithence the End of the said Session, and by what Warrant.'[330] The committee easily accomplished the second task, for Selden soon reported to the Commons that, in addition to the Petition of Right, 'his Majesties speech made the last day of the last Session in the upper House is also entered' in the Journals of the House of Commons 'by his Majesties command.'[331] Normally, the Journals of the House of Lords recorded the speeches of a monarch, so the committee was enlarged and asked also to investigate the precedents for such a procedure.[332] In addition, the House called the 'King's Printer,' Mr William Norton, before the Bar, 'to know from him by what Warrant he entered his Majesty's first Answer to the Petition of Right, and his Majesty's Speech in the End of the last Session of Parliament; and whether he did not first print the Petition of Right, with his Majesty's last Answer only.'[333] When Norton offered an evasive answer, the Commons established another committee, which included Selden, to investigate.[334]

On 22 January, Selden 'reporteth from the Committee' that they discovered that 'the Clerk of the Lords House had sent unto' the printers 'the original Petition of Right, with the King's second Answer' of which the Norton and Bill 'printed about 1500' copies, most of which remained uncirculated.[335] This, of course, fulfilled the understanding reached at the time between the king and the two Houses. However, Selden continued,

about One Day after the End of the Session, Mr Attorney sent for Mr. *Byll* to his Chamber, and told him (as by his Majesty's own Command, as he said) that those should not be published; and that the Lord Privy Seal told him as much: And that, upon the *Sunday* following, he was sent for to *Whytehall*, by Mr. Attorney, and was there told by him, that they must print the Petition of Right, with the first Answer, and his Majesty's Speech. These contained in divers Papers, and written in several Papers; and upon the last of them a Warrant.[336]

Since both Houses had spent considerable time and effort in obtaining what they judged to be the proper answer to the Petition of Right, the disclosure of this unilateral change must have caused feelings of considerable shock and betrayal.

If the recording and printing of the Petition of Right increased friction between royal servants and members of Parliament, the question of its contravention would remain a source of controversy. When this issue arose on 21 January, Selden seized the opportunity to press for a remonstrance to the king:

For this Petition of Right, it is known to some how it hath been lately violated since our last meeting; the liberties for life, person, and freehold, how have they been invaded? Have not some been committed contrary to that Petition? Now we, knowing this invasion, must take notice of it. For liberties in estate, we know of an order made in the Exchequer, that a sheriff was commanded not to execute a replevin; and mens goods are taken away, and must not be restored; and also no man ought to lose life or limb, but by the law, and hath not one lately lost his ears (meaning Savage that was censured in the Star Chamber by an arbitrary judgment and sentence)? Next they will take our arms, and then our legs, and so our lives. Let all see that we are sensible of these customs creeping upon us. Let us make a just representation hereof to his Majesty.[337]

Over the summer and autumn of 1628, Selden's discernment of danger had so deepened that his criticisms had become quite gratuitous.

The Exchequer, in its judgment on the cases mentioned, had deliberately left the decision on tonnage and poundage for Parliament. The inflammatory mention of illegal punishment sought to transform the not unreasonable fear of new, dangerous customs into a peremptory strike against legally proper procedures. As Selden well knew, good precedents existed for the Star Chamber order to sever an ear, for the law did not consider ears to be limbs; it could not touch arms, legs, or lives. The full meaning of these purported grievances would only become clear in succeeding days, when petitions came into the Commons from the merchants to whom Selden so obliquely referred.

Religion and Tonnage and Poundage

On 23 January Mr John Rolle, 'a merchant and member of the House, informed the House, that his goods were seized by the customers for refusing to pay the custom by them demanded, although he offered security to pay what was due by law or adjudged by parliament ...'[338] It became clear from Rolle's account that he was the person to whom Selden had referred as having had his replevin stayed by the Exchequer. When Secretary Coke and Sir Benjamin Rudyard suggested that Rolle may not have told the whole truth and opposed the appointment of a committee to consider the matter, Selden attacked Sir John for his unparliamentary language (in questioning the word of a fellow member) and neatly separated the question of parliamentary privilege from that of Rolle's liberty as a subject.[339]

His [Rolle's] information consists of two parts; first that which toucheth him as a parliament man, his privilege ought not to be referred to a committee, but for the House to take it upon the relation of the member: and whereas it was said that it may be untrue, that is not parliamentary. And for the other I think it fit to be referred to the committee, as it is a wrong to the subject.[340]

Following the lead of Selden and Eliot rather than the advice of the privy councillors, the House appointed a committee (including Selden) to investigate 'wherein the Subject's Liberty, in general, hath been invaded' in Rolle's Case and it ordered the customs officials involved 'to be sent for to the House to answer their contempt to the House, in the Particular concerning Mr. Rolles.'[341] Parliamentary privilege was cleverly transformed into a weapon for punishing those who had dared to enforce the collection of tonnage and poundage without statutory authority. Clearly, it would take a great deal of effort to bring about a reasonable accord between the king's servants and their supporters and the leadership of the Commons.

In his speech to both Houses delivered on Friday, 24 January, King Charles tried to take a step in the direction of amity, but even it contained some barbs. Declaring a desire 'to remove all obstacles that may hinder the good correspondency betwixt me and this Parliament' and, to answer the 'complaint' raised lately in the Lower House, the king confessed that those who believed that 'I have taken these duties as appertaining to my hereditary prerogative ... are much deceived; for it ever was and still is my meaning, by the gift of my people to enjoy' tonnage and poundage.[342] For Charles, this represented a great concession, for he had not made such a claim during the last session. It came too late. A hostile reference to the motion of Eliot and Selden to investigate Rolle's Case did not help to forward the healing professed in his speech. The effectiveness of the royal intervention came to light on the next Monday. When Secretary Coke 'moved that the bill of Tonnage and Poundage might be read,' he received the rude reply from Selden: 'That this Bill is a Subsidy Bill and it is against our liberties to have a Bill of Subsidy to come into this house by the Kings recomendacion, and therefore though he shall with all respect reverence whatsoever comes from his Majestie he would not have this Bill now read, for it hath bene against the course of parliament to beginne with a Bill of Subsidy.'[343] Secretary Coke had moved a subsidy in the Parliament of 1625, but that was before he held high royal office; an experienced member of the Commons, he should have known better than to have taken an initiative in the name of the king now. Still, Selden's sharp rebuke must have stung. Nor did amity resume when the House dropped discussion of tonnage and poundage and turned instead to religion. Powerful speeches by such effective orators as Rous, Kirton, Seymour, Sherland, and Phelips not only pointed the finger at the increase of Roman Catholicism, but also drew attention to 'new opinions ... brought in by some of our Churchmen' as a step towards a return to Rome.[344] Despite several attempts by Secretary Coke deflect discussion back to the passage of tonnage and poundage, the House voted that 'the Matter of Religion shall have the Precedence of all other Business; and the House, being presently resolved into a Committee, to take Consideration of Popery and Arminianism.'[345] This committee of the whole would meet regularly under the chairmanship of

John Pym and carry out a rigorous investigation of its agenda.

A clear pattern emerged during the first week of the new session. Relations between the Lower House and royal servants reached a degree of discomfort that made the earlier session look like a love feast. Selden's persistent barbs directed at Secretary Coke helped to establish a less than collegial atmosphere. Determined to set their own agenda, members of the Commons not only ignored the king's persistent requests for tonnage and poundage, but pursued grievances into sensitive areas. Neither side showed a realistic sense of reciprocity. When King Charles sent a message on 28 January asking, once more, that the House give precedence to the voting of customs, the Commons responded by working out four headings for a contrary position and striking a committee (including Selden) to 'pen an Answer herein to his Majesty.'[346] Selden may well have influenced the drafting of this reply, for it contained his argument that the 'manner' of moving the bill in the House was 'disagreeable to our orders and privileges'; in it, however, the greatest stress came upon the 'extreme dangers wherewith our Religion is threatened.'[347] Charles responded by challenging the assertion that the manner of presenting the bill had offended against the privileges of the House and by stressing derisively about religion, 'you must either think I want power (which cannot be), or that I am very ill counselled, if it be in so much danger as you affirm.'[348] The second alternative hit the nail on the head. The investigation into religion had proceeded at such a rapid pace, however, that the Commons could afford to ignore the provocative tone of the message. Indeed, by establishing committees to examine the printing of the Petition of Right, the seizure of Rolle's goods by customs officials, the growth of popery and Arminianism, and other concerns, the Commons showed that it would cooperate with royal servants only on their own terms. One need not read later events back into the early stages of this session to see that the king and the leaders of Commons had charted and seemed determined to maintain a collision course.

Selden made no small contribution to the outcome of the session. As a prominent figure in the House, he kept his hand in a great variety of parliamentary business. On several occasions, he participated in the discussion in the committee of the whole on religion, commenting accurately and moderately upon what could be defined as the public acts of the Church of England (Selden excluded the Lambeth Articles and the decrees of the Synod of Dort as not confirmed by public authority), for example, and serving on a subcommittee that looked into the failure to prosecute a number of Catholic priests.[349] From the Seymour connection in the Commons, however, Seymour and Kirton made the rousing speeches on the dangers posed to the Church of England from its external and internal enemies, while Selden turned his research and legal skills to advantage, sitting on and sometimes reporting from the subcommittee on the pardons of Manwaring and Montague and chairing a subcommittee investigating the attack made upon Parliament by another Arminian divine, Henry Alleyne.[350] Both of these subcommittees turned up grievances listed in that unfinished remonstrance being prepared by the committee on religion.

Rolle's Case

Throughout the session, Selden devoted much of his energy to the case of John Rolle, the member whose goods were seized for non-payment of tonnage and poundage. This involved both the liberties of the subject and the privilege of Parliament. As the champion of Sir Robert Howard in the Parliament of 1626, Selden had already established such a reputation as a determined advocate of the parliamentary privileges that the Commons arranged for him to attend two meetings on the same day, first the committee on Alleyne, 'till such time, as they have agreed upon the Matter of the Privilege of the House; and then Mr. *Selden* to go to the committee for Mr. *Rolles'* Business.'[351] For the first fortnight, investigation of this case moved slowly. Then, on 5 February, Rolle dramatically informed the House that one of the attorney general's messengers had 'served him with a *Subpoena* into the Star-chamber, for his Appearance there this Day,' even though he knew that Rolle 'was a Parliament-man'; almost parenthetically, he added that Attorney General Heath had later sent a letter, 'excusing this, by the Mistake of his Messenger, and promising the withdrawing of the Information.'[352] Sir Humphrey May, Chancellor of the Duchy of Lancaster, explained to the Commons that 'he believes that the serving of' the first 'subpoena is without the knowledge or privity of the King or Councell and that it proceeds from some great error and mistake.'[353] Challenging the attempt of May to smooth over any breach, Selden demanded strong punishment on the disputable grounds:

That this subpoena is served not only on Mr. Rolles who is a member of this house, but on some others, as Chambers etc. whose busines depending in this Court of parliament are under the protecion of this house, for every Court in Westminster hath power to protect the suyters in it: This violacion of our liberties he doth not beleeve to be an error or mistake but to proceede from the mildnes of our proceedings against such as have offered violacions to the privilidges and therefore would have us proceede rudly against them without delay.[354]

On an analogy with the central common-law courts, this attempted to extend the protection of parliamentary privilege beyond members to include non-members whose complaints were being considered by a committee of the Commons. Weighing the debate, the House passed a six-point resolution which ruled that Rolle should have his privilege and took positive steps to enforce it; these included the calling of those involved to the bar of the House and the appointing of a select committee (upon which Selden sat) to examine the matter.[355] Adding to the impact of Rolle's revelation came the appearance of Sheriff Acton of London.

Called before the House as a delinquent by the committee for 'refusing to answer some Particulars, indirect answering others, Contrariety in others, and a scornful casting in an impertinent Paper,' Acton excused his behaviour 'by the Shortness of his Memory' and claimed that he 'Desireth the good Opinion of this House,' but he forebore to testify or to apologize.[356] Placed within the context of the earlier discussion, his offence may have seemed more grave than it might have upon a more favourable occasion. Long moved that the sheriff 'be sent to the Tower,' and Seymour followed with a call for more lenient action by suggesting that 'he may now be referred back to the committee to be re-examined; if then he deal not clearly, this House may proceed to further punishment,' but Selden coarsely asserted that Sheriff Acton 'regarded no more to kneele here then sitt upon his stoole at home' and found a precedent for his commitment from the reign of Henry VIII.[357] At least seven knights spoke against this solution, including royal servants and courtiers, members of the former Buckingham network, and members of the Pembroke connection.[358] Selden's solution, however, also received able support from some members, including Kirton, who persuasively proclaimed: 'I came into this House with as good a heart to this man, as any man, for whom I was intreated to stand for him as I came in, and I promised to do him whatsoever favour I could; but if he were my brother he should go to the Tower ... We need not fear any rascallity report to the King; nor nede to feare our own justice.'[359] From the moderate speech of Seymour and the revelation made by Kirton, the Seymour network had originally intended that Sheriff Acton be given one more chance to clear himself before the committee. Clearly, Selden broke with this aim during the debate and Kirton followed; so did the majority of the Commons, who voted to send Acton to the Tower.[360]

The internment of the sheriff and the Star Chamber subpoena combined to revive interest in Rolle's predicament. On the next day, Selden reported from the committee that the subpoena 'was made out, by Warrant, under Mr. Attorney's Hand,' 'the Process delivered Mr. Attorney's Man on *Sunday* Morning,' and, 'upon *Monday* Night, a Discharge, under Mr. Attorney's Hand' was finally given to Rolle.[361] However, he continued, 'The Bill' from the Star Chamber against the other merchants who had complained to the Commons 'came in on Monday, and finding it doth express in the preamble his Majesties dede to Customers: the procedings in the Exchequer: a combinacion agaynst the geting forth the Replevins: a narracion of the Kings right to take the same,' it was read in the House; among other crimes, it charged that 'the merchants did plot, practice, and combine together against the peace of the Kingdom.'[362] At the conclusion of the report, Kirton noted: 'That wee heard the King say he took not nor did clayme the Subsidy of Tonnage and poundage as his right, and yet by the informacion exhibited in the Star Chamber we see his Majesties Ministers doe proceede otherwise.'[363] This raised an embarrassing problem, as had the whole report presented by Selden, so the House decided to meet on the next day as a committee of the whole on tonnage and poundage and to discuss these matters under that rubric; Selden moved and the House agreed that the select committee appointed to investigate the subpoena should also 'look into the Informations in the Court of Pleas, in the Exchequer, against Merchants, for taking away their Goods, without paying the Duties demanded.'[364]

When the committee of the whole met on 12 February, it opened with the reading of a petition from Chambers, Fowkes, and Gilman, the merchants called before the Star Chamber for refusal to pay tonnage and poundage. Selden suggested 'that it is highe tyme to consider how the merchants may get restitucion of their goods the

Terme being now even at an end'; this started a debate in which May pressed strongly for passage of the duties, and such powerful orators as Coryton, Phelips, and Noy pushed for the redress of grievances before voting supply.[365] For once appearing to be searching for a way out of the dilemma, Selden separated the actions of the king's servants from the desires of King Charles and then sought to outline a technicality upon which the Court of the Exchequer might modify its earlier judgment.

It appeares not by any immediatt [command] of the King that his Majestie doth meddle by any of these proceedings, but that it hath bene only the acts of his Majesties Ministers for ought we know without his Majesties privitie. In the matter of seizing of the merchants goods it doth not appeare that the King was knowing of it. It is apparent by the Comission granted to the farmers, and by the relacion of the proceedings of the Councell Board that they still said and intended that the parliament should determyne this busines of the Customes; and that the only stopp and cause why the merchants goods are kept from them is the decree in the Exchequer, which was grounded on the affidavitt which was falsifyed by the word duties, and now since those that made the affidavitt have affirmed that they intended by the word duties the Subsidy of Tonnage and poundage. Would have us therefore send by order of the house to the Judges of the Exchequer to acquaint them that the parties that made the affidavitt doe affirme that they meant Tonnage and poundage which we conceave to be mistaken duties, and therefore to move them to call the said parties before them againe and on oath to examyne them what duties they meant, and if it appeare to be mistaken duties, then they may alter their decree: and he doubts not but they will.[366]

This long, complex speech outlined a compromise by which the Judges of the Exchequer could bring in a new decision without admitting any error in their previous judgment (viz., because of new information). The merchants, then, could receive back their seized goods and this would allow the Commons, at last, both to uphold the liberties of the subject and to vote tonnage and poundage. Solicitor Shelton raised some (as it turned out, valid) objections, but the House decided 'to send a message,' drafted by Selden, Littleton, Glanville, and Noy, 'to the Court of Exchequer.'[367] On the next day, Selden formally sought to protect the merchants from prosecution in the Star Chamber by extending to them the privilege of Parliament; the House carried his motion and various orders to put it into action.[368]

When the answer came back from the Exchequer that their decision did not 'any ways trench upon the right of Tonnage and Poundage, and so they did declare openly in Court at the making of the said orders,' Selden's hopes proved hollow; as Kirton put it: 'We looked for satisfaction, but now we see a justification of their actions.'[369] When Selden called for an examination of the precedents for such actions by the Court of the Exchequer, the House appointed a committee (upon which he sat) for this purpose.[370] Before it could report, however, the customs farmers who had seized the goods of Rolle appeared before the House.

On 19 February, the Customers, Mr Dawes and Mr Carmarthern, stood at the bar of the Commons, where each experienced a full, separate interrogation. Both testified that they had taken 'Mr. Rolles goods for such duties as were paid in King James his tyme' and both admitted that they knew that Rolle was a member of Parliament, but Dawes pointed out that 'he never did heare that a parliament mans goods was free, but only for their persons; he did not acquaint the Lords of the Councell till the 20th of January that Rolles did demaund the priviledge of parliament.'[371] In making the distinction between the person and the goods of a member, the customs collectors might have had some coaching, but this raised a principle of serious consequences. In the long debate that followed, Kirton urged punishment of the Customers as delinquents and adding: 'We can not sitt here, if wee doe not this'; Pym wished 'to forbeare a debate question att this time'; Solicitor Shelton pleaded 'not to call them as delinquents'; Selden argued that it was 'fit and high tyme to proceede' and strongly supported punishment of the Customers, despite the advice of the privy councillors.[372]

And ... until we vindicate ourselves in this, it will be in vain for us to sit here. What we doe in a right way and justly will not displease his Majestie. If any ministers misrepresent us to him let the curse lyght upon them and not on us. In former tymes: when priviledge came in question, noe matter proceeded till that was determined: if not they will come shortly and take the mace from before you ...; he would have it put to question whether we should now proceede against these men as delinquents for breach of previledge.[373]

This called for the House to put aside all other parliamentary business until it received a just recognition of its privileges and warned that any other procedure would end in dissolution without satisfaction. When Rich and Digges wondered whether the privilege of Parliament applied to goods and favoured a delay of the decision, Seymour replied: 'If we finde not priviledge here we shal not finde it elsewhere, but he is doubtfull whether to take it into consideracion now will not disadvantage us att this tyme.'[374] Although firm, this sounded more conciliatory than had Kirton and Selden. However, the strong upholders of privilege persuaded the House to carry over the debate to a committee of the whole scheduled for the following day.[375]

The complex ramifications of Rolle's Case continued of occupy much of the time of the Commons until the end of the session. On 20 February, the House questioned Sir John Wostenholme, another Customer, and then moved into a committee of the whole for a full consideration of the issue; Selden opened with a long speech in which he differentiated the cases of the three Customers, noted that none had 'any power to seize but only to take and levy,' and suggested that the committee proceed case by case in its discussion.[376] The commission for collecting tonnage and poundage was then read, and most of the rest of the meeting was spent in trying to decide whether the seizures of goods had been carried out for the benefit of those farming the duties or for that of the king.[377] On the next day, Rolle produced a witness to testify that 'at the taking of his goods Mr. Rolles demanded his priviledge.'[378] This set off a long, bitter debate upon the appropriate application of the privilege of Parliament to this case, with members such as Seymour arguing 'that these customers have not made good that there was any right, here is only art used to entitle the King' and privy councillors such as May and Shelton replying that the Customers had taken the goods, 'not in their own right, but in the right of the King.'[379] Selden finally entered the debate with a lecture on the nature of parliamentary privilege.

Previledge of parliament is to keepe a parliament man free from any disturbance that he may freely attend the busines of parliament and the Kingdome, and there is noe doubt but it is as great a disturbance for a man to have his goods seized as his person arrested: the lords as they are lords have previledge for their persons, and if they have not previledge for their goods they have noe previledge at all. The Comission to the Farmers and officers is to take and levy, and this doth not give them any Comand or direccion to seize all a mans goods, but to take and levy a smaller proporcion: if the duties mencioned in the lease were due to the King then by that lease the interest was wholly in them, and if he had none then he hath none yet, and then they have done wrong and trespassed ...; that not ma[teri]all whether there were right or not right to seize Rolles his goods but whether he being a parliament [man] ought to have them free from arrest etc. 31 Henry 6 a parliament man ought to have previledge in all Cases, but for matter of suertie of peace, murther, fellony or treason, and if a parliament man ought not to have previledge for his goods against the King it would then have bene excepted. The ground of previledge of parliament proceedes from our attendance in parliament.[380]

This powerful speech represented Selden's parliamentary oratory at its best, clear in argument, reasonable in approach, with concrete evidence displayed to tie down the point. When Rich followed with the news that 'it was recorded the last Session in the Lords House, and citeth other precedents in this House, that the servant of a member of Parliament ought to have privilege in his goods,' he clinched the argument; subsequently, the committee of the whole voted 'that every member of this house ought to have priviledge for his goods and estate.'[381]

Some further debate followed, as the privy councillors tried to save some part of their case, but the committee of the whole decided that Rolle 'ought to have privilege of parliament for his goods seized 30 October, 5 January, and all times since.'[382] When these resolutions came up at the next sitting of the committee of the whole House, the privy councillors made a last-ditch attempt to stop the punishment of the Customers, May pleading in the committee of the whole with his colleagues to pour oil, not vinegar, on the wound, and Secretary Coke reporting, first in the committee, and then in the House:

I must speak plain English; his Majesty took notice of our labour last Saturday, and that we endeavoured to sever the act of the customers from his Majesties command. His Majesty commanded me to tell you, that it concerns him in an high degree of justice and honour; that the truth be not concealed, which is that what they did was either by his own direct order and command, or by order of the Council-board, himself being present and assisting, and therefore he will not have it divided from his act ... He will not have us proceede against them for that he conceaveth it doth highly concerne him in point of government which he doubteth not but this house will take into consideracion.[383]

The message cut through Selden's carefully laboured distinction and extended royal protection to the Customers. Once again, King Charles refused to allow royal servants to suffer for following his personal commands. When the committee reported back to the House about the violation of Rolle's privilege, the rereading of this message by Secretary Coke did not suffice in dissuading a majority of members from voting in favour of three resolutions supporting the extension of the parliamentary privilege of freedom from arrest to include goods, particularly Rolle's goods seized for non-payment of tonnage and poundage.[384] In order to enforce this resolution, the House still needed to decide how to proceed against the customs officials who had seized Rolle's goods. When Coke read the king's message again, many members, realizing the consequences of a division of the king from the two Houses, floundered in their reactions.[385] However, Selden remained analytic, presented the issues at stake, and suggested that the House adjourn for a full day to consider them rationally:

There are in the Kings Message 2 questions of soe highe a Nature as the foundacions of the liberties of the Kingdome and this house are in question. For seing we have fond these men delinquents; we have his Majesties message that this concernes his honor and justice if we procede agaynst them. 1. Whether a Crime committed by a subject as it is his act, yet whether he procuring the Kings command shal stay us from procedinge. This may stay all our procedinge here in this house. 2. Whether any kind of Command in our procedinge here shal stay us from giving one ... Any other Court in Westminster may and ought to procede, whatsoever comandes is receaved, and we are in this point to consider our previledge to be noe lesse. Moved to take tyme to consider the height of these questions til wednesday.[386]

Despite the consequences of disobeying a direct message from King Charles, Selden proposed a careful consideration of proceeding against the customs collectors. As a privy councillor in the House, May underlined the impasse by noting 'that we take this as a highe point of previledge, and his Majestie takes it as a highe point of a Soveragnty, and therefore would not have us thinke soe much of the previledge of this house as to neglect that of the Soveragnty.'[387] Without considering any motion on how to uphold Rolle's privilege, the House adjourned, with no committee meetings, until 25 February; on that day, the king adjourned the Parliament again, calling it together on 2 March for another adjournment.[388]

The Last Day of the Session

The last day for the Commons in this session witnessed the stormiest sitting in either House during the 1620s, with Eliot attempting to present a number of resolutions drawn from the anti-Arminian work of a subcommittee of the committee on religion and from the work done by the committee on merchants (that is, those who refused to pay tonnage and poundage). A small number of members had planned the radical step of forcing the Speaker, if necessary, to put these motions. However, the substance of the cause pushed by this clique reflected, if not a consensus (for the privy councillors and some other members had not given their approval), at least the will of what looks like a majority. After all, the issues of parliamentary privilege and religion had received a full investigation and debate in the committees of the whole and had resulted in a concrete position passed by majority votes. When Speaker Finch worked against the will of the House by refusing to allow a reading of Eliot's resolutions on the grounds that the king had commanded him to allow no business to reach the floor, all sorts of advice came from the benches. In the hubbub, Selden stood among those who grasped the lasting significance of the Speaker's refusal and developed this point in a dramatic, reasoned speech:

This that hath bene this day in question concerneth the whole body of the House of Commons whether they be any thing at all or no: I am not ready for voting any thing now; I heare some matters worthy of consideracion, but I know them not: Therefore now to come backe againe to the question of not putting the question: Without doubt (Mr. Speaker) as you are our Servant you ought to put it, when you are commanded by us: If wee must proceede here according to the particular commaund brought to us by you from his Majestie; and you will not putt it to question when you are commaunded, nothing shall bee henceforth doon amongst us but what and when you will. We are called together by his Majesties great Seale; and he sitting in his throne giving us leave to chuse a Speaker, you were presented by us to the King, and you by him returned back to us; then wee begg of him our privileges, freedome of persons and goods, and libertie of speech: all which (though it be meere matter of forme) he graunteth us; If then we have free libertie of speach, and you are our Speaker, and it be your duetye to put what we shall debate and resolve to the question (notwithstanding any private command contrary to what his Majestie hath publikely graunted us); what have you done in refusing to doe this, but indeede refused to be our Speaker: And it is agreeable to the liberties and orders of the House, that in this case, or in others (as if our Speaker should be sicke, or the like, as sometimes it hath happened) we should make choice of a new Speaker: But for the present, all I shall move shallbe, that since you have refused to put the reading of this paper in question, the Clarke may be commanded to read it.[389]

Clearly aware of the need for a close working relationship between the king and the Commons as revealed by his recounting of the writs of election and the selection of the Speaker, Selden nevertheless pointed to the necessity of the Speaker following the wishes of the Commons during a session, not the private commands of the monarch. Without that independence, freedom of speech and vote became a mockery. By suggesting that the House could elect a new Speaker and by moving that the Clerk read the resolutions, however, even Selden stepped outside of the bounds of his beloved precedent and custom; significantly, in proposing these actions, he omitted his usual historical appeal. Surely such solutions undermined any pragmatic functioning of Selden's ideal of mixed monarchy, for the king, the Lords, and the Commons had to work together in such a system. Ironically, since Eliot had burned the paper, the Clerk could not read it anyway.[390] Without convincing the king and his chief advisers that Selden's (or Coke's) version of the ancient constitution represented the truth, the attempt to force royal servants to govern within these boundaries had made compromise increasingly difficult and, therefore, had made King Charles 'out of love' with parliaments.

The Polarization of Parliament

Following out unfinished business from the session of 1628, Selden and Eliot championed the defence of the liberties of the subject and the privilege of Parliament from what, in their eyes, constituted a conspiracy by royal servants to change the ancient constitution; Pym and Rich led just as vigorous a campaign against the perceived Arminian threat. However, throughout the 1629 session, Selden acted more like an ideologue possessed than a practical politician. At times in his earlier parliamentary career (for example, in pushing the case of Sir Robert Howard, in managing the impeachment of the Duke of Buckingham, in agitating against discretionary imprisonment and martial law, and in continuing to press for a bill instead of a petition of right), he had displayed similar tendencies, but not so consistently. For the first time, he frequently, gratuitously insulted or tried to humiliate privy councillors. Selden often pressed for the most extreme alternative available and seldom tried to work out a compromise or reach a consensus on important issues. Frequently named as the first member to select committees, he had reached too high a standing in the House to accept much of a bridle. Strong, moderate members, including Sir Francis Seymour on occasion, failed to temper Selden's vigorous form of advocacy politics. Although Seymour sometimes tried to work for accommodation, he and Kirton took uncompromising positions as well, especially on religion. The committed leadership of the Commons helped to polarize even moderate members. Paradoxically, then, Selden's success as a leader in the Lower House played an important part in the failure of the session.

When King Charles observed his powers and his servants rudely challenged by such fiery spirits, the king reacted by sending a large number of commands and messages to the Lower House, and by taking uncompromising stands of his own. Members tended to take sides, and the two leading sides became increasingly rigid and more than slightly paranoid about the motives and aims of others. If Selden feared the introduction of arbitrary government, Charles I distrusted those 'evil spirits' who sought to undermine his 'sovereignty,' that is, his ability to rule as a sovereign.[391] The replacement of reciprocity of mutual respect and favour by mutual suspicion made parliaments look like less than beneficent assemblies and brought about a dissolution on 10 March. In his speech to the Lords on that occasion, King Charles excused the peers from any responsibility in the breakdown; instead, he lashed out at 'the undutiful and seditious Carriage in the Lower House' caused by 'some few Vipers amongst them that did cast the Mist of Undutifulness over most of their Eyes' and led them astray, 'that hath caus'd the Dissolution of this Parliament.'[392] Although he ominously underestimated the fears of the majority for the health of the Established Church and seriously misunderstood the view of the ancient constitution which Selden and his colleagues had sought to uphold, the king voiced an interpretation not fully lacking in truth. It was a one-sided truth, however. Charles could only see that many of the leaders of the Commons had presented a saucy face to royal servants and had made little effort to work out a reasonable provision for the fiscal needs of the realm in the session of

1629. He could not comprehend that he had made little attempt to show respect for the views on religion and law expressed in the earlier session of the Parliament of 1628. The interpretations of the ancient constitution and of the reformed Church of England favoured by the king and his leading advisers did not agree with those held by powerful Lords and leading members of the Commons. Mixed monarchy had reached an impasse in England.

SELDEN'S INTERROGATION AND IMPRISONMENT, 1629–1634

The anger and disappointment of the king and his leading servants became apparent in actions started before the dissolution; on 3 March, the privy council summoned nine members of the Commons, William Coryton, Sir John Eliot, Sir Peter Hayman, Sir Miles Hobart, Denzil Holles, Walter Long, John Selden, William Strode, and Benjamin Valentine, to explain their part in 'the undutiful and seditious Carriage in the Lower House' of the previous day.[393] Suspecting a conspiracy, Attorney General Heath had prepared elaborate sets of questions for each of the individuals under suspicion.[394] Most refused to answer on the grounds of parliamentary privilege.[395] Interrogated on 18 March, Selden provided more answers than the rest of the prisoners combined. Concerning his speech demanding that the Speaker allow a reading of the Eliot resolutions, he was asked whether 'he did not say, that this nowe did concerne the whole body of the house, wheather they be any thing at all or not; he answereth that he verily beleeveth he said noe such words.'[396] Asked 'wheather he did not use thos or like words, that the Speaker was the servant of the house, and ought to put it to the question, which the house commanded; he awnswereth he did not use those words or to the like effect.'[397] Asked 'wheather he did not use thies words, we begg our liberty of free speech of the kinge, which he grauntith us, though it be but matter of forme; he awnswereth that he remembereth well he spake somewhat of freedome or liberty of speech, but what he spake he cann not more remember but he spake not the words last mentioned that it was but a matter of form.'[398] Asked 'whether he did not move that the Clerk might reed it [the Eliot resolutions] because the Speaker did not; he answereth that he did not move that the clerk might reed it, nor moved any thing for the reeding of that paper.'[399] Instead, he claimed that he only wished to dampen the confusion in the House. Since these answers contradicted the accounts of his speech found in the parliamentary diaries, it becomes difficult to escape the conclusion that Selden had deliberately refused to tell the truth.[400]

The concluding paragraph strengthens the view that Selden appeared willing to use any means in attempting to escape imprisonment. Claiming not to have understood the Eliot resolutions on 2 March, Selden now strongly dissented from Eliot's position:

the particulars whereof were as they were nowe opened to him that such as should advise or assist the king to take Tunnadg and poundage, before it was graunted by parliament should be accounted a capitall enemye to the king and kingdome: and that if any Merchant should pay this duty to the king before it were graunted in parliament, they should be accounted as accessorye to the rest and traitors to the libertye of the subjecet, he saith, that if he had then understood those to have been the positions Sir John Eliot held or expounded, he would absolutely have dissented from him and saith that he is clerely of another opinion.[401]

This hardly reflected Selden's actions, whether on the day of commotion in the Commons or throughout the recent session; after all, he had taken a leading part in defending the liberty of Rolle and in attacking the customs agents who had collected tonnage and poundage. The statement, signed with Selden's own hand and with that of the privy councillors present, left no doubt that he had lost his will to resist. Attorney General Heath must have felt some relief at watching his talented adversary squirm under pressure. Before the end of the month, however, Selden had begun to work out a careful plan for bail.

The Bail Hearing in the King's Bench

After some hesitation, Attorney General Heath began proceedings against the prisoners. In a meeting of the justices of the common-law courts called by the king for 25 and 28 April, Heath formally put a series of questions about the prosecution of members of Parliament outside of their respective Houses. The justices replied with a series of carefully worded answers which allowed for a limited prosecution of members of Parliament after the end of the session, for something 'done exhorbitantly' if 'not punished for it in parliament.'[402] On 7 May, Heath laid an information against the nine in the Star Chamber.

In his plea and demurrer, Selden displayed a regained confidence and effectively attacked Heath's information.[403] On 6 May, Long, Strode, and Selden sought bail through writs of *habeas corpus*, and on 7 May, the King's Bench received a return of a warrant under the king's hand which specified that the commitment was for 'notable contempte committed by them against ourselfe and our government and for stirreing up sedition against us.'[404] It appeared that the attorney general wished to test the restraints placed upon the Crown's powers of discretionary imprisonment by the Petition of Right. This occasioned proceedings before the King's Bench which continued the earlier constitutional debates discussed in this chapter. The arguments broke new ground only in the accusation of sedition made by the Crown and in the attempt by the defence to apply the Petition of Right.

On 15 May, in Paschal term, Richard Ask presented the case for granting bail to Strode, John Mason for Long, while Sergeant Robert Berkeley and Sir Humphrey Davenport, King's Sergeant, replied for the Crown.[405] After opening with technicalities, Ask argued that the charges appeared too 'general and uncertain' and of too minor a nature for imprisonment without bail; for example, the word 'sedition' appeared in the common law 'adjectively, as seditious books, seditious news' in the 'Statute of the 1st and 2nd Philip and Mary, cap. 3,' where 'the penalty imposed upon such sedition is but a fine.'[406] In his defence, Mason developed this point, stressing that 'sedition is not any determined offence within our law; our law gives definitions or descriptions of other offences, to wit, of treason, murder, felony, etc., but there is no crime in our law called Sedition.'[407] Although sedition signified division in the civil law (indeed, Bracton and Glanville had used the word with that meaning) ever since the statute of 25 Edward III, cap. 2, had defined treason, only the adjective 'seditious' had remained at use in common law and applied to various sorts of 'treason, trespass, or other offences'; a careful examination of relevant statutes from the reigns of Henry IV, Phillip and Mary, and Elizabeth, none of which remained in force, demonstrated the point.[408] Arguing that 'this case' was 'within the Petition of Right' and repeated 'the very grief intended to be remedied by this statute,' Mason concluded with the request 'that Mr Long might be discharged from his imprisonment.'[409] Either Thomas Widdrington of Gray's Inn took particularly brief notes of the speeches made by Ask and Mason or the attorneys for the defence anticipated little difficulty in obtaining the release of their clients on bail. The latter would not prove easy.

Challenging the reasons and precedents presented by the defence, the king's sergeants argued strongly that the return to the writ of *habeas corpus* contained a charge sufficient for the further detention of the prisoners. Arguing that 'sedition is a special contempt' and that 'in a case of return upon *habeas corpus*, no precise certainty is required,' Berkeley pointed out that there were 'many writs which are more uncertain than this return here is, and yet good,' especially those concerning the taking of an apostate, the 'amoving of a leper,' the 'burning of an heretic,' and the 'burning of an ideot.'[410] In addition, he stressed the prerogative of the Crown in specifying charges and insinuated that sedition implied a serious offence: 'Perhaps the sedition mentioned in this return is high treason; and yet the king may make it an offence finable, for he may prosecute the offender in what course he pleaseth; and if it be treason, then the prisoners are not bailable by the statute of Westminster.'[411] Furious men needed to remain in prison, stressed Davenport, and sedition was 'always ranked and coupled with treason, rebellion, insurrection, or such like.'[412] Both Sergeants concluded by threatening an indictment of treason on the grounds that Strode and Long had attempted to divide the king from his people.[413] However, the charge remained that of 'stirreing up sedition against us,' as listed in the king's return.

Littleton's Case for the Defence

Nearly a month later, in Trinity term, these arguments became more fully developed and polished in the presentations of Edward Littleton and Sir Robert Heath. Selden and Heath had met before in the Five Knights' Case, while Selden, Littleton, and Heath had faced one another in that dramatic conference of both Houses which took place on 16–17 April 1628; each knew the other's probable position quite well.[414] The passage of the Petition of Right had done more to support Selden's view of the ancient constitution than that of the attorney general. Charging Selden and the other members provided Heath with a propitious opportunity to test the limits of the provisions contained in the Petition of Right, perhaps to vindicate his vision of constitutional monarchy created by kings. By the time that the bail hearing took place, Selden had regained his confidence. Apart from his own discomfort, he saw the importance of this test case in wide terms. Working closely together and considering the arguments previously put forward by both sides, Littleton and Selden wrote separate draft defences and merged them together for the formal presentation to the King's Bench.[415] The additional time also helped Heath to strengthen the arguments for the Crown.

On 5 June, Littleton opened his speech by cutting away some of the weak arguments of Ask and Mason, placing the case in context, and outlining the substance of the issue, the insufficiency of the cause for refusing bail:

1. I will admit, that the king may commit a man. 2. That a man committed by the king is not replevisable by the sheriff, but he is bailable by this court, notwithstanding the statute of Westminster 1, c. 15. And that he shall not be bailable is against the Petition of Right; I will not dispute it, for it is established by the answer of the king to the said Petition. And the arguments made to this purpose in the said parliament and in the Painted Chamber before both the houses are recorded in parliament, to which every one may resort. But I will lay as a ground of my following argument, that as offences are of two natures, capital, or as trespasses; so they are punished in two manners, to wit, capitally, or by fine or imprisonment ... That no Freeman that is imprisoned only for misdemeanors before conviction, may be detained in prison without bail, if it be offered, unless it be in some particular cases, in which the contrary is ordained by any particular statute.[416]

Concentrating upon the sufficiency of the cause for denying bail, this passage conceded the undoubted right of the king and privy council to imprison, cleverly attempted to establish the arguments presented by the spokesmen of the Commons in the Parliament of 1628 as binding evidence for the meaning of the Petition of Right, and attempted to establish the Journals of the House of Commons and the House of Lords as records at law in the King's Bench.[417] Although the warrant of the privy council was sufficient for commitment, 'it is no ground for the detaining of the prisoner without bail; and this the king himself hath acknowledged as the ancient right of the subject in the Petition of Right.'[418] This meant that all hinged upon the warrant of the king. Capital offences allowed for imprisonment without bail; less serious breaches did not. Did the warrant contain a capital charge or one of trespass or misdemeanour? This relatively simple question brought forth complex answers.

Dividing the warrant of the king into two parts, Littleton relatively rapidly disposed of the first portion, '"for notable contempts by him committed against ourself and our government,"' by reiterating that 'all contempts are against the king, mediately or immediately, and against his government' and noting that this made too general and vague a charge on which to hold a party without bail before conviction.[419] The second part, '"stirring up of Sedition against us,"' included the more difficult task of sorting out 'the nature of this offence, which is called "sedition,"' specifically, whether it 'ought to be understood ... as trespass or as High Treason,' the only feasible alternatives.[420] The word had no precise meaning at common law: 'For Sedition, it is not found in the division of offences in our law, but as it is mingled and coupled with other offences. No indictment of sedition only was ever seen, nor can be shewn; routs, riots, and unlawful assemblies, are much of the same nature with it, and do well express the nature of sedition.'[421] Pointing out that the 'English word is drawn from the word *seditio* in Latin,' drawing upon examples of its use 'in the Bible, in poets, histories, and orators, for tumult, or hurly-burly, or uproar, or confused noise,' and showing how it had come to indicate discord, Littleton recommended Bacon's essay 'Of Seditions and Tumults' for the 'natural signification of the word'; a detailed analysis of statutes and cases from the fifteenth and sixteenth centuries showed that the 'natural' meaning applied as well in the use of the term in relatively recent examples from the common law.[422]

Since Sergeants Berkeley and Davenport had indicated that sedition might involve treason, Littleton explored their references to early commentators on the common law. Granting that Bracton, Hengham, and Glanville 'reckon sedition amongst the crime *læsæ majestatis*, yet that is not to be regarded, for they are obsolete Authors ... but they may be used for ornament, and they are good marks to shew to us, how the law was then taken, but not to declare how the law is at this day; they are no binding authority ...'[423] Just as important, the view put forward by these early writers came from the civil law, which did not apply to England: 'sedition by the Civil Law is treason, "crimen læsæ majestatis." But it was resolved 11 Richard 2 n. 24, we are not governed by the Civil Law.'[424] Indeed, slightly later authorities, such as Britton and the author of the 'Mirrour of Justices,' did not have 'the word *Seditio* in them. And I affirm confidently, that there cannot be shewn any record, book, or statute, after the making of the statute of 25 Edward 3., in which *Seditio* is taken as a capital offence.'[425] As all admitted, the modern law of treason applied or built upon the statute of 25 Edward III. With this elegant application of an historical interpretation of the common law, Littleton closed off any reasonable opportunity of using 'sedition' to mean treason.

Lecturing the attorney general on his duty, Littleton suggested that, if the offence were treason, then 'the king would have so expressed it by the word Treason: for, as in his gracious disposition, he will not extend a fault beyond the magnitude thereof, so he will give to every offence the true and genuine name.'[426] In practice, this meant that the king's servants had the duty of returning an indictable offence. Had the return specified 'against our person,' then it might have implied something different, for actions against the person of the king were treasonous by the statute of 25 Edward III. Since it said 'against us,' however, the return fit into a normal pattern: 'Every breach of the peace is against the king'; contempts against courts, 'riots, illegal assemblies, may well be said and called, "Sedition against Us:" and for such offences, a man shall not be restrained of his liberty upon an "it may be."'[427] Returning to the Petition of Right and the proceedings in Parliament which led to its passage, Littleton argued that 'out of the Return, the substance of the offence ought always to appear, which appears not here' and explained the 'grievance complained of in the Petition of Right,' that 'upon such return no cause was certified,' as meaning 'no such cause upon which any indictment might be drawn up,' a point made by Selden several times during the debates.[428] This carefully eliminated any implication of treason being read into the return on king's warrant and raised further doubts upon the precision and sufficiency of the charge for denying bail.

In the concluding section of his speech, Littleton rehearsed the precedents in favour of his client and rebutted the objections raised by Sergeants Berkeley and Davenport. From 9 Henry III, Peter Russel's Case showed that a person accused of sedition was bailed and from 1 Henry VIII, Harrison's Case showed that 'a man committed by the command of the king is bailable.'[429] The resolution of the justices from 33 Elizabeth I, as recorded in Chief Justice Anderson's notebook, demonstrated that 'all men committed by the privy council are bailable, if the commitment be not for High-Treason.'[430] Displaying a deep grasp of the details of the precedents cited in the cases of Long and Strode, and building upon the arguments presented by Ask and Mason, Littleton poured scorn upon the objections to bail raised by the spokesmen for the Crown.[431] Returning to a positive statement of the case, he concluded with a strong expression of two additional points:

1. The return is here for Sedition; and there is an information in the Star-chamber against the prisoner, for seditious practices against the king and his government. I will not affirm, that they are the same offence, but there is some probability that they are the self-same; and if they be the same offense, then the sedition here intended is not Treason, and so the party is bailable.[432]

Since the Star Chamber could not deal with capital offences, any charge laid there clearly fit into a lesser category and bail must be provided before conviction. The second point deduced the nature of the charge from the lack of speed with which it was prosecuted:

2. This prisoner was ready at this bar the last term, and here was a grand-jury at bar the last term, and here was the king's counsel present, who are most watchful for the king; and yet an indictment was not preferred to them against this prisoner. Which things induce me to be of opinion, that the offence here mentioned in this Return is not Treason, or so great as is pre-tended on the other side.[433]

The refusal of the Crown to prefer an indictment after a good deal of delay told strongly against the gravity of the offence. With his con-centration upon the liberties supported by the Petition of Right and the meaning of sedition at common law, Littleton had built a strong case in support of bail for his client, so strong that Hobart, Holles, and Valentine agreed that they 'would rely upon this Argument made by Mr. Littleton.'[434]

Attorney General Heath's Case for the Crown

On 13 June, Sir Robert Heath replied. In the Five Knights' Case, he had presented a powerful case for the Crown, one built a positive vision of the Crown's discretionary powers. Perhaps he had grown tired of fighting the issue, or had received too much pressure from Charles I, or realized the weakness of attempting to set aside the Petition of Right, but the attorney general sounded stale and carping upon this occasion, for example, noting that imprisonment 'by the command of the lord the king ... in former times was held a very good return, when due respect and reverence was given to government; but, *tempora mutantur.*'[435] Although this represented an unjustifiably rosy and authoritarian view of the past, the times had changed indeed. After emphasizing the importance of the case for the 'Liberty of the Subject' and the 'safety and sovereignty of the king,' Heath argued for the validity of the return.[436] The warrant of the privy council, while general, was sufficient for commitment, but for continued imprisonment 'something ought to be expressed to which the party may answer.'[437] The returns clearly deserved, and would receive, a detailed discussion, but even more pressing was the need to separate the present cases from the context and contents of the Petition of Right.

In order to accomplish this difficult task, the attorney general went over the sections of the petition on imprisonment, recounted both the first and second forms of the royal assent, and claimed that the statement of Charles I to both Houses on 26 June 1628, '"that I have granted no new, but only confirmed the ancient Liberties of my Subjects"' expressed the king's 'intention and meaning in the said Answer.'[438] During the period between sessions, Heath had ordered the printing of the Petition of Right with the first, unsatisfactory, answer of the king and with the king's speech as a gloss on its meaning without the permission of either House; in the session of 1629, this action had stirred up a great deal of heated discussion which had resulted in the suppression of that printed version.[439] Ignoring these objections and actions, the attorney general continued to spell out an interpretation which severely limited the application of the Petition of Right.

A Petition in parliament is not a law, yet it is for the honour and dignity of the king, to observe and keep it faithfully; but it is the duty of the people not to stretch it beyond the words and intention of the king. And no other construction can be made of the Petition, than to take it as a confirmation of the antient liberties and rights of the subjects. So that now the case remains in the same quality and degree, as it was before the Petition.[440]

This passage questioned the status of the Petition of Right as a law, asserted that its recital of grievances, charters, and statutes had made no significant changes in the working of the common law, and elevated the 'words and intention of the king' into a rather unusual (and potentially subjective) standard for interpreting an act of Parliament. From this point of view, however, recent events had little impact upon the case of the Crown.

Building upon this foundation, the attorney general could argue for the sufficiency of the returns. First came the elimination of learned presentations made at several joint conferences by Coke, Digges, Littleton, and Selden as spokesmen for the Commons in the Parliament of 1628. 'It is true, that it was confidently urged in parliament, in 3 Carolus that general returns, that were committed by the command of the lord the king, are not good: and that those arguments remain as monuments on record, in the upper house of parliament; but I will not admit them for law.'[441] This turned an argument made by Selden in the Parliament of 1628 against him.[442] Second followed a repetition of arguments and precedents used to show that 'repleviable' in the first Statute of Westminster meant 'bailable' and that 'the constant opinion hath always been, that a man committed by the command of the king is not bailable.'[443] This section included a reference to 'the opinion in this court' not to bail those imprisoned in the Five Knights' Case, which urged that 'after the said time the law is not altered; and so, I hope, neither are your opinions.'[444] Despite the attorney general's attempt to enter a judgment to this effect in the roll of the King's Bench, the justices had not decided in favour of the Crown's prerogative of discretionary imprisonment without bail. Third ensued a lengthy examination of the cause, 'stirring up of Sedition against Us,' which was interpreted as meaning 'Sedition against the king, in his politic capacity.'[445] The examples of *seditio* cited by Littleton from the Bible and from ancient sources took on more threatening meanings in the mouth of Heath; the fact that Bracton ranked 'sedition amongst the crimes *læsæ majestatis*' (which 'cannot be a felony, but it may be treason'), and that sedition was 'always coupled with insurrection or rebellion' in the statutes cited by Littleton, led to the conclusion 'that Sedition is a word well known in the law, and of dangerous consequence ... Wherefore, as to the nature of the offence, I leave it to the court. But out of these statutes it appears that there is a narrow difference between it and Treason, if there be any at all.'[446] This innuendo suggested a crime more serious than a trespass, but failed to name a specific, indictable offence and tried to shift the duty of laying a charge from the Crown to the King's Bench!

In completing the case for the Crown, the attorney general stressed that one reason for imprisonment was to prevent a person from doing 'harm in the interim during his trial'; argued that the 'infection of sedition is as dangerous as' leprosy or madness, for which persons normally were imprisoned without bail; and concluded with an appeal to the discretion of the Justices, tempered by the wisdom of the monarch: '... I am confident that ye will not bail them, if any danger may ensue; but first ye are to consult with the king, and he will shew you where the danger rests.'[447] By attempting to bypass the Petition of Right and by insinuating that 'sedition,' although not a felony, came close to treason, Attorney General Heath had presented the best possible case, but even his able legal mind could not find a way around the fact that 'sedition' did not exist as a customary offence and that earlier statutes against 'seditious' behaviour, even if they remained in force, had treated such offences as misdemeanours and, therefore, allowed for bail as a standard procedure.

Having had the best of the argument, Selden and the other prisoners did not receive the judgment of the King's Bench regarding their application for bail. On 24 June, the night before the day set by the Justices for rendering their decision on the cases of Hobart, Long, and Strode, letters from the king arrived ordering the commitment of these prisoners in the Tower of London. Selden and Valentine followed later that evening, with King Charles explaining to the justices of his bench: 'That all of them shall receive the same treatment, and that none shall come before you, until we have cause given us to believe they will make a better demonstration of their modesty and civility, both towards us and your lordships, than at their last appearance they did.'[448] When the Court met on the next day, with the prisoners not at the bar, the Justices commanded 'the Keepers of the several prisons to bring in their Prisoners, but none of them appeared, except the Marshal of the King's Bench, who informed the Court, that Mr Stroud, who was in his custody, was removed yesterday and put in the tower of London by the king's own warrant'; with no prisoners to bail, deliver, or remand, the Justices could not deliver their decisions.[449] For the first time in this whole dispute over discretionary imprisonment, the prisoners lay beyond the reach of the common law.

Aware that he would remain in the Tower during the summer vacation, Selden petitioned to have his study unsealed on 29 July, so that he could return to work on his scholarly interests.[450] In the autumn, the issue of bail clearly would arise once more. As term aproached, when King Charles polled the judges and found that they favoured bailing the prisoners, he decided to 'proceed against them by the Common Law in the King's Bench, and to leave his proceeding in the Star Chamber.'[451] He recommended that the prisoners be bailed by letters patent, with securities for their good behaviour. At the opening of Michaelmas term, the court ruled 'that they are now content that they should be bailed, but that they ought to find sureties also for the good behaviour.'[452] This the prisoners refused, on the grounds argued by Selden: 'We demand to be bailed in point of Right; and if it be not grantable of right, we do not demand it: but the finding of Sureties for the good behaviour, is a point of discretion merely; and we cannot assent to it without great offence to the parliament, where these matters which are surmised by return were acted; and by the statute of 4 Henry 8, all punishments of such nature are made void, and of none effect.'[453] Selden stood fast for parliamentary privilege, but to no avail. In 1630, the Crown proceeded against Eliot, Holles, and Valentine in the King's Bench, where they were found guilty of sedition for their parts in the events of the last day of the Parliament.[454] A case in the Star Chamber against the earls of Bedford, Clare, and Somerset, Sir Robert Cotton, Oliver St John, and Selden for 'publishing a seditious and scandalous writing' collapsed when it turned out that the pamphlet in question had been written in Italy by Sir Robert Dudley during the reign of James I and had nothing to do with the situation in 1629.[455] Offering an apology, Coryton and Hayman had made their peace with the king before the summer of 1629, Holles, after paying his fine, a year later. Hobart agreed to surety and was released in 1631. Through the intervention of Sir Toby Matthew and the Earl of Portland, Selden was allowed to visit the Earl of Kent at Wrest in the summer of 1630, but was remanded back into prison by the judges in the autumn. In 1631, he obtained greater freedom in order to deal with a case involving the earls of Arundel and Pembroke. Through the persuasion of Archbishop Laud, Selden finally made his peace through a 'humble petition' of apology to the king and was released without bail in 1634.[456] Eliot died in prison; Strode and Valentine remained there until released in 1640.

CONCLUSION: SELDEN'S PARLIAMENTARY CAREER
IN THE 1620S

A number of points emerge from this study of John Selden's career in the parliaments of the 1620s. Selden came to Westminster in 1621 with a developed and refined historical model of the English constitution as a mixed monarchy, an interpretation which he wished to put into action. Clearly, the great antiquary also enjoyed the thrust and parry of debate, whether in the courts or in the Commons, and meticulously prepared for his major speeches, as the outlines remaining in his papers show. He also thrived in committee work, as his many appointments and his frequent employment as a spokesman for committees and subcommittees demonstrated. A great deal of his reputation, first as a consultant for the Lords and later as a member of the Commons, derived from his legal and historical expertise. Another portion of his power came from his aristocratic connections; as a person from a modest background, with no standing in the countryside, he could not have won a seat without such support. Although Selden had lasting ties with the Earl of Kent and transcribed the inscriptions on the Earl of Arundel's famous collection of marbles in the 1620s, he owed his seat in the parliaments of 1626 and 1628–9 to the Earl of Hertford. Selden was not the first intellectual who advised and spoke for a wealthy, powerful peer, nor would he be the last. His aims and actions fit into and probably influenced those of his patron. Since Hertford spoke only sparingly in the Lords, his political agenda must be inferred from the much fuller speeches of his brother and his estate agent in the Commons, and from the fact that he found a seat for a scholar who had published books containing controversial views. As part of the Seymour network in the Commons, Selden worked closely with Edward Kirton in 1626, and with Sir Francis Seymour and Kirton in 1628–9. An admirable weapon for attacking the Duke of Buckingham, his articulate interpretation of mixed monarchy suited the political concerns of the Seymour connection. Like other clients with notable talent, Selden was no puppet; he expected his advice to carry great weight.[457] As he became more prominent in the Commons, his independence and his value to Hertford increased together. In the 1620s, however valued, Selden remained a client. When he disagreed on as important a matter as the shift from statute to Petition of Right, Selden remained silent during the decisive discussions in the House, most probably on orders. He may have attempted to take a more independent role in the session of 1629, but this remains conjectural.[458] Because Hertford provided a seat, Selden could put his constitutional vision and legal talents to work at upholding the liberties of Parliament and of free-born English subjects.

Selden fought for 'liberties,' specific privileges upheld by custom or statute: for example, the parliamentary privilege of freedom from arrest coming to and going from Westminister, as well as in the Houses, for merchants appearing before a committee of the Commons, as well as for members; the privilege or liberty of indictment or presentment for a crime as a condition for extended imprisonment; the privilege or liberty of following customary or statuatory common-law procedures for controlling troops within the realm. He did not support some abstract ideal of 'liberty'; indeed, his historical mind could find little place for such theoretical constructions until they became concrete within a specific temporal/spatial context. In this, Selden both led and reflected the views of most of his contemporaries in the House of Commons; common lawyers did not revel in the sort of general principles favoured by such civil lawyers as Sir Henry Marten.[459] The fight for liberties had its unsavoury side, as seen in the case of Sir Robert Howard in 1626, when Selden suppressed evidence, intimidated the Commoners on the High Commission, and expanded the coverage parliamentary privilege beyond responsible limits. The impeachment of the Duke of Buckingham on largely trumped-up charges in 1626 and the case of John Rolle and the other merchants who refused to pay tonnage and poundage in 1629, although more above board, had some similar resonances. Even the struggle for the Petition of Right involved some distortion of evidence and the unfair bullying of royal servants.[460] The champions of liberties did not always operate within the spirit of fair play. Of course, neither did King Charles and his advisers, as seen in the imprisonment of Selden and his colleagues in 1629. This means, of course, that the historian must beware of taking the interpretation of events, or even of the ancient constitution, of either side as the unvarnished truth.

The parliaments of the 1620s, especially those of 1626 and 1628-9, witnessed a series of struggles for power between the moderates and hard-liners on the privy council (and their relatives, clients, and political friends) and between privy councillors and those who wanted royal office (and their supporters). Recently, historians have started to re-examine these rivalries, but they need much more study before a full, clear account can emerge.[461] The Seymour network participated in this contest for power and prestige, especially with their attacks upon the duke. In addition, a clash over the principle and practice of emergency war measures based upon the royal prerogative involved a larger portion of the political nation and became a contest between different interpretations of the English constitution in the

Five Knights' Case and in the session of 1628. The Seymour network took a leading role in these debates. Sometimes involving the same people, disputes over the nature of the reformed Church of England became heated, as well, a contest in which Seymour and Kirton played an active part. The leading rivals in all of these contests both sought power for themselves and fought for particular religious and political programs. As the competition encompassed both court and country, all factions came to draw upon professionals to articulate their shared beliefs about the church and the ancient constitution. Just as the struggle between the Arminians and the Reformed was not one of 'Catholic versus Protestant,' or even 'Anglican versus Puritan,' neither was that between the free and mixed monarchists one of 'absolute versus constitutional monarchy,' 'liberty versus tyranny,' or even 'the rule of law versus lawless rule.'[462] Sir Edward Coke, John Selden, and Attorney General Heath supported the rule of law and drew moderately upon Continental treatises and deeply upon the traditions of the common law to construct their rival versions of the ancient constitution. No single interpretation, however, reflected the full experience of the past; each assembled only a portion of the available evidence (itself often the product of earlier disputes) into a coherent pattern which contained elements of continuity and discontinuity. Heath probably came closer to the letter, Selden to the spirit of Elizabethan theory and practice; the most powerful statement of Coke's interpretation would not appear until the publication of *The Second Part of the Institutes* (London, 1642). During the 1620s, no single spokesman – not Heath, not Sir John Coke – not Selden, not even Sir Edward Coke, could create an interpretation of such power and force as to amass consensus support from contemporaries.

Under Charles I, the breakdown of religious and constitutional consensus led each side to attempt to impose its positions upon the whole. Naturally, the king and his ministers held the stronger position in this competition, but their actions increasingly polarized the political nation and broke down the personal ties between the monarch and the natural rulers of the countryside, as seen in the experience of the Earl of Hertford and his brother. In an age of interpersonal politics, not only the ideas, but the character of the people involved played a part in the outcome. Convinced that his own views represented the truth, Selden rarely displayed the ability to see more than one side to a question and showed little hesitation to ride roughshod over those who disagreed. In the parliaments of 1626 and 1628, but especially in the session of 1629, his style of vigorous advocacy wreaked havoc, first with the reality, and then even with the ideal of consensus politics. Selden's career reflected the trend towards adversarial politics and his actions – his uncompromising press for liberties and his eventual unwillingness to show a modicum of courtesy to the privy councillors in the Lower House – helped to strengthen the pattern and to assure that he would not receive royal office from Charles I. The Seymour network, by seeking power and prestige through management of business in the Commons, may also have helped to work out what would become a pattern of gaining and holding power in the age of adversarial politics. Of course, the king and some of his servants showed a similar unwillingness to compromise, based upon a similar conviction that their religious and constitutional interpretations represented the truth, and Charles may well have initiated a new adversarial intensity by pricking leading opponents of his favourite as sheriffs in 1626, by excluding those who did not cooperate with the forced loan from office in 1627 onward, and by imprisoning those he saw as 'evil spirits' in the Commons after the session of 1629.[463] By 1629, the 'depth of incomprehension' dividing King Charles and some of his leading advisers from such office seekers as the Earl of Hertford and John Selden or the Earl of Bedford and John Pym had become a lasting part of the political scene.[464] Memories and justifications of the positions taken up in the late 1620s carried over into the next decades; indeed, they continued to influence the ideas and the actions of the participants throughout their lifetimes, and not always in expected ways.[465] By trying to enforce his vision of mixed monarchy upon an unwilling monarch in the 1620s, Selden ironically helped to damage those reciprocal relationships among king, peers, and people which made such an ideal a working reality. Given his views, however, he should not have remained silent. Although the arguments he presented annoyed King Charles, and even such moderate royal councillors as Secretary Coke, Selden also helped to establish the value of his version of the ancient constitution for preserving both the rightful prerogatives of the Crown and the just liberties of the subject in the rough world of everyday politics. Ironically, the victory of the Petition of Right did not protect him from imprisonment by the command of a vindictive monarch.

CHAPTER THREE

John Selden's Interpretations of History and Law in the 1630s

SELDEN'S HISTORICAL METHOD

Just before John Selden began to obtain the political experience often considered a requisite for historical writing in ancient, medieval, and early modern Europe, he had put forward a new definition of 'history.' As Daniel Woolf has shown, the development of Selden's articulation of what constituted valid 'history' took place in a series of stages, starting with a few remarks in the preface of *Jani Anglorum Facies Altera*; continuing with a statement on 'synchronism' in the illustrations to Drayton's *Poly-Olbion* (1612); developing in some prefatory remarks and the hierarchical, chronological format, marginal notes, and indices of the first edition of *Titles of Honor* (1614); breaking through in the title, preface, and text of *The Historie of Tithes* (1618), the first work in English to apply the title 'history' to an account of laws and customs based largely upon primary sources; clarified in the methological characterization of 'true history' in Selden's preface to a book by Augustine Vincent; and exemplified in the historical practice of the second edition of *Titles of Honor* (1631). Historians of historical writing in England, from Frank Fussner through Daniel Woolf, have long seen Selden as a key figure in the creation of 'modern' history. Richard Tuck's recent situating of Selden within the sceptical new humanism of late-sixteenth-century Europe has opened further insights into his historical research and writing.[1] As with many early modern scholars, Selden saw his publications, not as something detached from the world, but as a means of gaining influence in the affairs of the realm. As the earlier chapters of this book have shown, *Jani Anglorum* voiced an interpretation of the ancient constitution which challenged that articulated by King James earlier in 1610; the notes to Selden's critical edition of Sir John Fortescue's *De Laudibus Legum Angliæ* (London, 1616) and Selden's brilliantly contentious *Historie of Tithes* (London, 1618) further supported his model of England's mixed monarchy; and his political career in the 1630s attempted to put it into effect through decisions in the courts and parliamentary actions. The search for a perfect history also involved a search for useful history.

In these quests, Selden wrestled with many of the problems which beset all historians, including the basic questions of how to articulate an accurate representation the past and what sources best provide the basis for a reliable account. Chronology formed the basic format for most of Selden's early books, with the notes to *Poly-Olbion* and to Fortescue's *De Laudibus Legum Angliæ* (1616) providing the clear exceptions, and *Jani Anglorum Facies Altera* (1610) and *The Duello or Single Combat* (1610) adding the twist of dealing with customs, *Analecton Anglobritannicon* (Frankfurt, 1614) following a regnal format, both editions of *Titles of Honour* advancing hierarchically by title and chronologically within a particular title, and *The Historie of Tithes* and *Mare Clausum* (1635) moving chronologically through European and English laws, both devoting less space to the Continent than to England.

Philosophical scepticism examined and cleared away improperly accepted principles or conclusions, so that humanist philology could provide the tools for building a new representation on the basis of a critical use of primary sources and secondary works. A full statement of the role of scepticism would not appear until the preface of *The Historie of Tithes*, but more than hints of the importance of philology surfaced in Selden's earliest works. A rather immature reference to his humanist philological method appeared in the preface of the *Jani Anglorum*, with the claim that the author had 'transcribed others faithfully' and the note that '*I have applyed my self not only to the meaning of the Writers, or to their historical account, but even to the very words and syllables, which they spoke, and have inserted them printed in a different character,*' including medieval texts which, despite their 'barbarous' language, '*do very well agree with the Records and Reports of Law, which we converse with.*'[2] In other words, he had quoted his sources accurately, printed quotations in italic to distinguish them from rest of the text, and compared some medieval chronicles and histories with some medieval legal documents to test their veracity. In practice, *Jani Anglorum* drew most of its evidence from secondary works and collections of printed sources, and sometimes cheated by quoting primary sources from such works as William Camden's *Britannia* (London, 1590 ff.) without acknowledgment. A tone of critical scepticism permeated the articulation of Selden's historical method voiced in the preface to his notes on *Poly-Olbion*, with its advocacy of 'Synchronisme (the best Touch-stone in this kind of Triall)' – making sure that sources came from as closely as possible to the events that they purported to describe and that they fit together with other authenticated contemporary sources – and its stress upon the avoidance of 'intollerable Antichronismes' and other 'impostures.'[3] Although brief and still somewhat cryptic, this discussion brought together many of the elements which would distinguish the more sophisticated philological approach of Selden's later works.

The first edition of *Titles of Honor* drew largely upon recent legal treatises for its evidence and used this material in a critical manner. In his dedication to Edward Heyward, Selden spoke of this book as 'dealing with *Verum* chiefly, in matter of *Storie* [history] and *Philologie*' and noted that his true patron was not his chamber fellow, but '*Truth* in my References, *Likelyhood* in my Conjectures, and the whole *Composture* ...' Claiming to have '*used Autorities of best choice, without the vain ambition of citing more than I needed*' and to have provided '*reference to the Reporter*' in the marginal note, he promised to '*vent to you nothing quoted at second hand, but ever lov'd the Fountain, and, when I could come at it, usd that Medium only, which would not at all, or at least, deceive by Refraction.*'[4] This hardly was an idle boast. As promised, the ubiquitous marginal notes directed the reader both to historical sources and to recent critical commentaries, complete with a reference to the section, chapter, page, or line cited. This allowed the inquisitive reader to examine the basis for Selden's interpretations. The preface privileged recent humanist legal historians as positive examples of philology in action – Andreas Alciato, Barnabé Brisson, Guillaume Budé, Jacques Cujas, Alberico and Scipio Gentili, François Hotman, and Matthæus Wesenbeck – but the text just as often cited such contemporary classical philologists as Justus Lipsius and Joseph-Juste Scaliger. Although addressed in part to the curious, to whom he promised '*much of what they never before met with, not without reformation of divers errors, possessing them with the vulgar; Perhaps with the Learned,*' this treatise did not attempt to represent all past practices of honour, but only those titles, however obscure, where *'the knowledge whereof may help to the understanding of those in present use.'* Lack of relevance, therefore, dictated the deliberate omission of an account of the long hair of the early kings of the Franks.[5] The correction of 'divers errors' of the 'vulgar' and the 'Learned' had informed all of Selden's work and would continue to do so, as would the concern that learning about the past inform decisions in the present. Near the end of *Titles of Honor*, Selden provided indices to the sources cited in the marginal notes, to Greek words, and to items touching the English common law. Still, nearly all of the works cited were treatises, chronicles, and printed editions of sources. In contrast, *The Historie of Tithes* included a bibliography of manuscripts, categorized according to the collections in which they resided.[6] In between, a leap of considerable historical imagination had occurred.

The title, preface, text, and bibliography of *The Historie of Tithes* marked a major refinement in Selden's theory and practice of history. In part, this appeared in the dedication to Sir Robert Cotton, whose 'inestimable Library (which lives in you) assures a curious Diligence in seach after the inmost, least known and most usefull parts of Historicall truth both of Past and Present Ages.' In these words, Selden elevated that detailed analysis of surviving written and material evidence from earlier ages which several generations of antiquaries had practised without claiming the title 'historian' into the proper foundation for the writing of history. The redefinition of 'Historicall truth' as the reconstruction of the past on the basis of a diligent study of surviving sources from the period under analysis (a refinement on synchronism) had practical moral consequences, as well. If other scholars had followed Cotton's example, 'so much head-long Error, so many ridiculous impostures would not be thrust on the too credulous'; in short, the demolition of false representations of the past helped to free people from the enforcement of improper behaviour.[7] To give contemporaries genuinely 'usefull' advice, histories needed the accuracy which came primarily from the careful study of manuscripts.

The borderline between truth and error, however, had not always seemed this precise for all of Selden's immediate predecessors and contemporaries, especially for such voices from the elder generation as Justus Lipsius, Michel de Montaigne, and, sometimes, Francis Bacon. Savants such as Bodin and Bacon sought to establish a firm method for the discovery of truth based upon humanist legal studies.

Others feared the dangers of moral relativity and epistemological Pyr-
honnianism lurking in the intense scepticism of Montaigne. Selden's
books also addressed these problems, albeit more in practice than in
theory. Daniel Woolf has noted that 'Selden believed that the pursuit
of truth knew no disciplinary boundaries: or, at least, that whatever
the nature of such boundaries in theory, they were not unpassable in
practice.'[8] In the preface of *The Historie of Tithes*, both Woolf's insight
into Selden's transcendence of 'disciplinary boundaries' and Tuck's
into Selden's moderate scepticism received considerable confirmation. Concerned about examining 'the truth which Patient Idleness
too easily takes for cleer and granted,' Selden recommended the scru-
tinizing of earlier interpretations and of all evidence through the lens
of a searching, but moderate philosophical scepticism:

For the old Sceptiques that never would professe that they had found a Truth,
shewd yet the best way to search for any, when they doubted aswell of what
those of the Dogmaticall sects too credulousy receivd for infallible Principles, as they did of the newst Conclusions. They were indeed questionlesse
too nice, and deceivd themselves with the nimblenesse of their own Sophis-
mes that permitted no kind of established Truth. But plainly, he that avoids
their disputing Levitie, yet, being able, takes to himselfe their Libertie of
Inquirie, is in the only way that in all kindes of studies leads and lies open
even to the Sanctuarie of Truth, while others, that are servile to common
Opinion and vulgar suppositions, can rarely hope to be admitted neerer then
into the base court of her Temple which too speciously often counterfaits her
inmost Sanctuarie. and to this purpose also is that of *Quintilian*, most worthy of memory, *Optimus est in discendo, patronus incredulus.*[9]

Unlimited scepticism merely devoured itself, but a restrained variety
helped to clear away unsound old and new interpretations and
thereby provide a foundation for soundly based truth. Selden tested
both the interpretations and the sources of his predecessors. He also
encouraged other scholars to verify his own representations of the
past against the sources cited, for example, to point out if he had
'omitted any thing in the *Historie* or the *Review*, that deserved place
in them' and he promised that 'who ever shall admonish me of it
shall have a most willing acknowledgment of his learning and courtesie.' The marginal notes, with their careful references, and the full
bibliography of manuscript sources provided means for a scrutiny of
detail and of micro-interpretations. Not encouraged, however, was a

sceptical examination of his overall interpretation or of his philological method. Hence, Selden protested against those who dismissed *The Historie of Tithes* on the basis of what he saw as old, now discarded interpretations.

The key to Selden's conception of representations of the truth stemmed from his great respect for 'true *Philologie*' and 'her two Hand-maids *Curious Diligence* and *Watchfull Industrie*' who discover 'many hidden Truths' not really accessible to 'any one restraind Profession,' for 'every Profession takes from' philology 'some necessary part not elswhere to be sought for, not much otherwise then as the Subaltern sciences do from their Superiors, or as they all do from that *Universalitie* or *First Philosophie*, which is but the more reall part of true *Philologie*, and establishes principles to every Facultie that coulde not of it selfe alone know how to get them.'[10] This complicated sentence elevated philology to the highest realms of philosophy, by making it comparable to the highest or '*First Philosophie*' of a hierarchical metaphysic which contained universal principles applicable to the pursuit of all knowledge. The mastery of philology allowed a common lawyer to transcend his profession by writing about matters normally disputed among Roman or canon lawyers. In practice, Selden's pairing of scepticism and philology meant that, once the scholar had carried out a sceptical assessment of previous interpretations and the closest available evidence, then diligence and industry, the assiduous seeking out and interpreting of new sources and the building of new micro- and middle-range interpretative patterns, took over to create an accurate representation of the truth. This fruitfully joined a metaphysical critical method to an epistemological creative method.

The new view of history announced in the dedication and preface of *The Historie of Tithes* – new not only for Selden, but also for England – received a systematic professional explication in his preface to Augustine Vincent's 'discovery' of errors made by Ralph Brooke, who himself had claimed to correct William Camden. In the midst of this dispute among those normally called antiquaries, Selden drew upon the discourse of 'true Philology' to commend Vincent for his 'exceeding *Industry* in Reading, and curious *Diligence* in Observing not onely the *published Authors* which conduce to your purpose, but withall, the more abtruse parts of *History*, which ly hid either in privat *Manuscripts*, or else in the publique *Records* of the Kingdome.'[11] Contrasting the numerous scholarly editions of early manuscripts recently printed in other states with the paucity of such publications for England, Selden stressed the need of historians to base their accounts upon such sources. Systematically discussing the major private and public collections of English manuscripts, he privileged those 'Acts of the State' preserved in the public records as the most extensive and reliable sources available: 'Those publique Acts are a just Touch for the triall, and a large Treasurie, for the increase of what we receive in our common *Histories*, as well of the latter as elder times.' This moved beyond his earlier praise of manuscripts and created an exacting standard for judging the validity of ancient or modern historical works. Evidence from public records (the more the better) provided the test for the authenticity of any history. Although English historians displayed a particular reluctance to base their accounts upon the administrative records of royal and ecclesiastical officials, Selden argued, a rich treasury awaited their efforts:

But what a world of Historicall matter both of our Church and State, lyes hid in the Records kept in the severall Offices of the *Exchequer*, in the *Tower* with you, in the *Chappell of the Rols*, in the *Paper Chamber* (which is also an Office of *Records of State*) in the *Journals of Parliament*, in the *Registers* of the Archbishop of *Canterburie*, *Winchester*, *Lincolne*, and in some other places of obscurer name, whereof ther is not so much as any memory in our common Histories?[12]

The 'Historicall matter' contained in these public records of church and state offered a better 'memory' of past events and customs than early chronicles, the 'common Histories' which provided most of the sources used by traditional historians (including the younger Selden).

Few available histories measured up to these exacting standards; those historians deserving mention included such ancients as Polybius, Livy, Suetonius, Tacitus, and Thucydides; such modern writers of history as Carlo Sigonio, Juan de Mariana, Cherubino Ghirardacci, and Prudencio de Sandoval; such modern editors of historical manuscripts as Melchior Goldast, Augustin du Paz, Gilles Brie, and Joannes Georgius Herwart ab Hohenburg; and one medieval English chronicler, Henry of Knighton.[13] Clearly, such famous Italians as Niccolo Machiavelli and Francesco Guicciardini lacked the proper qualifications, as did all but two modern Englishmen: 'For except onely the Annals of Queene *Elizabeth* and the life and raigne of King *Henry* the VII. lately set forth by learned men of most excelling abilities, we have not so much as a publique piece of the *Historie of England* that tastes enough either of the *Truth* or *Plenty* that may be gained from the records of this Kingdome.'[14] This referred to William Camden, *Annales rerum Anglicarum, et Hibernicarum, regnante Elizabetha ad annum M.D. LXXXIX.* (London, 1615), and Francis Bacon, Viscount St Albans's *History of the Reign of King Henry the Seventh* (London, 1622). Since Selden had long acknowledged his intellectual debt to Camden and had provided Bacon with some of the evidence used in the writing of *Henry the Seventh*, the English examples contained more than a trace of self-interest. Apart from *The Historie of Tithes*, which Selden could hardly mention, Camden's *Annales* provided the better example. Bacon's *Henry the Seventh* came closer to the old conception of history as the acts of great men; under Selden's new grid for valid history, the archival foundation of Camden's *Annales* gave it the edge.

For Selden, the content of historical writing held more importance than its form. Beautiful prose, and even clever organization, meant less than research in primary sources. 'And to labour with the fancie of a fairer language, or better order for the Composition of our storie or any part of it (as divers have done) without the carefull searching of these kinde of helps, is but to spend that time and cost in plastering onely, or painting of a weake or poor building, which should be imployed in provision of timber and stone for strengthening and inlarging it.'[15] Better to write an accurate history than a beautifully decorated one. This sacrificed the 'art' of historical writing for the 'science' of accurate representation. The stress upon the 'Plenty' (the extent and richness of public records) implied a new quantitative element in the equation, the need to examine as much surviving evidence as possible on a given topic. Historians had to base their accounts on private and archival manuscripts because these provided the widest available range of sources close to the events under analysis. In working out his mature conception of proper historical method, Selden added to the earlier criteria of 'synchronism' (or the employment of contemporaneous evidence and the writing of history forward from the earliest recoverable point) and moderate scepticism, the new measure of an exhaustive employment of the relevant surviving primary sources. The more contemporary and complete the sources, the more that sources and old or new interpretations came under careful sceptical examination, the more truthful the historical account. This revised theory of what constituted proper historical method, with its moderate scepticism, elevation of philology into a method for the search for truth, and praise of diligence and industry in research, provided a model for all scholarly disciplines. It also had practical philosophical and moral implications. Only by a secure understanding of past practices could any political participant offer wise advice.

Fulfilling the promise announced in earlier works, the second edition of *Titles of Honor* (1631) addressed the 'inmost, least known' and the 'most usefull parts of Historicall truth' and drew its evidence '*out of rich and most select Stores and Cabinets of* Civill Learning.' Systematically applying the dicta of synchronism, scepticism, and completeness to a subject of great complexity, this massive tome exemplified Selden's new definition of history. In his dedication to Edward Heyward, Selden addressed his friend's scientific studies and returned to his concern for the wholeness of truth: '*I confesse, Sir, your Nobler Contemplations, of* Nature *and the* Mathematiques, *are farre remote from the Subject I give you. Yet there is habitude even betweene it and them also. States themselves are from Nature, and the Supreme and Subordinate Powers and Honors in them, from the example of it.*' From these remarks, the reader may have expected a repeat of the *wunderkammer* eccentricity of the preface of the first edition. Instead, he discussed the sources and purpose of the following treatise. Modestly, the preface announced: '*The* Materialls *have beene principally taken out of severall* Autors *that have purposely writen of Parts of the Subject, out of the* Histories *of severall States and Ages, and out of their* Constitutions *and* Customes.'[16] 'Autors' included those who had written on gentility, a few ancients and many moderns who, after 'Bartol, *that great Lawyer (who flourished about MCCCXL of our Saviour) wrote something of* Armes *and* Gentry,' had produced numerous treatises on nobility and gentility in many parts of Europe. 'Histories' extended beyond the chronicles and narratives of great deeds normally associated with the term to include scholarly accounts of past practices with a more specialized focus:

Under Histories, *I comprehend here not only the Numerous store of* Histories *and* Annalls *of severall States and Ages, wherein the Actions of them are put together in some continued discourse or thred of time, but those also that otherwise, being writen for some narrow particulars, and sometimes under other names, so shew us in example what was done in erecting or* granting or otherwise, concerning the Titles here medled with, that we may thence extract what conduces to the representation of the Formes and Patents of Erections and Grants and of the Circumstances and Nature of the Being of them.

The examples listed on these pages largely embraced regional and genealogical studies, which included the *Histoire généalogique de ... Bretagne* by Augustine du Paz, which Selden had praised in his preface to Vincent's book. These provided the sources for much of his material on 'Forrein Nations; *whose Records indeed or publique Acts have in good Measure, for this purpose, beene by those and the like Writers communicated to us who, living at home only, cannot have accesse to them.*'[17] 'Constitutions *and* Customes,' the laws '*of Severall States and Ages,*' came partly '*out of those* Autors *of* Treatises *and* Histories *before spoken of, but principally out of Volumes that purposely contain them,*' including the codes of Justinian and Theodosius, and the edicts, ordinances, and customs of the rulers and provinces in France, Germany, Italy, and Spain:

... Justinians *Bodie of the Lawes,* Theodosius *his Code, and the* Constitutions *joyned usually with either of them, the Volumes of the* Imperiall Constitutions *of the* French *and* German Empires, *the* Codex Legum Antiquarum, *the* Bullary *of the See of* Rome, *the* Councels, Ritualls *and* Ceremonialls *aswell of the* Easterne *as the* Westerne Church, *the Constitutions and Customs of* Naples *and* Sicily, *and some other that belong to some States that are or have beene in the later ages parts of the* Empire; *out of the* Partidas *and* Recompilacions *and* Pragmatacas *of* Castile, *the* Ordinances *of* Portugall, Navarre *and such more, the* Edicts *and* Ordinances, *and the* Custumier *of* France, *the Statutes of* Scotland *and* Ireland, *and the Statutes and Customes of* England, *besides divers* Decisions *that more peculiarly and respectively belong to those Nations.*[18]

Having praised the published editions of Continental manuscript sources in the preface to Vincent's book, Selden now drew heavily upon them for his revised and expanded edition of *Titles of Honor.*

On the other hand, his profound understanding of the English past derived from what in his day was the mastery of a prodigious number of English medieval manuscripts (including such royal records as Domesday Book, the patent rolls, the close rolls, and the Rolls of Parliament, and numerous others in private collections, especially that of his good friend Sir Robert Cotton).[19] His sections on English and Irish titles drew extensively upon royal and ecclesiastical manuscripts:

But for Titles erected or granted by the Kings of England and Ireland; the Records or Rolls themselves of the Chancerie of England sufficiently enough stored me with whole Formes of the Charters or Patents of them, though withall, some testimonies concerning those of Ireland I have received out of the Records of that Kingdome also. With those Records or Rolls of the Chancerie, I have used also such as give helpe here in the Treasuries of the Exchequer, besides the Registers of the Vicar Generall of the Archbishop of Canterbury, some of the Bishoprique of Winchester, divers Originall Charters, with as many other such pieces and passages, aswell in Verse as Prose, as are to be reckond for Historie or among the parts of it, and of necessary use in the search of it; though they beare other Titles, and are too much neglected chiefly by Compilers of Annalls and Historie, who for the most part seeke no other Materials or helps then what obvious Volumes that beare but such kind of Names as their owne shall, can easily afford them.[20]

If these state papers and private manuscripts provided the core of his English evidence, material remains such as coins, seals, and the inscriptions on funeral monuments established additional points.[21] In comparison, the evidential scholarship of Selden's earlier publications and of most chapters of *Mare Clausum* looked skimpy.

This rich, weighty documentation more than fulfilled the requirements for historical truth spelled out by Selden during the previous decade. The marginal notes contained reasonably precise citations to manuscripts, secondary works, and printed sources. Privately owned manuscripts *'most commonly'* had *'added in whose hands they remaine, or out of what Librarie or whence or where I had the use of them.'* Many came from Cotton's library, others from Selden's own collection, and some from those of others. Manuscripts in public collections had *'the places where they are kept ... rarely noted. Out of their own Nature, it is known to men that are acquainted with Records, where their are.'*[22] Although the text of *Titles of Honor* was in English, quotations appeared in the original languages: *'The Formes of Patents or Charters of Creation and the like are inserted at large in the tongues we find them; as Latin, French, Spanish ... and that without Translations.'* The English text either supplied a rendering of the passage or sufficient discussion for *'a fit Reader'* to understand its meaning: *'For I expect not here a Reader without such measure of knowledge as is usually had by Liberall Education.'*[23] This systematic scholarly apparatus made it easier for the educated reader to test the interpretations offered against the sources. All of this care made the second edition of *Titles of Honor* (1631) look and feel much more like a modern scholarly history than any of Selden's other publications analysed in this book.

As well as providing a model for true history, the revised edition of *Titles of Honor* also sought to establish a solid foundation for a new philosophy of politics, one based upon a systematic historical and comparative examination of 'modern' European political systems. For Selden, history continued to have its uses. Only systematic study of the laws and the 'Faces and Formes of Government' of the not too distant past could produce 'Precepts and Directions,' as soundly based as the *Laws, Politics,* and political writings of Plato, who used *'for his principall Materialls, the severall Frames, Constitutions, and Customes of the States that then flourished as well in Greece as in other parts of the World that were known to him.'* Plato had examined the 'Frames or Formes' of at least 158 '*Common Wealths*' of different sorts, '*some Popular, some Oligarchicall, some Optimacies, some Monarchies, with the various Mixtures of these.*' Theophrastus and other ancients had based their political advice on similar studies. In the intervening centuries, however, the constitutions of governments had changed from a preponderance of city-states to one of substantial monarchies. The scholarship of the ancients was seriously seriously out of date and so was any advice based upon it :

> ... It cannot doubted that if any of those great Writers of Greece were now living again, they would in recognizing and fitting their Politiques to Present use, first informe themselves of the severall Faces and Formes of Government, and the Constitutions and Customes of the Present ages (as they did of their owne times) and of their Grounds and Reasons, and according to them make Instaurations of divers of their Precepts and Directions, no otherwise then they would new examine the lame Astronomie of their ages with the later observations of Ptolemy, Copernicus, Tycho, Galileus, Kepler, and such more, or their learning of Generation, Corruption, Digestion, Transmutation and other like by the later experiments of the Chymiques.[24]

Of course, the 'observations' of Nicholas Copernicus, Tycho Brahe,

Galileo Galilei, and Johannes Kepler involved new theoretical conceptions of the heavens (as had those of Ptolemy in his day) and,
perhaps, Selden believed that 'modern' philology stood above the
scholarly principles of the ancient world as highly as did the methods
of modern astronomers and chemists. He did not say.

In these passages, 'Faces and Formes of Government' probably
meant what Selden had earlier called 'states,' that is, the distribution
of powers in a particular society at its foundation (what we could call
an 'original constitution'), and 'Constitutions' meant constitutio,
laws issued by Roman emperors and their successors (statutes, in
England), hence the frequent usage of 'Constitutions and Customes'
throughout the preface. The fertile passage comparing ancients and
moderns justified the extensive study of medieval and modern constitutions by arguing that, were they 'now living again,' ancient philosophers would follow their previous pattern and found their views upon
relatively contemporary evidence. Nor was there any reason why
modern philologists could not match the accomplishments of modern
astronomers and chemists. If based upon a systematic study of 'the
Constitutions and Customes of the Present ages' (i.e., the period since
the replacement of the Roman Empire in the West by successor
regimes), moderns could match or surpass the political advice of the
ancients.[25] For Selden, this involved devoting considerable diligence
and industry towards carefully charting the nature of contemporary
institutions as they had developed over time. Hence, the detailed
historical nature of his treatise and its strong reliance upon published
and manuscript sources. Exact history both led to and supported valid
political advice. While the advice offered by the second edition of
Titles of Honor remained partially hidden among the details of its
analytical narrative, that given by the last of this series of Selden's
books, Mare Clausum, stood clearly open to all who read Latin.

In several ways, Mare Clausum embodied both the historical
method outlined in the preface of The Historie of Tithes (and spelled
out in the preface to Vincent's book) and the relevance of 'modern'
studies for offering proper political advice indirectly promised in the
preface of Titles of Honor (1631). Mare Clausum contained a more
detailed theoretical clearing away of previous interpretations with
scepticism, a more systematic natural-law theory as the basis for its
historical and political interpretations than any of Selden's earlier
publications. However, it still turned to accurate philology as the
means for putting together an accurate representation of the past and

offering proper advice in the present. In the preface, Selden carefully emphasized the nature and location of his sources:

Among Testimonies, besides such as are in Print, and Manuscripts reserved in private men's Libraries, there are not a few (especially in the second Book [which dealt largely with England]) *brought out of Records or publick Monuments ... Those which lie in private men's Libraries, you will finde where they are kept, in the Margin* [i.e., in a marginal note]: *If omitted there, they are my own. But as to the Testimonies taken often out of publick Records, som likewise have the Place either of the Archive or* Rolls, *or the name of the Record-keeper's Office so noted in the Margin, that thereby you may know immediately where to find them.*

Once again, the privileging of public records as the true sources for history received great emphasis. The preface told the reader how to find manuscripts identified by regnal year in the *'Archive of the Tower of* London' and in the 'Chappel of the Rolls' (which contained all of the records of the *'English Chancerie'*) and noted how the diligent reader might conveniently examine these records: *'For the Record-keepers (who have a special care to preserv them safely) do usually give admittance, at seasonable hours, to all that pleas to consult them ...'*[26] In a work addressed to an international audience, Selden could no longer assume that scholars who might wish to consult the sources quoted or cited would know where they resided in the English archives, so he provided a better guide than ever before. Despite the sparsity of its scholarship in comparison to that displayed in *Titles of Honor* (1631), the last of Selden's treatises on England and Europe utilized the humanist philological method discussed and employed in his earlier histories.

Although he began to practise aspects of humanist philology in his earliest works and included some remarks on aspects of method in the preface for his notes on *Poly-Olbion*, Selden did not sketch out his mature historical method until the last of his earliest works, *The Historie of Tithes*. The very title, by applying the term 'history' to a narrative account of laws, marked a major turning-point in the definition of history in early modern England. The dedication and preface, with their commendation of moderate scepticism and philology and their praise for the consultation of manuscripts, and the body of the text, with its imaginative account put together largely from printed primary sources and manuscripts, provided both a statement and an example of Selden's conception of history as involving painstaking research into primary sources and careful philological analysis on any sort of a topic, rather than celebrating great deeds recorded in chronicles or histories from the past. Although the preface displayed some predilection towards moderate philosophical scepticism, Selden did not follow Montaigne in questioning the possibility of 'scientific' knowledge; instead, he based it upon the philology of humanist legal and classical scholars. The historical side of the *mos gallicus* remained paramount in Selden's approach to the finding and writing of truth. This became even more clear in the concept of history spelled out at some length in Selden's preface to Vincent's book. Here, Selden added to the earlier criteria of 'synchronism' (or the employment of contemporaneous evidence and the writing of history forward from the earliest recoverable point) and moderate scepticism, the new measure of an exhaustive employment of the relevant surviving primary sources and, in part because of their 'Plenty,' he privileged manuscript public records as the sources that historians most needed to consult. Although he more than once displayed a concern for the relevance of historical writing, of the ability of properly constructed history to instruct statesmen, lawyers, and others who lived in the present, Selden did not employ the teleological patterns seen in the works of even the most sophisticated French legal historians and writers on historical method.[27] The publication of the second edition of *Titles of Honor* (1631), with its careful references to sources and secondary works, its reliance upon collections of laws and state papers, especially in its sections on English honours, and its underlying interpretation of the 'frames' of European states since the collapse of the Roman Empire in the West as a series of unique, but related adaptions of Germanic laws to Roman offices, more than fulfilled the requirements for true history spelled out earlier. By offering useful political advice founded upon archivally based history, so did *Mare Clausum*. Together, they provided excellent models of somewhat different styles of representing the past for future historians.

SELDEN'S HISTORICAL SCHOLARSHIP IN THE 1620S

As detailed in the previous chapter, Selden attempted to put his constitutional ideas into action during the 1620s, largely after he had written the preface for Vincent. Although his parliamentary career, provided a public stage for political advice, it slowed the pace of his scholarly publication. Not that legal history and political advocacy formed separate enterprises; Selden's scholarly skills played an important part in his parliamentary career, and constitutional disputes excited archival research. His report to the House of Lords on the privileges of the baronage certainly evidenced a deep plunge into the public records of medieval England, and the drafting, passage, and support of what became the Petition of Right demanded a good deal of painstaking archival research (largely carried out by assistants). In the years surrounding and following the formulation of his new idea of history, Selden became involved in an impressive number of scholarly enterprises not directly related to political problems. By 1621, he had prepared a second edition of *Titles of Honor*, which probably drew upon a large number of manuscript and printed public records.[28] In 1623, his critical edition of Eadmer's history of the reigns of William I, William II, and Henry I displayed a more sophisticated familiarity with such key evidence as Domesday Book than his earlier writings and indicated continuing research in early English evidence.[29] It printed an important source for early Norman England and included an edition of the 'laws of William I' – which displayed a striking similarity to the *Leges Edwardi Confessoris* printed by William Lambarde – and extracts from the Lichfield chronicle and the history of the pseudo-Ingulf, cited so often in his earlier works.[30] These sources provided better documentary evidence than previously available for the continuity of the Anglo-Saxon constitution across the potential break of the Norman Conquest. Those portions of the text of *Mare Clausum* added during the 1620s probably drew upon archival evidence, as well; when it appeared in print in 1635, Selden acknowledged his use of manuscripts in public and private collections, stressed the location of each so that the reader could check his references, and privileged such '*Records or publick Monuments, whose credit I suppose every indifferent Judg of matters will, as once the Senate of Rome did, allow better than other Witnesses ...*'[31] The critical chronology accompanying his edition of the classical inscriptions in the collection of marbles assembled by Thomas Howard, Earl of Arundel, took a great deal of research, as well.[32]

Throughout the 1620s, Selden's correspondence with James Ussher, Bishop of Meath and Archbishop of Armagh, dealt with a wide variety of scholarly topics, including the siting of churches in antiquity, the Samaritan Pentateuch (especially interesting for its chronology in comparison with those contained in the Hebrew and Greek versions), and British historical materials; in addition, they exchanged books and manuscripts, including many from Cotton's library.[33] Selden's knowledge of Anglo-Saxon had improved to the degree that Ussher could suggest, when returning Cotton's 'two Saxon Annales' in August or September 1625, that 'there be some five of these Annales yet left: out of all which if you did compose one bodye of a Saxon Chronicle, and publishe it either in English or Latin, you should doe therein a gratefull worke unto all our antiquaryes.'[34] The letters indicate that Selden continued to work on a wide variety of evidence relevant to his revision of *Titles of Honor* throughout the 1620s.

Having received a copy of Sir Henry Spelman's *Archæologus in modum Glossarii ad rem antiquam posteriorem* (London, 1626) as a gift from the author, Selden somehow had to incorporate, or at least deal with, the new material and insights it contained, as well.[35] By 1629, Sir Henry Bourgchier (a regular purveyor of news from London) could report to Ussher 'the close imprisonment of your grace's friend and servant, Mr. Selden, for some offence given, or rather taken, at his carriage and deportment in parliament' and add that 'Mr. Selden's Titles of Honour is ready to come forth here, and his De Diis Syris at Leyden, both well enlarged; I wish he were so too, that his friends who much love him might enjoy him.'[36] The hope for publication of the new edition of *Titles of Honor* proved premature. On 21 January 1630, Bourgchier could pass on the more cheerful news that 'Mr. Selden is also a prisoner in the King's Bench, but goes abroad when he pleaseth, so that his friends enjoy him often; I hope we shall have his Titles of Honour very shortly.'[37] This time the wait was shorter. After the relaxation of his imprisonment, Selden could see his greatly expanded second edition of *Titles of Honor* through the press.

TITLES OF HONOR (1631)

The 'States' or 'Frames of Government' of Europe

As indicated by the title, the second edition of *Titles of Honor* attempted to explain the origin and development of the titles of monarchy, nobility, and gentility from the end of the Roman Empire in the West to the present. This meant unravelling the meaning of social and legal practices and institutions which had changed considerably during the course of centuries. Above all, it involved fashioning a solution to the puzzle of feudal customs and their relationship to the replacement of Roman by 'barbarian' rule. In the first edition of *Titles of Honor*, Selden had followed François Hotman to portray the feudal law as originating among the Franks and spreading to Germany and Italy by the conquests of Charlemagne, to England by the conquest of William I, and to the rest of Europe by imitation. Now he dissolved the unitary feudal-law interpretation of many civil lawyers into various national, provincial, or local feudal laws. With plentiful evidence, much of it from manuscripts, Selden portrayed these realms as having a series of ancient constitutions, each with its own 'state' – its own basic distribution of power and responsibilities – and its own feudal customs. Although Selden did not discuss the formation of 'states' in contractual terms, he noted that the process took place when a particular society arose in or succeeded to a particular geographical area. The notes to his edition of Sir John Fortescue's *De Laudibus Legum Angliæ* (London, 1616) described the 'state' as a 'limited law of nature' and compared it to the 'ship, that by often mending had no piece of the first materialls ... which yet ... is to be accounted the same still.'[38] The second edition of *Titles of Honor* (1631) applied that theory to the formation of the states of Europe.

To authenticate this pattern of many ancient constitutions, the treatise concentrated upon particular societies, especially national monarchies. Only the titles Emperor and King received Europeanwide treatment. The histories of such titles as Duke, Count, Baron, and Knight unfolded country by country, starting with the Empire and moving on to Sweden, Poland, Hungary, Bohemia, Naples, France, Spain, England, Ireland, and Scotland.[39] In each of these realms, rulers carried out their own adaptation of northern European customs to Roman offices. Selden's philological evidence of how the people from the 'northern nations' came to express their customs in Latin; his astute awareness of how titles, offices, and institutions varied over time and space; and his sophisticated representation of fealty, homage, service, and investiture with land, including the handling of subinfeudation and knights' fees in England, all helped to verify the overall interpretation. Fitting into European patterns, England also had a different 'state' from that in other European societies, a 'state' in which kings, nobles, clergy, and freemen had shared power from the very beginning through general councils, a 'state' in which the common law consisted of custom and statute. Of course, this strongly bolstered the interpretation of the ancient constitution of England that Selden had supported in Parliament during the previous decade. This represention of the history of European *Titles of Honor*, then, also fashioned a sophisticated, cosmopolitan, scholarly defence of the mixed nature of England's monarchy and of its continuity across the Norman Conquest.

Kings or Emperors

Evidence of greater knowledge and of a better historical understanding of the ancient world appeared early in the treatise. In the first edition of *Titles of Honor*, Selden had argued that people first lived together in extended families ruled by patriarchs, but that civil government originally placed all power in the hands of male heads of households; the usurpation of strong men or the common consent of those holding power eventually created monarchies. In the opening historical discourse of the second edition on 'that Supreme Title of KING OR EMPEROR,' he now argued that all civil government originated as monarchical: 'Either from the power of the Sword or CONQUEST ... or by some CHOICE proceeding from the opinion of the vertue and noblenesse of him that is chosen.'[40] There is little room for the people here, except in the election of kings, but considerable space for different sorts of 'states.' This interpretation helped to explain the variety of constitutions which existed in the ancient world and in medieval and early modern Europe. Kingdoms founded on conquest included Assyria, Rome, Castile, and Portugal, while those springing from choice included Greece, Media, the old kingdom of Rome, Poland, the German Empire, and Israel. Cautiously, this section contained no mention of the origins of the English constitution. The rejection of the popular origins of civil government meant that monarchy could naturally flow out of the rule of a father over his family; it no longer demanded the commanding figure of Nimrod, the image of rule by might.[41] Although not entirely certain about how the first monarchy started, Selden no longer clearly distinguished between patriarchical and monarchical rule; instead, he accepted the possibility of making '*Adam* the first King and Governour.'[42] This discussion concluded with a strong stress upon the historical priority of kingship over other forms of government; even the democracies and oligarchies of ancient Greece had devolved from monarchies:

although divers of the chiefest States of the old *Grecians* (and I think only of the *Grecians* in the elder Ages) were in their most flourishing times *Democracies* or *Optimacies*, yet the more ancient States there were in every place Monarchies ... For all other States which keep their names till this day, the common Stories of them plentifully shew both the beginnings and the particular propagation of Monarchie in them.[43]

The history of each particular state recorded its origins and the nature of its monarchy. Through these histories, through the experience of the past, rather than through abstract political theory, came the answers to questions about the origins and qualities of civil society. Selden's profoundly historical perspective proposed that scholars could discover the ancestry of government in general only through a careful study of the laws and histories of particular societies.[44]

The chapters on supreme and subordinate kings, while making wide reference to all European monarchies, also contained a good deal of evidence about the English Crown.[45] While that on King as a subordinate title added little new English material and merely repeated the section on the Anglo-Saxon heptarchy found in the edition of 1614, it was exceptional.[46] Selden displayed the results of his more recent research throughout most of the chapters. The section showing how the title of '*Emperor* or *Basileus*' denoted a monarch without a mortal superior, pointed out that, in addition to the ancient Greeks and Romans and their more modern European successors, 'The Kings of *England* or great *Britain*, have also justly used it and that from ancient Ages. For our *Edgar* frequently in his Charters, called himselfe *Albionis et Anglorum Basileus* ...'[47] This particular usage ceased with the Conquest, but the pattern continued. Throughout the Middle Ages, neighbouring kings by recognizing that 'the Kings of *England*, time out of mind, as Kings of *England*, had been in peaceable possession of the Sovereigne Lordship of the Sea of *England*,' thereby also acknowledged their Imperial status.[48] In the Act in Restraint of Appeals from the reign of Henry VIII and 'in other Parliaments of later times,' Selden added, 'the Crown of *England* ... is titled the *Imperiall Crown*.'[49] It was important to establish the ancient Imperial nature of the English Crown and of the common law, for 'divers Civilians, especially of *Italy* and *Germanie*, which professe the old Laws of *Rome*, tell us, that the Emperor is at this day of right LORD OF THE WHOLE WORLD OR EARTH ...'[50] The views of the civil lawyers, however, remained theoretical and contrary to the practice revealed by historical evidence:

But it is most cleer that neither anciently nor at this day is there any such title, as *Lord of the whole World*, really due to him, and that divers other Princes, as the Kings of *England, Scotland, France, Spain*, besides others, have their supremacie, acknowledging no Superior but God himselfe, and may every way as justly (as the Emperor of *Rome*) be stiled *Emperors*, or by any other name which expresses the fullest height of Honor and Dignitie.[51]

Thus, historical practice established the independence of English and Continental kings from any pretence of suzerainty or sovereignty made by the Holy Roman Emperor. This argument not only paralleled the structure used in *The Historie of Tithes* to rebut the claims of the canon lawyers and that used in *Mare Clausum* to establish the sovereignty of English monarchs over portions of the North Sea, it also illustrated the European perspective of Selden's approach. The attack upon the concept of universal Imperial rule undermined the perspective normally taken by some civil lawyers and supported Selden's historical interpretation that the laws of various European societies (including England) arose independently and adjusted to the shifting needs of particular 'states' through 'constitutions' and customs.

Ancient Constitutions and Feudal Laws

No impartial work of scholarship, the second edition of *Titles of Honor* documented an interpretation of European social and political institutions which dissolved the feudal law into a variety of local ancient constitutions. A complex representation of this pattern came in the midst of a detailed historical discussion of such titles as Duke (*Dux*), Count (*Comes*), and Baron (*Baro*), and such honours as knighthood.[52] In the first edition of *Titles of Honor*, Selden had argued that the offices of Duke and Count originated as honorifics in the late Roman Empire, but then became feudal and hereditary in the French and German empires.[53] While he still voiced a similar position, it now took a more complex historical relation to show how these titles which 'originally depend upon the ancient notions of *Dux* and *Comes* (as they were honorary or officiary, or both in the old Empire),' became 'for the most part Feudall'; it was 'therefore first necessary to shew the Nature and Notion of those names, and also the Nature and Beginning of Feuds, and the Annexing of Dignities to them.'[54] The section on the 'old Empire' paid greater attention to such Gothic kings as Theodoric, whose Chancellor Cassiodor was a Goth 'bred up in Roman learning'; indeed, these *'Romane-Gothique* Customes' provided some of the first tentative links between Roman titles and northern tenures.[55] Although the offices retained their Latin names, the tenures which became feudal originated among the northern peoples, not the Romans. Aware that the Romans had set-tled *foederati* on their borders, to whom 'Lands were given to bee possessed to them and their heires, under the tenure of militarie service to be performed by them,' Selden argued such arrangements explained neither the honorary nature nor the complexities of the feudal laws of medieval and early modern Europe.[56]

A sophisticated discussion of those practices that made up the heart of the medieval European feudal system – homage, fealty, ser-vice, and investiture with land – supported the thesis that these insti-tutions developed independently in different jurisdictions. Selden opened this portion of the discussion with a compact characteriza-tion of feudal holdings:

Feuds or *Feuda* (being the same which in our Lawes we call Tenancies or Lands held, and *Feuda* also; which is but the same word in our *feoda mili-taria*) are possessions so given and held, that the possessor is bound by hom-age or fealtie to doe service to him (or those which derive under him) from whom they were given. And the services that are to bee performed by the Tenants of these Lands are various. And frequently rents as well as other ser-vices are due out of them to the Lords of whom they are held. But although *Feudum* or *Feud*, bee taken to interpret the very word *Beneficium*, and of it selfe orginally to signifie no more, yet that which really gives it the Nature or Notion that is now fixt on it, is the bond of homage or fealtie between the Lord and the Tenant. Without that bond, no possession (though it pay rent or other satisfaction upon any Contract, either Censuall, Emphyteuticarie, or the like) can be a Feud.[57]

With its notable omission of perpetuity or inheritability and its firm emphasis upon homage and fealty, Selden's intricately shaded, rea-sonably clear sketch served both to include a wide variety of aristo-cratic relationships from medieval western Europe and to exclude preceding and succeeding usage of overlapping terminology for differ-ent social and political practices.[58] In early modern Europe, such definitions abounded (albeit in Latin), most of them not unrelated to a particular theory of the historical origins and nature of feudal laws.[59] Selden's served the purpose of defending a northern origin for feudal tenures.

And although there were some use of Feuds in the Empire before the incursions of those Northerne Nations in the declining times, yet we may more fitly attribute the Originall of the common use of Feuds through all the Westerne and Southerne parts of *Europe*, to those Nations. And to them also the first annexing of Feuds to the dignities of *Dux* and *Comes* is justly to bee referd. For those dignities, as they were Officiary, they found in all or most of the Provinces wher the *Romans* had bin, and they annexed them to Feuds, and so used those *Roman* names as they did otherwise the language of *Rome* in their Charters, Lawes and such like, though not without much abuse and spoil of the neatnesse of it.[60]

This added up to an intricate historical interpretation involving a continuity of names but a change in practices by the barbarian kings who succeeded to the Roman lands in western and southern Europe, an annexation of lands to titles and offices, so 'that from the title of *Comes*, so derived out of the old Empire into those Nations that joind it with Feuds, the title of *Comitatus* was made for the Territory or Feud, as also, in the abstract, for the dignitie of a Count; as *Ducatus* for a Duchy, from *Dux* also.'[61] The successor kings translated northern practices into the Latin language and employed the names of Roman offices for new purposes, not entirely unrelated to the old.

Continental Dukes, Counts, and Barons

Masses of evidence, especially from what became the Holy Roman Empire and the Kingdom of France, served to demonstrate this interpretation. From his intensive study of European evidence, including many collections of provincial customs, Selden managed to convey a subtle feeling for the myriad local differences without sacrificing the clarity of his overall interpretation. Although the title Duke sometimes indicated an 'absolute supremacy,' as in Venice, Muscovy, and parts of Germany, normally both Duke and Count indicated subordinate titles which went through the shift from an office at will (under the late Roman Empire) to feudal office (under early barbarian kings) to an inherited title (under later monarchs).[62] The Lombards, who adapted Roman titles to northern customs at an early date, preferred 'Duke' for leading magistrates, but most of the northern peoples took up either 'Dux' or 'Comes' without much partiality:

And as the Lumbards in Italy, chose Dux rather than Comes for their highest title under the King, so in some parts of France, of Germany, and of other Countries also, where those Northerne Nations planting themselves had found the Provinciall names of Dux and Comes, as they denoted Governours of Provinces) Comes being apprehended to bee every way, at least as honourable a title as Dux ... it was retaind also, among such as were subordinat, as a title of highest dignitie, and so annexed to Feuds, as Dux in Italy.[63]

This meant that feudal laws started to come into existence in each society as soon as leaders claimed or successor kings started to provide their leading subordinates with Roman titles and grants of land in return for homage and fealty. From these early fusions of northern customs and Roman titles, the Lombards initiated the next step: 'And the first joyning of the title of Dux with a Feud, and so making it perpetuall (being before temporary or at will only) was in that of Alboinus the first King of the Lumbards, his making Friuli and the Province about it a Duchie, and giving it to Gisulfe his Nephew.'[64] This became a widespread pattern: 'Thus under him and his Successors before Charles the great, began also the Duchies of Spoleto, Tuscanie, Benevento and others in Italie.'[65] By the late sixth century, the Lombard kings had established hereditary, feudal dukedoms as far south as Naples.[66] Although not providing as full documentation, Selden claimed that similar developments had started to take place in France and Germany before the end of the seventh century.[67] With its own variations, Spain followed a similar pattern; there the title of 'Comes or Conde' was 'used as an Officiarie or honorarie dignitie for a long time,' even by magistrates who exercised royal powers, 'as we see in the ancient Condes of Castile, Aragon, Portugall and Barcelona, three of which became thence to bee Kingdomes.'[68] The title became feudal at an early date 'among the Gothes for life' and hereditary at a late date during the reign of Ferdinand III in 1215.[69] Although this interpretation celebrated the differences in various societies, its coherence stood or fell upon the timing and nature of the spread of feudal laws across western and southern Europe.

Selden needed to exhibit early roots for the creation of feudal dukes and counts. If feudal customs had become established before the revival of the Empire by Charlemagne, then they could have diverse origins; if not, then the argument in favour of diffusion of a unified feudal law throughout the Empire by a dominant ruler remained persuasive. Crucial was the revival of the Empire in the west. Here Selden followed the centralist disposition of French and German civilians and portrayed provincial titles, however powerful, as derived from a national monarch, not as independent entitities with their own history. Although aware that, 'in the more ancient times,' there were 'severall Kings of Territories in *France*; as not onely the Chiefe that are knowne by the name of the Kings of *France*; but those of *Burgandie, Aquitaine, Bretagne*, and some such more,' Selden still portrayed the provincial titles of Count and Duke as derived from the kings of France: 'Those Dignities of *Comes* and *Dux*, being first at the Kings will and only Officiarie, became afterward to be joyned with Feudes, first for life. And at length they were also, with the Feudes, transmitted to heires.'[70] When Charlemagne became emperor, he and his imperial successors formalized and extended the range of such titles:

Since the Empire translated to the *French* in *Charles* the Great (under whom the use of Feudall dignities was common enough, as they were also before him in the Kingdomes of *France, Italie*, and *Germany*), Not only those titles of Duke and Count (or *Hertzog* and *Grave*, as the *Dutch* call them) but divers others also were annext to Feuds; the chiefest of them being made out of Duke or Count, or *Hertzog* and *Grave* by addition; as *Ertzhertzog*, Great Duke, *Pfaltsgrave, Landtgrave, Marcgrave*, or Marquess, and such more. And whereas those titles of Duke and Count, and some others were not commonly hereditary in the *French* Empire; after it was translated into *Germany*, into *Otho* the Great [m.n. 'circa A.D. 970'], they became both to bee more frequently given, and commonly also thus far hereditary, that the Feuds and dignities discended to the issue male of them that were first invested, and afterward under *Conrad* the II. [m.n. 'circa A.D. 1030'] the inhcritance of them was extended to the grand children, and since that time aswell to Females as Males generally of the bloud, and in perpetuall Succession to Prelates or otherwise according to the limits of the first grant.[71]

If strong emperors established a program of inheritable feudal titles in Germany, the creation of hereditary titles came about in France as part of a long lasting devolution of power by a weak Crown.[72] As noted in both editions of *Titles of Honor*, the chronology of hereditary feudal titles in France had produced considerable scholarly debate: 'Divers of the French place the beginning of the Transmission of them to heires, in the time of *Hugh Capet*, which falls about DCCCCL of our Saviour [A.D. 950].'[73] Although many feudal titles clearly had become hereditary under Hugh Capet, evidence pointed to the creation of a number of powerful hereditary counties and dukedoms at an earlier date. Charles the Simple had granted the County of Holland to Thierry in 813 and Normandy to Rollo in a similar manner, while '*Charles* the Bald, in DCCCLXIII [863] created *Baldwin* Count of *Flanders*, from whom the dignitie, as Feudall was derived to his heirs.'[74] The process continued until the resurrection of royal sovereignty in the later Middle Ages once again subordinated such nearly sovereign provinces to the Crown.

The genesis and evolution of Europe's lesser honours followed that of the greater, each varying somewhat from jurisdiction to jurisdiction, according to the custom of the people. Selden's systematic, hierarchical vision portrayed a host of titles, from Count through Baron and Vavasour, as bridging the gap between the great titles Duke and Count and the foundation of the honorary order, the knights. For example, the laws of the West Goths and the Ripurarians contained numerous references to inferior counts having charge over a city or a small part of a province.[75] Selden saw this as a lesser honour rather than a bridge between the '*comites*' who were the 'friends' of the late Roman emperors in the west and the counts of the eighth and ninth centuries. In France, he argued, minor counts held office under the greater feudal dukes and counts from an early time, as did viscounts, a title which became feudal in some places, but also retained its officiary nature in others.[76] As well, the title '*Baron*' encompassed a wealth of meaning, including '(at least in elder times) all the Lords' in France; or 'a Noble, Stout, Brave, or (more litterally) Manly Lord'; or 'a particular dignity' called a baron.[77] The last of these originally signified barons either 'originally and immediately holding of the Crowne, or mediately,' with those direct tenants of the Crown 'of the elder state of *France*.'[78] When sovereignty became dispersed among the nobility, those with great holdings who did not have the titles Duke or Count were called barons. During the high Middle Ages, barons who held mediately through dukes or counts became the most common rule:

The beginning of these kind of Barons, were for the most part either by Creation (which was solemnly done by the old Dukes and Counts) or by assumption of the Title, which was the ancienter course. The assumption was especially used by the young sonnes of Counts, that receiving part of their Fathers Inheritance, as it were in appenage, without the honorarie Title of Count, that went only with the eldest, stiled themselves Barons of that Patrimonie.[79]

This account of the division of large holdings among members of the same family also provided some notion of subinfeudation, but this concept was not systematically developed in the Continental portion of Selden's treatise. In the late Middle Ages, the Crown began to create barons by patent and eventually the title became quite common.[80]

From France, the title Baron later spread to England under the Normans. While in Germany it retained some of the old characteristics and lost others. The 'Barons or *Freyherrn*, of the Empire are principally such as possesse Territories and Jurisdiction from the Emperor' (that is, hold their titles immediately); however, since some barons held the title without lands or duties, the title had escaped from the feudal laws.[81] In Italy especially, the title Vavasour came to signify those who held land, but not great titles; the 'division anciently of Feudall dignities among the *Lombards* was generally into *Capitanei* and *Valvasores*, the first comprehending all those great titles, the other all such as had Territory and Jurisdiction by Feudall right without those titles.'[82] In Naples, the title Vavasour not only indicated barons, but '*Vavasor* more particulary was a Feudall dignitie of it selfe also, that is, the dignitie of him that hath a fiefe with Jurisdiction from the soveraigne or any other of the greater dignities, without any of those titles.'[83] With a more diverse usage than among the greater titles, the murky host of lesser titles varied considerably from state to state, but eventually made its way down to the basic honorary status of knight.

Continental Knights

In his chapters on Continental titles of honour, Selden never explicitly put together knight service with feudal tenures; however, he did trace knighthood back to northern European roots and stress its connection with the bearing of arms. After dismissing the origin of military knights from the *Equites* of Rome, he supported a derivation from the 'Germans, and the customes exercised among the Germans and other warlike Nations of the North. Their use was, in publike assemblies by a solemne giving a Lance or Target to conferre such kind of honor. An[d] this was done somtimes by some prince of the State, somtimes by a Father or Kinsman. Tacitus is a witnesse of it.'[84] The ancient custom continued into the migration age, as seen in its employment by Theodoricus, King of the East Goths, in Italy, and into the Middle Ages: 'From this use of those Northern Nations came the fashion of Knighting in the Empire, which under Charles the Great, and after him, consisted of none else but of those Northern, or of such as had upon their incursions been mixt with them, and so received most of their customes.'[85] France, Italy, and Spain provided excellent examples of Latin countries which practised this northern custom. So high was the status of warriors that the roll of honour extended down to 'all such Gentlemen as were either imployed in Militarie service ... or attended on other great Souldiers as their servants, having not received the order of Knighthood, [who] were called Escuyers, Scutarij, Scutiferi, and Armigeri, which since also (as at this day) in times of peace have been given to all Gentlemen of the better note, to set a title of action, or of hope upon them.'[86] So strong became the reputation of bearing arms that even civil officials sought the prestige of titles derived from military honour. From the great feudal titles down to the honour of knighthood, then, the customs of the northern peoples combined with Latin titles to form the offices of the new 'states,' each with its own feudal laws fitting the needs and mixture of the inhabitants. The pattern worked out by Selden for the Continental successor kingdoms applied equally well to Britain.

Anglo-Saxon Ealdormen, Earls, and Thegns

Sufficient evidence did not exist to reconstruct the honours and offices which flourished in England under the Britons, nor did those under the Romans receive attention here. Anglo-Saxon kings shaped the new state of England where 'under the Saxons, the subordinate Titles of Temporall Honour, were that of Etheling, Ealdorman, and Thane or Thegen.'[87] Each of these titles merited and obtained considerable attention. In 1614, Selden had serious difficulties in understanding Anglo-Saxon titles, equating, for example, Duke with Eorle and Alderman with Ealdorman; by 1631, his better knowledge of the language and the evidence, especially of Anglo-Saxon charters, allowed him to put together a splendid, shaded pattern of meanings, including an indication of how titles changed over time. Etheling, '*Ætheling, Atheling* or *Adeling*,' originally meant noble, but 'about *Athelstan's* time,' *Eorle* 'came into England with the Danes' as a 'synonymie to *Etheling*, and so denoted here the sonnes and brothers to the King.'[88] Etheling, then, indicated royal blood. Ealdorman, on the other hand, began as and remained officiary. At first, ealdormen 'were such as had Provinces or Counties or other Territories under their government.'[89] Scribes translated this office into Latin by a number of terms:

The name is sometimes expressed by *Subregulus* and *Regulus*, sometimes by *Patricius, Princeps, Dux*, and in *Saxon* also by ɲeþtoʒa; By *Comes* also and *Consul*; nor is it without example that they are called *Reges* ... But that *Princeps* is most frequent for *Ealdorman* both in the Charters of Kings of that time, and in the subscriptions to those Charters and to other Instruments; as also is the title of *Dux*.[90]

The various translations attempted to capture the extensive flexibility in the functions performed by ealdormen. In some contexts, this title seemed to apply to people holding military power, 'as *Duces*' under the Romans had, while in others '*Ealdorman* denoted the civill dignitie in such sense as *Senator, Senior*, or *Seigneur* hath done through many ages in most parts of *Europe*.'[91] Although usually only officiary, the title Ealdorman or Earl of Northumberland remained 'both Feudall and inheritable' from 'the age of the first comming of the *Saxons* into *England*, which is commonly placed in CCCCXLVIII [448] ... until DLXVII [567]' and at that time was 'held of the Kings of *Kent*.'[92] Eventually, even it became a normal late-Saxon earldom. This subtle explanation, with its representation of rich variety of Anglo-Saxons usage, clearly exemplified the pattern of northern people employing Latin titles for offices of their own invention.

The late-Saxon period witnessed a shift in terminology. Under King Cnut, 'the word €oɲle, by which the *Danes* called men of like dignitie, was attributed to them [ealdormen]; and the *Saxon Æthelings* were no longer stiled Earles ... And the word *Ealdorman* in the former sense soone grew out of use'; from henceforth, it applied to those lesser officials, the aldermen of municipalities.[93] Also during the reign of Cnut, *Comes* came into use as a translation for ealdorman or *Eorle*, but it also continued to denote 'men of an Officiary dignitie or Counsellours of State only, or personall Counts whom they usually called (as I thinke) ȝeꝛiþeꝛ or ȝeꝛiþmonneꝛ, that is *Socij* or *Comites* literally.'[94] After the Conquest, the trend towards a simplified roster of titles continued, but 'the name of Earle was in that age of such dignitie that *William* the first, in his *Saxon* stile of *Normandy*, called himself only Earle of it, which in that age was translated *Princeps Normannorum*. But hee used also the same name for those that were then the *Comites* of *England*.'[95] The latter soon came to monopolize the title: 'And from that age to this day those two words only, the *Latin Comes*, and the *Danish* word Eorl or *Earl* have expressed with us this title.'[96] Despite the change of terminology and the disappearance of 'etheling,' the high office of ealdorman or earl retained its basic character as an officiary, non-hereditary title under the Anglo-Saxons, one that had an impact upon later titles, as well.

Various complications entered into Selden's new account of the pattern of honorary governance. 'Ealdorman' represented only one high office, held apart from or together with other positions. Plentiful evidence indicated that Saxon kings appointed such powerful officeholders, such as 'Shiregereeves,' 'Highgereeves,' and 'Holds,' each exercising particular functions as a royal servant:

The *Holds* were Captaines or Commanders in the Warres. The *Highgereves* were but the High Sheriffs of Shires, or such Territories as were committed to their custody and change by the King, in such sort as the *Custordia Comitatus* is at this day given to the Sheriffs. *Shire-reeve*, or *Shire gereeve* is but the same word as *Shrive* or *Sheriffe*.[97]

These men derived their considerable powers directly from the king. Although the Saxons translated Sheriff as '*Vicecomites*' or '*Vicedomini*,' this meant that they held their positions under kings, not as subordinates of an ealdorman or earl, a *comites*. Kings also provided supplies and revenues for important offices. Late Saxon Earldoms had:

one or more shires committed to them. Sometimes their possessions consisted in some particular Territories, the bodies of the Shires remaining in the crowne. And they had also sometimes a Third or some other customary part of the profits of certaine Cities, Boroughs, or other places within the Earldome.[98]

Although Selden argued that only the ealdordom of Northumberland remained both feudal and hereditary during the early Anglo-Saxon period, he also knew that it became an independent kingdom for many years and, at last, reverted to a late Saxon earldom, now held at the pleasure of the king.[99] At least one other example existed of an hereditary grant; Ethelred had all of Mercia 'to his use as an Ealdordom and fiefe given him in marriage with *Ethelfled* by her Father, King *Alfred*.'[100] Even this exception, however, revealed the unusual nature of the grant, for King Edward took back the whole of Mercia from his sister upon the death of her husband. Despite all of the complications and subtleties, then, the title Ealdorman or Earl had become neither hereditary nor feudal, but had retained its officiary status throughout the Saxon period.

According to Selden, however, feudal tenures flourished in Anglo-Saxon England, especially among those who held the title Thane or Thegn. Also covering a complex pattern of relationships, this title:

denoted a Servant or Minister generally (and so divers had the title, as it was meerely Officiarie and personall) yet those that were the Kings immediate Tenants of faire possessions, which they held by personall service as of his person ... were, I conceive, the *Thanes* that had the honorary dignitie, and were part of the greater Nobility of that time ... That is, they were all the Kings feudall *Thanes*, and the land held so was called *Tainland* or *Thane land*, as afterwards the Lands held that made a Baron were called a Barony, as also they are called to this day.[101]

Thegns, the service nobility of Anglo-Saxon England, could obtain that title personally as a servant or minister of a king, but they also came to hold lands from the Crown on feudal tenures. Each feudal thegn held at least five hides of land.[102] The five-hide unit, found in various law codes, charters, and Domesday Book, related to the provision of service. Selden drew upon Cotton's manuscript of the 'Laws of Athelstan' to make this point firmly: 'I cannot understand here the five Hides but for so much land held of the King by the service of that office or some military attendance.'[103] In 1614, Selden had a very shaky understanding of the hide. In 1631, fortified by a careful examination of Domesday Book, he provided a sophisticated definition:

Now a Hide of Land Regularly is and was (as I thinke) as much Land as might be manured with one Plough, together with Pasture, Medow, and Wood competent for the maintenance of that Plough, and the servants of the Family. I know divers of the Ancients make it C [100] Acres. Others give otherwise a certaintie to it. But doubtless it was uncertaine, and justly is by others called only a plough-land, or so much as belongs to the tillage, whence it must of necessitie be various according to the soile and custome of husbandry in every County.[104]

The hide with its supply of rents in kind and money, provided the foundation for the Anglo-Saxon feudal system. To those who argued that Domesday Book reflected new tenures introduced by the Conqueror, Selden replied that:

... In *Lincolnshire*, wee have *Consuetudines Regis et Comitis*, rememberd in *Domesday*, which must, it seemes, be referd to the *Saxon* times. For that booke was begun and ended between the XIV and XX yeere of *William* the first, and comprehends among other things those ancient customes, which could not have so late a beginning as the comming of the *Normans*.[105]

In other words, twenty years could not a custom create.[106] Selden argued that historians could trust such documents as Domesday Book as detailed guides to the military and fiscal obligations due from across the realm under the Anglo-Saxon kings. The same evidence also showed how the highest officers in the land, ealdormen and earls, held land from the king on feudal tenures.

Such nobles and officials governed Anglo-Saxon England. Twice a year, ealdormen or sheriffs and bishops presided over the shire court.[107] Various officers and the king's thegns witnessed royal charters.[108] Occasionally the great men of the realm gathered together as a 'wiᴛenaȝemoᴛ or ᴔicel sẏnoð ... which afterward was from the *Romance* Dialect stiled a Parliament.'[109] Here lay the origins of that institution that gave life to the mixed monarchy of the Anglo-Saxons and provided the pattern for the Norman gatherings of tenants-in-chief of the Crown. Selden admitted that 'most parts of the state of the *Saxon* government are so obscure that we can see only steps or torne reliques of them, rather then so much as might give a full satisfaction.'[110] However, a careful look at Saxon laws led to the conclusion: 'That their *Jurisdiction* in the greatest Court or Councell, or the wiᴛenaȝemoᴛe, consisted either in a *deliberative power* which concerned their assenting to new Lawes, and advising in matter of state, or in *Judiciall*, which was, of giving judgement upon suits or complaints in the same Court.'[111] In other words, such assemblies advised in matters of state and both assented to and judged laws. Reference to the Laws of Ine, Ethelbert, Alfred, Cynewulf, and others supported this carefully developed, coherent explanation of the offices, feudal nobility, and institutions of Anglo-Saxon England.

Norman and Later Earls and Barons

After the Conquest a number of shifts in terminology took place as the king's thegns became barons and the middle thegns became vavasours, 'a name that never was honorary here, but only feudall.'[112] The feudal and hereditary payment of heriot by thegns now became the reliefs paid by barons.[113] However, the thegns and their provision by five-hide units was the key to the continuity of Anglo-Saxon tenures into the early Norman period; the functions and positions remained the same, but, after a time, the names changed: 'For after some yeares that followed the comming of the *Normans*, this title of *Thane* grew out of use, and that of *Baron* and *Barony* succeeded for *Thane* and *Thainland* ...'[114] Although the feudal tenures of the Saxons had survived the Norman Conquest, most of the nobles who held thegn lands under Harold lost them under William I:

William the first, after his victorie against King *Harold* and the English Earles or *Thanes* that tooke part with *Harold* (whence it fell out that they forfeited their estates to King *William* that pretended at least, by the just Titles both of gift and Inheritance, a right to the Crowne of *England*) gave most of the *Earldomes* and *Baronies*, or *Tainlands* to his *Normans*, though some also to the *English*, and to such as had right derived from the *English*, that were Earles in the *Saxon* times; as wee see in that example of *Gospatric* Earle of *Northumberland* before cited; but so large was his bounty towards his *Normans* that (as *Ingulphus* sayes who lived in Court with him) *Comitatus et Baronias, Episcopatus et Prælatus totius terræ suis Normannis Rex distribuit.*[115]

In this passage which both echoed and modified his earlier accounts of distribution of land by William I, Selden cleverly portrayed Norman Conquest both as a major change and as one more stage of continuous development for the ancient constitution of England. The ambiguities no longer arose from indecision, but from an attempt both to reflect the subtleties found in a wide range of documents and to show how this evidence cohered to his theory of law as custom and statute.

The transformation of Anglo-Saxon titles and institutions into those of the early Normans was an extremely complex process which both began at once and extended over several centuries. Following the standard format, Selden's account started out with Earl, then moved on to Baron and Knight. Ironically, the title that seemed to herald a continuity in Anglo-Saxon usage changed the most. 'The title of *Earle*, since the time of the *Normans*, is either *Locall* or *Personall. Locall* we call that which is denominated from any Countie or other territory. As Earle of *Chester*, or *Arundell*, of *Kent*, and the like. *Personall*, that which hath its being in some great office only, as in that of *Earle Marshall*.'[116] Personal Earls only came into existence under King John.[117] The nature of local earls changed at a much earlier date, however, for only the '*Locall Earls Palatin* were of the same nature with those of the *Saxon* time that had both their Earldomes to their owne use, and also, under the King, all Regal Jurisdiction or *merum et mixtum Imperium*, in so much as that the Kings Writ of ordinary Justice did not runne there.'[118] Three of these, 'the Bishop of *Durham*, and the Earles of *Chester* and *Pembroke*, were together acocounted under Henry III, three especiall Lords of the Kingdome, that had like Regall Jurisdiction.'[119] For the most eminent, Cheshire, the 'speciall rights the Earles there had before the comming of the *Normans*, may be observed out ... of *Domesday*,' but neither these rights nor the designation of County Palatine appeared there before the reign of Henry II.[120] County Durham seemed to provide an exception, however, for some evidence suggested that it may have held a special status from an early date: 'There is colour to thinke that the Palatin Jurisdiction began there in Bishop *Walcher* whom King *William* the first made both *Episcopus* and *Dux Provinciæ*,' although even here a note of scepticism intruded: 'But I thinke rather that *Dux Provinciæ*, denotes there only the Sheriffe of the Countie ...'[121] '*Comitatus*' indicated an Earldom under the early Normans, while '*Provincia*' stood for a sheriffdom.[122] Evidence for the Palatine earldoms which most resembled those of the Anglo-Saxons started only in the reign of Henry III, well over a century after the Conquest, which more than suggested that a major change had taken place.

Throughout the early Norman period, however, Earl (*Comes*) remained an important honorary title, as attested by a wide variety of evidence:

The *Nature* of *Local Earles* that being *not Palatin* were made since the comming of the *Normans*, will best appeare by their *Charters* or *Patents* of Creation, Confirmation, Restitution, or livery, with some ancient testimonies of that kind; the Observation of their *honorarie possessions* or *Earldomes*, with their *Reliefs*, and of the *chiefe Ornaments used* at the *Investiture* or otherwise *mentioned* as belonging to them.[123]

The earliest charters of creation existed from the reign of Queen Maud and King Stephen made many earls 'and wasted the Crowne Revenue on them.'[124] Numerous charters creating or confirming earldoms existed from the time of Henry II onward, as shown in examples cited from the reigns of John, Henry III, Edward I, Edward II, Richard II, Edward IV, Henry VII, and Edward VI.[125] In a passage which left little doubt about the nature of major change undergone by the title from the late Anglo-Saxon to the early Norman period, Selden pointed out that earls no longer normally ruled counties or provinces: 'And to conclude this point, it will be plaine by the Lawes and Rolls of those ancient times, that Sheriffes of the Counties had the government and custodie of them, and not the Earles (unlesse they were Palatin) otherwise then in cases where they had the Sheriffe-wicks joyned with their dignities.'[126] Under William I, Earl had became a feudal title, held in knight service from the Crown. Selden correctly saw those holdings and privileges which made up an earl's honour as the key to this title under the early Norman kings:

The *honorary possessions* of an ancient Earle of this kind, or his *Earldome*, was called his *Honour* in such a sense as at this day we use the word *Honour* for a prediall possession; as we say *Honours, Castles, and Mannors.* And *Honor Comitis Gloucestr., Honor Comitis Eustachij, Honoris Comitum,* and the like, to this purpose, occure in *Domesday,* in the olde Pipe Rols, and elsewhere frequently. It is the same with *Comitatus* ... Such an Earldome of that age is stiled also sometimes *Baronia* or *honor Capitalis.* For the word *Baro* likewise, in a more comprehensive signification, denotes an Earle also; whereof more anon in the title of Barons. These honorary possessions consisted usually of Castles, Mannors, and other Lands held in chiefe by common Knight Service, or Grand Serjanty, or both.[127]

Although earls paid their reliefs 'in Armes and Horse for the most part' under William I, as they had paid their heregates in Anglo-Saxon times, this hint of continuity proved more misleading than symptomatic.[128] In the transformation of titles at the Conquest, Baron replaced Thegn, and Earl indicated a particularly prestigious Baron; the difference became one of degree, not kind, for both held their lands directly from the Crown on feudal tenures. After the Conquest, it became difficult to discuss the title Earl without involving that of Baron.

Nowhere in the second edition of *Titles of Honor* (1631) did Selden better show his remarkable skills as an historian than in the lengthy section on post-Conquest barons. These chapters offered clever and highly sophisticated solutions for a number of complicated historical puzzles (including English feudal practices).[129] Profoundly aware of and able to accommodate changes over time, Selden divided the ages 'betweene the beginning of *William* the first and this day into three parts': 1 / from William I to near the end of John's reign; 2 / from the later part of John's reign to the middle of Richard II's, and 3 / from the middle of Richard II's reign to that of King James.[130] Displaying a great sensitivity towards the unhurried adjustments of people, even to major changes, Selden noted that at the beginning of this period:

The name [Baron] succeeded, after the *Normans*, into the roome of Cýninȝeꞃ Đane ða him nihꞃt ꞃýnðon, *A Kings Thane that was next him*, among the *Saxons*; however, in the beginning of the *Norman* state, that of *Thane* was often also retained. Nor is it likely that the use of language could have beene so sodainly altered that the Title of Baron only should have presently expressed it. Thence is it that in *Domesday*, and the Lawes attributed to *Henry* the first, *Thanus* is so used.[131]

Contemporary evidence established both the change and continuity of the title and the continuity of its nature. Although Baron encompassed a wide variety of rich usage from early in the Norman period, in its most important meaning it 'denoted all kind of Lords of Parliament, as well Earles as others, and the word *Baronage*, as a collective, hath in like sense, comprehended them.'[132] Not suprisingly for the author of 'The Privileges of the Baronage,' parliamentary barons provided the focus for the ensuing discussion.

Whether as a result of reading Spelman's *Archæologus* or independently, Selden had come to the important conclusion that, during the first century and one half of Norman rule, 'all Honorary Barons ... were (for aught appeares) Barons only by tenure and created by the Kings gift or Charter of good possessions (without the title of Earle) whereby hee reserved to himselfe a tenure in chiefe by Common Knights Service, or by Grand Serjentry, or both.'[133] Other historians and common lawyers knew this, of course, but as Pocock has pointed out, with the notable exception of Spelman, early-seventeenth-century English legal writers tended to read the feudal tenures of their own day back into those of the early Norman period.[134] They failed to grasp the fact that William I expected payment in armed knights, not in money, and thereby missed the essential nature of the Norman feudal law as it applied to England.

In contrast to the readings put forward by most of his contemporaries came the subtle, detailed discussion of the distinctive nature of feudal tenures during the early Norman period in *Titles of Honor* (1631):

These possessions given, were their Baronies or *Baroniæ Capitales*, as the Baronies both of Earles and Barons were sometimes called. And the Knights Service reserved was of no certaine number of Knights, or men to doe Knights service, but according to the pleasure of the King or to the contract had with him. And by the Knights or Military men expressed in the service reserved, the land given was esteemed more or fewer Knights Fees ...[135]

With a reasonably good sense of anachronism, Selden broke through the barrier of reading the meaning of 'knight's fee' from his own day back into the early Norman period and pointed out that barons held their land from the king on the condition of providing a stipulated number of fighting men, that the number varied depending upon the agreement reached between the king and any individual baron, and that each knight's fee actually supported a professional warrior. This not only underlined the personal, reciprocal nature of feudal relationships, it stressed their military nature. In addition, he noted, 'there were two kinds of Knights Fees':

Those that were held in chief of the King, and those that were held by a mean tenure, called also anciently *Vavasories*. Of the first kind only, these Baronies (as also the Baronies or honors of Earles) were made; and they, by sub-infeudation for the most part, made the second. And by themselves and others provided at their owne charge, or by their Tenants (whom they made by such sub-infeudation) they performed the services reserved by the King. As if the King gave XX Knights Fees to be held in Chiefe ..., if the Patentee infeoffed others of part to be held under him (for example) by the service of fifteene Knights, then the King was served at the charge of his Baron the Patentee with five Knights, and the other fifteene were supplied by those that held the rest by meane tenures ...[136]

By stressing the contractual nature of feudal relationships and by presenting a well-thought-out concept of subinfeudation, Selden managed to pack two key insights into the feudal laws of the early Norman kings into a relatively short compass. The descriptions quoted above represented a considerable accomplishment of historical imagination and representation. Integrating some of Spelman's insights into early Norman tenures into his own interpretation of the English constitution in a critical manner, Selden presented the results in a readily available, easily understood, original form and illustrated it with concrete examples.[137]

The greatest change in this system of military feuds involved the holders of what became ecclesiastical lordships. Even in his earlier edition, Selden had noted the differences for the great churchmen and now he stressed the point even more strongly:

The Bishops, Abbots, and other Ecclesiasticall persons of the *Saxon* times, held their lands free from all Secular service besides *trimoda necessitas* ... *Expeditio, Pontium et Arcium extructio* or *refectio* (or supply for the warres, and for the building or repairing of *Castles* and *Bridges*) were the three, which were commonly excepted in the Kings grants of Church-lands ...[138]

Under Anglo-Saxon kings, however, these reservations of specific services did not constitute a tenure; the church did not hold its lands as a feudal tenant of the Crown, nor did leading churchmen sit in Micel Synods or Witenagemotes on the basis of their lands or temporalities, but 'they had place and voice there as Bishops and as they were Spirituall only.'[139] Selden argued that the momentous shift of church lands to feudal tenure commenced during the fourth year of William I, 'when he made the Bishopriques and Abbeyes subject to Knights Service in chiefe, by creation of new tenures, and so first turned their possessions into Baronies, and thereby made them Barons of the Kingdom by tenure.'[140] Plenty of evidence, from Domesday Book, the aid collected by Henry II, and the Pipe Rolls and other documents from the reign of John, proved that the clergy provided the required knights.[141] Selden argued that since temporal lords (the thegns) had already held their lands on the basis of military (or other) services, the changes ushered in by the Conqueror marked a much greater burden upon churchmen.[142] Only in one respect did the spiritual barons differ from their colleagues; in Parliament, they did not sit in judgment in matters involving the death penalty:

... All Bishops, Abbots, Priors, and the like that held in chiefe of the King, had their possessions as Baronies, and accordingly to doe all services, and to sit in judgement with the rest of the Barons in all cases, saving cases of bloud. The exception of cases of bloud proceeded from the Canon Lawes, which prohibited Clergie men to assent to such judgements. And the Clergie of the Parlament of *England* hath somtimes, by reason of those Canon Lawes, absented themselves from such judgements, and committed their whole interest for the time to a lay proxie.[143]

Although uncertain about the means by which the Conqueror had carried through this creation of ecclesiastical lordships, Selden pointed out that William I had held a Parliament in his fourth year and speculated that 'perhaps this innovation of their tenures was done by an act of that Parliament also.'[144] Of course, this fit into Selden's theory that English law derived either from custom or statute.

Parliaments and Parliamentary Barons

The case for continuity across the barrier of the Conquest depended strongly upon evidence that the early Norman kings had followed the example of their Anglo-Saxon predecessors in holding regular meetings of assemblies for legal advice and judgment. Since neither writs nor Rolls of Parliament remained from this period, this posed a serious test. Selden could not use contemporary archival sources, but had to rely upon such early historians as Roger of Hoveden, Matthew Paris, and Eadmer. Hoveden related that William I, in his fourth year, had called together an assembly of his Barons, English nobles, and those learned in the laws of the English: 'And XII were returned out of every Country who shewed what the customes of the Kingdome were, which being writen by the hands of *Aldred* Archbishop of *Yorke*, Hugh Bishop of *London*, were with the assent of the same Barons for the most part, confirmed in that assembly which was a Parliament of that time.'[145] To Selden this demonstrated that the Conqueror had expended considerable effort to hear, record, and confirm the customs of the Anglo-Saxons, as expounded by legal experts from every county. Rarely does one find the transition from oral to written law, the intermingling of custom and statute, depicted so vividly. In confirming old and making new laws, even the Conqueror did not act alone, but held a Parliament for these purpose.

Selden carefully marshalled other evidence to show that similar parliaments were assembled in the seventh year of William II, at the coronation of Henry I, in the tenth and twenty-third years of Henry II, the first and second years of Richard I, and the second and sixth years of John.[146] Candidly admitting that he found no evidence for parliaments meeting from after the death of Henry I until well into the reign of Henry II, Selden also noted that 'the Ancientest Writ of Summons that I have seene is no elder than the sixt of King *John*.'[147] Although careful to note the distinct terms, such as '*consilium Baronum*,' and '*generale Consilium*,' used in his evidence to describe these gatherings, Selden argued that all royal tenants-in-chief could attend these 'assemblies of the Earles and Barons, as well Spirituall as Temporall of all *England*.'[148] Painfully aware of the tentative nature of the evidence, Selden had put together a sensitive representation of the feudal structure of early Norman England and a credible case for the continuity of Anglo-Saxon laws and institutions across the barrier of the Conquest. During the first century and a half of Norman rule, all titles of honour were feudal grants from the king and all tenants-in-chief sat in Parliament by virtue of their tenures.

This early equality at law of royal tenants-in-chief passed away sometime during the second phase of development, perhaps as early as the latter part of King John's reign. A hierarchy of status arose among the barons and changed the membership of parliaments:

... Whereas in the time of the first part, every tenant in chiefe, as is before shewed, was indifferently an honorary or Parliamentary Baron by reason of his tenure or lands held, which made his Barony; about the end of King *John*, some only that were most eminent of those tenants in chief (sometimes stiled *Majores Regni Barones*) were summoned by severall [i.e., individual] Writs directed to them. And the rest ... were summoned also, not by severall writs, but by one generall Summons given by the Sheriffes in their severall Counties. What speciall kind of place and voice different from the other, they that were thus summond by the Sheriffe had, I find not.[149]

Spelman had briefly sketched this general reading in the *Archæolo-*

gus, but Selden added to it evidence and interpretations of his own.[150] As well as stressing a growing differentiation among the barons, it provided a key for explaining the individual writs sent to members of the Lords and the general summons, through the sheriff, for representatives of the Commons in the later thirteenth century. This supposed that the barons called by a general summons somehow lost this right and gave way to elected knights of the shire during the reign of Henry III. Not writing about the history of Parliament as such in this treatise, Selden did discuss the transformation of minor barons into knights, but did not show how the barons called by a general summons sent to the sheriff turned into the elected knights of the shire. However problematic it may look to twentieth-century historians, this account of the differentiation among barons and shift in the criteria for the parliamentary baronage provided a neat solution to a major historical problem, the rise of parliaments out of the assemblies of royal tenants-in-chief, and another excellent example of how the law and constitution adjusted to important social shifts.

Arguing that the ravages of time and the quarrels of John's reign, especially the escheats shortly before Magna Carta, had ruined the standing of some barons, Selden attempted to sort out the emergence of major and minor barons:

Divers Barons also were perhaps so decayed in their estates that they were not able honorably any longer to support their Titles. Now the other Barons which were of ancient foundation or bloud, or of great revenue, or the *Majores Barones*, forseeing, it semes, how their dignitie and power might suffer much diminuation, if the new tenants in Chiefe, or Patentees of those Escheated Baronies and the rest that were decayed ... should have equallity with them ..., procured (so we may justly thinke) a Law in some of those Parlaments that preceded that Grand Charter, by which themselves only should hereafter be properly stiled and be Barons, and the rest tenants in chiefe only, or Knights, or *Milites*, which titles should be given them as distinct names from Barons.[151]

With its slightly worldly-wise Tacitean tone and its frank speculation that the great magnates looked after their own interests by pushing through acts of Parliament, this passage provided a plausible explanation of how magnates came to monopolize titles of nobility and individual summons to parliaments which at least as well reflected Selden's own experience in the parliaments of the 1620s as evidence from the reign of King John. According to Selden, Magna Carta established degrees in the payment of reliefs which gave the Crown and smaller landholders a stake in the change:

For whereas formerly while those Tenants in chiefe ... were in the ordinary state of Barons ... their Reliefes were payable uncertainly, sometimes in Armes, sometimes in mony ... and the Reliefes of the ancient and greater *Barons* were now, by the grand Charter, assessed at C markes; the Reliefes of these Tenants in chiefe were made payable, not as for Baronies, but now only as those of *Vavasors* anciently were ... That is that they were to pay five pounds only for every Knights Fee ...[152]

This helped to explain how the magnates had marshalled support behind the laws which created their new status; the king received more money, and ordinary tenants-in-chief paid less.

The emergence of an individual summons to parliaments as the test for the baronial status, not the distinction between major barons and other tenants-in-chief, was crucial for this reading: 'For it was in it selfe much more honorable to receive Writs of Summons directed from the King, then to be summoned by the generall name only in the County by the Sheriffe.'[153] According to Selden, this innovation produced long-lasting consequences. The nature of the title Baron also changed, so that 'no tenure, in that alone, should any longer make a *Baron* of the Kingdome; but that now the Writ of Summons only, might make one.'[154] Barons by feudal tenure alone had ceased to exist. In this critical feature, the feudal laws of William lasted only for a century and a half. Out of the social shifts and political struggles of John's reign arose the new criterion for membership in the baronage, the receipt of an individual summons to Parliament.

Probably on the basis of Spelman's speculation, Selden had put together a brilliant, if sometimes wordy, historical account, one which plausibly explained a good deal of evidence and related shifts in the law to changes in society. However, it remained largely largely conjectural. Because of this, Selden felt impelled to defend his construction. No statutes survived to mark these momentous innovations:

In what yeare either that Law, which we suppose made the first distinction betweene the greater *Barons* and those Tenants, passed, or when the other was made, which we conceive hereafter utterly excluded those Tenants from their place which by the Grand Charter they had upon the generall Summons in the County, appeares not. But it seemes the first was in some parlament held not long before King *Johns* grand Charter was made; and the other, I thinke not long after it.[155]

An old writer cited by William Camden dated the confining of the baronage to those who received an individual summons to Parliament to the end of the reign of Henry III or the early part of that of Edward I, but Selden could not accept such a late date.[156] Instead he indulged in a lengthy discussion on the fragility of the records of ancient laws:

Neither let it be imputed that we seeme too confident in the conjecture, that such Lawes, as we have supposed, were made in those times, because wee have neither Roll nor History that expresly mentions them. The common Histories of those obscure times, have many that the Rols have not. The Rols that remaine (as the Patents and Close Rols especially) have divers that the Histories want. Neither have all. And it is a wonder rather that they have so many. For the proper place of the Lawes as well of those times (as of ours) was in their Rols of Parlament, all of which are lost. And such Lawes as we find in those other Rols of those times came but accidentally into them. Whence it is also that neither the Grand Charter of King *John*, nor of *Henry* the third, is in the Rols of either of those Kings, though we have that of *Henry* the third elsewhere, both in Rols of later time and in good Writers that are neere as ancient as the Charter. And that of King *John* is extant only in some originalls and in some stories as *Matthew Paris, Roger of Wendover, Thomas of Rudborne,* and some other, but not in any Roll that remaynes now. Nor is it strange, that the memory of the making such Lawes of so great moment should be utterly lost. ... And, in the old *Roman* Monarchie, that famous *Lex Regia* ... was, it seemes, made about the beginning of the same Monarchie, yet no man hath fund either the time or the words of it ... The like might be said of the *Lex Regia,* in the *German* Empire, and of some other ancient Lawes, in every state, of whose being we are certaine by the circumstances of matter, but for the just time of their making, and of the formes of them, we are left wholy to conjecture for want of those ancient testimonies of them which have perished.[157]

Only someone as familiar as Selden with the records of the thirteenth century could have written such an eloquent defence.

In the hands of many other early-seventeenth-century common

lawyers, a similar defence would have turned into a discussion of immemorial custom which reconstructed the past on the basis that written legal documents recorded practices that had already existed from time out of mind.[158] Selden firmly resisted the temptation of immemoriality and used the problems caused by presumably perished documents to justify filling in the gaps with historical imagination. The comparative method helped to bolster the point that the historian, in order to make a plausible representation of the past, had to move from the known to the unknown by conjecture. Selden, while careful to seek for the most contemporary evidence for his history, certainly displayed and appreciated the need for historical imagination. The description of the chance survival of important documents, such as Magna Carta, not only rang true but also reflected a good deal of expertise in the manuscript sources for the period. The comparison with other European societies showed that the problem was not confined to England alone. Anachronism intruded, however, in the assumption that Rolls of Parliament had existed for the early Norman period. Here and indeed in his ardent concern to find parliaments in the Anglo-Saxon and early Norman periods, Selden could not escape from the tendency to read history backwards from some future date; however, we need to remember that these social and institutional changes still pose problems for historians. After all, a shift in the usage of 'Baron' had taken place in the thirteenth century. Displaying a degree of insight rare in the early seventeenth century, Selden offered a coherent, plausible historical interpretation.

With the intricacies of the Anglo-Saxon and early Norman periods sorted out, the rest of the account flowed more freely. During the second period, which lasted from late in John's to the middle of Richard II's reign, Selden saw two kinds of barons: *'Barons by Writ and Tenure, and Barons by Writ only.'*[159] The first included the ancient, major barons, the second those newly raised to the honour by kings. Those old royal tenancies-in-chief which did not measure up to magnate status, might 'abusively' be called baronies, but they were esteemed 'Knights Fees only.'[160] To show the new criterion at work, Selden quoted writs of summons from the parliaments of Henry III's reign. To fill out his account of the baronage, he also charted the shifting make-up of the ecclesiastical membership (with bishops always summoned and abbots sometimes called and sometimes not) and noted that from the reign of Edward I onward, kings summoned some (such as the judges, the attorney general, and the king's sergeants) who had place but not voice in the Lords.[161] This also illustrated the growing complexity of parliaments.

The third period opened with the creation of barons by letters patent and the introduction of new titles in the middle of the reign of Richard II. Plentiful documentation marked these innovations. Selden quoted the patent of John Beauchamp, Steward of the Household to Richard II, the first temporal baron created in this way, and printed another patent from the reign of James I to show the continuity.[162] Edward III revived the title Duke for his sons, while Richard II 'invested' the first non-royal duke in his ninth year by raising Edmund, Earl of Cambridge, and Thomas, Earl of Buckingham and Essex, to that honour.[163] Richard II also introduced the title Marquess when 'he Created *Robert de Vere* Earl of *Oxford*, Marquesse of *Dublin* in *Ireland* for life.'[164] Henry VI completed the roll of English noble titles by raising John, Lord Beaumont, to the new honour of Viscount Beaumont.[165]

Selden's representation of the history of the title Baron, apart from its great interest as an example of an accomplished historical imagination, strongly immersed in contemporary evidence, provided a major reassessment of the changing, yet continuous, nature of the English constitution. From the beginning to the end of the account, Selden insisted that the variety of titles should not cloak the unity of the parliamentary baronage: 'They are all comprehended under the name of *Magnates,* or *Les Grandes, Proceres, Domini,* Lords (anciently hlaɣonðeɣ and *Louerds*), *Seigneurs, Pares Regni,* or *Peeres of the Realme.*'[166] Indeed, dismissing the *cinq pers* story from Jean Froissart, he strengthened this point by noting that the Rolls of Parliament often refer to all of the Lords as '*jus paritatis*' and that they often appeared in records and histories as peers.[167] Tying up the last possible strand, Selden ended this section with a discussion of the courtesy titles held by the sons of lords during the lifetime of their father.[168] In the course of this long discourse on barons, Selden had demonstrated the feudal and military character of the early Norman baronage, established the nature of the knight's fee as a grant of land designed to provide the service of a professional warrior, and illustrated the transformation of a baronage by tenure into one defined by receiving an individual summons to parliaments and, later, one created by letters patent. In comparison to historiography on these questions of his own day, this marked a major accomplishment.[169] It also contained profound constitutional implications. Given the changing character of titles throughout the Saxon, Norman, and medieval periods, the Conquest took on the appearance of one of many fairly major periods of innovation, rather than a unique, catastrophic turning-point for English government and law. Throughout, the centrality of assemblies for judgment and advice, the *consilia* or parliaments of the Normans and their successors, received great stress. The complexity and length of the section on Baron made possible a more compact discussion of the history of English knighthood, one which needed only to establish the nature of the honorary title, not its feudal function.

Knights and Gentlemen

With the title Knight, the Saxon influence, while paradoxically more in sound than substance, became readily apparent: '*Knight*, or Cniht or Cnӯht (as it was written in the *Saxon*) signified *puer*, *servus*, or an attendant.'[170] In Saxon times, the term sometimes denoted 'a Souldier,' while after the Conquest the military meaning became exclusive:

... Tenants by Knights Service were ... called *Knights*, *Milites*, or *Chivalers*, because their service was militarie, which most especially occurres in the ancient Rols of Escuages, and in the Pipe Rols where Escuages and Aides are accounted for, and in our writs of attaint.[171]

This seemed to indicate a major shift in meaning, but continuities in practice existed as well, for 'in the *Saxon* times (if wee may beleeve, as I thinke we may; that *Miles* denoted this dignity) wee have frequent mention of it.'[172] Having established the general meaning of the title and dismissed the 'fabulous tales' of Arthur and the Romans, Selden turned to the history of knights bachelors, the earliest manifestation of the title and the one from which bannerets and such orders as the Knights of the Garter and the Knights of Bath had derived.[173] As in the Empire and France, the Anglo-Saxons continued to practice the old northern custom of girding a young man of royal or aristocratic birth with a sword as a sign of his coming of age. This formed the basis for knighthood.

The ancientest mention of any Courtly Ceremonies used at the creation of a Knight with us, is that of King *Alfred* his Knighting his grand child *Athelstan*, that was afterward King ... Here was a purple Robe and a Sword given.

In the stories of the following times, often mention is of making Knights. But other Ceremonies of the Court, besides Feasts and the giving of Armes or the girding on of a Sword (and those generally expressed) are but seldom remembered.[174]

Later evidence revealed more elaborate ceremonies. From the pseudo-Ingulf came a description of the 'Sacred Ceremonies, anciently used' by the 'English *Saxons* before his time,' which included 'a solemne Confession, a Vigil in the Church, Receiving the Sacrament after an Offering of the Sword on the Altar and redemption of it, and the Bishops, Abbots, Monkes or other Priests putting it on him that was to be created ...'[175] Selden argued that this practice fit into the general pattern of local development of northern customs and had become well established before the arrival of the Normans.

As noted above, William I made the provision of armed warriors the basis of his grants of land under knight service to his lay and religious barons. Under the Normans the ceremonies noted by Ingulf continued and the tenants of a lord paid a feudal aid to help to cover the cost of the ceremony of knighthood:

For our Feudall Laws ..., there is frequent mention in our Law Bookes of *Reasonable aide a faire fits Chivaler*, that is, certaine summes of money levied on the Tenant to make the sonne and heire apparent of the Lord a Knight. For the Ceremonies, Preparations and other circumstances were such anciently at the receiving of the dignitie (as before shewed) that such an aide might have place enough in the charge of it.[176]

Arbitrary before the reign of Edward I, this aid was stabilized for the vassals of lords at 2s per knight's fee by a parliamentary statute passed in 3 Edward I and applied to royal lands by a statute of 25 Edward III.[177] After establishing that knights bannerets in England were the same as in France, but not hereditary, Selden detailed the origins and development of the Order of the Garter (including a history of St George) and the Order of Bath.[178] Overall, the title Knight displayed a history similar to more prestigious honours, including a northern origin, a changing definition, and minor variations from one society to another. Although containing a discussion of neither Parliament nor the emergence of knights of the shire, this section ended with a brief look at the newly created title Baronet (invented by

Selden's friend Sir Robert Cotton) and that of Esquire or Armiger, which, in turn, led back to Continenal customs.

The most ancient use of Esquire came from the days of William I, where it signified young heirs waiting to be knighted, but it came to apply to 'the most eminent sort of Gentlemen.'[179] So prominent did the profession of arms stand in later ages that landowners with any strong social pretensions sought to claim honour by usurping the title:

Now as in those elder times of military action, such Gentlemen as wer employed in service receiving their dignitie, either at home or abroad, were frequently, it seemes, for distinction from the rest, and as a note of honor, called Esquires ..., so at length, especially in the times of peace, when military service could make but litle distinction, they that by or birth or other eminencie were commonly thought worthy of some note of distinction above the ordinary ranke of Gentlemen, have had the same title given unto them.[180]

A full discussion of the attributes of gentility, however, awaited another occasion. Almost as an afterthought and accompanied by relatively brief chapters on precedence, feminine titles, and the attributes of honour, appeared a short section on the various ways used to create gentry.[181] This section barely touched the surface of a vast topic, considering the abundance of evidence and treatises available on the minor nobility; 'for Armes and Crests, the severall wayes of ennobling, by Feuds, by employment, by degrees in learning, or the like, according to the Lawes of severall Countries, and the great harvest of other particulars touching Gentrie, the store of former Writers, is so great of them' that one could easily write as lengthy a book on gentlemen alone.[182] The title Gentleman also arose among the northern successors to the Roman Empire, later involved the legal right to bear and inherit a coat of arms, and eventually made the shift from warrior to prestigious landholder:

And thus in the customes of *Europe* (which for the most part came immediatly from those Northern Nations, that about declining the Empire planted themselves almost throughout it) the right of having Armes hath been from ancient time an Ensigne of Gentrie, and that almost as the right of having Images was in the old *Roman* State. Those warlike Nations and the rest with whom they are mixt in *Europe*, so esteemed the noble office of a Souldier, and were so much all Souldiers, that from what belonged to the warres only rather then from any thing else they would take the Ensignes of Gentry, whence also *Miles, Chevalier, Cavaliero and Escuyer* also, or *Scutarius*, or *Armiger*, all being names framed first as proper for the warres, are used sometime in a notion that means only a Gentleman as may be observed out of what is already delivered touching them.[183]

A similar pattern followed by more formal titles applied to the lower ranges of honour, with northern customs working themselves out in various societies; this time, however, without taking over old Roman but creating new Latin titles.

Concluding Remarks on *Titles of Honor* (1631)

Selden's representation of the history of English titles provided a major reassessment of the changing, yet continuous, nature of the English constitution. The second edition of *Titles of Honor* presented the most sophisticated interpretation of Anglo-Saxon governance and social institutions available at the time, demonstrated the feudal and military character of the early Norman baronage, established the nature of the knight's fee as a grant of land designed to provide the service of a professional warrior, speculated on the transformation of a baronage by tenure into one defined by receiving an individual summons to parliaments, illustrated the later creation of nobles by letters patent, and showed how Knight had shifted from a title indicating a warrior into one that provided prestige to lesser landholders. Supported by evidence from public and private manuscripts contemporary with the periods under analysis, these interpretations represented a major scholarly accomplishment and one more easily accessible than the incomplete but impressive volume so far published by Spelman. From the perspective of Selden's history of the changing character of titles and laws throughout the Saxon, Norman, and medieval eras, the Conquest of 1066 looked more like one of many major moments of innovation, or one additional adjustment of northern customs to Latin offices, rather than a unique, catastrophic turning-point for English government and law. Throughout these scholarly narratives, Selden stressed the centrality of assemblies for judgment and advice, the Micel Synods or Witenagemots of the Anglo-Saxons, the *consilia* or parliaments of the Normans and their successors.[184] Mixed monarchy proved more lasting than changes of dynasty and social customs.

A complex work of great scholarship and historical imagination, the second edition of *Titles of Honor* (1631) interpreted European titles of monarchy, nobility, and gentility as a series of local adaptions of northern customs to Latin offices within the those kingdoms which succeeded to the Roman Empire in western and southern Europe. With plentiful evidence, much of it from manuscripts contemporary or nearly contemporary to the events under analysis, Selden portrayed these societies as a series of ancient constitutions, each with its own 'state' (or basic distribution of power and responsibilities) and its own feudal customs. The feudal law of the civil lawyers became a series of national, provincial, or local feudal laws. Selden's philological evidence of how the people from 'northern nations' came to express their customs in Latin; his astute awareness of how titles, offices, and institutions varied over time and space; and his sophisticated representation of fealty, homage, service, and investiture with land, including the handling of subinfeudation and knights' fees in England, helped to establish his overall interpretation. Although fitting into the European pattern, England had a different 'state' from that of other countries, a 'state' in which monarchs, nobles, clergy, and freemen shared power from the very beginning through general councils, a 'state' in which the law consisted of communally created custom and statute. Selden created a sophisticated, scholarly, cosmopolitan defence of the mixed nature of England's monarchy. His demonstration of considerable change in Anglo-Saxon laws, offices, and institutions before the Norman Conquest; of the continuity of the Anglo-Saxon feudal tenures, offices, and institutions across the potential divide of the Conquest; and of the shifting nature of the Norman baronage during the first two centuries of the new regime, created a solid alternative to those who argued that William I had imposed the feudal law of the Continent upon England. If English common lawyers found it difficult to see the Norman Conquest as a decisive break in constitutional development before the publication of the second edition of *Titles of Honor* in 1631, the barrier became even greater after Selden had employed the weight of his learning to absorb feudal laws into the ancient constitutions of various European societies.

Mare Clausum

The subtle, complex historical imagination displayed in the second edition of *Titles of Honor*, however, became considerably more directed in the last published of Selden's early historical treatises on English and Continental laws. *Mare Clausum* (London, 1635) managed to combine a lengthy, sophisticated theoretical discussion of law – which translated the integrationist theory of the common lawyers into the discourse of natural law – with a partisan and reasonably well-documented history of the exercise of dominion over the seas surrounding the British Isles from the days of the Roman Empire onward. Long recognized as one of the foundational works for modern international law and now seen as an early example of 'modern' natural law, *Mare Clausum* has remained the best-known and probably the most frequently studied of Selden's early works.[185] First written around 1619, and then revised and expanded for publication in 1635, it took an extreme stand within an ongoing dispute over claims to portions of the sea.

Although the debate between those who supported freedom of the seas and those who favoured some sort of dominion had raged since ancient times, first Spanish and Portuguese colonial expansion – vindicated by claims to huge tracts of land and water – and then the vigorous growth of Dutch trading and fishing – upheld by wide-ranging claims to the freedom of the seas – intensified it during the sixteenth and early seventeenth centuries. The academic positions argued largely by jurists trained in the Roman law defended positions on international trade with important economic consequences, the attempts of the Portuguese to monopolize sea routes for trade between Europe and the Far East, of the Spanish to monopolize trade with the new world, and of the Dutch to trade anywhere in the world (including the Far East and the Spanish colonies) and to fish anywhere (including off the coast of Scotland and England). As king of Scotland, James VI had made fitful resistance to what he saw as the unlicensed intrusions of the huge Dutch herring fleet into Scots waters and had rewarded William Welwood, the professor of law at St Andrews University, for his treatise *The Sea Law of Scotland* (Edinburgh, 1590), a defence of royal dominion over the seas stretching for eighty miles from the coast of Scotland. Soon after becoming king of England, James VI and I stepped up the pressure with a proclamation requiring the purchase of a royal licence by all foreign ships who wished to fish in British waters. Although it applied to fishermen from France, various German jurisdictions, Portugal, and Spain, this scheme weighed most heavily upon the Dutch. Originally written as a chapter in an unpublished treatise attacking the Portuguese claim for a monopoly of trade in the Far East, Hugo Grotius's famous anonymous brief treatise on the freedom of the seas, *Mare Liberum* (Leiden, 1609), was fortuitously published at the start of the English campaign to license boats engaged in the herring fishery. In a series of fierce disputes and negotiations which took place between 1609 and 1619, Grotius developed the principles contained in *Mare Liberum* into a strong natural-law case for the Dutch position that the seas were free for all to fish. King James longed for a powerful reply to the principles and evidence presented by the spokesmen of the United Provinces of the Netherlands. Rather early into the fray, Welwood attacked *Mare Liberum* in two treatises: *An Abridgement of All Sea Lawes* (London, 1613) and *De Dominio Maris* (Cosmopoli [London], 1615).[186] Chapter twenty-seven of the former, 'Of the Communitie and Proprietie of the Seas,' and the whole of the latter provided a reasonably traditional defence of dominion over coastal waters. Hence, Welwood frequently quoted and cited the books of Moses to reject the notion of an original community of property and the esteemed medieval Roman lawyers Baldus and Bartolus to establish respectively the view that 'waters became divisible ... in like manner with the earth' (i.e., by occupation) and that the dominion of 'Princes and people at the sea side' extended for 'an hundred miles of sea forth from their coasts.'[187] However, Welwood's rather brief chapter and treatise did not challenge the freedom of waters beyond the hundred-mile limit nor did he provide more than scanty evidence for the historical exercise of dominion in European waters.

The way lay open for the original version of *Mare Clausum*, which Selden wrote in 1619. It probably attacked the natural-law case for freedom of the seas made in such works as D. Fernandus Vasquius's *Controversiæ Illustres* (Venice, 1564), Alberico Gentili's *De Jure Belli* (London, 1588), and [Grotius's], *Mare Liberum*, and defended British claims over the North Sea with historical evidence. This treatise remained unpublished, however, and has not survived in any manuscript version. When Charles I began to reassert royal sovereignty over the seas surrounding the British Isles and to attempt to license the herring fleets fishing in those waters in the early 1630s, the time seemed auspicious for the publication of a treatise defending maritime dominion. At the time, Selden was beginning to enjoy a limited freedom from his imprisonment in the Tower and probably viewed this project as part of making his peace with King Charles. Although the final version may well have retained much of the gen-

eral format of the earlier treatise, Selden thoroughy revised the theoretical section of *Mare Clausum* and presented additional arguments
and evidence elsewhere. The strong impact of Hugo Grotius's *De Jure
Belli ac Pacis* (Paris, 1625) transformed the early chapters and made
this into the first of Selden's works to reflect and wrestle with the
consequences of the minimalist reinterpretation of natural law carried out by Grotius. To support particular points, Selden also added
arguments from such other recent works as Franciscus de Ingenius's
Epistola de Jurisdictione Venetæ Reipublicæ in Mare Adriaticum
(Geneva, 1619). In addition, the sections on the counts of the Saxon
shore and on Anglo-Saxon and Norman kings reflected the more
sophisticated understanding of late Roman, Anglo-Saxon, and Norman sources displayed in the second edition of *Titles of Honor*
(1631). All of these clearly marked recent additions and revisions to
the original treatise. Where and when other revisions or additions
took place, however, remains largely a matter of conjecture.[188] By
publishing this substantial defence of sovereignty over the sea in theory, and over British waters in particular, Selden intentionally made
a political move for royal favour and offered political advice based
upon archival historical research. What started out as a gift to James
VI and I finally reached print in a strengthened and expanded rendi-
tion as a peace offering dedicated to Charles I.[189]

Although it was published in 1635, much of the format, style, and
marshalling of evidence in the historical portions of *Mare Clausum*
hearkened back to such earlier works as the *The Historie of Tithes*
(1618). Indeed, many similarities united the agendas of these two
treatises. Both used historical evidence to stave off the universalist
pretensions of civil and canon lawyers. Both provided concrete historical illustrations of the theory of law sketched in one of the
lengthy notes to Fortescue's *De Laudibus Legum Angliæ*. The *Historie of Tithes* had expanded a focus on tithes into an interpretation of
the relationship of the law of God and the canon law to the laws of
particular communities, while *Mare Clausum* broadened the history
of British dominion over the surrounding seas into an interpretation
of the relationship of the laws of nature and nations to Roman law
and the laws of particular states. Both offered openly polemical interpretations of controversial topics. Despite these parallels, however,
Mare Clausum contained one substantial difference in format from
the rest of Selden's early treatises; by including an extensive theoretical section on the nature of social relations (with a tight definition of

terms) and highly focusing its analysis and discussion of historical evidence to conform to these definitions, *Mare Clausum* took up the challenge of systematic analysis and organization posed by the treatises of Grotius.

Selden divided *Mare Clausum* into two books, each dealing with a major theme, the first: 'That the Sea, by the Law of Nature or Nations, is not common to all men, but capable of private Dominion or proprietie as well as Land,' and the second 'That the King of *Great Britain* is Lord of the Sea flowing about, as an inseparable and perpetual Appendant of the British Empire.'[190] Book one dealt with the theoretic capability of exercising dominion over the sea and with international practice recognizing this principle. It included eight chapters of introductory and theoretical discussion, eleven chapters on the 'Customs and Constitutions *of the more civilized and more noble* Nations, both antient and modern,' and seven chapters answering various objections from writers who had argued in favour of the communal nature of the sea. Book two employed historical evidence to demonstrate that both Roman officials and the successor rulers of England, Ireland, Scotland, and Wales had exercised an effective lordship over the adjoining seas. It contained thirty-two chapters largely chronologically arranged. In terms of its coverage, the major portion of *Mare Clausum* – forty-three out of fifty-eight chapters – could have appropriately received the title 'A History of Dominion over the Seas, with special reference to those surrounding Europe and the British Isles.' Because it addressed a question openly contested among natural-law writers and after the new approach to natural law taken by Grotius, *Mare Clausum* needed to have a systematically developed theoretical structure. Selden could hardly have hoped to refute Vázquez de Menchaca, Gentili, and Grotius on the basis of history alone. Turning this structural demand into a positive attribute, Selden stressed the interrelationship of theory and evidence by arguing that 'the point of *Law*' (the capability of dominion over the sea) 'hath many things mingled with it, which manifestly arise from matter of *Fact*' (the evidence of dominion exercised over the sea in the past); 'so this of *Fact* comprehends not a few which relate to that of *Law*.'[191] Not only was *Mare Clausum*, in the words of Richard Tuck, 'a deeply Grotian work,' especially in its discussions of natural law, it was also a deeply Gentilian work, especially in its derivation of an international law of the sea from the practice of European states and its concentration of 'modern' history.[192] This stress on theory expressed a shift in focus towards a foundation in the natural-law tradition which would become increasingly evident in later tomes such as John Selden's *De Jure Naturali et Gentium Juxta Disciplinam Ebræorum* (London, 1640).[193]

Definitions of Law and Dominion

In order to undermine arguments in favour of the freedom of the seas, Selden challenged some of the basic interpretations put forward by Vázquez de Menchaca, Gentili, and Grotius. Along with many of the ancients, they had argued that the whole world originally had belonged to everyone, and that occupation of various portions of the land had created property. This Selden accepted, but systematically made the move of applying the principle of occupation to the seas, as well. What he rejected was the basic premise shared by Gentili and Grotius that the sea (like the air) 'is not susceptible of occupation,' but that 'its common use is destined for all men,' and the distinctions made by Gentili between 'dominium,' on the one hand, and 'territorium' and 'jurisdictio,' on the other.[194] Gentili had allowed permitted 'dominium' to extend over the waters adjoining a coast as part of the 'territorium' of a state which included both land and water, but the high seas remained communal and not capable of 'dominium,' only that 'jurisdictio' which permitted the punishment of crimes committed at sea; since 'jurisdictio' included the enforcement of the laws of a particular state and of international law, it included most conceivable crimes on the high seas.[195] Building upon an even firmer stress on the communal nature of the sea in his *Mare Liberum*, Grotius had denied any specific claims of 'dominium,' 'territorium,' and 'jurisdictio' over the sea.[196]

Any attempt to refute the premise of community and the distinction of territory and jurisdiction from dominion had to involve a careful scrutiny of basic terms. Grotius had begun *De Jure Belli ac Pacis* with definitions of 'war' and 'law.' Selden opened *Mare Clausum* with definitions of 'sea' and 'dominion' (which involved 'law'). Providing broad a broad definition of 'sea' did not prove difficult: 'By SEA wee understand the whole Sea, as well the main Ocean or Out-land Seas, as those which are within-land, such as the *Mediterranean, Adriatick, Ægean* or *Levant, British, and Baltick* Seas, or any other of that kinde,' which included the great oceans and contiguous enclosed bodies of water.[197] In contrast, a delineation of the meaning of 'dominion' involved a complicated discussion of 'law' ('*Ius*'); this opened with a basic distinction between the binding and neutral portions of the laws of God and nature. The '*Obligatorie*' or '*Preceptive*' ('*Obligativum*' or '*Præceptivum*') part was 'known by such things as are commanded or forbidden,' while the '*Permissive*' or '*Concessive*' ('*Permissivum*' or '*Concessivum*') part included such actions as 'buying, selling, infranchisement, framing conditions of contract according to the will of the contractors, and many more of the same nature.'[198] Clearly subverting any claim that the laws of God and nature had only a universally binding ('obligatory') character, this opening move also mapped out a wide area (including all matters of property) for those neutral ('permissive') laws instituted by the constitutions, customs, laws, and treaties of and among individual states. Both the binding and neutral portions of natural law could concern either 'mankinde in general, that is all Nations; or not all.'[199] This meant that not even the obligatory laws of God and nature applied universally, and that those which did still needed interpretation and application within the context of the systems of law accepted in or among particular states.

Although paying lip-service to the commonplace that the law 'which relates to the generalitie of mankind, or *all Nations*, is either *Natural* or *Divine*,' Selden could now reject a number of the conclusions traditionally drawn from this premise.[200] Universal natural law was discovered by 'the light of nature or the use of right reason' and made up what the Roman or civil lawyers called the '*Primitive Law of Nations*' ('*Ius Gentium Primævum*'), while the holy Scriptures revealed the law of God.[201] Both involved interpretation and application by human beings who lived in particular societal settings, which opened the enforcement of such laws to human error. Nor was this only a theoretical problem, for Selden had demonstrated in *The Historie of Tithes* that early church fathers had misread the divine laws revealed by the Scriptures and medieval canonists had sometimes deliberately misinterpreted the nature of their binding force and application. Not every aspect of divine or natural law was binding, and both had to be interpreted and supplemented by judges when applied in actual cases under dispute. Although 'reputed by men to be unchangable,' those binding laws of God and nature became enforceable only through what Selden termed '*Additions* or *Inlargements*,' which included the interpretations of judges and commentators. This meant that even the most unchanging and binding laws of

God and nature varied in their enforcement in existing societies. The *'Permissive* Law, whether Natural or Divine' posed fewer problems to Selden's agenda; by the very neutrality of its nature, permissive law changed over space and time to relate to the shifting needs of societies, 'according to the judgment and pleasure of persons in power.'[202] In theory and practice, natural and divine laws that dealt with property came under the same constitutional strictures as any other laws made and interpretated within an individual society.[203]

Selden cleverly employed 'additions' to obligatory law and the normal changes created by societal differences over time and place to permissive law as the means of moving from divine and natural law to the 'positive' laws that governed both particular societies and international relations. Although exclusive to one society or a number of states, positive law (embodied in such forms as customs, statutes, contacts, and treaties) transformed abstract universals into concrete and enforceable laws.

Out of such *Additions* as are made to that is *Obligatorie*, and *Alterations* of that which is *Permissive*, another kinde of *Law* takes its rise, which is of a more narrow Sens and Acceptation, and relates, not to all Nations or the Universalitie of mankinde, but onely to som particulars thereof, and it is ordinarily well termed *Positive* (as beeing positively ordained either by God or men;) Somtimes also it is termed *Civil*, and an Addition of right Reason. This *Positive Law* may bee divided into that which is singular and peculiar to any one particular Nation or Societie ... or into that *which is received by divers Nations*. Again this last is divided into two parts: either into that which *binds divers Nations jointly, equally, and indifferently, by som common obligation*; or els into that which *binds divers Nations or people, not jointly and equally, or by any common obligation, but singly and by Accident*. And of this three-fold kinde of *Positive Law*, wee may call the first the *Law purely Civil*, as it relates to any one particular civil societie. The second the *Common Law of divers Nations*, so named from som common tie or obligation betwixt them. The third the *Law of som* or *divers Nations, Civil* or *Domestick* ... whereby they are bound singly among themselvs, without any obligation to each other in common.[204]

Most existing legal systems fit into the first two categories: 'civil law' (the laws of particular societies) and the 'common law of divers nations' (laws jointly accepted by more than one state); the third, the 'law of some or divers nations, civil or domestic' (international law accepted as binding by a one or more states), opened a place for the exercise of dominion over the sea.

Selden illustrated each of these types with concrete examples. That of *'Civil'* law (*'Ius simpliciter Civile'*) fit the common law of England or the laws of any individual state. The *'Common Law of divers Nations'* (*'Ius plurium Gentium commune'*) was either *'Imperative'* (*'Imperitavum'*), commanded by God or by a human lawmaker, or *'Intervenient'* (*'Interveniens'*), binding by compact or custom. Even the former was imperative only in the recognition of a command by particular societies, for example, as 'when any Nations, in obedience to the *Pope's* Autoritie and command, do alike submit to one and the same Law' (in this case, the canon law), while international treaties and European customary laws best exemplified the negotiated nature of the latter. The reception of Roman law by various European societies provided an outstanding instance of the *'Law of som* or *divers Nations, Civil* or *Domestick'* (*'Ius Gentium aliquot seu Plurium Civile seu Domesticum'*), but the coincidental claims of dominion over the sea made by such states as Venice, Portugal, and England also typified this sort of international law.[205]

This carefully crafted discussion served more than one purpose. The close definition of potentially ambiguous terms increased the coherence of Selden's argument and contributed to debates over the nature of law by helping to separate the law of God from canon law and the law of nature from Roman law. For Selden, canon law commanded on a voluntary basis, that is, only in so far as nations agreed to submit to it 'in obedience to the *Pope's* Authority,' and, therefore, drew its force from the decisions of human lawmakers, not the commands of God. The 'Imperial Law' (*'Jus Cæsareum'*), ironically, no longer held imperative power. In so far as it agreed 'with the Universal Law of Nations, Natural or Divine,' the Roman law become a part of the intervenient *'Primitive Law of Nations,'* but it held no favoured position. In so far as it agreed with 'the Universal Law of Nations,' the common law of England, or the law of any other state, also became part of the intervenient *'Primitive Law of Nations.'* Since a number of societies had accepted the Roman law, however, it also became absorbed into the *'Law of som Nations'* and the *'Civil'* law of particular nations.[206] Canon and Roman law entered any realm only through being integrated into the 'civil' law of that state. This meant that the canon law gained any universality it possessed through consent, and that the Roman law (long accepted as universally imperious by its practitioners) held no status, even by agreement or custom, as a 'common law of divers nations.' This move deftly eliminated canon law from considerations of dominion and deflated Roman law to a status inferior to international treaties and equal to other national laws. By deliberately building the integrationist argument of English common lawyers into the definition of law, Selden clearly attempted to subvert the universalist pretentions of most canon and Roman lawyers.

Having resolved some of the complexities of *jus*, Selden turned to another crucial term *dominium* (dominion), which he defined in societal terms and as either communal or private:

Dominion, which is a Right of Using, Enjoying, Alienating, and free Disposing, is either Common to all men as Possessors without Distinction, or *Private* and peculiar onely to som; that is to say, distributed and set apart by any particular States, Princes, or persons whatsoever, in such a manner that others are excluded, or at least in som sort barred from a Libertie of Use and Enjoiment.[207]

Noting that such ancient pagans as Virgil, Seneca, and Cicero had argued in favour of a community of property in the earliest times (an argument vital for the advocates of freedom of the seas) and that the Bible had seemingly contradicted this assumption by revealing that Adam held a 'universal dominion,' and Noah and his sons 'som universal or common interest in Things' (thus marking private dominion as the original form of propriety), Selden concluded that 'neither the Law Natural nor Divine ... hath expresly commanded or forbidden ... [either] a common enjoiment' or 'a private dominion or possession of the Things of this life.'[208] The mode of which first prevailed made little difference in theory or practice, however, because both divine and natural law remained neutral on the topic of property; for Selden the parcelling of lands and goods derived from a covenant involving the 'consent of the whole bodie or universalitie of mankinde.'[209] As people occupied uninhabited portions of the earth, explicit or implicit contracts created private dominion and made it capable of distribution through allocation or inheritance.[210]

This strong sense of contract was crucial to Selden's argument and also provided a means of joining his definition of *dominium* with his categories of *jus*.

By the introducing of *private Dominion*, in the aforesaid manner, it came to pass, that the same Territorie or Field, whose use before was free for all men alike in Tillage, Building, Pasturage, cutting of wood, gathering of Fruits, egress and regress, was either by distribution or occupation so peculiarly appropriated unto the possessor, that hee might lawfully hinder such a Communitie of use and injoyment, nor might any other man use it lawfully without his permission. And from this Original sprang every Dominion or Proprietie of things, which either by Alienation, or any other kinde of Cession, is transferred upon others, or held by continued possession; respect beeing alwaies had to those particular Forms and Qualifications, which usually relate unto Dominion, either by Law, Custom, or compact, according to the various Institutions of several people: For by these, the free and absolute power of the Proprietor, in what hee enjoies, is lesned and restrained; but when this Reason wholy ceaseth, then what the Proprietor possesseth is so his own, that it cannot lawfully in any wise, without his consent, becom another man's. And all these things are derived from the alteration of that *Universal* or *Natural Law of nations* which is *Permissive*: For thence came in private Dominion or Possession, to wit from the *Positive Law*. But in the mean while it is established by the *Universal Obligatorie Law*, which provides for the due observation of Compacts and Covenants.[211]

The binding character of covenants transformed what may have remained putative occupation into a secure claim of private dominion. Even before the formation of societies, occupiers could establish a preponderant use over particular pieces of land. When people formed societies, they transformed these often implicit agreements into the distinct property laws of particular societies. Solid contracts, then, instituted private dominion and transformed the universal permissive law of nature into the local laws through which particular states governed property.

So far Selden's argument had mentioned only the relatively uncontroversial question of dominion over land. The derivation of dominion from the effective occupation of uninhabited lands had the support of a distinguished company of natural-law scholars. Extension of analogous claims to the sea that into what had become a highly defended barrier; it would take considerable skill for Selden to coordinate the theoretical and historical weapons for his assault upon the argument that the same laws of nature did not apply to the sea that did to the land. The discussion opened by asking whether 'those more antient distributions of Territories' included the seas or whether 'they might not lawfully bee acquired afterwards by Title of occupation' as could vacant lands? To answer this question, Selden argued that the 'Law of divers Nations, Common or Civil' was, 'in matters of this nature ... the best Interpreter of the natural Law which is Permissive.'[212] This move from an abstract obligatory natural law to a concrete permissive natural law recorded in such documents and customs as the Corpus Juris Justiniani, treaties between independent states, and the laws of individual realms transformed a knotty theoretical dispute into a potentially demonstrable historical hypothesis of dominion over the sea: 'if by the Positive Law of Nations, such a Dominion of the Sea, as wee intend, hath been introduced or admitted by the consent of the more famous Ages and Nations; then (I suppose) it will not bee doubted, but that the Seas are, by all manner of Law, every way capable of private Dominion, as is the Land.'[213] Historical practice would answer the theoretical question. What 'the more famous Ages and Nations' had done in the past and continued to do in the present would decide the legitimacy of dominion over the sea.

Having already eliminated any serious intrusion from the imperative laws of God and nature into the question of private dominion as a matter of theory, Selden brought forward evidence in chapter six to prove that the 'Law of God, or the Divine Oracles of holy Scripture' allowed dominion of the sea as a matter of fact.[214] This left for chapter seven the much more contestable argument that 'the natural-Permissive Law ... is to bee derived out of the Customs and Constitutions of the more civilized and more noble Nations, both antient and modern,' an interpretation defended with historical evidence.[215] Because national customs served the interests of distinct societies and suited 'the humor and disposition of the people whom they are to rule,' Selden admitted, the 'right use of humane Reason' in such matters as 'about things Divine or such as relate to Divine Worship' could not 'well bee gathered from the Customs of several Nations.'[216] Restrained in these religious matters by the Scriptures, the 'Law Natural' in merely human issues such as 'the Dominion of Territories' – issues 'wholly grounded upon the consent of men' – was 'rightly determined by the Laws, Placarts, and received Customs of divers Ages and Nations.'[217] The strong consent of Selden's definition of dominion now became revealed in the laws of various historical communities. The alternative to this discovery of the permissive law of nature in the laws of nations was the absurd proposition that the 'more famous Nations' had 'for so many Ages erred against Nature.'[218]

Of course, not even the most erudite scholar could or even needed to consult the laws of all nations. The laws of states without coasts contained little of relevance to the topic and those of the 'uncivilized' peoples had little to add: 'Therefore wee must have recourse here unto the more civilized and more eminent Nations of the past and present Age, and of such whose Customs wee are best acquainted with.'[219] In practice, this meant a relatively limited, but still extensive body of evidence. The 'Testimonies' of lawyers, historians, and 'Leagues and Treaties' from the maritime nations of the ancient Mediterranean and of medieval and early modern Europe, would establish 'what the *Civil Law of Nations* ..., the *Common Law of divers Nations*, and lastly, what the *natural permissive Law* ... hath determined touching private Dominion of the Sea.'[220] Once again, theory resolved into practice.[221]

Ancient and Modern Dominion over European Seas

Having elaborated this theoretical foundation, Selden could now turn to the presentation of historical evidence. Setting aside the 'fabulous' ages for which no reliable evidence existed, he began with: '*The first* Dominion of the Sea *among the* Greeks *in the* Historical age; *that is, the Dominion of King Minos, or the Cretan*,' moved through the ancient Greeks, 'Eastern *Nations*,' Romans, and Byzantines up to such moderns as the Venetians, Portuguese, Spanish, French, Danes, Swedes, and Norwegians; in all of these countries, he argued, claims over the adjoining seas 'hath been received into Custom, as a thing very usual, and agreeable to Law.'[222] Venice provided an excellent example of a modern 'Common-weal' which had defended a theory of maritime sovereignty and had exercised dominion over the Adriatic Sea for centuries. Here Selden relied upon a defence of Venetian claims written by '*Franciscus de Ingenuis*,' who cited such prominent medieval civil lawyers as Bartolus, Baldus, and Angelus to show that

this Sea doth so properly belong to the *Venetians*, that it is not lawful for any other to use or enjoie the same without their permission; forasmuch as they have right to prohibit any to pass, to impose custom upon those whom they permit, to do any other thing in order to the raising of benefit

and advantage out of the water, as any man may do in his proper possessions by Land.[223]

Leaning heavily upon these legal writers, Selden actually offered
little historical evidence to demonstrate the fact of Venetian occupation of the Adriatic.

Moving from such relatively enclosed bodies of water as the Adriatic, Baltic, and Mediterranean, the focus turned to those who
extended claims of dominion over oceans, such as the Portuguese and
some Spanish lawyers.[224] Although the chapter on Scandinavia cited
a number of treaties, it proved an exception; on the whole, Selden
cited very little direct evidence to illustrate these European historical
claims. One of the few explications of a particular law in these chapters cited a decree of the Byzantine emperor Leo, 'by virtue of which
that stale opinion of the communitie of the Sea, beeing utterly cash-
iered, as not agreeing with equitie, that ancient one of the lawfulness
of a possession and private Dominion in the neighboring Sea, backed
with the Autoritie of other eminent Lawyers, was entertained
again.'[225] This served to undermine the interpretation of Ulpian that
Roman law upheld a common ownership of the seas and to lay the
grounds for refuting those modern lawyers who based their arguments for communal ownership of the seas upon the authority of the
Corpus Juris Justiniani.

Objections to Dominion over the Sea

Part one ended with a seven chapters dealing with specific objections
to private dominion over the seas put forward by such writers as
Vázquez de Menchaca, Gentili, and Grotius. By citing the limitations
already placed upon the movements of merchants and mariners by all
European princes, chapter twenty purported to refute the argument
of freedom of passage, without really dealing with the careful distinctions made by Gentili which allowed for such actions within a theory
of freedom of the high seas. That based upon the fluid, ever-changing
nature of water proved more complicated; Selden extended the general recognition of private dominion over rivers, which also consisted
of fluid water, into the plausible reply that

in Substance, Nature, and Name, the Seas, Rivers, and other Bodies of Waters
(so far as concerns the Point in question) are all the same, that whatsoever

may bee said of these, may bee applied in like manner also to the other; save that there may som difference bee alleged onely from the largeness of the one and the narrowness of the other, which in the Point of Dominion (as it relates to Possession) is of no account.

Since the Roman law recognized 'the Dominion and Possession of that space which confines a Hous from the Foundation upward,' this meant it allowed private dominion over the 'whirling Aër,' an element even more mobile than water.[226] This took care of the objection that the fluid nature of air and water made property claims over them inadmissable. As for the supposedly limitless and abundant nature of the sea (a point stressed by Grotius), Selden offered three rebuttals: first, that the surveys which used latitude and longitude to mark the land boundaries of European colonies in America could just as easily apply to the sea; second, that nations had long exercised dominion over waters which produced pearls and coral (as well as over mines in the land); and third, that such maritime resources as fish clearly existed in finite numbers. As well as presenting plausible abstract points, all of these refutations drew upon historical experience, especially European countries, as embodied in laws and treaties.

This left the writings of ancient, medieval, and early modern Roman lawyers as the main surviving obstacle. Although Selden had to admit that many prominent ancient advocates had favoured a communal ownership of the seas, he also managed to find some others who supported private dominion. More troublesome to his argument, however, were the universalist assumptions of those many Roman-law scholars who identified the Justinian as the most complete statement of the law of nature and nations. A passage quoted from Gentili's *De Jure Belli* provided a short summary of the perspective: '*That the Law prescribed in those Books is not the Law onely of a Citie, but even of Nations and nature; and that the whole is so fitted unto nature, that after the Empire was extinct, though the Law was a long time buried; yet it rose again, and spread itself through all the world.*'[227] Gentili and his colleagues went on to argue that those national laws which held other positions offended against reason and justice.

In order to subvert the magnification of the *Corpus Juris Justiniani* into the law of nature and nations, Selden stressed that the decrees and customs in the '*Romane-Germane* Empire it self and other places abroad have extremly altered many things conteined in those Books' and that the kings of Spain and France had prohibited the use of the law of Justinian in their courts of justice. This helped to undermine the universalist pretensions of Roman lawyers. In addition, Selden noted that those early modern European states which had received Roman-law principles and practices had not accepted all portions of the ancient texts as still applicable and, indeed, drew the bulk of their laws from their own customs: 'there are truly som things in the very Law of the Nations of *Europe* (who receiv those Books ... both into their Schools and Courts, so far as the particular Laws of their Kingdoms will permit) I mean in their Law Common, or Intervenient, which are not grounded upon the Law of *Justinian*, but have had their original from Customs quite contrarie thereto.'[228] This meant that local customs integrated and limited the purportedly universal provisions of the *Corpus Juris Justiniani*, not vice versa. Selden's response to the universalist challenge of the Roman lawyers transformed the integrationist argument of the English common lawyers into a coherent theory of law.

Two telling issues established the proposition that medieval and early modern states had actually changed and improved the Roman law: first, the fact that Europeans no longer enslaved prisoners of war, a point which took up 'a Title in the *Digests*'; and, second, the fact that shipwrecks, considered to remain the property of the owners or of the 'First finders' by the *Corpus Juris Justiniani*, now became the property of the prince in England, Brittany, Sicily, and in parts of Italy. To further support the latter point, Selden noted that this law not originated not in 'rude and barbarous Ages,' but was received by 'divers Princes' out of 'the most ancient Maritim Laws of the *Rhodians*.'[229] In addition, evidence showed that Justinian himself may not have practised the principle of freedom of the seas, for Procopius mentioned that the emperor had 'appropriated the *Hellespont* to himself in such a manner, that he would not permit Merchants and Sea-men to enjoy a freedom of that Sea and Ports, but at an extraordinarie rate.'[230] In practice, then, even the Roman emperor whose laws supposedly supported the freedom of the seas had collected dues and exercised dominion over a portion of the sea! Once again, historical practice subverted and limited a purported 'law of nature.'

The appeals to ancient authority made by Gentili and his colleagues allowed Selden to characterize early modern Roman lawyers as having 'pinned their Faith ... upon the sleev of *Ulpian*, or som other such antient Autor.' Anticipating or reflecting that modernist voice used in the preface to the second edition of *Titles of Honor*, he poured scorn upon scholars who relied solely upon the controverted authority of the ancients:

Just in the same manner, as if a man should so discourse upon *Aristotle's* Astronomie, or the opinion of *Thales* touching the Earth's floating, like a Dish in the Sea, and that of the Stoicks of its encompassing the Earth like a Girdle, with that of the Antients concerning an extreme heat under the Equinoctial, and other opinions of that kinde, which are rejected and condemned by the observation and experience of Posteritie ...[231]

The experience and observations of modern Europeans, with astronomy as a model, had modified and made obsolete many of the theories of the ancients and undermined the interpretations based upon them. This applied to law as well as astronomy and seriously subverted the authority the ancients, especially those who favoured an interpretion of the seas as communal. It followed then, that 'the Autoritie of those antient Lawyers beeing removed out of the way, all the determinations of the modern which are supported by it, must be extremely weakned.'[232]

In his detailed attack upon those moderns who defended the community of the seas, Selden dealt mainly with the arguments presented by Ferdinand Vázquez de Menchaca and Hugo Grotius. Vázquez de Menchaca he dismissed as supporting the empirically absurd position that people had always held the seas in common (easily refuted by historical evidence) and the unsound theory that prescriptive law should 'ceas betwixt Foreigners in relation to each other' and not to have a 'place in the Law of Nations.' To sustain the latter position, Vázquez de Menchaca had attempted to limit prescription to what Selden called 'civil law' (the internal laws of individual nations).[233] Since Selden included such European customs as ransom according to rank and the agreement not to enslave Christian prisoners of war among the '*Intervenient Law of Nations*,' he had strong theoretical reasons for resisting this move, but a serious practical reason also stood in the way. By the 'long consent of persons using them' an international customary law of nations had come into existence on a series of issues and 'prescription or antient Custom' had established its provisions. It followed that the attempt of Vázquez de Menchaca 'to deny a Title of prescription wholly among

Princes, is plainly to abrogate the very intervenient Laws of Nations.'[234] Selden could argue with some force that the position advocated by Vázquez de Menchaca clearly would undermine international law as it existed in early modern Europe and, therefore, threatened to create a chaotic situation.

Showing more outward respect for Grotius as 'a man of great learning' from whom he had learned how to organize a treatise on natural law and with whom he shared a general definition of dominion, Selden concentrated upon their agreements and differences as to whether private dominion applied to the sea.[235] Contradictory positions on the freedom of the seas seemed to occur in the works of the Dutch scholar; the *Mare Liberum* appeared to depart from the principle of the community of the sea in several places, while *De Jure Belli ac Pacis*, in its discussion of the 'received Customs of Nations,' allowed private ownership of creeks, rivers, straits, and narrow seas, and 'more than once' mentioned 'the proprietie or private Dominion of the Sea, as a thing somtimes to bee yielded without Controversie.'[236] These criticisms were not unfair; Grotius had made a number of shifts in his position between 1609 and 1625. He would never attack *Mare Clausum*, in part because he was in the employ of Sweden in the 1630s and that country claimed dominion over the Baltic.[237] A slight departure from the principle of freedom of the seas in *De Jure Belli ac Pacis* and the seeming contradictions between theory and practice in both works allowed Selden to mount an effective challenge to the consistency of Grotius's position. Combined with the telling points raised against Vázquez de Menchaca, upon whom Grotius had strongly drawn, these arguments appeared to answer the objections of contemporary critics.

Ancient and Modern British Dominion over the Sea

Having maintained that the sea was 'capable of private Dominion as well as the Land, and that by all kindes of Law, whether wee seriously consider the *Divine*, or *Natural*, or any *Law of Nations* whatsoever,' Selden turned to the longest portion of his book, the demonstration with historical evidence that successive rulers of portions of the British Isles had enjoyed varying degrees of dominion over the surrounding seas:

from all Antiquitie, down to our times without interruption, that those, who by reason of so frequent alterations of the State of Affairs have reigned here, whether *Britains, Romans, Saxons, Danes,* and *Normans,* and so the following Kings (each one according to the various latitude of his Empire) have enjoied the Dominion of the Sea by perpetual occupation, that is to say, by using and enjoying it as their own after a peculiar manner, as an undoubted portion either of the whole bodie of the estate of the *British* Empire, or of som part thereof, according to the state and condition of such as have ruled it; or as an inseparable appendant of this Land.[238]

The bodies of water under examination included the '*British* Sea' between Britain and France, Aquitaine, and northern Spain; the North Sea up to Iceland and west to an unknown degree; the '*German* Sea' between Britain, Germany, and Scandinavia; and the British sea to the west of England, Scotland, and Ireland, with the waters between England and the Low Countries and France receiving the greatest attention.

The Britons and Romans

The writings of such ancient historians as Caesar and Tacitus contained 'clear passages' showing that the ancient Britons had claimed 'Ownership and Dominion of the Sea flowing about them, especially of the South and East part of it, as a perpetual Appendant of the Soveraigntie of the Island.' Not disdainful of these 'ancient testimonies,' Selden placed more confidence, however, in 'the continued and more certain usage and Custom of later times' as revealed in the records of the kings of Anglo-Saxon, Norman, medieval, and early modern England.[239] The account of the petty kings of ancient Britain reflected that in the *Jani Anglorum* and showed why a single dominion did not exist over the surrounding seas until after the Roman Conquest. Although noting that Caesar reported that the ancient Britons exerted some dominion over the sea from small boats made out of twigs and ox hides, Selden critically discussed the partiality of early Roman accounts and conjectured that the Britons probably had oaken vessels like those ascribed to the continental *Veneti* by Caesar.[240] Their rule came to an end with the Roman conquest of much of Britain.

The defence of Britain by sea during the last years of the Empire received the greatest attention in the section on Roman dominion. Selden drew upon mature Continental and English scholarship on the fourth and fifth centuries (probably carried out originally for the second edition of *Titles of Honor*) to document the sovereignty wielded over the seas to the south and east of Roman Britain by the '*Count of the* Saxon *Shore.*' Unlike most other late Roman counts or Dukes who held command over a limited district or a province, this official commanded the sea from shore to shore through 'Garrisons and Fortifications placed upon the South and Eastern Shore of *Britain.*'[241] The testimony such ancient geographers and historians as Ptolemy, Marcianus Heracleotes, and Zosimus confirmed the maritime nature of the office:

[The] Territorie or Province subject to this particular *Dignitie* or Command, reached through the very *British* Sea, from the Shore of *Britain* to the Shores on the other side of the Sea, or those which lie over against our Isle of *Britain*, in *France*, the *Low Countries*, *Holland*, and *Denmark*; so that what Sea or Islands soever lay between near the *British* Shore, appertained all to the Command of the aforesaid *Count*, as to the charge of an Admiral belonging to a Province or Territorie.[242]

With his seats in 'either of those Garrisons, Towns, or nine Maritim Cities ... seated upon the Shores of *Sussex*, *Kent*, *Essex*, and *Norfolk*,' identified in *Mare Clausum* by their Roman and English names, the count of the Saxon shore commanded a fleet which patrolled the adjacent seas.[243]

Earlier scholars had mistakenly identified the command of the count of the Saxon shore not with the sea itself, but either with a portion of the coast of Britain guarded by the Saxons invited over by Vortigern or with the shores on both sides of the sea from Britain to Denmark to France. Since the office existed as early as A.D. 370, long before the arrival of the Saxons in England, Selden easily refuted the first of these interpretations. The second – which had garnered support from such eminent scholars as Abraham Ortelius and William Camden – demanded considerable discussion and a careful sifting of evidence from Ammianus Marcellinus, Gregory of Tours, the late Roman *Brevarie of Dignities*, and coins from the reign of Antoninus Pius (which 'signified that *Britain* had Dominion over the sea about it, and the *Roman* Emperor over *Britain*') in order to establish this new interpretation.[244] Once established, however, the maritime rule of the count of the Saxon shore served both to demonstrate the exercise of Roman dominion over the waters to the east and south of Britain and to provide a firm precedent for later royal claims of sovereignty over the same seas.

The Saxon and Danish Kings

With the collapse of Roman power, the 'Southern *Britains*' invited the Anglo-Saxons 'to assist them against the *Scots* and *Picts*' and 'at length' these European warriors 'got the whole Power here into their own hands,' replaced the Romans as rulers over southern Britain and lords of the 'British Sea.' The Saxons established seven kingdoms with one pre-eminent monarch over the whole: 'And so in that famous Heptarchie of theirs, the Kingdom was ever accounted of in such a manner, that even before the time of King *Egbert*, it was under the Power of som one King, which all the rest acknowledged as Supreme ... Questionless, they both had a Dominion by Sea conjoined with that upon Land.'[245] Since the Saxons possessed an 'admirable ... acquaintance with the Sea and Sea-affairs,' including a sophisticated knowledge of tides, it hardly seemed surprising that they asserted their power over the adjoining seas 'newly deserted by the *Roman* Navie.'[246] Indeed, the '*English-Saxons*' and their successors, the Danes, raised considerable naval forces and revenue for the protection of the seas.

Evidence from such medieval historians as William of Malmesbury, Henry of Huntingdon, and Roger Hoveden established the large size of the rowing-ships built by King Alfred; even better, an Anglo-Saxon chronicle for A.D. 897 proved that these ships had sixty or more oars. Various Cottonian manuscripts and Domesday Book showed that the holders of hides were 'rated proportionably' towards the building of warships, a fleet estimated by Selden to number 785 ships. Medieval historians, several Anglo-Saxon chronicles, and the Dialogue of the Exchequer detailed the payment of Danegeld from the days to the Saxons until 'the name of *Danegeld* grew out of use' in 'the Reign of King *Henrie* the second.'[247] Domesday Book also provided examples of military service at sea and monetary payments in lieu of service provided by towns under the Anglo-Saxons.[248] As to the extent of this dominion, King Edgar's title, '*Soveraign Lord of all* Albion, *and of the Maritim or Insular Kings inhabiting round about*,' extended to all the kingdoms 'in the *British* Sea,' and a charter in Worcester Cathedral demonstrated that it extended as far north as Norway and incorporated the greater part of Ireland. Other reliable evidence showed that Cnut and other kings of England exercised similar dominion.[249] All of this added up to a sophisticated case for the systematic organization of naval defence and for the exercise of sovereignty over the surrounding seas under the Anglo-Saxon and Danish kings of England. Most probably, Selden had drawn upon his recent researches into the late Roman Empire and his newly found mastery of Anglo-Saxon and early Norman sources to put together these portions of *Mare Clausum*.

The Admirals of the English Sea

Having established the principle of dominion over the sea as historical 'fact' in his chapters on the Romans, Anglo-Saxons, and Danes, Selden could treat the six centuries from the Norman Conquest forward as a discrete period. In order to establish the continuing nature of English sovereignty over the British Sea, *Mare Clausum* discussed the admirals of the English Sea, dominion over islands near the French shore, the '*Libertie of Fishing* therein allowed upon courtesie to Foreiners and Neighbors and the *Protection* given to Fisher-men,' the 'Proscribing of *Laws* and *Limits* to *Foreiners*,' the acceptance such claims in the records of English kings and parliaments, and the testimony of the '*Commentaries of the Law of the Land, and common customs of the Nation,* which do either assert or at least allow such a Dominion.'[250] Each of these topics filled at least one chapter and involved considerable interpretation of historical evidence, much of it from manuscripts.

Copious sources from contemporary 'publick Records and Histories' demonstrated that the 'Guard or Government instituted for the defence and guarding of the Sea' by Anglo-Saxon kings survived after the Norman Conquest.[251] Domesday Book provided proof of the existence of such a guard under the late Saxon kings, while both Florence of Worcester and Roger Hoveden mentioned that Henry I '*gave order to his* Butsecarli *to guard the Sea*,' drawing once again upon his improved knowledge of Anglo-Saxon, Selden equated these with '*Butescarles,* in the old English Language,' who were 'Officers belonging to the Navie, or Sea-souldiers, as *Hutesecarli,* were Domestick Servants or Officers in Court.'[252] Lamenting the loss of public records which would have documented such officers from 'betwixt the coming in of the *Normans,* and the Reign of K. *John,*' Selden rejoiced that manuscripts survived from the reign of Henry III to record the appointment of Thomas de Moleton as '*Captain and Guardian of the Sea*' of the Eastern Shore and Hugh de Crequer as '*Warden of the Cinque-ports and of the Sea of those parts*' and from the patent rolls of Edward I, Edward II, Edward III, Richard II, Henry IV, Henry V, and Henry VI to demonstrate that 'the title of Guardians or Wardens very often changed into that of Admirals' in later centuries.[253] Since a philological examination of the language of command employed in thirteenth and fourteenth centuries revealed that the terms 'guardian' and 'keeper' of the sea were frequently applied to what later came to be styled the '*Governors, Keepers* or *Captains*' of such territories as the Islands of Jersey and Guernsey, as well as to other more general offices, Selden argued that the Kings of England evidently used the same terms for custody over the sea as for provinces on land.[254] The step from the fifteenth to the seventeenth century took little effort; during this period 'the Universal Custodie of the Sea ... was committed by our Kings to the *high Admirals of England*' who commanded the surrounding seas in person or through deputies.[255] Although practice varied somewhat over the centuries, a lengthy quotation from the commission of great or high admiral granted to the Earl of Warwick in the reign of Edward VI served to establish the general nature of this command.

Some of the most significant evidence for the means of extending dominion over the seas came from the '*Tributes* or *Customs* that were wont to bee imposed, paid, and demanded, for the *Guard of the English Sea*' after the Norman Conquest.[256] The levying of Danegeld continued into the reign of King Stephen, as shown in the comments of medieval historians and the early accounts in the Exchequer. Eventually other means of providing revenue and supplies, such parliamentary subsidies (cited from the reign of Edward III) and parliamentary grants of customs (cited from the reign of Richard II), came to replace Danegeld. Citing the published *Acts of Parliament*, Selden concluded that

wee very often finde it, as a thing asserted by the Estates of the Realm in Parliament, that the Kings of *England* have time out of minde, by autoritie of Parlament, taken large sums of monie, by way of Subsidie or Custom, upon Merchandise either imported or exported, *For the defence of the Realm, and the keeping and saufegard of the Seas, for the entercourse of Merchandise safely to come into and to pass out of the same* (which is the usual form of words).[257]

Numerous acts and actions of parliaments, including the accusation of William de la Pole, Duke of Suffolk, for converting 'Subsidie monie' voted '*For the Defence and tuycion and saife keeping of the Sea*' to 'other uses' during the reign of Henry VI, subsidies voted '*For the defence of the Realm, and the keeping and saufegard of the Seas*' from the reigns of Edward VI, Mary, Elizabeth I, and James I, and statutes of tonnage and poundage passed in a number of reigns, demonstrated that the defence of the realm included not just the land, but the sea as well.[258]

Citing the letters patent which commissioned the admirals of England with command over the seas adjoining the 'Western, Southern, and Northern Coasts,' Selden noted that the early title of '*Guardian of the Sea* ("*Custodes Maris*"), was taken from the Sea it self, whereof he was Governor as of a Province.' The 'Catalogue' of such officers 'set down by that eminent man Sir *Henrie Spelman* in his Glossarie' provided considerable evidence of the continuity of this command.[259] From the reign of Henry IV onward, one man was 'appointed Admiral not onley of the Fleets or Navies, but of *England and Ireland* ... yea and in express words also Admiral of *Aquitain* and *Picardie*.'[260] Specific examples demonstrated the genesis of this form of commission, which lasted into the reign of Henry VIII, who added the terms '*Calais and the Marches thereof*' to the command of admirals, a change still included in patents from the reign of Charles I.[261] Marking the geographical borders of English claims, these additions represented more than the historical exercise of jurisdiction by the admirals of England over the 'Courts of Admiraltie in those Provinces.' Just as the names of England, Wales, and Ireland served to indicate the limits 'on this side of the Sea,' Selden argued, so the additions of Aquitaine, Gascony, and Picardy marked the limits on the other side.[262] An analogy between of the command of the admirals of England with that of the Roman count of the Saxon shore helped to define the extent of these boundaries:

Therefore as in that Roman dignitie of the *Count of the Saxon shore throughout Britain*, the shore was the transmarine bound or limit of that dignitie, so also in the Command of the high Admiral of *England* (so far onely as hee hath a Province or Jurisdiction by Sea, as a Governor of a Territorie) those opposite shores or transmarine Provinces, named in his Commission, are to bee reckoned the Bounds of the Sea under his Charge or Protection.[263]

The exercise of maritime dominion meant that, even after the French drove the English out of the land portions of Aquitaine, Gascony, and Normandy, the kings of England could continue to command the adjoining seas and rightfully retain the names of these provinces in their commissions.

A lack of evidence that the kings of France had seriously challenged the exercise of English sovereignty over the seas off their coasts only strengthened the claims derived from English sources. True to his strictures about proper historical method, Selden had based his interpretation upon his reading of 'the antient publick Records of those times.'[264] His search of the Admiralty commissions of the kings of France from the same period, starting with officers appointed by Charlemagne, moving through the medieval dispersion of sovereignty to powerful provinces, and on to the revival of royal power in the later Middle Ages, revealed that they had never claimed jurisdiction over the seas flowing between France and England. Any honest historian observing the 'deep silence of antient Testimonies, touching such a kind of Dominion among the French,' the weakness of the French Crown for so many centuries, the 'most ample Power alwaies exercised throughout the Sea and the shore lying about it, under the sole command of the English,' and 'the late addition of the Sea-Coast to the Kingdom of *France*,' Selden argued, could only reach the conclusion that no such jurisdiction had existed.[265] The continued dominion of the kings of England over the Channel Isles of Jersey, Guernsey, and Aureney, which 'though they used different Customs, constitute one entire Bodie of Empire with the Kingdom of *England*,' served to strengthen the point.[266]

Foreign Recognition of English Dominion

English Imperial dominion over these seas had not gone unrecognized. Considerable evidence existed to demonstrate that, at least from the time of Edward II forward, the kings of England had issued passports to the subjects of other realms 'for leav to pass through this Sea' with

innumerable other Letters of Passport (called *safe Conducts*) in the Records, especially of *Henrie* the fift and sixt, whereby safe Port and Passage was usually granted *as well by Sea as by Land and Rivers* ... And it is worthy of observation, that this kinde of Letters were usually superscribed and directed by our Kings to their Governors of the Sea, Admirals, Vice-Admirals, Sea-Captains, to wit, the Commanders appointed by the King to take care of his Territorie by Sea ...[267]

Such recognition of English rule over the Channel continued into the late sixteenth and early seventeenth centuries. During the recent wars with Spain, 'the Kings both of *Denmark* and *Sweden*, together with the *Hans Towns*, very often and earnestly begged of Queen *Elizabeth*, that they might have free passage through the English Sea with Provisions towards *Spain*,' but she had denied these requests and the English had seized Hansiatic ships accused of transporting necessities to the enemy.[268] Although Gentili and Grotius had argued that, according to the law of nations, a neutral ship made a neutral cargo, Elizabeth I had insisted that even neutrals could not transport 'Warlike Necessaries and Corn' to Spain without danger of reprisal, a practice with firm precedents from as early as the passports issued by Edward I during his war with France.[269] A similar exercise of dominion also applied to the licences granted to foreigners to fish in English waters – for example, those granted to Dutch herring fishermen by Elizabeth I and James I (a highly contested issue not treated as such by Selden) – and to the letters of safe passage to citizens of the United Provinces and subjects of the King of Spain after the peace of 1604.[270] If the granting and refusal of passports to foreigners furnished at least a tacit recognition of the '*Sea-Dominion of the Kings of* England,' more active proofs came from the actions of naval officers commissioned by various rulers and states, not least by 'the usual striking of the Top-sails, by every Ship of any Forein Nation whatsoever, if they sail near the King's Navie or any Ship belonging to the same Navie in the Sea,' a recognition traced back to the reign of Edward I.[271]

Recognition of Royal Maritime Dominion by English Parliaments

In making his case for English ownership of the surrounding seas, Selden had cited many legal and parliamentary records. Now he turned to a specific discussion of the recognition of royal dominion over the seas by parliaments and the common law. To combine the delicate themes of royal sovereignty over the sea argued so strongly throughout the *Mare Clausum* with the constitutional position of mixed monarchy that he had defended in print and speech since 1610 took both interpretative care and scholarly expertise. The discussion

of a 'notable Testimonie touching this business in the Parliament-
Records of *Henrie* the Fifth' brought forth a remarkable passage
which provided a technical explanation of why a petition from the
Commons which had received a royal answer must have been a bill:

For, most certain it is, that, according to Custom, no Answer is given either
by the King or in the King's name, to any Parliamentarie Bills, before that the
Bill, whether it bee brought in first by the Lords or by the Commons, hath
passed both Houses, as it is known to all that are verst in the Affairs and
Records of Parliament. And when the name of either of them is left out in
the draught of the Bill, (as the Lords in that before alleged) it was wont to bee
supplied, as it is also at this day, by the brief form of Assent, which is added
by that House, to whom the Bill is sent and transmitted. For, that Hous
which first prefers it, transmits it to the other, who either gives an assent, or
rejects it. And when both Houses have so given their assent, then after a
while, either the King gives his assent (whereby it becomes an Act or Law) or
els hee laies it aside, and (as I have alreadie shewn) takes time to advise;
Neither of which is ever don by the King, according to the cours of Parlament, till both Lords and Commons have given their assent. But the whole
form of the afore-mentioned Bill, which is full of all kinde of storie concerning things transacted in Parlament, is taken out of the very Schedules
annexed to the Bill, (wherein the Forms of this kinde of assent were wont
expressly to bee added) and registered according to antient Custom, among
the Records of Parliament, in the very same words wherein it was at first
exhibited; no express mention beeing made of the assent both of Lords and
Commons which is annexed to the Body of the Form ... and the Kings assent
onely or intent of deliberation beeing added by way of subscription, as I have
shewn. But most of those Schedules annexed to that kinde of Bills which
relate to the more antient times are lost; whereas notwithstanding the
Records wherein they were wont to be registered have been carefully preserved in the *Tower* for above CCC years.[272]

Only a thorough understanding of procedure and of the records of
Parliament could have produced such an outline of the technicalities
of English parliamentary procedure. Few if any contemporaries had
the expertise to dispute what we would now see as Selden's faulty
interpretation of medieval parliamentary petitions. Indeed, his considerable knowledge of parliamentary records and procedure had
helped to empower Selden during his career in the Commons in the
1620s. In this context, however, this expertise served to underline

the crucial necessary role of parliaments in the making and modification of English law.

Selden argued that this document contained three important messages about the nature of dominion over the waters between England and France; the first of these more than touched on the nature of the English constitution.

First, that the Estates in Parlament, according to the Custom of their Ancestors, that is to say, both Houses of Lords and Commons, beeing well-informed of the matter perhaps from som antient Testimonies whereof wee are bereft by the injurie of time, did with one consent affirm it as a thing unquestionable, that the King of *England* is Lord of the Sea ...[273]

The assumption that the 'Houses' of Parliament had drawn upon 'ancient Testimonies' appeared nowhere in the document, but the conclusion that the 'Estates in Parlament' recognized and did not confer royal sovereignty over the seas followed the source more closely. The second message underlined one of the major interpretations of the *Mare Clausum*, that dominion extended from coast to coast: '*Secondly*, that the Sea whereof they speak is the whole that flows between *France* and *England*,' including '*the Coasts* or *Shores on both sides of the Sea* ...' The third, by reserving the authority for taxation to Parliament, revealed a crucial limit to unaided royal power:

Thirdly, that those *Estates* did not question but that Tributes might bee imposed by autoritie of Parlament, upon all strangers whatsoever, wheresoever they pass through this Sea; as well as Customs in Port; And that they did not at all conceiv, that a Bill ought to bee presented touching that business unto the King, as hee was at that time King of *France*, but onely as King of *England*, that is, as Lord of the whole Sea flowing between.

Although sovereignty over the seas between England and France pertained to the royal prerogative, taxation of subjects and strangers alike belonged to the 'autoritie of Parliament.' Stressing the ever responsible behaviour of members of Parliament throughout this section (hardly an uncontentious issue after the session of 1629), Selden also noted both the deliberative nature of this bill and the fact that it applied to 'a place that was not subject, as a part of the Roial patrimonie, to the King of *England*, as King of *England*.'[274] This meant that English parliaments exercised an imperial sovereignty, as well.

Not without some seeming irony for a supporter of mixed monarchy, the very next passage used the ship money writs recently issued by Charles I as another valid example of assertion and recognition of royal sovereignty over these seas:

From hence it was also, that our present King *Charls* did this last year declare, *that himself and his progenitors the Kings of* England *have in all times hitherto, by and antient and most just title, been Lords of this Sea;* to wit, in his Letters Patents sent to the Maritim Counties of *England*, whereby ship-monie was imposed for the defence of his Dominion by Sea.[275]

However, Selden did not argue in favour of ship money here, nor did he challenge parliamentary control over taxation; he merely supported the royal claim of dominion made in the writ of October 1634. This writ applied only to ports and maritime counties, as accorded with precedent, and therefore posed few or no constitutional problems. Throughout this portion of *Mare Clausum*, Selden carefully avoided the contested question of impositions or, indeed, any claims to collect duties by royal prerogative alone. The evidence from the reigns of the late Anglo-Saxon, Danish, and early Norman kings of England – especially in their collection of Danegeld – could have supported such claims, but Selden refrained from making that argument.[276] Nor could such early precedents still hold. As the account explicitly noted, since the reigns of Edward III and Richard II at the latest, parliamentary taxes had replaced earlier general levies such as Danegeld and had secured the principle of parliamentary control of general taxation over the neighbouring seas. Parliamentary recognition of this aspect of royal sovereignty posed no threat to England's mixed monarchy.

Recognition of Royal Maritime Dominion
by the English Common Law

Having dealt specifically with parliamentary recognition of royal dominion over the sea, Selden turned to the 'Law-Books, and the received Customs therein, which prove it from the most antient times.'[277] These posed some serious problems, since early treatises on the common law, especially that by Henry Bracton, followed the Roman-law argument that the sea was held in common in accord with the law of nature:

Which wee find likewise in som other of our Law-Books of that Age, as a passage that fell from som Writers (of whom I spake at large in the former Book) that were more affected than was meet with the words of *Ulpian* and *Justinian*, in the general division of things. But these very men in other places, shewing the Customs of our Countrie, do sufficiently admit the King's Dominion by Sea.[278]

Selden countered this general theory by a technical discussion showing that the same common-law treatises accepted royal dominion over the sea, especially in sections dealing with '*Pourprestures*,' those procedures 'whereby detriment is done to any publick place belonging to the Patrimonie of the Crown, as a publick thorow-fare, a River, and the like' which applied equally to the inclosure or possession of 'any kinde of salt-waters' by 'any subject.'[279] In addition, a ruling of the 'whole Bench of Judges' made in the reign of Edward III, traced back '*the antient superioritie of the Sea*' to laws '*interpreted, declared, and published in the Isle of* Oleron' in France by Richard I. This codification 'declared as a thing most received and certain, that the King of *England* hath, by antient right, been Lord of the Sea, of the same name, or that which flows about it,' that is, the English sea and provided further support for Selden's interpretation.[280]

Several technicalities of the common law also demonstrated a general recognition of English Imperial dominion over portions of the sea. For example, fines levied by common-law courts did not jeopardize people outside of the country, but did recognize that people within the kingdom included those

within the four Seas, to wit, the Southern, Western, Eastern, and that Northern Sea which washeth both the sides of that neck of Land whereby *Scotland* is united to *England*. That is to say, within the outmost bounds of the *English* Empire in those four Seas, or within the opposite Shores of the Eastern and Southern Sea or Ports belonging to other princes, and within the bounds of the Northern and Western Sea ..., that is, according to the extent of possession West-ward beyond the Western Shores of *Ireland*, and by the first beginning of that Sea, which is of the Scotish name and jurisdiction.[281]

This passage also spelled out some of the geographical limits of English rule which would be discussed at greater length in the last chapters of *Mare Clausum*. Related to this legal definition of '*within the four seas*' was the temporal excuse or '*Essoin ... de ultra Mare*' that a defendant could not appear in court when summoned because he lived 'beyond the Seas, belonging to the English Empire,' which applied to Ireland as well as France or Spain.[282] Similar procedures were applied in the Court of Admiralty for dealing with a person accused of a capital crime at sea:

In the antient Records also concerning the Customs of our Court of Admiraltie, wee read it was an usual Custom in the time of King *Henrie* the first (who died *Anno Dom.* MCXXXVI.[1136]) and of other Kings both before and after him, That, if any man accused of a capital crime don by Sea, beeing publickly called five times by the voice of the Crier, (after so many several daies assigned) did not make his appearance in the Court of Admiraltie, hee was banished out of *England* and *de mer appurtenant au Roy d'Angleterre*, or out of the Sea belonging to the King of England, for fourtie years, more or less, according to the pleasure of the Admiral.[283]

All of these customs and procedures, including the provision that jurisdiction over 'this Sea-Province' belonging by 'antient recieved Custom, to the high Admiral, or his Deputies,' demonstrated how the common law had dealt with the royal exercise of maritime dominion.

Despite the arguments of Bracton and John Cowell in favour of 'that antient communitie of the Sea, and of Fishing also in Rivers, according to the Books of *Justinian*; as if such a kind of communitie were admitted in our Law,' the weight of evidence, including the procedures of the common law, pointed to the opposite conclusion. 'So that at length it is manifest, that the Sea-Dominion of the King of *England*, is without controversie admitted and asserted also, both by the Determinations and Customs of the Law of the Land, and by the express words of the Writs and Forms of the Actions themselvs.'[284] As with the bills and acts of Parliament, the 'Determinations' of judges and 'Customs,' which, together with statutes, made up the common law of the land, firmly recognized and provided means for enforcing the maritime dominion of the kings of England.

British Dominion over the Western and Northern Seas

Having devoted some twenty-nine chapters to demonstrating the dominion of the kings of England over 'the *English* or *British* Sea' which lay primarily to the east or south of the island, Selden alloted a mere three chapters to a historical demonstration of the *'Dominion of the King of Great Britain'* over the Irish, western, Scottish, and North seas.[285] The change in terminology from the kings of England to the king of Great Britain marked the shift in historical perspective and documents. Stressing their geographical unity, Selden argued that Great Britain, Ireland, and all of the neighbouring islands were called British: 'just as if the narrow Seas flowing between, like Rivers or turnings of Rivers, did disjoin those Banks or Shores from great *Britain,* as *Fragments* of the same. Whereby it appears, that the narrow Seas themselvs with the Isles, even as Rivers with their Banks, are to bee reckoned a part of the *British* Territorie.'[286] This comparison of the waters between the British Isles to rivers extended the well-known Roman-law recognition of dominion over inland waters by analogy into the seas between islands. This was a clever move, but, historically, the issue was more problematic. In 'the latter time of the *Anglo-Saxon* Empire, the *Norwegians* or *Danes'* had 'seized both' the Isle of Man 'and the *Hebrides,* and held them almost two hundred years,' during which time the king of Man had often exercised dominion over the Irish Sea.[287] During the reigns of Henry II and John, however, 'when *Ireland* was subdued' and *'Reginald* King of *Man'* conquered by King John, 'there is no reason at all to doubt, but that the neighboring Sea round about was taken also into the Dominion of the *English.'* Shortly thereafter, 'Alexander the Third, King of *Scots,'* drove the Norwegians out of the Hebrides and, henceforth, the kings of Scotland 'enjoied the Northern part of this *Western* Sea.'[288] On the grounds of continual exercise of dominion for four centuries, Selden concluded that these western islands and seas 'ought now also to bee accounted the antient Patrimonie of the King of *great Britain.'*[289]

To the west of Ireland washed the North Atlantic, a huge body of water over which to exercise effective sovereignty. Here, Selden confined himself to dominion by the 'King of *Great Britain'* over 'a verie large extent upon the Shore of *America.'* The English claim to Newfoundland derived from its discovery by *'Sebastian Chabot,* in the time of *Henrie* the Seventh'; during the reign of Elizabeth I, Sir Humphrey Gilbert reinforced English sovereignty there. Since Selden confessed that he had 'as yet made but little enquirie' about: 'How far our *English* Colonies lately transported into *America,* have possessed themselvs of the Sea there' and continual possession of portions of the North American coast had started only very recently, he defended this dominion on the grounds that the same principles that applied to the occupation of land – namely, that those taking posses-sion of a field needed only '*enter any part of that Field*' to obtain the whole and that those entering unoccupied land not only occupied as much as they could till, '*but they reserved as much as they were in hope they might bee able to till.*'[290] So stretched, the kings of England could lay claim to the western sea from the coast of Ireland to that of North America.

To the north of Britain, the sovereignty claimed by the monarchs of England and Scotland conflicted with that exercised continually by the the kings of Norway and Denmark over such islands as Ice-land, the Faeroes, Shetlands, and Orkneys and the adjoining sea. Since all of these realms normally supported the principle of domin-ion over the sea and tried to remain on friendly terms with each other on these matters (Selden virtually ignored the wars between England and Scotland throughout this treatise), their disputes and treaties dealt with conflicting interpretions of rights and boundaries. On the basis of the evidence presented by William Welwood, Selden argued that the kings of Scotland had long levied duties on the fisher-men of all nations (and especially those from the Netherlands) and, thereby, exercised an effective dominion over the waters off the coast of Scotland. Although the kings of Norway and Denmark had long possessed the Orkneys and Shetland, and the 'people of the *Orcades* speak the *Gothish* Language to this day,' these island had come into the possession of the kings of Scotland in lieu of the dowery of '*Ladie* Margarite *daughter of the King of* Denmark,' who married '*James the third, King of Scotland*,' in 1468.[291] This treaty and that negotiating the marriage of James VI to Anne of Denmark confirmed the rule of the kings of Scotland over this portion of the North Sea.

The 'main and open Sea of the North' remained a different matter. Although Gentili had argued that it belonged to the '*King of* Great Britain' and an Icelandic bishop had lent some support, the Kings of Denmark stoutly denied any such claim and, instead, 'this more Northerly Sea which belongs to *Island*, they challenge to themselvs, as they are Kings of *Norway*, and that by antient right.'[292] In other words, the kings of Denmark had inherited their sovereignty over Iceland, Greenland, and the surrounding seas as successors to the kings of Norway. Although various treaties between the monarchs of Denmark and England from the fifteenth, sixteenth, and seventeenth centuries governed English rights to trade in the North Sea ports of the Dano-Norwegian monarchy, Queen Elizabeth I had refused to abandon English rights to fish freely in the waters off Iceland.[293] Selden also supported the English whale fishery off the coast of Greenland on the familiar grounds of the discovery and possession of unoccupied territory and made a key restatement of this principle:

The use of a Sea never entered by Occupation and such a kinde of profit bee-ing first discovered doth according to the manner of the claim, give a Domin-ion to the discoverer who claims it in the name of another (as here in the name of the Soveraign of *England*) as well by a corporal as intentional posses-sion, no otherwise than doth the first both natural and civil possession of any other things whatsoever that were never yet possessed.[294]

Appropriately this statement stood near the end of the book as a summary of the argument it presented. The universal application of the principle of effective occupation, normally confined to possession of the land, had formed the most effective theoretical foundation for Selden's historical demonstration of the dominion exercised by suc-cessive rulers of Britain from the times of the Romans to the reign of Charles I. Although ending on an ironic note by quoting a poem of Grotius which celebrated the accession of James I to the English throne and recognized his lordship over the seas surrounding Britain, *Mare Clausum* closed as it had opened, by carefully combining argu-ments based on natural-law theory and history into a powerful case for royal sovereignty over the seas surrounding Britain.

Concluding Remarks on *Mare Clausum*

At its most obvious, *Mare Clausum* presented a well-organized and well-argued lawyer's brief justifying before an international audience the principle of dominion over the high seas and the historical exer-cise of dominion over the adjoining seas by the rulers of Britain. Both echoing and challenging arguments presented in earlier European treatises, Selden articulated what became a classic statement of one extreme of the ongoing dispute over the nature of maritime gover-nance. Both in its theoretical statements and its historical accounts, *Mare Clausum* also made a significant move in the continuing debate between customary and Roman lawyers over the nature of law and the relationship of 'municipal' laws to the laws of God and nature. In order to demonstrate that English common law permitted and supported royal dominion over the seas and that the kings of England had exercised an effective power over the seas flowing from their island to the opposite shores, Selden drew upon a sophisticated historical method and portions of his deeply technical legal historical learning. Reaching an international audience of jurists, however, necessarily involved writing in Latin and moving more thoroughly into the discourse of natural law than was normal in Selden's works on medieval and early modern Europe. The tight definitions of dominion and of the laws of God, nature, nations, and individual realms offered in the early chapters of *Mare Clausum* built upon the natural-law discourse of Grotius to enforce closure on the competing interpretation of freedom of the seas and to undermine the universalist pretensions of Roman judicature. In order to meet potential arguments based upon the positions of Vázquez de Menchaca, Gentili, Grotius, and even Welwood, Selden presented a reasonably coherent theory of law and society based largely upon binding contracts which articulated universalist claims not at all dissimilar in scope to those contained in Grotius's *De Jure Belli ac Pacis*. This marked the first great impact of the arguments of Grotius on the nature of property, governance, and international relations on Selden's publications. Despite the importance of this foray into theory, when it came to constructing an enforceable system of natural law, Selden built more upon the existing laws of 'Civilized nations,' both ancient and modern, than upon abstract, 'self-evident' universal principles.[295] Hence, even book one of *Mare Clausum* often supported its interpretations with historical evidence.

Book two of *Mare Clausum* – by far the longest portion of the text – provided a historical account based upon a variety of primary sources from public and private collections to establish the continuous existence of British dominion, especially over the seas between England and France from ancient times to the present. Sections of this history, especially the chapters on the counts of the Saxon shore and on the Anglo-Saxon and early Norman kings, displayed the sophisticated grasp of ancient and medieval sources which characterized the second edition of *Titles of Honor* (1631), but these looked like later additions to the less refined historical scholarship of the text as a whole, although drawing upon a wide variety of primary sources in an imaginative manner. Although *Mare Clausum* resembled more a partisan lawyer's brief than an impartial work of scholarship, it was not unique among Selden's early works at putting forward controversial interpretations supported by what contemporaries would have seen as considerable historical evidence. As a work of history, *Mare Clausum* more closely resembled Selden's treatises from the decade in which it was originally written than that from the decade in which it was finally printed.

Still, Selden did not revitalize and publish this treatise primarily as a paradigm of historical learning and only an uncharitable critic would judge it solely from that perspective. The moment and purpose of its appearance and the intellectual and political commitments of its author meant that *Mare Clausum* combined a complex number of potentially contradictory or subversive interpretative moves. Significant in the depth of its theoretical and historical subversion of the universalist pretensions of civil or Roman lawyers and in its provision of a stronger theoretical foundation for that particularist interpretation of law which had envigorated *The Historie of Tithes* and the second edition of *Titles of Honor* (1631), *Mare Clausum* articulated in sophisticated natural-law discourse a highly contractual vision of human societies which spoke to Continental theorists at a level rarely reached by English common lawyers in the early seventeenth century.[296] The relationship of natural law to the laws of particular societies would continue to exercise Selden's imagination and research throughout the 1630s and beyond. In a treatise which so obviously laid great stress upon royal power by asserting and upholding the sovereignty of English (and British) monarchs over portions of the seas, it took a major effort of restraint, imagination, and selection of evidence to refrain from subverting that vision of England as a mixed monarchy which Selden had upheld from 1610 onward. The historical chapters of *Mare Clausum* carefully balanced royal sovereignty with the powers of Parliament and the common law in a manner which managed both to please King Charles and to preserve the integrity of mixed monarchy. This also marked a major accomplishment. The relative ease with which Selden managed a series of intricate open and hidden agendas within the pages of *Mare Clausum* more than made up for its relative lack of historical sophistication.

CONCLUSION

The publication of *Titles of Honor* (1631) and of *Mare Clausum* (1635) brought an end to one phase of John Selden's career as a scholar and politician, one that drew upon an increasingly deep historical understanding of the legal systems and institutions of medieval and early modern Europe as a basis for offering political advice. Not one to shy away from controversial or even extreme interpretations, he built upon the reputation created by his historical treatises of the 1610s to establish his political career in the 1620s and defended his political positions of the 1620s indirectly in his historical treatises of the 1630s. As his scholarship matured, Selden acquired an unrivalled mastery of English printed and manuscript sources; Continental printed sources; and British and European treatises which strengthened his discourse on history, law, and governance. A twentieth (or late-nineteenth)-century historian looking back at these books from the perspective of archivally based 'scientific' history would probably award pride of place to the second edition of *Titles of Honor* (1631). Certainly, recent historians of historical research and writing have singled out Selden as a crucial figure in what one of them has called a 'historical revolution.'[297] As a example of modern scholarly history, with its exacting critical analysis of sources within the context of their own time and its subtle sense of interpretation, *Titles of Honor* (1631) set a standard rarely surpassed before the late nineteenth century. This was not its sole purpose, however; nor was was its author a detached academic historian.

As with other Renaissance savants, Selden became a scholar to make an impact upon events. Both *Titles of Honor* (1631) and *Mare Clausum* spoke to contemporary political disputes by drawing upon evidence from the past. As political advice, however, the detailed, cosmopolitan account of the major titles in Europe since the collapse of Rome followed an extraordinarily oblique approach which opened the way for what the author would have seen as gross misinterpretation and misapplication. As we shall see, at least one such misappropriation took place before the end of the 1630s. In part, Selden was too good a historian for his audience. Few of his contemporaries had a strong enough sense of anachronism to understand the sophisticated account of feudal tenures presented in *Titles of Honor* (1631). Few either then or since have grasped the firm support for the common law and for English mixed monarchy embedded in the overwhelming detail of its pages. In the dense, oblique analytical narrative of *Titles of Honor* (1631), Selden the scholar subverted the hope that Selden the political adviser might rival the fame of Plato and Aristotle.

During the late 1620s and early 1630s, another active member of the Commons in 1628, the ancient Sir Edward Coke, also worked on a comparable work of political advice, *The Second Part of the Institutes of the Lawes of England* (London, 1642). This extensive commentary upon Magna Carta and succeeding statutes and judgments also represented an indirect but less oblique reply to the absolutist and royal constitutionalist spokesmen of 1628. Seized with other papers from Coke's study after his death by command the privy council, it finally appeared with the blessing of the House of Commons on the eve of England's Civil War. With his concern to find and publish the truth, Selden may well have agreed with his elder contemporary that 'our Expositions or Commentaries upon *Magna Charta*, and other Statutes,' based upon 'the resolutions of Judges in Courts of Justice in judiciall courses of proceeding, either related and reported in our Books, or extant in judiciall Records, or in both, and therefore being collected together, shall (as we conceive) produce certainty, the Mother and Nurse of repose and quietnesse.'[298] Both claimed to believe that accurate scholarship, based upon public records, would produce a consensus political vision for the distribution of power and the proper behaviour of royal servants. However, neither succeeded in converting either King Charles or his leading legal advisers to their interpretations of mixed monarchy and constitutional monarchy limited by the common law, at least not during the 1620s and 1630s. Indeed, the failure of the Petition of Right to prevent the privy council from imprisoning Selden and others after the dissolution of Parliament in 1629 displayed for some the futility of the hope that legal-historical scholarship would win the political battles of the day.

Selden's historical scholarship in *Titles of Honor* (1631) displayed a far more sophisticated historical understanding of English medieval public records than did that of Coke in *The Second Part of the Institutes*. Coke, however, wrote a more effective political treatise which made a stronger impact upon the parliamentarian discourse on governance during the 1640s and beyond. A glance at the pamphlets of John Lilburne or the tracts of the American Revolution could illustrate this point. As we shall see, Selden's interpretation of mixed monarcy helped to shape the voices of constitutional royalists in the 1640s. During the later seventeenth century, Selden's writings on natural law probably had a greater impact upon political theorists than his histories; although *Titles of Honor* was one of the few books mentioned by author and title in the *Leviathan* of Thomas Hobbes, this came during a discussion distinctions of worthiness and honour by sovereigns, not one attacking the coherence of theories of mixed government.[299] Still, Selden's interpretation of the English constitution as a mixed monarchy remained part of the vocabulary of cosmopolitan legal professionals, especially in such key works as Sir Matthew Hale's *The History of the Common Law of England* (London, 1713) or Sir William Blackstone's *Commentaries on the Laws of England*, four volumes (Oxford, 1765–69). In these ways, *Titles of Honor* made a modest and ambiguous, but lasting contribution to discourse on governance in England.

A far more effective piece of political advice, *Mare Clausum* more than made up for a relative diminution in historical subtlety by a resolute, direct focus upon one relevant issue, the nature and extent jurisdiction over the seas, especially those surrounding the British Isles. For the first time since his dedication of *Jani Anglorum* to the Earl of Salisbury, Selden took the courtier's perspective of presenting advice which sought to please and guide. The detailed discussions of ancient and medieval military and diplomatic affairs, which paid equal attention to the royal appointment of admirals and to parliamentary statutes, sugared the pill of mixed monarchy for Charles I with the sweetness of royal maritime sovereignty. Again, only a careful reader would have discovered this unsubversive paradox. Selden's experience in the handling of patrons (gained from his long relationship with the Earl of Kent and more recent dealings with the Earl of Hertford) combined with the discomforts of imprisonment to produce some of the interpretive complexities of this seemingly direct text, but the integration of natural-law discourse with historical evidence played a major role as well. Written in Latin for an international audience, *Mare Clausum* paradoxically provided a firmly contractual theoretical basis for the common lawyer's reduction of all law to the 'states' or original constitutions and customs of particular jurisdictions, a most English interpretation. Successfully combining theory and practice, Grotian natural law and philological history, *Mare Clausum* has remained a classic defence for the extreme position that states can claim and exercise claims of sovereignty over the high seas. It also provided a fitting finish to the strictly European historical phase of Selden's scholarship and, with its introductory section on the definition of *jus* and *dominium*, a transition to Selden's weighty tome on natural law.

Ironically, as Selden's powers as a historian of medieval and early modern Europe reached their peak, he focused his scholarship on other areas of research and other sources, especially the Torah and the Talmud.[300] The extraordinary effort needed to carry out historical research into a huge number of manuscript and printed sources and treatises needed for the attempts to place limits on the actions of royal servants in the 1620s, and for the production of *Titles of Honor* (1631) and *Mare Clausum* (1635), may well have exhausted Selden's desire to continue on a similar path. Perhaps the bitter disappointment of failing to persuade royal servants to accept the constitutional practices of mixed monarchy, reflected in his abrasiveness in the session of 1629, and the failure of the Petition of Right to protect even members of the House of Commons from arbitrary imprisonment in the aftermath of the dissolution of Parliament in 1629, also shook his belief in the power of historical truth to make an impact upon political affairs. Whatever the reason, the fascination with natural law, which found its earliest sophisticated voice in the opening chapters of *Mare Clausum*, became Selden's preferred mode of political discourse for the rest of his life and shifted his concerns from governance in England and Europe (especially from the common law and customary laws, but also from the canon law and Roman law), to natural law and universalist political theory. In the twenty-three years which remained in his life, Selden published no more treatises which drew their evidence from English and European history; indeed, no comparable work in English and only a scholarly edition of an early source in Latin, *Ad Fletam Dissertatio* (London, 1653), ever appeared again from his pen on a related topic. For all of its accomplishment, this phase of Selden's scholarship and political career both reached its peak and came to a bittersweet end in the mid-1630s.

Conclusion

This study has provided a close reading of John Selden's public discourse on history, law, and governance during the period from 1610 through 1635 as articulated in his legal and parliamentary speeches, his few surviving letters, and his published histories dealing with European and English topics. Selden's changing interpretations of English and Continental legal history, including his attempts to work out the relationship between the English common law and the laws of God, nature, and nations, has received considerable attention, as has his historical method and practice, including his increasingly sophisticated mastery of medieval primary sources and early modern legal and historical studies. As shown in the text and in the summaries at the end of each chapter, the interpretations articulated in the first two decades of the century formed the basis for the positions on governance voiced during his parliamentary career in the 1620s and defended in his major relevant publications from the 1630s. Throughout this period, Selden's trust in humanist philology continued as basic and firm. Although he carefully modified (and sometimes radically changed) some of his medium-range and micro-historical interpretations, especially in light of his increasingly sophisticated grasp of historical primary sources, his reduction of all law to the 'frame' of governance, 'constitutions,' and customs of a particular state and his model of the English constitution as a mixed monarchy in which monarchs, nobles, clergy, and representatives of freemen shared sovereignty remained constant from at least 1616 onward. Since the details of Selden's interpretations and of his dialogue with the competing voices of contemporaries has received considerable attention in the previous chapters, this conclusion offers a few final general reflections on Selden's public contribution to English historical, legal, and political discourse during this portion of his career.

Both as a theorist and a practitioner, Selden helped to shape the conception, research, and writing of history in England for his contemporaries and for later generations. Of course, other historians took from his theory and example those aspects which they perceived as best suiting their own needs, as he had done from earlier and contemporary English and Continental scholars. Drawing deeply upon the traditions, studies, editions, and collections of such earlier and contemporary English antiquaries as William Camden (his mentor and model), Sir Robert Cotton, William Lambarde, Archbishop Matthew Parker, Sir Henry Savile, and Archbishop James Ussher, Selden embraced the meticulous search for detailed sources which characterized their work, added a commitment to sophisticated humanist philology (with its well-developed sense of chronology and anachronism), and fashioned a new conception of history which started from a relevant point in the past and moved forward to the present. Especially with the publication of *Titles of Honor* (1614), *The Historie of Tithes* (1618), and the preface to Vincent's book, the definition of history as an account of a portion of the past based upon as many primary sources and reputable recent studies as possible laid out a new theory and practice of how historians should properly represent the events, laws, customs, offices, and institutions of the past. *Titles of Honor* and *The Historie of Tithes* also served as practical working examples of how to research and write a new genre, a social history of a practice, office, institution, or custom. Especially after Selden published his highly successful *Historie of Tithes*, his contemporaries could and did apply similar techniques of research and composition to other topics, as seen in Peter Heylyn's, *The History of the Sabbath* (London, 1636), which charted the attitudes of Christians towards activities on Sunday through the ages, and in Sir William Dugdale's, *The History of St. Paul's Cathedral* (London, 1658), which extended the format to a single institution. As with any historical genre, once it becomes established, anyone can use it. The privileging of public records articulated in the preface to Vincent's book, and especially in the sections of the second edition of *Titles of Honor* (1631) dealing with England, inspired a host of followers, even in the partisan historical studies unleashed by the British civil wars of the mid-seventeenth century (such as the less sophisticated, but detailed historical works by William Prynne) and in the later, deeper (and committed) scholar-ship of Dugdale and Sir Matthew Hale. Although the conception of history as a well-told tale of great deeds never disappeared (and even revived in the eighteenth century), Selden's scholarly definition remained widely available in the reprints of various works in the 1670s and 1680s, and in the edition of his complete works edited by David Wilkins and published in 1726.[1] Crucial to the research and writing of all of Selden's histories from this period were traditions of scholarship derived from the publications of Continental Roman and customary lawyers.

Well read in the treatises produced by medieval, sixteenth-, and seventeenth-century canon and civil or Roman lawyers, Selden exemplified a new, cosmopolitan style of scholarship made possible by printing. The margins of his books abounded with references to printed editions, commentaries, and treatises; except for *The Historie of Tithes* and portions of *Titles of Honor* (1631) and *Mare Clausum*, which drew strongly upon manuscripts, as well. Learned in a human-ist philology largely derived from civil lawyers who practised the French method (*mos gallicus*), Selden also appreciated and absorbed aspects of the neo-Bartolist Italian method (*mos italicus*), especially as a means of addressing current social and political problems. Apply-ing this mastery of Continental methods to English legal sources made a unique impact upon early-seventeenth-century English legal discourse. Trying to pry apart the common from the civil lawyer in John Selden would subvert a balanced interpretation of his work. In these and many other ways, 'Selden belonged to a plurality of discur-sive communities' and constructed his identity and his scholarship not only '*within* particular forms and communities,' but 'also *across* them.'[2] Some of his contemporaries had supplemented their civil-law learning by a more than superficial study of the English common law (for example, Dr John Cowell, Sir Henry Marten, and William Ful-becke), and others learned in the common law had enriched their learning by a more than superficial study of Roman law (for example, Lord Chancellor Ellesmere, Sir John Davies, and Sir John Doderidge). Only Selden displayed equal fluency in both discourses; only Selden possessed such a deep mastery of the scholarship, hermeneutical tra-ditions, and sources of civil law, Continental customary law, canon law, and English common law; and only Selden so skilfully applied the discourse of common lawyers to the study of canon and civil law and the discourse of civil lawyers to the study of the English common law. Clearly, he did not conform to J.G.A. Pocock's pattern of an 'insular common-law mind.'

The contrast between Selden's cosmopolitanism and the relative insularity of his common-law colleagues becomes even more clear in reading such roughly contemporary works of jurisprudence as the manual of Sir John Doderidge (with its stress upon maxims drawn from outside of the common law), the *Reports* of Sir Edward Coke (with their historical sketches in the prefaces and discussions of individual cases in the text), the Irish *Report* of Sir John Davies (with its defensive preface and clever use of the civil law in individual cases), the first of Coke's *Institutes* (with its detailed marginal glosses on Littleton's treatise on English tenures), and even the second of Coke's *Institutes* (with its focus on Magna Carta and subsequent statutes). Although they often contained references to the past and sometimes cited Continental learning, these treatises centred on contemporary common-law practice, and their historical interpretations read the practices of their own day back into the past.[3] Ironically, however, both the format and the European-wide scope of Selden's books may have diffused some of their impact as treatises concerned with the common law of England. Most common lawyers probably wanted something more practical and less philological and historical. As a lawyer, then, Selden left an ambiguous legacy: he enriched the practice of the common law with a method and interpretations derived from the civil law; he enriched the literature of the civil law with interpretations founded in the common law; and he showed the practicality of these approaches in common-law courts and in parliaments, but the wide and sophisticated nature of his learning spoke beyond the comprehension of most contemporaries and set a standard of scholarship which few of his successors could hope to emulate.

Rather than providing guides for practising common lawyers, Selden published histories which commented briefly and indirectly upon the 'frame' of governance in England and European states and extensively and directly upon the statutes and customs of these jurisdictions. The insights gained from the comparative study of legal systems allowed Selden to reduce all law to the original constitution of a particular society as interpreted by subsequent statutes and customs which applied the 'frame' of governance to changing needs and circumstances. Paradoxically, some of his strongest insights into Continental legal history – for example, the interpretation of the laws of

European successor states to the Roman Empire as a discrete series of ancient constitutions – derived from the interpretations of English common lawyers, while many of his strongest insights into English legal history – his whole philological, historical treatment of the English constitution – derived from the comparative interpretations of civil lawyers, especially from the *Francogallia* of François Hotman. Few contemporaries so successfully practised this mutually enriching interchange. Among English common lawyers who published in the early seventeenth century, Davies used Roman-law principles to introduce the English common law into Ireland, and Spelman matched Selden's absorption of Continental historical scholarship; the former demonstrated his wizardry in the text of his Irish *Report*, and the latter displayed his learning in his glossary – neither wrote a history. In good humanist fashion, Selden's histories enriched and informed his legal and political practice; his readings of medieval laws became the basis for his advice on seventeenth-century governance.[4] In *The Historie of Tithes*, Howard's Case in the Commons, the Five Knights' Case, the debates leading up to the Petition of Right, Rolle's Case, the bail hearing for Selden's arrest in 1629, and, as we shall see, the Irish Case of 1637, Selden's philological approach impacted strongly upon the highest realms of English common-law and political discourse.

During the first four decades of the seventeenth century, political debates in England took place largely within the discourse of the common law, as Margaret Judson and J.G.A. Pocock pointed out long ago.[5] Since common-law courts provided the primary means of enforcing governance in early modern England, this should hardly cause any great surprise. Our concept of the 'common-law mind' as a unitary voice was assembled by Pocock from the discrete interpretations of Coke in the prefaces to his *Reports* and of Davies in the preface to his *Irish Report*.[6] Although modifying Pocock's interpretation in other ways, Glenn Burgess has also tended to see the politics of the ancient constitution as a unitary, not multiple discourse.[7] Indeed, in his recent 'retrospect,' Pocock pressed the issue by arguing that the 'ancient constitution' arose not as a response to historical moments but as a habit of mind, a *mentalité*, which stretched back into the Middle Ages and forward into the eighteenth and nineteenth centuries.[8] In a recent essay, 'The Place of Magna Carta and the Ancient Constitution in Sixteenth-Century English Legal Thought,' however, Christopher Brooks challenged Pocock's assumption of continuity by demonstrating that Tudor writers did not employ the concept of an ancient constitution. Brooks has suggested that this interpretation emerged in the prefaces to Coke's *Reports*.[9] My own research has pointed to a particular moment in the first decade of the seventeenth century when concerns over the distribution and exercise of power came to the fore in debates over impositions and the union of England and Scotland as the time when competing interpretations of the ancient constitution became articulated in a coherent manner. Within what Burgess has called 'the Jacobean consensus,' plenty of room remained for creative tensions springing from different empha-ses.[10] More than one voice spoke about the ancient constitution of England.

Tensions between theological, civil-law, and common-law concep-tions of governance came into the open in the first decade of the seventeenth century and remained a not always hidden agenda for debate in the following decades. Arguing that the differing 'claims and principles' of common lawyers, theologians, and civilians nor-mally moved 'like ships that pass in the night,' Burgess has recently explained how a 'consensus' in political discourse during this period came about 'not in the absence of conflict, but in a shared set of con-ventions for the theoretical resolution of conflict, and for the non-controversial employment of a variety of languages.'[11] As shown in this book, the muted conflict between common and both canon and civil lawyers sometimes flashed up more strongly than Burgess's image would allow, and many common-lawyers perceived a threat in the universalist perspective of civil or Roman lawyers who derided common law principles and practices as merely 'municipal,' those of one jurisdiction. Selden spent a great deal of thought and energy on protecting the common law from this and other perceived threats from the civil, canon, and natural laws. Extended a bit to take account of these rivalries, however, Burgess's interpretation remains more persuasive than its competitors. The Tacitist discourse of 'necessity' and 'reason of state' recently emphasized by Richard Tuck, although getting some play during the 1620s, rarely intruded into disputes over governance before 1642, and even the discourse of natural law stressed by Tuck and by Johann Sommerville found little articulation outside of the voices of clergymen and civil or Roman lawyers before the 1630s.[12] Indeed, common-law discourse domi-nated debates over governance, whether carried on by barristers, solicitors, or country gentlemen in the courts or in parliaments, while the discourses of theology and civil law normally addressed other audiences attuned to different issues.

Even had James I or Charles I wished to introduce some form of absolutism, he would have had to enforce it in the King's Bench (a common-law court) through charges laid by the attorney general (a common lawyer) or else change the whole legal system of the realm. Neither seriously contemplated these options. For all of his expressed respect for Roman-law principles and his plans for legal codification, James I recognized that his powers and initiatives as an English monarch drew their strength from the common law and he worked within its boundaries. Charles I sometimes displayed an annoyance with the ancient channels of precedent, as seen in his orders to Attorney General Heath to register a decision of the roll of the King's Bench without that judgment having received the consent of the justices, but he did not attempt any major change of existing practices or institutions and always took his legal advice from ministers trained in the common law. In early-seventeenth-century England, then, the alternative was not between 'French absolutism' or 'Dutch' republicanism, as argued years ago by Christopher Hill, nor between *Divine Right and Democracy*, as argued more recently by David Wooton; rather, the dispute took place between different versions of the ancient constitution.[13]

John Selden stood in the centre of these early-seventeenth-century debates, first as an author, and later as a lawyer and member of the House of Commons. During the years before 1642, most English political theorists remained constitutionalists, as had many in Germanic lands before the outbreak of the Thirty Years War. In addition, disputes in England dealt largely with issues of governance, how royal servants should govern the realm, not with such abstract, formal, natural-law political theories as those of absolutism or mixed monarchy.[14] Dangers lurked in not very hidden ways for those who published, whether in print or in circulated manuscript, what might have seemed criticisms of the reigning monarch, or even of such established institutions as the church, as Selden found both in the suppression of his *Historie of Tithes* and in a case brought before the Star Chamber by Attorney General Heath in 1629. Along with the earls of Bedford, Clare, and Somerset; Sir Robert Cotton; his librarian Richard James; and others, Selden was named in a bill of information before this court in November 1629 for alleging in a piece of writing found in Cotton's library that 'your sacred majesty has a purpose to alter the ancient laws of this kingdom ... and to draw all things to be disposed of at your sacred majesty's absolute will and pleasure'; even the discovery that the pamphlet was written in Italy by Sir Robert Dudley and sent to Sir David Foulis in 1614 did not immediately stop the prosecution of Selden and others.[15] Clearly, Charles and his advisers wanted contemporaries to perceive the Crown as upholding the ancient constitution – but, of course, their own version. The dangers of seeming to contradict the monarch may provide a clue to the indirection of some of Selden's published works and to his failure to follow through with publishing a full, revised version of *Jani Anglorum* in English.[16] His harassment in 1629 certainly helps to explain why the pages of *Titles of Honor* (1631) only obliquely supported the principle of mixed monarchy which he had employed so effectively against the interpretations of leading legal advisers of the Crown in the Parliament of 1628–9. On the other hand, this indirection allowed Selden's history to appear in print during the 1630s. The manuscripts of the more direct second *Institutes* of Coke suffered a different fate; seized shortly before Coke's death in 1634 by a fearful privy council, it was not printed until so ordered by the House of Commons in 1642.[17] Outside of parliaments, direct discussions of governance, unless published anonymously, remained problematic.

The privilege of free speech, however, extended to members of the Lords and Commons gave them a much greater freedom than other subjects to discuss both general and particular issues of governance (including the improper behaviour of powerful royal servants) inside the Houses and their committees. Much of the censorship and self-censorship which impeded frank discussion of issues in the press and in writings did not apply to voices raised in parliaments.[18] Hence, Selden's attacks upon the High Commission and the Duke of Buckingham, the royal favourite, in the Parliament of 1626, while no doubt distasteful to the king and many of his leading servants, produced no penalties. Parliaments provided important arenas where leading magistrates from across the realm could exchange views and bring together local grievances in order to formulate them into more general issues of governance. Here, common lawyers, the primary generators of ancient constitutional discourse, could communicate their interpretations to leading users of that discourse in the court and countryside, to nobles, country gentlemen, and members of urban élites. Despite their relatively small output of statutes, the parliaments of early-seventeenth-century England remained important places for wide-ranging discussions of governance, not least because they constituted the largest existing assembly where the political, social, and economic élite in the realm could speak freely about any issues of governance. The Sir Geoffrey Elton who wrote about parliaments as a point of contact would appear to have more application to these parliaments than the Elton who saw statutes as the primary business of parliaments, and the Earl Russell who wrote about 'Westminster and the Wider World' more validity than the Russell who argued in favour of the powerlessness of early-seventeenth-century parliaments.[19] No assembly which could enforce limits upon the behaviour of royal servants, however reluctantly accepted by the monarch, lacked significant power.

Because Selden did not have the power or social prestige needed to obtain a seat in the House of Commons on his own, he sought election as part of a team. In the Parliament of 1624, he may have received the support of Sir Humphrey May, the Chancellor of the Duchy of Lancaster and an experienced member of the Commons, who may have wished to recruit Selden as a supporter of his group within the privy council. During the parliaments of 1626 and 1628–9, Selden represented a borough controlled by the Earl of Hertford and gave every indication of sitting as a member of the Seymour network. His dislike of the Duke of Buckingham and his advocacy of mixed monarchy, plus his aristocratic connections with the Earl of Kent and his affinity, helped to bring Selden and Hertford together and helped the Seymours to put together one of the most effective networks in the Commons in 1628–9. Both in the Parliament of 1626, with attacks upon the Duke of Buckingham, and that of 1628–9, with the debates leading to the Petition of Right, the impeachment of Manwaring, the attack upon the duke, and the dismissive treatment of royal servants, the leadership in the Commons was exercised by the clients and allies of peers, not least by such active members of the Seymour network as Sir Francis Seymour, Edward Kirton, and John Selden. Even the network of the Earl of Pembroke, so active against Buckingham in 1624 and arrayed in support of the war effort in 1628, could not deflect the aggressive attacks upon the actions of royal servants made by the networks of such other peers as the earls of Bedford, Hertford, and Warwick.[20] Although a good deal more research needs to be done to detail the operation of various aristocratic networks and their goals, a good deal of evidence from the parliaments of 1626 and 1628–9 suggests that the early stages of what became party politics, with its typical contests for power and office by at least two reasonably organized groups, may well have started with the attempts of various peers both within and outside of the privy council to contain the actions of royal servants and shape policy.[21] Certainly this interpretation looks more promising than the alternative suggested by Derek Hirst and, in a rather different manner, by Brian Manning, that the pressure for such politics came from below the ranks of the gentry.[22]

Although not quite the 'man of business' in the Commons for the privy council or a peer portrayed by Michael Graves and J.S.A. Adamson, nor even the intellectual in politics portrayed by Lisa Jardine and Anthony Grafton, Selden clearly used his skills as a common lawyer, antiquary, and political adviser to good effect in the management of the House of Commons.[23] The influence he exerted as an active participant in debates and a member frequently named to committees and subcommittees probably reached a peak during the sessions of 1628 and 1629. During the session of 1628, Selden's model of mixed monarchy became a significant means for attempting to control the actions of royal servants, both in the debates leading up to the Petition of Right and in those leading to the impeachment of Manwaring. In these causes his motto, with its advocacy of liberty, transformed into the more concrete task of upholding the historical liberties of English freemen. His sometimes brutal handling of the Howard Case in 1626 and his gratuitous insults of privy councillors in 1629 revealed an adversarial style more attuned to victory at almost any cost rather than to fair play. Both sets of skills made Selden a valuable client or ally in the House of Commons, a person worthy of receiving a seat. Ironically, the adversarial way in which they sometimes came into play also helped to engender the strong disputes between royal servants and the leading managers of the House of Commons, especially in 1629, which led to that breakdown of cooperation between the king, Lords, and Commons which alone could sustain a successful mixed monarchy.

In more than one way, Selden replied to the arguments of royal spokesmen and his own imprisonment after the session of 1629 with his strongest defence of mixed monarchy in the second edition of *Titles of Honor* (1631), just as Sir Edward Coke replied posthumously in *The Second Part of the Institutes of the Lawes of England* (1642). Unlike the former chief justice, however, Selden also began the quest for natural-law political arguments in the 1630s with the publication of *Mare Clausum* (1635) and this mode of argument became more prominent in the years that followed in his own political discourse as well as that of others. Nor, as we shall see in the case from Ireland in 1637, were elements of Selden's interpretation of the ancient constitution confined only to the applications which he supported. The bitter experience of the weakness of ancient constitutionalism in the debates of the late 1620s, from his imprisonment in 1629 through the early 1630s, and in this application from the 1630s – of the inability of 'true' histories of the ancient constitution to prevent perverse applications of the common law by royal servants – may well help to explain Selden's desertion of English and European historical studies and his turn to natural-law discourse in the late 1630s and of the growing scepticism which characterized his table talk in the 1640s.

Once published, the interpretations and evidence contained in books become open to interpretations well beyond that put forward by their authors. Before leaving the 1630s, a glance at one application of Selden's scholarship in the courts should dispel any notion that the publication of *Titles of Honor* (1631) and *Mare Clausum* had actually enforced closure upon rival interpretations of the ancient constitution. Paradoxically, in '*The Case of Tenures upon the Commission of Defective Titles argued by all the judges of Ireland*' in 1637, the judges rejected Spelman's argument that William I had introduced feudal tenures into England on the basis of Selden's account for continuity, but they also used Selden's interpretation of the ancient constitution to buttress an extension of royal claims which seriously undermined previously secure land tenures.[24] Perhaps a collusive action brought against Robert Lord Dillon of Kilkenny-West, a close associate of Sir Thomas Wentworth in Ireland (Lord Dillon's son James married Elizabeth Wentworth, the sister of the Lord Deputy, in 1636), the suit sought to set aside as void letters patent issued in 1608 by the commission of defective titles because they did not grant the land on knighthood tenure *in capite*, which would have established the primacy of a royal title and made the tenant-in-chief liable to rents and wardship.[25] When the attorneys for the defence cited the early Selden and Spelman to prove that feudal tenures came in with the Norman Conquest, the justices drew upon Selden's later works to reply that

we find he was of another Opinion; and that this Tenure was in Use in *England*, in the times of the *Saxons*.

What were those *Thani Majores*, or *Thani Regis* among the *Saxons*? But the King's immediate Tenants of Lands, which they held by Personal Service, as of the King's person by Grand Serjeantry, or Knight's Service in *Capite* ...

After some years that followed the coming of the *Normans*, the Title of *Thane* grew out of Use, and that of *Baron* and *Barony* succeeded for *Thane* and *Thaneland*.[26]

Bolstered by references to Selden's notes in his editions of Eadmer and Fortescue, this represented a fair summary of the arguments that he made there and in the second edition of *Titles of Honor* (1631). The justices then used Selden's interpretation to argue that 'Sir *Henry Spelman* was mistaken, who in his *Glossary verbo Feudum*, refers to the Original of *Feuds* in *England*, to the *Norman* Conquest.'[27] In other words, the historical interpretation of tenures presented by Selden carried the day over that of his fellow antiquary.

Moving well beyond the careful interpretation of Selden, however, the argument in this portion of the judgment took up the interpretative method of Sir Edward Coke to read Norman tenures back into the period before the Conquest: 'It is most manifest, that *Capite Tenures*, Tenures by *Knights service*, Tenures in *socage*, Frankalmoigne, etc. were frequent in the Times of the Saxons.'[28] Working forward from the earliest recoverable past rather than adopting this backward perspective, Selden had argued that the forms of tenures commonly used by Norman monarchs had developed from earlier military tenures, that Thegn gave way to Baron, not that the latter had existed in Anglo-Saxon England! The anachronistic extension made by the judges subverted the forward-moving chronological pattern which had characterized all of Selden's historical interpretations the English constitution. The application of portions of Continental legal philology to common-law cases did not necessarily challenge the patterns of immemorial-ity and reading back of later offices, institutions, and tenures into the past which characterized the ancient constitution of Coke. Thus, Selden's historical interpretations became just one more weapon in the armoury of common lawyers to be used when the occasion demanded. In this case, it allowed the justices to invali-date royal patents from the previous reign in which the commis-sioners on defective titles had not reserved a tenure *in capite* to the Crown.[29] Ironically, Selden's defence of mixed monarchy thereby became a means for extending the power of the Crown in Ireland, the opposite purpose for its creation, thereby turning into a sort of Frankenstein's monster of learning.

The ironies of Selden's legal, historical, and political discourse continued into the 1640s. During the summer of 1642, as royalists and parliamentarians scrambled to attract supporters for the armies which they had started to assemble, a wide-ranging debate over the shape of English governance took place in print – in ordinances or proclamations of one or both Houses, royalist answers, petitions, and pamphlets. In the dispute over the parliamentary militia ordinance versus the royalist commissions of array, Selden reluctantly took the side of his colleagues who continued to sit in the House of Commons in Westminster and remained there himself, despite a plea from his old patron, the Earl of Hertford, to join him with King Charles at York. Hertford, obtaining office as governor of the Prince of Wales and raised to the rank of Marquess in early 1642, had become a leading constitutional royalist.[30] In order to advance the royalist position in the summer of 1642, the royal spokesmen who wrote *The Answer to the XIX Propositions* (London, 1642) took the high ground of mixed monarchy and defended a constitution in which the shared and separate powers of the king, Lords, and representatives of freemen gathered together in Parliament represented a mixture of monarchy, aristocracy, and democracy. This carefully written appeal sought to subvert the Nineteen Propositions presented to the king by the Lords and Commons as unprecedented and dangerous. Particularly telling was the accusation that the 'Cabalists of this businesse' had

thought fit to remove a troublesome Rub in their way, *The Law*; To this end, (that they might undermine the very foundations of it) a new Power hath been assumed to interpret and declare Laws without Us by extemporary Votes, without any Case judicially before either House, (which is in effect the same thing as to make Laws without Us) Orders and Ordinances made onely by both Houses (tending to a pure arbitrary power) were pressed upon the people as Laws, and their obedience required of them.

This reversed the accusation of plotting to undermine the ancient constitution and erect an arbitrary authority, long made against royal servants, by applying it against the leaders of the two Houses. The Militia Ordinance represented just one such attempt to 'erect an upstart Authority without us.' The accusation that parliamentary leaders aimed at making this 'Kingdom a Republique' and a 'new *Utopia* of Religion and Government' complemented warnings of the disastrous consequences of imbalance among the 'three estates.' Through their appeals for a defence of the 'ancient, equall, happy, well-poised and never-enough commended Constitution of the Government of this Kingdom,' the king's advisers sought to subvert the appeal of the Nineteen Propositions.[31] As stances reversed, such parliamentary spokesmen as Henry Parker replied in the discourse of Tacitean necessity.[32] Even after the strong force of natural-law political theories became apparent during the mid-seventeenth century, however, ancient constitutionalism retained considerable importance in discussions of law and governance. Treatises of advice, or even histories, can only attempt to persuade by example, they cannot enforce enclosure on later readers. Although strongly challenged and competing increasingly with natural-law theories, the mixed monarchy so strongly defended by John Selden during the first four decades of the seventeenth century continued to enrich the legal, historical, and political discourse in unforeseen ways, including the advocacy by significant royal servants of an interpretation of the ancient constitution which stressed the legitimate and enduring powers of the peers and representatives of the people in shaping governance in England.

Notes

1 For this branch of theological discourse, see J. P. Sommerville, 'James I and the Divine Right of Kings: English Politics and Continental Theory.'

2 For the range of books available, many of them in Latin, and the positions argued, see such recent surveys as: Glenn Burgess, *The Politics of the Ancient Constitution: An Introduction to English Political Thought, 1603–1642*; J.H. Burns and Mark Goldie, eds., *The Cambridge History of Political Thought, 1450–1700*; Quentin Skinner, *The Foundations of Modern Political Thought*, 2 vols.; J.P. Sommerville, *Politics and Ideology in England, 1603–1640*; and Richard Tuck, *Philosophy and Government, 1572–1651*.

3 For example, see the arguments and evidence presented in Anthony Fletcher, *Reform in the Provinces: The Government of Stuart England*, and Mark Kishlansky, *Parliamentary Selection: Social and Political Choice in Early Modern England*.

4 For a stress upon the natural-law tradition, see Richard Tuck, *Natural Rights Theories: Their Origin and Development* and *Philosophy and Government, 1572–1651*; the relevant portions of Skinner, *Foundations of Modern Political Thought*, Sommerville, *Politics and Ideology in England*, and John Tully, *A Discourse on Property: John Locke and His Adversaries*; cf. J.G.A. Pocock, *The Machiavellian Moment: Florentine Political Thought and the Atlantic Republican Tradition*. The foundational role of Hugo Grotius in the 'modern' theory of natural law was established in Richard Tuck, 'The "Modern" School of Natural Law,' and reinforced in his *Philosophy and Government*, pp. 205–21. In England, 'civil' lawyers were those who studied the Roman-law traditions based

upon the *Corpus Juris Justiniani* and, to a lesser extent, Theodosian Code at the universities of Oxford and Cambridge (or abroad) and practised especially in the ecclesiastical courts and the Admiralty. As part of an international fraternity, they tended to see Roman-law principles as universal, and national legal systems as inferior 'municipal' laws. I subsequently refer to these practitioners as 'Roman lawyers.'

5 Burgess, *Politics of the Ancient Constitution*, ch. 5, passim.

6 Ibid., p. 168. For an articulation of competing traditions of common-law discourse, see Paul Christianson, 'Royal and Parliamentary Voices on the Ancient Constitution, ca. 1604–21,' and 'Ancient Constitutions in the Age of Sir Edward Coke, and John Selden.'

7 In chronological order, see Margaret Judson, *The Crisis of the Constitution: An Essay in Constitutional and Political Thought in England*; J.G.A. Pocock, *The Ancient Constitution and the Feudal Law: English Historical Thought in the Seventeenth Century*; Sommerville, *Politics and Ideology in England*; and Burgess, *Politics of the Ancient Constitution*.

8 From a host of studies, see Martin Butler, *Theatre and Crisis, 1632–1642*; Jonathan Goldberg, *James I and the Politics of Literature: Jonson, Shakespeare, Donne and Their Contemporaries*; Oliver Millar, *The Age of Charles I*; David Norbrook, *Poetry and Politics in the English Renaissance*; Stephen Orgel, *The Illusion of Power*; Stephen Orgel and Roy Strong, eds., *Inigo Jones: The Theatre of the Stuart Court*, 2 vols.; Per Palme, *Triumph of Peace: A Study of the Whitehall Banqueting House*; Kevin Sharpe, *Criticism and Compliment: The Politics of Literature in the England of Charles I*; Kevin Sharpe and Peter Lake, eds., *Culture and Politics in Early Stuart England*; R. Malcolm Smuts, *Court Culture and the Origins of a Royalist Tradition in Early Stuart England*; and Roy Strong, *Van Dyck: Charles I on Horseback* and *Britannia Triumphans: Inigo Jones, Rubens and Whitehall Palace*.

9 See Paul Christianson, 'The Causes of the English Revolution: A Reappraisal'; the moral nature of criminal justice at the formal level has recently received a good deal of attention in Cynthia B. Herrup, 'Law and Morality in Seventeenth-Century England' and *The Common Peace: Participation and the Criminal Law in Seventeenth-Century England*, while other scholars, including Martin Ingram, 'Ridings, Rough Music, and the "Reform of Popular Culture" in Early Modern England' and 'Ridings, Rough Music, and Mocking Rhymes in Early Modern England'; Joan R. Kent, '"Folk Justice" and Royal Justice in Early Seventeenth-Century England: A Charivari in the Midlands' and *The English Village Constable, 1580–1642: A Social and Administrative Study*; and David Underdown,

'The Taming of the Scold: The Enforcement of Patriarchal Authority in Early Modern England' and *Revel, Riot and Rebellion: Popular Politics and Culture in England, 1603–1660*, have dealt with popular rituals for enforcing 'proper' behaviour at the local level.

10 Cf. the call for contextual readings in Quentin Skinner, 'Meaning and Understanding in the History of Ideas,' 'Motives, Intentions, and the Interpretation of Texts,' 'Some Problems in the Analysis of Political Thought and Action,' and 'A Reply to My Critics'; J.G.A. Pocock, *Virtue, Commerce, and History: Essays on Political Thought and History, Chiefly in the Eighteenth Century*, ch. 1; and the 'deconstructionist' critique of both in David Harlan, 'Intellectual History and the Return of Literature.' Clearly, I do not agree with those literary critics who dissolve authorship into intertextuality. Nor does the stress upon communities of interpreters in my 'Patterns of Historical Interpretation' aim at subverting Skinner's emphasis upon authors and their intentions; the readings articulated in this book owe a considerable debt to Pocock and Skinner.

11 Clearly, Selden broke the mould of the 'common-law mind' modelled by Pocock, a point which has received some recognition in the retrospect of J.G.A. Pocock, *The Ancient Constitution and the Feudal Law: English Historical Thought in the Seventeenth Century: A Reissue with a Retrospect*, and considerable discussion in Burgess, *Politics of the Ancient Constitution*, chs. 1 and 2.

12 For the best short account of Selden's life and works, see D.S. Berkowitz, 'SELDEN, John (1584–1654).' The early part of Selden's career was detailed in David S. Berkowitz, 'Young Mr. Selden, Essays in Seventeenth-Century Learning and Politics, being Prolegomena to Parliament' and *John Selden's Formative Years: Politics and Society in Early Seventeenth-Century England*; also see Richard A. Filloy, 'The Religious and Political Views of John Selden: A Study in Early Stuart Humanism.' In his thesis, Berkowitz includes a chronological bibliography of Selden's writings.

13 Arthur B. Ferguson, *Clio Unbound: Perception of the Social and Cultural Past in Renaissance England*, chs. 4, 7, and 8; F. Smith Fussner, *The Historical Revolution: English Historical Writing and Thought, 1580–1640*, ch. 11; Daniel Robert Woolf, 'Erudition and the Idea of History in Renaissance England' and *The Idea of History in Early Stuart England: Erudition, Ideology and 'The Light of Truth' from the Accession of James I to the Civil War*, ch. 7; Donald R. Kelley, 'History, English Law and the Renaissance' and 'A Rejoinder'; Christopher Brooks and Kevin Sharpe, 'Debate: History, English Law and the Renaissance'; Tuck, *Natural Rights*, ch. 4; Martha A. Ziskind, 'John Selden: Criticism and Affirmation of the Com-

mon Law Tradition'; Paul Christianson, 'Young John Selden and the
Ancient Constitution, ca. 1610–1618' and 'Political Thought in Early Stuart England'; Tuck, *Philosophy and Government*, pp. 205–21; and J.P. Sommerville, 'John Selden, the Law of Nature, and the Origins of Government.'
14 Berkowitz, *John Selden*; Burgess, *Politics of the Ancient Constitution*,
pp. 37–40, 63–8; Colin G.C. Tite, *Impeachment and Parliamentary Judicature in Early Stuart England*, ch. 2; Stephen D. White, *Sir Edward Coke
and 'The Grievances of the Commonwealth,' 1621–1628*; Linda S. Popofsky, 'Habeas Corpus and "Liberty of the Subject": Legal Arguments for
the Petition of Right in the Parliament of 1628'; and Paul Christianson,
'John Selden, the Five Knights' Case, and Discretionary Imprisonment in
Early Stuart England' and 'Ancient Constitutions'; also see David S.
Berkowitz, 'Reason of State in England and the Petition of Right, 1603–
1629.' For all of its merits, Berkowitz's book on Selden does not provide a
systematic reading of Selden's early books, nor do his concept of 'humanism,' interpretation of Selden's constitutional ideas, and chapters on
Selden's parliamentary career reflect the concerns of recent historiography, including and moving forward from Pocock, *Ancient Constitution*;
Paul Oskar Kristeller, *Renaissance Thought*; Donald R. Kelley, *Foundations of Modern Historical Scholarship: Language, Law, and History in
the French Renaissance*; and Conrad Russell, *Parliaments and English
Politics, 1621–1629*, respectively.

CHAPTER ONE Young John Selden and the Ancient Constitution,
ca 1610–1618

1 For the common lawyers, see Pocock, *Ancient Constitution: A Reissue*,
chs. 2, 3, and 5, and retrospect, pp. 270–3, and Burgess, *Politics of the
Ancient Constitution*, chs. 1, and 2; references made to Pocock, *Ancient
Constitution*, are to the new edition, which retains the pagination of the
original. For the civil or Roman lawyers, see Brian P. Levack, *The Civil
Lawyers in England, 1603–1641: A Political Study*, ch. 4; Charles
Donahue, Jr, 'The Civil Law in England'; Daniel R. Coquillette, 'Legal
Ideology and Incorporation, I: The English Civilians, 1523–1607,' 'II: Sir
Thomas Ridley, Charles Malloy, and the Literary Battle for the Law Mer-
chant, 1607–1676,' and 'III: Reason Regulated – the Post-Restoration
English Civilians, 1653–1735'; and C.P. Rodgers, 'Legal Humanism and
English Law – the Contribution of the English Civilians'. Before 1620,
Selden wrote and published a number of relevant treatises, especially *Jani
Anglorum Facies Altera* (London, 1610), *The Duello or Single Combat*

(London, 1610), notes to Michael Drayton's, *Poly-Olbion* (London, 1613), *Titles of Honor* (London, 1614), *Analecton Anglobritannicon* (Frankfurt, 1615), an edition with notes and a translation of Sir John Fortescue's, *De Laudibus Legum Angliæ* (London, 1616), and *The Historie of Tithes* (London, 1618). An earlier version of this chapter appeared in *Proceedings of the American Philosophical Society* 128 (1984), 271–315.

2 See Tuck, *Philosophy and Government*, pp. 205–21. Tuck's suggestion that Selden 'repudiated the traditional Calvinist notion that the ancient constitution of European states was a limited monarchy or mixed government' has little foundation: ibid., p. 208. For Selden's citations, see notes 18 and 92, below; for the powerful impact of Grotius upon Selden's *Mare Clausum* (London, 1635), see chapter 3, below.

3 Cf. Burgess, *Politics of the Ancient Constitution*, pp. 37–48 (for the common law as reason) and p. 64 (for immemoriality); Burgess attempted to demonstrate a commitment to immemoriality on the basis of a quotation from the introduction to Selden's edition of *Ad Fletam Dissertatio*, where the common law was characterized as '"something immemorially fitted (*antiquitate adaptata*) to the genius of the nation."' The Latin posits a long period of time, but not necessarily one beyond memory. I have not found any reference to the common law or English constitution as 'immemorial' in any of Selden's early works.

4 The marginal notes of *The Duello* refer to numerous treatises on honour and duelling, including citations to John Ferne (4) from England, and Jean Bodin (4) and Guilliame de Roule (4) from France; cited even more frequently were Andreas Alciato (10), the Italian founder of the French legal-historical school, and Michael Beuther (7), the German historian. For Alciato, see note 91, below, and for Beuther, see *Algemeine Deutsche Biographie*, 45 vols. (Berlin, 1967–71) [hereinafter *ADB*]. For sources, Selden turned most often to the English Law Books (18); John Stow, *Annales* (7); Thomas Walsingham (5); William Lambarde, *Archaionomia* (5); Matthew Paris (4); Ranulf Glanville (4); Britton, and Henry de Bracton (3). Britton and Bracton were authors of thirteenth-century English common-law treatises; Glanville, a twelfth-century justiciar who also wrote a legal treatise; Matthew Paris, an early-thirteenth- and Thomas Walsingham an early-fifteenth-century historian. See Edgar B. Graves, ed., *Bibliography of English History to 1485*, pp. 441, 450–1, 455–6, 458, and also see note 34, below. *The Duello* presented a more sophisticated analysis than any of the papers on this topic read to the Society of Antiquaries in 1600 and 1601; see those published in Thomas Hearne, ed., *A Collection of Curious Discourses*, II, pp. 172–224.

5 François Hotman, *Francogallia*, collates the Latin editions of 1573, 1576, and 1586 and provides an English translation; Harvey's marginal note on his copy of Livy as quoted in Lisa Jardine and Anthony Grafton, '"Studied for Action": How Gabriel Harvey Read His Livy,' 43. For Hotman's life, see Donald R. Kelley, *François Hotman: A Revolutionary's Ordeal*. The historical section of [Arthur Hall], *A Letter Sent by F.A.*, sig. A1–E2^r, provided an English model which briefly traced the history of the common law and parliaments. Selden did not refer to this pamphlet, however, and the parallels with the more substantial *Francogallia*, to which he did refer, were much stronger.

6 Cf. Hotman, *Francogallia*, passim, and Selden, *Analecton Anglobritannicon*, passim; even a comparison of the tables of contents will reveal the similarities. The polities they described had marked differences as well.

7 Selden, *Analecton Anglobritannicon*, pp. 17, 20, and see pp. 76, 118–19, 123–4, and Tuck, *Philosophy and Government*, p. 208

8 Historians have not fully explored these patterns; the latter stages started with Catholic claims to the English succession such as that put forward in [Robert Persons] R. Doleman, *A Conference about the Next Succession to the Crowne of England*, which evoked such refutations as [King James VI], *The Trew Law of Free Monarchies*; Thomas Craig, *Concerning the Right of Succession to the Kingdom of England*; and [John Hayward], *An Answer to the First Part of a Certaine Conference*. The original of Craig's treatise, which apparently has disappeared, was dedicated in 1603. For a discussion of these works, see J.W. Allen, *A History of Political Thought in the Sixteenth Century*, pp. 251–62, and James VI and I, *The Political Works of James I*, pp. xxxv–xlvii; for the importance of Catholic constitutional thought in the English setting, also see J.P. Sommerville, 'From Suarez to Filmer: A Reappraisal.' For debate in the House of Commons over the union and wardship, see Wallace Notestein, *The House of Commons, 1604–1610*, passim. For a wider perspective on the union, see Brian P. Levack, 'English Law, Scots Law, and the Union, 1603–1707,' 'The Proposed Union of English Law with Scots Law in the Seventeenth Century,' 'Toward a More Perfect Union: England, Scotland and the Constitution,' and *The Formation of the British State: England, Scotland, and the Union, 1603–1707*, chs. 1–3; and Bruce Galloway, *The Union of England and Scotland: 1603–1608*. Also see Bruce R. Galloway and Brian P. Levack, eds., *The Jacobean Union: Six Tracts of 1604*. For an overall view, see Glenn Burgess, 'Common Law and Political Theory in Early Stuart England.'

9 Pocock, *Ancient Constitution*, pp. 16–17. Also see J.H.M. Salmon, *The French Religious Wars in English Political Thought*. For cogent accounts of arguments made in England for 'the divine right of kings,' see James Daly, 'Cosmic Harmony and Political Thinking in Early Stuart England'; Sommerville, *Politics and Ideology*, ch. 1, 'James I and the Divine Right of Kings'; and chapter 2, below, note 462.

10 Julian Franklin, *Jean Bodin and the Rise of Absolutist Theory*, chs. 2 and 3; Skinner, *Foundations*; and Tuck, *Philosophy and Government*. Also see Burns and Goldie, eds., *The Cambridge History of Political Thought*; Julian Franklin, *Jean Bodin and the Sixteenth-Century Revoluton in the Methodology of Law and History*; Hotman, *Francogallia*; George Huppert, *The Idea of Perfect History: Historical Erudition and Historical Philosophy in Renaissance France*; and Kelley, *Foundations*.

11 See the development of this interpretation in Christianson, 'Royal and Parliamentary Voices' and 'Ancient Constitutions.' Also see Jenny Wormald, 'James VI and I, *Basilikon Doron* and *The Trew Law of Free Monarchies*: The Scottish Context and the English Translation.'

12 McIlwain, *Political Works of James I*, p. 309. For a similar reading of this speech, see Burgess, 'Common Law and Political Theory,' 13–14; for a reading representing this speech as embodying the 'Jacobean consensus,' see Burgess, *Politics of the Ancient Constitution*, pp. 152–6. My reading places greater weight upon the initiatives retained by monarchs to create, modify, and administer the law.

13 Elizabeth Read Foster, *Proceedings in Parliament, 1610*, II, p. 175. Hedley sat for the borough of Huntingdon and, according to Notestein, became a 'well-known judge': see Notestein, *Commons, 1604–1610*, p. 365. For more lengthy interpretations of Hedley's speech and its context, see Christianson, 'Royal and Parliamentary Voices,' pp. 78–82, and 'Ancient Constitutions,' pp. 99–103, and the notes for each.

14 Foster, *Proceedings in Parliament*, II, pp. 178–9.

15 Ibid., p. 180.

16 Ibid. Obviously, Hedley did not invent the concept of 'immemorial custom' – long before, both Glanville and Bracton had characterized the law of England as unwritten custom, and, in the debate over impositions, other members of Parliament had traced individual liberties or privileges back beyond memory – however, Hedley combined custom and immemoriality, applied the combination to the whole of the common law, and used it to support a particular version of the ancient constitution in which the common law distributed power to the Crown and Parliament. For Glanville, see *The Treatise on the Laws and Customs of the Realm of England*

Commonly called Glanvill, prologue, pp. 2–3; Bracton, see *Bracton on the Laws and Customs of England*, II, introduction, p. 19.

17 For the call for codification of the common law in the late sixteenth and early seventeenth centuries, see Richard Helgerson, *Forms of Nationhood: The Elizabethan Writing of England*, ch. 3, especially pp. 73–8; Louis A. Knafla, *Law and Politics in Jacobean England: The Tracts of Lord Chancellor Ellesmere*, ch. 5; Julian Martin, *Francis Bacon, the State, and the Reform of Natural Philosophy*, ch. 5; and Burgess, *Politics of the Ancient Constitution*, pp. 125–7.

18 Entered at the Stationer's Register on 26 November and dated in the preface at 25 December 1610, *Jani Anglorum* probably appeared in print early in 1610–11. The title page contained a woodcut of a Janus head, surrounded by the text 'Equibus hæc Populum spectat: at illa Larem.' One face looked at the 'Populum' and the other at the 'Larem.' With this emblem and the subtitle promising to provide memorials of Anglo-British profane law up to the reign of Henry II, Selden probably meant that one face of Janus represented the customary secular law (that is, the people) and the other face sacred law (that is, the household gods). This would explain the statement in the preface that the book deals with '*whatsoever concerns the* Civil *or* Profane Law' (sig. a 2ᵛ) and the absence of any systematic discussion of the canon law and church courts; *Jani Anglorum* looked only at the 'Populum.' The proposed union with Scotland raised fears about the primacy of the common law in England and reopened the debate about the relationship of the common to the canon and Roman or civil laws. For a receptionist view, see the dedication in William Fulbecke, *A Parallele or Conference of the Civill Law the Canon Law, and the Common Law of this Relame of England*, where he expressed the following aim for writing this dialogue: 'it seemed straunge unto me, that these three lawes, should not as the three *Graces* have their hands linked together, and their lookes directly fixed one upon the other, but like the two faces of *Janus*, the one should be turned from the other, and should never looke toward, or upon the other ...' In order to preserve the independence of the English common law, Selden may have turned Fulbecke's negative image into a positive emblem. I would like to thank Dr Gerald Aylmer for raising the question of the meaning of the title of *Jani Anglorum* with me, Dr Ross Kilpatrick for helping to provide an answer, and Dr Daniel Woolf for the reference to the Stationer's Register. The wide-ranging marginal notes of *Jani Anglorum* frequently cite such authorities as William Camden (13), Justus Lipsius (8), François Hotman (6), and Jean Bodin (5), none of whom should need an introduction, and such sources as

Plutarch (12), William of Malmesbury (11), Bracton (10), Ingulf of Croyland (9), Seneca (9), the English Law Books (8), the Old Testament (8),
Julius Caesar (7), Tacitus (7), and Matthew Paris (6), while numerous
references to Ovid (13) enliven the text. Malmesbury lived in the mid-
twelfth century, and the pseudo-Ingulf was a fourteenth-century forgery
that purported to come from the eleventh century: see Graves, ed., *Bibliography to 1485*, pp. 294, 436–7.

19 Hall's anonymous pamphlet seems to have had a very limited circulation,
and the historical section took up slightly more than a quarter of the text.
Most of the papers delivered at the Society of Antiquaries remained in
manuscript until the eighteenth century; for papers on the antiquity of
the common law and of parliaments, see Hearne, ed., *A Collection*, I,
pp. 1–10, 281–310. Many of the most telling arguments of Coke appeared
in the prefaces of his *Reports*. Speeches in parliaments often made passing
reference to the ancient constitution rather than expounding upon it at
length; see the examples cited in White, *Sir Edward Coke*, and in the next
chapter of this study. Massive histories of England or Britain, such as that
by John Speed, contained constitutional material, but did not expound an
articulated history of the constitution. A manuscript rival existed in Sir
Roger Owen's, 'Of the Antiquitie Amplenes and Excellence of the Common Lawes of England,' written in 1615–16, but this was not printed and
had only a limited circulation: see William Klein, 'The Ancient Constitution Revisited,' especially pp. 36–41. Only with the publication of such
works as William Prynne's, *The Soveraigne Power of Parliaments* did
substantial rival accounts appear for aspects of Selden's; a century later,
Jani Anglorum was finally replaced by Sir Mathew Hale's, *The History of
the Common Law of England*, a work that owed a great debt to Selden.
For a brief account of the relationship of Hale's *History* to the views of
Selden, see Tuck, *Natural Rights Theories*, pp. 132–9 and Alan Cromartie, *Sir Matthew Hale, 1605–1676: Law, Religion and Natural Philosophy*, chs. 2, 3, and 7.

20 John Selden, 'The Reverse or Back Face of the English Janus,' p. 8. Normally quotations in English that appear here are from this translation; in
a number of cases, however, where the translator misleads the reader – for
example, by consistently rendering 'concilium' as 'parliament,' a translation which begs the question of Selden's point of view – either a more
appropriate rendering is made or the word or phrase is quoted in Latin, or
both. For passages over which doubt might arise or for which the Latin
text adds clarity, reference is made to both *Jani Anglorum* and 'English
Janus.' Selden's interest in the biblical posterity of Noah would develop in

later writings. For Samothes, see T.D. Kendrick, *British Antiquity*, pp. 70–2. In light of his later treatises based upon the Talmud and Talmudic writers, the denigration here seems ironic.

21 Ibid., p. 16; see Kendrick, *British Antiquity*, chs. 7 and 8, and Arthur Williamson, *Scottish National Consciousness in the Age of James VI: The Apocalypse, the Union and the Shaping of Scotland's Public Culture*, ch. 5.

22 Selden, 'English Janus,' pp. 17, 93, and *Jani Anglorum*, pp. 25, 124: 'Reges neque insulæ Anglo Britanniæ monarchæ. Uni etenim præfuere simul Cantil Cyngotorix, Carvilius, Taximagulus, et Segonax; ad eum modum aliis. Pluribus id circo subjacuisse et aristocræ gubernationi, juxta quod Polydorus, Joannes Tuinus, David Pouelus atque alii edocuerunt, in qua versamur partem obtem perasse, non est curdubitemus.' Cf. *Analecton*, p. 20, and see the quotation cited to note 7, above.

23 Selden, 'English Janus,' p. 93, see pp. 13–16; cf. *Analecton*, ch. 4.

24 Selden, 'English Janus,' pp. 17–18, 93; on the latter page, Selden says that 'of ancient times the *Semnothei*, the *Kings*, and the *Druids* were *Lawgivers*; amongst the *Britans*,' but followed with the two passages quoted above which limited the jurisdiction of kings and stressed that of the Druids. Hotman severely limited the power of the ancient Gallic kings; see *Francogallia*, ch. 1, especially pp. 154–5, where he explained that the kingdoms of Gaul were not hereditary and that the kings were circumscribed by law. Although Selden favourably cited Coke's *Reports* on several occasions in this section, he must have made a deliberate break both in his attack upon Brutus and in his classification of the government of the Britons as an aristocracy. Since the polity of the Britons did not set the pattern for the common law, Selden probably had not reached as radical position as had Grotius in 1610, as suggested by Richard Tuck in a review in the *Journal of Modern History* 59 (1987), 570–2, and in *Philosophy and Government*, p. 208. For a derivation of law from royal grant, see [Hall], *A Letter*, sig. D2^r; in this section, Hall argued that the British kings governed 'without our forme of Parliament' because neither nobility and shires nor cities and boroughs existed to provide the members.

25 In his discussion of the major marks of sovereignty near the end of *Jani Anglorum*, Selden systematically dismissed any attempt to read a single lawmaking sovereign into the ancient constitution: *Jani Anglorum*, pp. 123–33, and 'English Janus,' pp. 93–9. The Trojan legend asserted a monarchical historical foundation and was revived in early-seventeenth-century France specifically to bolster the revival of royal power: see Huppert, *Idea of Perfect History*, pp. 75, 83–4, 87.

26 With references to Plato, to the British queens *'Boadicia'* and *'Chartis-mandua,'* and to the equality of the male and female gods of antiquity, Selden specifically defended the right of women to rule: see Selden, 'English Janus,' pp. 19–20.

27 Selden, 'English Janus,' p. 27; see pp. 24–8; cf. *Analecton*, ch. 6, and also see Glanmor Williams, 'Some Protestant Views of Early British Church History.' The Lucius account brought bishops into the ancient constitution at a very early date (as replacements for pagan priests) – indeed, before the arrival of the Saxons. Selden showed moderation on this point, compared with George Saltern, *Of the Antient Lawes of Great Britaine* who used King Lucius as a link for binding the laws of the Saxons to those of the ancient Britons. As Glenn Burgess pointed out: 'Saltern's aim was to show that the laws of England were genuinely Christian': *Politics of the Ancient Constitution*, p. 77. I would like to thank Dr Daniel Woolf for drawing Saltern's work to my attention.

28 Selden, 'English Janus,' p. 28; cf. Selden, *Titles of Honor* (1614), pp. 37–8, and see Winnefred Joy Mulligan, 'The British Constantine: An English Historical Myth.'

29 Selden, 'English Janus,' p. 95; cf. *Analecton*, p. 75, and see pp. 55, 58–9. Hotman argued that the Franks liberated the Gauls from Roman slavery and merged with them to form Francogallia. Selden saw the Saxons as conquering and replacing the Britons. For a recent account of Anglo-Saxon government, see H.R. Loyn, *The Governance of Anglo-Saxon England, 500–1087.*

30 Selden, 'English Janus,' p. 93. The translation accurately reflects Selden's lack of understanding of the office of 'ealdorman' in 1610.

31 Ibid., p. 94, and Selden, *Jani Anglorum*, pp. 124–5. For a less sanguine view, cf. [Hall], *A Letter*, sig. A3–B1^v, D2^v–3^v.

32 Selden, 'English Janus,' p. 32, and *Jani Anglorum*, p. 43; Selden quoted Tacitus here.

33 On the eve of the English Civil War, *The Aphorismes of the Kingdome* ([London, 1642]), a work sometimes wrongly attributed to William Prynne, and *Militia Old and New* (London, 2642 [1642]), employed the precedent of the election of local officials in Anglo-Saxon times to argue that the two Houses of Parliament possessed the right to appoint lords lieutenant. For the Levellers, see Don M. Wolfe, ed., *Leveller Manifestoes of the Puritan Revolution*, pp. 190–1.

34 At this time, Selden drew most of his knowledge of early laws from William Lambarde, *Archaionomia, sive de Priscis Anglorum Legibus* (London, 1568), a work that contained several early Norman forgeries, as

Pocock has pointed out: see Pocock, *Ancient Constitution*, pp. 42–3. For Lambarde's work as an antiquary, see Retha M. Warnicke, *William Lambarde: Elizabethan Antiquary, 1536–1601* chs. 4 and 9, and James D. Alsop and Wesley M. Stevens, 'William Lambarde and the Elizabethan Polity.' A printed edition of Bede appeared in [Jerome Commelin], *Rerum Britannicarum* ... *Scriptores Vetustiores*, of the pseudo-Ingulf and of William of Malmesbury in [Henry Savile], *Rerum Anglicarum Scriptores Post Bedam*. Not until the nineteenth century was it demonstrated that Ingulf of Croyland was a much later forgery. For a guide to these sources, see Graves, *Bibliography to 1485*, pp. 137, 143, 288–9, 294, 436–7; for the early Norman forgeries, also see H.G. Richardson and G.O. Sayles, *Law and Legislation from Æthelberht to Magna Carta*, pp. 120–31.

35 Selden, 'English Janus,' pp. 33, 36.
36 Ibid., pp. 32, 33, 36, and see pp. 30–6. The passage on military tenure had marginal notes to Jean Bodin, *De Republica*, and François Hotman, *De Feudis Commentatio Tripetita*, an acknowledgment by Selden that his insights into feudal institutions came from Continental legal historians.
37 Ibid., p. 36.
38 Ibid. Selden also discussed the Anglo-Saxon practice of trial by the ordeals of fire or water in a separate section; having noted that the laws of the Franks and the Lombards contained such ordeals and that 'a great many instances both of this way of trying by water and of that by fire are afforded by the histories of the *Danes, Saxons, Germans, Franks, Spaniards*, in a word of the whole Christian world,' he dismissed their constitutional significance by asserting that they 'do more appertain to sacred rites, than to civil customs': ibid., pp. 84, 86; see pp. 84–6, and *Analecton*, ch. 8.
39 Selden, *Jani Anglorum*, pp. 53–4, 126, 129; 'English Janus,' pp. 41, 95–6.
40 Selden, 'English Janus,' p. 37. Selden had no sense that this marked the beginning of all written law in Anglo-Saxon England: see Dorothy Whitelock, *The Beginnings of English Society: The Anglo-Saxon Period*, p. 134; cf. Richardson and Sayles, *Law and Legislation*, pp. 2–12, 157–69, who see Ethelbert's laws as essentially pagan and owing nothing to Roman example, and John Frederick Winkler, 'Roman Law in Anglo-Saxon England,' who sees an indirect impact.
41 Selden, 'English Janus,', p. 37.
42 Ibid., pp. 93, 97. Bishops played an essential role in the Saxon constitution. Since he deprecated the Norman creation of separate church courts and portrayed the Christianized Saxon interdependence of religion and government (of the sacred and the profane) in a positive manner, Selden

may have seen a return to the Saxon example as a reforming ideal for his own day.

43 Cf. John Speed, *The Historie of Great Brittaine under the Conquests of the Romans, Saxons, Danes and Normans*, pp. 391–408 and passim; William Camden, *Britain, or a Chorographicall Description of England, Scotland, and Ireland*, pp. 101–3; and [Hall], *A Letter*, sig. A3–4^r, D3. Selden paid greater attention to the Danes in *Analecton*, ch. 4–6.

44 Selden, 'English Janus,' p. 39.

45 Ibid., p. 38.

46 Foster, *Proceedings in Parliament, 1610*, II, p. 190. Pocock, *Ancient Constitution*, pp. 42–3, 53–5, 99–102, 149–50, passim; cf. Johann P. Sommerville, 'History and Theory: The Norman Conquest in Early Stuart Political Thought,' and Burgess, *Politics of the Ancient Constitution*, pp. 82–6.

47 For Coke's reliance on the *Modus* and the *Mirror*, also see Pocock, *Ancient Constitution*, p. 43; Ferguson, *Clio Unbound*, p. 272; and Christianson, 'Ancient Constitutions,' pp. 109–10. For assessments of these two works as evidence, see Graves, *Bibliography to 1485*, pp. 459, 509–10; Nicholas Pronay and John Taylor, eds., *Parliamentary Texts of the Later Middle Ages*, ch. 1; and Michael Prestwich, 'The Modus Tenendi Parliamentum.'

48 As early as 1610, Selden described the *Modus* as 'an old book, which pretends to more antiquity by far than it ought,' but he did not discuss its authenticity at length until 1631; see 'English Janus,' p. 88; *Jani Anglorum*, p. 118; *Titles of Honor* (1614), p. 274; and *Titles of Honor* (1631), pp. 739, 742–4.

49 Of these, William of Malmesbury was the source closest to the Conquest; Selden, as noted above, thought that Ingulf and the laws were contemporary and, therefore, gave them greater weight. Mathew Paris was available in Matthew Parker, ed., *Chronicles*, 4 vols., and Roger of Hoveden, in [Savile], *Rerum Anglicanum*. For the historians mentioned and these editions, see Graves, *Bibliography to 1485*, pp. 142, 143, 431, 441–2, and note 34, above.

50 Selden, 'English Janus,' pp. 47–8, and *Jani Anglorum*, pp. 61–2; cf. *Analecton*, p. 119. The word order of the quotation has been altered slightly from that in 'English Janus' to bring the emphasis of the English more closely into line with that in the Latin text.

51 As Pocock pointed out, scholars trained in the historical legal traditions of the Continent did not agree on the questions of the origin and nature of feudal institutions: see Pocock, *Ancient Constitution*, ch. 1, and Donald

R. Kelley, *'De Origine Feudorum:* The Beginnings of an Historical Problem.'

52 Selden, 'English Janus,' pp. 52, 55, 57–8.

53 Ibid., p. 48; the same passage is quoted in Camden, *Britain,* p. 170

54 Ibid.; the same passage appears in *Analecton,* p. 119, and in Camden, *Britain,* p. 153. Selden's wording in *Jani Anglorum* does not exactly fit that in the available Latin versions of William Camden's, *Britannia;* cf. *Jani Anglorum,* pp. 62–3, and *Britannia* (1590), p. 89, (1594), p. 94, and (1607), p. 123. However, these passages are so close that one suspects that Selden either mistranscribed them or found them in Camden, but then took the quotation from another version of the source; in either case, he owed a considerable debt to Camden. For Gervase of Tilbury's *Otia Imperialia,* written in 1212, see Graves, *Bibliography to 1485,* p. 446.

55 Selden, 'English Janus,' p. 48; by 'lawyers' in this passage, Selden meant 'civil lawyers.'

56 Ibid., p. 98; see pp. 94–9.

57 Ibid., sig. a 3^{v}-4^{r}; see Tuck, *Natural Rights,* p. 83, for a shortened version of this quotation taken slightly out of context; for a similar passage, also derived from Machiavelli, cf. *Analecton,* pp. 123–4.

58 The theme of a break at the Conquest, strongly articulated in Samuel Daniel, *The First Part of the Historie of England,* became more pronounced in Selden's publications, as we shall see, up to and including the first edition of *Titles of Honor* (1614), but receded thereafter and was rejected in *The Historie of Tithes* (1618). For Daniel's interpretation of the Norman Conquest, see D.R. Woolf, 'Community, Law and State: Samuel Daniel's Historical Thought Revisited,' 78–80, and *The Idea of History,* pp. 95–9.

59 Selden, 'English Janus,' pp. 58–91.

60 Ibid., pp. 61–5.

61 Ibid., pp. 60–1. For a recent interpretation which posits a breakdown of Saxon traditions in the reign of Henry I, see W.L. Warren, *The Governance of Norman and Angevin England, 1086–1272,* ch. 3.

62 Selden, 'English Janus,' p. 68. Much later, Selden would give a much more sophisticated interpretation of the relationship of the Roman to the common law in Norman and Angevin England: see *Ioannis Seldeni Ad Fletam Dissertatio,* chs. 7 and 8.

63 Selden, 'English Janus,' p. 68.

64 Ibid., pp. 51–2; earlier, Arthur Agard had established this point in his presentation to the Society of Antiquaries: see Hearne, ed., *A Collection,* II, pp. 314–15.

65 Tuck, *Natural Rights*, p. 83; this apt phrase may underestimate Selden's ability to deal with major historical shifts, however.

66 Selden, 'English Janus,' p. 94; *Jani Anglorum*, p. 126. As one who doubted the authenticity of *Modus Tenendi Parliamentum*, Selden, of course, did not use its terminology of 'gradus' for 'estates,' but used the normal medieval term of 'ordines.' Selden may have obtained this image from the paper given at the Society of Antiquaries by Francis Tate: see Hearne, ed., *A Collection*, I, pp. 299–300. For a lengthy discussion of the origins and application of this image of mixed monarchy, see Michael Mendle, *Dangerous Positions: Mixed Government, the Estates of the Realm, and the Making of the Answer to the XIX Propositions*. This characterization would become very popular in the 1640s and beyond.

67 See G.R. Elton, 'Arthur Hall, Lord Burghley and the Antiquity of Parliament'; Mendle, *Dangerous Positions*, passim; Pocock, *Machiavellian Moment*, pp. 66–80, passim; Corinne Comstock Weston, *English Constitutional Theory and the House of Lords*; and Weston and Jannelle Renfrow Greenberg, *Subjects and Sovereigns: The Grand Controversy over Legal Sovereignty in Stuart England*. As I argue in this study, Selden's view of mixed monarchy did not depend upon the formula that parliaments consisted of the three estates of king, Lords, and Commons. On the basis of conjecture, Mendle has strongly overstated the 'dangerousness' of such a position in late Elizabethan and Jacobean England.

68 See A.W. Pollard and G.R. Redgrave, revised by W.A. Jackson, F.S. Ferguson, and Katherine F. Pantzer, *A Short-Title Catalogue of Books Printed in ... 1475–1640*, 3 vols., nos. 14396, 14396.3, 14396.7.

69 For the articulation of 'constitutional monarchy created by kings' by such major royal servants as Lord Chancellor Ellesmere and Attorney General Sir Robert Heath, see Knafla, *Law and Politics*, introduction, pp. 65–92, and the tracts on the royal prerogative and on the case *post-nati*, pp. 197–254, and Christianson, 'John Selden, the Five Knights' Case, and Discretionary Imprisonment'; 'Royal and Parliamentary Voices,' pp. 85–9; and 'Ancient Constitutions,' pp. 114–15, 127–8, 143–6. Hall saw kings as originating law, but as gradually sharing this power with nobles under the Anglo-Saxons, and with commoners starting under Henry III. Thus, kings bound themselves to make law with the consent of the realm and gradually created Parliament for this purpose: [Hall], *A Letter*, sig. D4^{v}–E1^{r} and passim.

70 Burgess, *Politics of the Ancient Constitution*, ch. 5. While Burgess has noted the more than nuanced differences among common lawyers on such issues as the rational, mutable, and customary nature of the com-

mon law (including the eccentricity of Sir Edward Coke's historical representation of an immutable, immemorial constitution), he included nothing analogous to 'constitutional monarchy created by kings.' Finding a place for a common-law tradition often voiced by the early Stuart kings and many of their chief legal officers helps in understanding many of the constitutional debates which took place in England during the first four decades of the seventeenth century. For example, the differences between 'constitutional monarchy created by kings' and 'constitutional monarchy governed by the common law' outlined above should help to clarify our understanding of the different attitudes towards the 'reform' of the common law voiced by King James and Sir Francis Bacon versus Sir Edward Coke. See the works cited in note 17, above, especially, Helgerson, *Forms of Nationhood*, ch. 2.

71 Michael Drayton, *Poly-Olbion*, sig. A2^r. See the nuanced reading by Anne Lake Prescott, 'Marginal Discourse: Drayton's Muse and Selden's "Story."'

72 Drayton, *Poly-Olbion*, sig. A2^r. This was one of the few explicit statements made by Selden about his philological historical method.

73 Ibid., pp. 93–4. This represented a continuation of the Renaissance debate between history and poetry: see Hershel Baker, *The Race of Time*, ch. 1; Arthur Ferguson, *Utter Antiquity: Perceptions of Prehistory in Renaissance England*, ch. 7; and Prescott, 'Marginal Discourse.'

74 Drayton, *Poly-Olbion*, sig. A2^r.

75 Ibid., sig. A2^v. This attack upon the legend of Brutus had a long history in England, going back at least as early as the history of Polydore Vergil; see Kendrick, *British Antiquity*, ch. 6.

76 Drayton, *Poly-Olbion*, sig. A2^v.

77 Ibid., sig A3^r. After Caesar, these included '*Tacitus* and *Dio* especially, *Vopiscus, Capitolin, Spartian* ... afterward *Gildas, Nennius* (but little is left of them, and that of the last, very imperfect), *Bede, Asserio, Ethelwerd* ... *William of Malmesbury, Marian, Florence of Worcester* ... and the numerous rest of our Monkish and succeeding Chronographers': Ibid., sig A2^{v}–3^r.

78 Ibid., sig A3^v and marginal note. For just a few examples, cf. p. 129 with 'English Janus,' p. 27; p. 194 with 'English Janus,' p. 39; and p. 74 with *Jani Anglorum*, pp. 61–2.

79 Drayton, *Poly-Olbion*, pp. 151–2, 167–9; for Selden's use of British coins, see p. 127; in this, he followed the lead of Camden.

80 Ibid., see pp. 126, 194, 211–12, for the Danes; for Anglo-Saxon society, see pp. 184–91, 194; cf. *Analecton*, pp. 89–90, 102–12, 119.

81 Drayton, *Poly-Olbion*; for Drayton's point of view, see pp. 28, 63–4, 139, 256–60; for Selden's response, see pp. 74, 181, 188–91, 268.

82 Ibid., p. 268. In the marginal note to the quoted passage, Selden cited three works: François Hotman's, *Quæstionum Illustrium Liber* (Geneva, 1573 ff.), Alberico Gentili's, *De Jure Belli* (London, 1588), and Sir Edward Coke's, *La Sept Part des Reports* (London, 1608). Alberico Gentili held the regius professorship of Civil Law at Oxford from 1587 to 1608 and was a leading Bartolist; his *De Jure Belli Libri Tres* (London, 1588–9) dealt with the international law of warfare as practised in Europe: see the *Dictionary of National Biography* (hereinafter *DNB*) and Coquillette, 'Legal Ideology and Incorporation, I,' 31–5, 54–63.

83 Drayton, *Poly-Olbion*, p. 126; cf. the passage quoted above at note 45, which mentioned the laws of earlier kings but not the laws of different kingdoms.

84 Ibid., pp. 271–2. This account derived from John Foxe, *Actes and Monuments*, I, pp. 252–60, or a later edition of Foxe.

85 Drayton, *Poly-Olbion*, p. 272.

86 Ibid.; Selden had compared the texts; Speed, for example, noted no differences.

87 Ibid., pp. 273, 274. Selden's knowledge of King John's Magna Carta stemmed from the hybrid version printed in Matthew Paris's, *Angli Historia Maior, à Guilielmo Conquaestore, ad ultimum annum Henrici tertii*. For this version, see Faith Thompson, *Magna Carta: Its Role in the Making of the English Constitution, 1300–1629*, pp. 292–3, and J.C. Holt, *Magna Carta*, p. 290.

88 Prescott, 'Marginal Discourse,' 317.

89 Selden, *Titles of Honor*, sig. a 3^v–4^r.

90 A Latin treatise of some thirty-two folios on the subject exists in the Selden papers among Hale manuscripts at Lincoln's Inn: see Lincoln's Inn, Hale MS 12, f. 16–48. After a brief introduction, starting with the Romans (f. 16–21) and moving through Byzantium (f. 21^v–22^v), the Lombards (f. 22^v–23^r), and Charlemagne and the later Empire (f. 23–4), this treatise devotes most of its space to England, working forward from the Anglo-Saxons (f. 25^r) through to the Elizabethan period, and quoting the patents creating William Cecil as Lord Burghley, John Beaumont as Viscount Beaumont, Walter Devereux as Earl of Essex, Thomas Grey as Marquess of Dorset, Anna Rochford as Marquise of Pembroke, Edward Seymour as Duke of Somerset, and Edward, the son of Henry VI, as Prince of Wales (f. 28–36); included are also some statements quoted in Saxon, English, and Latin, which indicate a not very extensive familiarity with

Saxon (f. 47^v). If this is an early draft of *Titles of Honor* written around the same time as his early Latin works (*ca* 1607-10), the production of the much more sophisticated edition of 1614 within a few years represented a major accomplishment.

91 Selden, *Titles of Honor*, sig. c 4^v, d 3^v-4^r. Guillaume Budé was an early, and Jacques Cujas the greatest, philological civil lawyer in France; Matthæus Wesenbeck edited and commented upon Justinian's *Institutes*, and Barnabé Brisson, president of the Parlement of Paris, wrote on numerous relevant topics, including Persia. For Wesenbeck, see the *ADB*. For Brisson, see the *Nouvelle Biographie Universelle*, 46 vols. (Paris, 1852-66) [hereinafter *NBU*]. For Budé, Alciato, and Cujas, see Kelley, *Foundations*, chs. 3 and 4. For Alberico Gentili, see note 82, above; his father and brother were also civil lawyers.

92 Selden made numerous marginal references to various writers. The most frequent were as follows – ancient: Old Testament (40), Cassiodorus (20), Josephus (15), Pliny (15), Cicero (13), Plutarch (9), Tacitus (9), Herodotus (7), Lampridius (7), Macrobius (7), Polybius (6), Seneca (6), Suetonius (6), Tertullian (6), Ulpian (6), and Virgil (6); English: Camden (25), Year Books (21), Patents and Statutes (19), Rotuli Parliamentorum (17), Malmesbury (15), Plea Rolls (15), Bracton (13), Hakluyt (11), Hoveden (11), Laws of Cnut (11), and Matthew Paris (11); Continental: Scaliger (23), Lipsius (20), Leunclavius (14), Bodin (13), Casaubon (13), the Constitutions of the Civil Law (13), Bignon (10), Cantacuzeni (9), Constantine Porphyrogenetus (9), Crantzius (8), Alciato (7), and L'Oyseau (7). Bodin, Camden, Casaubon, Lipsius, and Scaliger should need no introduction; all but Camden appear in the biographical section of Burns and Goldie, eds., *Cambridge History of Political Thought*. Jérôme Bignon was a French jurist who wrote a weighty treatise on the powers of the kings of France and another on the election of popes: see *NBU*. Charles L'Oyseau published several weighty treatises on the orders, offices, and institutions of France: see H.A. Lloyd, 'The Political Thought of Charles Loyseau (1564–1610).' Albertus Krantz gathered sources for the history of the early Germans and Scandinavians, all published posthumously, and Joannes Leunclavius translated numerous works on the Ottoman Turks into Latin; both appear in *ADB*. Joannis V Cantacuzeni and Constantine VII Porphyrogenetus were Byzantine emperors whose works were published in Latin translation in the sixteenth and seventeenth centuries.

93 For a more traditional approach which included chapters on the topics left out by Selden and a moral code for 'every knight and gentleman,' see Sir William Segar, *Honor, Military, and Civil*, pp. 53-5, 60, 65-108, passim.

94 Selden, *Titles of Honor*, sig. b 3^v. The favourable citation of Bartolus, the medieval jurist who adapted the Justinian Code of Roman law to contemporary circumstances, indicated the scope of Selden's allegiance, that is, to both the humanist and historical *mos gallicus* and the more practical *mos italicus*. From among the rich bibliography on these traditions of civil or Roman lawyers and their impact upon England, see Donald R. Kelley, 'Law,' and 'Civil Science in the Renaissance: The Problem of Interpretation,' the relevant articles collected in Donald R. Kelley, *History, Law and the Human Sciences*; and Coquillette, 'Legal Ideology and Incorporation, I,' 22–35.

95 Selden, *Titles of Honor*, sig. A 1^r and c 1^r.

96 Ibid., c 1.

97 Ibid., sig. c1^v–2^r.

98 Ibid., sig. c 2^r.

99 Ibid., sig. c2^v–3^r.

100 Ibid., sig. c3^r–4^r; also see d2–3.

101 Ibid., pp. 5, 5–14. For remarks about the image of Nimrod, see Pocock, *Ancient Constitution*, pp. 283–5, 326–7.

102 Selden, *Titles of Honor*, p. 2. For an account which places Selden's ideas in different perspective, cf. Sommerville, 'John Selden, the Law of Nature, and the Origins of Government,' especially 443–5.

103 For absolutist arguments, see Sommerville, *Politics and Ideology*, ch. 1, especially pp. 27–34.

104 Selden, *Titles of Honor*, pp. 4–5; cf., p. 5: 'Well I allow, that a Family, being in nature before a publique societie or common-welth was an exemplary Monarchie, and, in that regard, a Monarchie is ancienter then any State: but as it applied to a common societie of many families and to what we now call a Kingdome, it cannot but presuppose a popular State or Democracie.'

105 Ibid., pp. 2–3. Selden hardly saw the transformation of a 'popular state' into a 'monarchy' as a 'radical transformation'; changes of this sort took place in a number of ways, including unthreatened choice: cf. Tuck, *Philosophy and Government*, pp. 208–9.

106 Selden, *Titles of Honor*, p. 3.

107 Ibid., p. 5.

108 Tuck, *Natural Rights*, ch. 4; '"The Ancient Law of Freedom": John Selden and the Civil War' and *Philosophy and Government*, pp. 214–21; cf. Sommerville, *Politics and Ideology*, pp. 60–4, 'John Selden,' 437–47. The first two chapters of Sommerville's *Politics and Ideology* provide a valuable summary of the major natural-law arguments available to early-

seventeenth-century English political philosophers. Tuck's, *Natural Rights* draws primarily from Selden's *Mare Clausum* and *De Jure Naturali et Gentium Juxta Disciplinam Ebræorum* (London, 1640), and, to a lesser extent, upon the posthumously published *Table Talk*, while '"The Ancient Law of Freedom"' adds material related to Selden's activities in the Long Parliament; both also cite other works by Selden.

109 Selden, *Titles of Honor*, p. 15.

110 Ibid.

111 Ibid., pp. 182–3; see pp. 182–6.

112 Ibid., p. 184; see p. 219.

113 Ibid., p. 187; see pp. 186–7.

114 Ibid., p. 188; for a recent examination of the complexities of this process in France, see Edward James, *The Origins of France: From Clovis to the Capetians, 500–1000.*

115 Selden, *Titles of Honor*, pp. 189–90.

116 Ibid., p. 190.

117 Ibid., p. 191.

118 Ibid.

119 Ibid., p. 195. Selden often displayed an unusual talent for summarizing complex historical changes in relatively brief passages.

120 Ibid., p. 196; he did not stress the role of the civil lawyers and the Parlement of Paris in this 'recovery' of royal privileges. His account here differed fundamentally with Hotman's *Francogallia*, a sign of Selden's wider reading in French legal-historical accounts since his completion of the *Jani Anglorum*.

121 Selden, *Titles of Honor*, p. 202 (misnumbered as 206).

122 Ibid., p. 203 (misnumbered as 207); see p. 205 and note for wergild; cf. *Jani Anglorum*, pp. 129–30, or 'English Janus,' pp. 96–7.

123 Selden, *Titles of Honor*, pp. 227–8.

124 Ibid., pp. 223–4. The title Earl, used in the early Kentish law codes, was revived to replace that of Ealdorman in the reign of King Cnut. Selden read too much of a jurisdictional difference and too little of a temporal one into his sources on this point. For a recent account, see H.R. Loyn, *Anglo-Saxon England and the Norman Conquest*, pp. 213–14.

125 Selden, *Titles of Honor*, p. 224.

126 Ibid., p. 226. Selden had improved his understanding over that expressed in the *Jani Anglorum*; cf. the passage cited to note 30, above.

127 Selden, *Titles of Honor*, p. 227.

128 Ibid., pp. 224–5; cf. note 60, above.

129 Ibid., p. 228.

130 Ibid.; cf. the passage cited to note 56, above.
131 Selden, 'English Janus,' p. 98; *Jani Anglorum*, p. 131.
132 Selden, *Titles of Honor*, p. 265.
133 Ibid., p. 267.
134 Ibid.
135 Ibid., p. 269.
136 Ibid., pp. 270–1. For a brief introduction to modern interpretations of the hide, see Warren, *Governance of Norman and Angevin England*, pp. 27–9, 36–8; cf. Frederic W. Maitland, *Domesday Book and Beyond*, pp. 357–520; R. Welldon Finn, *An Introduction to Domesday Book*; C. Hart, *The Hidation of Cambridgeshire* and *The Hidation of Northamptonshire*; and C. Warren Hollister, *Anglo-Saxon Military Institutions on the Eve of the Norman Conquest*.
137 Selden, *Titles of Honor*, p. 272. The Saxon fragment to which Selden referred was printed in William Lambarde, *A Perambulation of Kent*, pp. 500–1.
138 Selden, *Titles of Honor*, p. 273.
139 Ibid., pp. 273–4. He compared these parliamentary barons to the senators of ancient Rome; ibid., p. 275. Cf. Selden, 'English Janus,' p. 94, and *Jani Anglorum*, pp. 125–6.
140 Selden, *Titles of Honor*, p. 278; cf. [Hall], *A Letter*, sig. D3^v–E1^r.
141 Selden, *Titles of Honor*, pp. 278–9; in lines four and five of the quotation, 'to omit' means 'not to mention.'
142 Ibid., p. 282.
143 Ibid., p. 281; cf. p. 278, where Selden cited Camden to this effect. Cf. 'English Janus,' p. 83, and *Jani Anglorum*, pp. 111–12.
144 Selden, *Titles of Honor*, p. 344.
145 Ibid., p. 305. In the 1631 edition of *Titles of Honor*, this ancient northern origin of military knighthood would provide the starting-point for the derivation of feudal tenures: see chapter 3 below.
146 Selden, *Titles of Honor* (1614), p. 308.
147 Ibid., pp. 308–9.
148 Ibid., p. 312.
149 Ibid., p. 313.
150 Ibid.
151 Ibid., p. 321.
152 Ibid., p. 332. On the same page, however, Selden did draw attention to the cognate 'Knecht' in German.
153 Ibid., p. 319.
154 For the foundation for the more recent discussions of this topic, see J.H.

Round, *Feudal England*; for recent interpretations and a refutation of Round's argument that William introduced knight service, see John Gillingham, 'The Introduction of Knight Service into England.'

155 Selden, *Titles of Honor*, p. 319.

156 Ibid., p. 319; see p. 320.

157 Ibid., pp. 320–1. This section contained enough precedents to provide a justification for the revival of distraint of knighthood in England.

158 Ibid., p. 334.

159 Ibid., p. 335.

160 Cf. Pocock, *Ancient Constitution*, chs. 1 and 4, and Kelley, '*De Origine Feudorum*.' Kelley brings out the ongoing nature of this dispute. The topic still remains controversial; for example, see E.A.R. Brown, 'The Tyranny of a Construct: Feudalism and the Historians of Medieval Europe.'

161 Selden, *Titles of Honor*, p. 294. For a classic account, see F.L. Ganshof, *Feudalism*, and cf. Marc Bloch, *Feudal Society*. A number of more recent accounts avoid the term 'feudal' in dealing with early medieval Europe: see James, *Origins of France*, and Susan Reynolds, *Kingdoms and Communities in Western Europe, 900–1300*.

162 Selden, *Titles of Honor*, p. 295. Selden would discuss the relationship between the English common law and the civil or Roman law at greater length in his *Historie of Tithes*.

163 Ibid., p. 296. On the previous page, Selden reported that in these matters he followed 'the conceit of the learned Hotoman.' Selden's argument in this section was correct, but for the wrong reasons. That presented in the discussion of dukes came closer to the chronology of such modern specialists as Ganshof.

164 Ibid.

165 Ibid., p. 297.

166 Ibid.; see pp. 297–9. This was one of those Isidorian etymologies so frequently seen in medieval and Renaissance works of scholarship.

167 Ibid., p. 300. The Romanist thesis garnered several prominent supporters, including such great scholars as Budé, Cujas, Etienne Pasquier, and Ulrich Zasius: see Kelley, '*De Origine Feudorum*,' 215–19, 226–8.

168 Selden, *Titles of Honor*, pp. 300–1. This passage clearly brings out the shift in tenure.

169 Ibid., p. 301.

170 Ibid., pp. 301–2.

171 Ibid., pp. 302–3.

172 Sir John Davies, *Le Primer Report des Cases et Matters en Ley Resolves*

et Adjudges en les Courts del Roy en Ireland, sig. 3[r], and Sir Edward
Coke, *La Huict^{me} Part des Reports*, preface; there is no signature mark
for this section. This preface portrayed the common-law side of Davies;
ironically, a side strongly influenced by the civil law emerged in the
cases reported; see Hans J. Pawlisch, *Sir John Davies and the Conquest
of Ireland: A Study in Legal Imperialism.* For a fuller discussion of these
works by Coke and Davies, see Christianson, 'Ancient Constitutions,'
97–9, 105–11; Burgess, *Politics of the Ancient Constitution*, ch. 2; and,
for Coke, Helgerson, *Forms of Nationhood*, ch. 2.

173 Fortescue, *De Laudibus*, 'To the reader,' sig iii[v]. In this edition, Fortescue's text and Selden's notes follow different pagination, the first in
folios and the second in pages. In preparing the Latin text, Selden probably used the 'M.S. volume of *Fortescue's* works (Otho B1)' in Cotton's
library, which contained 'both the *Praise of the Laws of England* and the
Governance but not the *Nature of the Law of Nature*': Berkowitz, 'Reason of State,' 171 n. 29.

174 Fortescue, *De Laudibus*, f. 38–9[r]; for a history similar to and derived
from that of Fortescue, see Saltern, *Ancient Lawes*, sig. K1[r]–2[v], L3[v].

175 Sir Edward Coke, *La Size Part des Reports*, sig. ¶ 3.

176 Fortescue, *De Laudibus*, Selden's notes, pp. 9–14.

177 Ibid., pp. 7–9; this passage added considerable nuance and sophistication
to his earlier account, which had cited a passage from Gervase of Tilbury
noting that, when William I '"resolved to govern his Subjects ... by Laws
and Ordinances in Writing,"' he examined the '"*English* Laws according
to their Tripartate or threefold distinction, that is to say, *Merchenlage*,
Danlage, and *Westsaxonlage*,"' some of which '"he disliked and laid
aside; others he approved of, and added to them, some from beyond the
Sea out of *Neustria* (he means *Normandy*)"': 'English Janus,' p. 48. In
1616, Selden now translated *Neustria* as 'Norway' and understood that
the Danelage, Mercenlage, and Westsaxonlage represented three legal
jurisdictions in Anglo-Saxon England. Saltern, *Antient Lawes*, sig. B3[r],
cites the appropriate passage from Fortescue with uncritical approval
and uses it as a framework for his account.

178 Sir Edward Coke, *Le Tierce Part des Reportes*, sig. D1[r].

179 Fortescue, *De Laudibus*, Selden's notes, p. 9.

180 Ibid., pp. 11–12.

181 Ibid., p. 12.

182 Ibid., pp. 17–20. Although Tuck quotes most of this passage in *Natural
Rights*, p. 84, it needs repetition in this context. The point here was that
the ship, despite its changes, was 'to be accounted the same still,' not, as

Tuck would have it, that 'it returned home quite different in substance from how it had left port originally': Tuck, *Philosophy and Government*, p. 209. For a more theoretical application of the idea of 'additions' and 'alterations' to the law of nature, see the passages in chapter 3, below, cited to notes 196–8. As Tuck pointed out elsewhere, Sir Matthew Hale would use the image of the ship of the Argonauts as the foundation for his history of the common law: see Tuck, *Natural Rights Theories*, pp. 132–3, and Hale, *History of the Common Law*, p. 40; cf. Gray's introduction, pp. xxi, xxii, xxxiv, xxxvi. One executors of Selden's estate and heir to many of his papers, Hale combined Selden's historical model of the common law with Coke's model of the common law as 'refined reason.' See Cromartie, *Sir Matthew Hale*, chs. 1, 2, 3, 6, and 7.

183 For the full historical demonstration of the theoretical defence of this interpretation in John Selden, *Titles of Honor* (London, 1631) and *Mare Clausum*, see chapter 3, below.

184 Selden returned to this theme in the appendix to *The Historie of Tithes*. For the debate, see F.W. Maitland, *English Law and the Renaissance*; Samuel E. Thorne, 'English Law and the Renaissance'; Levack, *Civil Lawyers*, ch. 4; Louis A. Knafla, 'The Influence of Continental Humanists and Jurists on English Common Law in the Renaissance'; J. H. Baker, 'English Law and the Renaissance'; and Christianson, 'Political Thought in Early Stuart England.'

185 Fortescue, *De Laudibus*, Selden's notes, pp. 20–1.

186 Ibid., p. 21.

187 Selden, *Titles of Honor* (1614), pp. 295–6; see the quotation cited to note 162, above.

188 Fortescue, *De Laudibus*, Selden's notes, pp. 21–2.

189 See Graves, *Bibliography to 1485*, no. 6857, p. 896.

190 Selden, *Historie of Tithes*, sig. a2; previously, he had dedicated the *Analecton* to Cotton. For their friendship, see Berkowitz, 'Young Mr. Selden,' ch. 3; Filloy, 'Views of John Selden,' ch. 3; Sharpe, *Sir Robert Cotton*, passim, and Colin G.C. Tite, 'A "Loan" of Printed Books from Sir Robert Cotton to John Selden.' Lengthy accounts of *The Historie of Tithes* and its critics appear in Edith Bershadsky, 'Controlling the Terms of the Debate: John Selden and the Tithes Controversy'; Filloy, 'Views of John Selden,' ch. 4; Fussner, *Historical Revolution*, ch. 11; Kathleen Loncar, 'John Selden's "History of Tithes": A Charter for Landlords?'; and Woolf, *Idea of History*, ch. 7. I would like to thank Dr Bershadsky for making a copy of her paper available to me before publication and for helping me come to a better understanding of the complexity of the dis-

pute over tithes. I have not had the opportunity to consult her doctoral thesis.

191 For this campaign and for the question of tithes in general, see Christopher Hill, *Economic Problems of the Church, from Archbishop Whitgift to the Long Parliament*, chs. 5, 6, and 12; Roland G. Usher, *The Reconstruction of the English Church*, I, pp. 229–37, 337–9, and II, pp. 53–73. 230–45, 256–8; Peter Lake, 'Presbyterianism, the Idea of a National Church and the Argument from Divine Right'; and Andrew Foster, 'The Clerical Estate Revitalised.'

192 Sir Henry Spelman, *De Non Temerandis Ecclesiis: A Tract, of the Rights and Respect Due unto Churches*, preface. Neither *The Larger Treatise* nor the collection of Spelman's papers published as *Tithes Too Hot to be Touched* took account of Selden's arguments or evidence; if he had worked on the topic after 1618, Spelman could hardly have hoped to avoid the points raised by Selden. Therefore, these look like works composed before the publication of *The Historie of Tithes*.

193 For a recent account of the sorting out of 'teinds' in Scotland, see Maurice Lee, Jr, *The Road to Revolution: Scotland under Charles I, 1625–1637*, ch. 2. The Continental situation would bear careful examination.

194 For the Tudor background and early Stuart debates, see Bershadsky, 'Controlling the Terms of the Debate,' pp. 187–97, and Lake, 'Presbyterianism and the Argument from Divine Right.'

195 *Tithes and Oblations according to the Lawes established in the Church of England*, pp. 2–3.

196 Ibid., 'Of Fruits,' pp. 12–53, 'Of Composition,' pp. 54–69; quotations from the statutes appear on pp. 62–8.

197 William Fulbecke, *The Second Part of the Parallele or Conference*, 'Of Prohibitions and Consultations,' f. 1^r–15^v. For Fulbecke, see Coquillette, 'Legal Ideology and Incorporation, I,' 63–70.

198 George Carleton, *Tithes examined and proved to bee due to the Clergie by a divine right*, fol. 1; this work drew its inspiration from the recently published attack upon 'sufficient maintenance' by Franciscus Junius and was dedicated to the recently elevated Archbishop George Bancroft. Carleton became Bishop of Llandaff in 1618, and later Bishop of Chichester: see *DNB*.

199 Ibid., sig. Az^v, fol. 8^r; in this section, Carleton drew upon the authority of John Calvin to establish that Abraham paid a tithe of his own goods, not of his recently acquired spoils (fol. 7^r)

200 Ibid., fol. 11^v.

201 Ibid., fol. 21^v.

202 Ibid., fol. 28^v.
203 Ibid., fol. 33^v.
204 Ibid., fol. 33^r.
205 Ibid., sig. A3^v; from the dedication to Bancroft.
206 Thomas Ridley, *A View of the Civile and Ecclesiastical Law*, pp. 125–6, 129–32; this work was dedicated to James I. For Ridley's praise of the arguments of Junius, see pp. 162, 163 mn. Ridley obtained his LL.D. from Cambridge in 1583, assisted Bancroft with the Canons of 1604, and, after a series of lesser posts, ended his career as vicar general to the Archbishop of Canterbury (1609–29) and member of the High Commission (1611–29); see Levack, *Civil Lawyers*, pp. 265–6, passim, and Coquillette, 'Legal Ideology and Incorporation, II,' 323–4, 336–46.
207 Ridley, *A View of the Civile and Ecclesiastical Law*, pp. 160, 170–1.
208 Spelman, *De Non Temerandis*, pp. 22, 72–3.
209 Ibid., pp. 86–7; see sig. A3, pp. 27–9, 33, 36, 38, 65–6, 67–78, 87–8, 91. I would like to thank Dr Bershadsky for pointing out that *De Non Temerandis* made little substantial scholarly contribution to the controversy over tithes in 'Controlling the Terms of the Debate,' pp. 199–200; the present account corrects that presented in Christianson, 'Young John Selden and the Ancient Constitution,' 299–300.
210 Foulke Robartes, *The Revenue of the Gospel is Tythes, due to the Ministerie of the Word, by that Word*; dedicated to John, Bishop of Norwich, Sir Edward Coke, and the 'Mayor, Sherifes, and Commons ... of Norwich.' Robarts appears in the *DNB* Cf. Richard Eburne, *The Maintenance of the Ministerie*.
211 Robartes, *Revenue of the Gospel*, pp. 9, 13.
212 Ibid., p. 59; see pp. 65–70.
213 Ibid., pp. 74–5.
214 Ibid., p. 76.
215 Ibid., p. 19.
216 Ibid., pp. 81–102.
217 Ibid., p. 80.
218 Ibid., pp. 102–42.
219 Of the 448 pages of text in *The Historie of Tithes*, the first 45 deal with the period A.D. 1000, the next 150 with Europe after A.D. 1000, and the last 253 with England from A.D. 1000 to the present.
220 See Richard Montague, *Diatribæ upon the First Part of the Late History of Tithes*; [Sir James Sempill], *Sacrilege Sacredly Handled*; and Richard Tillesley, *Animadversions upon M. Seldens History of Tithes and His Review Thereof*. These do not exhaust the subject. A clever controver-

sialist in his own right who later became Bishop of Chichester and Norwich, Montague attacked Selden's lack of charity, learning, and authorities. An Archdeacon of Rochester, Tillesley more conventionally deprecated the innovation of Selden's argument. See Bershadsky, 'Controlling the Terms of the Debate,' pp. 198–9, 207–8; Fussner, *Historical Revolution*, pp. 293–6; and Woolf, *Idea of History*, pp. 230–5.

221 Selden, *Historie of Tithes*, pp. xv, i, sig. a3. Comparing himself to Roger Bacon, Budé, Desiderius Erasmus, and Johannes Reuchlin as scholars attacked by the 'lazy' and ignorant clergy of their day who could not match their mastery of Greek and Hebrew, Selden noted that 'the World hath never wanted store of such blockes laid in the way of Learning' and made his appeal to those 'that both can judge and doe wish for all light to Truth': p. xvi.

222 Ibid., p. xx. The praise of philology in this section articulated some of the principles already put into practice in his earlier publications. For Brisson, Budé, and Cujas, see note 91, above; both Pithou and Pasquier, leading legal historical scholars in sixteenth-century France, appear in biographical section of Burns and Goldie, eds., *Cambridge History of Political Thought*. For their impact upon Selden, see Woolf, *Idea of History*, pp. 209–10. This marked the first praise of Grotius in Selden's published works.

223 Selden, *Historie of Tithes*, p. vi. In the context of his discussion of the various theories of tithes held during the Middle Ages, Selden asked: 'Whether, by Gods immediat Morall Law, the Evangelicall Priesthood have a right to Tithes, as to their Inheritance in equal degree as the Lay man hath to his Nine; or if they have them only as by human Positive Law, and so given them for their spiritual labor?': ibid., pp. 156–7. By posing a scholarly question capable of more than one answer, Selden subverted the closure attempted by Carleton and Robarts with their argument that tithes had always belonged to parish priests by divine right.

224 Ibid., p. xiii; cf. other sections of this passage quoted in Tuck, *Philosophy and Government*, p. 210.

225 Selden, *Historie of Tithes*, pp. 1–4. This was a crucial point; both Carleton and Robarts had insisted that Abraham had offered one-tenth of all of his increase and had used his example as the foundation for their argument that tithes were due by the moral law of God. See Carleton, *Tithes examined*, f. 7^r, and Robartes, *Revenue of the Gospel*, p. 32; cf. Bershadsky, 'Controlling the Terms of the Debate,' pp. 203–5, 215–16, n. 75.

226 Selden, *Historie of Tithes*, pp. 6, 10–24.

227 Ibid., pp. 24–34. By arguing that the custom of such extraordinary tithing may have spread from Abraham's example to other cultures, Selden sought to foreclose the view put forward by Carleton that tithes were due the law of nations as well as to the law of God; ibid., p. 34, and Carleton, *Tithes examined*, f. 6–10

228 Selden, *Historie of Tithes*, pp. 36, 35. Since Robarts had pressed for the Apostolic origin of Christian tithes and Carleton had dated their establishment to approximately A.D. 266, Selden had to prove his interpretation from a careful, philological examination of passages from the New Testament and of the records of the early councils.

229 Ibid., pp. 48, 53–6. Carleton and Robarts had used the testimony of these fathers as proof of the existence of a system of parochial tithes.

230 Ibid., p. 48.

231 Ibid., pp. 49, 67; see pp. 49–67, 82–7. As Loncar has pointed out, Selden did not relate the building and endowment of parish churches with 'the change in Western Europe from a predominantly city-based economy to a situation where more people were living upon country estates, grouped around a landowner for protection, and living on the produce of the estate': Loncar, 'John Selden's "Historie of Tithes,"' 221.

232 Selden, *Historie of Tithes*, p. 44.

233 Ibid., p. 87. Such lay dedications received no mention in any of the treatises mentioned in sketching the background to Selden's *Historie*; indeed, all had explained the monastic holdings of tithes as the result of 'annexations' of parish churches. For the creation of such rural 'parish' churches, see Loncar, 'John Selden's "Historie of Tithes,"' 221–3.

234 Selden, *Historie of Tithes*, pp. 69–70.

235 Ibid., p. 158.

236 Ibid., pp. 160, 167.

237 Ibid., p. 176; see pp. 168–76.

238 Ibid., p. 141. For a discussion of the disputes among the canonists, monks, and friars, see Bershadsky, 'Controlling the Terms of the Debate,' pp. 201–3.

239 Selden, *Historie of Tithes*, pp. 215, 203. This refuted Ridley's suggestion of a British origin. An excellent example of Selden's method came in his handling of an 'ancient collection of divers *Canons*' in the library of his friend Sir Robert Cotton, attributed to '*Ecbert* ... Archbishop of *York* from the yeer DCCXLIII. [743] to DCC.LXVII. [767]'; comparing these to the heads of a synod held in Canterbury during Egbert's time and noting that the constitutions on tithes mirrored those of Charlemagne, made after Egbert's death, Selden concluded that the collection had been made

during the reign of Henry I, a time when a considerable number of forgeries of Anglo-Saxon laws took place: ibid., p. 197, see pp. 196–8. Selden's argument that enforced tithes only began under Charlemagne may have clouded his assessment of this document, but the arguments presented made good philological sense within the limits of his knowledge of these documents and the philological method of his day: cf. Loncar, 'John Selden's "Historie of Tithes,"' 223.

240 Selden, *Historie of Tithes*, p. 260.
241 Ibid., p. 257.
242 Ibid., p. 280.
243 Ibid., pp. 289, 290–1. For a fuller discussion of this process, see Loncar, 'John Selden's "Historie of Tithes,"' 223–6.
244 See his statement in the 'Review': 'This of arbitrarie Consecrations, I presume, is like strange Doctrine to most men; it well may be; for the truth of it, I think, was never before so much as pointed at by any that hath writen of any part of our subject': ibid., p. 470.
245 Selden, *Historie of Tithes*, pp. 488–9. This argument severely undermined the moral authority of the medieval canonists.
246 Ibid., p. 285.
247 Ibid., p. 486; see pp. 486–8 and the preface.
248 Ibid., p. 170.
249 Ibid., p. 469. This indignation over clerical fraud did not, however, add up to anticlericism: cf. Woolf, *Idea of History*, pp. 221–2, and Tuck, *Philosophy and Government*, pp. 209–11.
250 Selden, *Historie of Tithes*, p. 478.
251 See the quotation cited to note 182, above, and the discussion in note 184, above. For England, lawmaking meant custom or parliamentary statute; in other jurisdictions, the prince or nobility or people might create new and amend old laws.
252 Selden, *Historie of Tithes*, p. 479; for the gap also see sig. d 4 and the quotation cited to note 185, above. This denigration of the status of Roman law would receive a theoretical justification in the early chapters of John Selden, *Mare Clausum*; see chapter 3, below, the section bound by notes 199–200.
253 Selden, *Historie of Tithes*, p. 479. Three decades later, Selden would deal in a more lengthy and sophisticated manner with the employment of the Theodosian Code in parts of western Europe during the early Middle Ages and the impact of the importation of the Justinian Code from the twelfth century onward; see his *Ad Fletam Dissertatio*, ed. Ogg, chs. 5 and 6.

254 Selden, *Historie of Tithes*, p. 481. The reference to Ireland contained a probably unintended irony, for at the time that Selden was writing, Sir John Davies was using civil-law arguments to introduce the English common law to Ireland: see Pawlisch, *Sir John Davies*, chs. 1, 4, 5, 8, 9.

255 Selden, *Historie of Tithes*, p. 478.

256 Ibid., p. 482. This accords with contemporary civil-law interpretations of the law of conquest, see Pawlisch, *Sir John Davies*, pp. 8–14.

257 Selden, *Historie of Tithes*, p. 484; see the discussion and quotations cited to notes 49, 81, and 82, above.

258 For the natural rights side of this argument, see Tuck, *Natural Rights*, ch. 4.

259 Selden, *Historie of Tithes*, p. 482.

260 John Selden, 'A Letter to the Marquess of Buckingham,' in *Opera Omnia*, col. 1394; for the whole letter, dated 5 May 1620, see cols. 1393–6. Also see Filloy, 'The Religious and Political Views of John Selden,' pp. 59–65, and Berkowitz, 'Young Mr. Selden,' ch. 4, pp. 18–24, and ch. 5, pp. 11–13, 16–17.

261 Berkowitz, *John Selden*, pp. 54–5, 308–9, n. 8–10.

CHAPTER TWO John Selden's Parliamentary Career, 1621–1629

1 Berkowitz, 'Young Mr. Selden,' ch. 5, pp. 17–28, and *John Selden*, pp. 58–64; his role as a consultant to the Lords left a lasting public impact.

2 Lady de Villiers, ed., 'The Hastings Journal of the Parliament of 1621,' p. 7, and *Journals of the House of Lords* [hereinafter *L.J.*], III, p. 10. For privileges of the Lords, see Elizabeth Read Foster, *The House of Lords, 1603–1649: Structure, Procedure, and the Nature of Its Business*, pp. 137–9, ch. 8; for the Parliament of 1621, see Russell, *Parliaments*, ch. 2, and Robert Zaller, *The Parliament of 1621*. The Commons displayed a similar concern for their privileges and developed some procedural innovations in this Parliament: see G.A. Harrison, 'Innovation and Precedent: A Procedural Reappraisal of the Parliament of 1625.' For disputes between the king and the Commons during this Parliament, see also Christianson, 'Royal and Parliamentary Voices,' pp. 87–94.

3 *L.J.*, III, pp. 17, 21, 65, 74; de Villiers, 'Hastings Journal,' pp. 15, 21, and Helen Relf, ed., *Notes of the Debates in the House of Lords*, pp. 1–2.

4 Relf, *Debates*, p. 48; Elsyng's notes mention John Selden and William Hakewill as the researchers. A well-known common-law attorney, Hakewill had belonged to the Society of Antiquaries and sat in the parliaments of 1601, 1603–10, 1614, 1621, 1624, and 1628–9. For Elsyng, see

Elizabeth Read Foster, *The Painful Labour of Mr. Elsyng*, and for the 'Defenders of Old English Honour,' see Vernon Snow, *Essex the Rebel*, ch. 5.

5 Maurice F. Bond, ed., *Manuscripts of the House of Lords*, X: 1712–1714, pp. 1–6, prints this draft; pages 1–11 contain all of the standing orders for the period before 1660. Lady de Villiers thought that the standing orders in the 'Remembrances for Order and Decency' were part of the report made on 7 February: de Villiers, 'Hastings Journal,' pp. vi–vii, 8, and 8 n. 3. Since the committee had just started to meet, however, this seems very unlikely. Disputes over procedure broke out on several occasions during the early months of this Parliament; see Relf, *Debates*, pp. 8–10, 18–23, for two examples. For the later date, see also Tite, *Impeachment*, p. 32, n. 24; portions of my account of Selden's parliamentary career draw upon Tite's monograph.

6 Quoted in Berkowitz, *John Selden*, p. 61. Bishop John Williams, recently appointed Lord Keeper as the successor of Sir Francis Bacon, wrote to Buckingham to get Southampton and Selden released, and Selden was free again on 20 July. For this whole affair, see Berkowitz, *John Selden*, pp. 58–63. Berkowitz sometimes seems to confuse [Henry Elsyng], *Of the Judicature of Parliament* (London, 1681), with the report to the Lords in this section. For the authorship of *Judicature*, see Elizabeth Read Foster, 'Henry Elsyng, "Judicature in Parliament."'

7 *L.J.*, III, pp. 196–7. Months before the report was formally presented, the Lords began to exercise their jurisdiction: see James S. Hart, *Justice upon Petition: The House of Lords and the Reformation of Justice, 1621–1675*, pp. 7, 15. Arrested in the middle of June on a warrant from the privy council alleging 'speciall causes and reasons of State knowne unto' the king and held incommunicado in the house of one of the sheriffs of London, Selden wrote to Secretary Calvert requesting his papers and release: see the copies of the warrant and letter in British Library, Harley 286, fol. 288–9. It appears that Selden was suspected, along with Sir Edwin Sandys, of conspiring with the Earl of Southampton against the Crown: see the copy of the interrogation of the three in Inner Temple, Petyt MS 598, fol. 1–3. Selden was asked whether he did not wish that the House of Commons had the power of judicature.

8 Since the official manuscript version in the House of Lords Record Office contains some significant variations from the printed version, I quote from the former. Berkowitz, 'Young Mr. Selden,' ch. V, p. 48 n. 85, lists some fifteen manuscript copies; see pp. 28–48 for his detailed account of Selden's work for the Lords, and see also Foster, *House of Lords*, pp. 138–9. Presumably individual peers had copies made.

9 John Selden, 'The Priviledges of the Baronage in England,' fol. 2^v, 98^r.
10 For Selden's letter to Vincent, see chapter 3, below.
11 Selden, 'Priviledges,' fol. 3^v.
12 Ibid.
13 Ibid., fol, 4^r.
14 Ibid., fol. 6^r.
15 Bond, *Lords Manuscripts*, X, pp. 8–9; see Vernon F. Snow, 'The Arundel Case, 1626,' for the limitations made in 1626.
16 Selden, 'Priviledges,' fol. 9^v–10^r
17 For the judicature of the Lords, see Foster, *House of Lords*, ch. 9, and Hart, *Justice upon Petition*. Among the works cited in the next note, those of Flemion, Foster, Horstman, Russell, and Tite have stressed the complex nature of the revival of judicature; earlier historians tended to concentrate upon impeachment to the exclusion of other areas, but Hart clearly redresses the balance.
18 In varying degrees, Jess Stoddart Flemion, 'Slow Process, Due Process, and the High Court of Parliament: A Reinterpretation of the Revival of Judicature in the House of Lords in 1621'; Menna Prestwich, *Cranfield: Politics and Profit under the Early Stuarts*, ch. 7; Relf, *Debates*, pp. ix–xxxii; Clayton Roberts, *The Growth of Responsible Government in Stuart England*, p. 25 and ch. 1; Tite, *Impeachment*, ch. 4; White, *Sir Edward Coke*, pp. 142–64; and Zaller, *Parliament of 1621*, pp. 59–61, 69–70, and ch. 2, all concentrate upon the role of the Lower House in the revival of parliamentary judicature. For accounts more solicitous of the Lords, see Vernon F. Snow, 'Essex and the Aristocratic Opposition to the Early Stuarts'; Allen Henry Horstman, 'Justice and Peers: The Judicial Activities of the Seventeenth-Century House of Lords,' pp. 139–51, ch. 3; Foster, *House of Lords*, ch. 9; and Hart, *Justice upon Petition*, introduction and ch. 1. Russell, *Parliaments and Politics*, pp. 15–7, 103–14, places this development in a complex political context.
19 *L.J.*, III, pp. 176, 196–7, and Tite, *Impeachment*, pp. 31–6.
20 Cf. Berkowitz, *John Selden*, p. 85; Filloy, 'Views of John Selden,' pp. 83–4; Berkowitz, 'Young Mr. Selden,' ch. V, pp. 50–1, and Russell, *Parliaments and Politics*, pp. 200–1. Selden's connection with the Henry Grey, Earl of Kent, seems to have had only an indirect political importance. Since Selden did not sit on the committee on 'An act to enable *William* earl of *Hertford*, and Sir *Francis Seymour* Knight, to make sale of certain lands, for payment of his debts,' it seems likely that his association with the Seymour connection had not yet started. See note 35, below, and *Journals of the House of Commons* [hereinafter *C.J.*], I, pp. 730, 731–2, 747, 757.

For a fuller account of Selden's career in the Parliament of 1624, see Berkowitz, *John Selden*, ch. 6, and for the background to and business of this Parliament, see Thomas Cogswell, *The Blessed Revolution: English Politics and the Coming of War, 1621–1624* and Robert E. Ruigh, *The Parliament of 1624.*

21 *C.J.*, I, pp. 670, 739, 744, 798, British Library, Additional Manuscripts 46,191 (Parliamentary diary of Sir Walter Earle), fol. 90^r, and Wiltshire Record Office, Unnumbered MSS (parliamentary diary of John Hawarde), p. 211. My notation to parliamentary diaries cites, first the particular manuscript quoted, and then other versions of the same speech; the first citation refers to the manuscript and subsequent ones to the name of the diarist. For the problem of how to quote from early Stuart parliamentary diaries, see J.H. Hexter, 'Quoting the Commons, 1604–1642.' All of my references to unpublished parliamentary diaries for this Parliament come from the transcripts so generously put at my disposal by the staff of the Yale Center for Parliamentary History, to whom, and especially to Dr Maija Jansson and Dr William B. Bidwell, I would like to express my thanks.

22 British Library, Harleian MSS 6383 (parliamentary diary of John Holles), fol. 108^r.

23 Public Record Office, State Papers 14/166 (parliamentary diary of Edward Nicholas), fol. 95, and Houghton Library, Harvard University, English MSS 980 (parliamentary diary of Sir William Spring), p. 139.

24 *C.J.*, I, p. 744.

25 Ibid., p. 749. Selden reported on two occasions to the committee of privileges from a subcommittee established to find out how many parliamentary boroughs had been revived by the Commons: Northamptonshire Record Office, Finch-Hatton MSS 50 (parliamentary diary of John Pym), fol. 51^v, 87. For his other committee work, see *C.J.*, I, p. 752; Earle, fol. 179; and Nicholas, fol. 103^r, 114^r, 122^r, 174^v.

26 Nicholas, fol. 103^r; see *C.J.*, I, p. 744 and Pym, fol. 36. For Selden's good friend, Sir Robert Cotton, see Sharpe, *Sir Robert Cotton.*

27 Nicholas, fol. 174^v.

28 *C.J.*, I, pp. 755–6. For Coke, see White, *Sir Edward Coke.* Called to the bar in 1602 and made a bencher at Lincoln's Inn in 1618, Noy sat in the parliaments of 1604–11, 1614, 1624, 1625, and 1628–9, and became attorney general in 1631: see *DNB.*

29 Ibid., pp. 691, 776; see also Berkowitz, *John Selden*, pp. 90–2, 94–5.

30 *C.J.*, I, pp. 692, 707, 713, 777, 791; Nicholas, fol. 212–14^r, 230^v, 232; and Earle, fol. 186^v.

31 *C.J.*, I, pp. 704, 789, and Nicholas, fol. 215. The son of a former Speaker of the House of Commons and Master of the Rolls, Phelips was a leading gentleman in Somerset and experienced member of the Commons who had sat in every Parliament since 1604: see the *DNB* and Thomas Garden Barnes, *Somerset, 1625–1640: A County's Government during the 'Personal Rule,'* pp. 20, 22–3, 24, 26, 28, 29–30, 38–9.

32 Pym, fol. 38ᵛ; only Pym noted this speech.

33 Nicholas, fol. 151ʳ, and *C.J.*, I, p. 765. For the incident involving Hall, see *C.J.*, I, pp. 111–13, 125–7, J.E. Neale, *Elizabeth I and Her Parliaments, 1559–1581,* pp. 333–45,407–10; and Elton, *Studies,* III, pp. 254–73. For the investigation of Fowles by the Lords in 1621, see *L.J.*, III, pp. 63, 65, 91, 92, 123, and Samuel Rawson Gardiner, ed., *Notes of the Debates in the House of Lords ... 1621,* pp. 1, 24–35, 131.

34 *C.J.*, I, pp. 765, 772, 773, 782, 792.

35 Pym, fol. 77ʳ; for the context, see *C.J.*, I, p. 751, Nicholas, fol. 167ᵛ, and Bodleian Library, Tanner MSS 392 (parliamentary diary of Sir Thomas Holland), fol. 86v. Lord Keeper John Williams placed Selden in his debt by helping to obtain his release from prison in 1621; for the relationship between the two men, see Berkowitz, *John Selden,* pp. 28–9, 61–2.

36 Selden's precise connections could use some further study; for the longest account, see Berkowitz, *John Selden,* pp. 97–100. For suggested ties with the Howard network and the Herbert connection, see Russell, *Parliaments and Politics,* p. 281 n. 5, and Brian O'Farrell, 'Politician, Patron, Poet: William Herbert, Third Earl of Pembroke, 1580–1630,' pp. 191, 194. For Ilchester and Great Bedwin, see Evangeline [Lady] de Villiers, 'Parliamentary Boroughs Restored by the House of Commons 1621–41,' p. 188; Vivienne Jill Hodges, 'The Electoral Influence of the Aristocracy, 1604–1641,' p. 431; and John K. Gruenfelder, *Influence in Early Stuart Elections, 1604–1640,* p. 162.

37 For the concept of a 'man of business' in the House of Commons for higher authorities, see M.A.R. Graves, 'Thomas Norton the Parliament Man: An Elizabethan M.P., 1559–1581,' 'The Management of the Elizabethan House of Commons: The Council's Men of Business'; and J.S.A. Adamson, 'Parliamentary Management, Men-of-Business and the House of Lords, 1640–49,' ch. 1. For intellectuals as political advisers, see Jardine and Grafton, '"Studied for Action"'; and Sharpe, *Sir Robert Cotton.*

38 Violet Rowe, 'The Influence of the Earl of Pembroke on Parliamentary Elections 1625–1641'; Russell, *Parliaments and Politics;* and Cogswell, *Blessed Revolution;* for the patronage of the court, individual peers, and

individual gentry, see Gruenfelder, *Influence in Early Stuart Elections*, and Hodge, 'Electoral Influence.'

39 Mark Kishlansky, 'The Emergence of Adversary Politics in the Long Parliament, 'Consensus Politics and the Structure of the Debate at Putney,' and *Parliamentary Selection*, and Victor L. Stater, *Noble Government: The Stuart Lord Lieutenancy and the Transformation of English Politics*.

40 Respectively, Edward Nicholas, Richard Oliver, Edward Savage, John Ashburnham, Sir William Becher, Sir Robert Pye, Sir Ralph Freeman, Sir Francis Cottington, Sir Thomas Badger, Sir John Hippisley, Sir James Bagg, John Harrison, and Sir William Twysden. An early version of this research was read as a paper – 'Politics, Patronage, and Conceptions of Governance in Early Stuart England: The Duke of Buckingham and His Supporters in the Parliament of 1628' – at the conference 'Remapping the History of Early Modern Britain' held at the Henry E. Huntington Library, San Marino, California, 2–3 June 1995.

41 See Samuel Rawson Gardiner, ed., *Debates in the House of Commons in 1625*, pp. 112, 118; the first of these attacked the report from Buckingham delivered by Sir Robert Heath in the Commons: ibid., pp. 94–102.

42 For aspects of their early troubles with the court and their later careers as 'constitutional royalists,' see David L. Smith, *Constitutional Royalism and the Search for Settlement, c. 1640–1649*, pp. 42–7, passim.

43 *C.J.*, I, pp. 818, 819, 820, 821, 822, 824, 826, 829, 831, 832, 833, 834, 836, 837, 839, 840, 858, 863, 865. In this Parliament, Selden made twenty-six speeches and nine reports from committees or subcommittees; Kirton made forty-three speeches, many of them short or only briefly noted. A long-time confidant of Hertford, Kirton had sat in the parliaments of 1621, 1624, and 1625, and was a justice of the peace in Somerset. For a fuller account of Selden's activities in the Parliament of 1626, see Berkowitz, *John Selden*, ch. 7, and for this Parliament as a whole, see Russell, *Parliaments and Politics*, ch. 5. Digges received his BA from University College, Oxford, in 1601; was knighted in 1607; served as a diplomat to Russia and Holland; and was a very experienced member of the Commons. Later, he became a member of the High Commission in 1633 and Master of the Rolls in 1636: see Thomas Kiffin, 'Sir Dudley Digges: A Study in Early Stuart Politics,' ch. 11. Eliot attended Exeter College, Oxford; was knighted in 1618; was vice-admiral of Devon from 1622 to 1628; and was an experienced member of Parliament: see Harold Hulme, *The Life of Sir John Eliot, 1592 to 1632*, chs. 6 and 7. For Kirton, see Mary Frear Keeler, *The Long Parliament, 1640–1641: A Political Study*,

pp. 241–2. For the sources for this Parliament, see William B. Bidwell and Maija Jansson, eds, *Proceedings in Parliament 1626*, 3 vols. [herinafter *Lords 1626; Commons 1626*, II; and *Commons 1626*, III]. My research for this section was originally done in the printed *Journals* of both Houses and the transcripts of parliamentary diaries made by the Yale Center for Parliamentary History. As the volumes of *Proceedings in Parliament* have become available, I have changed the references made to the diaries and some references to the *Journals* to the pages of this edition. I would like to thank Maija Jansson and William Bidwell for their help and encouragement.

44 *Commons 1626*, II, p. 36. A former lieutenant of the Tower of London with continuing court connections, More sat in five Elizabethan and all of the Jacobean parliaments: see *DNB*.

45 *Commons 1626*, II, p. 40; see pp. 36, 12, 16–17. The request for a new writ arose on 10 February; the debate took place on 14 February.

46 Ibid., pp. 40, 36. This passage seems to argue that the writ commanded the sheriff to conduct free and indifferent elections so as not to hinder the king's business. Selden's friend Cotton had a collection of writs of summons (and other materials) for the years of 4–51 Edward III from which he could have drawn his sources: see Colin G.C. Tite, 'The Cotton Library in the Seventeenth Century and Its Manuscript Records of the English Parliament,' 129.

47 *Commons 1626*, II, pp. 33, 134. For a report from the subcommittee to the committee made by Selden on 21 February in which he admitted that sheriffs had been excluded in writs from 14 Henry IV onward, see ibid., pp. 83–4.

48 Ibid., pp. 134–5. The issue was postponed to 3 March, and then to 10 March, for resolution, but did not reappear on the latter date, which did witness a report from the committee on privileges: ibid., pp. 186, 246–7. Made a bencher at Grey's Inn and recorder of Canterbury in 1617, Finch was knighted and became Attorney General to the Queen in 1626, Speaker of the House of Commons in the Parliament of 1628–9, and Chief Justice of the Common Pleas in 1634: see *DNB*.

49 Ibid., p. 60; for other claims of privilege, see pp. 12, 45, 53–4; cf. Berkowitz, *John Selden*, pp. 114–15. Since Sir Robert Cotton did not sit in the Parliament of 1626, Selden may have taken up the cause of Howard, in part as a favour to his friend.

50 Ibid., p. 61.

51 Ibid.

52 Ibid., p. 65. For earlier extensions of the privilege of freedom from arrest

by substituting adjournments for prorogations, see Harrison, 'Innovation and Precedent.'

53 For a brief account of Lady Purbeck and her child, see Antonia Fraser, *The Weaker Vessel: Woman's Lot in Seventeenth-Century England*, pp. 13–21.

54 *Commons 1626*, II, p. 328. For Howard, see *DNB* and N.E. McClure, ed., *The Letters of John Chamberlain*, II, pp. 599, 601, 605, 607–8. One of the members of the High Commission, Sir Henry Marten, sat for Sir John Eliot's borough of St Germans (Cornwall) in the parliaments of 1625 and 1626: see Levack, *Civil Lawyers*, p. 252, and Hodges, 'Electoral Influence,' p. 434.

55 *Commons 1626*, II, p. 61, see pp. 63, 65.

56 Ibid., p. 68.

57 Ibid., pp. 327–9. For news and rumours about the prerogations, see Chamberlain, *Letters*, II, pp. 581, 587, 603. Son of a York alderman, Brooke made his career as a lawyer and poet in London; made a bencher at Lincoln's Inn in 1614, he sat in the parliaments of 1604–11, 1614, 1621, 1624, and 1626: see *DNB*. Suckling, the father of the poet, began his career as a courtier in the service of Sir Robert Cecil; knighted in 1616, he became a Master of Requests in 1620, Comptroller of the Royal Household in 1622, and a Secretary of State; he sat in the parliaments of 1614, 1624, 1625, and 1626: see *DNB*.

58 Ibid., p. 333; see pp. 332–4.

59 *Commons 1626*, III, p. 99.

60 Ibid.; for Marten, see note 54, above.

61 Ibid. The privilege of freedom from arrest included twenty days before and after the sitting, as well as during adjournments.

62 Ibid., p. 100.

63 Ibid., pp. 141–2. For Hayward, Mottershed, and Pope, see Levack, *Civil Lawyers*, pp. 237–8, 257, and 262–3. Lord President Montagu studied at Christ's College, Cambridge, and the Middle Temple; he was appointed Recorder of London in 1603, a king's sergeant in 1611, Chief Justice of the King's Bench in 1616, Lord Treasurer in 1620, Lord President of the Council in 1621, Master of the Wards in 1624, and Lord Privy Seal in 1628; he sat in the Commons in the parliaments of 1601, 1604–11, and 1614, was raised to the peerage as Lord Kimbolton in 1620, and elevated to Earl of Manchester in 1624: see *DNB*.

64 Ibid., p. 142.

65 Ibid., p. 144.

66 Ibid., p. 150.

67 Ibid., p. 152. Lowther was a leading gentleman in Westmorland.

68 Ibid., p. 142.

69 Ibid., p. 414; for the order of 14 June, see p. 445.

70 The most detailed accounts appear in Roger Lockyer, *Buckingham: The Life and Political Career of George Villiers, First Duke of Buckingham, 1592–1628*, ch. 8; Tite, *Impeachment*, ch. 7; Russell, *Parliaments and Politics*, ch. 5; and Hulme, *Sir John Eliot*, ch. 6 and 7, but see also J.N. Ball, 'The Impeachment of the Duke of Buckingham in the Parliament of 1626'; Berkowitz, *John Selden*, pp. 102–13; Roberts, *Growth of Responsible Government*, ch. 2; and Kevin Sharpe, 'The Earl of Arundel, His Circle and the Opposition to the Duke of Buckingham, 1624–28.' Foster, *House of Lords*, pp. 162–7, deals with the cases of the Earl of Bristol and the Duke of Buckingham in 1626 under the category of 'trial by peers,' a very useful distinction. For the background of these events, see Thomas Cogswell, 'Foreign Policy and Parliament: The Case of La Rochelle, 1625–1626,' and Michael B. Young, *Servility and Service: The Life and Work of Sir John Coke*, ch. 10.

71 *Commons 1626*, II , p. 109; for the three speeches made by Marten on 22 February, see pp. 88, 90, 92, 91, 95, and for the testimony of the Lieutenant of the Tower and the Lieutenant of Dover Castle on 23 February, see pp. 102–3, 104–5, 107, and 103, 105, 107–8, respectively. Reporting from a committee established on 18 February to investigate 'the seizure and arrest of our goods and ships in Fraunce,' Sir John Eliot opened the question of the *St Peter* on 22 February; Marten had testified on the case and was cleared by a general vote of the House on the latter date: ibid., pp. 68, 86–9. From the Seymour network, Kirton sat on this committee from the beginning.

72 Ibid., p. 103; for subsequent actions on the *St Peter*, see pp. 159–61, 162–3, 164–6, 167–71, 171–2 (1 March); pp. 177, 178, 180–2 (2 March).

73 Ibid., pp. 256–7, 259–61. As early as 24 February, Kirton supported an inquiry into the lack of military success before voting any taxes: 'We have given money, men, ships – all miscarried. Shall we not see what the cause of this is?' He was probably aiming at Buckingham, whose name clearly entered the debate over the *St Peter* on 1 March, when he was asked by the Commons to show why 'after a legal discharge of the *St. Peter*, the same was again stayed': see ibid., pp. 122, 162, 194–6, 197, 201–2, 204–5, 210–11.

74 Ibid., pp. 261–3, 268; see also Berkowitz, *John Selden*, pp. 107–8, 320 n. 47–8. For Turner, see Keeler, *The Long Parliament*, pp. 367–8.

75 *Commons 1626*, II, p. 285; see pp. 278, 282, 284–5. Clement was the son of Sir Edward Coke.

76 Ibid., pp. 282, 299.

77 Ibid., pp. 293–4.

78 Ibid., p. 323; see pp. 307–8, 322–3.

79 Ibid., p. 343.

80 Ibid., pp. 360, 362; see pp. 357–62.

81 Ibid., p. 381, 375; see pp. 376–82.

82 Ibid., pp. 391–5.

83 Ibid., pp. 399–403, 404–13.

84 Ibid., pp. 433, 434; see pp. 432–4.

85 *Lords 1626*, p. 284; see Foster, *House of Lords*, p. 166. The willingness of Bristol to accuse the favourite contrasted with the procedure by common fame taken by Turner in the Commons.

86 *Commons 1626*, III, p. 50; see also p. 46. For Malet's and other speeches, see pp. 45–7, 48–51. Malet had sat in the parliaments of 1614, 1621, 1625; in 1626, he had the support of Buckingham: see David Harris Willson, *The Privy Councillors in the House of Commons, 1604–1629*, pp. 86, 143 n. 25, 156 n. 49, 190 n. 48. Most of the precedents cited in this debate were discussed later in *Of the Judicature of Parliaments*.

87 *Commons 1626*, III, p. 47.

88 Ibid., p. 38. This took place on 21 April.

89 Ibid., pp. 53–4.

90 Ibid., pp. 83–4, 89–90.

91 Ibid., p. 108; for the debate on this issue, see pp. 109–16.

92 Ibid., p.121; for his full report and the debate that it produced, see pp. 121–2, 122–4, 126–31, 131–3, 133–5.

93 Ibid., p. 140. For Jones, the son of William Jones, Justice of the Common Pleas and then the King's Bench, see Hodges, 'Electoral Influence,' p. 437, and Wilfrid R. Prest, *The Rise of the Barristers: A Social History of the English Bar, 1590–1640*, pp. 28, 373–4.

94 *Commons 1626*, III, p. 183; see pp. 182, 184. May attended St John's College, Oxford, and the Middle Temple; held a number of Crown offices; was made a privy councillor and a member of Gray's Inn in 1625; and was a very experienced member of the Commons: see *DNB*.

95 Ibid., pp. 192.

96 Ibid., p. 191.

97 Ibid., p. 192; see p. 195.

98 Ibid., pp. 192–3, 195; and John Selden, *Opera Omnia*, III, cols. 1931–2; see also *L.J.*, iii, 594–608.

99 Selden, *Opera*, III, col. 1932.

100 *Commons 1626*, III, p. 193.

101 Selden, *Opera*, III, col. 1934.
102 *Commons 1626*, III, pp. 219, 223; see *Lords 1626*, pp. 460–3, and Hulme, *Sir John Eliot*, pp. 141–2.
103 Ibid., p. 201; see pp. 202–3, 207–12, 213–16.
104 Ibid., pp. 235–98. This took up all of the sitting of the Commons from 12 through 20 May.
105 Ibid., pp. 404, 406, 407–8, 409, 410, 415–20.
106 Ibid., p. 416.
107 Ibid.
108 Ibid., p. 418.
109 Ibid., p. 415; see pp. 416–17, 419–20, 420.
110 Ibid., p. 433, see pp. 432, 433–4, 435, 436–41.
111 Bodleian Library, Selden MS, supra 108, fol. 101^r; cf. Berkowitz, *John Selden*, p. 120. For the whole process, see Paul E. Kopperman, *Sir Robert Heath, 1575–1649: Window on an Age*, pp. 159–60, and Hulme, *Sir John Eliot*, pp. 150–1.
112 In general, see Derek Hirst, 'Court, Country and Politics before 1629,' ch. 4, and 'The Privy Council and Problems of Enforcement in the 1620s'; Paul Slack, 'Books of Orders: The Making of English Social Policy, 1577–1631'; Kevin Sharpe, 'Crown, Parliament and Locality: Government and Communication in Early Stuart England'; and, at greatest length and depth, Richard Cust, *The Forced Loan and English Politics, 1626–1628*. For the circulation of news and its role in political disputes, see Richard Cust, 'News and Politics in Early Seventeenth-Century England,' and Thomas Cogswell, 'The Politics of Propaganda: Charles I and the People in the 1620s.'
113 Sommerville, *Politics and Ideology*.
114 See Burgess, *Politics of the Ancient Constitution*, and Christianson, 'Royal and Parliamentary Voices' and 'Ancient Constitutions'; for a greater stress upon natural-law theories, see Sommerville, *Politics and Ideology*, chs. 1 and 2; 'From Suarez to Filmer'; 'John Selden, the Law of Nature, and the Origins of Government'; and 'History and Theory: The Norman Conquest in Early Stuart Political Thought.' The largest portion of Sommerville's examples come from clergymen or men drawing upon Roman-law traditions.
115 Recent accounts of the Five Knights' Case and its bearing upon actions taken in the Parliament of 1628 appear in Berkowitz, 'Reason of State,' and *John Selden*, chs. 8 and 9; Linda S. Popofsky, 'Habeas Corpus and "Liberty of the Subject": Legal Arguments for the Petition of Right in the Parliament of 1628'; J.A. Guy, 'The Origins of the Petition of Right

Reconsidered'; and Christianson, 'John Selden, the Five Knights' Case, and Discretionary Imprisonment.' For the political context, see Cust, *Forced Loan*; for the constitutional debate, see Judson, *Crisis of the Constitution*; for the parliamentary setting, see Russell, *Parliaments and Politics*; and for the role of Heath, see Kopperman, *Heath*, pp. 161–4.

116 For a full account of these measures, see Cust, *Forced Loan*; Lindsay Boynton, 'Martial Law and the Petition of Right'; Thomas Garden Barnes, 'Deputies not Principals, Lieutanants not Captains: The Institutional Failure of Lieutenancy in the 1620s,' and Victor Stater, 'War and the Structure of Politics: Lieutenancy and the Campaign of 1628.' I would like to thank Dr Fissell for bringing the last two essays to my attention.

117 Quoted in Guy, 'Origins of the Petition of Right,' 291; Erle had petitioned the council for a hearing, and Hampden had petitioned for a relaxation of his imprisonment on grounds of health; see the *Calendar of State Papers, Domestic Series, of the Reign of Charles I, 1627–1628*, pp. 205, 299, 336.

118 Guy, 'Origins of the Petition of Right,' 291–2. Guy has worked out the correct chronology on the basis of the records of the King's Bench.

119 T. B. Howell, ed., *A Complete Collection of State Trials*, III, p. 50; cf. Burgess, *Politics of the Ancient Constitution*, pp. 192–3, who interprets Heath's position as more absolutist. For normal and unusual seventeenth-century usage of one of the terms employed by Heath, see Janelle Greenberg, 'Our Grand Maxim of State, "The King Can Do No Wrong."'

120 For a fuller discussion, see Christianson, 'John Selden, the Five Knights' Case, and Discretionary Imprisonment,' 65–72.

121 Roger Manwaring, *Religion and Allegiance* (London, 1627), as quoted in Cust, *Forced Loan*, p. 64, and see pp. 62–7; Sommerville, *Politics and Ideology*, pp. 127–31; and Burgess, *Politics of the Ancient Constitution*, pp. 173–8.

122 Howell, *State Trials*, III, p. 17; cf. Bodleian Library, Selden MSS, supra 123, fol. 203^r. Selden prepared a detailed outline of this argument in a small hand on thinly folded sheets of paper (*ca* 4 by 14 inches); such a brief served to organize the speech and act as an aid to the memory: see Bodleian Library, Selden MSS, supra 123, fol. 203^r–13; for some preparatory notes on Hampden's case, see fol. 192–3. Since the report of the speech printed in *State Trials* follows the manuscript outline closely, the latter is used to cross-reference the former.

123 Howell, *State Trials*, III, p. 17; cf. Bodleian Library, Selden MSS, supra

123, fol. 203^r. See also Popofsky, 'Habeus Corpus and "Liberty of the Subject,"' 262, and Berkowitz, 'Reason of State,' pp. 184–5.

124 Howell, *State Trials*, III, p. 18. Selden quoted only this shortened version of the chapter numbered twenty-nine in the confirmation of 1225, and thirty-nine in the charter of 1215. These two versions vary considerably, but not in the words afforded special attention by Selden. The version of 1215 reads: '*Nullus liber homo capiatur, vel imprisonetur, aut desseisiatur, aut utlagetur, aut exuletur, aut alizuo modo distruatur, nec super eum ibimus, nec super eum mittemus, nisi per legale judicium parium suorum vel per legem terre*': Holt, *Magna Carta*, p. 326; cf. p. 355, for the version of 1225. Holt translates the above as: 'No free man shall be taken or imprisoned or disseised or outlawed or exiled or in any way ruined, nor will we go or send against him, except by the lawful judgement of his peers or by the law of the land': ibid., p. 327.

125 Howell, *State Trials*, III, p. 18.

126 Ibid.

127 Ibid.; cf. Bodleian Library, Selden MSS, supra 123, fol. 203^v: 'This is the meaning of it in Magna Charta and so it hath relation truly to. For plainly In the other sense, a villain hath equal relation to it. For he can not be imprisoned but [by] *per legum terræ* in the first sense ... And in that time *liber homo* had his appeale of delivery.'

128 Ibid. See Popofsky, 'Habeas Corpus and "Liberty of the Subject,"' 262–3.

129 Howell, *State Trials*, III, p. 18.

130 Ibid.; cf. Bodleian Library, Selden MSS, supra 123, fol. 203^v: 'The Statut of Mag. ch. is 17 Joh. R. *nec eum incarcere mittimus* Matth. Paris pag 345.' Selden first used this reading in his notes to Sir John Fortescue's, *De Laudibus Legum Angliæ* pp. 29–30. The standard version printed the confirmation made by Henry III in 1225; a different version, based in part on that of John's reign, appeared in Paris, *Angli Historia Maior*, p. 345. For the chapter in question, Matthew Paris followed the version of 1225 in everything except the words '*nec eum in carcere mittemus*,' which he substituted for '*nec super eum mittemus*,' as reported by Selden. For a thorough discussion of the printing and the interpretation of Magna Carta during the Tudor and early Stuart period, see Thompson, *Magna Carta*, chs. 6–12. For assessments of the version found in Matthew Paris, see Thompson, *Magna Carta*, pp. 292–3, and Holt, *Magna Carta*, p. 290.

131 Howell, *State Trials*, III, pp. 18–19.

132 Ibid., p. 19. My interpretation here may prove somewhat exaggerated. The question of the impact of civil-law humanist philology upon interpretation of the common law has only recently started to receive some

attention: see Christianson, 'Political Thought in Early Stuart England'; for a fascinating practitioner who employed a fairly sophisticated understanding of Continental civil law to attack the 'ancient liberties' of the Irish, see Pawlish, *Sir John Davies*.

133 Howell, *State Trials*, III, p. 35.

134 Ibid.

135 Ibid., p. 37. This derived all justice from the king, a commonplace, but remained ambiguous about the 'rules' used by the king 'to govern himself by'; did these include the law of God, the law of nature, or the law of the land? The judges had to follow the common law, but did the monarch? Later in the speech, Heath opened the possibility that royal discretionary powers were not unlimited, only to dismiss the question as one not under discussion (see the passage quoted to note 142, below).

136 Ibid. This almost implied that even in ordinary circumstances, the king could allow his servants to list *'per speciale mandatum domini regis'* alone on the return to a writ of *habeas corpus*. Selden's point on this part of the issue was that returning a specific cause of imprisonment to a writ of *habeas corpus* was no longer a matter of grace, to be granted or withheld as circumstances seemed to warrant, but a liberty, binding upon royal servants, guaranteed by Magna Carta.

137 Ibid.

138 Ibid., p. 38. Heath quoted some of the crucial phrases in Latin, but also quoted an English translation of the whole chapter 29 in the version of 1225.

139 Ibid.

140 Ibid. Ironically, given the lack of sophistication in paleography indicated by his statement, Heath was correct and Selden was incorrect about the wording.

141 Ibid.

142 Ibid., p. 44; the common-law maxim that 'the king can do no wrong,' of course, also made royal servants responsible for any wrongs which took place.

143 Ibid., pp. 44–5. For different interpretations of Heath's position, see Berkowitz, 'Reason of State,' pp. 185–7; Burgess, *Politics of the Ancient Constitution*, pp. 191–4; and Popofsky, 'Habeas Corpus and "Liberty of the Subject,"' 263–4. My view builds upon those of Judson, *Crisis of the Constitution*, chs. 1 and 4, and James Daly, 'The Idea of Absolute Monarchy,' especially 233.

144 Howell, *State Trials*, III, p. 50.

145 For brief overviews, see Julian H. Franklin, 'Sovereignty and the Mixed

Constitution: Bodin and His Critics,' J.P. Sommerville, 'Absolutism and Royalism'; and Peter Burke, 'Tacitism, Scepticism, and Reason of State,' chs. 10, 12 and 15. Neither a consistent political theoretician nor a scholar steeped in the works of Continental theorists, Heath hardly qualified as a disciple of Bodin or Botero. Taking account of the ambiguity of his language, 'sovereign' and 'sovereignty' seem to have retained the medieval meaning relating to the power exercised by the uppermost lord in the realm, while 'reason of state' seems to have indicated only a rational organization of a state, in this case a monarchy.

146 See Burgess, *Politics of the Ancient Constitution*, pp. 193–4.

147 Guy, 'Origins of the Petition of Right,' 292. Guy quotes the judgment in the King's Bench: '*Ordinatum est quod defendentes rimittuntur separalibus prisonis ubicunque antæ fuerunt salvo custodiendo quosque, etc.,*' expands the contraction into '*quosque secundum legum deliberanti fuerint,*' and provides the translation printed above.

148 Robert C. Johnson, Maija Jansson Cole, Mary Frear Keeler, and William B. Bidwell, eds., *Proceedings in Parliament 1628*, 6 vols.: *Commons Debates 1628*, vols. I–IV; *Lords Proceedings 1628*, vol. V; and *Appendices and Indexes*, vol. VI, [hereinafter *Commons 1628*, I–IV; *Lords 1628*; and *Parl. 1628*], *Commons 1628*, II, pp. 28–9, passim. Recent studies of the Petition of Right and the Parliament of 1628 include Russell, *Parliaments and Politics*, ch. 6 (the standard account); J. Norman Ball, 'The Petition of Right in the English Parliament of 1628'; Berkowitz, 'Reason of State,' and *John Selden*, chs. 9 and 10; Christianson, 'John Selden, the Five Knights' Case, and Discretionary Imprisonment,' 72–82 and 'Ancient Constitutions,' pp. 118–43, 289–91; Richard Cust, 'Charles I, the Privy Council and the Parliament of 1628'; Jess Stoddart Flemion, 'The Struggle for the Petition of Right in the House of Lords: The Study of an Opposition Party Victory,' and 'A Savings to Satisfy All: The House of Lords and the Meaning of the Petition of Right'; Guy, 'Origins of the Petition of Right,' 296–312; Hulme, *Sir John Eliot*, chs. 10 and 11; Judson, *Crisis of the Constitution*, ch. 6; Kiffin, 'Sir Dudley Digges,' ch. 13; Lockyer, *Buckingham*, ch. 11; Popofsky, 'Habeas Corpus and "Liberty of the Subject"'; and White, *Sir Edward Coke*, ch. 7; see also Helen Relf, *The Petition of Right*. Large portions of my account of the session of 1628 appeared in Christianson, 'Ancient Constitutions.'

149 Gruenfelder, *Influence in Early Stuart Elections*, p. 163. In 1628, the Seymour connection also included Sir Francis Seymour and Edward Kirton, the earl's steward.

150 *Commons 1628*, II, pp. 42, 45, 47.

151 Ibid., pp. 54–75. For the plans of Charles and his moderate councillors, see Cust, 'Charles I and the Parliament of 1628,' 25–6, 30–6. For the linking of supply and the redress of grievances, see T.E. Cogswell, 'A Low Road to Extinction? Supply and Redress of Grievances in the Parliaments of the 1620s.' To avoid too much repetition of first names, I normally refer to Sir John Coke as 'Secretary Coke' and employ 'Coke' for Sir Edward.

152 *Commons 1628*, II, 65, 56, 60, 62, 70. The opening critics were all leading country gentlemen and experienced members of Parliament. Phelips had sat in every Parliament since 1604; Seymour was the brother of the Earl of Hertford; Wentworth had spent some time at the Inner Temple in his youth; all appear in *DNB*. A graduate and fellow of Trinity College, Cambridge, Sir John Coke made a career in naval administration before becoming secretary in 1625; he was knighted in 1624 and was an experienced member of Parliament: see Young, *Servility and Service*.

153 *Commons 1628*, II, pp. 85–7, 89, 92–3. For attacks on the Arminians in this and other parliaments, see Hillel Schwartz, 'Arminianism and the English Parliament, 1624–1629.'

154 *Commons 1628*, II, p. 109, see pp. 99–100, 106, 113; cf. Seymour's speech which pressed for a petition of right to uphold the liberties of the people, pp. 104, 111, 115.

155 Ibid., p. 135, see pp. 125, 132.

156 Ibid., p. 149; see pp. 146–50, 153–4, 157–8, 160–1, 163–4.

157 Ibid., pp. 150–1; see pp. 150–2, 154–5, 158–9, 161–2, 164–5; cf. Berkowitz, *John Selden*, pp. 142–3. An outline for this speech in Selden's hand shows how he marshalled his points under the general categories '1 Reason,' '2 Acts of parliament,' '3 Book cases,' '4 Records,' and '5 Objections,' and included such details as crucial words from the Matthew Paris version of Magna Carta: see Bodleian Library, Selden MSS, supra 123, fol. 244^r.

158 *Commons 1628*, II, p. 159. Of course, Selden had devoted much effort on preparing a second, greatly expanded edition of *Titles of Honor* (London, 1631) at this time, and this project involved, among other things, considerable additional research into Continental law collections. For the impact of Continental legal historians upon his earlier work, see chapter 1, above. For the whole question, see also Ziskind, 'John Selden: Criticism and Affirmation of the Common Law Tradition.'

159 *Commons 1628*, II, p. 162, see pp. 152, 155–6, 159–60, 165; for the effect of Shelton's speech, see that of Wentworth, p. 198. Shelton studied at Clement's Inn and the Inner Temple, was called to the bar in 1606, and

became a bencher in 1622; a client of Buckingham, he was appointed
Solicitor General in 1625; he also served as a justice of the peace and was
an experienced member of the Commons: see *DNB*.

160 *Commons 1628*, II, p. 165, and Guy, 'Origins of the Petition of Right,'
296.

161 *Commons 1628*, II, pp. 171–85, 188–209.

162 Ibid., pp. 172, 183, 173; cf. pp. 173–4, 176, 180, 183. The maxim quoted
by Nethersole appeared in Sir Edward Coke, *La Dix^{me} Part des Reports*,
fol. 139. See Christianson, 'Ancient Constitutions,' p. 120.

163 *Commons 1628*, II, p. 191; see pp. 193, 200–2. For Selden's notes from
subcommittee meetings, see ibid., VI, pp. 94, 105.

164 *Commons 1628*, II, pp. 173–4, 176–7, 185, 193, 202.

165 Guy, 'Origins of the Petition of Right,' 296; see 296–312.

166 *Commons 1628*, II, pp. 211–12; see pp. 217–18, 219–20, 222–3.

167 Ibid., p. 212 n. 3, a translation of the Latin of the draft judgment.

168 Ibid., pp. 212–13, 218–19, 220–2, 223.

169 Ibid., pp. 229, 232, 234, 238.

170 Ibid., pp. 231, 239, 240 for the resolutions; pp. 236–7 for the drafting.

171 *Lords 1628*, pp. 137–44. For a fuller discussion of this issue, see Paul
Christianson, 'Arguments on Billeting and Martial Law in the Parliament of 1628'; see also Boynton, 'Martial Law and the Petition of Right';
Barnes, 'Deputies not Principals'; and Stater, 'Lieutenancy and the Campaign of 1628.'

172 *Commons 1628*, II, p. 254, see pp. 252–4, 263–4; for another attack upon
billeting by Kirton, see pp. 253, 260, 268, 272. Giles attended Exeter College, Oxford, and the Middle Temple, was knighted in 1603, and was a
very experienced member of Parliament: see *Athenae Oxonienses*,
p. 566. Rodney studied at Magdalen College, Oxford, and Middle Temple; served as a justice of the peace and deputy lieutenant; and was an
experienced member of the Commons: see Keeler, *The Long Parliament*,
pp. 324–5. Wallop received his BA from St John's College, Oxford, in
1588; attended Lincoln's Inn; had estates and experience in Ireland; and
was a very experienced member of Parliament: ibid., pp. 376–8.

173 *Commons 1628*, II, p. 254; see pp. 255, 264. George Browne studied at
Magdalen College, Oxford, and the Middle Temple, receiving his BA in
1602, being called to the bar in 1609, and becoming a bencher in 1628; he
was also a justice of the peace, the Recorder of Lyme Regis and Taunton,
and an experienced member of Parliament: see Prest, *Rise of the Barristers*, p. 348.

174 *Commons 1628*, II, pp. 279–80; cf. pp. 286–7, 290–1, 292. In notes pre-

pared on this topic, he stressed that 'Tenures by knight service some testimony is in the Book of Ely and in the laws of the Saxons,' but that there were 'Divers more such' after William I became king; he had 'Conquered not the kingdome so much as the king only' and 'made laws in 'Parliament'; Bodleian Library, Selden MSS, supra 123, fol. 210.

175 Commons 1628, II, p. 280.

176 Ibid., p. 281.

177 Ibid., pp. 281, 287–8, 291, 292–3. See also Christianson, 'Arguments on Billeting and Martial Law in the Parliament of 1628,' 545–8.

178 Commons 1628, II, p. 288.

179 Ibid., p. 293.

180 Ibid., p. 276.

181 Ibid., p. 296.

182 Ibid., p. 333. For this speech, see also Berkowitz, John Selden, pp. 150–2; Christianson, 'Ancient Constitutions,' p. 123; and Popofsky, 'Habeas Corpus and "Liberty of the Subject,"' 268–70.

183 Commons 1628, II, p. 334.

184 Ibid., pp. 333–58.

185 Ibid., pp. 334–42.

186 For Selden's speech of 27 March, see ibid., pp. 150–2, 154–5, 158–9, 161–2, 164–5; Bodleian Library, Selden MSS, supra 123, fol. 244[r]; and note 133, above. In this speech, he cited Magna Carta, c. 29; 3 Edward I, c. 15; 5 Edward III, c. 9; 25 Edward III, c. 4; 28 Edward III, c. 3; 36 Edward III, no. 9; and 42 Edward III, c. 13. A narrowly folded outline, 'Report from the subcommittee for records &c. touching Personell Liberty,' in the Selden papers added 36 Edward III, no. 20, and 42 Edward III, no. 12, and Littleton added 37 Edward III, c. 8: see Bodleian Library, Selden MSS, supra 123, fol. 216[r]. The attorneys in the Five Knights' Case had cited six of these ten charters, statutes, and petitions. For another account of this conference, see White, Sir Edward Coke, pp. 137–42.

187 Commons 1628, II, pp. 344, 348; see pp. 342–56; this edition incorporates the draft of the speech from 7 April and the account of the conference of 16–17 April in Bodleian Library, Selden MSS, supra 123, fol. 245–72. The outline 'Report from the subcommittee for records' contains a full listing of the precedents discussed in Selden's speech: see Bodleian Library, Selden MSS, supra 123, fol. 216–18. On the basis of these manuscripts, it is difficult to determine whether the written draft of the speech or the outline aide memoire was written first, but these outlines are so full that they seem to have been prepared afterward; folded into a long, narrow shape which could fit up one's sleeve; and brought into the House or

court so that Selden could remember all of the points and precedents for long speeches. Berkowitz has drawn attention to the important role played by Selden during the early stages of the attempt to uphold the liberties of the people: see 'Reason of State,' 192, and *John Selden*, pp. 137–52. Popofsky stressed the key role of Coke, but paid a great deal of attention to Selden's speeches: see 'Habeas Corpus and "Liberty of the Subject,"' 258, passim; so did White, *Sir Edward Coke*, ch. 7. Ball hardly mentioned Selden and centered his account upon Sir Thomas Wentworth: see 'Petition of Right,' passim.

188 *Commons 1628*, II, p. 354.

189 Ibid., pp. 354–6; by 'authentic copies,' he meant accurate transcriptions of the original documents.

190 Ibid., p. 356.

191 Ibid., 356, 357–8; for Coke's earlier speech, see pp. 191–2; for Selden's earlier speeches, see pp. 150–2, 154–5, 158–9, 161–2, 164–5, and Howell, *State Trials*, III, pp. 16–19

192 *Commons 1628*, *II*, p. 358. For a fuller version of the sixth reason, see Christianson, 'Ancient Constitutions,' p. 125.

193 *Commons 1628*, II, pp. 360–71.

194 For the interrogation of Baber, see ibid., pp. 383–4, and cf. pp. 377, 385, 392–3, 393; for Seymour's speech, see pp. 377, 384, 388, 392; for Selden's speech, see pp. 378, 385, 388, 392.

195 Ibid., for Baber's suspension, see p. 375; for Rich's speech, see p. 391; for the passage of the petition, see pp. 376, 397. Later in the session, Selden supported the readmission of Baber into the House: see *Commons 1628*, IV, p. 19.

196 *Commons 1628*, II, p. 452; for the text of the petition, see pp. 451–2.

197 Ibid., p. 453.

198 *Lords 1628*, p. 186.

199 Ibid., p. 208.

200 Ibid., p. 206; see pp. 199–200, 210–11.

201 Ibid.

202 Ibid., p. 213; see 200–3, 211–13.

203 Ibid., p. 203; for Heath's report, see pp. 197–203, 206, 208–13.

204 Ibid., p. 203.

205 Ibid., pp. 222, 223, 228, 225; for the report by the Justices of the King's Bench to the Lords, see pp. 217, 219–20, 222–6, 228–32, 234–40, and Guy, 'Origins of the Petition of Right,' 301.

206 *Lords 1628*, p. 198; see pp. 205, 208, 210; for the debates of the Lords over when and whether to hold a conference with the Commons, see

pp. 204–14, 232–3, 235–7. See also Christianson, 'Ancient Constitutions,' pp. 127–9.

207 *Commons 1628*, II, p. 500; for full reports of the conference, see pp. 490–503, 524–38, and *Lords 1628*, pp. 249–52, 268–92, 293–300, 301–4, 306–8. For other accounts, see Berkowitz, *John Selden*, pp. 157–9, and White, *Sir Edward Coke*, pp. 245–51.

208 *Commons 1628*, II, p. 500; see *Lords 1628*, pp. 268–9.

209 *Commons 1628*, II, p. 500; see *Lords 1628*, pp. 269–70.

210 *Commons 1628*, II, p. 501; see *Lords 1628*, pp. 270–1.

211 *Commons 1628*, II, p. 495; for a less detailed account of the exchange over precedents between the attorney general and the spokesmen of the Commons, see *Lords 1628*, pp. 249–52. Selden took the lead for his side in this dispute.

212 *Commons 1628*, II, p. 496.

213 Ibid., p. 497.

214 *Lords 1628*, p. 257. The Lord Treasurer, the Earl of Marlborough, had raised the point earlier: see pp. 204–6, 207–8, 209–10.

215 *Commons 1628*, II, p. 534; cf. *Lords 1628*, pp. 273–81, for a full account of Heath's speech.

216 *Commons 1628*, II, p. 527, and *Lords 1628*, p. 274; cf. *Commons 1628*, II, pp. 529, 534–5. For the points raised by Heath, see also Berkowitz, 'Reason of State,' 195–6.

217 *Commons 1628*, II, p. 527; see *Lords 1628*, p. 275.

218 *Commons 1628*, II, p. 528; see *Lords 1628*, pp. 275–8.

219 *Commons 1628*, II, p. 530; see *Lords 1628*, pp. 282–3. For an extended account of Ashley's interpretation, which draws upon his reading of 1616 on Magna Carta, c. 29, at the Middle Temple, see Thompson, *Magna Carta*, pp. 286–93, 343–5.

220 *Commons 1628*, II, pp. 528–9; see *Lords 1628*, pp. 283–4. The Lords clearly thought that Sergeant Ashley had ruined any remaining chances of accommodation by his ill-timed and provocative speech, for they questioned and censured him on 19 April: see *Lords 1628*, pp. 293, 300–1, 303, 311, 315, 316. Ashley's petition to Buckingham displayed little regret: see *Parl. 1628*, p. 217.

221 *Commons 1628*, II, p. 284. Ironically, in his 1616 reading on Magna Carta, Ashley had alluded to the need to '"restrain the swelling and exhorbitant power of ecclesiastical or any other jurisdiction which by way of encroachment seeks to impeach the vigour of our municipal laws"': quoted in Prest, *Rise of the Barristers*, p. 266 n. 78.

222 *Commons 1628*, II, pp. 536–8, and *Lords 1628*, pp. 284–9. The various

accounts do not always agree upon the order of the speeches, nor on the speaker; I have followed the order in Harleian MSS 2313 and the MSS Journals of the House of Lords as those which seem most accurate for the overall view, but have drawn upon other accounts for details.

223 *Commons 1628*, II, p. 525.

224 Ibid., p. 530.

225 For this point, see Christianson, 'Young John Selden and the Ancient Constitution,' 297–9, 305–8, and chapter 1, above.

226 *Commons 1628*, II, p. 526; the quotation modifies the word order of the original.

227 Ibid., pp. 527, 526–7.

228 Ibid., p. 527. Of course, Coke had already said as much in earlier debates.

229 Ibid.

230 Ibid., p. 534; see *Lords 1628*, pp. 291–2.

231 *Commons 1628*, II, p. 538; see *Lords 1628*, pp. 292–3.

232 *Commons 1628*, II, p. 538. The account in the Journals of the House of Lords presents a condensed and moderated version of the exchange; cf. *Lords 1628*, p. 292.

233 *Commons 1628*, II, p. 538.

234 Ibid. The speaker may have been Noy, who was credited with a different intervention in the Journals of the House of Lords: see *Lords 1628*, p. 292.

235 *Commons 1628*, II, pp. 538, 529; see also White, *Sir Edward Coke*, pp. 250–1.

236 *Commons 1628*, II, p. 445; see pp. 446, 453–4, 456, 457–8; see also Berkowitz, *John Selden*, pp. 153–6.

237 *Commons 1628*, II, p. 445, see pp. 448–9, 454–5, 456, 458.

238 Ibid., p. 446; both Seymour and Kirton sat on this committee! For the 'Instructions,' see pp. 424–6.

239 *Lords 1628*, pp. 217, 220–1, 223, 225, 233, 259–62.

240 Ibid., pp. 221, 259–62.

241 *Commons 1628*, II, pp. 460, 466, 469, 475, 476, 508–9, 511–12, 514–16, 517–19, 519–20, 522, and 522–3.

242 Ibid., pp. 541–61.

243 Ibid., pp. 542–3; see pp. 548–9, 552–3, 556–7, 558–9, 560–1.

244 Ibid., p. 543.

245 Ibid., p. 558.

246 *Commons 1628*, II, pp. 565, 568, 572; this quotation is a composite text drawing mainly upon the versions found in proceedings and debates and in Stowe MSS 366.

247 Ibid., pp. 569, 573, 577. For a more detailed account of this debate, see Christianson, 'Arguments on Billeting,' 549–53.

248 *Commons 1628*, III, pp. 72, 79, 83, 86, 88. For a similar judgment, see White, *Sir Edward Coke*, pp. 224–6.

249 *Commons 1628*, III, p. 81. After censuring Sergeant Ashley for the 'unfitting speeches' which he had made at the conference, the Lords spent two full days of fierce debate on the resolutions of the Commons. Unable to reach agreement in the House, they appointed a committee on 23 April to work out suggestions for an accommodation; it produced the propositions sent to the Commons on 25 April, 'in writing with liberty for to add, alter, or take away any part of it': *Lords 1628*, pp. 293, 345; see pp. 293, 300, 303, 311–18, 330–1, 333–7, 339–41, 344–7. For the disputes in the Lords and over the five propositions, see Flemion, '"A Savings to Satisfy All"'; cf. Cust, 'Charles I and the Parliament of 1628,' 42 n. 68; see also Berkowitz, 'Reason of State,' pp. 196–8, 204–7, and *John Selden*, pp. 161–4: Flemion, '"A Savings to Satisfy All,"' 199–202, 205–8; and David L. Smith, 'The 4th Earl of Dorset and the Politics of the Sixteen-Twenties,' 46–9.

250 *Commons 1628*, III, pp. 94–119. Rich was a relative of the Earl of Warwick, Digges closely connected to his former tutor, the Archbishop of Canterbury, and Pym a client of the Earl of Bedford; for Rich, see the *DNB*, and Gruenfelder, *Influence in Elections*, p. 157; for Digges, see Kiffin, 'Sir Dudley Digges,' chs. 11 and 13, pp. 362–71; and for Pym, see Conrad Russell, 'The Parliamentary Career of John Pym, 1621–9.'

251 *Commons 1628*, III, p. 95.

252 Ibid., pp. 110, 105; the quotation combines the two accounts. See also Berkowitz, *John Selden*, pp. 164–6, and Guy, 'Origins of the Petition of Right,' 304–5.

253 *Commons 1628*, III, p. 101.

254 Ibid., p. 110.

255 *Commons 1628*, III, pp. 96–7. For Coke's role, see White, *Sir Edward Coke*, pp. 253–6.

256 Ibid., p. 125.

257 Ibid., pp. 126–7. The reference was to the speech made by James on 21 March 1610.

258 Ibid., p. 130.

259 Ibid., pp. 152, 176; see also White, *Sir Edward Coke*, pp. 256–8. Meticulous in his concern to cite the manuscript, Selden searched through the rolls of Parliament for each relevant statute and petition.

260 *Commons 1628*, III, p. 189.

261 Ibid., pp. 189–92, 195–9, 201–5, 210–12; cf. Berkowitz, *John Selden*, pp. 166–8.

262 *Commons 1628*, III, pp. 210–12. For these events, see Guy, 'Origins of the Petition of Right,' 305–11; White, *Sir Edward Coke*, pp. 258–64; Elizabeth Read Foster, 'Petitions and the Petition of Right,' 35, 37–8, 40–3; Michael B. Young, 'The Origins of the Petition of Right Reconsidered Further'; and Berkowitz, *John Selden*, pp. 169–73. Young suggests that Secretary Coke first broached the procedure of a petition of right.

263 *Commons 1628*, III, pp. 136, 252, 258, 262–3, 265.

264 Sir Francis Seymour favoured proceeding by petition as early as 1 May and on 6 May. Selden clearly disagreed, but could not directly oppose his patron in public: ibid., pp. 187, 191, 194, 202, 204, 211, 212, 215, 220, 222, 223, 225, 226, 227, 235, 237, 240–1, 244, 272, 277, 283, 286, 290, 296. Since Seymour strongly advocated a detailed procedure and would not accept the general answers propounded by King Charles as sufficient, the disagreement appears to have been tactical, not strategic. Nor did this difference of approach arise late in the session. As early as 25 March, Seymour had said in the House that 'many particulars concerning the subject are fitter for a petition to the King than to be put into a bill': ibid., p. 111. This may have applied the the particular issue, however.

265 *Commons 1628*, III, p. 317; for reports on the conferences, see pp. 302, 311, 317.

266 Ibid., pp. 302–17, 326, 327, 329.

267 Ibid., pp. 325–31; see also *Lords 1628*, pp. 394–7.

268 *Commons 1628*, II, p. 372; see pp. 369, 371–3, 374, 378–9, 379–80, 382; for the consideration of the petition by the peers, see *Lords 1628*, pp. 399–403, 405–6, 409–13, 421–36, 438–42, 445, 447–8, 451–7, 460–9, 473, 475–7, 479–87, 489–96, 499–500, 507–17, 520–8, 532–3, 536; see also Flemion, '"A Savings to Satisfy All,"' 37–42.

269 *Commons 1628*, III, pp. 387–401.

270 Ibid., p. 407; see pp. 404, 406–9, 411–14, 417, and *Lords 1628*, pp. 409–13, 422–3, 424–36.

271 *Commons 1628*, II, p. 452; see *Lords 1628*, pp. 445, 447–8, 451–7, 475–6, 479–80, 483–4, 486–7.

272 *Commons 1628*, III, p. 464; see pp. 464, 465, 467–8, 470–1, 475–8, 482–7, 491–2, 493–508, 512, 515–16, 517–18, 520, 527–54, 558–90, 595–98, 599–600, 601–4, 604–7, 611, 612–13, 614–15, 618, 623–5, and *Lords 1628*, pp. 507–8, 509–13, 515–17, 520–1, 522–4, 526–7, 527–8, 532, 540.

273 *Commons 1628*, III, pp. 369, 387, 390, 397, 400, 404–9, 411–14, 448, 451, 454, 456, 457, 465, 491 (where Selden was specifically spared from being a reporter), 535, 544, 547, 549 (the membership of this subcommittee to

draft the reasons of the Commons against the proposed addition was not recorded), 522, 557, 611, 618, 623, 625, 631.

274 Ibid., p. 533; see pp. 538, 543, 546, 547, 548, 552.

275 Ibid., p. 534; see pp. 533–4, 538, 543–4, 547, 548–9, 552; see also the outline for this speech on a narrowly folded paper, Bodleian Library, Selden MSS, supra 123, fol. 292–3. Selden's speech calling for the rejection of the addition came on 22 May and supported the policy then favoured by the Earl of Hertford. After originally approving of Lord Weston's suggestion for an addition mentioning the liberties of the subject and the prerogatives of the Crown, Hertford withdrew his support for the additional clause passed by the Lords: see Lords 1628, p. 453 (for the support on 17 May), and pp. 484, 487 (for his change of heart on 20 May). On 20 May, Seymour strongly attacked the addition in the Commons: see Commons 1628, III, pp. 496, 501.

276 Commons 1628, III, pp. 534, 543, 552.

277 Ibid., p. 534.

278 Ibid., pp. 535, 535 n. 43, 544.

279 Ibid., pp. 535, 538, 539, 544, 546, 547, 549, 552, 557–60, 582–5. For another assessment of Selden's speech, see Popofsky, 'Habeas Corpus and "Liberty of the Subject,"' 271–2. Coke also opposed the addition; see White, Sir Edward Coke, pp. 266–7; and Berkowitz, 'Reason of State,' pp. 206–7, and John Selden, pp. 176–86.

280 Commons 1628, III, pp. 491–508, 512–17, 520, 522–3, 526–54, 557–60, 562–90, 594–607, 612–18, 620.

281 Ibid., pp. 560–71, for Glanville's speech. As one of the most effective speakers on rejection and as one of Glanville's assistants, Selden probably sat on the subcommittee established to draw up the case presented by the Commons for their rejection of the addition proposed by the Lords. None of the references to this subcommittee, however, lists its membership.

282 Ibid., pp. 623–34; Commons 1628, IV, pp. 3, 4, 7, 8, 9, 11–12; and Lords 1628, pp. 539–40, 542–3, 554, 556, 559. For the various answers given by the king and their significance, see Relf, Petition of Right, pp. 47–51; Foster, 'Petitions and the Petition of Right,' 22–6, 43–4; and Berkowitz, 'Reason of State,' pp. 208–11.

283 For an argument that the Petition of Right held the status of a statute, see L.J. Reeve, 'The Legal Status of the Petition of Right.'

284 Commons 1628, IV, pp. 60–6, 68–9, 72–3, 77–8. Considerable discussion followed. For the genesis and completion of this remonstrance, see Russell, Parliaments and Politics, pp. 377–85.

285 *Commons 1628*, IV, pp. 85, 88, 92, 94, 96, 99.

286 Ibid., p. 113; see pp. 118, 122, 129, 131.

287 Ibid., p. 114; see pp. 118, 122–3, 129, 131.

288 Ibid., p. 119; see pp. 114, 117, 123, 129.

289 Ibid., pp. 123, 124; Kirton prepared the way for Selden's motion: see pp. 123–4.

290 Ibid., p. 124, see pp. 114–15, 119; cf. Berkowitz, *John Selden*, pp. 188–94.

291 *Commons 1628*, IV, p. 124, see pp. 115, 119, 129–30, 132. See White, *Sir Edward Coke*, pp. 271–3.

292 *Commons 1628*, IV, pp. 117, 121, 126–7, 133; the quotation is a composite text put together from all of these diaries. For Kirton's attack upon the favourite, see ibid., pp. 115–16, 119–20, 124–5, 130, 132.

293 Ibid., pp. 117, 128, 131, 133.

294 Ibid., p. 117; see pp. 128, 131.

295 Ibid., pp. 140–51, 154–74, 200–6, 208–17; Seymour and Kirton, however, kept up the attack: see pp. 146, 148, 160, 165, 171, 173.

296 Ibid., pp. 221, 212; the latter includes a list of the headings. Neither diary lists the membership of the subcommittee.

297 Ibid., pp. 252, 266; see pp. 242–5, 252–6, 257–60, 263–72, 274–7.

298 Ibid., pp. 243–4; see pp. 258, 264, 271; for Seymour's support of Selden on this point, see p. 264.

299 Ibid., p. 244.

300 Ibid., p. 245; see pp. 254, 259, 265, 271–2, 276.

301 Ibid., pp. 248, 266; the quotation contains portions of each account; both Seymour (who thought that others also deserved punishment) and Kirton supported the attack upon the Duke: see pp. 247, 251, 255, 267.

302 Ibid., p. 266.

303 Ibid., p. 256.

304 Ibid., pp. 237–8, 256, 269.

305 Ibid., p. 310; see pp. 320, 322, 327.

306 Ibid., p. 310; see pp. 320, 322, 327, 328.

307 Ibid.

308 Ibid., pp. 311, 316, 323; see pp. 321–3, 327; for the full text of the remonstrance, see pp. 311–17.

309 Ibid., p. 352; for the passage of the subsidy through the Commons and the presentation of the remonstrance, see pp. 331, 332, 334, 336, 338–40, 351–2, 356; for the king's answer, see pp. 352, 354, 356, 357; and for the passage of the subsidy through the Lords, see *Lords 1628*, pp. 653, 654, 655, 656.

310 *Commons 1628*, IV, pp. 361, 366, 369, 371, 378, 388, 390–400, 403, 404,

406–8, 411–12, 414–15, 418–19, 420, 427, 442, 447–51, 453–8, 461–2, 468, 470–3, 474–7; for a text of the remonstrance on tonnage and poundage, see pp. 470–1. See Linda S. Popofsky, 'The Crisis over Tonnage and Poundage in Parliament in 1629,' 65.

311 *Commons 1628*, IV, pp. 450–1; see pp. 458, 462. The arguments presented in this speech later appeared in the remonstrance mentioned above.

312 For Bowdler's Case, see ibid., pp. 360 and n. 1, 362, 363, 365, 367, 368, 447, 451 and n. 45, 451–3, 460–4, 468 and n. 10; and note 317, below; for this portion of the debate over Holland's patent, see pp. 425–30, 432–4, 436, 438, 440–2.

313 Ibid., p. 431; see pp. 431–2, 438–9, 441–2; this patent was voted a grievance: see p. 433.

314 Ibid., pp. 360, 362–3, 365, 367–8. For a full account, see Charles M. Gray and Maija Jansson Cole, 'Bowdler's Case: The Intestate Bastard.' A brief treatise by Selden, 'Of the disposition or administration of intestates goods,' appeared in several collections in the 1680s, including *Tracts written by John Selden* (London, 1683).

315 *Commons 1628*, IV, pp. 367, 363; the quotation draws portions from each account and omits references to various statutes and precedents.

316 Ibid., p. 360: see pp. 363, 367.

317 Ibid., pp. 447, 462; see pp. 390, 404, 427.

318 Ibid., p. 447; see pp. 451, 462.

319 Ibid., p. 476; see pp. 469, 473.

320 Ibid., p. 475.

321 Ibid., p. 480; see pp. 481–3.

322 Cf. Cust, 'Charles I and the Parliament of 1628,' 42, 45–6, and Flemion, '"A Savings to Satisfy All,"' 43–4.

323 See Burgess, *Politics of the Ancient Constitution*, pp. 179–80, where he interpreted the dispute over the meaning and fear of the effectiveness of the common law as part of the breakdown of the 'Jacobean consensus' over the ancient constitution.

324 For the 'constitutionalist' nature of the case put by Selden, Sir Edward Coke, and other common lawyers, see J.G.A. Pocock, 'The Commons Debates of 1628.' Guy sees the arguments put by the spokesmen of the Commons as less than persuasive and writes of the change from bill to petition: 'The truth was that Selden and the commons' lawyers had failed to vindicate the interpretation of English law they had evolved on 1 April; the four resolutions were worthless unless translated into legislative form. M.P.s were now going round in circles, undoubtedly because they were no longer working within an accepted procedural framework':

Guy, 'Origins of the Petition of Right,' 309. Selden had evolved his interpretation of the common law much earlier, but it did not always agree in perspective and detail with that held by his allies. My account provides a more favourable reading of the case presented by the spokesmen of the Commons.

325 *Commons 1628*, II, p. 309; for Selden's letter of 1620 to the Marquess of Buckingham, see Selden, *Opera*, III, cols. 1393–6.

326 These statistics come from my database on committee memberships in the Commons during the session of 1628. During the course of the session, Seymour, Kirton, and Selden shared three committee memberships (*Commons 1628*, II, pp. 28–9; III, pp. 3–4, 448), while Seymour and Selden shared eight (ibid., II, pp. 29, 78, 398, 428–9; III, pp. 43–4, 355, 386; IV, p. 390), Selden and Kirton seven (ibid., II, pp. 41, 277, 411, 460, 479; III, p. 446; IV, p. 178), and Seymour and Kirton three (ibid., II, pp. 168, 446; III, pp. 123–4). For examples of teamwork among Seymour, Selden, and Kirton, see notes 137, 157, 222, 261, 291, 294, 297, 300, and 303, above, and *Commons 1628*, II, pp. 245, 251, 256, 258, 261, 265, 266, 270, 272, 299, 300, 301, 305, 306, 307, 309, 310, 311, 312, 315, 317, 318, 319, 401; III, 226, 327, 328, 329, 330, 332, 386, 388, 393, 419, 421, 424, 425, 426; IV, 181, 184, 185, 188, 190, 294, 295, 298, 300–1, 302, 333, 472, 473, 477, 348, 351, 356, 380, 450, 468. Upon occasion, members of the Seymour connection disagreed on issues or tactics: see note 257, above, and ibid., III, pp. 235, 237, 240–1, 242, 244, 245, 246, 247, 359, 362, 363, 432, 437, 439, 441, 442, 596, 599, 600, 602, 603–4, 605, 606.

327 See Popofsky, 'The Crisis over Tonnage and Poundage in Parliament,' 58–61.

328 Manwaring's book was suppressed by royal proclamation on 24 June 1628, but in terms which left the main arguments intact: see Berkowitz, *John Selden*, pp. 200–1; L.J. Reeve, *Charles I and the Road to Personal Rule*, 58–72; and Sommerville, *Politics and Ideology*, pp. 127–31. The sermon by Manwaring did not defend 'Arminian' theology, nor did a clear link between the 'Arminians' and the defence of absolute monarchy exist in the 1620s: see especially Burgess, *Politics of the Ancient Constitution*, pp. 174–90. For the 'Arminians,' see especially Nicholas Tyacke, *Anti-Calvinists: The Rise of English Arminianism, c. 1590–1640*, ch. 6; for challenges to Tyacke's interpretation, see Julian Davies, *The Caroline Captivity of the Church: Charles I and the Remoulding of Anglicanism, 1625–1641*, and Peter White, *Predestination, Policy and Polemic: Conflict and Consensus in the English Church from the Refor-*

mation to the Civil War; see also the essays in Kenneth Fincham's, *The Early Stuart Church, 1603–1642.*

329 Selden served on twelve select committees: see *C.J.,* I, pp. 921 (3 committees), 922, 923, 924, 925, 926, 929, 930 (2 committees), 931; in addition, he served on at least three subcommittees. For this session, see Russell, *Parliaments and Politics,* ch. 7; Berkowitz, *John Selden,* ch. 11; Hulme, *Sir John Eliot,* ch. 13; Reeve, *Road to Personal Rule,* ch. 3; and Christopher Thompson, 'The Divided Leadership of the House of Commons in 1629.' Since this session witnessed little interaction between the Lords and the Commons, my account makes little reference to the Upper House.

330 *C.J.,* I, p. 920; Selden had moved the formation of this committee; see Wallace Notestein and Francies Helen Relf, eds., *Commons Debates for 1629* [hereinafter *Commons 1629*], p. 6 n. For this whole dispute, see Berkowitz, *John Selden,* pp. 204–8; Reeve, 'The Legal Status of the Petition of Right'; and Elizabeth Read Foster, 'Printing the Petition of Right.'

331 *Commons 1629,* p. 4.

332 *C.J.,* I, p. 920; precedents did occur from the previous reign.

333 Ibid.

334 Ibid., pp. 920–1; see *Commons 1629,* pp. 5–6, 6 n. Elsyng's account shows that the committee knew that King Charles had endorsed the warrant authorizing the destruction of the first printing and the publication of the second: see Foster, 'Printing the Petition of Right,' 83.

335 Ibid., p. 921; see *Commons 1629,* pp. 8, 9 n.

336 *C.J.,* I, p. 921; see *Commons 1629,* pp. 9, 9–10 n. In light of Elsyng's account, Selden's report was less than candid; of course, members of the Commons could not blame the king.

337 *Commons 1629,* p. 5; see p. 6 n.

338 Ibid., pp. 7, 9 n.; the quotation draws upon accounts in two diaries.

339 Ibid., pp. 7–8. The Earl of Pembroke, Rudyard's patron, would not have supported the refusal to pay tonnage and poundage.

340 Ibid., p. 9 n.

341 *C.J.,* I, p. 921.

342 *Commons 1629,* pp. 10–11.

343 Ibid., pp. 12, 108; see 108 n.

344 Ibid., p. 14, from Kirton's speech; see pp. 12–16, 109–10.

345 *C.J.,* I, pp. 922–3, and *Commons 1629,* pp. 18–21, 110, 111–12, 111 n. For these opening moves, see Popofsky, 'TheCrisis over Tonnage and Poundage in Parliament,' 61–3.

346 *C.J.,* I, p. 923, and *Commons 1629,* pp. 22–3, 112–13.

347 *Commons 1629*, p. 29; see pp. 29–30, and *C.J.*, I, p. 925.

348 *Commons 1629*, p. 32; see pp. 31–2.

349 Ibid., pp. 117, 118 n., 119–20, 70, 145, 205, 79–80, 152–3, 215–16, 154, 219; see also his speech there on printing, pp. 58–9.

350 Ibid.; for the pardons, see pp. 36, 45, 131 and n., 175, 49–50, 179; for the remarks of Alleyne, see pp. 48–9, 132, 178, and *C.J.*, I, pp. 925–7; and for the remonstrance, see *Commons 1629*, pp. 95–101. Since Selden was to receive the papers involved in this case, it seems reasonable to assume that he acted as chair of the subcommittee: *C.J.*, I, p. 925.

351 *C.J.*, I, p. 926.

352 Ibid., p. 928; see *Commons 1629*, pp. 55, 186.

353 *Commons 1629*, p. 136; see pp. 55–6, 187.

354 Ibid., p. 136; see pp. 56, 187.

355 *C.J.*, I, p. 928; see *Commons 1629*, pp. 56, 136, 187.

356 *Ibid.*, p. 928; see *Commons 1629*, pp. 56, 136, 187–8.

357 *Commons 1629*, pp. 56, 188; see pp. 136–7.

358 Ibid., pp. 188–9; Sir Miles Fleetwood and Sir Henry Mildmay, Master of the Jewel House, belonged to the Buckingham network, while Sir Robert Mansell was a client of the Earl of Pembroke; Sir Humphrey May had helped his kinsman, the courtier Sir Thomas Jermyn, obtain a seat in earlier parliaments, but Jermyn probably used his own family's influence in 1628; Sir John Maynard was a courtier and a Knight of Bath. For the connections, see Russell, *Parliaments and Politics*, pp. 16–17, 174, 434, and Gruenfelder, *Influence*, pp. 81–2, 114, n. 54, 126–7, 146, 150, 178, n. 52.

359 Ibid., pp. 57, 188; the quotation combines portions of two accounts.

360 *C.J.*, I, p. 928; see pp. 57, 137, 189.

361 Ibid., p. 929; see *Commons 1629*, p. 190.

362 *Commons 1629*, pp. 190, 57.

363 Ibid., pp. 137–8. Kirton made reference to the king's speech of 24 January.

364 *C.J.*, I, p. 929; see *Commons 1629*, pp. 58, 138, 190.

365 *Commons 1629*, p. 141, see pp. 141–4, 60–3, 196–201.

366 Ibid., p. 143; see pp. 62, 199. For these events, see Popofsky, 'The Crisis over Tonnage and Poundage in Parliament,' 64–6.

367 *C.J.*, I, p. 929; see *Commons 1629*, pp. 143, 199, 200. For a reasonable presentation of this complex issue, see Thompson, 'Divided Leadership,' pp. 264–6.

368 *C.J.*, I, p. 929, *Commons 1629*, p. 202.

369 *Commons 1629*, pp. 73, 74; *C.J.*, I, pp. 929, 930.

370 *Commons 1629*, pp. 147–8, 74, 207; *C.J.*, I, p. 930.

371 *Commons 1629*, p. 155; see, 155–6, 83–4, 221–2.

372 Ibid., pp. 222, 156–7, 223. For May's denial of privilege, see pp. 155, 222.

373 Ibid., pp. 85, 223, 157. The quotation draws from three diaries.

374 Ibid., p. 157.

375 *C.J.*, I, p. 931.

376 *Commons 1629*, p. 159; see 87, 158–9, 227, and *C.J.*, I, p. 931

377 *Commons 1629*, pp. 86–7, 158–61, 226–8.

378 Ibid., p. 228; see p. 162.

379 Ibid., pp. 89–90; see pp. 164–5, 230–1; for this lengthy debate, see pp. 88–93, 162–6, 228–34.

380 Ibid., p. 165; see pp. 90–1, 231–2.

381 Ibid., pp. 91, 232; see p. 165.

382 Ibid., p. 93; see pp. 166, 234; for the concluding debate, see pp. 91–3, 165–6, 232–4.

383 Ibid., pp. 94, 168; for May, see pp. 193, 167, 235, and for Coke, see pp. 94, 167–8, 236.

384 *C.J.*, I, 932; see *Commons 1629*, pp. 168, 237.

385 *Commons 1629*, pp. 94–5, 168–9, 237–9, and *C.J.*, I, p. 932. See Popofsky, 'The Crisis over Tonnage and Poundage in Parliament,' 67.

386 *Commons 1629*, pp. 169, 238.

387 Ibid., p. 169; see p. 238.

388 *C.J.*, I, p. 932; *Commons 1629*, pp. 101, 169–70, 239.

389 *Commons 1629*, pp. 264–5; see pp. 101–6, 170–2, 239–44, 252–67; see also Berkowitz, *John Selden*, p. 225.

390 *Commons 1629*, pp. 171, 265.

391 'The King's Declaration showing the Causes of the Dissolution of the Late Parliament, 1629,' printed in Samuel Rawson Gardiner, *Constitutional Documents of the Puritan Revolution, 1625–1660*, pp. 83–99; the original draft in the State Papers 'is in Heath's hand': Berkowitz, *John Selden*, p. 232.

392 *L.J.*, IV, p. 43.

393 For the imprisonment and trials of these members, see the thorough accounts in Berkowitz, *John Selden*, chs. 12 and 13, and Reeve, *Road to Personal Rule*, ch. 5; for other aspects, see Kopperman, *Sir Robert Heath*, pp. 175–87; John Reeve, 'The Arguments in the King's Bench in 1629 concerning the Imprisonment of John Selden and Other Members of the House of Commons,' 257–77, and 'Sir Robert Heath's Advice for Charles I in 1629'; for the interrogation, see Ian H.C. Fraser, 'The Agitation in the Commons, 2 March 1629, and the Interrogation of the Anti-Court Group.'

394 For the first draft of the elaborate set of questions drawn up by Heath, some addressed to all and some to particular defendants, see British Library, Egerton MSS 2978, 'Interrogatory to be ministered to the prisoners to be examined concerninge the late disorders in the commons house of parliament 2° March. 1628[/9],' fol. 39–42.

395 Public Records Office, State Papers, 16/139/8, as quoted in Fraser, 'Agitation in the Commons,' 94. The biographies of Coryton and Hobart appear in *DNB*; for Eliot, see Hulme, *Sir John Eliot*, chs. 14–16; for Holles, see Patricia Crawford, *Denzil Holles, 1598–1680: A Study of His Political Career*, pp. 23–6; for Long, Strode, and Valentine, see Greaves and Zaller, ed., *Biographical Dictionary*, II, pp. 201–2, and III, pp. 213–14 and 259.

396 Public Records Office, State Papers, 16/139/8; these words did appear in the account of the speech cited to note 384, above.

397 Ibid., fol. 15^r; similar words appear in the speech cited to note 384, above.

398 Ibid.; these words do not appear in the accounts, so this may have been accurate.

399 Ibid.; Selden may have made no formal motion, but he did suggest that the Clerk might put the question in the speech cited to note 384, above.

400 In his answers, Selden appeared to show less and less confidence. English Protestant casuists of the early seventeenth century did not approve of lying in such circumstances: see Camille Wells Slights, *The Casuistical Tradition in Shakespeare, Donne, Herbert, and Milton*, chs. 1 and 2, Keith Thomas, 'Cases of Conscience in Seventeenth-Century England'; and, from a different point of view, Perez Zagorin, *Ways of Lying: Dissimulation, Persecution and Conformity in Early Modern Europe*.

401 Public Records Office, State Papers, 16/139/8, fol. 15^v. Of Selden's performance, Gardiner remarked that 'the falsehood was so unblushing that it can hardly be reckoned as a falsehood at all. He could never for an instant have expected to be believed. All he meant was to intimate that he had no intention of allowing himself to be made a victim for any opinion whatever': Samuel R. Gardiner, *History of England from the Accession of James I. to the Outbreak of the Civil War, 1603–1642*, VI, p. 80; cf. Berkowitz, *John Selden*, pp. 236–8.

402 Howell, ed., *State Trials*, III, pp. 237–8; see Berkowitz, *John Selden*, pp. 234–5, 238–42, and Reeve, *Road to Personal Rule*, pp. 120–4.

403 See Berkowitz, *John Selden*, pp. 243, 246–51.

404 King's Bench controlment roll as quoted by Reeve, 'Arguments in the King's Bench in 1629,' 269.

405 Ask read at the Inner Temple and was called to the bar in 1614; under

the commonwealth, he became a Justice of the Upper Bench: see Edward Foss, *The Judges of England*, VI, pp. 417–18. One of the managers of the impeachment of the Duke of Buckingham in the Parliament of 1626 and a frequent participant in the debates which led to the Petition of Right in the Parliament of 1628, Mason became the Recorder of London in 1634. Sir Robert Berkeley would become a Justice of the King's Bench in 1632, while Sir Humphrey Davenport would become a Justice of the Common Pleas in 1630 and President of the Court of the Exchequer in 1631: all three appear in *DNB*.

406 Howell, ed., *State Trials*, III, pp. 241–2.

407 Ibid., p. 242.

408 Ibid., pp. 243–4.

409 Ibid., p. 244.

410 Ibid., p. 248. In general, this represented a refinement of the argument earlier presented to the Lords by Attorney General Heath that the law demanded a general, but not a particular cause in the return to a writ of *habeas corpus*: see the passages cited to notes 193–5 and 209–11, above.

411 Ibid., p. 250.

412 Ibid., p. 252.

413 Ibid., pp. 249, 252.

414 For Littleton, see notes 164, 183, 195, and 207, above. A distinguished common lawyer, Littleton was almost as well read in the French legal-historical tradition as Selden: see J.H. Baker, 'The Newe Littleton,' in his *The Legal Profession and the Common Law: Historical Essays*, pp. 231–241.

415 A comparison of Littleton's draft, in Cambridge University Library, MS, Mm. 6.63(4), fol. 1^v, 3^r–28^v, and Selden's draft, in Howell, ed., *State Trials*, III, pp. 264–80, with the record of Littleton's presentation, in ibid., pp. 251–64, would indicate something like the procedure noted above. Since Attorney General Heath answered Littleton's arguments, it seems best to deal with them in the text and to quote or cite appropriate portions of Littleton's and Selden's drafts in the footnotes.

416 Howell, ed., *State Trials*, III, pp. 252–3; Littleton's more lengthy draft varied in wording, but not in substance; Cambridge University Library, MS, Mm. 6.63(4), fol. 4–5. The same was true of Selden's draft: 'That persons committed by command of the king are not replevisable, and out of Stamford, fol. 73. as if he interpreted "bailable" (which indeed he doth not, if he be observed) to be understood in that statute by "replevisable," and the like, are directly against the very body of the petition of right, and were so fully cleared in the debates, out of which the petition of

right was framed, that to dispute them again, were to question what the whole parliament had already resolved on as the certain and established law of the kingdom'; and 'All offences, by the laws of the realm, being of two Kinds: the first, punishable by loss of life or limb; the second, by fine, or some pecuniary mulct, or damage and imprisonment, or by one of them; and those of the first kind being treason, murder, felonies of less nature, and some more; and of the second kind, bloodsheds, affrays and other trespasses: If any prisoner stand committed (though before conviction) for treason or murder; the Judges, for aught appears in the Books, have not often used to let him to bail ... But if a prisoner before conviction ... stand committed for trespasses only, as all offences of the second kind are ... there, by constant course (unless some special act of parliament be to the contrary in some particular case) upon offer of good bail to the court, he is to be bailed ...': ibid., pp. 265, 265–6.

417 The distinction between the meaning of 'repleviable' in the first Statute of Westminster and 'bailable' had arisen in the Five Knights' Case; Selden continued to pursue it in the parliamentary debates and stressed that the two terms did not have the same meaning. In his speech to the Lords of 7 April, Littleton had underlined Selden's distinction, while in the joint conference of 17 April, Heath had replied by stressing that the two terms had the same meaning at law; see the passage cited to notes 178 and 210, above. The point had considerable substance; Heath's reading severely weakened the case for bailing the prisoners.

418 Howell, ed., State Trials, III, p. 253; cf. Cambridge University Library, MS, Mm. 6.63(4), fol. 5^{v}.

419 Howell, ed., State Trials, III, p. 253; cf. p. 276, for Selden's draft: '... all Contempts, of what kind soever, that are punishable by the laws of the realm, are "against the king and his government," immediately or mediately. And though the latitude of them be such, as that some may vastly exceed others; yet they are all, as Contempts, only trespasses, etc. punishable only by fine or imprisonment or both, but not until conviction of the parties ... unless the contempt be in the face of some court, against which it is committed, which supplies a conviction.' See also Cambridge University Library, MS, Mm. 6.63(4), fol. 6.

420 Howell, ed., State Trials, III, pp. 253–4; for the same points, see Selden's draft, p. 267, and Littleton's draft, Cambridge University Library, MS, Mm. 6.63(4), fol. 6^{v}-8^{r}; the latter contains numerous marginal notes spelling out many of the specific cases eventually mentioned in the speech.

421 Howell, ed., State Trials, III, p. 254; this follows the wording of Selden's draft quite closely; cf. pp. 267–8.

422 Ibid., pp. 254–5, 254–7; in this section, Littleton dealt more with cases, mentioning statutes from the reigns of Henry IV, Henry VIII, Philip and Mary, and Elizabeth I, and cases from the reign of Edward III onward; these are found in his draft, as well: Cambridge University Library, MS, Mm. 6.63(4), fol. 8–10; Selden did not recite as many examples, but he examined the statutes from the reigns of Richard II, Henry IV, Henry VI, Edward VI, Philip and Mary, and Elizabeth I; analysed at length the treason act from 35 Edward III; and concluded that the 'words "sedition" and "seditious" ... in all these places ... denoted in our language ... such an offence as was not punishable (without some special provision by act of parliament) otherwise than by fine and imprisonment at the utmost ...': Howell, ed., *State Trials*, III, p. 269; see pp. 269–77.

423 Ibid., p. 257, citing Coke as the authority, as in his draft, Cambridge University Library, MS, Mm. 6.63(4), fol. 12; cf. Selden's draft, pp. 277–8, where he noted that Bracton, Glanville, and Hengham were 'learned and famous Judges in their ages, yet they lived so long since, and the rest of the particulars of which they write are so different ... from the practice and established laws of ensuing ages, that their authority is of slight or no moment for the direction in judgment of the law at this day, though it be very considerable in examination of what the law was in their times: and that way it sometimes is used as an ornament in argument only, as it is said in the Commentaries of them.' The opening portion of this quotation appears as a marginal note in Littleton's draft, which would indicate that it incorporated material from Selden's draft: Cambridge University Library, MS, Mm. 6.63(4), fol. 12^v mn.

424 Howell, ed., *State Trials*, III, pp. 257–8; cf. Cambridge University Library, MS, Mm. 6.63(4), fol. 14^r: 'everybody knoweth the solemn resolution in parliament 11 Richard 2 that this kingdome was never governed by the civill lawe nor never should be ...' In his draft, Selden made reference to particular sections of the the Roman law; however, he did not mention the resolution of 11 Richard II, regarding the civil law, even though he had cited it more than once in his earlier works.

425 Howell, ed., *State Trials*, III, p. 258; for the same points, see Cambridge University Library, MS, Mm. 6.63(4), fol. 14^r.

426 Howell, ed., *State Trials*, III, p. 258.

427 Ibid., p. 259; this closely follows Littleton's draft, Cambridge University Library, MS, Mm. 6.63(4), fol. 17. See also Reeve, 'Arguments in the King's Bench in 1629,' 275.

428 Howell, ed., *State Trials*, III, p. 259. Of course, Littleton did not mention that the Lords did not recognize the validity of this particular interpretation.

429 Ibid., pp. 260–1; cf. Cambridge University Library, MS, Mm. 6.63(4), fol. 20^v–21^v; cf. Selden on Russell's case, pp. 275–6.

430 Howell, *State Trials*, III, p. 261; all of these precedents had received extensive discussion in the debates and joint conferences which led to the Petition of Right.

431 Ibid., pp. 262–3; cf. Cambridge University Library, MS, Mm. 6.63(4), fol. 24–7.

432 Howell, *State Trials*, III, pp. 263–4; for Heath's proceedings in the Star Chamber, see Public Record Office, State Papers, 16/142/62–5.

433 Howell, *State Trials*, III, p. 264.

434 Ibid.

435 Ibid., p. 281.

436 Ibid.

437 Ibid.

438 Ibid.

439 See Foster, 'Printing the Petition of Right,' and Reeve, 'Legal Status of the Petition of Right,' 262–3 and n. 36.

440 Howell, ed., *State Trials*, III, pp. 281–2; for the whole question of the legal position of the petition of right, see Reeve, 'Legal Status of the Petition of Right,' 257–77.

441 Howell, ed., *State Trials*, III, p. 282.

442 In attacking as a precedent a speech in support of discretionary imprisonment made in the Parliament of 1621 by Sir Edward Coke, Selden had noted that the Journals of the House of Commons did not constitute a valid record at law; see the passage cited to note 217, above.

443 Howell, ed., *State Trials*, III, p. 282.

444 Ibid., pp. 282–3.

445 Ibid., p. 283.

446 Ibid., pp. 283–4. This presentation ignored Littleton's points that Bracton no longer held any authority and that none of these statutes remained in force.

447 Ibid., pp. 284, 286. For even less favourable representations of Heath's position, see Reeve, 'Arguments in the King's Bench in 1629,' 279–82, and Berkowitz, *John Selden*, pp. 254–5.

448 Howell, ed., *State Trials*, III, p. 287; for a full account of these manoeuvrings, see Berkowitz, *John Selden*, pp. 255–9.

449 Howell, ed., *State Trials*, III, p. 286. Reeve, *Road to Personal Rule,*

p. 127, comments: 'This device deserves to be considered nothing less than a despicable and "dirty" trick.'

450 *Acts of the Privy Council of England, 1629–1630*, 352; a full account of these later proceedings appear in Berkowitz, *John Selden*, pp. 259–80 and Reeve, *Road to Personal Rule*, pp. 128–64.

451 Howell, ed., *State Trials*, III, p. 288.

452 Ibid., p. 289.

453 Ibid.

454 Ibid., pp. 294–310; see Berkowitz, *John Selden*, pp. 267–8, 276–8.

455 Howell, ed., *State Trials*, III, pp. 310–15; see Berkowitz, *John Selden*, pp. 268–76, 279–80, and Reeve, *Road to Personal Rule*, pp. 158–64.

456 John Selden, *Vindiciæ Secundum Integritatem*, pp. 43–9; for a full documentation, see Berkowitz, *John Selden*, pp. 281–91. Earlier, the Earl of Essex, Earl of Bath, Sir Robert Cotton, and Thomas Cotton, his son, had agreed to stand surety for Selden's release: see *Vindiciæ*, pp. 37–8, and Selden's letter of thanks and promise of future service to the Earl of Essex of 26 July 1631, British Library, Add. MSS 46,188, fol. 133^r.

457 Professor J.H. Hexter has implied that historians have argued that 'the political conflicts in the House of Commons are reducible to faction fights among puppets of the peers of the realm': see J.H. Hexter, 'Power Struggle, Parliament, and Liberty in Early Stuart England, ii; see also p. 19, n. 31. For the quite different view that reciprocal interpersonal relationships of political friendship, kinship, patronage, and clientage supplied the *method*, and the preservation of 'proper order' defined the *aim* of governing in early modern England, see Christianson, 'The Causes of the English Revolution: A Reappraisal,' 62–7 and 'The Peers, the People, and Parliamentary Management in the First Six Months of the Long Parliament,' 576–82.

458 In the Long Parliament, Selden sat for Oxford, probably through the help of Archbishop Laud, not for one of Hertford's seats: see Berkowitz, 'SELDEN, John (1584–1654),' p. 157. If so, this may have followed from an earlier rupture. Hertford tried to draw upon their old relationship in June 1642 by extending to Selden an invitation to join the king at York, but Selden declined, remarking that his going thither would constitute a 'disservice, by which name I call whatsoever will at this time (as this necessarily would) doubtless occasion some further differences "twixt his majesty and that house of commons"': quoted in Richard Tuck, '"The Ancient Law of Freedom,"' p. 137; for the letter, see Bodleian Library, Selden MSS, supra 123, fol. 159^r.

459 For the fascinating debate over the militia which pitched Marten against

a host of common lawyers, see *Commons 1628*, II, pp. 541–61, 567–76. As Richard Tuck has shown, Selden became more interested in theoretical constructs during the 1630s; see his *Natural Rights Theories*, ch. 4. Cf. Sommerville, 'John Selden, the Law of Nature, and the Origins of Government,' which raises a number of valid points about Selden's views on the law of nature and the origins of civil government; after 1614, however, the question of the hypothetical starting-point of society received no attention in Selden's English works. For constitutionalist and absolutist natural-law arguments, see Sommerville, *Politics and Ideology*, chs. 1 and 2, and for the relationship between common and civil law in early-seventeenth-century England, see Christianson, 'Political Thought in Early Stuart England,' and Burgess, *Politics of the Ancient Constitution*, ch. 5.

460 For example, cf. Boynton, 'Martial Law and the Petition of Right,' and the treatment accorded to John Baber and to various deputy lieutenants by the Commons in 1628.

461 For the struggles for power and disputes within the privy council and outsiders seeking office for themselves, see Cust, *Forced Loan*; Cogswell, *Blessed Revolution*; Russell, *Parliaments and Politics*; Sharpe, 'Earl of Arundel and the Opposition to Buckingham'; and Christopher Thompson, 'Court Politics and Parliamentary Conflict in 1625.'

462 For the religious dispute, see Tyacke, *Anti-Calvinists*; Peter Lake, 'Calvinism and the English Church 1570–1635,' and 'Anti-Popery: The Structure of a Prejudice'; and most of the essays in Fincham, ed., *Early Stuart Church*. Cf. Davies, *Caroline Captivity*, chs. 1–3, and White, *Predestination, Policy and Polemic*, chs. 11–14. While a few absolutists did exist in early-seventeenth-century England, Sommerville, *Politics and Ideology*, tends to collapse 'divine right' arguments into absolutist ones (a tendency largely remedied in Sommerville, 'Absolutism and Royalism') and to underestimate the key importance of common-law discourse in English disputes over governance; for criticisms, see Glenn Burgess, 'The Divine Right of Kings Reconsidered,' and Conrad Russell, 'Divine Rights in the Early Seventeenth Century.' Over a decade ago, Hexter argued that, before the Parliament of 1628, Charles I 'had ruled lawlessly. And the courts of law had not stopped him': J.H. Hexter, 'Power Struggle, Parliament, and Liberty in Early Stuart England,' 46. For a more charitable view, cf. Francis Wormuth, *The Royal Prerogative, 1603–1649*, and Judson, *Crisis of the Constitution*, chs. 1 and 4; W.J. Jones, *Politics and the Bench: The Judges and the Origins of the English Civil War* has upheld their judgment. Attorney General Heath, of

course, became that Chief Justice Heath whom Charles I removed from the bench in 1634 for his reformed religious views: see Reeve, 'Heath's Advice.'

463 See Stater, *Noble Government*, p. 17. 'Charles's unprecedented actions pointed the way toward a political style that would flourish a generation later ...'

464 The term comes from Russell, *Parliaments and Politics*, p. 416.

465 Of course, between 1629 and 1642, the political positions of such people as Charles I, Hertford, and Selden changed several times, but that is another story. See Mendle, *Dangerous Positions*, chs. 1, 5–8, and Smith, *Constitutional Royalism*, pp. 44–5, 86–91, 94–5, 97, 98–102.

CHAPTER THREE John Selden's Interpretations of History and Law in the 1630s

1 D.R. Woolf, 'Erudition and the Idea of History in Renaissance England,' and *Idea of History*; for Selden, see 32–43 of the article and ch. 7 of the book; for experienced politicians writing history, see 25 of the article; see also Fussner, *Historical Revolution*, ch. 11. This section owes a great deal to the work of Professor Woolf and to the pioneering essay by H.D. Hazeltine, 'Selden as Legal Historian'; cf. Berkowitz, *John Selden*, ch. 3. I would like to thank Professor Woolf for our many discussions on Selden's historical method and related matters.

2 Selden, 'English Janus,' sig. a3^r.

3 Drayton, *Poly-Olbion*, sig. A2H^r; for Selden's 'Illustrations' or antiquarian notes for this chorological poem, see chapter 1, above.

4 Selden, *Titles of Honor* (1614), sig. a2^v, a3^v, c4; also see chapter 1, above.

5 *Ibid.*, sig. d1^r, d 2^r, and see the passages cited to chapter 1, above, notes 91 and 92.

6 Selden, *The Historie of Tithes*, unpaginated; these included the records in the Tower of London; Office of the Receipt of the Exchequer; Office of the King's Remembrancer; the public library of Oxford; and the libraries of the Inner Temple, St Paul's Cathedral, the Prince, Sir Robert Cotton, Mr Thomas Allen, Mr Patrick Young, and his own collection. The largest number of manuscripts came from the famous library of his friend Sir Robert Cotton.

7 *Ibid.*, sig. a2^r; italics in the original.

8 Woolf, 'Erudition and the Idea of History,' 35; for the French writers on method in this context, see James L. Darroch, 'Method and History: The Importance of Dialectic, Rationalism and Skepticism in the Develop-

ment of Historical Consciousness and Methodology in Early Modern France, 1555–1700,' and for the relationship between Bacon's proposals of reforms for the English common law and for science, see Martin, *Francis Bacon*. For Selden's explicit analogies between the science of his day and his own studies, see the passages cited to notes 25 and 44, below.

9 Selden, *Historie of Tithes*, p. xiii; also quoted in part in Tuck, *Philosophy and Government*, p. 210; also see chapter 1, above, note 224.

10 Selden, *Historie of Tithes*, pp. xii, xix.

11 John Selden, 'To My Singular Good Friend, Mr. *Augustine Vincent*,' in Augustine Vincent, *A Discoverie of Errours in the first Edition of the Catalogue of Nobility Published by Raphe Brooke, Yorke Herald, 1619*, sig. a1^r. For a discussion of this key statement, see Woolf, 'Erudition and the Idea of History,' 41–2.

12 Selden, 'To My Singular Good Friend, Mr. *Augustine Vincent*,' sig. a1^v. Ironically, most of the evidence used in this preface came, not from public records, or from private manuscripts, but from printed medieval histories! In fairness, however, one should add that, prior to writing this preface, Selden had constructed much of *The Historie of Tithes* and all of his report to the House of Lords from public records.

13 See Carlo Sigonio, *Historiarum de regno Italiæ*, 2 parts (Venice, 1591); Cherubino Ghirardacci, *Della Historia di Bologna* (Bologna, 1596); Juan de Mariana, *Historiæ de rebus Hispaniæ* (Toledo, 1592); Melchoir Goldast, *Collectio consuetudinum et legum imperialium* (1613) and *Politica imperiala* (Frankfort, 1614); Augustin du Paz, *Histoire généalogique de plusveurs maisons illustres de Bretagne* (Paris, 1619); and Johannes Georgius Herwart ab Hohenburg, *Ludouicus quartus Imperator defensus* (Munich, 1619); Knighton had used a number of medieval English rolls of Parliament that no longer existed.

14 Selden, 'To My Singular Good Friend, Mr. *Augustine Vincent*,' sig. a1^v. Since Selden had carried out some of Bacon's research, he knew about the quality of his account: see Daniel R. Woolf, 'John Selden, John Borough and Francis Bacon's *History of Henry VII, 1621*,' and Berkowitz, *John Selden*, p. 311 n. 53. Even after carefully considering the criteria, Selden's list contains what may seem like some surprising omissions.

15 Selden, 'To My Singular Good Friend, Mr. *Augustine Vincent*,' sig. a 2^r.

16 Selden, *Titles of Honor* (1631), sig. †3^v, †4^r, §2^v.

17 Ibid., sig. §4^r, 4^v.

18 Ibid., sig. §4^v–¶1^r; see §4 for a list of eight of these specialized works.

19 For a full discussion of the evidence used in this treatise, see ibid., sig. §4^r–¶3^v.

20 Selden, *Titles of Honor* (1631), sig. §4^v. Selden had mentioned many of these collections in his preface to Vincent's book.

21 For an illustrated discussion of such honorary headgear of rulers as 'fillets,' diadems, and crowns, see Selden, *Titles of Honor* (1631), pp. 156–72.

22 Ibid., sig. ¶3. Most pages of the text display this system in operation.

23 Ibid., sig. ¶3^v.

24 Ibid., sig. ¶1^v, 2^r; the 'Chymiques' mentioned here were, of course, the Paracelsian alchemists of his day. Selden refers to the relevant works of Plato: see sig. ¶1.

25 Political philosophy involved as careful and painstaking research as natural philosophy; for Selden's attitude towards the latter, see Mordechai Feingold, 'John Selden and the Nature of Seventeenth-Century Science.'

26 John Selden, *Of the Dominion, Or, Ownership of the Sea*, sig. (e)1, (e)2^r.

27 For the teleology of the French, see Zachary Syre Schiffman, 'An Anatomy of the Historical Revolution in Renaissance France,' 'Etienne Pasquier and the Problem of Historical Relativism,' and 'Renaissance Historicism Reconsidered.'

28 In a letter of 24 May 1621, Selden reported to James Ussher, Bishop of Meath, that 'my Titles of Honour are in the press, and new written, but I hear it shall be staied; if not, I shall salute you with one as soon as it is done': *The Whole Works of the Most Rev. James Ussher D. D.*, XV, p. 170, letter 48. The second edition would not appear until 1631. In the preface of John Selden, *Titles of Honor* (London, 1631), sig. q3^v–4^r, he mentions that this edition had been delayed at the press for a long time. During the course of the 1620s, he added other materials, some after the research carried out in the session of 1628 and others, including those contained in the additions and amendments (pp. 916–41), after 1629. For example, the reference to Magna Carta from the reign of King John being 'extant only in some originalls and in some stories as *Matthew Paris, Roger of Wendover, Thomas of Rudborne*, and some other, but not in any Roll that remaynes now' (p. 713) must have been written after Sir Robert Cotton received his two manuscripts of John's Magna Carta in 1629 and 1630: see Berkowitz, *John Selden*, p. 324 n. 34.

29 See *Eadmeri monachi Cantuariensis, Historia Novorum ... sub Guilielmis I et II et Henrico I Angliæ Regibus* (London, 1623), pp. vi, 170.

30 For these various law codes, see Corinne C. Weston, 'England: Ancient Constitution and Common Law.'

31 Selden, *Of the Dominion, Or, Ownership of the Sea*, sig. e1^v, originally published in Latin as *Mare Clausum* (London, 1635): see Selden, *Titles of Honor* (1631), pp. 19, 917, for the claim that he had written *Mare*

Clausum around 1620; portions appeared in English in appropriate parts of the text of *Titles of Honor* (1631), as well.

32 John Selden, ed., *Marmora Arundeliana* (London, 1628). This work and others from the 1620s which did not deal with the European past are not discussed here.

33 For this correspondence, see Ussher, *Works*, XV, pp. 170, 175–6, 290, 302–3, 380–7; Bodleian Library Library, Selden MSS, supra 108, f. 93–4, 174–5, 184–5, 217. These letters remind us of the incredible breadth of scholarship practised by learned people in seventeenth-century Europe. Selden did not always return the works borrowed: see Tite, 'A "Loan" of Printed Books.'

34 Bodleian Library, Selden MSS, supra 108, f. 93^r. The first edition of a composite Anglo-Saxon chronicle would appear as an appendix to Abraham Wheelocke's edition of an Anglo-Saxon translation of Bede, *Historiæ Ecclesticæ Gentis Anglorum* (Cambridge, 1644).

35 The copy in the Bodleian Library contains Spelman's note of presentation to Selden. The primary dedications of Spelman's work were to James Ussher, Archbishop of Armagh, and John Williams, Bishop of Lincoln, with Cotton, Selden, and a host of Continental scholars as secondary dedicatees: Sir Henry Spelman, *Archæologus in modum Glossarii ad rem antiquam posteriorem*, ms. note and dedication.

36 Ussher, *Works*, XVI, p. 430, letter 144. Selden's book on the gods of the ancient Syrians first appeared in 1617; Daniel Heinsius shepherded the expanded second edition through the press in Leiden in 1628; for his relationship to Selden, see Paul R. Sellin, *Daniel Heinsius and Stuart England*, pp. 103–9.

37 Ussher, *Works*, XVI, p. 461, letter 159.

38 Fortescue, *De Laudibus*, pp. 19–20; see the passage cited to note 182 in chapter 1, above.

39 Topical chapters on the status of gentlemen and creation of nobles, feminine titles and the transmission of titles, honorary attributes, and precedents, and a section on amendments, additions, and errata, rounded out this folio tome of nearly one thousand pages.

40 Selden, *Titles of Honor* (1631), p. 3. The means remained the same.

41 See Pocock, *Ancient Constitution*, pp. 283–5.

42 Ibid., p. 4. This demoted Nimrod from his earlier position as the first monarch to that of the first king after the Flood.

43 Ibid., p. 11; see pp. 3–11. For Greece, of course, this was correct.

44 Sommerville, 'John Selden, the Law of Nature, and the Origins of Government,' has suggested that the change from a popular derivation of govern-

ment to those mentioned above came about because of Selden's desire to court Charles I. Since Selden would not write the apology to Charles needed to gain his full freedom until 1634, this seems unlikely in 1631. Selden's increased knowledge, gained from his chronological studies of the 1620s, as seen in the charts of his *Marmora Arundeliana*, seems a more reasonable explanation. I would like to thank Dr Mordechai Feingold for drawing to my attention the extent of Selden's chronological interests in his paper 'John Selden and the Nature of Seventeenth-Century Science,' pp. 67–8; this interest also appeared in Selden's correspondence with Ussher.

45 Selden, *Titles of Honor* (1631), pp. 18, 53, 161–2, 171–2.
46 Ibid., p. 25; cf. *Titles of Honor* (1614), pp. 30–1.
47 Selden, *Titles of Honor* (1631), p. 18. This led to an excursus of several pages in which Selden, drawing upon his '*Mare Clausum*, writen some two yeers since,' used English sovereignty over the sea to demonstrate the imperial power of the English Crown: ibid., pp. 18–19.
48 Ibid., p. 18. Significantly, this section made no mention of the vassalage of the kings of England to the Pope.
49 Ibid., p. 19.
50 Ibid., p. 20.
51 Ibid., p. 21.
52 The chapter on the Empire opened with the title 'King of the Romans' before moving on to Duke and Count; this section served as a bridge between the 'old' Roman Empire and that revived by Charlemagne: see ibid., pp. 275–94. The meanings of such terms as *Rex, Dux*, and *Comes* in the fourth, fifth, sixth, and seventh centuries still pose serious problems for historians; for example, see J.M. Wallace-Hadrill, *Early Germanic Kingship in England and on the Continent*, especially chs. 1 and 3, and P.S. Barnwell, *Emperor, Prefects and Kings: The Roman West, 395–565*, pp. 33–40, passim, and index, under *comes, comes ciuitatis, comes domesticorum, comes palatii, comes patimonii, comes prouinciae, comes rei militaris, comes rerum priuatarum, comes sacrarum largitionum, comes stabuli*, and *dux*.
53 Cf. the section in chapter 1, above, bounded by notes 111 and 120, with Selden, *Titles of Honor* (1631), pp. 295–327.
54 Selden, *Titles of Honor* (1631), pp. 294–5.
55 Ibid., pp. 302–18.
56 Ibid., p. 332. No unreflective Germanist on this matter, Selden attacked those scholars who argued that the Romans had obtained the office of *Comes* 'from the *Germans* by imitation': see pp. 330–1. For recent looks

at this complex development and reinterpretations of the 'hospitality' extended by the Romans, see Walter Goffart, *Barbarians and Romans A.D. 418–584: The Techniques of Accommodation,* and Barnwell, *Emperor, Prefects and Kings.*

57 Selden, *Titles of Honor* (1631), p. 332; the marginal note referred to Jacques Cujas, *Observationum et emendationum libri XXVIII* (Colonæ Agrippa, 1598), and Jean Bodin, *De Republica;* for the ceremony of investiture in 'elder times,' see p. 338. Emphyteusis was a form of property holding practised in ancient Rome, which medieval European civil lawyers adapted to new uses. Although Selden had derived his overall interpretation of the feudal law in *Titles of Honor* (1614) largely from Hotman, the discussion in that edition indicated very little understanding of such matters as homage, fealty, and the performance of military and other services. Since Spelman, *Archæologus,* contained substantial entries under: *'De Fidelium et fidelitatis generibus, fusè,'* pp. 266–71, and *'De Homagio et Homine feodali,'* pp. 356–62, Selden could hardly avoid such matters in 1631.

58 Selden's willingness to countenance non-military services may have come from his familiarity with such provisions in England. Cf. F.L. Ganshof, *Feudalism;* Ganshof stressed the primacy of military service and argued that the feudal law originated in the northern part of the Frankish kingdom and spread from there to other parts of Europe; this Frankish origin and spread of feudal practices more closely reflected the position held by Hotman and taken over by Selden in 1614.

59 See Kelley, *'De Origine Fendorum.'* For example, Spelman, *Archæologus,* p. 256 (misnumbered as 254), quoted definitions of *Feudum* and *Beneficium* from Jacques Cujas, *Feud. Tit.* [*De feudis* (1588)]; the former read: *'Feudum est ius in prædio alieno, in perpetuum utendi, fruendi, quod pro beneficio dominus dat ea lege, ut qui accipit sibi fidem et miltia munus, aliuduè seruitium exhibeat.'* When Spelman later wished to exclude Saxon England from feudal society, he started with a brief definition from Cujas not unlike that of Selden's: *'A Feud* is said to be *Usus fructus quidam rei immobilis sub conditione fidei,'* only to attack it as too broad and then to quote from Cujas the following definition: *'"A Feud is a right which the Vassal hath in Land, or some immoveable thing of his Lords, to use the same and take the profits thereof hereditarily: rendring unto his Lord such feodal duties and services as belong to military tenure: the meer propriety of the soil always remaining unto the Lord."'*: Spelman, *Reliquiæ Spelmannianæ* (Oxford, 1698), 'The Original, Growth, Propagation and Condition of Feudes and Ten-

ures by Knight-Service in England,' p. 2. To the inheritability basic to this definition, Spelman added the necessity of the aids of wardship, marriage, and relief. By privileging the practices of twelfth-century England as the 'proper' model for feudal relationships, Spelman's second definition downplayed the continuities between the landholding customs of late Anglo-Saxon and early Norman England. Like many later historians, Spelman probably overestimated the systematic coherence of Norman feudal practices in 1066: cf. David Bates, *Normandy before 1066*, pp. 122–7, 133–5, 168–70.

Recently a strong reaction against any discussion of 'feudalism' has challenged the views of such earlier historians as Bloch and Ganshof; see Brown, 'The Tyranny of a Construct: Feudalism and the Historians of Medieval Europe.' Such works as James's *Origins of France* and Reynolds's, *Kingdoms and Communities* eschew any discussion of 'feudal' relationships.

60 Selden, *Titles of Honor* (1631), pp. 333–4. For his discussion of feuds, Selden could draw upon the lengthy, sophisticated analysis in Spelman, *Archæologus*, pp. 255–63; Spelman favoured the Germanic origin of feuds: see pp. 256–7 (misnumbered as 254 and 158).

61 Selden, *Titles of Honor* (1631), p. 336.

62 Ibid., p. 295.

63 Ibid., p. 334; for the various Imperial counts in Germany, see pp. 376–425.

64 Ibid., p. 334.

65 Ibid.

66 Ibid., p. 471.

67 Ibid., p. 335. In 1614, Selden had followed Hotman to argue that hereditary feudal titles had spread from France to Italy and Germany with the conquests of Charlemagne: see the quotation cited to note 163, chapter 1, above.

68 Ibid., p. 568.

69 Ibid.

70 Ibid., pp. 493–4; see pp. 493–5. For a recent portrayal of this process which attempts to avoid a centralist perspective, see James, *Origins of France*. Selden had little understanding of the complex and varied nature of kingship in the successor societies; for example, see the papers in P.H. Sawyer and I.N. Wood, eds., *Early Medieval Kingship*.

71 Selden, *Titles of Honor* (1631), p. 336; in 1614, Selden had argued that Otto the Great had created inheritable titles in *ca* 940 (see the citation to note 117, chapter 1, above); now he saw those creations as just a systematic extension of a practice already customary at an earlier date.

72 Ibid., pp. 494–5. This only slightly modified the view presented in 1614: see the passage in chapter 1, above, cited to note 120.

73 Ibid., p. 494 (misnumbered as 492).

74 Ibid.

75 Ibid., p. 335. For Imperial and early Frankish and Visigothic *comes ciuitatum*, see Barnwell, *Emperor, Prefects and Kings*, pp. 35–6, 80–1, 108–11; cf. James, *Origins of France*, p. 58.

76 Selden, *Titles of Honor* (1631), pp. 510–35; for a passage on differentiation among the French feudal nobility, not unlike that on the English tenants-in-chief of the early thirteenth century, see pp. 510–13.

77 Ibid., pp. 535–6; cf. Spelman, *Archæologus*, pp. 77, 80–1. Selden captured the often amorphous meaning of the title here: see David Crouch, *The Image of Aristocracy in Britain, 1000–1300*, pp. 107–9.

78 Selden, *Titles of Honor* (1631), p. 536; note the similarity of this interpretation with that which Selden would offer for the shift in the English nobility in the early thirteenth century later in this edition.

79 Ibid., pp. 538–9.

80 Ibid., pp. 539–40.

81 Ibid., p. 425.

82 Ibid., p. 435.

83 Ibid., p. 473; sceptical about the derivation of 'Vavassor' from 'vassal' by Hotman, Selden confessed his ignorance of how 'Vavassor' had changed into 'Baron' in Italy: pp. 435, 473.

84 Ibid, p. 438. In 1614, Selden had observed that these customs formed the basis for an explanation of the practices of medieval European knighthood, but he had not used them as a basis for deriving the feudal law from the ancient northern peoples; see chapter 1, above, the section bounded by notes 145–52.

85 Ibid., p. 440.

86 Ibid., p. 556.

87 Ibid., p. 603; for the offices and titles of the Anglo-Saxons, see Loyn, *Governance of Anglo-Saxon England*.

88 Selden, *Titles of Honor* (1631), pp. 600, 604; see pp. 600–4 and cf. the markedly inferior understanding displayed in Spelman, *Archæologus*, pp. 10–11 ('*De nomine & dignitate Adelingi*').

89 Selden, *Titles of Honor* (1631), pp. 604–5.

90 Ibid., p. 605; cf. Spelman, *Archæologus*, pp. 28–31 ('*Aldermannus*').

91 Selden, *Titles of Honor* (1631), p. 605; a point stressed by Spelman, *Archæologus*, p. 28.

92 Selden, *Titles of Honor* (1631), p. 616.

93 Ibid., p. 609; cf. Spelman, *Archæologus*, pp. 241–2 (misnumbered as 231–2) ('*Eorla, Erle*'). Selden collapsed the time period over which these changes took place and did not realize the degree to which the family of Earl Godwine came to dominate landholding and power: see Robin Fleming, *Kings and Lords in Conquest England*, chs. 1–3, and Crouch, *Image of Aristocracy*, pp. 46–50.

94 Selden, *Titles of Honor* (1631), p. 607; cf. Loyn, *Governance of Anglo-Saxon England*, pp. 47–50.

95 Selden, *Titles of Honor* (1631), p. 610.

96 Ibid.; cf. Loyn, *Anglo-Saxon England*, pp. 213–14 and Crouch, *Image of Aristocracy*, pp. 56–72.

97 Selden, *Titles of Honor* (1631), p. 611.

98 Ibid., p. 614. Much of this information came from Domesday Book; for the variety of lands and dues held by the sons of Godwine, see Fleming, *Kings and Lords*, ch. 3.

99 Selden, *Titles of Honor* (1631), pp. 616–17.

100 Ibid., p. 615.

101 Ibid., p. 612; cf. Loyn, *Anglo-Saxon England*, pp. 211–19. Selden did not have much grasp of the importance of kinship and lordship among the Anglo-Saxons: see Maitland, *Domesday Book*, pp. 66–79, and Fleming, *Kings and Lords*, pp. 138–44.

102 Selden, *Titles of Honor* (1631), p. 621; since the Anglo-Saxon laws did not contain any feudal contracts, this represented a clever extrapolation from the sources, especially Domesday Book.

103 Ibid., p. 622.

104 Ibid.; in this passage, 'Ancients' signified medieval writers. For a less sophisticated understanding which made no reference to Domesday Book, cf. Spelman, *Archæologus*, pp. 352–3 ('*De Hidis et Hidagiis Anglo-saxonicis*'). For recent definitions and discussions, cf. Loyn, *Governance of Anglo-Saxon England*, pp. 34–9, 119–21, 167–8; Marjorie Chibnall, *Anglo-Norman England, 1066–1166*, p. 106, n. 1, and Warren, *Governance of Norman and Angevin England*, pp. 27–9, 36–8.

105 Selden, *Titles of Honor* (1631), p. 621.

106 Although Domesday Book included information on landholders and obligations before the Conquest, it also demonstrated a vast change in those who held these lands between 1066 and 1086; for a brief introduction to Domesday Book, see Chibnall, *Anglo-Norman England*, pp. 105–14; cf. Peter Sawyer, '1066–1086: A Tenurial Revolution?,' who

argues for continuity of estates, and Robin Fleming, 'Domesday Book and the Tenurial Revolution' and *Kings and Lords*, chs. 4–7, who argues for a combination of continuity and reorganization.

107 Selden, *Titles of Honor* (1631), p. 628; Selden cites the Laws of Ethelred for this point.

108 Ibid., p. 612.

109 Ibid., p. 613. Selden strongly attacked the *Modus Tenendi Parliamentum* as a guide to Saxon practice: see pp. 613, 738–44.

110 Ibid., p. 628.

111 Ibid., p. 632; for his citations, see pp. 632–3.

112 Ibid., p. 625. For a recent definition of 'vavasour,' see Crouch, *Image of Aristocracy*, pp. 171–2.

113 Selden, *Titles of Honor* (1631), p. 625. Spelman correctly disputed this equivalence of heriots and reliefs at length in 'The Original of Feudes,' pp. 31–3.

114 Selden, *Titles of Honor* (1631), p. 612.

115 Ibid., p. 636; cf. Spelman, *Archæologus*, p. 80 ('*Feudalium*'), which portrayed William I as 'disposing all England' under feudal tenures. Athough differing in detail and lacking the rich evidential and critical base of recent historical writing on the subject, Selden's interpretation took a perspective not entirely unlike that presented in Chibnall, *Anglo-Norman England*; Crouch, *Image of Aristocracy*; and portions of Fleming, *Kings and Lords*.

116 Selden, *Titles of Honor* (1631), pp. 638–9.

117 Ibid., p. 685.

118 Ibid., p. 639.

119 Ibid., p. 643.

120 Ibid., p. 640; see pp. 640–1.

121 Ibid., p. 642.

122 Ibid., pp. 674–6.

123 Ibid., p. 645.

124 Ibid., p. 650; see pp. 647–50. Warren argues for a revival of the Anglo-Saxon style of earldoms in the reign of Stephen: see Warren, *Governance of Norman and Angevin England*, ch. 4; cf. Chibnall, *Anglo-Norman England*, pp. 89–90, and Crouch, *Image of Aristocracy*, pp. 63–4; the latter sees Stephen's new earldoms as drawing upon Carolingian traditions, but notes that they were hereditary.

125 Selden, *Titles of Honor* (1631), pp. 650–66.

126 Ibid., p. 676. Crouch, *Image of Aristocracy*, p. 65, points out that 'after 1154 the earls no longer had any innate political function.'

127 Selden, *Titles of Honor* (1631), p. 666; this built upon his earlier work
(see chapter 1, above, the passages cited to note 131). Having studied a
much larger number relevant documents by 1631, Selden had reached a
more sophisticated understanding of the early Norman honour; see
Chibnall, *Anglo-Norman England*, passim, and Sir Frank Stenton, *The
First Century of English Feudalism, 1066–1166*, ch. 2.

128 Selden, *Titles of Honor* (1631), p. 672.

129 For this section, he built upon his earlier explanation (see chapter 1,
above, the section bounded by notes 132–43) and also could draw upon the
lengthy, sophisticated discussion in Spelman, *Archæologus*,
pp. 76–88 ('*Ditribe de Baronibus*'); for a discussion of this section of
Spelman, see Pocock, *Ancient Constitution*, pp. 108–14. The type of
baron under consideration was classified by Spelman as '*Baro pro vassallo
capitali* in genere.' According to Spelman, these barons as immediate vassals were 'devised by ancient kings of France' and introduced to England
by William I, as seen in Domesday Book: Spelman, *Archæologus*, p. 79.

130 Selden, *Titles of Honor* (1631), p. 690; Selden's discussion extends for
more than eighty folio pages. For a recent reading which stresses the
flexibility of the early usage of 'Baron' in England and argues that it
became an individual title only after 1200, see Crouch, *Image of the
Aristocracy*, pp. 108–14.

131 Selden, *Titles of Honor* (1631), p. 687; for an account which stresses the
continuity of governance over the Conquest, see Warren, *Governance of
Norman and Angevin England*, ch. 2.

132 Selden, *Titles of Honor* (1631), p. 688; cf. Spelman, *Archæologus*, p. 79.

133 Selden, *Titles of Honor* (1631), pp. 690–1; cf. 'English Janus,' p. 94; *Jani
Anglorum*, pp. 125–6; and *Titles of Honor* (1614), pp. 273–4, as cited in
chapter 1, above, to note 139. For an argument that William I did not
introduce military services to England, see Gillingham, 'Introduction of
Knight Service,' pp. 53–64.

134 See Pocock, *Ancient Constitution*, pp. 65–8. In *Titles of Honor* (1614),
Selden had come close to this interpretation; clearly, he knew about feudal tenures and the provision of actual fighting before the Parliament of
1628: see chapter 2, above, the passages cited to notes 167–9. This may
suggest that Selden probably obtained his understanding of knight service from Spelman's *Archæologus*. The relationship between the scholarship of the two men was extremely complex and varied over time. By
1631, Selden had a better grasp of Anglo-Saxon offices and titles than
that displayed by Spelman in the first volume of *Archæologus*. Selden
also argued for much more continuity over the Conquest than did the

elder antiquary. Indeed, from his studies of the Anglo-Saxon thanes, Selden may have independently worked out the notion of military service as a part of feudal tenures, but this seems unlikely. The explanation of the parliamentary baronage contained in the first edition of *Titles of Honor* (1614) probably stimulated the especially fertile section on '*Barones*' in Spelman, *Archæologus*, pp. 79–80: see Spelman, 'The Original of Feudes,' p. 26. In preparing the interpretation put forward in *Titles of Honor* (1631), Selden not only developed his earlier explanation, but probably drew upon that in Spelman, *Archæologus*. The starkly stated and fully worked out explanation contained in Spelman, *Reliquiæ Spelmannianæ*, 'Of Parliaments,' pp. 58–65, carried the argument much further (for the purported transformations of the early thirteenth century in this work, see pp. 62–5); probably written around 1630, this essay did not appear in print until 1698.

135 Selden, *Titles of Honor* (1631), p. 691; Selden seems to have put this interpretation of the knight's fee together on his own, if only because the entry under '*Militum, Milites*' did not appear in the *Archæologus*, which only reached the letter 'L,' but in Sir Henry Spelman, *Glossarium Archaiologicum* (London, 1664), pp. 410–11. The concept of a knight's fee was more appropriate to the twelfth than to the eleventh century: see Chibnall, *Anglo-Norman England*, pp. 2–3, 114–15, 130–1, and Sally Harvey, 'The Knight and the Knight's Fee in Medieval England.'

136 Selden, *Titles of Honor* (1631), pp. 691–2; Selden projected the twelfth-century meaning of the word back into the eleventh century: see Stenton, *English Feudalism*, pp. 16–25. He also assumed that a written instrument marked the assignment, whereas William made assessments by word of mouth; Selden spent a good deal of effort trying to puzzle out how many knights were provided by these arrangements; after noting that Ordericus Vitalis claimed that William I raised 60,000 knights from England and that other sources listed 60,215, he placed greater credence in the estimate of 32,000 made by Alexander, Archdeacon of Shrewsbury (who lived at the time of Kings John and Henry III): see pp. 692–4. The estimate of 60,215, by a monk of St Augustine's, Canterbury, probably came from Spelman, *Archæologus*, p. 258. Since Selden had mentioned the figure of 60,000 knights in his speech of 1628 (see the passage cited to chapter 2, above, note 168), he had changed his judgment, probably because of further research. For these numbers, see Gillingham, 'Introduction of Knight Service,' pp. 56, 58–9. Cf. Crouch, *Image of Aristocracy*, pp. 120–1.

137 Spelman's essays on knight service in England and on Parliament would

not appear in print until sixty-seven years later, in the *Reliquiæ Spelmannianæ*; the essay on knight service was written in 1639; that on Parliament probably was written around 1630. I know of no evidence to suggest that Selden had read either of these essays; clearly, he would have strongly disagreed with that on Parliament.

138 Selden, *Titles of Honor* (1631), p. 697. For an argument against this interpretation, see Gillingham, 'Introduction of Knight Service,' pp. 58–60; for the lending-out of church lands as thegnland, see Fleming, *Kings and Lords*, pp. 127–8.

139 Selden, *Titles of Honor* (1631), pp. 695–6. Ancient precedent could justify the continued membership of the bishops in the Lords on more than one basis.

140 Ibid., p. 699.

141 Ibid., pp. 700–1; cf. Chibnall, *Anglo-Norman England*, pp. 27–34, and Warren, *Governance of Norman and Angevin England*, ch. 2.

142 For a more complex picture, see Chibnall, *Anglo-Norman England*, pp. 32–3.

143 Selden, *Titles of Honor* (1631), p. 704.

144 Ibid., p. 699.

145 Ibid., p. 701; of course, this represented a later extrapolation of what must have happened, not a contemporary account of what had happened.

146 Ibid., pp. 702–6.

147 Ibid., pp. 707–8; this writ was addressed to the Bishop of Salisbury.

148 Ibid., p. 703; see pp. 702–6. Of course, the argument lumped these different kinds of meetings together under the category 'parliament.' Cf. Spelman, *Archæologus*, pp. 79–80. Spelman's discussion of parliaments came under the sections headed '*Baro, pro Vassallo capitali majore*' and '*Baro pro simplici Magnate*' and, therefore, made no reference to the Commons: cf. Tuck, *Philosophy and Government*, p. 266.

149 Selden, *Titles of Honor* (1631), p. 708; cf. Spelman, *Archæologus*, p. 80, and see the passages from *Titles of Honor* (1614) in chapter 1, above, cited to notes 140–3. Selden had expressed an early, less sophisticated form of this argument in *Jani Anglorum*, pp. 125–6, 'English Janus,' p. 83.

150 Spelman supported his interpretation with a quotation from the *Modus Tenendi* which stipulated that a baron of Parliament needed to have either the equivalent of a whole earldom (that is, twenty knights' fees, or £400 per annum in rents) or a whole barony (that is, thirteen and one half knights' fees, or 400 marks per annum in rents): Spelman, *Archæologus*, p. 80. Selden correctly assigned a much later date to the *Modus* and, therefore, could not use it as evidence of this shift.

151 Selden, *Titles of Honor* (1631), pp. 710–11; of course, no such law existed.
152 Ibid., p. 711.
153 Ibid.
154 Ibid., p. 712.
155 Ibid.
156 Ibid., p. 713.
157 Ibid., pp. 713–14.
158 A stress upon immemoriality did not necessarily exclude a sophisticated historical approach, but did built a strongly anti-historical principle into the accounts produced: see Burgess, *Politics of the Ancient Constitution*, pp. 4–7, 66–7, and 58–78.
159 Selden, *Titles of Honor* (1631), p. 715.
160 Ibid.
161 Ibid., pp. 720–31.
162 Ibid., pp. 744–7.
163 Ibid., p. 754.
164 Ibid., p. 759.
165 Ibid., pp. 762–3.
166 Ibid., p. 767.
167 Ibid., pp. 767–8.
168 Ibid., pp. 768–9.
169 Only Spelman, most of whose work remained unpublished during his lifetime, approached the historical imagination, learning, and freedom from anachronism displayed by Selden.
170 Selden, *Titles of Honor* (1631), p. 769; see Crouch, *Image of Aristocracy*, pp. 130–1. Selden noted the linguistic relationship to the German 'Knecht.'
171 Selden, *Titles of Honor* (1631), p. 769.
172 Ibid., p. 770. This argument stood on shaky grounds, as Selden admitted, because the manuscripts in which it appeared generally were later transcripts which used the abbreviation 'M.,' which could stand for 'Minister' as easily as 'Miles.' Cf. Spelman, *Glossarium*, pp. 410–11 ('*Militum, Miles*').
173 Selden, *Titles of Honor* (1631), p. 770; bannerets and knights bachelor had made their appearance in the section on France, pp. 542–56; cf. Spelman, *Archæologus*, pp. 70–2 ('*De Banaretto*').
174 Selden, *Titles of Honor* (1631), p. 773; this developed the argument made in *Titles of Honor* (1614); see chapter 1, above, the section bounded by notes 144–59. For these early practices and for knights, see Crouch, *Image of Aristocracy*, pp. 136–8, ch. 4.

175 Selden, *Titles of Honor* (1631), p. 779.

176 Ibid., p. 782.

177 Ibid., p. 782–3.

178 Ibid., pp. 790–820.

179 Ibid., p. 835; for Baronet, see pp. 821–30; cf. Spelman, *Archæologus*, pp. 50–1 ('*De Armigeris*') and 88–92 ('*De Baronetto*'). See Crouch, *Image of Aristocracy*, ch. 5.

180 Selden, *Titles of Honor* (1631), pp. 836–7.

181 Ibid., pp. 866–915. The chapter on precedence repeated his earlier reduction of all law to the 'state' and customs of that jurisdiction and his strictures that 'the whole body of the old Imperiall Law is no where in force:' ibid., p. 899; see pp. 896–915.

182 Ibid., p. 855.

183 Ibid., cf. the passage from *Titles of Honor* (1614) cited to chapter 1, above, note 152.

184 However, apart from some remarks on the form of summons for Norman tenants-in-chief, Selden did not detail the membership of any of these assemblies; as Richard Tuck has pointed out: 'there is no passage' in the second edition of *Titles of Honor* 'which is incompatable with the view that the Commons had always been a separate part of Parliament, though equally no passage which states that they had been': Tuck, *Philosophy and Government*, p. 267. Debates over the origins of the Commons became common and pressing only in the 1640s.

185 Quotations in the text are from Selden, *Of the Dominion*, with cross-references or citations of the Latin text where this seems helpful. For discussions of *Mare Clausum* within the context of the international law of the sea, see Thomas Wemyss Fulton, *The Sovereignty of the Sea: An Historical Account of the Claims of England to the Dominion of the British Seas, and of the Evolution of the Territorial Waters: with special reference to the Rights of Fishing and the Naval Salute*, ch. 9; Pitman B. Potter, *The Freedom of the Seas in History, Law, and Politics*, ch. 4; and Frans De Pauw, *Grotius and the Law of the Sea*, pp. 12–13; both Fulton and Potter draw strongly upon Selden's references for their earlier chapters, as well. For Selden's place in early modern natural-law theories, see Tuck, 'The "Modern" School of Natural Law,' pp. 99–122, and *Philosophy and Government*, pp. 205–21, passim.

186 For the theoretical and practical fisheries disputes between the English and Scots and the Dutch, see Fulton, *Sovereignty of the Sea*, and George Edmundson, *Anglo-Dutch Rivalry during the First Half of the Seventeenth Century*.

187 William Welwood, *An Abridgement of All Sea Lawes* pp. 62, 63, 69, and see also his *De Dominio Maris*, pp. 2–3 (for his attack upon a community of property), 4 (for the quotation from Baldus), 5 (for the hundred-mile limit from Bartolus); other references to Baldus and Bartolus appear on pp. 5, 9, 10, 13, and 23. The relevant section of *An Abridgement* extended to 12 pages, and the text of *De Dominio Maris* to 28; neither contained extensive historical evidence; in contrast, the text of the first printed edition of *Mare Clausum* filled 309 pages. For Welwood, see *DNB*; Fulton, *Sovereignty of the Sea*, pp. 352–5; and J.K. Oudendijk, *Status and Extent of Adjacent Waters*, pp. 67–70. Welwood aroused Grotius sufficiently to pen an answer, but it remained in manuscript until the nineteenth century.

188 Selden could have used the a revised edition of Grotius's, *De Jure Belli*, published in 1631. Vasquez de Menchaca was a Spanish jurist, and Gentili was an Italian Protestant who became regius professor of civil law at Oxford and later a practitioner in the Admiralty Court of England. Not only Selden saw these three as important defenders of the freedom of the high seas; Grotius drew up both *Mare Liberum* and *De Jure Belli ac Pacis* in relation to works by Gentili and drew very heavily upon Vázquez de Manchacha or Vasquius (who received some seventy-four references in the greater work from which *Mare Liberum* was taken): see Peter Haggenmacher, 'Grotius and Gentili: A Reassessment of Thomas E. Holland's Inaugural Lecture,' pp. 146, 151, 133–76. For the positions of Gentili and Grotius, also see Gesina H.J. van der Molen, *Alberico Gentili and the Development of International Law: His Work and Times*, and Oudendijk, *Adjacent Waters*, chs. 1 and 3. Although Selden cited Grotius twice in *Titles of Honor* (1614) and mentioned him as an example of a Continental scholar who had applied the philology of the *mos gallicus* to the study of the customary laws of his own society in the preface of *The Historie of Tithes* (1618), the opening section of *Mare Clausum* saw the first impact of Grotius's theory of natural law on Selden's publications.

189 See Berkowitz, *John Selden*, pp. 51–4, 291. For the claim and assertion of sovereignty over the seas surrounding Britain by Charles I during the 1630s, see Fulton, *Sovereignty of the Sea*, chs. 6–9; Kenneth R. Andrews, *Ships, Money and Politics: Seafaring and Naval Enterprise in the Reign of Charles I*, ch. 6, especially pp. 134–7, 155–6, 158; and B.W. Quintrell, 'Charles I and His Navy in the 1630s.'

190 Selden, *Of the Dominion*, sig. e2^v; *Mare Clausum* (1635), sig. b2^r: 'Mare ex Iure Naturæ seu Gentium omnium hominum non esse commune, sed Dominii Privati seu Proprietatis capax æquè ac Tellurem; *altera* Serenis-

simum Magnæ Britanniæ Regem Maris curcumflui, ut individuæ ac per-
petuæ Imperii Britannici appendicis, Dominum esse.' I quote from the
translation published by Nedham in 1652, with cross-references to the
Latin text of 1635 when appropriate. In places, the translation varies
from the text.

191 Selden, *Of the Dominion*, p. 2; *Mare Clausum*, p. 1: 'Tam enim id quod
Juris est, alterum *Facti* ... quàm id quod *Facti* est, quæ sunt *Juris* non
pauca.'

192 Tuck, *Philosophy and Government*, p. 213. Although *Mare Liberum* discussed contemporary problems, *De Jure Belli ac Pacis* drew almost all of
its examples from the ancient world; Gentili's projects were much more
up-to-date in their focus.

193 See Tuck, *Natural Rights Theories*, ch. 4, and *Philosophy and Government*, pp. 214–21. Of course, even *De Jure Naturali* remained far more
historical in focus and evidence than most natural-law treatises: see
Michael Bertram Crowe, 'An Eccentric Seventeenth-Century Witness to
the Natural Law: John Selden (1584–1654).'

194 Hugo Grotius, *The Freedom of the Seas*, p. 28; the facing Latin text
reads: 'tum qui accupari non potest, tom quia usum promiscuum hominibus debet.' Gentili made these distinctions first in his *De Jure Belli*
and applied and developed them further in *Hispanicæ Advocationis
Libri Duo*: see Van der Molen, *Alberico Gentili*, pp. 163–5. Following
Baldus, Welwood had applied the principle of occupation to the sea, but
had not developed it as radically as would Selden. See note 187, above,
and the passage in the text cited to it.

195 Van der Molen, *Alberico Gentili*, pp. 164–5. Territorial waters could
extend out one hundred miles from the coast. Since Selden would claim
that English dominion over the seas between England and the Netherlands and France had extended from coast to coast, he could not admit
Gentili's principle of territoriality.

196 Grotius, *Freedom of the Sea*, pp. 33–6: e.g., 'nullam Maris in territorio
populi alicuius posse censeri'; p. 34. For cxample, even the punishment
of pirates came not from any private exercise of jurisdiction, but 'by the
common right which' all 'free peoples' enjoyed 'upon the sea'; p. 35.

197 Selden, *Of the Dominion*, p. 12; *Mare Clausum*, pp. 7–8: '*Mare* intelligi-
mus universum, et tam Oceanum apertum seu Exteriora quæ sunt
Maria, quám quæ Interiora sunt, veluti Mediterraneum, Adriaticum,
Ægæum, Britannicum, Balticum, et quæ sunt id genus alia ...' Note how
he begs the question here by slipping in the 'British' sea, which was not
as enclosed as the others.

198 Selden, *Of the Dominion*, p. 12; *Mare Clausum*, p. 8: 'quemadmodum in ipso Emtionis, Venditionis, Manumissionis actu in contrahentium conditionibus, pro eorum arbitratu, contractui adjici solitis, ad genus aliis.' In the interest of clarity, some of the Latin terms appear in the text here rather than in the notes. Within the context of Selden's early works, it seems best to translate 'jus' in these passages as 'law,' rather than 'right': cf. Tuck, *Natural Rights Theories*, ch. 4, and Sommerville, 'John Selden, the Law of Nature, and the Origins of Government.' My discussion of this portion of *Mare Clausum* owes a strong debt to Tuck's books.

199 Selden, *Of the Dominion*, p. 12; *Maxe Clausum*, p. 8: '... Id est *Gentes universas* spectat, aut *non universas*.'

200 Ibid.; 'Quod universum spectat genus humanum seu *Gentes universas*, aut *Naturale* est aut *Divinum*.'

201 Selden, *Of the Dominion*, pp. 12–13; *Mare Clausum*, p. 8.

202 Selden, *Of the Dominion*, p. 13; *Mare Clausum*, p. 8. By 'persons in power' he meant those people constitutionally empowered by that particular 'state.' Selden had already written about 'additions and interpretations'; see the quotation from his notes to Fortescue, *De Laudibus*, cited to note 182 of chapter 1, above.

203 Selden had argued this point at some length in the '*Review*' of *The Historie of Tithes*: see pp. 478–81 and see chapter 1, above, the section bounded by notes 250–4.

204 Selden, *Of the Dominion*, pp. 13–14; *Mare Clausum*, p. 9: 'Ex *Obligativi* hujusmodi *Additionibus et Permissivi Mutationibus* conflatum est alterum illud Jus, quod angustius est, et ad *Gentes non universas* seu non ad totum genus humanum, sed ad aliquas ejusce tantùm partes, spectat, atque rectè *Positivum* (sive scilicet à *Numine* sive ab *Hominibus* positum) nuncupari solet, interdum etiam *Civile*, et rectæ Rationis Naturalis additatmentum. *Positivum* hoc jus dispertire liceat in illud *quod unicæ alicui Genti Populóve* in societatem coalescenti proprium fuerit et singulare ... et illud, *quod in usu Pluribus*. Hoc rursum quod pluribus in usu, bifariam dividimus: in id *cui plures simul, pariter, ac communiter, seu ex Communi aliqua Obligatione Gentes Populive subsunt*; atque *id cui gentes populive plures non simul, pariter, aut ex Obligationis Communione aliqua subsunt, sed singulatim atque ex accidente*. Triplicis hujus speciei *Juris Positivi* primam *Ius simpliciter Civile* nominemus, putà ad Civitatem aliquam unicam attinens; Secundam *Ius plurium Gentium commune*, ob communionem Obligationis ita dicendum; Tertiam *Ius Gentium aliquot* seu *Plurium Civile* seu

Domesticum, propter obligationem quâ tenentur tantùm domesticam, atque sibi singulis, sine Obligationis Communione civilem.'

205 Selden, *Of the Dominion*, pp. 14–16; *Mare Clausum*, pp. 9–10.

206 Selden, *Of the Dominion*, p. 16; *Mare Clausum*, p. 10.

207 Selden, *Of the Dominion*, p. 16; *Mare Clausum*, p. 11: '*Dominium*, quod est Jus utendi fruendi, alienandi, liberè disponendi, aut omnium hominum, pro indiviso possidentium, *Commune* est, aut aliquorum tantùm *Privatum*; id est, inter Universitates singulares, Principes, Personas qualescunque, privatìm ita tributum, ut libertas utendi fruendi aliis aut intercludatur aut saltem minuatur.'

208 Selden, *Of the Dominion*, p. 20; *Mare Clausum*, p. 13: 'nec vetuit Jus sive Naturale sive Divinum quod Universal erat ... sed permisit Utrumque; tam nempe rerum communionem, quàm privatum dominium.' In contrast to Selden, Welwood had interpreted the Bible as supporting private dominion; see note 187, above. Cf. Sommerville, 'John Selden, the Law of Nature, and the Origins of Government,' 439–40, n. 25.

209 Selden, *Of the Dominion*, p. 21; *Mare Clausum*, p. 14: 'consensus veluti humani generis Corpis sev Universitatis.' As Tuck has shown, Selden's theory of property builds strongly upon that of Grotius; see especially Tuck, *Philosophy and Government*, pp. 213–14.

210 Selden, *Of the Dominion*, pp. 22–3; *Mare Clausum*, p. 15.

211 Selden, *Of the Dominion*, pp. 24–5; *Mare Clausum*, p. 16: 'Ex Dominio, ad modum jam dictum, privato introducto evenit, ut Territorii seu Agri, cujus usus anteà universis pariter erat in arando, ædifucando, depascendo, arbores cædendo, fructus percipiendo, transeundo liber, Proprietas ita possidenti, sive per Distributionem sive per Occupationem, privatim acquirerentur, ut is liberum ejusmodi usum jure posset impedire, nec ejus injussu alius licitè uti posset. Atque ab hâc origine manavit omnis rerum Proprietas seu Dominium quod sive alienatione, seu quacunque aliâ cessione, in alios transfertur, sive possessione continuâ retinetur; Habita semper ratione specialium modorum ac temperamentorum quæ, sive ex Legibus moribusque sive ex pacto, dominio solent, pro variis populorum institutis accedere. Nam hisce restringitur et minuitur libera, in re, domini potestas. Quæ ubi prorsus definit, ita suum est quod privatim possidet dominus, ut alîus esse, ejus injussu, omnino jure esse nequeat. Atque hæc omnia ex Mutatione *Iuris Gentium Universalis* seu *Naturalis* quod *Permissivum* est, orta sunt. Inde enim introductum Dominium privatum; es *iure* nempe *Positivo*. Sed interea stabliltum est ex *Iure Universali Obligativo*, quo Pactis standum est et servanda fides.'

212 Selden, *Of the Dominion*, pp. 26–7; *Mare Clausum*, p. 18: 'vetustiores illas Territoriorum distributiones'; 'titulo Occupationis, ut res vacuæ ac derelictæ, potuerint jure postmodùm adquiri'; 'sive *Iure Gentium plurium* seu *Communi* seu *Civili'*; and 'sive *Iure Naturali* sive *Divino Universali* quod *Permissivum* est.'

213 Selden, *Of the Dominion*, p. 27; *Mare Clausum*, p. 18: 'si *ex Iure Positivo Gentium*, Marinum dominium, quale quærimus, fuerit seculorum populorumque illustriorum suffragiis introductum ac admissum; dubitandum (puto) non erit, quin Iure quidem omnimodo dominii privati Maria sint, ut Tellus, undiquaque capacia.'

214 Selden, *Of the Dominion*, p. 27; *Mare Clausum*, p. 18: 'Jus Divinum, *seu* Divina *in sacris Literis* effata, *dominio Maris privato favere.'* Here, Selden built upon one of the arguments voiced by Welwood.

215 Selden, *Of the Dominion*, p. 42; *Mare Clausum*, p. 29: '*Jus* Naturale Permissivum ... *è* Gentium *illustriorum civiliorumque, tum prisci tum recentis ævi*, Moribus placitisque *esse eliciendum.'*

216 Selden, *Of the Dominion*, pp. 42–3; *Mare Clausum*, pp. 29–30: 'commodis suis aut Populorum (qui imperio contendi)' and 'rectum Humanæ rationis, quæ pro Naturalis Iuris indice haberi solet, usum circa res Divinas seu quæ ad Numinis attinent cultum, ex plurimarum gentium moribus non ritè edifici.'

217 Selden, *Of the Dominion*, p. 43; *Mare Clausum*, p. 30: 'Territoriorum Dominii distinctio ejusque ratio, quæ hominum consensu tota nititur' and 'rectè descernitur ex plurium Gentium ac seculorum veterum recentiorumque scitis, placitis, moribusque receptis.' In *Mare Liberum*, Grotius had attempted to prevent such a position by arguing that the treaties between states bound only the contracting parties, that prescription or custom applied only to the laws of particular societies, and that the law of nature or nations was always stronger than the laws of a particular society: pp. 35, 47.

218 Selden, *Of the Dominion*, p. 44; *Mare Clausum*, pp. 30–1: 'aut tot gentes easque illustriores per tot secula contra Naturam commisisse ... pronuntiandum.'

219 Selden, *Of the Dominion*, p. 45; *Mare Clausum*, p. 31: 'Ad Gentes igitur præteriti præsentisque ævi illustriores civilioresque et quorum mores habemus exploratiores, heic recurrendum.'

220 Selden, *Of the Dominion*, pp. 45–6; *Mare Clausum*, p. 32: 'tum quid *Civile Gentium jus*, tum quid *Gentium Commune plurium*, quid denique *Ius Naturale Permissivum* ... de Dominio Maris Privato statuerit, simul erit apertissimum.' Since this theoretical material laid the

foundation for the later historical argument, it probably had existed in some form in the draft written for James VI and I.

221 The division between morality in theory and fact, so strongly made by Immanuel Kant in the eithteenth century, had not yet been devised in early-seventeenth-century Europe; the past was supposed to speak to the moral and legal concerns of the present: see Burgess, *Politics of the Ancient Constitution*, pp. 7–11.

222 Selden, *Of the Dominion*, p. 53, and see chs. 10–19; *Mare Clausum*, pp. 36–7. On this point, Welwood derived ancient sea laws from those of Rhodes, and medieval western European ones from 'the lawes of *Oleron*,' an island off the coast of France: Welwood, *An Abridgement*, pp. 11–14.

223 Selden, *Of the Dominion*, p. 99b (this edition contains two pages numbered '99'); *Mare Clausum*, p. 67. This was Franciscus de Ingenius, *Epistola de Jurisdictione Venetæ Reipublicæ in Mare Adriaticum* (Geneva, 1619), written in reaction against the *Mare Liberum*: see Fulton, *Sovereignty of the Sea*, p. 351 and n. 1. Arguing on behalf of Venetian claims, Ingenius hardly took an impartial position!

224 Selden, *Of the Dominion*, ch. 17.

225 Ibid., p. 96; *Mare Clausum*, p. 64.

226 Selden, *Of the Dominion*, p. 132; *Mare Clausum*, p. 89.

227 Selden, *Of the Dominion*, p. 152; *Mare Clausum*, p. 102: '*Ius illis præscriptum libris non civitatis tantum esse sed et Gentium et Naturæ; et aptatum sic esse ad Naturam universum, ut Imperio extincto ipsum jus diu sepultum, surrexerit tamen et in omnes se effuderit gentes humanas.*' Selden also pointed out that Gentili had attacked the decree of the Byzantine emperor Leo for making 'a change against reason of Law.' For the way in which Welwood shared some of these universalist assumptions, see *An Abridgement*, pp. 4–5.

228 Selden, *Of the Dominion*, pp. 152–3; *Mare Clausum*, p. 103: 'nonulla sanè sunt in ipso jure Gentium Europæarum (quibus recepti sunt ... in Scholas tum in forum libri illi, quà singularia regnorum jura permisserint) jure inquam earum communi, scu Interveniente, quæ non omnio jure nituntur Justinianeo, sed ex morbus ei planè adversis, justitiæ tamen ad trutinam satis exactis, sunt orta.'

229 Selden, *Of the Dominion*, pp. 153–4; *Mare Clausum*, pp. 103–4. Selden devoted the whole of chapter twenty-five to demonstrating that the Emperor Antoninus Pius made the Rhodian law, already received in many portions of Greece, his law of the sea.

230 Selden, *Of the Dominion*, p. 155. This did not appear in the first edition of *Mare Clausum*: see p. 104.

231 Selden, *Of the Dominion*, p. 169; *Mare Clausum*, p. 112: 'Perinde ac
sequis Astronomica Aristotelis, Thaletis sententiam Terram Mari, ut
discum, innatare, Stoicorum hoc illam ut cingulum ambire, Veterum de
immenso sub Æquatore calore, et quæ sunt ejusmodi alia à Posteritate,
cui illuxit observationum experienta, rejecta damnataque ita explicaret
...' Ironically, Selden built upon the innovative, 'modern' refoundation of
natural-law theory carried out by Grotius!

232 Selden, *Of the Dominion*, p. 169; *Mare Clausum*, p. 122.

233 Selden, *Of the Dominion*, p. 170; *Mare Clausum*, pp. 112–13.

234 Selden, *Of the Dominion*, pp. 170–1; *Mare Clausum*, p. 113: 'Omnia ferè
Iuris Gentium Intervenientis capita ex Præscriptione seu inveteratâ con-
suetudine, annoso utentium consensu stabilita, pendent'; 'Et præscrip-
tionis sanè titulum prorsus inter Principes negare, est ipsa Iura Gentium
intervenientia planè tollere.' This also attacked Grotius, *Freedom of the
Seas*, ch. 7, which opened with the assertion that prescription applied
only to national, not to international law: 'Nam praescriptio a jure est
civili, unde locum habere non potest inter reges, aut inter populos
liberos'; p. 47.

235 See Tuck, *Natural Rights Theories*, pp. 86–7. Crucial here was Grotius,
De Jure Belli ac Pacis.

236 Selden, *Of the Dominion*, pp. 174–5; *Mare Clausum*, p. 116: 'Sed tandem
receptis populorum moribus se dedit, et de Maris proprietate seu
dominio privato, ut re extra controversiam interdum condedenda, non
semel loquitur.'

237 See De Pauw, *Grotius and the Law of the Sea*, especially pp. 67–9; Tuck,
Philosophy and Government, ch. 5 and p. 213; and C.G. Roelfsen, 'Grotius and the International Politics of the Seventeenth Century.' For a
more sympathetic reading of Grotius's consistency, see Oudendijk,
Adjacent Waters, pp. 40–52.

238 Selden, *Of the Dominion*, pp. 181–2; *Mare Clausum*, pp. 119–20: 'Mare
pariter ac Tellurem dominii privati capax esse, idque ex Jure omnimodo,
sive Divinum, sive Naturale, sive Gentium qualecunque accuratiùs per-
pendamus' and 'Dominium Maris illius perpetuâ occupatione, id est
utendo privatim et fruendo, signatum, propagatumque velut nunquam
non individuam sive Corporis totius patrimonii regni Britannici, sive
partis ejus, pro ratâ dominantium, protionem, seu ut Telluris appen-
dicem, nunquam disjunctam, eos, qui per toties mutantes rerum status
heic regnarunt, sive Birtannos scilicet, sive Romanos, sive Anglosaxo-
nes, sive Danos, Normannos, adeóque Reges insequentes (quoslibet pro
diversa Imperii amplitudine) obtinuisse. Regum denique Magnæ Britan-

niæ, Maris curcumflui, ceu termini eorum imperii non terminatis sed terminati (ut agrimensorum verbis utar) dominium, perinde ac ipsius Insulæ cæterarumque quas possident circumvicinarum, esse proprium.'

239 Selden, *Of the Dominion*, p. 189; *Mare Clausum*, p. 125.

240 Selden, *Of the Dominion*, pp. 189–200; *Mare Clausum*, pp. 125–33. Some of this scepticism derived from a treatise by Petrus Ramus, *De C. Julius Cæsaris Militiâ*.

241 Selden, *Of the Dominion*, p. 217; *Mare Clausum*, p. 144: 'Comes litoris Saxonici per Britanniam, præsidiis in litore Australi et Orientali Britanniæ dispositis, Mari universo quod Gallias, Bataviam, et Cimbricam Chersonesum, et Magnam Britanniam interfluit.'

242 Selden, *Of the Dominion*, pp. 218–19; *Mare Clausum*, p. 145: 'Iam verò protensum est territorium illud seu provincia huic dignitati singulari subjacens per Mare ipsum Britannicum, à Britannico litore usque in litora transmarina, seu quæ in Galliâ, Belgiâ, Bataviâ, Cimbricâ Chersoneso, Britanniæ nostræ adversa sunt. Ita ut quicquid à Britannico litore sive Maris sive Insularum interjaceret, Comitis (quem diximus) præfecturæ, veluti Admiralli provincialis seu territorialis administrationi, accederet.'

243 Selden, *Of the Dominion*, p. 221; see pp. 220–5; *Mare Clausum*, p. 146; see pp. 146–9. The translation contained additional information from the Theodosian Code and other sources that the Roman fleet included 'certain Barks or nimble Vessels call[ed] *Losoriæ* or *Lusoriæ* (in *English* wee may call them *Flie-boats*),' as well as larger sailing and rowed warships, with which 'they scouted out as far as the remotest Banks and the Castles built upon them, to guard the Bounds of Empire': *Of the Dominion*, p. 226.

244 Selden, *Of the Dominion*, p. 245, see chs. 7 and 8; *Mare Clausum*, p. 157: 'Britanniam cricumambienti Oceano imperare ita notabant, et Romanum Imperatorem Britanniæ.'

245 Selden, *Of the Dominion*, p. 248; *Mare Clausum*, p. 159.

246 Selden, *Of the Dominion*, pp. 249–50; *Mare Clausum*, p. 160.

247 Selden, *Of the Dominion*, pp. 249, 271; see chs. 10–12, *Mare Clausum*, pp. 167, 176: 'Sub Henrico autem II Rege, nomen Danegeldi in desuetudinem abiit.' From Archbishop Ussher's letter of 1625, we know that Ussher returned what look like Cotton's manuscripts of the Anglo-Saxon Chronicles to Selden; I know of no evidence that Selden knew these in 1619; the discussion on the Anglo-Saxon section of *Titles of Honor* (1631) above should have made evident the greatly increased sophistication of Selden's understanding of the language between 1614 and 1631. The sophisticated use of Domesday and the Anglo-Saxon

chronicles throughout this section were much closer to the second than to the first edition of *Titles of Honor*, which suggests considerable revision or additions made in the late 1620s or early 1630s. For Ussher's letter, see the passage quoted to note 16, above.

248 Selden, *Of the Dominion*, pp. 271–3; *Mare Clausum*, pp. 176–7. There was no mention here of the similar principles used in the collection of ship money in the sixteenth and early seventeenth centuries.

249 Selden, *Of the Dominion*, p. 273, see pp. 273–9 (the page numbering skips from 274 to 279); *Mare Clausum*, p. 177; see pp. 177–8: '*totius Albionis Basileus nec non maritimorum seu Insulanorum Regum circumhabitantium*' and '*in mari Britannico.*'

250 Selden, *Of the Dominion*, pp. 285–6; *Mare Clausum*, p. 183.

251 Selden, *Of the Dominion*, p. 287; *Mare Clausum*, p. 184.

252 Selden, *Of the Dominion*, pp. 287–8; *Mare Clausum*, p. 184: '*Butsecarlis suis præcepit mare custodire et observare*' and '*Butsecarli seu Butescarles sunt Ministri Nautiei seu classiarii ut Husecarli ministri domestici seu aulici, linguâ Anglorum veteri.*'

253 Selden, *Of the Dominion*, pp. 288, 289, see pp. 288–90; *Mare Clausum*, pp. 185, 186: '*Captaneus et Custos Maris*' and '*Custos erat Quinque portuum et Maris in partibus illis.*' As in the second edition of *Titles of Honor* (1631), Selden had used the fiction of 'lost' documents to explain why he could not demonstrate the shift from barons who held their titles as tenants-in-chief of the Crown to parliamentary barons who received an individual writ of summons.

254 Selden, *Of the Dominion*, p. 293, see pp. 293–4; *Mare Clausum*, p. 188: '*Gubernatores, Custodes, et Capitanei.*'

255 Selden, *Of the Dominion*, p. 294; *Mare Clausum*, p. 189: '*Postea verò omnimoda maris Custodia ... summis Admirallis Angliæ ... à Regibus nostris permissa ...*'

256 Selden, *Of the Dominion*, p. 295; *Mare Clausum*, p. 189: '*De Tributis seu Vectigalibus ad Maris Anglieani Custodiam indictis, pendi solitis, postulatis, testimonia sunt amplissima, vetustissima, omnisque ævi cis Normannorum tempora.*'

257 Selden, *Of the Dominion*, p. 303; see pp. 296–302; *Mare Clausum*, p. 194; see pp. 190–4; to make the point, Selden quoted at length in Norman French from the statute from the reign of Richard II.

258 Selden, *Of the Dominion*, pp. 303; *Mare Clausum*, p. 194.

259 Selden, *Of the Dominion*, pp. 306, 308; *Mare Clausum*, pp 196, 197, 198.

260 Selden, *Of the Dominion*, p. 308; *Mare Clausum*, p. 198.

261 Selden, *Of the Dominion*, p. 309; see pp. 309–10; *Mare Clausum*, p. 198; see pp. 198–200: '*Calesiæ et marchiarum ejusdem.*'
262 Selden, *Of the Dominion*, p. 313; *Mare Clausum*, p. 201.
263 Selden, *Of the Dominion*, p. 314; *Mare Clausum*, p. 203: 'Ut, igitur in Romana illa dignitate *Comitis litoris Saxonici per Britanniam*, litus Dignitatis limes erat transmarinus, ita etiam in Admiralli Angliæ summi præfectura (quà provinciam tantum fortitur Marinam, ut præficientis territorium) litora illa adversa seu provinciæ, quæ scodicillis nominantur, transmarinæ Maris tutandi limites censendi sunt.'
264 Selden, *Of the Dominion*, p. 318; *Mare Clausum*, p. 206.
265 Selden, *Of the Dominion*, p. 326; *Mare Clausum*, p. 211.
266 Selden, *Of the Dominion*, p. 342; *Mare Clausum*, p. 222.
267 Selden, *Of the Dominion*, pp. 344–5; *Mare Clausum*, p. 223.
268 Selden, *Of the Dominion*, p. 346; *Mare Clausum*, p. 224. Selden cited correspondence with Christian IV of Denmark, John of Sweden, and the Hansiatic League from manuscripts in Sir Robert Cotton's library to establish this point.
269 Selden, *Of the Dominion*, pp. 347–51; *Mare Clausum*, pp. 225–8.
270 Selden, *Of the Dominion*, pp. 355–75; *Mare Clausum*, pp. 230–46.
271 Selden, *Of the Dominion*, p. 398; see pp. 398–428; *Mare Clausum*, p. 263; see pp. 263–81. Even in these chapters on external acknowledgment of English dominion over the British sea, most of the evidence came from English, not European sources.
272 Selden, *Of the Dominion*, pp. 378, 379–80; *Mare Clausum*, p. 248. This argument revealed both the depth of Selden's knowledge of the records and the limits of his understanding of Parliament during the Middle Ages. He knew what records would prove that this had been a bill, but he assumed that only bills brought forth a royal answer. Rather than asking whether parliamentary procedure had changed since the fifteenth century, whether royal consideration of petitions from either the Lords or the Commons alone might reach the record of the Rolls of Parliament, Selden read the procedure of his own day back into the past and made recourse to purportedly lost records to buttress his interpretation. For an account of English medieval parliaments, see George O. Sayles, *The King's Parliament of England*.
273 Selden, *Of the Dominion*, p. 380; *Mare Clausum*, p. 250: 'Primò ex jure à Majoribus accepto, Maris dominum esse Regem Angliæ uno ore Ordines Parlamentarios, id est, et proceres universos et plebis universitatem indubitanter, utpote rei ex veterum etiam testimoniis forte aliquot.'
274 Selden, *Of the Dominion*, p. 381; *Mare Clausum*, pp. 250–1: 'Secundò

Mare de quo loquuntur esse totum quod Gallias et Angliam interluit';
'litorum utriusque partis Maris'; and 'Tertiò, Ordines illos non dubitasse
quin exertis quibuscunque, per mare hoc ubicunque transeuntibus, Par-
lamenti Anglicani autoritate vectigalia irrogari potuissent; ut in portu
portoria. Nec cogitâsse omninò, Regem, quà Rex erat tunc Galliarum,
sed quà Angliæ tantum, id est quà totius interluentis Maris dominus, ea
de re esse rogandum.'

275 Selden, *Of the Dominion*, p. 381; *Mare Clausum*, p. 251: 'Hinc etiam
Serenissimus et potentissimus Carolus Rex noster anno superiore, titulo
avito et justissimo, *Se* pronunciavit *et progenitores suos Reges Angliæ
dominos Maris hujus, semper bactenus extitisse;* in literis nimirum ad
provincias Angliæ maritimas datis, quibus Navium subsidiariarum in
domini sui Marini tutelam constructio irrogatur.' The dispute over ship
money during the 1630s did not begin until the unprecedented step was
taken of extending it to counties without sea coasts.

276 The royal power to levy impositions, upheld by the Court of Exchequer
in Bate's Case, was contested at length in the session and in a number of
subsequent parliaments, including the session of 1629; see Popofsky,
'The Crisis over Tonnage and Poundage in Parliament.' By making no
mention of this hot dispute, Selden begged the question and refused to
uphold this prerogative right, hardly the position of those tender of royal
power in the 1630s: cf. Sommerville, 'John Selden, the Law of Nature,
and the Origins of Government,' 445.

277 Selden, *Of the Dominion*, p. 382; *Mare Clausum*, p. 252: 'de Iuris Patrii
Commentariis et moribus in eo receptis, qui illud à vetustissimis seculis
adstruant.'

278 Selden, *Of the Dominion*, p. 383; *Mare Clausum*, p. 252: 'Quod itidem in
aliis aliquot illis ævi Iurisconsultorum nostratium libris occurrit, ut id
quod exciderat scriptoribus Ulpiani et Justiniani verborum (de quibus
abundè dictum est in libro superiore) quàm par erat, in generali rerum
divisione, amantioribus. Ceterùm hi ipsi aliis in locis, mores Patrios
indicantes, Regis in mari dominium satis admittunt.'

279 Selden, *Of the Dominion*, p. 384; *Mare Clausum*, p. 253; enquiry about
such matters was carried out by the Court of Admiralty. Selden's discussion on pourprestures covered citations from Bracton and Fleta; the
reigns of Richard II, Henry VIII, and Elizabeth I; and Sir Edward
Coke.

280 Selden, *Of the Dominion*, p. 386; *Mare Clausum*, p. 254. For Welwood's
position on the laws of Oleron, see note 222, above.

281 Selden, *Of the Dominion*, pp. 387–8; *Mare Clausum*, pp. 255–6.

282 Selden, *Of the Dominion*, pp. 389–90 (misnumbered as 400); *Mare Clausum*, pp. 256–7.

283 Selden, *Of the Dominion*, pp. 390–1; *Mare Clausum*, pp. 257–8.

284 Selden, *Of the Dominion*, pp. 392, 391; *Mare Clausum*, p. 258: 'de Maris illa veteri in libris Justianeis etiam et in fluminibus piscandi communione, obiter effutierint; ac si in jure nostro djusmodi communio locum haberet' and 'Adeò tandem ut manifestum sit, etiam ex juris Patrii tum sententiis tum moribus, instituendarúmque in ea actionum olim formulis, dominium Regis Angliæ marinum citra controversiam admitti asserique.'

285 Selden, *Of the Dominion*, pp. 433, 443; *Mare Clausum*, chs. 30–2.

286 Selden, *Of the Dominion*, pp. 433–4; *Mare Clausum*, p. 285: 'perinde ac si freta interfluentia eas, non aliter atque flumina aut aquarum diverticula ripas, à Magnâ Britanniâ disjungerent, velut ejusdem ... *fragmenta*. Quo indicatur ipsa freta cum insulis, ut flumina cum ripis, territorii Britannici partem esse censendam.'

287 Selden, *Of the Dominion*, p. 439; see pp. 434–40; *Mare Clausum*, p. 290: 'Citeriore autem Anglo-saxonici imperii ævo; Norwegi seu Dani, quorum latrociniis frequentioribus mare et hoc et boreale habebatur infestissimum, et hanc insulam et Hebridas involabant easque ducentos fermè annos obtinuere.'

288 Selden, *Of the Dominion*, pp. 440–1; *Mare Clausum*, pp. 290–1.

289 Selden, *Of the Dominion*, p. 441; *Mare Clausum*, p. 291.

290 Selden, *Of the Dominion*, pp. 441–2; *Mare Clausum*, pp. 291–2. The first of these principles Selden cited to Paulus, the third century A.D. Roman jurist, and the second from Siculus Flaccus, *De Conditionibus Agrorum*. Welwood had made good use of Paulus in *An Abridgement*, p. 67.

291 Selden, *Of the Dominion*, pp. 446–7; *Mare Clausum*, pp. 294–5.

292 Selden, *Of the Dominion*, pp. 447–8; *Mare Clausum*, p. 296.

293 Selden, *Of the Dominion*, pp. 448–56; *Mare Clausum*, pp. 296–303.

294 Selden, *Of the Dominion*, pp. 456–7; *Mare Clausum*, p. 303: 'Maris ita nondum occupati usus et ejusmodi quæstus primò repertus, repertori tam corpis quàm animi possessione id sibi alterius (ut heic Angliæ Principis) nomine vendicanti, ad modum vendicationis dominium tribuit non aliter atque aliarum quarumcunque rerum nondum possessarum prima et naturalis et civilis possessio.'

295 For an interpretation which draws a firm line between the natural-law tradition of the scholastics (including such neo-scholastics as Francisco Suarez) and the 'modern' tradition of natural law founded by Grotius (which attempted to answer the objections of the sceptics), see Tuck, 'The "Modern" Theory of Natural Law,' pp. 99–119.

296 For differing interpretations of this success which do not concentrate upon the issue of the relationship of the law of nature to the laws of particular societies, compare Tuck, *Natural Rights Theories*, chs. 4 and 5, and Sommerville, 'John Selden, the Law of Nature, and the Origins of Governments.'

297 See especially, Ferguson, *Clio Unbound*, chs. 4, 7, and 8; Fussner, *Historical Revolution*, ch. 11; and Woolf, *Idea of History*, ch. 7.

298 Sir Edward Coke, *The Second Part of the Institutes of the Lawes of England*, p. 8^v.

299 Thomas Hobbes, *Leviathan* (London, 1651), p. 46. For the impact of Selden's theory of natural law, cf. Tuck, *Natural Rights Theories*, ch. 6, and Johann P. Sommerville, *Thomas Hobbes: Political Ideas in Historical Context*, pp. 39, 42–5, 72, and 'John Selden, the Law of Nature, and the Origins of Government.'

300 For this phase of Selden's scholarly career, see Jason P. Rosenblatt, 'Milton's Chief Rabbi,' 43–71; *Torah and Law in 'Paradise Lost'* pp. 79–82, 85–91, 94–103, 122–29; and the introduction to *John Selden on Jewish Marriage Law: The Uxor Hebraica*, translated with a commentary by Jonathan R. Ziskind (Leiden, 1991).

CONCLUSION

1 Two editions of *Jani Anglorum* appeared in 1681 and a translation was printed alone in 1682 and twice in a collection of tracts in 1683; the second edition of *Titles of Honor* was reprinted three times in 1672; at least one edition of *The Historie of Tithes* appeared in 1681 (dated 1618); a translation of *Mare Clausum* was printed in 1652 and reprinted in 1662; and the complete works finally appeared in Selden, *Opera Omnia*, in 1726.

2 Rosenblatt, *Torah and Law*, p. 82, and Helgerson, *Forms of Nationhood*, p. 300.

3 For Doderidge, see Burgess, *Politics of the Ancient Constitution*, pp. 40–2, 50–1, and Christianson, 'Ancient Constitutions,' p. 287 n. 16. For Coke and Davies, see especially Christianson, 'Ancient Constitutions,' 97–9, pp. 105–11; Helgerson, *Forms of Nationhood*, ch. 3; and Pawlisch, *Sir John Davies*.

4 This was also part of the humanist legacy: see Jardine and Grafton, '"Studied for Action."'

5 See Judson, *Crisis of the Constitution*, and Pocock, *Ancient Constitution*.

6 For a different reading of these *Reports*, see Christianson, 'Ancient Constitutions,' pp. 105–11.

7 See Burgess, *Politics of the Ancient Constitution*, chs. 1 and 2.

8 Pocock, *Ancient Constitution*, pp. 277–80.

9 Christopher W. Brooks, 'The Place of Magna Carta and the Ancient Constitution in Sixteenth-Century English Legal Thought.'

10 See Christianson, 'Royal and Parliamentary Voices,' 'Ancient Constitutions,' and chapter 1, above. Cf. Burgess, *Politics of the Ancient Constitution*, chs. 5 and 6.

11 Burgess, *Politics of the Ancient Constitution*, pp. 18–19.

12 Tuck, *Philosophy and Government*, *Natural Rights Theories*, and '"Modern" School of Natural Law,' and Sommerville, *Politics and Ideology*. chs. 1 and 2, and 'John Selden, the Law of Nature, and the Origins of Government.'

13 Christopher Hill, *The Century of Revolution, 1603–1714*, p. 5, and David Wooton, *Divine Right and Democracy: An Anthology of Political Writing in Stuart England*.

14 For all of his support for 'mixed monarchy,' Selden never became an English natural-law equivalent of Johannes Althusius: cf. *Politica Methodice Digesta of Joannes Althusius reprinted from the Third Edition of 1614*, ed. Carl Joachim Friedrich (Cambridge, MA., 1932); Otto Friedrich von Gierke, *The Development of Political Theory* (New York, 1939); Peter Jochen Winters, *Die 'Politik' des Johannes Althusius und ihre zeitgenössischen Quellen* (Freiburg, 1963); and Joannes Althusius, *Politics*, trans. Frederick S. Carney (London, 1964).

15 Public Record Office, State Papers 16/151/69, fo, 137^v, as quoted in Berkowitz, *John Selden*, p. 271; for this whole incident, see pp. 268–80.

16 For a clearly unfinished draft of such a treatise, see *England's Epinonmis*, published in 1683, along with the English translation of *Jani Anglorum* and other brief works, in his *Tracts*.

17 See J.H. Baker, 'Coke's Notebooks and the Sources of his Reports,' in his *Legal Profession*, pp. 196–8.

18 See Annabel Patterson, *Censorship and Interpretation: The Conditions of Writing and Reading in Early Modern England*.

19 G.R. Elton, 'Tudor Government: The Points of Contact; I, The Court; II, The Council; III, Parliament,' 'The Business of the House,' and *The Parliament of England, 1559–1581*; Russell, *Parliaments and English Politics*, ch. 1, and 'Parliamentary History in Perspective.'

20 Both John Pym, the client of Bedford, and Sir Nathaniel Rich, the man of business for his relative Warwick, were among the top five members named to committees and subcommittees during the session of 1628 and

very active participants in the debates of the House and the committee of the whole House. For the impact of peers upon elections to the Commons, see Gruenfelder, *Influence in Early Stuart Elections,* and Hodges, 'The Electoral Influence of the Aristocracy.'

21 For the creation of contested politics in the mid and later seventeenth century, see Kishlansky, *Parliamentary Selection,* and Fletcher, *Reform in the Provinces.*

22 Cf. Derek Hirst, *The Representative of the People? Voters and Voting in England under the Early Stuarts,* and Brian Manning, *The English People and the English Revolution* and 'The Nobles, the People, and the Constitution.'

23 See their respective articles and papers: Graves, 'Thomas Norton and the Parliament Man' and 'The Management of the Elizabethan House of Commons'; Adamson, 'Parliamentary Management'; Jardine and Grafton, '"Studied for Action."'

24 William Molyneux, *The Case of Ireland's Being Bound by Acts of Parliament in England Stated,* pp. 119–92.

25 For the establishment of this commission, see Pawlisch, *Sir John Davies,* pp. 67–70, 89; for its revenue uses in the 1630s, including the extension of the jurisdiction of the Court of Wards, see Aidan Clarke, *The Old English in Ireland, 1625–1642,* pp. 111–18. For Lord Dillon and his connections to Wentworth, see *The Complete Peerage,* Cockayne, s. XI, pp. 125–6. The connections between Lord Dillion and the lord deputy and the connections of one of Dillon's lawyers, Sergeant Nicholas Catlin, a former Speaker of the Irish House of Commons who had acted as Crown counsel in Wentworth's proceedings in 1635 to find the king's title to County Roscommon, lead to the presumption of a collusive suit; however, Nicholas Plunkett, Lord Dillon's principal lawyer, had taken an active role in defending a number of Old English landowners against the claims of the Crown pressed by Wentworth; for Catin and Plunckett, see Clarke, *Old English,* pp. 93, 84, 102.

26 Molyneux, *Case of Ireland,* pp. 161–2.

27 Ibid., p. 163; for another attack upon Spelman, see p. 166.

28 Ibid.

29 Ibid., pp. 167–9.

30 See Smith, *Constitutional Royalism,* pp. 44–5, 94–5, 97, 98–102. Selden declined Hertford's request, 'remarking that his going thither would constitute a "disservice, by which name I call whatsoever will at this time (as this necessarily would) doubtless occasion some further differences 'twixt his majesty and that house of commons"': quoted in Tuck, '"The Ancient

Law of Freedom,'" p. 137; for the letter, see Bodleian Library, Selden MSS, supra 123, f.159ʳ.

31 *His Majesties Answer to the XIX propositions* [E151.25; 18 June], pp. 1, 2, 8, 17; see pp. 4–5, 17–22. See especially, Mendle, *Dangerous Positions;* Weston and Greenberg, *Subjects and Sovereign;* and Smith, *Constitutional Royalists,* pp. 86–91.

32 See Tuck, *Philosophy and Government,* pp. 224–32.

Bibliography

PRIMARY SOURCES

Manuscripts

Bodleian Library, Selden MSS, supra 108 and 123
British Library, Additional MSS 46, 188; Harley MS 286
Cambridge University Library, MS, Mm. 6.63(4)
House of Lords Record Office, John Selden, 'The Priviledges of the Baronage
    in England'
Inner Temple, Petyt MS 598
Lincoln's Inn, Hale MS 12
Public Record Office, State Papers 16/139–42

Printed Editions, Pamphlets, and Treatises

Acts of the Privy Council of England, 1613–32, 32 vols. London, 1929–64
The Aphorismes of the Kingdome. [London, 1642])
Bidwell, William B., and Maija Jansson, eds. *Proceedings in Parliament,*
    1626, 6 vols. New Haven, 1991–3
Bond, Maurice F., ed. *Manuscripts of the House of Lords,* XI vols. London,
    1953
Bracton on the Laws and Customs of England, ed. George E. Woodbine,
    trans. with revisions and notes by Samuel E. Thorne, 4 vols. Cambridge,
    MA, 1968
Calendar of State Papers, Domestic Series, of the Reign of Charles I, 1627–
    1628, ed. John Bruce. London, 1858
Camden, William. *Britain, or a Chorographicall Description of England,*
    Scotland, and Ireland. London, 1610

– *Britannia*. London, 1590, 1594, 1607

Carleton, George. *Tithes examined and proved to bee due to the Clergie by a divine right*. London, 1605

Charles I. *His Majesties Answer to the XIX propositions*. London, 1642

Coke, Sir Edward. *La Dix^{me} Part des Reports*. London, 1614

– *La Huict^{me} Part des Reports*. London, 1611

– *La Size Part des Reports*. London, 1607

– *Le Tierce Part des Reportes*. London, 1602

[Commelin, Jerome]. *Rerum Britannicarum ... Scriptores Vetustiores*. Heidelberg, 1587

Craig, Thomas. *Concerning the Right of Succession to the Kingdom of England*. London, 1703

Daniel, Samuel. *The First Part of the Historie of England*. London, 1612

Davies, Sir John. *Le Primer Report des Cases et Matters en Ley Resolves et Adjudges en les Courts del Roy en Ireland*. Dublin, 1615

de Villiers, Lady, ed. 'The Hastings Journal of the Parliament of 1621.' In *Camden Miscellany*, XX (Camden Society, third series, vol. LXXXIII) London, 1953

Drayton, Michael. *Poly-Olbion*. London, [1612]

Eburne, Richard. *The Maintenance of the Ministerie*. London, 1609

Foster, Elizabeth Read. *Proceedings in Parliament, 1610*, 2 vols. New Haven, 1966

Foxe, John. *Actes and Monuments*, 2 vols. London, 1576

Fulbecke, William. *A Parallele or Conference of the Civill Law the Canon Law, and the Common Law of this Relame of England*. London, 1601

– *The Second Part of the Parallele or Conference*. London, 1602

Gardiner, Samuel Rawson, ed. *Constitutional Documents of the Puritan Revolution, 1625–1660*. Oxford, 1889

– ed. *Debates in the House of Commons in 1625* (C.S., new ser., VI). London, 1873

– ed. *Notes of the Debates in the House of Lords ... 1621* (C.S., CIII). London, 1870

Grotius, Hugo. *The Freedom of the Seas*, ed. James Brown Scott. New York, 1916

– *The Treatise on the Laws and Customs of the Realm of England Commonly called Glanvill*, ed. G.D.G. Hall. Edinburgh, 1965

Hale, Sir Mathew. *The History of the Common Law of England*. London, 1713

[Hall, Arthur]. *A Letter Sent by F.A.* London, [1579?]

[Hayward, John]. *An Answer to the First Part of a Certaine Conference*. London, 1603

Hearne, Thomas, ed. *A Collection of Curious Discourses*, 2 vols. London, 1771

Hotman, François. *Francogallia*, ed., with an introduction by Ralph E. Giesey and J.H.M. Salmon. Cambridge, 1972

Howell, T.B., ed. *A Complete Collection of State Trials*. London, 1809

[James VI]. *The Trew Law of Free Monarchies*. Edinburgh, 1598

James VI and I. *The Political Works of James I*, ed., with an introduction by Charles Howard McIlwain. Cambridge, MA, 1918

Johnson, Robert C., Maija Jansson Cole, Mary Frear Keeler, and William B. Bidwell, eds. *Proceedings in Parliament 1628*, 6 vols. New Haven, 1977–83

Journals of the House of Commons. London, 1803+

Journals of the House of Lords. London, 1767+

Lambarde, William. *Archaionomia, sive de Priscis Anglorum Legibus*. London, 1568

– *A Perambulation of Kent*. London, 1596

McClure, N.E., ed. *The Letters of John Chamberlain*, 2 vols. Philadelphia, 1919

Militia Old and New. London, 2642 [1642]

Molyneux, William. *The Case of Ireland's being bound by Acts of Parliament in England stated*. Dublin, 1725

Montague, Richard. *Diatribæ upon the First Part of the Late History of Tithes*. London, 1621)

Paris, Matthew. *Angli Historia Maior, à Guilielmo Conquæstore, ad ultimum annum Henrici tertii* [ed. Matthew Parker]. London, 1571

Parker, Matthew, ed. *Chronicles*, 4 vols. London, 1567–74

[Persons, Robert] R. Doleman. *A Conference about the Next Succession to the Crowne of England*. Antwerp?, 1594

Pronay, Nicholas, and John Taylor, eds. *Parliamentary Texts of the Later Middle Ages*. Oxford, 1980

Prynne, William. *The Soveraigne Power of Parliaments*. London, 1643

Relf, Helen, ed. *Notes of the Debates in the House of Lords* (C.S., third ser. XLII). London, 1929

Relf, Frances Helen, ed. *Commons Debates for 1629*. Minneapolis, 1921

Ridley, Thomas. *A View of the Civile and Ecclesiastical Law*. London, 1607

Robartes, Foulke. *The Revenue of the Gospel is Tythes, due to the Ministerie of the Word, by that Word*. Cambridge, 1613

Saltern, George. *Of the Antient Lawes of Great Britaine*. London, 1605

[Savile, Henry]. *Rerum Anglicarum Scriptores Post Bedam*. London, 1596 ff.

Segar, Sir William. *Honor, Military, and Civil*. London, 1602

Selden, John. *Analecton Anglobritannicon*. Frankfurt, 1615
– *De Jure Naturali et Gentium Juxta Disciplinam Ebræorum*. London, 1640
– *The Duello or Single Combat*. London, 1610
– *Eadmeri monachi Cantuariensis, Historia Novorum ... sub Guilielmis I et II et Henrico I Angliæ Regibus*. London, 1623
– *The Historie of Tithes*. London, 1618
– *Jani Anglorum Facies Altera*. London, 1610
– *John Selden on Jewish Marriage Law: The Uxor Hebraica*, trans. with a commentary by Jonathan R. Ziskind. Leiden, 1991
– *Ioannis Seldeni Ad Fletam Dissertatio*, reprinted from the edition of 1647 with parallel translation, introduction, and notes by David Ogg. Cambridge, 1925
– *Mare Clausum*. London, 1635
– 'Of the Disposition or Administration of Intestates Goods.' In *Tracts written by John Selden*. London, 1683
– *Of the Dominion, Or, Ownership of the Sea*, trans. by Marchamont Nedham. London, 1652
– Opera Omnia, ed. David Wilkins, 3 vols. in 6 London, 1726
– 'The Reverse or Back Face of the English Janus.' In *Tracts written by John Selden*, trans. Redman Westcot [Dr Adam Littleton]. London, 1683
– *Table Talk*. London, 1689
– *Titles of Honor*. London, 1614
– *Titles of Honor*, 2d ed. London, 1631
– 'To My Singular Good Friend, Mr. *Augustine Vincent*.' In Augustine Vincent, *A Discoverie of Errours in the first Edition of the Catalogue of Nobility Published by Raphe Brooke, Yorke Herald, 1619*. London, 1622
– *Tracts written by John Selden*. London, 1683
– *Vindiciæ Secundum Integritatem*. London, 1653
– ed. Sir John Fortescue, *De Laudibus Legum Angli*. London, 1616
– Notes in Michael Drayton, *Poly-Olbion*. London, 1613
[Sempill, Sir James]. *Sacrilege Sacredly Handled*. London, 1619
Speed, John. *The Historie of Great Brittaine under the Conquests of the Romans, Saxons, Danes and Normans*. London, 1623
Spelman, Sir Henry. *Archæologus in modum Glossarii ad rem antiquam posteriorem*. London, 1626
– *De Non Temerandis Ecclesiis: A Tract, of the Rights and Respect Due unto Churches*. London, 1613
– *Reliquiæ Spelmannianæ*. Oxford, 1698
– *Tithes Too Hot to be Touched*. London, 1646
Tillesley, Richard. *Animadversions upon M. Seldens History of Tithes and*

His Review Thereof. London, 1619

Tithes and Oblations according to the Lawes established in the Church of England. London, 1595

Ussher, James. *The Whole Works of the Most Rev. James Ussher D.D.*, 17 vols., ed. Charles Richard Elrington. Dublin, 1847

Welwood, William. *An Abridgement of All Sea Lawes.* London, 1613

– *De Dominio Maris.* Cosmopoli [London], 1615

Wolfe, Don M., ed. *Leveller Manifestoes of the Puritan Revolution.* New York, 1944

SECONDARY SOURCES

Adamson, J.S.A. 'Parliamentary Management, Men-of-Business and the House of Lords, 1640–49.' In *A Pillar of the Constitution: The House of Lords in British Politics, 1640–1784*, ed. Clyve Jones, ch. 1. London, 1989

Allen, J.W. *A History of Political Thought in the Sixteenth Century.* London, 1928; reprt 1961.

Alsop, James D., and Wesley M. Stevens. 'William Lambarde and the Elizabethan Polity.' *Studies in Medieval and Renaissance History* 8 (1987), 233–66

Andrews, Kenneth R. *Ships, Money and Politics: Seafaring and Naval Enterprise in the Reign of Charles I.* Cambridge, 1991

Baker, Hershel. *The Race of Time.* Toronto, 1967

Baker, J.H. 'Coke's Notebooks and the Sources of His Reports.' In *The Legal Profession and the Common Law: Historical Essays*, pp. 177–204. London, 1986

– 'English Law and the Renaissance.' In *The Legal Profession and the Common Law: Historical Essays*, pp. 461–76. London, 1986

– 'The Newe Littleton.' In *The Legal Profession and the Common Law: Historical Essays*, pp. 231–41. London, 1986

– *The Legal Profession and the Common Law: Historical Essays.* London, 1986

Ball, J.N. 'The Impeachment of the Duke of Buckingham in the Parliament of 1626.' *Melanges Antonio Marongiu: Studies presented to the International Commission for the History of Representative and Parliamentary Institutions*, XXXIV, pp. 35–48. Palermo, 1968

– 'The Petition of Right in the English Parliament of 1628.' In *Album E. Lousse*, IV, 45–64. Louvain, 1964

Barnes, Thomas Garden. 'Deputies not Principals, Lieutanants not Captains: The Institutional Failure of Lieutenancy in the 1620s.' In *War and Government in Britain, 1598–1650*, ed. Mark Charles Fissell, pp. 58–86. Manchester, 1991

– *Somerset 1625–1640: A County's Government during the 'Personal Rule.'* Cambridge, MA, 1961

Barnwell, P.S. *Emperor, Prefects and Kings: The Roman West, 395–565.* London, 1992

Bates, David. *Normandy before 1066.* London, 1982

Berkowitz, David S. *John Selden's Formative Years: Politics and Society in Early Seventeenth-Century England.* Washington, DC, 1988

– 'Reason of State in England and the Petition of Right,1603–1629.' In *Staatsräson: Studien zur Geschichte eines politschen Begriffs*, ed. Roman Schnur, pp. 191–207. Berlin, 1975

– 'SELDEN, John (1584–1654).' In *Biographical Dictionary of British Radicals in the Seventeenth Century*, eds. Richard L. Greaves and Robert Zaller, III, pp. 153–60. Brighton, 1984

– 'Young Mr. Selden, Essays in Seventeenth-Century Learning and Politics, being Prolegomena to Parliament.' PhD thesis, Harvard University, 1946

Bershadsky, Edith. 'Controlling the Terms of the Debate: John Selden and the Tithes Controversy.' In *Law, Literature and the Settlement of Regimes*, eds. Gordon J. Schochet, Patricia E. Tatspaugh, and Carol Brobeck, pp. 187–220. Washington, DC, 1990

Bloch, Marc. *Feudal Society*, 2d ed., 2 vols. London, 1962

Boynton, Lindsay. 'Martial Law and the Petition of Right,' *English Historical Review*, 79 (1964), 255–84

Brooks, Christopher W. 'The Place of Magna Carta and the Ancient Constitution in Sixteenth-Century English Legal Thought.' In *The Roots of Liberty: Magna Carta, Ancient Constitution, and the Anglo-American Tradition of Rule of Law*, ed. Ellis Sandoz, pp. 57–88, 279–84

Brooks, Christopher, and Kevin Sharpe. 'Debate: History, English Law and the Renaissance.' *Past and Present* 72 (1976), 139–40

Brown, E.A.R. 'The Tyranny of a Construct: Feudalism and the Historians of Medieval Europe.' *American Historical Review*, 79 (1974), 1063–88

Burgess, Glenn. 'Common Law and Political Theory in Early Stuart England.' *Political Science* 40 (1988), 4–17

– 'The Divine Right of Kings Reconsidered,' *English Historical Review*, 425 (1992), 837–61

– *The Politics of the Ancient Constitution: An Introduction to English Political Thought, 1603–1642.* London, 1992

Burke, Peter. 'Tacitism, Scepticism, and Reason of State.' In *The Cambridge History of Political Thought, 1450–1700*, eds. J.H. Burns and Mark Goldie, ch. 15. Cambridge, 1991

Burns, J.H., and Mark Goldie, eds. *The Cambridge History of Political Thought, 1450–1700*. Cambridge, 1991

Butler, Martin. *Theatre and Crisis, 1632–1642*. Cambridge, 1984

Chibnall, Marjorie. *Anglo-Norman England, 1066–1166*. Oxford, 1986

Christianson, Paul. 'Ancient Constitutions in the Age of Sir Edward Coke and John Selden.' In *The Roots of Liberty: Magna Carta, Ancient Constitution, and the Anglo-American Tradition of Rule of Law*, ed. Ellis Sandoz, pp. 89–146, 284–292. Columbia, 1993

– 'Arguments on Billeting and Martial Law in the Parliament of 1628.' *Historical Journal* 37 (1994), 539–67

– 'The Causes of the English Revolution: A Reappraisal,' *Journal of British Studies* 15 (1976), 40–75

– 'John Selden, the Five Knights' Case, and Discretionary Imprisonment in Early Stuart England.' *Criminal Justice History*, 6 (1985), 65–87

– 'Patterns of Historical Interpretation.' In *Objectivity, Method and Point of View: Essays in the Philosophy of History*, eds. W.J. van der Dussen and Lionel Rubinoff, pp. 47–71. Leiden, 1991

– 'The Peers, the People, and Parliamentary Management in the First Six Months of the Long Parliament.' *Journal of Modern History* 49 (1977), 575–99

– 'Political Thought in Early Stuart England.' *Historical Journal* 30 (1987), 955–70

– 'Royal and Parliamentary Voices on the Ancient Constitution, ca. 1604–21.' In *The Mental World of the Jacobean Court*, ed. Linda Levy Peck, pp. 71–95; 289–98. Cambridge, 1991

– 'Young John Selden and the Ancient Constitution, ca. 1610–1618,' *Proceedings of the American Philosophical Society* 128 (1984), 271–315

Clarke, Aidan. *The Old English in Ireland, 1625–42*. London, 1966

Cogswell, Thomas. *The Blessed Revolution: English Politics and the Coming of War, 1621–1624*. Cambridge, 1989

– 'Foreign Policy and Parliament: The Case of La Rochelle, 1625–1626.' *English Historical Review* 199 (1984), 241–67

– 'A Low Road to Extinction? Supply and Redress of Grievances in the Parliaments of the 1620s.' *Historical Journal* 33 (1990), 283–303

– 'The Politics of Propaganda: Charles I and the People in the 1620s.' *Journal of British Studies* 29 (1990), 187–215

Coquillette, Daniel R. 'Legal Ideology and Incorporation, I: The English
    Civilians, 1523–1607'; 'II: Sir Thomas Ridley, Charles Malloy, and the Lit-
    erary Battle for the Law Merchant, 1607–1676'; and 'III: Reason Regulated –
    the Post-Restoration English Civilians, 1653–1735.' *Boston University
    Law Review* 61 (1981), 1–89, 315–71; 67 (1987), 289–361
Crawford, Patricia. *Denzil Holles, 1598–1680: A Study of His Political
    Career*, London, 1979
Cromartie, Alan. *Sir Matthew Hale, 1609–1676: Law, Religion, and Natural
    Philosophy*. Cambridge, 1995
Crouch, David. *The Image of Aristocracy in Britain, 1000–1300*. London,
    1992
Crowe, Michael Bertram. 'An Eccentric Seventeenth-Century Witness to the
    Natural Law: John Selden (1584–1654).' *Natural Law Forum* 12 (1967),
    184–95
Cust Richard. 'Charles I, the Privy Council and the Parliament of 1628.'
    Transactions of the Royal Historical Society, sixth ser., II (London, 1992),
    pp. 25–50
– *The Forced Loan and English Politics, 1626–1628*. Oxford, 1987
– 'News and Politics in Early Seventeenth-Century England,' *Past and
    Present*, 112 (1986), 60–90
Cust, Richard, and Ann Hughes, ed. *Conflict in Early Stuart England: Stud-
    ies in Religion and Politics, 1603–1642*. London, 1989
Daly, James. 'Cosmic Harmony and Political Thinking in Early Stuart
    England.' *Transactions of the American Philosophical Society*, LXIX, part
    7 (Philadelphia, 1979), pp. 1–40
– 'The Idea of Absolute Monarchy.' *Historical Journal*, 21 (1978), 227–50
Darroch, James L. 'Method and History: The Importance of Dialectic, Ratio-
    nalism and Skepticism in the Development of Historical Consciousness
    and Methodology in Early Modern France, 1555–1700.' PhD thesis, Univer-
    sity of Toronto, 1980
Davies, Julian. *The Caroline Captivity of the Church: Charles I and the
    Remoulding of Anglicanism, 1625–1641*. Oxford, 1992
de Villiers, Evangeline [Lady] 'Parliamentary Boroughs Restored by the
    House of Commons 1621–1641.' *English Historical Review* 67 (1952),
    175–202
Donahue, Charles, Jr. 'The Civil Law in England.' *Yale Law Journal*, 84
    (1974), 167–81
Edmundson, George. *Anglo-Dutch Rivalry during the First Half of the Sev-
    enteenth Century*. Oxford, 1911
Elton, G.R. 'Arthur Hall, Lord Burghley and the Antiquity of Parliament.' In

Studies in Tudor and Stuart Politics and Government, III: Papers and Reviews, 1973–1981, pp. 254–73. Cambridge, 1983

– 'The Business of the House,' *Times Literary Supplement* 3/928 (1977), 763–4

– *The Parliament of England, 1559–1581*. Cambridge, 1986

– 'Tudor Government: The Points of Contact. I, The Parliament.' *Transactions of the Royal Historical Society*, series 5, 24 (1974), pp. 183–200

– 'Tudor Government: The Points of Contact. II, The Council.' *Transactions of the Royal Historical Society*, series 5, 25 (1975), pp. 195–211

– 'Tudor Government: The Points of Contact. III, The Court.' *Transactions of the Royal Historical Society*, series 5, 26 (1976), pp. 211–28

Feingold, Mordechai. 'John Selden and the Nature of Seventeenth-Century Science.' In *In the Presence of the Past: Essays in Honor of Frank Manuel*, eds. Richard T. Bienvenu and Mordechai Feingold, pp. 55–78. Dordrecht, 1991

Ferguson, Arthur B. *Clio Unbound: Perception of the Social and Cultural Past in Renaissance England*. Durham, NC, 1979

– *Utter Antiquity: Perceptions of Prehistory in Renaissance England*. Durham, NC, 1993

Filloy, Richard A. 'The Religious and Political Views of John Selden: A Study in Early Stuart Humanism.' PhD thesis, University of California at Berkeley, 1977

Fincham, Kenneth. *The Early Stuart Church, 1603–1642*. London, 1993

Finn, R. Welldon. *An Introduction to Domesday Book*. London, 1963

Flemion, Jess Stoddart. '"A Savings to Satisfy All": The House of Lords and the Meaning of the Petition of Right.' *Parliamentary History* 10 (1991), 27–44

– 'Slow Process, Due Process, and the High Court of Parliament: A Reinterpretation of the Revival of Judicature in the House of Lords in 1621.' *Historical Journal* 17 (1974), 3–16

– 'The Struggle for the Petition of Right in the House of Lords: The Study of an Opposition Party Victory.' *Journal of Modern History* 45 (1973), 193–210

Fleming, Robin. 'Domesday Book and the Tenurial Revolution.' In *Anglo-Norman Studies, IX, Proceedings of the Battle Conference 1986*, ed. R. Allen Brown, pp. 86–102. Woodbridge, 1987

– *Kings and Lords in Conquest England*. Cambridge, 1991

Fletcher, Anthony. *Reform in the Provinces: The Government of Stuart England*. New Haven and London, 1986

Foss, Edward. *The Judges of England*, 9 vols. London, 1848–64

Foster, Elizabeth Read. 'Henry Elsyng, "Judicature in Parliament,"'*Parliamentary History* 9 (1990), 158–62
– *The House of Lords, 1603–1649: Structure, Procedure, and the Nature of Its Business*. Chapel Hill, 1983
– *The Painful Labour of Mr. Elsyng*. Philadelphia, 1972
– 'Petitions and the Petition of Right.' *Journal of British Studies* 14 (1974), 35, 37–8, 40–3
– 'Printing the Petition of Right.' *Huntington Library Quarterly* 38 (1974), 81–3
Foster, Andrew. 'The Clerical Estate Revitalised.' In *The Early Stuart Church, 1603–1642*, ed. Kenneth Fincham, pp. 150–2. London, 1993
Franklin, Julian. *Jean Bodin and the Rise of Absolutist Theory*. Cambridge, 1973
– *Jean Bodin and the Sixteenth-Century Revolution in the Methodology of Law and History*. New York, 1963
– 'Sovereignty and the Mixed Constitution: Bodin and His Critics,' In *The Cambridge History of Political Thought, 1450–1700*, ed. J.H. Burns and Mark Goldie, ch. 10. Cambridge, 1991
Fraser, Antonia. *The Weaker Vessel: Woman's Lot in Seventeenth-Century England*. London, 1984
Fraser, Ian H.C. 'The Agitation in the Commons, 2 March 1629, and the Interrogation of the Anti-Court Group.' *Bulletin of the Institute of Historical Research* 30 (1957), 86–95
Fulton, Thomas Wemyss. *The Sovereignty of the Sea: An Historical Account of the Claims of England to the Dominion of the British Seas, and of the Evolution of the Territorial Waters: with Special Reference to the Rights of Fishing and the Naval Salute*. Edinburgh and London, 1911
Fussner, F. Smith. *The Historical Revolution: English Historical Writing and Thought, 1580–1640*. London, 1962
Galloway, Bruce. *The Union of England and Scotland: 1603–1608*. Edinburgh, 1986
Galloway, Bruce and Brian P. Levack, eds. *The Jacobean Union: Six Tracts of 1604*. Edinburgh, 1985
Ganshof, F.L. *Feudalism*, transl. Philip Grierson. London, 1952
Gardiner, Samuel R. *History of England from the Accession of James I. to the Outbreak of the Civil War, 1603–1642*, 10 vols. London, 1884
Gillingham, John. 'The Introduction of Knight Service into England.' In *Ango-Norman Studies, IV: Proceedings of the Battle Conference, 1981*, ed. R. Allen Brown, pp. 53–64. Woodbridge, 1982

Goffart, Walter. *Barbarians and Romans, A.D. 418–584: The Techniques of Accommodation.* Princeton, 1980

Goldberg, Jonathan. *James I and the Politics of Literature: Jonson, Shakespeare, Donne and Their Contemporaries.* Baltimore, 1983

Graves, M.A.R. 'The Management of the Elizabethan House of Commons: The Council's Men of Business.' *Parliamentary History* 2 (1983), 11–38

– 'Thomas Norton the Parliament Man: An Elizabethan M. P., 1559–1581.' *Historical Journal* 23 (1980), 17–35

Gray, Charles M., and Maija Jansson Cole. 'Bowdler's Case: The Intestate Bastard.' *University of Toronto Law Journal* 30 (1980), 46–74

Greenberg, Janelle. 'Our Grand Maxim of State, "The King Can Do No Wrong."' *History of Political Thought* 2 (1991), 209–28

Gruenfelder, John K. *Influence in Early Stuart Elections, 1604–1640.* Columbus, 1981

Guy, J.A. 'The Origins of the Petition of Right Reconsidered.' *Historical Journal* 25 (1982), 289–312

Haggenmacher, Peter. 'Grotius and Gentili: A Reassessment of Thomas E. Holland's Inaugural Lecture.' In *Hugo Grotius and International Relations*, eds. Hedley Bull, Benedict Kingsbury, and Adam Roberts, ch. 4. Oxford, 1990

Harlan, David. 'Intellectual History and the Return of Literature.' *American Historical Review* 94 (1989), 581–609

Harrison, G.A. 'Innovation and Precedent: A Procedural Reappraisal of the Parliament of 1625.' *English Historical Review* 102 (1987), 31–62

Hart, C. *The Hidation of Cambridgeshire.* Leicester, 1974

– *The Hidation of Northamptonshire.* Leicester, 1970

Hart, James S. *Justice upon Petition: The House of Lords and the Reformation of Justice, 1621–1675.* London, 1991

Hazeltine, H.D. 'Selden as Legal Historian.' In *Festschrift Heinrich Brünner*, pp. 579–630. Weimar, 1910

Helgerson, Richard. *Forms of Nationhood: The Elizabethan Writing of England.* Chicago, 1992

Hexter, J.H. 'Power Struggle, Parliament, and Liberty in Early Stuart England.' *Journal of Modern History* 1 (1978), 1–50

– 'Quoting the Commons, 1604–1642.' In *Tudor Rule and Revolution: Essays for G.R. Elton from His American Friends*, eds. Delloyd J. Guth and John W. McKenna, pp. 369–91. Cambridge, 1982

Herrup, Cynthia B. *The Common Peace: Participation and the Criminal Law in Seventeenth-Century England.* Cambridge, 1987

– 'Law and Morality in Seventeenth-Century England.' *Past and Present* 106 (1985), 102–23

Hill, Christopher. *The Century of Revolution, 1603–1714*. Edinburgh, 1961

– *Economic Problems of the Church, from Archbishop Whitgift to the Long Parliament*. Oxford, 1956

Hirst, Derek. 'Court, Country and Politics before 1629.' In *Faction and Parliament: Essays on Early Stuart History*, ed. Kevin Sharpe, ch. 4. Oxford, 1978

– 'The Privy Council and Problems of Enforcement in the 1620s.' *Journal of British Studies* 18 (1978), 46–66

– *The Representative of the People? Voters and Voting in England under the Early Stuarts*. Cambridge, 1975

Hodges, Vivienne Jill. 'The Electoral Influence of the Aristocracy, 1604–1641.' PhD thesis, Columbia University, 1977

Hollister, C. Warren. *Anglo-Saxon Military Institutions on the Eve of the Norman Conquest*. Oxford, 1962

Holt, J.C. *Magna Carta*. Cambridge, 1969

Horstman, Allen Henry. 'Justice and Peers: The Judicial Activities of the Seventeenth-Century House of Lords.' PhD thesis, University of California at Berkeley, 1977

Hulme, Harold. *The Life of Sir John Eliot, 1592 to 1632*. London, 1957

Huppert, George. *The Idea of Perfect History: Historical Erudition and Historical Philosophy in Renaissance France*. Urbana, 1970

Ingram, Martin. 'Ridings, Rough Music, and Mocking Rhymes in Early Modern England.' In *Popular Culture in Seventeenth-Century England*, ed. Barry Reay, ch. 5. London, 1985

– 'Ridings, Rough Music, and the "Reform of Popular Culture" in Early Modern England.' *Past and Present* 105 (1985), 99–113

James, Edward. *The Origins of France: From Clovis to the Capetians, 500–1000*. London, 1982

Jardine, Lisa, and Anthony Grafton. '"Studied for Action": How Gabriel Harvey Read His Livy.' *Past and Present* 129 (1990), 30–78

Jones, W.J. *Politics and the Bench: The Judges and the Origins of the English Civil War*. London, 1971

Judson, Margaret. *The Crisis of the Constitution: An Essay in Constitutional and Political Thought in England*. New Brunswick, NJ, 1948

Keeler, Mary Frear. *The Long Parliament, 1640–1641: A Political Study*, Philadelphia, 1954

Kelley, Donald R. 'Civil Science in the Renaissance: The Problem of Interpretation.' In *The Languages of Political Theory in Early Modern Europe*, ed. Anthony Pagden, pp. 57–78. Cambridge, 1987

– '*De Origine Feudorum*: The Beginnings of an Historical Problem.' *Speculum* 39 (1964), 207–28

– *Foundations of Modern Historical Scholarship: Language, Law, and History in the French Renaissance*. New York, 1960

– *François Hotman: A Revolutionary's Ordeal*. Princeton, 1973

– 'History, English Law and the Renaissance.' *Past and Present* 65 (1974), 47–50

– *History, Law and the Human Sciences*. London, 1984

– 'Law.' In *Cambridge History of Political Thought, 1450–1700*, eds. J.H. Burns and Mark Goldie, ch. 3. Cambridge, 1991

– 'A Rejoinder.' *Past and Present* 72 (1976), 143–6

Kendrick, T.D. *British Antiquity*. London, 1950

Kent, Joan R. *The English Village Constable 1580–1642: A Social and Administrative Study*. Oxford, 1986

– ' "Folk Justice" and Royal Justice in Early Seventeenth-Century England: A Charivari in the Midlands.' *Midland History* 8 (1983), 69–85

Kiffin, Thomas. 'Sir Dudley Digges: A Study in Early Stuart Politics.' PhD thesis, New York University, 1972

Kishlansky, Mark. 'Consensus Politics and the Structure of the Debate at Putney.' *Journal of British Studies* 20 (1981), 50–69

– 'The Emergence of Adversary Politics in the Long Parliament.' *Journal of Modern History* 49 (1977), 617–40

– *Parliamentary Selection: Social and Political Choice in Early Modern England*. Cambridge, 1986

Klein, William. 'The Ancient Constitution Revisited.' In *Political Discourse in Early Modern Britain*, eds. Nicholas Phillipson and Quentin Skinner, ch. 3. Cambridge, 1993

Knafla, Louis A. 'The Influence of Continental Humanists and Jurists on English Common Law in the Renaissance.' In *Acta Conventus Neo-Latini Bonensis Proceedings of the Fourth International Congress of Neo-Latin Studies*, ed. R. Schoeck, pp. 60–71. Binghamton, 1985

– *Law and Politics in Jacobean England: The Tracts of Lord Chancellor Ellesmere*. Cambridge, 1977

Kopperman, Paul E. *Sir Robert Heath, 1575–1649: Window on an Age*. Wolfeboro, 1989

Kristeller, Paul Oskar. *Renaissance Thought*. New York, 1961

Lake, Peter. 'Anti-Popery: The Structure of a Prejudice.' In *Conflict in Early Stuart England: Studies in Religion and Politics, 1603–1642*, eds. Richard Cust and Anne Hughes, ch. 3. London, 1989

– 'Calvinism and the English Church, 1570–1635.' *Past and Present* 114 (1987), 32–76

– 'Presbyterianism, the Idea of a National Church and the Argument from Divine Right.' In *Protestantism and the National Church in Sixteenth-Century England*, eds. Peter Lake and M. Dowling, pp. 211–13. London, 1987

Lee, Maurice. Jr. *The Road to Revolution: Scotland under Charles I, 1625–1637*. Urbana, 1985

Levack, Brian P. *The Civil Lawyers in England, 1603–1641: A Political Study*. Oxford, 1973

– 'English Law, Scots Law, and the Union, 1603–1707.' In *Law-Making and Law-Makers in British History: Papers Presented to the Edinburgh Legal History Conference, 1977*, ed. Alan Harding, pp. 105–19. London, 1980

– 'The Proposed Union of English Law with Scots Law in the Seventeenth Century.' *Juridical Review*, new series, 20 (1975), 99–115

– 'Toward a More Perfect Union: England, Scotland and the Constitution.' In *After the Reformation: Essays in Honor of J.H. Hexter*, ed. Barbara C. Malament, pp. 57–74. Philadelphia, 1980

– *The Formation of the British State: England, Scotland, and the Union, 1603–1707*. Oxford, 1987

Lloyd, H.A. 'The Political Thought of Charles Loyseau (1564–1610).' *European Studies Review* 11 (1981), 53–80

Lockyer, Roger. *Buckingham: The Life and Political Career of George Villiers, First Duke of Buckingham, 1592–1628*. London, 1981

Loncar, Kathleen. 'John Selden's "History of Tithes": A Charter for Landlords?' *Journal of Legal History* 11 (1990), 218–37

Loyn, H.R. *Anglo-Saxon England and the Norman Conquest*. London, 1962

– *The Governance of Anglo-Saxon England, 500–1087*. London, 1984

Maitland, Frederic W. *Domesday Book and Beyond*. Cambridge, 1897

– *English Law and the Renaissance*. Cambridge, 1901

Manning, Brian. *The English People and the English Revolution*, London, 1976

– 'The Nobles, the People, and the Constitution.' *Past and Present* 9 (1956), 42–64

Martin, Julian. *Francis Bacon, the State, and the Reform of Natural Philosophy*. Cambridge, 1992

Mendle, Michael. *Dangerous Positions: Mixed Government, the Estates of* the Realm, and the Making of the Answer to the XIX Propositions. University, AL, 1985

Millar, Oliver. The Age of Charles I. London, 1972

Morill, John, Paul Slack, and Daniel Woolf, eds. Public Duty and Private Conscience in Seventeenth-Century England: Essays Presented to G.E. Aylmer. Oxford, 1993

Mulligan, Winnefred Joy. 'The British Constantine: An English Historical Myth.' Journal of Medieval and Renaissance Studies 8 (1978), 257–79

Neale, J.E. Elizabeth I and Her Parliaments, 1559–1581. New York, 1953

Norbrook, David. Poetry and Politics in the English Renaissance. Oxford, 1984

Notestein, Wallace. The House of Commons, 1604–1610. New Haven, 1971

O' Farrell, Brian. 'Politician, Patron, Poet: William Herbert, Third Earl of Pembroke, 1580–1630.' PhD thesis, University of California at Los Angeles, 1966

Orgel, Stephen. The Illusion of Power. Berkeley, 1975

Orgel, Stephen, and Roy Strong, eds. Inigo Jones: The Theatre of the Stuart Court, 2 vols. London, 1973

Oudendijk, J.K. Status and Extent of Adjacent Waters. Leyden, 1970

Palme, Per. Triumph of Peace: A Study of the Whitehall Banqueting House. London, 1957

Patterson, Annabel. Censorship and Interpretation: The Conditions of Writing and Reading in Early Modern England. Madison, 1984

De Pauw, Frans. Grotius and the Law of the Sea, trans. P.J. Arthern Brussels, 1965

Pawlisch, Hans J. Sir John Davies and the Conquest of Ireland: A Study in Legal Imperialism. Cambridge, 1985

Pocock, J.G.A. The Ancient Constitution and the Feudal Law: English Historical Thought in the Seventeenth Century. Cambridge, 1957

– The Ancient Constitution and the Feudal Law: English Historical Thought in the Seventeenth Century: A Reissue with a Retrospect. Cambridge, 1987

– 'The Commons Debates of 1628.' Journal of the History of Ideas 29 (1978), 332–4

– The Machiavellian Moment: Florentine Political Thought and the Atlantic Republican Tradition. Princeton, 1975

– Virtue, Commerce, and History: Essays on Political Thought and History, Chiefly in the Eighteenth Century. Cambridge, 1985

Popofsky, Linda S. 'The Crisis over Tonnage and Poundage in Parliament in 1629.' Past and Present 126 (1990), 44–75

- 'Habeas Corpus and "Liberty of the Subject": Legal Arguments for the Petition of Right in the Parliament of 1628.' *Historian* 41 (1979), 257–75
Potter, Pitman B. *The Freedom of the Seas in History, Law, and Politics.* London, 1924
Prescott, Anne Lake. 'Marginal Discourse: Drayton's Muse and Selden's "Story." ' *Studies in Philology* 88 (1991), 307–28
Prest, Wilfrid R. *The Rise of the Barristers: A Social History of the English Bar, 1590–1640.* Oxford, 1986
Prestwich, Menna. *Cranfield: Politics and Profit under the Early Stuarts.* Oxford, 1966
Prestwich, Michael. 'The *Modus Tenendi Parliamentum.*' *Parliamentary History* 1 (1982), 221–5
Quintrell, B.W. 'Charles I and His Navy in the 1630s.' *Seventeenth Century* 3 (1988), 159–79
Reeve, L.J. 'The Arguments in the King's Bench in 1629 Concerning the Imprisonment of John Selden and Other Members of the House of Commons.' *Journal of British Studies* 25 (1986), 264–87
- *Charles I and the Road to Personal Rule.* Cambridge, 1989
- 'The Legal Status of the Petition of Right.' *Historical Journal* 29 (1986), 257–77
- 'Sir Robert Heath's Advice for Charles I in 1629.' *Historical Research* 40 (1986), 215–24
Relf, Helen. *The Petition of Right.* Minneapolis, 1917
Reynolds, Susan. *Kingdoms and Communities in Western Europe, 900–1300.* Oxford, 1984
Richardson, H.G., and G.O. Sayles. *Law and Legislation from Æthelberht to Magna Carta.* Edinburgh, 1966
Roberts, Clayton. *The Growth of Responsible Government in Stuart England.* Cambridge, 1966
Rodgers, C.P. 'Legal Humanism and English Law – the Contribution of the English Civilians.' *Irish Jurist*, new series, 14 (1984), 115–36
Roelfsen, C.G. 'Grotius and the International Politics of the Seventeenth Century.' In *Hugo Grotius and International Relations*, eds. Hedley Bull, Benedict Kingsbury, and Adam Roberts, ch. 3. Oxford, 1990
Rosenblatt, Jason P. 'Milton's Chief Rabbi.' *Milton Studies* 24 (1988), 43–71
- *Torah and Law in 'Paradise Lost.'* Princeton, 1994
Round, J.H. *Feudal England.* London, 1895
Ruigh, Robert E. *The Parliament of 1624.* Cambridge, MA, 1971
Russell, Conrad, Earl. 'Divine Rights in the Early Seventeenth Century.' In

Public Duty and Private Conscience in Seventeenth-Century England: Essays Presented to G.E. Aylmer, eds. John Merill, Paul Slack, and Daniel Woolf, ch. 7. Oxford, 1993

– 'The Parliamentary Career of John Pym, 1621–9.' In *The English Commonwealth, 1547–1640: Essays in Politics and Society Presented to Joel Hurstfield*, eds. Peter Clark, Alan G.R. Smith, and Nicholas Tyacke, ch. 8. Leister, 1979

– 'Parliamentary History in Perspective.' *History* 61 (1976), 1–27

– *Parliaments and English Politics, 1621–1629*. Oxford, 1979

Salmon, J.H.M. *The French Religious Wars in English Political Thought*. Oxford, 1959

Sawyer, Peter. '1066–1086: A Tenurial Revolution?' In *Domesday Book: A Reassessment*, ed. Peter Sawyer, pp. 71–85. London, 1985

Sawyer, Peter, ed. *Domesday Book: A Reassessment*. London, 1985

Sawyer, Peter, and I.N. Wood, eds. *Early Medieval Kingship*, Leeds, 1977

Sayles, George O. *The King's Parliament of England*. New York, 1974

Schiffman, Zachary Syre. 'An Anatomy of the Historical Revolution in Renaissance France.' *Renaissance Quarterly* 42 (1989), 507–33

– 'Etienne Pasquier and the Problem of Historical Relativism.' *Sixteenth Century Journal* 18 (1987), 505–17

– 'Renaissance Historicism Reconsidered.' *History and Theory* 24 (1985), 170–82

Schwartz, Hillel. 'Arminianism and the English Parliament, 1624–1629.' *Journal of British Studies* 12 (1973), 41–68

Sharpe, Kevin. *Criticism and Compliment: The Politics of Literature in the England of Charles I*. Cambridge, 1987

– 'Crown, Parliament and Locality: Government and Communication in Early Stuart England.' *English Historical Review* 100 (1986), 321–50

– 'The Earl of Arundel, His Circle and the Opposition to the Duke of Buckingham, 1624–28.' In *Faction and Parliament: Essays on Early Stuart History*, ed. Kevin Sharpe, pp. 209–44. Oxford, 1978

Sharpe, Kevin, ed. *Faction and Parliament: Essays on Early Stuart History*. Oxford, 1978

Sharpe, Kevin, and Peter Lake, eds. *Culture and Politics in Early Stuart England*. London, 1994

Skinner, Quentin. *The Foundations of Modern Political Thought*. 2 vols. Cambridge, 1978

– 'Meaning and Understanding in the History of Ideas.' *History and Theory* 8 (1969), 3–53

- 'Motives, Intentions, and the Interpretation of Texts.' *New Literary History* 3 (1972), 393–408
- 'A Reply to My Critics.' In *Meaning and Context: Quentin Skinner and His Critics*, ed. John Tully, ch. 14. Cambridge, 1989
- 'Some Problems in the Analysis of Political Thought and Action.' *Political Theory* 23 (1974), 277–303

Slack, Paul. 'Books of Orders: The Making of English Social Policy, 1577–1631.' *Transactions of the Royal Historical Society*, fifth series, XXX (1980), pp. 1–22

Slights, Camille Wells. *The Casuistical Tradition in Shakespeare, Donne, Herbert, and Milton*. Princeton, 1981

Smith, David L. *Constitutional Royalism and the Search for Settlement, c. 1640–1649*. Cambridge, 1994
- 'The 4th Earl of Dorset and the Politics of the Sixteen-Twenties.' *Historical Research* 65 (1992), 37–53

Smuts, R. Malcolm. *Court Culture and the Origins of a Royalist Tradition in Early Stuart England*. Philadelphia, 1987

Snow, Vernon. 'The Arundel Case, 1626.' *Historian*, 26 (1964), 32
- 'Essex and the Aristocratic Opposition to the Early Stuarts.' *Journal of Modern History* 32 (1960), 226–8
- *Essex the Rebel*. Lincoln, 1970

Sommerville, Johann P. 'Absolutism and Royalism.' In *The Cambridge History of Political Thought, 1450–1700*, eds. J.H. Burns and Mark Goldie, ch. 12. Cambridge, 1991
- 'From Suarez to Filmer: A Reappraisal.' *Historical Journal* 25 (1982), 525–40
- 'History and Theory: The Norman Conquest in Early Stuart Political Thought.' *Political Studies* 34 (1986), 249–61
- 'James I and the Divine Right of Kings: English Politics and Continental Theory.' In *The Mental World of the Jacobean Court*, in ed. Linda Levy Peck, ch. 4. Cambridge, 1991
- *Politics and Ideology in England, 1603–1640*. London, 1986
- 'John Selden, the Law of Nature, and the Origins of Government.' *Historical Journal* 27 (1984), 437–47
- *Thomas Hobbes: Political Ideas in Historical Context*. London, 1992

Stater, Victor. *Noble Government: The Stuart Lord Lieutenancy and the Transformation of English Politics*. Athens, GA, 1994
- 'War and the Structure of Politics: Lieutenancy and the Campaign of 1628.' In *War and Government in Britain, 1598–1650*, ed. Mark Charles Fissell, pp. 87–109. Manchester, 1991

Stenton, Sir Frank. *The First Century of English Feudalism, 1066–1166*, 2nd ed. Oxford, 1961

Strong, Roy. *Britannia Triumphans: Inigo Jones, Rubens and Whitehall Palace*. London, 1980

– *Van Dyck: Charles I on Horseback*. London, 1972

Thomas, Keith. 'Cases of Conscience in Seventeenth-Century England.' In *Public Duty and Private Conscience in Seventeenth-Century England: Essays Presented to G.E. Aylmer*, eds. John Morill, Paul Slack, and Daniel Woolf, pp. 29–56. Oxford, 1993

Thompson, Christopher. 'Court Politics and Parliamentary Conflict in 1625.' In *Conflict in Early Stuart England: Studies in Religion and Politics 1603–1642*, eds. Richard Cust and Ann Hughes, ch. 6. London, 1989

– 'The Divided Leadership of the House of Commons in 1629.' In *Faction and Parliament: Essays on Early Stuart History*, ed. Kevin Sharpe, ch. 8. Oxford, 1978

Thompson, Faith. *Magna Carta: Its Role in the Making of the English Constitution, 1300–1629*. Minneapolis, 1948

Thorne, Samuel E. 'English Law and the Renaissance.' In *La storia del diritto nel quadro delle scienze storiche*, pp. 437–45. Firenze, 1966

Tite, Colin G.C. 'The Cotton Library in the Seventeenth Century and Its Manuscript Records of the English Parliament.' *Parliamentary History* 14 (1995), 121–38

– *Impeachment and Parliamentary Judicature in Early Stuart England*. London, 1974

– 'A "Loan" of Printed Books from Sir Robert Cotton to John Selden.' *Bodleian Library Record* 13 (1991), 486–90

Tuck, Richard. '"The Ancient Law of Freedom": John Selden and the Civil War.' In *Reactions to the English Civil War, 1642–1649*, ed. John Morrill, pp. 137–61. New York, 1982

– *Natural Rights Theories: Their Origin and Development*. Cambridge, 1979

– 'The "Modern" School of Natural Law.' In *The Languages of Political Theory in Early-Modern Europe*, ed. Anthony Pagden, pp. 99–122. Cambridge, 1987

– *Philosophy and Government, 1572–1651*. Cambridge, 1993

Tully, John. *A Discourse on Property: John Locke and His Adversaries*. Cambridge, 1980

Tully, John, ed. *Meaning and Context: Quentin Skinner and His Critics*. Cambridge, 1989

Tyacke, Nicholas. *Anti-Calvinists: The Rise of English Arminianism, c. 1590–1640*. Oxford, 1987

Underdown, David. *Revel, Riot and Rebellion: Popular Politics and Culture in England, 1603–1660*. Oxford, 1985

– 'The Taming of the Scold: The Enforcement of Patriarchal Authority in Early Modern England.' In *Order and Disorder in Early Modern England*, eds. Anthony Fletcher and John Stevenson, ch. 4. Cambridge, 1985

Usher, Roland G. *The Reconstruction of the English Church*, 2 vols. New York, 1910

van der Molen, Gesina H.J. *Alberico Gentili and the Development of International Law: His Work and Times*, 2d ed. Leyden, 1968

Wallace-Hadrill, J.M. *Early Germanic Kingship in England and on the Continent*. Oxford, 1971

Warnicke, Retha M. *William Lambarde: Elizabethan Antiquary, 1536–1601*. London, 1973

Warren, W.L. *The Governance of Norman and Angevin England, 1086–1272*. London, 1987

Weston, Corinne Comstock. 'England: Ancient Constitution and Common Law.' In *The Cambridge History of Political Thought, 1450–1700*, eds. J.H. Burns and Mark Goldie, pp. 379–87. Cambridge, 1991

– *English Constitutional Theory and the House of Lords*. London, 1965)

Weston, Corinne Comstock, and Jannelle Renfrow Greenberg. *Subjects and Sovereigns: The Grand Controversy over Legal Sovereignty in Stuart England*. Cambridge, 1981

White, Peter. *Predestination, Policy and Polemic: Conflict and Consensus in the English Church from the Reformation to the Civil War*. Cambridge, 1992

White, Stephen D. *Sir Edward Coke and 'The Grievances of the Commonwealth', 1621–1628*. Chapel Hill, 1979

Whitelock, Dorothy. *The Beginnings of English Society: The Anglo-Saxon Period*. Harmondsworth, 1952

Williams, Glanmor. 'Some Protestant Views of Early British Church History.' *History*, new series, 38 (1953), 229–31

Williamson, Arthur D. *Scottish National Consciousness in the Age of James VI: The Apocalypse, the Union and the Shaping of Scotland's Public Culture*. Edinburgh, 1979

Willson, David Harris. *The Privy Councillors in the House of Commons, 1604–1629*. New York 1971; originally Minneapolis, 1940

Winkler, John Frederick. 'Roman Law in Anglo-Saxon England.' *Journal of Legal History* 13 (1992), 101–27

Woolf, Daniel Robert. 'Community, Law and State: Samuel Daniel's Histori-
cal Thought Revisited.' *Journal of the History of Ideas* 49 (1988), 61–83
- 'Erudition and the Idea of History in Renaissance England.' *Renaissance
Quarterly* 40 (1987), 11–48
- *The Idea of History in Early Stuart England: Erudition, Ideology and 'The
Light of Truth' from the Accession of James I to the Civil War.* Toronto,
1990
- 'John Selden, John Borough and Francis Bacon's *History of Henry VII,
1621.' Huntington Library Quarterly* 47 (1984), 47–53
Wooton, David. *Divine Right and Democracy: An Anthology of Political
Writing in Stuart England.* Harmondsworth, 1986
Wormald, Jenny. 'James VI and I, *Basilikon Doron* and *The Trew Law of Free
Monarchies*: The Scottish Context and the English Translation.' In *The
Mental World of the Jacobean Court*, ed. Linda Levy Peck, ch. 3. Cam-
bridge, 1991
Wormuth, Francis. *The Royal Prerogative, 1603–1649.* Ithaca, 1939
Young, Michael B. 'The Origins of the Petition of Right Reconsidered Fur-
ther.' *Historical Journal* 27 (1984), 449–52
- *Servility and Service: The Life and Work of Sir John Coke.* Woodbridge,
1986
Zagorin, Perez. *Ways of Lying: Dissimulation, Persecution and Conformity
in Early Modern Europe.* Cambridge, MA, 1990
Zaller, Robert. *The Parliament of 1621.* Berkeley, 1971
Ziskind, Martha A. 'John Selden: Criticism and Affirmation of the Common
Law Tradition.' *American Journal of Legal History* 19 (1975), 22–39

REFERENCE WORKS

Algemeine Deutsche Biographie, 45 vols. Berlin, 1967–71
Athenae Oxonienses. New York, 1967; originally London, 1813–20.
The Complete Peerage, ed. George Edward Cokayne, 13 vols. London,
1910–49
Dictionary of National Biography, eds. Sir Leslie Stephen and Sir Sidney Lee.
London, 1885–1904
Graves, Edgar B., ed. *Bibliography of English History to 1485.* Oxford, 1975
Nouvelle Biographie Universelle, 46 vols. Paris, 1852–66
Pollard, A.W., and G.R. Redgrave, eds. *A Short-Title Catalogue of Books
Printed in ... 1475–1640*, revised by W.A. Jackson, F.S. Ferguson, and
Katherine F. Pantzer, 3 vols. London, 1976–86

Index